LIBERTY HALL.

A
CONSTITUTIONAL VIEW
OF THE LATE
WAR BETWEEN THE STATES;
ITS
CAUSES, CHARACTER, CONDUCT AND RESULTS.
PRESENTED IN A
SERIES OF COLLOQUIES
AT LIBERTY HALL.

BY

ALEXANDER H. STEPHENS.

Times change and men often change with them, but principles never!

IN TWO VOLUMES.

VOL. I.

NATIONAL PUBLISHING COMPANY,
PHILADELPHIA, PA.; CINCINNATI, OHIO; ATLANTA, GA
ZEIGLER, McCURDY & CO.,
CHICAGO, ILL.; ST. LOUIS, MO.

S. A. GEORGE,
STEREOTYPER AND PRINTER, 124 NORTH SEVENTH STREET,
PHILADELPHIA.

DEDICATION.

TO

All true friends of the Union under the Constitution of the United States, throughout their entire limits, without regard to present or past party associations; and to all true friends of Constitutional Liberty, the world over, now and forever,—especially to all, everywhere, who may, now or hereafter, look to the Federative System, between neighboring Free Democratic States, as the surest means of saving Mankind from ultimate universal Monarchical Rule,—this Work, with all the earnestness of his nature, which the great subject thoroughly awakens, is hereby, not formally, but most solemnly and sacredly, dedicated by the

AUTHOR.

Liberty Hall,
Crawfordville, Ga.,
16 Dec'r, 1867.

LIST OF ILLUSTRATIONS.

CONTENTS.

COLLOQUY IV.

COLLOQUY V.

COLLOQUY VI.

COLLOQUY VII.

COLLOQUY VIII.

COLLOQUY IX.

COLLOQUY X.

COLLOQUY XI.

COLLOQUY XII.

APPENDIX A.

APPENDIX B.

APPENDIX C.

APPENDIX D.

APPENDIX E.

APPENDIX F.

APPENDIX G.

INTRODUCTION.

THE purpose of the writer of this work is to present a Constitutional view of the late War between the States of "the Union," known as the "United States of America."

The view is intended to embrace a consideration of the causes, the character, conduct and results of this War, in relation to the nature and character of the joint Government of these States; and of its effects upon the nature and character of this Government, as well as of its effects upon the separate Governments, Constitutions and general internal Institutions of the States themselves. The subject is one that does not fall clearly within the domain of History, in the usual acceptation of that word. The design is rather to deal with the materials of History than to supply them. It is not so much to present any portion of American History, as it is, by Historical analysis, to show what are the principles embodied in those systems of Government established, by the Anglo-Saxons, on this Continent, and to illustrate their singularly happy adaptation, so long as adhered to, to the situation and character of the North American States.

The chief usefulness of all History consists in the lessons it teaches, in properly estimating the compound result of the action of the principles of any system of Government upon human conduct, and the counter-action of human conduct upon these principles, in effecting those moral and political changes which mark the type, as well as progress, of civilization, at all times, and in all countries. Mankind cannot live without Society or Association. Organized communities, with Governments of some sort, are no more universal than essential to the existence of the *Genus Homo*, with all its Species and Varieties, in every age and clime. The organic laws, which enter into the

Structure of any such Association, Society, Community, Commonwealth, State, or Nation, by whatever name it may be designated, form what may be styled the Constitution of that particular Organism. These are the elementary principles, from which spring the vital functions of the Political Being, thus brought into existence, and upon which depend, mainly, the future development of the Organism, and the character, as well as standard, of its civilization. But, while these Structural laws act upon Society, in its *embryo* state, as well as in shaping its subsequent development, Society is also constantly acting back upon them. As individual life, in all its forms and stages, is said to be the result of a war between opposing agencies, so it is with the political life or existence of every body politic.

Between the primary laws, from which Society first springs, and takes its first form and shape, and the internal movements of Society itself, in its progress, there are continued action and counter-action, producing endless changes, from slight innovations or alternations to entire Revolutions. With these come, either for better or worse, entire changes of the type, as well as standard, of civilization.* History, for the most part, has con-

* "The Institutions of a people, political and moral, are the matrix, in which the germ of their organic structure quickens into life, takes root, develops in form, nature and character. Our Institutions constitute the basis—the matrix—from which spring all our characteristics of development and greatness. Look at Greece! There is the same fertile soil; the same blue sky; the same inlets and harbors; the same Ægean; the same Olympus;—there is the same land, where Homer sung; where Pericles spoke;—it is, in nature, the same old Greece; but it is 'living Greece no more!'

"Descendants of the same people inhabit the country; yet, what is the reason of this mighty difference? In the midst of present degradation, we see the glorious fragments of ancient works of art—temples, with ornaments and inscriptions that excite wonder and admiration—the remains of a once high order of civilization, which have outlived the language they spoke! Upon them all, Ichabod is written—their glory has departed! Why is this so? I answer this, their Institutions have been destroyed! These were but the *fruits* of their *forms of Government*—the matrix from which their grand development sprung. And when once the Institutions of our people shall have been destroyed, there is no earthly power that can bring back the Promethean spark, to kindle them here again, any more than in that ancient land of eloquence, poetry and song!"—*Author's Union Speech*, 14 November, 1860.

fined itself, from the earliest times, to presenting but one side of this complex subject. It has devoted itself so exclusively to the consideration of human action only, that this has become, in general estimation, if not by common consent, its peculiar Province. Hence, it treats chiefly of men, their deeds, their achievements, their characters, their motives, their patriotism or ambition, and the impress their actions make upon Society.

The opposite workings and effects of principles, or *the results of their neglect*, upon the very actions of men, of which they treat so largely, receive but slight, if any attention, even in the most graphic descriptions of the most terrible convulsions, which, if traced to their origin, would often, and most frequently, perhaps, be found to arise, as effect follows cause, from these very principles or organic laws themselves. Those writings upon such subjects, whether considered as Historical or otherwise, are most to be prized as contributions to the general stock of knowledge, which treat of both of these elements of human destiny, together; and, in the progress of any political organism, trace, with Philosophic hand, the connection between them, and the reciprocal bearing they have upon each other.

In the prosecution of the design of the writer, it has not been his purpose to treat, at all, of men or their actions, civil or military, further than they relate to, or bear upon, those principles which are involved in the subject under consideration. Principles constitute the subject-matter of his work. Times change, and men often change with them, but principles never! These, like truths, are eternal, unchangeable and immutable!

Most of the diseases with which the human system is afflicted, proceed, as natural and inevitable consequences, from the violation or neglect of some one or more of the vital laws of its organization. All violent fevers and convulsions have their origin in this, though the real cause may be too occult to be ascertained by the most skilful Pathologist. So with political organizations, whether simple or complex, single or Federal. No great disorders ever occur in them without some similar real cause.

It is a postulate, with many writers of this day, that the late War was the result of two opposing ideas, or principles, upon the subject of African Slavery. Between these, according to their theory, sprung the "irrepressible conflict," in principle, which ended in the terrible conflict of arms. Those who assume this postulate, and so theorize upon it, are but super ficial observers.

That the War had its origin in *opposing principles*, which, in their action upon the *conduct of men*, produced the ultimate collision of arms, may be assumed as an unquestionable fact. But the opposing principles which produced these results in physical action were of a very different character from those assumed in the postulate. They lay in the organic Structure of the Government of the States. The conflict in principle arose from different and opposing ideas as to the nature of what is known as the General Government. The contest was between those who held it to be strictly Federal in its character, and those who maintained that it was thoroughly National. It was a strife between the prin ciples of Federation, on the one side, and Centralism, or Consolidation, on the other.

Slavery, so called, was but *the question* on which these antagonistic principles, which had been in conflict, from the beginning, on divers *other questions*, were finally brought into actual and active collision with each other on the field of battle.

Some of the strongest Anti-slavery men who ever lived were on the side of those who opposed the Centralizing principles which led to the War. Mr. Jefferson was a striking illustration of this, and a prominent example of a very large class of both sections of the country, who were, most unfortunately, brought into hostile array against each other. No more earnest or ardent devotee to the emancipation of the Black race, upon humane, rational and Constitutional principles, ever lived than he was. Not even Wilberforce himself was more devoted to that cause than Mr. Jefferson was. And yet Mr. Jefferson, though in private life at the time, is well known to have been utterly opposed to the Centralizing principle, when *first* presented, on *this question*, in the attempt to impose conditions and restrictions on the State of Missouri, when she applied for admission into the Union, under the Constitution. He looked upon the movement as a political manœuvre to bring this delicate subject (and one that lay so near his heart) into the Federal Councils, with a view, by its agitation in a forum where it did not properly belong, to strengthen the Centralists in their efforts to revive their doctrines, which had been so signally defeated on so many other questions. The first sound of their movements on this question fell upon his ear as a "fire bell at night." The same is true of many others. Several of the ablest opponents of that State Restriction, in Congress, were equally well known to be as decidedly in favor of emancipation as Mr. Jefferson was. Amongst these, may be named Mr. Pinkney and Mr. Clay, from the South, to say nothing of those men from the North, who opposed that measure with equal firmness and integrity.

It is the fashion of many writers of the day to class all who opposed the Consolidationists in *this*, their *first* step, as well as all who opposed them in all their subsequent steps, on *this question*, with what they style the Pro-Slavery Party. No greater injustice could be done any public men, and no greater violence be done to the truth of History, than such a classification. Their opposition to that measure, or kindred subsequent ones, sprung from no attachment to Slavery; but, as Jefferson's, Pinkney's and Clay's, from their strong convictions that the Federal Government had no rightful or Constitutional control or jurisdiction over such questions; and that no such action, as that proposed upon them, could be taken by Congress without destroying the elementary and vital principles upon which the Government was founded.

By their acts, they did not identify themselves with the Pro Slavery Party (for, in truth, no such Party had, at that time, or at any time in the History of the Country, any organized existence). They only identified themselves, or took position, with those who maintained the Federative character of the General Government.

In 1850, for instance, what greater injustice could be done any one, or what greater violence could be done the truth of History, than to charge Cass, Douglas, Clay, Webster and Fillmore, to say nothing of others, with being advocates of Slavery, or following in the lead of the Pro-Slavery Party, because of their support of what were called the adjustment measures of that year?

Or later still, out of the million and a half, and more, of the votes cast, in the Northern States, in 1860, against Mr. Lincoln, how many, could it, with truth, be said, were in favor of Slavery, or even that legal subordination of the Black race to the White, which existed in the Southern States?

Perhaps, not one in ten thousand! It was a subject, with which, they were thoroughly convinced, they had nothing to do, and could have nothing to do, under the terms of the Union, by which the States were Confederated, except to carry out, and faithfully perform, all the obligations of the Constitutional Compact, in regard to it.

They simply arrayed themselves against that Party which had virtually hoisted the banner of Consolidation. The contest, so commenced, which ended in the War, was, indeed, a contest between opposing principles; but not such as bore upon the policy or impolicy of African Subordination. They were principles deeply underlying all considerations of that sort. They involved the very nature and organic Structure of the Government itself. The conflict, on *this question* of Slavery, in the Federal Councils, from the beginning, was not a contest between the advocates or opponents of that peculiar Institution, but a contest, as stated before, between the supporters of a strictly Federative Government, on the one side, and a thoroughly National one, on the other.

It is the object of this work to treat of these opposing principles, not only in their bearings upon the *minor question* of Slavery, as it existed in the Southern States, and on which they were brought into active collision with each other, but upon others (now that this element of discord is removed) of far more transcendant importance, looking to the great future, and the preservation of that Constitutional Liberty which is the birthright of every American, as well as the solemnly-guaranteed right of all who may here, in this new world, seek an asylum from the oppressions of the old.

The general scope of the work is intended to embrace:—

First. An inquiry into the nature of the Government of the

United States, or the nature of that Union which exists between the States under the Constitution, with the causes, or conflict of principles, which led to a resort to arms; and the character of the War, thus inaugurated.

Secondly. The conduct of the War on both sides, so far as it affected Constitutional principles, with its final results upon the organic structure of the entire system of American Democratic Free Institutions.

It was the writer's intention, at first, to embody the whole in one volume; but, as he progressed, he found the materials so massive, and the subject so vast, that it was utterly impossible to do justice to the great theme in so small a compass.

He finds quite enough for one volume wrought up under the first part of his design. This he has concluded to give to the public in advance of what may follow hereafter; especially, as what is now prepared is perfectly complete in itself, upon the general head on which it treats; that is, the nature of the Government of the United States, and those organic principles from which the conflict arose. The remaining portions of his design will be embraced in an additional volume, to be issued as soon as circumstances will permit.

As to the manner of execution, or the form in which the view is presented, a few words may be proper. The method adopted is the Colloquial style. This manner of treating subjects of this character is, as far as he knows, without precedent in this age and country. He was aware, therefore, of the difficulties to be encountered on this score. He felt the risk attending putting forth any thing, in the form of a Book, which, in its departure from the usual mode of treating subjects of the character in hand, might not be in accordance with the ruling taste of the day. He remembered, however, that such subjects, in remoter times, were thus treated by the master writers of antiquity.

Plato and Cicero are illustrious examples. Without any purpose to imitate these classic models, it was enough for him to know that the plan adopted by him, in this particular, was not without well-established precedents in other ages and countries.

But the real controlling reason which determined his course in the matter was that it was in strict accordance with nature. If writing be an art, and if art, in this line, consists in presenting to the mind real images of nature, through the medium of language, as painting does by colors, then he has not deviated from a proper rule of taste, so far as relates to the method adopted. For these Colloquies are but an elaboration of conversations actually had at his residence, as they purport, in substance, to be.

It so happened, in the spring, and early part of the summer, of 1867, while the writer was at his home, devoting his mind, in that quiet retreat, to the general subjects herein discussed, with a view to the preparation of a work of some sort, upon them, for publication, that he was visited, at different times, by great numbers of his old friends, from the Northern States, representing almost every shade of opinion upon the present state of public affairs. During these visits, conversations were had, and very thoroughly indulged in, with perfect good temper, on all sides, upon all these subjects. These actual Colloquies, with rare exceptions, began just as the following pages begin; and they usually took the same course.

As this was so general, and almost universal, it seemed to indicate that line or mode of writing, on the same subjects, which would be the most natural for the entertainment of the great majority of those who might be disposed to read any thing that might be written upon them.

Hence the conclusion as to the mode of treatment now presented. Whether it will be acceptable to modern taste, the test of experiment must disclose. It certainly enabled the writer to present the views of both sides more clearly and forcibly, upon many points, than he could have done in a more stately or didactic form.

The only fiction in the machinery is in the names of the parties, and in connecting the whole discussion with the same persons. The real names of the parties, for obvious reasons, are not given. Others, and entirely *fictitious* ones, are substituted. For unity in the general plan, three representative characters, thus selected, are retained throughout the discussion.

Judge Bynum, from Massachusetts, represents, throughout, that class of visitants who belong to what is called the Radical branch of the Republican Party. Professor Norton, from Connecticut, represents, in like manner, those of that class known as the Conservative branch of the same Party; while Major Heister, from Pennsylvania, represents those of that class known as War Democrats.

The living prototypes of each of these fictitious representatives were in the actual conversations had; and the writer trusts, when the real characters shall see, if they ever do, the reports, now given to the public, of the actual Colloquies which took place, and the parts they took in them, that they will not feel that any injustice has been done to them or their positions.

With this explanation, let the reader imagine all the parties in the Portico, at Liberty Hall, the day after the arrival of the guests, and after the usual salutations and inquiries, upon the reunion of old acquaintances and personal friends—especially upon such a re-union, after years of separation, and these years marked by such scenes as marked those of the separation in this case—and he will be fully prepared for the curtain to rise, and to be entertained, or not, with what follows in the Colloquies, according to his taste and judgment.

CONSTITUTIONAL VIEW OF THE WAR

COLLOQUY I.

MR. STEPHENS'S UNION SPEECH OF 1860 THE SUBJECT ON WHICH THE DISCUSSION BEGINS—THE MOST THOROUGH DEVOTION TO THE UNION CONSISTENT WITH THE RECOGNISED SOVEREIGNTY OF THE SEVERAL STATES—THE UNION ITSELF IS A UNION OF SOVEREIGN STATES—THE WHOLE SUBJECT OF THE WAR, ITS CAUSES, NATURE, AND CHARACTER, OPENED UP BY A QUESTION PROPOUNDED, HOW MR. STEPHENS WITH HIS SENSE OF DUTY COULD GO WITH HIS STATE ON SECESSION AGAINST THN UNION ?—BEFORE GOING INTO A FULL ANSWER TO THIS QUESTION, TWO PRELIMINARY OBSERVATIONS MADE, ONE RELATING TO CITIZENSHIP, THE OTHER TO THE SUPREME LAW OF THE LAND—CITIZENSHIP PERTAINS TO THE STATES—OBEDIENCE IS DUE TO THE SUPREME LAW WHILE IT IS LAW, BUT ALLEGIANCE IS DUE TO THE PARAMOUNT AUTHORITY—OBEDIENCE TO LAW WHILE IT IS LAW, AND ALLEGIANCE WHICH IS DUE TO THE PARAMOUNT AUTHORITY WHICH CAN RIGHTFULLY MAKE AND UNMAKE ALL LAWS, CONSTITUTIONS AS WELL AS OTHERS, ARE VERY DIFFERENT THINGS—THE QUESTION PROPOUNDED REQUIRES A THOROUGH INQUIRY AS TO WHERE, UNDER OUR SYSTEM, THIS PARAMOUNT AUTHORITY RESIDES.

Judge Bynum. We were all at the North very much surprised as well as disappointed, Mr. Stephens, at your course on Secession.

Mr. Stephens. Why so?

Judge Bynum. Because we were led to believe, from your speech against that measure on the 14th of November, 1860, before the Legislature of your State in Milledgeville, that you were really and thoroughly for the Union. We regarded your speech on that occasion as one of the best Union speeches ever made. There was a tone of earnestness and sincerity in it which created that impression. It was published in all our leading papers, and was almost literally spread broadcast throughout the whole country. From that speech especially, as well as from your course in 1850—and indeed from your whole course from the time you entered public life—we thought that, when the crisis came, if it ever should come, you would certainly go for the Union.

Mr. STEPHENS. It is quite as surprising to me that any such conclusion touching my course, in case Secession should be resorted to, should have been drawn from the speech you allude to, or from my course in 1850, or from any act of my life, as you say my actual course was to you when the event occurred. I was indeed thoroughly for the Union. This the speech referred to fully attested, as well as my whole public course. No words were ever uttered with more earnestness or greater sincerity than were the words of that speech. No stronger or more ardent Union man ever lived than I was. Not a man in the Convention which framed the Constitution of the United States, which sets forth the terms of "the Union," was or could have been more devoted to it than I was. But what Union? or the Union of what? Of course, the Union of the States under the Constitution. That was what I was so ardently devoted to. The Union is a phrase often used, I apprehend, without considering its correct import or meaning. By many it is used to signify the integrity of the country as it is called, or the unity of the whole people of the United States, in a geographical view, as one Nation.

JUDGE BYNUM. Certainly; that is what I mean by it.

MR. STEPHENS. Well, allow me then to say that there

never was in this country any such union as you speak of; there never was any political union between the people of the several States of the United States, except such as resulted indirectly from the terms of agreement or Compact entered into by separate and distinct political bodies. The first Union so formed, from which the present Union arose, was that of the Colonies in 1774. They were thirteen in number. These were distinct and separate political organizations or bodies. After that the Union of States was formed under the Articles of Confederation, in 1777; and then, the modifications of the terms of this Union by the new Compact of 1787, known as the present Constitution. To this last Union, at first, only eleven of the original thirteen States became parties. Afterwards the other two (North Carolina and Rhode Island) also acceded and became members. The last of these (Rhode Island) rejoined her former associates in 1790. Subsequently, twenty new members were admitted into the association, on an equal footing with those first forming it. Whatever intimate relationships, therefore, existed between the citizens of the respective thirty-three States constituting the Union in 1860, they were created by, or sprung from, the terms of the Compact of 1787, by which the original States as States were united. These terms were properly called the Constitution of the United States; not the Constitution of one people as one society or one nation, but the Constitution of a number of separate and distinct peoples, or political bodies, known as States. The absolute Sovereignty of these original States, respectively, was never parted with by them in that or any other Compact of Union ever entered into by them. This at least was my view of the subject. Georgia was one of these States. My allegiance therefore was, as I considered it, not due to the United States, or to the people of the United States, but to Georgia in her Sovereign capacity. Georgia had never parted with her right to command the ultimate allegiance of her citizens. In that very speech this doctrine, or these principles, were clearly asserted and distinctly maintained. However strongly opposed I was to the policy of Secession, or whatever views I gave against it as a policy, or wise measure, yet in that very speech, which you considered so strong a Union speech, I declared my convictions to be, that if the people of Georgia, in their majesty, and in the exercise of their resumed full Sovereignty, should, in a regularly-constituted Convention called for that purpose, withdraw from the Compact of Union, by which she was confederated, or united, with the other States under the Constitution, that it would be my duty to obey her high behest. That speech was made mainly, it is true, against the policy of Secession for then existing grievances complained of, but also against the unconstitutionality of measures proposed to be passed by the State Legislature, with a view of dissolving the Union. The Sovereign power of the people of the State, which alone could regulate its relations with the other States, was not vested in the Legislature. That resided with the people of the State. It had never been delegated either to the State authorities, or the authorities created by the Articles of Union. It could be exercised only by the people of the State in a regularly-constituted Convention, embodying the real Sovereignty of the State—just such Convention as had agreed to and adopted the Constitution of the United States. It required the same power to unmake as it had to make it.* Hence, I said—"Let the sove-

* "*Unum quoque dissolutur eo modo quo colligatur*"—"Every thing is dissolved by the same means it is constituted."—*Noy's Maxims*, p. 11.

reignty of the people of Georgia be first heard on this question of severing the bonds that united them with the other States;" and that, whatever decision the State might thus and then make, "my fortunes would be cast with hers and her people."

I indulged a strong hope that when the Sovereignty of the people should be so invoked that it would take the same view I did of the policy of Secession or Disunion. In this hope, however, I was disappointed. The Convention was called; it was regularly and legally assembled; the Sovereign will of the State, when expressed through its properly constituted organ, was for Secession, or a withdrawal of the State from the Union. The Convention passed an Ordinance repealing and rescinding the State Ordinance of the second of January, 1788, by which Georgia became one of the United States under the constitutional Compact of 1787. I was in this Secession Convention, which assembled on the sixteenth day of January, 1861. The rescinding Ordinance passed that body on the nineteenth day of that month; I voted against that Ordinance. It was an Ordinance repealing and rescinding the Ordinance of a similar Sovereign Convention of the people of the State, passed the second day of January, 1788, as before stated, and placed Georgia just where she was, or would have been, if her Convention in 1788 had not passed the Ordinance by which she acceded to the Union under the Constitution of 1787. Such were my convictions.

After the passage of this Ordinance by the State Con-

Or, as the Institutes and Broom have it—"*Nihil tam conveniens est naturali æquetati quam unum quoque dissolvi eo ligamene quo ligatum est*"—"Nothing is so consonant to natural equity as that every contract should be dissolved by the same means that rendered it binding."—*Broom's Legal Maxims*, p. 407; 2 *Inst.* 360.

vention on the nineteenth day of January, 1861, withdrawing from the Union, I obeyed the high and Sovereign behest of my State, as I felt bound in duty and patriotism to do, and as I had on all occasions declared that I should do. My position, in that Convention and after, was the same that it would have been if I had been in the State Convention of 1788. Had I been in that Convention, I should have been warmly in favor of Georgia's entering into the Union under the Constitution; but if she had decided otherwise, I should, as a good citizen, have felt myself bound to obey her Sovereign will.

This is a short statement of that matter, and how you, or any person who read that speech, could have drawn any other inference as to what my course would be, in case the people of Georgia, in Sovereign Convention, should determine to Secede, I cannot well imagine, but upon the supposition that I did not mean what I said.

Moreover, however general the surprise and disappointment you speak of, may have been at the North, as to my course, yet it certainly was not universal; for Mr. Greeley, in his American Conflict, very clearly shows that he was not either surprised or disappointed at my course from any thing expressed in that speech. After quoting with commendation several extracts from it, he says: "This was frank and noble, yet there was a 'dead fly in the ointment' which sadly marred its perfume. That was a distinct avowal of the right of the State to overrule his own personal convictions and to plunge him into treason to the Nation."*

However Mr. Greeley and I may differ as to what constitutes treason, and as to what he is pleased to call "the Nation," this shows conclusively that he at least was

* *American Conflict*, vol. i, page 343.

clearly and fully apprized of my position in case the State of Georgia should Secede, even against my earnest entreaty and utmost exertions in opposition to the measure.

Judge Bynum. That part of the speech, I must confess, escaped me; at least it was lost in the deep impression which the fervid appeals for the Union in other parts made upon my mind.

Major Heister. I recollect that part of the speech well, but I could not well reconcile it with your speech in the Secession Convention of Georgia, in January, 1861, in which you characterized Secession as the "height of madness, folly and wickedness, that could never get either your vote or sanction."

Mr. Stephens. I am not surprised at your difficulty in this respect. The ready solution to it, however, is this: no such speech as that you quote from was ever made by me. I did regard Secession as an unwise measure, but never questioned its Rightfulness. I thought the State had ample cause to justify her in Seceding, but I thought that a redress of her wrongs might be better secured by another line of policy.

Major Heister. Why, the speech is in Lossing's History* of the War, and in the Rebellion, by Botts.†

Mr. Stephens. I know that. I have read it in both; it may be in many other similar works, but it is an entire fabrication from beginning to end. No such speech was ever made by me in that Convention or anywhere else; I made but one speech on the subject in that Convention, which was extensively published in the newspapers of the day, and can be seen in the volume of my speeches which has been recently published. This speech was against the

---

* *The Civil War in America*, by Lossing, vol. i, page 57.

† *The Great Rebellion*, by John M. Botts, page 326.

policy of Secession, as the one before the Legislature in November was; but it expressed the same sentiments as the other, touching my course in case the State should go against my judgment. It had the same "dead fly in the ointment," as Mr. Greeley would express it. Other speeches I see attributed to me in Mr. Lossing's, as well as in several other Histories of the War, which are as groundless as this. Of this class are those quoted from by Mr. Lossing, representing me as raising the cry of "on to Washington,"* in April, 1861. No such sentiments were ever uttered by me as are given in these reported speeches. This shows what kind of materials histories are sometimes made of.

JUDGE BYNUM. But, Mr. Stephens, allow me to ask you, how you could reconcile it with your sense of duty, to go with your State against the Union, or against the Constitution, which you admit was the foundation of the union of the States, and which, on its face, is declared to be the supreme law of the land? How could you consider what you style your ultimate allegiance as due to your State and not to the United States? You were a citizen of the United States; allegiance and citizenship go together; they cannot be separated. Allegiance and Paramount authority, it seems to me, necessarily go together under our institutions. The first follows the latter, as a matter of course. Pardon me, therefore, for asking you, if you will not consider it obtrusive or impertinent, how you could possibly do otherwise than consider, not only your ultimate, but present and ever absolute allegiance due to the General Government, when there was a combination to overthrow it, and which you declared, in your speech of November 14th, 1860, to be,

* *The Civil War in America*, by Lossing, vol. i, pages 379, 382.

in your opinion, the best Government in the world? Was not your allegiance due to that Government?

Mr. Stephens. By no means. Allegiance, as we understand that term, is due to no Government. It is due the power that can rightfully make or change Governments. This is what is meant by the Paramount authority, or Sovereignty. Allegiance and Paramount authority do go together; we agree in that. But there is a great difference between the supreme law of the land and the Paramount authority, in our system of government, as well as in all others. Obedience is due to the one, while allegiance is due to the other. Obedience to law, while it is law, or the Constitution, which is an organic law for the time being, and allegiance to the Paramount authority, which can set aside all existing laws, fundamental laws, Constitutions, as well as any others, are very different things.

Your question, however, my dear sir, opens up the whole subject of the late war, its causes, nature, and character. It involves all the questions of right and wrong, in its beginning, conduct, and conclusion. This, too, necessarily involves an inquiry into and a correct understanding of the nature of the Government of the United States; the relations of the States to it; and the nature and character of that Union of which we have spoken, and about which we often hear so much. In a word, it involves a solution of the great question, where the Paramount authority or ultimate Sovereignty, under our system of Government, resides. If these matters had been properly discussed, and properly understood, and settled by reason, in accordance with truth and justice, before a resort to arms was had, our once happy and prosperous country would have been saved the widespread desolation that now broods over so large a section of it, and the far greater evils which I seriously apprehend still threaten the whole of it. The million of lives that were sacrificed in this fratricidal strife, and the billions of treasure that were expended in it, as well as the untold suffering which attended it, would have been saved.

We have many Histories of this war, which, from the bench of the Supreme Court of the United States, has been pronounced to be "the greatest civil war known in the history of the human race,"* and "the din of conflict" in which, says Mr. Lossing, the author of one of these Histories, "was heard all over the world; and people of all nations were spectators of the scene!"†

Most of these Histories, that I have read, treat mainly of the current, or passing events, preceding and during its continuance. They are but the records and chronicles, and imperfect ones too, of the excited passions, imbittered prejudices, and extravagant utterances, of the public men, as well as of the masses of the people on both sides. Their most entertaining parts are chiefly devoted to a portrayal of the terrible conflict of arms, scenes of battle-fields, the marshalling of hosts in hostile array, the skill of Generals, and deeds of valor and prowess on one or the other, or both sides, which excite the highest admiration with those who take pleasure in such descriptions; but none of them have taken any thing like an unimpassioned and Philosophical view of the real causes of this great scourge; or how it might have been and ought to have been prevented, or how like results and calamities, under like circumstances, may hereafter be avoided.

The only exceptions to this remark of all the works of the kind, that I have seen, are, "A Youth's History of the Great Civil War," published by Van Evrie, Hor-

* 2d *Black's Reports*, 669. † *Lossing*, vol. i, p. 3.

ton & Co., New York, and a work entitled, "The Origin of the late War," by Mr. George Lunt, of Boston.* Mr. Lunt has treated his subject with great truthfulness and rare ability; but still he does not go quite to the bottom of the subject. He does not go into an inquiry into the nature of the Government of the United States, and the character of the Union, by which the States were united. Herein alone can be discovered the remote, but real causes of the war. Such an inquiry did not lie, it seems, within the scope of his object. The Youth's History barely glances at what I allude to. There has been as yet, as far as I have seen, no history entering into an exposition of those great fundamental laws, governing our complicated system of political organization, from a violation of which, all these troubles resulted. Resulted as inevitable consequences: just as the most malignant

* Since the preparation of these sheets for the press, the writer has seen, for the first time, a copy of the first volume of "The Civil War in America, by John W. Draper, M. D., LL. D., of the University of New York." This, perhaps, should be also excepted from the remarks of the text. There is a very profound philosophy running through this book, somewhat of the Buckle School; but its philosophy, as to the causes of the war, is very well condensed, by the author himself, in one sentence, on page 25. That sentence is in these words: "There is a political force in ideas which silently renders protestations, promises, and guarantees, no matter in what good faith they may have been given, of no avail, and which makes Constitutions obsolete. Against the uncontrollable growth of the anti-slavery idea the South was forced to contend."

This kind of Philosophy accounts for the war, as it might very readily account for most of the evils which afflict mankind, by simply assigning it and them to the general depravity of human nature.

This is the Philosophy of Fatalism—which assigns consequences to antecedents, over neither of which human will has any control; and for either of which it would be difficult to assign any just responsibility or accountability. A better and sounder philosophy is that which teaches men their errors, and which, by inculcating sound and correct principles, enables those who study it, in the exercise of virtue, to become wiser, truer, and better, politically as well as morally.

diseases often do, from a neglect or violation of the vital laws of physical organism. From such an investigation and exposition alone, can be known the nature and character of the war itself, and on which side the right or wrong attending it, or the right or wrong of the conduct of any of the actors in it, is to be placed for the enlightenment of mankind, and the benefit of posterity. We have books upon books about "Negro Slavery," "The Slave Power," "Slave Drivers," and about "An Oligarchy of Slave Holders," etc., but none of them attempt to show that these subjects, even according to their fancies, came within the purview of the powers of the General Government.

Mr. Greeley, one of the ablest and fairest writers of the class I have alluded to, in his "American Conflict," treats the whole war as the culmination of a strife, for more than half a century, about "Negro Slavery," without scarcely giving a passing word upon the subject of the nature of the Government of the United States, or attempting to show that it had any rightful authority whatever over the subject matter of this strife. He writes as if it were conceded that the United States is one great Nation, one people, divided in sentiment upon the subject of African Slavery, or the *legal status* of the African race in some of the States. He traces and treats the discussion of this question just as a British historian might treat the discussions on the Corn Laws, or the extension of the franchise in his country. All this manner of treatment of the subject is radically defective. It utterly ignores the true causes of the war, on which alone its Rightfulness depends. Slavery, so called, or that legal subordination of the black race to the white, which existed in all but one of the States, when the Union was formed, and in fifteen of them when the war began, was unquestionably the occasion of the war, the main exciting proximate cause on both sides, on the one as well as the other, but it was not the real cause, the "*Causa causans*" of it. That was the assumption on the part of the Federal authorities, that the people of the several States were, as you say, citizens of the United States, and owed allegiance to the Federal Government, as the absolute Sovereign power over the whole country, consolidated into one Nation. The war sprung from the very idea you have expressed, and from the doctrine embraced in the question propounded to me. It grew out of different and directly opposite views as to the nature of the Government of the United States, and where, under our system, ultimate Sovereign power or Paramount authority properly resides.

Considerations connected with the *legal status* of the Black race in the Southern States, and the position of several of the Northern States toward it, together with the known sentiments and principles of those just elected to the two highest offices of the Federal Government (Messrs. Lincoln and Hamlin), as to the powers of that Government over this subject, and others which threatened, as was supposed, all their vital interests, prompted the Southern States to withdraw from the Union, for the very reason that had induced them at first to enter into it: that is, for their own better protection and security. Those who had the control of the Administration of the Federal Government, denied this right to withdraw or secede. The war was inaugurated and waged by those at the head of the Federal Government, against these States, or the people of these States, to prevent their withdrawal from the Union. On the part of these States, which had allied themselves in a common cause, it was maintained and carried on purely in defence of this great Right, claimed by them, of State Sovereignty and Self-government, which they with their associates had achieved in their common struggle with Great Britain, under the Declaration of 1776, and which, in their judgment, lay at the foundation of the whole structure of American free Institutions.

This is a succinct statement of the issue, and when the calm and enlightened judgment of mankind, after the passions of the day shall have passed off, and shall be buried with the many gallant and noble-spirited men, who fell on both sides in the gigantic struggle which ensued, shall be pronounced, as it will be, upon the right or wrong of the mighty contest, it must be rendered in favor of the one side or the other, not according to results, but according to the right in the issue thus presented.

I should take pleasure, though a melancholy pleasure it would be, in giving you my views in full on this subject, if it would be agreeable to you and the other gentlemen present. Not so much, however, with a view to a personal vindication, as with a view to the vindication of the truth of History. But, in doing so, I think I should be able to make it appear very clearly to you why I acted as I did in going with my State, as I did. At least I am not at all averse to giving "the reason of the faith that is in" me, which thoroughly impresses me with the conviction not only of the correctness of my own course, but, also, of the Rightfulness in itself, or Justifiableness on the part of the State in the adoption of a policy that I did not approve; and that if the History of this most lamentable and disastrous conflict, disastrous I fear to all the great principles of Self-government, established or attempted to be secured by the Constitution of the United States, shall ever be written, the Right and

Justice of the cause will be found to be on the side of those, with whom my fortunes were cast, and with whom, in all their heroic struggles and unparalleled sacrifices, my feelings and sympathies were ever thoroughly enlisted, and my utmost exertions put forth for their success. Whatever errors in policy they may have committed, either in the inception of the difficulties or in their subsequent management, the real object of those who resorted to Secession, as well as those who sustained it, was not to overthrow the Government of the United States; but to perpetuate the principles upon which it was founded. The object in quitting the Union was not to destroy, but to save the principles of the Constitution. The form of Government therein embodied, I did think, and do still think, the best the world ever saw, and I fear the world will never see its like again.

Judge Bynum. Be assured I should like very much to hear you, otherwise I should not have introduced the subject as I have. The same I feel warranted in saying for my friends. We came to spend a few days with you, not only to see you, and to revive the friendship of former years, but to talk with you, and to hear your views generally upon the present state of public affairs. We know your opinions on some matters differ widely from ours. But we cheerfully accord to you perfect sincerity in your convictions. You must not, though, indulge the hope or expectation of producing such a change in ours as you seem to think you can. That, indeed, would be a Herculean undertaking.

Mr. Stephens. You mean simply to verify what is said in the old quaint lines:

> "Convince a man against his will,
> He's of the same opinion still."

Or, as Butler, in Hudibras, has it:

> "He that complies against his will,
> Is of his own opinion still."

Prof. Norton. He rather intimates, one might infer, that the roots of his Radicalism would be more difficult to exterminate than were the roots of the hundred heads of the Lernæan Hydra, which even Hercules was unable to destroy without the assistance of Iolas. Is that your idea, Judge?

Judge Bynum. No. I was not thinking of the Hydra, its heads or their roots. I was only giving utterance to the consciousness I feel of the impregnable position of Truth, Justice and Right, upon which my principles are founded; and, these being so founded, I meant only to say that I did not think that either they or my opinions in regard to them can possibly be changed.

Mr. Stephens. Well, be that as it may. I did not mean to say that I thought that I could change your opinions on these subjects, but only that I could make it appear clearly to you, why I, with my convictions, acted as I did, under the circumstances. Our ideas of Truth, Justice and Right, in political as well as social matters, and all the relations of life, depend very much upon circumstances. This seems to be owing partly to the infirmities of human nature. There ought, however, to be no difference between intelligent minds as to Truth, which rests simply and entirely upon matters of fact; but, in practical life, there are great and wide differences, even on this, owing to a disagreement or a different understanding as to the facts merely. Justice and Right, depending on the Truth of the facts, must, of course, be the subjects of much wider differences in all cases where the facts are not first settled, or where the Truth is not admitted by both sides. Men's convictions as to Truth, or what they receive as the Truth, depend entirely upon their understanding of facts. Convictions are always sincere. There may be insincere professions of opinions, but there can be no insincere convictions, as to Truth, Justice, or Right, in any matter relating to human conduct. These depend upon laws of mind, over which voli tion has no control. There is as much sound, genuine Philosophy, as wit, in the couplets quoted. There is no such thing as convincing a man against his will. Galileo *complied* with the exactions of torture, by renouncing his belief in the rotatory motion of the earth; but his convictions of this great truth remained as firm as ever, notwithstanding. Belief and conviction are results with which the will has nothing to do, except in collecting and ascertaining the facts upon which depend the truth, or what is considered the truth, to which alone the mind yields its assent. Hence, the necessity of a very liberal charity in all discussions of this nature.

The question you submit relates to Government—one of the most intricate, as well as interesting, subjects that can engage the attention of reflecting minds. Cicero maintains, that nothing connected with human affairs can more properly or profitably occupy the attention of thinking men, in their moments of leisure, or periods of holiday, than matters concerning the good of the Commonwealth. Your question opens a wide field for interchange of views upon topics of this kind, and it will be quite as agreeable to me, with the qualification before stated, as it can be to you, to have a full, free and social talk on these and kindred matters, whether for bare entertainment only, and nothing else, or whether with a view to the chances of mutual profit, each agreeing to disagree throughout, where our convictions differ, or where, to state it differently, our understanding of the facts differ. Is it agreeable all round, that we should have such a talk, upon these terms and conditions?

JUDGE BYNUM. Perfectly so, to me; and I will undertake to vouch for the others. You see the Professor and the Major both nod their assent.

MR. STEPHENS. Well, then, before undertaking to answer your question, Judge, "how I could reconcile it with my sense of duty, to go with my State against the Union," which opens such a field of inquiry, allow me to premise, by making an observation or two on your remark about my being a citizen of the United States, and, as such, being bound by allegiance, as a *loyal citizen* (to use a popular phrase, so current just now), to obey the acts of that Government, as the supreme law of the land.

I agree with you in this, that allegiance and Paramount authority go together; that the first follows the latter. We shall have much to say on that, hereafter.

But, first, as to citizenship. Is there any such thing as citizenship of the United States, apart from citizenship of a particular State or Territory of the United States? To me it seems most clearly that there is not. We are all citizens of particular States, Territories, or Districts of the United States, and thereby only, citizens of the United States. I was a citizen of Georgia; being a citizen of Georgia, I became, thereby, a citizen of the United States, only because Georgia was one of the United States under the Constitution, which was the bond, or compact, of the Union between the States thus united. Had Georgia never united with the other States, her people would never have been, in any sense of the word, citizens of the United States.

JUDGE BYNUM. You do not mean to say that there is no such thing as being a citizen of the United States, except as a citizen of some one of the States or Territories?

Mr. Stephens. Yes; that is exactly what I mean to say.

Judge Bynum. That is, certainly, a strange idea. What do you do with naturalized foreigners, who are, by the laws, made citizens of the United States?

Mr. Stephens. They are, as you and I are, citizens of the United States, because of their being, under the laws, admitted to citizenship of some one of the States or Territories of the United States. The only power Congress has, under the Constitution, on this subject, is to make uniform rules of naturalization. That is, to prescribe uniform rules, which are to be the same in all of the States, by which foreigners may be permitted to become citizens of the several States or Territories. Before this power was delegated to Congress, each State, as all other Sovereign, independent nations, had the uncontrolled right to admit foreigners to citizenship, upon such terms as each, for itself, saw fit. In order that the same terms or conditions might exist in all the States, each State, in the Constitution, agreed to delegate the power to Congress, to make the rules on the subject of naturalization uniform in all of the States. This is the view of all writers upon the subject.

Mr. Rawle, in his admirable treatise on the Constitution of the United States, has well said, on the subject of citizenship, generally:* "It cannot escape notice that no definition of the nature and rights of citizens appears in the Constitution." And then, on the subject of naturalization, and the reason of giving power to Congress over the subject, he says:† "In the second section of the fourth article, it is provided that the citizens of each State shall be entitled to all the privileges

---

* *Rawle on the Constitution*, p. 85. † *Id.*, p. 84.

and immunities of citizens in the several States; and the same rule had been ambiguously laid down in the Articles of Confederation. If this clause is retained, and its utility and propriety cannot be questioned, the consequence would be that, if each State retained the power of naturalization, it might impose on all other States such citizens as it might think proper. In one State, residence for a short time, with a slight declaration of allegiance, as was the case under the former Constitution of Pennsylvania, might confer the rights of citizenship; in another, qualifications of greater importance might be required: an alien, desirous of eluding the latter, might, by complying with the requisites of the former, become a citizen of a State in opposition to its own regulations; and thus, in fact, the laws of one State become paramount to that of another. The evil could not be better remedied than by vesting the exclusive power in Congress." That is, of making the rule for admission to citizenship in each State uniform in all the States. The same view is clearly and strongly expressed by Judge Curtis, of the Supreme Court of the United States, in a very able and elaborate opinion upon questions of as much importance as were ever decided by that Court. I refer to the Dred Scott case, 19 *Howard's Reports*, 393. Here is what he says:—

"It appears, then, that the only power Congress has concerning citizenship is confined to the removal of disabilities of foreign birth."

Judge Curtis, in support of his position, cites numerous authorities—*The Federalist*, No. 42; 12*th Wheaton*, 259, 269; 3*d Washington*, 313, 322; 12*th Wheaton*, 277; 3*d Story on Constitution*, 1–3; *Rawle on the Constitution*, 84–88; 1*st Tucker's Blackstone*, App., 255, 259.

When a foreigner, therefore, wishes to become a citizen

of any one of the States or Territories, he has to file his petition to this effect, according to the uniform rules established by Congress; and the Courts, in the State or Territory, whether Federal or State, have to conform to these rules, in admitting to citizenship, where the application is made. He then becomes possessed of all the rights, privileges and immunities pertaining to citizenship which are possessed by native-born citizens in that State or Territory, and no more. He then and thereby only becomes a citizen of the United States as native-born citizens so become, and no more. He cannot enter suit, in any of the United States Courts, for a redress of any wrong within their jurisdiction, any more than a native-born citizen, without stating distinctly that he is a citizen of some one of the States, and of which one. He is, in every respect, after being naturalized in conformity to the uniform rules, as stated, on the same footing with native-born citizens. Of this class, Judge Curtis, further on in the same opinion, says: "The necessary conclusion is, that those persons, born within the several States, who, by force of their respective constitutions and laws, are citizens of the State, are thereby citizens of the United States." This covers the whole question. There is no such thing as general citizenship of the United States under the Constitution.

Judge Bynum. That is not the general understanding upon this subject.

Mr. Stephens. That may be, but it is certainly the understanding of the Supreme Court of the United States in repeated decisions, as well as the understanding of the ablest writers upon the subject; and it is very clear to my mind that it is the only true constitutional understanding of the subject. So much then for citizenship and its necessary legitimate consequences, by way of premise, barely at this time.*

Secondly. Another observation now in the same way upon what you call the supreme law of the land. The Constitution does declare that "this Constitution and the laws of the United States made in pursuance thereof, and all treaties made or which shall be made under the authority of the United States, shall be the supreme law of

* Mr. Calhoun, in the United States Senate, expressed himself upon the subject, as follows :—

"The Senator from Delaware (Mr. Clayton), as well as others, had relied with great emphasis on the fact, that we are citizens of the United States. I, said Mr. C., do not object to the expression, nor shall I detract from the proud and elevated feelings with which it is associated; but he trusted that he might be permitted to raise the inquiry, in what manner we are citizens of the United States, without weakening the patriotic feeling with which he trusted it would ever be uttered. If by citizen of the United States he meant a citizen at large, one whose citizenship extended to the entire geographical limits of the country without having a local citizenship in some State or Territory, a sort of citizen of the world, all he had to say was, that such a citizen would be a perfect nondescript; that not a single individual of this description could be found in the entire mass of our population. Notwithstanding all the pomp and display of eloquence on the occasion, every citizen is a citizen of some State or Territory, and, as such, under an express provision of the Constitution, is entitled to all privileges and immunities of citizens in the several States; and it is in this, and in no other sense, that we are citizens of the United States. The Senator from Pennsylvania (Mr. Dallas), indeed, relies upon that provision in the Constitution which gives Congress the power to establish a uniform rule of naturalization; and the operation of the rule actually established under this authority, to prove that naturalized citizens are citizens at large, without being citizens of any of the States. He did not deem it necessary to examine the law of Congress upon this subject, or to reply to the argument of the Senator, though he could not doubt that he (Mr. D.) had taken an entirely erroneous view of the subject. It was sufficient that the power of Congress extended simply to the establishment of an uniform rule by which foreigners might be naturalized in the several States or Territories, without infringing, in any other respect, in reference to naturalization, the rights of the States as they existed before the adoption of the Constitution." *Niles's Register*, vol. xliii, Supplement 166.

the land, and the Judges in every State shall be bound thereby, any thing in the Constitution or laws of any State to the contrary notwithstanding."

Judge Bynum. Exactly so; and, this being so, is not everybody in the States—judges, legislators and people, whether citizens of the United States, in the usual acceptation of that term or not—bound to obey them?

Mr. Stephens. Most certainly; so long as the Paramount authority over them shall so ordain and order, but no longer; so long as it is law, and no longer. There is a wide difference, as I stated at first, between the supreme law of the land and the Paramount authority. Obedience is due to the one as long as it is the law, and allegiance is due to the other when it declares, as it can, that the law no longer exists. In our Government, as in all Governments, there must be a supreme law-making power on the subjects within its jurisdiction; that is, the supreme power of making laws to be obeyed on these subjects must be lodged somewhere. It is not an absolute power in any Government founded upon the principles of ours. It is a power exercised in trust only. This supreme power, moreover, or the delegation of its exercise, emanates from Sovereignty or the Paramount authority, but it is not Sovereignty itself. All laws therefore passed in pursuance of the rules prescribed by the Sovereign or Paramount authority, are supreme, and to be obeyed so long as they remain of force by the continued authority of the Sovereign power. This is universally admitted; no one disputes it. In this country it is equally admitted on all hands that Sovereignty, which is the Paramount authority, resides with the People. All government, according to our axioms and maxims, is but the exercise in trust of delegated powers. The exercise of supreme or Sovereign powers may be by delegation. In this country it is entirely by delegation; but whatever is delegated may be resumed by the authority delegating. No postulate in mathematics can be assumed less subject to question than this. The exercise of supreme law-making power, even over the authority delegating it, may be legitimate so long as the delegated power is unresumed. Obedience to laws passed under such delegation of power, is, as I have said, a very different thing from allegiance which is due to the authority delegating the exercise of the supreme law-making power. Whenever the delegated powers are resumed, allegiance must be due to the resuming Sovereign power; to that which can rightfully make and unmake Constitutions.

The Government of the United States was created by the States. All its powers are held in trust by delegation from the States. These powers are specific and limited. They are supreme within the sphere of their limitations—supreme so long as the authorities delegating them continue the trust even over the authorities delegating them; but being held entirely by delegation, they exist no longer than the party or parties delegating see fit to continue the trust. In this sense alone is the authority of the General Government supreme, even over the subjects which lie within the sphere of the powers with which it was intrusted by delegation. The Paramount authority in this country, Sovereignty, that to which allegiance is due, is with the People somewhere. There is no Sovereignty either in the General Government or the State Governments. These are permitted to exercise certain Sovereign powers so long only as it shall suit the Sovereign will that they shall so do, and no longer. Sovereignty itself, from which emanates all political power, I repeat, remains and ever resides with the People somewhere. And with what People? Why, of necessity, it appears to me, with the same People who delegated whatever powers the General Government has ever been intrusted with; that is, the People of the several States; not the whole People of the United States as one mass, as can be most conclusively demonstrated.

In addition to this, I remark that this clause of th Constitution contains no grant or delegation of power in itself. It only declares what would have been the effect of the previously delegated powers without it. All Treaties or Covenants between Sovereigns are the supreme law over their subjects, or citizens, so long as they last. Indeed, so far from containing any new or substantive power, upon its very face this clause shows that it was intended as a limitation of powers. So far from showing that absolute Sovereignty was thereby vested in the General Government, such Sovereignty as is entitled to the allegiance of anybody, it shows conclusively that even obedience is due to such laws, treaties, etc., only, as may be made in pursuance of the Constitution. This, by itself, shows the Government to be one of limited powers —and so far from allegiance being due to it in any sense, that even obedience is due only to a limited extent.

This was the opinion of Alexander Hamilton, who was one of the extremest of the Nationals of his day, and who never failed to claim all acknowledged, as well as some doubtful, or questionable powers, which tended to strengthen the Federal Government. While the Constitution was before the several States, for their consideration before its adoption, he unequivocally declared, on several occasions, that this clause conveyed no grant of power, and was entitled to no such construction as that which would claim under it the allegiance of the citizens of the several States. Let us see what he wrote on the subject at that time. In a note to the 27th number of the *Federalist*, wherein he had alluded to this clause, he says "the *sophistry*," as he called it, which had been employed to give it the construction you would put upon it, would, "in its proper place, be fully detected." And then, in the 31st number of the *Federalist* (*Dawson's Edition*), page 206, he thus detects and exposes this sophistry: "But," says he, "it is said that the laws of the Union are to be the supreme law of the land. But what inference is to be drawn from this, or what would they amount to, if they were not supreme? It is evident that they would amount to nothing. A law, by the very meaning of the term, includes supremacy. It is a rule which those, to whom it is prescribed, are bound to observe. If individuals enter a state of society, the laws of that society must be the supreme regulator of their conduct. If a number of political societies enter into a larger political society, the laws which the latter may enact, pursuant to the powers intrusted to it by its Constitution, must necessarily be supreme over those societies, and the individuals of whom they are composed."

And further in the same paper—"But it will not follow from this doctrine that acts of the larger societies, which are not pursuant to its constitutional powers, but which are invasions of the residuary authorities of the smaller societies, will become the supreme law of the land. These will be merely acts of usurpation, and will deserve to be treated as such. Hence we perceive that the clause which declares the supremacy of the laws of the Union, like the one we have just before considered, only declares a truth which flows immediately and necessarily from the institution of a Federal government. It will not, I presume, have escaped observation, that it expressly confines this supremacy to the laws made pursuant to the Constitution, which I mentioned merely as an instance of caution in the Convention, since that limitation would have been to be understood, though it had not been expressed."

This shows conclusively that Mr. Hamilton, one of the extremest of the Nationals in his day—he who did wish a National government instituted instead of a Federal one, but who gave a cordial support to the Federal plan when the National one was abandoned, as we shall hereafter see—did not claim any delegation or grant of power from this clause of the Constitution, but expressly states that it was intended as a limitation, as its words fairly import, of other powers which had been delegated, and that this limitation had been inserted out of abundant caution on the part of the Convention. He maintained the same position in the State Convention of New York. This is quite enough I think to show in this place, by way of premise, that the allegiance of the citizens of the several States was never intended to be transferred to the United States, or to the Government of the United States, by this clause of the Constitution. And from what has been said, without going into a history of this clause, or explaining how it came to be introduced, which would strengthen the views given, it very clearly appears, as well as from the language of the clause itself, that the Government of the United States is not, by virtue of it, supreme or Sovereign in the sense in which you use that term; and so far from being entitled thereby to claim the ultimate or any sort of allegiance of the citizens of the several States, it is not entitled even to claim their obedience to its laws except within the strict limit of its specifically-delegated powers. Thus far, it appears clearly, that a thorough inquiry into and a full investigation of the nature of the Government of the United States, as well as the character and extent of its delegated powers, are essential to a correct understanding of the subject presented in the question propounded. Without this, there can be no correct knowledge or sound judgment as to the nature and character of the war, whether an Insurrection, a Rebellion, a Civil war, or a war of Aggression for unjust power and Dominion on one side—while one purely in defence of ancient and well-established Sovereign Rights on the other. Without this there can be no correct judgment as to whether I acted properly or improperly in the course I took, or as to the conduct or rectitude of any of the various actors therein, on one side or the other. To this inquiry we will therefore now proceed.

Professor Norton. Without wishing to interrupt you, allow me a word at this point. What you have read from Mr. Hamilton's article in the Federalist was new to me. I was not aware that he took any such view of that subject. I was always of opinion that Mr. Hamilton claimed absolute Sovereignty for the United States, and I supposed it was with him, as with most others who do, mainly under this clause of the Constitution. In this it seems that I was wrong. You stated that the history of this clause of the Constitution, or the facts connected with its introduction, would strengthen the view you take of it, and in which it appears you are sustained by Mr. Hamilton. I should like, before you proceed further, to know the facts and circumstances attending its introduction, to which you refer, if it will not too much interfere with the line of your remarks.

Mr. Stephens. Not at all. But allow me first to set you right with regard to Mr. Hamilton's position as to the absolute Sovereignty of the United States over the several States. You are quite mistaken in supposing that he ever held that doctrine. He advocated the Constitution as *Federal* in its character, as we shall see. In this 27th number of the *Federalist* he speaks of "the laws of the Confederacy." He styles the Government a "Confederacy."

But, without digressing further on that point now, I will proceed to reply to your question. The history of this clause of the Constitution is this. It is well known, or, at least, it may be here stated, as it will be established without question, that, in the Convention that formed the Constitution, there was a party who were strongly in favor of doing away with the Federal system that existed before that time, and substituting, in its stead, a General National Government over the whole people of all the States, as one body politic. This party wished to do away entirely with the Sovereignty of the several States. Their object was to give the Central National Government Paramount authority over the Sovereignty of the States. With this view, a proposition was brought forward, to give the National Government power "to negative all laws, passed by the several States, contravening, in the opinion of the National Legislature, the articles of Union, or any treaties subsisting under the authority of the Union." This proposition, if it had been adopted, would have greatly favored the object of the Nationals, but it was rejected by a decided vote. Here is the journal of the Convention.* Only three States voted for it, while seven voted against it. It was then immediately afterwards that Luther Martin, of Maryland, the strongest States-Rights man, perhaps, in the Convention—one who would, under no circumstances, consent to any infringement upon the ultimate Sovereignty of the States, or

---

* *Elliot's Debates*, vol. i, p. 207.

agree to any thing tending to change the character of the Federal system, offered a proposition in these words: "That the legislative acts of the United States, made by virtue and in pursuance of the articles of Union, and all treaties, made and ratified under the authority of the United States, shall be the supreme law of the respective States, as far as those acts or treaties shall relate to the said States, or their citizens and inhabitants; and that the Judiciaries of the several States shall be bound thereby in their decisions, any thing in the respective laws of the individual States to the contrary notwithstanding."

This proposition expressly restricted the authority of the United States, in all cases within the sphere of its delegated powers. It refused to confer upon the General Government the power or the right to judge of infractions upon the Articles of Union on the part of the States. It was a limitation against any construction by implication to that effect, and simply declared a truth, as Hamilton said of it. It simply asserted what would have been the result under fair construction without it; but it was offered from abundant caution, and was unanimously agreed to, as appears from the Journal on the same page. It was subsequently put in the form in which it is now found in the Constitution, by the committee on style and revision. There was no change in substance. And that it did not answer the purpose of the Nationals, as now contended for by many, appears conclusively, not only from the opinion of Hamilton cited; but from the action of the Nationals themselves in the Convention afterwards. For, notwithstanding this clause was agreed to, as stated, on the 17th of July, yet we find that the very identical original proposition was again offered on the 23d day of August afterwards, as appears on the Journal, page 260. It then met with no greater favor than it did at first. The Convention refused to entertain it, and it was withdrawn. Moreover, I will here add, that no truth is better established than that the general view and understanding of the advocates of the adoption of the Constitution in that day, in reference to this clause, were in conformity with those given by Mr. Hamilton. That is, that no power was granted by the clause—that it simply declared a truth—that it was intended as a limitation of powers delegated, and only announced a principle that would have been recognized by the Courts, even if it had not been made, or in other words, that this clause did not in the least change the character of the former Government in this respect, and that the acts of the General Government, under the present Constitution, are no more binding on the States, or the citizens of the States, by virtue of it, than they were under the Confederation. This was the opinion of Mr. Madison. Here, in a number of the *Federalist*, written by him (No. 37), he shows that "treaties made by Congress, under the Articles of Confederation, had been declared by Congress, and recognized by most of the States, to be the supreme law of the land," without any such declaration to that effect in the Articles of the Union. And further, if further argument be necessary to show the prevailing opinion at that time, I refer you to a decision of the Supreme Court of the United States, made in 1796. In this case, *Ware, etc.* vs. *Hilton, etc.*, 3*d Dallas*, 199, Judge Chase says: "It seems to me that treaties made by Congress, according to the Confederation, were superior to the laws of the States, because the Confederation made them obligatory in all of the States. They were so declared by Congress, on the 13th of April, 1787, were so declared by the Legislatures and Executives of most of the States, and were so decided by the judiciary of the General Government, and by the judiciaries of some of the State Governments." So it appears conclusively from the language of the clause, from the opinions of Mr. Hamilton, and Mr. Madison, and Judge Chase of the Supreme Court of the United States, that the proposition offered by Mr. Martin, and incorporated substantially in the Constitution, conferred no more power under the new Constitution than existed without the declaration under the Confederation.

PROF. NORTON. Your position, then, is simply this: that this clause in the Constitution effected no radical or substantial change in the character of the General Government from what it was before. That if it was not vested with complete Sovereignty over the State authorities, and entitled to the allegiance of the citizens of the several States under the Confederation, that it did not become so vested by virtue of this clause of the Constitution.

MR. STEPHENS. Exactly so. That is my position, and I will add that Judge Chase, in the same opinion from which I have just read, and to which we may have occasion to refer again, held that under the Confederation the States severally were clothed with all the attributes of perfect sovereignty. And yet the Articles of Confederation were the Supreme law of the land as much as the Constitution now is. All compacts between sovereigns are the supreme law over their subjects or citizens so long as they continue. This is the doctrine of Vattel. General Pinckney, in the South Carolina Convention, when this clause of the Constitution was under discussion, after quoting Vattel to this effect, goes on: "Burlamaqui, another writer of great reputation on political law, says, 'that treaties are obligatory on the subjects of the powers who enter into treaties; they are obligatory as *conventions between the contracting powers;* but they have the *force of law* with respect to their subjects.' These are his very words: '*Ils ont force de loi a l'egard des sujets, considèrès comme tels;*' and it is very manifest, continues he, 'that two sovereigns, who enter into a treaty, impose, by such treaty, an obligation on their subjects to conform to it, and in no manner to contravene it."* Every treaty existing, to-day, between the United States and every other Government or Governments is the Supreme law over the subjects of such Government or Governments, as well as over the citizens of the several States of this Union. That is, every such treaty is a law, Superior to all other local laws in both countries, over which it operates. Their Courts are bound to so hold, and do so hold. This no more affects the allegiance of the subjects of those Governments than it does the allegiance of the citizens of these States. These treaties are Compacts between the Parties to them, and *laws* as to their subjects or citizens.

This clause in the Constitution, therefore, settles nothing on the question of allegiance. The Constitution may be a bare *convention or compact* between the States as Sovereigns, and yet be the supreme law while it continues over their citizens, without affecting their ultimate allegiance in the slightest degree. So we will proceed with our inquiry as to the nature of the present Government of the United States, and enter into an examination of the vexed question, where, under it, the ultimate Sovereign power resides. These are essential facts first to be ascertained and settled.

---

* *Elliot's Debates*, vol. iv, page 279.

COLLOQUY II.

INQUIRY INTO THE NATURE OF THE UNION—A BRIEF HISTORICAL SKETCH—THE DECLARATION OF INDEPENDENCE—THE FIRST CONFEDERATION—A COMPACT BETWEEN SOVEREIGN STATES—JUDGE STORY REVIEWED.

MR. STEPHENS. The object of our immediate inquiry, is the nature of the Government of the United States, and where under it dwells or resides that Paramount authority which in the last resort can rightfully and peaceably make and unmake Constitutions, and to which allegiance is due. Is it in the whole mass of the people of the United States, territorially considered as one Nation, or in the People of the States, severally and separately, each for itself, untramelled by any obligations or restrictions incurred or imposed by any Articles of Union existing between them?

To understand and decide this question correctly, a brief historical review is necessary. From what has been said and assented to, it clearly appears that something exists in this country which by all sides is called "the Union." This must have parties of some sort. It requires parties to make any thing bearing the designation of Union. Who are the parties to this Union? Are they the whole mass of the People, or are they States?

It also appears in the same way, that what is called the Constitution of the United States sets forth the terms of this Union, so admitted to exist on all sides. Now, to understand the force and meaning of the terms used in this written instrument called the Constitution, it is essential to know the state of things existing, and the relations which the Parties to the Union under it bore toward each other before its formation or adoption. To understand the force and effect of a new law, it is often necessary to inquire into the old law upon the same subject-matter, in order to see the evils under the operation of the old one, and the objects aimed at in the remedies provided by the new. To understand properly the present Supreme law, we must look into what was the Supreme law before. The present is not the first Constitution of the United States. "The Union" existed *under an old Constitution.* The main object of the present Constitution, as appears in its preamble, was to make "the Union" then existing more perfect. It was not to make a new one, or to change the fundamental character of the one then existing; no such purpose at least is declared on the face of the instrument; it was only to make the previous "Union" more perfect, or better adapted to secure the great objects for which it had been originally formed.

PROF. NORTON. The first Union to which you refer was nothing but a Confederation between States. The terms of that Union were called Articles of Confederation. They were not called a Constitution. I cannot concede the propriety of styling the Articles of Confederation a Constitution. Daniel Webster on some occasion said—"If there is one word in the English language that the people of the United States understand, it is the word Constitution. It means," said he, "the fundamental law," and nothing like League, or Compact, or Articles of Confederation. I have often thought of the point and force of his illustration on that occasion, of the importance and the power of words barely.

MR. STEPHENS. Mr. Webster did say something like what you quote him as saying. I remember it well, and perhaps may have something more to say about him and his position in the exposition of the Constitution he made on the occasion to which you allude, before we get through. But were not the Articles of Confederation a Constitution even according to his own definition? Did they not constitute the fundamental law of the Union of the States under the Confederation of which you speak? Being the fundamental law for their government for the *time being*, is it not perfectly proper to style them a Constitution upon the authority of Mr. Webster himself? In so styling them, I use the same term that has been applied to them by the highest authority, not only of that day, but since. As you question its propriety, however, we had better settle all points of difference as we go along, especially as a great deal often depends upon words barely, which are frequently, as Mr. Webster says, much more than sounds, being real things within themselves. Let me therefore just here refer to some authorities which I think clearly justify the use of the term as made by me. Mr. Curtis, in his *History of the Constitution of the United States*, volume i, page 139, says these Articles of Confederation were "the first written *Constitution* of the United States." Here is *Marshall's Life of Washington*, volume ii, page 83. In it is Washington's letter to the Governors of the several States, dated 8th of June, 1783, in which he speaks of the Articles of the then existing Confederation as "*the Constitution*" of the States. Here is the first volume of *Elliot's Debates;* on page 96, is given, in full, a letter from the then Congress to the several States, making several recommendations to them. It is dated 18th of April, 1783. In this letter, on page 98, these words occur: "The last object recommended is a

Constitutional change of the rule by which a partition of the common burthens is to be made." This shows that the men of that day understood the Articles of "the Union" then existing to be a *Constitution*. Changes in these Articles they characterized as *Constitutional* changes. Here is the ninth volume of *Sparks's Writings of Washington*. In this are given quite a number of letters written by him in 1788, after what I call the new Constitution had been agreed to by a Convention of the States in 1787, of which we shall have much to say perhaps hereafter. In these letters, Washington called this instrument, as I did, the *new Constitution*. Here is a letter written on the 23d of February, 1789, to Mr. Monroe, in which Washington says: "I received, by last night's mail, your letter dated the fifteenth of this month, with your printed observations on the *new Constitution*," etc. Here is another letter written by Washington to Henry Lee, under date 22d September, 1788, in which he also calls it the *new Constitution*. Another to Benjamin Lincoln, on the 26th of October, 1788, in which he uses the same language. These letters (and I refer to but few of them) show, beyond cavil, that Washington considered the old Articles of "Union," as much as the new, a *Constitution*. Besides this, the writers in the *Federalist* usually designated the paper then before the States for their consideration as the *new Constitution* in contradistinction to the old or the Articles of Confederation. I cite but a few of them: Numbers 22, 39, 41 and 44, pages 147, 255, 296 and 324, in *Dawson's edition of the Federalist*. Moreover, two of the States at least, Massachusetts and New Hampshire, in their Ordinances adopting and ratifying the present Constitution, expressly style it a *new Constitution*. Is more authority needed on this point to justify my use of the term Constitution in applying it as I did to the Articles of Confederation, as well as to the Articles of the present "Union," whatever they may be. The first was a fundamental law as long as it lasted as much as the other.

MAJOR HEISTER. No farther authority, I think, is necessary. The Professor, from the expression of his countenance, seems to be gracefully giving it up.

MR. STEPHENS. Well, then, if the old Articles of Union were a Constitution, the new Constitution is but new Articles of Union between the same parties; unless the new Constitution changes fundamentally the character of "the Union" then existing between them. The bare change of name, of course, does not affect any change of substance.

Preliminaries being settled thus far, let us proceed with the historic sketch, which I said was necessary for a clear understanding of the subject.

Thirteen of those bodies now known as States of "the Union," were originally, or before the date of our common history, Colonies of Great Britain. Some of them were known as Provincial Colonies, some Proprietary, and some Charter Colonies, but all Colonies of Great Britain. These thirteen Colonies were New Hampshire, Massachusetts, Connecticut, Rhode Island, New York, New Jersey, Delaware, Pennsylvania, Maryland, Virginia, North Carolina, South Carolina, and Georgia. These were all distinct political organizations, having no connection whatever between each other, except that the inhabitants of all were common subjects of the Government of Great Britain. They were all planted at different times, and had different forms of government; that is, the Constitutions or Charters of no two of them were alike, though all were founded upon the representative principle. They were all free Democratic Governments. The Charter of the Virginia Government was the oldest; it dates back to 1606. The charter of the last of these Colonies was that of Georgia; it was granted in 1732. These Colonies, as stated, were all separate and distinct political bodies, without any direct permanent political connection between them until 1774. It is true, in 1643, a Convention or Union of some sort for their own mutual protection, was formed between two or more of the New England Colonies, a name given to all those lying East of New York, which lasted until 1683–4,* when it was dissolved by the abrogation of their original charters by the British Government. No farther notice, therefore, for our present object need be taken of that "Union" or its character. Subsequently, in 1754 and 1765, attempts were made by certain Colonies to form some sort of a general Union or Confederation of all these Colonies for their better protection, in combined efforts against the Indians, as well as for joint consultation between themselves on questions of policy adopted by the mother country touching their common interests. These efforts failed. No Union of any sort resulted from them. The last and successful effort was made in 1774. This was at the instance of Virginia. This was after what is known as the Boston Port Bill passed the British Parliament, and after the act of Parliament again changing the Charter of the Massachusetts Colonial Government, and against her consent. These measures awakened a profound sensation in all the Colonies, though the blow was aimed directly at one of them only, yet they all saw that the principle involved the rights and liberties of each severally. Virginia appealed to all to send up delegates to a General Convention or Congress, for joint consultation

---

* *Bancroft's History United States*, vol. ii, p. 127.

and concert of action. Mr. Webster once said that the American Revolution was fought on a Preamble—on the Preamble of the act of Parliament, which, while it reduced the tax on tea to a nominal amount, yet declared the right of the British Parliament to tax the Colonies in all cases whatsoever. This statement has in it much more of the exuberance of a figure of rhetoric than the exact accuracy of historical statement. The *first* moving cause which aroused all the Colonies to that concert of action which ended in the Revolution, was the direct assault of the British Government upon the *chartered Rights of Massachusetts.** This, and not the tax on tea, or what was contained in the Preamble to that act, is what caused the Colonial Legislature of Virginia to pass an order appointing a day for fasting, humiliation and prayer, to implore the Divine interposition for averting the heavy calamity which threatened their civil rights, and which caused them, when dissolved on account of this Resolution by their Royal Governor, to call for a Congress of all the Colonies.†

It was then that the cry went up, from the St. Croix to the Altamaha, "the cause of Boston is the cause of all." The violation of the chartered rights of Massachusetts, prompted the call for a general Congress. This was the moving cause. This appeal, made by Virginia, was responded to by the Colonies generally. The result was the assemblage of deputies from twelve Colonies, which met at Philadelphia on the fifth of September, 1774. This is the first Convention or Congress of the Colonies from which the present "Union" sprung. The first thing settled in this Congress was the nature of its

---

* *Curtis's History of the Constitution*, vol. i, p 6.

† *Id.* vol. i, p. 11.

own character and organization. It was determined to be a Congress of separate, distinct political bodies. In all its deliberations each Colony was to be considered as equal, and each was to have an equal vote and voice upon all questions coming before it, without reference to the number of delegates sent up by the respective Colonies; for the object of all was the defence and preservation of what was claimed to be the inalienable right of each.*

This Congress, so organized and so constituted, after making a declaration of the indefeasible Rights of all the Colonies, made several recommendations to the Governments of the Colonies respectively, as to the course which should be adopted by them in common, for a redress of the wrongs of each in particular. After this action, this body was dissolved, with a recommendation to the Colonies to

---

* *Elliot's Debates*, vol. i, p. 42, *et sequens*. The object of the meeting of this Congress may be seen from some of the powers conferred on their delegates in several of the Colonies:

VIRGINIA: "To consider of the most proper and effectual manner of so operating on the Commercial connection of the Colonies with the Mother country, as to procure redress for the much-injured Province of Massachusetts Bay, to secure British America from the ravage and ruin of arbitrary taxes, and speedily to procure the return of that harmony and union so beneficial to the whole empire, and so ardently desired by all British America."

MARYLAND: "To attend a General Congress to assist one general plan of conduct operating on the Commercial connection of the Colonies with the mother country, for the relief of Boston and the preservation of American Liberty."

SOUTH CAROLINA: "To consider the acts lately passed, and bills depending in Parliament with regard to the Port of Boston and Colony of Massachusetts Bay; which Acts and Bills, in the precedent and consequence, affect the whole Continent of America. Also the grievances under which America labors, by reason of the several acts of Parliament that impose taxes or duties for raising a revenue, and lay unnecessary restraints and burdens on trade, etc." The defence of the rights of Massachusetts was a leading object with all. Note on page 21 of Judge Upshur on the Nature of the Federal Government.

meet in Congress again by deputies, on the tenth of May, 1775. The Colonies did accordingly send up deputies to another Congress as recommended, which assembled on the tenth of May, 1775, as recommended. All the thirteen Colonies, above stated, were represented by delegates in this Assemblage. This is the Congress by which the first permanent "Union" between the Colonies was formed. At first, as their predecessor, they adopted various measures and recommendations for the relief of grievances, which failing, they came to the conclusion finally, on the fourth day of July, 1776, that the only hope for the inalienable as well as chartered liberties of each was for all to throw off their allegiance to the British Crown and to declare their separate Independence of it. This is the Congress, or body of men, that formed the Articles of Confederation to which you referred, and which Mr. Curtis styles, as I have shown, the first written Constitution of the United States. This was the first "Union." And after this brief historical review, with these further preliminaries settled, I proceed to assert, as a matter of history, that the former "Union," or "the Union" under the Articles of Confederation, the first Constitution, was a "Union" of separate, distinct, Sovereign and Independent States. In other words, that the thirteen States, formerly British Colonies, after they asserted their Independence as Sovereign States, entered into "a Union" as separate Sovereignties, and that it was a Union of States, as States. This "Union" was formed in 1777, during the common struggle of all the States for the separate and several Independence and Sovereignty of each. Eleven States, to wit: New Hampshire, Massachusetts, Rhode Island, Connecticut, New York, Pennsylvania, New Jersey, Virginia, North Carolina, South Carolina, and Georgia, ratified that "Union" in the year 1778.

Delaware entered it in February 1779, and Maryland in March 1781.* Each of these States entering into it did so as a distinct, separate, Sovereign political body. This was "the Union" of the Confederation, as you styled it. Mr. Curtis, in his *History of the Constitution of the United States*, to which I have just referred, in speaking of "this Union," says: "the Parties to this instrument (the Articles of Confederation) were free, Sovereign, political Communities—each possessing within itself all the powers of Legislation and Government over its own citizens, which any political Society can possess."†

This, I assume, then, as an unquestionable truth or fact in our History, from which we may start in our inquiry.

Judge Bynum. I am not prepared to grant that. If I recollect correctly, Judge Story, in his *Commentaries on the Constitution of the United States*, utterly overthrows and refutes the facts upon which that assumption is based. He denies that the States were ever separate distinct Sovereign, political Societies or bodies. He maintains that the people of the United States became one Nation even before the Articles of Confederation were entered into, and that the Sovereignty of the whole was merged into one during the joint struggle of all for independence, which was achieved by the whole for the whole, and not for parts separately. Have you *Story on the Constitution?* I am a disciple of Story on this question, as well as on all other questions of Constitutional law! I think Motley, the historian, also takes the same view of this subject as Story. Have you at hand what these writers have said on this point?

Mr. Stephens. Yes; I have *Story's Commentaries on*

---

* *Elliot's Debates*, vol. i, p. 78.

† *Curtis on the Constitution of the United States*, vol. i, p. 142.

the Constitution, and also Mr. Motley's article to the *London Times*, to which, I suppose, you refer. I am quite familiar with both. Here is what you refer to in *Story*, I suppose. Volume i, Book ii, Chap. i, § 210.

JUDGE BYNUM. Yes, this is it. Now hear what he says: and see how completely he disproves the fact upon which your whole argument is about to be founded.

"Now it is apparent, that none of the colonies before the Revolution were, in the most large and general sense, independent, or Sovereign communities. They were all originally settled under, and subjected to the British crown Their powers and authorities were derived from, and limited by their respective charters. All, or nearly all, of these charters controlled their legislation by prohibiting them from making laws repugnant, or contrary to those of England. The Crown, in many of them, possessed a negative upon their legislation, as well as the exclusive appointment of their superior officers; and a right of revision, by way of appeal, of the judgments of their courts. In their most solemn declarations of rights, they admitted themselves bound, as British subjects, to allegiance to the British Crown; and, as such, they claimed to be entitled to all the rights, liberties, and immunities of free born British Subjects. They denied all power of taxation, except by their own Colonial Legislatures; but at the same time they admitted themselves bound by acts of the British Parliament for the regulation of external commerce, so as to secure the commercial advantages of the whole empire to the mother country, and the commercial benefits of its respective members. So far, as respects foreign States, the Colonies were not, in the sense of the laws of nations, Sovereign States; but were dependencies of Great Britain. They could make no treaty, declare no war, send no ambassadors, regulate no intercourse or commerce, nor in any other shape act, as Sovereigns, in the negotiations usual between independent States. In respect to each other, they stood in the common relation of British subjects; the legislation of neither could be controlled by any other; but there was a common subjection to the British Crown. If in any sense they might claim the attributes of Sovereignty; it was only in that subordinate sense, to which we have alluded, as exercising within a limited extent certain usual powers of Sovereignty. They did not even affect to claim a local allegiance.

"In the next place, the Colonies did not severally act for themselves, and proclaim their own independence. It is true, that some of the States had previously formed incipient Governments for themselves; but it was done in compliance with the recommendations of Congress. Virginia, on the 29th of June, 1776, by a Convention of Delegates, declared 'the Government of this Country, as formerly exercised under the Crown of Great Britain, totally dissolved;' and proceeded to form a new Constitution of Government. New Hampshire also formed a Government, in December, 1775, which was manifestly intended to be temporary, 'during,' as they said, 'the unhappy and unnatural contest with Great Britain.' New Jersey, too, established a frame of Government, on the 2d of July, 1776; but it was expressly declared that it should be void upon a reconciliation with Great Britain. And South Carolina, in March, 1776, adopted a Constitution of Government; but this was, in like manner, 'established until an accommodation between Great Britain and America could be obtained.' But the Declaration of the Independence of all the Colonies was the united act of all. It was 'a Declaration by the Representatives of the United States of America, in Congress assembled;' 'by the Delegates, appointed by the Good People of the Colonies,' as in a prior Declaration of Rights they were called. It was not an act done by the State Governments, then organized; nor by persons chosen by them. It was, emphatically, the act of the *whole People* of the United Colonies, by the instrumentality of their Representatives, chosen for that, among other purposes. It was an act, not competent to the State Governments, or any of them, as organized under their Charters, to adopt. Those Charters neither contemplated the case, nor provided for it. It was an act of original, inherent Sovereignty, by the People themselves, resulting from their right to change the form of Government, and to institute a new Government, whenever necessary for their safety and happiness. So the Declaration of Independence treats it. No State had presumed, of itself, to form a new Government, or to provide for the exigencies of the times, without consulting Congress on the subject; and when they acted, it was in pursuance of the recommendation of Congress. It was, therefore, the achievement of the whole for the benefit of the whole. The People of the United Colonies made the United Colonies free and independent States, and absolved them from all allegiance to the British Crown. The Declaration of Independence, has, accordingly, always been treated as an act of Paramount and Sovereign authority, complete and perfect, *per se;* and, *ipso facto,* working an entire dissolution of all political connection with, and allegiance to, Great Britain. And this, not merely as a practical fact, but in a legal and Constitutional view of the matter by Courts of Justice.

"In the debates in the South Carolina Legislature, in January, 1788, respecting the propriety of calling a Convention of the People, to ratify or reject the Constitution, a distinguished Statesman used the following language: 'This admirable manifesto [*i. e.*, the Declaration of Independence] sufficiently refutes the doctrine of the individual Sovereignty and Independence of the several States. In that Declaration, the several States are not even enumerated; but, after reciting, in nervous language, and with convincing arguments, our right to Independence, and the tyranny which compelled us to assert it, the Declaration is made in the following words: "'We, therefore, the Representatives of the United States, etc., do, in the name, etc., of the Good People of these Colonies, solemnly publish, etc., that these United Colonies are, and of right ought to be, free and independent States.'" The separate Independence and individual Sovereignty of the several States were never thought of by the enlightened band of patriots who framed this Declaration. The several States are not even mentioned by name in any part, as if it was intended to impress the maxim on America, that our freedom and independence arose from our Union, and that, without it, we could never be free or independent. Let us, then, consider all attempts to weaken this Union by maintaining that each State is separately and individually independent, as a species of political heresy, which can never benefit us, but may bring on us the most serious distresses.

"In the next place, we have seen that the power to do this act was not derived from the State Governments; nor was it done generally with their co-operation. The question, then, naturally presents itself, if it is to be considered as a National act, in what manner did the Colonies become a Nation, and in what manner did Congress become possessed of this National power? The true answer must be that, as soon as Congress assumed powers, and passed measures, which were, in their nature,

National, to that extent, the People, from whose acquiescence and consent they took effect, must be considered as agreeing to form a Nation."

Judge Story here maintains and clearly shows that the whole people of the United States became one people, one political society, and bound together in one National Government, by the Declaration of Independence, which was one Supreme Sovereign National act, done by the Paramount authority, or Sovereignty of the whole people of all the Colonies, as one Nation, and that all idea of separate State Sovereignty, or of the States ever having been separate, Independent Sovereign powers at any period of their history, is utterly unfounded. That the separate Independence and individual Sovereignty of the several States were never thought of by the enlightened band of patriots, who framed the Declaration of Independence. To my mind his positions are unassailable, and his arguments unanswerable. I should like to hear what you have to say against them. We will postpone Mr. Motley's article until we hear from you in reply to Judge Story.

MR. STEPHENS. Perhaps we had better take up Mr. Motley first. The one is a complete answer to the other, on the question directly now before us; that is, whether the States of our "Union" were ever separate Independent Sovereignties. On this point he fully agrees with Mr. Curtis. Judge Story wrote in 1833. He was a much better lawyer than a historian, as we shall see. In his preface to these *Commentaries*, he says: "In dismissing the work, I cannot but solicit the indulgence of the public for its omissions and deficiencies. With more copious materials it might have been made more exact as well as more satisfactory. With more leisure and more learning, it might have been wrought up more in the spirit of political philosophy. Such as it is, it may be not wholly useless as a means of stimulating abler minds to a more thorough review of the subject," etc.*

Mr. Curtis, who went much more elaborately into the subject, wrote in 1854. Mr. Motley's article appeared in 1861. Here is that article in the *Rebellion Record*, volume i, page 210. In it, he, like Judge Story, attempts to show, that the whole people of the United States now constitute one Nation. He arrives at this conclusion, however, by a very different chain of reasoning. That chain, and its links, we shall, perhaps, have occasion to examine in detail hereafter. Just here, I refer only to that part bearing directly upon the question now in issue. This is what he says:

"The body politic, known for seventy years as the United States of America, is not a Confederacy, not a compact of Sovereign States, not a co-partnership; it is a Commonwealth, of which the Constitution, drawn up at Philadelphia, by the Convention of 1787, over which Washington presided, is the organic, fundamental law. We had already had enough of a Confederacy. The thirteen rebel provinces, afterwards the thirteen original independent States of America, had been united to each other during the Revolutionary War, by articles of Confederacy. '*The said States* hereby enter into a firm *league* of friendship *with each other*.' Such was the language of 1781, and the league or treaty thus drawn up was ratified, not by the *people* of the States, but by the State Governments,—the legislative and executive bodies namely, in their corporate capacity.

"The Continental Congress, which was the central

* Preface to *Commentary*, p. 7.

administrative board during this epoch, was a diet of envoys from Sovereign States. It had *no power* to act on *individuals*. It could not *command* the States. It could move only by requisitions, and recommendations. Its functions were essentially diplomatic, like those of the States General of the old Dutch Republic, like those of the modern Germanic Confederation. We were a league of petty Sovereignties."

This is quite enough of this article just now. I quote from him no further for the present. We may have to refer to other portions of his article again on another point as we advance. Mr. Motley, in that portion which I have quoted, fully admits and distinctly asserts that the first "Union" was "a Union" of States. Of Sovereign States. So much by way of setting off one of these high authorities against the other.

Now what I have to say in reply to Judge Story's argument, is, that it would be conclusive of the question if it were sustained by the facts; but being so directly in opposition to the great unquestionable facts of our history—facts which Mr. Motley could not venture to gainsay—facts as well established as that America was discovered by Columbus, or that the colonies were subject to the British Government at the time of their Declaration of Independence—it is utterly untenable.

JUDGE BYNUM. Do you question his facts?

MR. STEPHENS. Some of them I most certainly do. Indeed, all of them, every one of them, that has any material bearing upon the question in issue. I do not question the fact that the Colonies, under their Charter Governments, were not Sovereign, or that they never pretended to be Sovereign, or that they did not claim a local allegiance. What has that to do with the question? Nor do I dissent from the statement that the Declaration of Independence was not made by these Charter Governments, nor that they were not competent or authorized to adopt it. No truth is better established than that—but what has that to do with the question? That the Declaration of Independence was entirely revolutionary in its character is also true. All admit it. The Declaration was made with a view to overthrow these very Governments, as they were then administered, and the authority of the British Crown, under whose auspices they had been established, or by which they were then attempted to be controlled. What need had Judge Story to state this fact in the line of his argument? I do most fully agree with him also where he says that those Charters neither contemplated the case or provided for it. It was an act of "original inherent Sovereignty by the people themselves, resulting from their right to change the form of Government, and to institute a new Government, whenever necessary for their safety and happiness." This I fully agree to. But this was done by the Paramount authority of the people of each Colony respectively for themselves. The Declaration itself was made by the people of each Colony, for each Colony, through representatives acting by the Paramount authority of each Colony, separately and respectively. The Declaration of Independence was, in this way, a joint act of all the Colonies, for the benefit of each severally, as well as for the whole. The Congress that made it was a Congress of States. The deputies or delegates from no State assumed to vote for it until specially instructed and empowered so to do. Massachusetts had instructed and empowered her delegation so to act as early as January before; South Carolina in March; Georgia in April; North Carolina in April; Rhode Island in May; Virginia in May; New Hampshire in June; Connecticut in June;

New Jersey in June; Maryland in June; Pennsylvania and New York were the last. The powers and instructions from these States did not arrive until after the 1st day of July, which caused a postponement of final action of the Congress on the Declaration until the 4th day of that month, when, full powers being received from all the States, it was then, after being voted upon by States and carried by States, unanimously proclaimed by all the States, so in Congress assembled.* The Declaration of Independence was, be it remembered, voted upon and carried by States, and proclaimed by and in the name of States.

This is the true history of the matter. But the statement adopted by Judge Story, of the reported remarks of Mr. Pinckney of South Carolina, is even more extraordinary still.

This statement is, "that the separate independence and individual Sovereignty of the several States were never thought of by the enlightened band of patriots who framed this Declaration."

That these men did look forward hopefully for a continued Union of the States, under a Compact to be formed securing the Independence and Sovereignty of each, I do not doubt; but that they did not then consider each as an Independent Sovereign power, is wholly at variance with all the attending facts. The very Declaration itself shows this conclusively without going farther into a detail of these facts. The very title shows how it was made. Here it is: "In Congress, July 4th, 1776, the unanimous Declaration of the thirteen United States of America."† It was the Declaration of States in Congress

* *Bancroft*, vol. viii, pp. 449, 450, 475; *Elliot's Debates*, vol. i, p. 60; *Curtis's His. Cons.*, vol. i, p. 51.

† *See Appendix* A.

assembled, by their deputies, empowered by the Paramount authority of each, to make it. The Declaration was not that they were to be *one State*, as New Hampshire had instructed her representatives to make it,* but, in their own language, "thirteen free, Sovereign and Independent States." This was in strict accordance with the instructions of their constituents. The people of the several Colonies would not consent for a Declaration to be made in any other way. This appears from the instructions of all the Colonies or States except New Hampshire. In their several instructions and powers for the Declaration of Independence, were instructions and powers for forming a Confederation of Independent States.† So universal was this sentiment, that Richard Henry Lee's first motion for the Declaration of Independence, early in June, was not only for Independence, but farther—for "a plan of Confederation, to be prepared and transmitted to the respective Colonies for their consideration and approbation."‡

The plan for a Confederation of separate Independent Sovereign States, was moved in the very resolution which

---

* *Bancroft*, vol. viii, p. 438. † *Bancroft*, vol. viii, pp. 378, 437.

‡ *Bancroft*, vol. viii, p. 389.

The following contains the instructions and powers given by Maryland to her deputies in Congress:

"*We, the Delegates of Maryland, in Convention assembled*, do declare that the King of Great Britain has violated his compact with this people, and that they owe no allegiance to him. We have, therefore, thought it just and necessary to empower our Deputies in Congress to join with a majority of the United Colonies in declaring them free and independent States, in framing such further Confederation between them, in making foreign alliances, and in adopting such other measures as shall be judged necessary for the preservation of their liberties:

"*Provided*, the sole and exclusive right of regulating the internal polity and government of this Colony be reserved to the people thereof.

We have also thought proper to call a new Convention for the purpose of establishing a Government in this Colony."

proposed the Declaration of their Independence. And subsequently, on the 24th of June, 1776, the Congress declared, by resolution, that "all persons abiding within any of the United Colonies and deriving protection from the laws of the same, owed allegiance to the said laws, and were members of such Colony; and that all persons passing through, or making a temporary stay in any of the Colonies being entitled to the protection of the laws, during the time of such passage, visitation, or temporary stay, owed, during the same, *allegiance* thereto.*

Hence, with these views and objects, after enumerating the causes which induced the people of each Colony, as a separate political body, or *one people*, to take the course they did, this unanimous Declaration of the thirteen United States, was in these words: "We, therefore, the Representatives of the United States of America in General Congress assembled (that is of the States thus united in Congress assembled), appealing to the Supreme Judge of all the world for the rectitude of our intentions, do, in the name and by the authority of the good people of these Colonies, solemnly publish and declare, that these United Colonies are, and of right ought to be, free and independent States; that they are absolved from all allegiance to the British Crown, and that all political connection between them and the State of Great Britain is, and ought to be, totally dissolved; and that, as free and independent States, they have full power to levy war, conclude peace, contract alliances, establish commerce, and to do all other acts and things which independent States may of right do. And for the support of this declaration, with a firm reliance on the protection of Divine Providence, we mutually pledge to each other our lives, our fortunes, and our sacred honor."

---

* *Journals*, ii. 216; *Curtis's History of the Constitution*, vol. i, p. 52.

The Declaration was then signed by the delegates from each Colony or State, separately, each delegation acting in behalf and by the Paramount authority of each State severally and respectively.

Judge Story says that this Declaration has always been treated as an act of Paramount and Sovereign authority, complete and perfect *per se*, and *ipso facto*, working an entire dissolution of all political connection with and allegiance to Great Britain. This is certainly true to the letter. He very cautiously, however, abstains from stating, by whose Paramount and Sovereign authority it was done, and to what Paramount authority allegiance under it was due, and declared to be due, by the States themselves in Congress assembled. We have seen that it was done by the authority of each State severally and respectively, and that the allegiance of the citizens of each was declared to be due to each severally and respectively.

Strange, indeed, is it, that Judge Story should assert, as he does, "that we have seen that the power to do this act was not derived from the State Governments, nor was it done generally with their co-operation." This language is exceedingly ambiguous. If he meant that it had been seen that the act was not done by the authority, nor with the co-operation of the Royal Charter Governments, no fact is more readily admitted; and none could be stated, less relevant, or less pertinent; but, if he meant to say that it was not done entirely by the authority of the new Revolutionary Governments, erected in each State by virtue of the asserted Sovereignty of the People thereof, respectively, then, his statement is utterly unsustained by the record itself, as well as in direct conflict with the whole history of the times. The Delegates themselves say, in the paper signed by them, that it was done in the name, and by the authority, of the People of the Colonies. That is, the Sovereign authority of the People of each Colony, respectively. For not one of them had any authority to speak for the People of any Colony, except the one he was delegated to represent; nor did any one assume or presume to speak for his own Colony, until empowered to do so. The object of Judge Story seems to have been to produce the impression, without positively stating the fact so in truth to be, that the Declaration of Independence was a National act. That it was not made by the States, as States, but by an assembly of men, assuming to speak for the American Colonists as one People or Nation; and that, too, without any authority whatever, except their own assumed powers. This is clearly the purport of the concluding part of what you read from him. The language used by him is most remarkable, coming from such a source. "The question," says he, "then naturally presents itself, *if it is to be* considered a National act [he does not affirm that it was, but says *if it is to be considered so*], in what manner did the Colonies become a Nation, and in what manner did Congress become possessed of this National power? The true answer [*that is, if it is to be considered so*, he goes on to say] must be that, as soon as Congress *assumed* powers and passed measures which were National, to that extent, the people, from whose acquiescence and consent they took effect, must be considered as agreeing to form a Nation!"

Such an argument and such a conclusion, founded upon such an IF, you must allow me to say, require all Judge Story's reputation, to entitle them to even a moment's notice, or to elevate them to the dignity of serious consideration.

You will please excuse me, Judge, for speaking so of an

argument presented by the founder of your school of Politics. I mean no detraction from his real merits. He was, truly, a very great man, in many respects. I knew him well, and esteemed him highly. He was a man of most charming manners, and of extraordinary attainments in many departments of learning; he was an accomplished lawyer and a profound Jurist. He was an ornament to the Supreme Court Bench, and an honor to the country and the age in which he lived. He had, however, little to do with Politics. He was, in no sense, a Statesman. The science of Government was not the one in which his abilities shone to advantage; and hard pressed, indeed, must he have been in his efforts to prove that the whole People of the United States now constitute one Nation, when he was compelled to resort to such logic, to establish so great and so important an historical fact! He was, however, lawyer enough to know that, if it could not be thus established, it could not be established at all. He knew that, if it be once admitted that the States severally were ever Sovereign, they are so still, or were up to the beginning of this war which was waged against the assertion of this right. He so frankly asserts in a subsequent part of his treatise, as we shall see as we advance. It was exceedingly important, therefore, for the establishment of his theory of a unity of the people now as one Nation, to get a conclusion somehow, that the States were never separately Sovereign. But nothing is easier to be done, than to show that his conclusion, so drawn, from premises of the imagination entirely, has not a solitary fact to stand upon.

Our history at this period rests not upon legends or fables. That Congress itself did not regard their act as the result of assumed, or unauthorized powers, their acts at the time abundantly show. That they did not consider the Declaration of Independence as a National act, or put any such construction upon it, as Judge Story has done, appears clearly from what they were then doing. At the very time the Declaration of Independence was made, a Committee, consisting of one delegate from each State, was organized to prepare articles of Confederation between the States, as separate, distinct Sovereign political Communities.* That Committee, which was appointed on the 11th of June, even before the Declaration of Independence was agreed to, and in anticipation of it, reported the Articles of Confederation, before referred to, which, Mr. Curtis says, was the first written Constitution of the United States. The title of these Articles speaks for itself. It is in these words: "Articles of Confederation and perpetual Union between the States of New Hampshire, Massachusetts-Bay, Rhode Island and Providence Plantations, Connecticut, New York, New Jersey, Pennsylvania, Delaware, Maryland, Virginia, North Carolina, South Carolina, and Georgia." After stating the style of the Confederacy to be "The United States of America," the very first clause in these Articles of Union is in these words: "Each State retains its Sovereignty, freedom and independence, and every power, Jurisdiction and right, which is not by this Confederacy expressly delegated to the United States, in Congress assembled." These Articles were reported on 12th day of July, eight days after the Declaration.† Moreover, this argument and conclusion of Judge Story are utterly inconsistent with the facts acknowledged and set forth in the treaty of Peace with Great Britain, in 1783. The very first article of that treaty is in these words:‡

* *Curtis's His. Con.*, vol. i, p. 53. † *Curtis's His. Con.*, vol. i, p. 53.
‡ *Statutes at Large*, vol. viii, p. 80.

"His Britannic Majesty acknowledges the said United States, *viz.:* New Hampshire, Massachusetts-Bay, Rhode Island and Providence Plantations, Connecticut, New York, New Jersey, Pennsylvania, Delaware, Maryland, Virginia, North Carolina, South Carolina, and Georgia, to be free, Sovereign and Independent States; that he treats with them as such; and for himself, his heirs, and successors, relinquishes all claim to the Government, propriety, and territorial rights of the same, and every part thereof."

The fifth article of the treaty clearly shows how the States, the other party to it, understood it. This is in these words:

"It is agreed that the Congress shall earnestly recommend it to the Legislatures of the respective States, to provide for the restitution of all estates, rights and properties, which have been confiscated, belonging to real British subjects, and also of the estates, rights and properties of persons resident in Districts in possession of his Majesty's arms, and who have not borne arms against the said United States. And that persons of any other description shall have free liberty to go to any part or parts of any of the thirteen United States, and therein to remain twelve months, unmolested in their endeavors to obtain the restitution of such of their estates, rights and properties, as may have been confiscated; and that Congress shall also earnestly recommend to the several States a reconsideration and revision of all acts or laws regarding the premises, so as to render the said laws or acts perfectly consistent, not only with justice and equity, but with that spirit of conciliation, which on the return of the blessings of peace should universally prevail. And that Congress shall also earnestly recommend to the several States, that the estates, rights and properties of such last mentioned persons, shall be restored to them, they refunding to any persons who may be now in possession, the *bona fide* price (where any has been given) which such persons may have paid on purchasing any of the said lands, rights or properties, since the confiscation. And it is agreed, that all persons who have any interest in confiscated lands, either by debts, marriage settlements, or otherwise, shall meet with no lawful impediment in the prosecution of their just rights."

So far from the Federal Government assuming a national character at that time, it would not presume to bind the States or enter into an obligation upon matters that related to their own separate Sovereign Jurisdiction. That Government only engaged to use its influence in recommending to the Sovereign States respectively certain stipulations. This statement of Judge Story is the more remarkable, because it is in direct conflict with numerous decisions of the Supreme Court of the United States.

This Court, in the case of *McIlvaine* vs. *Coxe, 2d Peters's Condensed Reports,* page 86, in 1805, held that, "on the 4th of October, 1776, the State of New Jersey was completely a Sovereign, Independent State, and had a right to compel the inhabitants of the State to become citizens thereof." In delivering the opinion of the Court in this case, Mr. Cushing says: "the Court deems it unnecessary to declare an opinion upon a point which was much debated in this case, whether a real British subject, born before the 4th of July, 1776, who never from the time of his birth resided within any of the American Colonies or States, can upon the principles of the common law take lands by descent in the United States; because Daniel Coxe, under whom the lessor of the plaintiff claims, was born in the Province of New Jersey, long before the Declaration of Independence, and resided there until some time in the year 1777, when he joined the British forces.

"Neither does this case produce the necessity of discriminating very nicely the precise point of time, when Daniel Coxe lost his right of election to abandon the American cause and adhere to his allegiance to the King of Great Britain; because he remained in the State of New Jersey, not only after she declared herself a Sovereign State, but after she had passed laws by which she pronounced him to be a member of, and in allegiance to the new Government. The Court entertains no doubt, that after the 4th of October, 1776, he became a member of the new Society, entitled to the protection of its Government, and bound to that Government by the ties of allegiance."

One of the points in this case was citizenship, and to what power allegiance was due; or in other words, where Sovereignty or Paramount authority under our system then resided—that is, under the Confederation. These, as we settled in the beginning, belong to Sovereignty and follow it. In this case the Supreme Court of the United States decided that both citizenship and allegiance, in 1776, after the Declaration of Independence, belonged to the States severally and respectively. Further on, in the same case, the Court say: "If then, at the period of the treaty of peace, the laws of New Jersey, which made Daniel Coxe a subject of that State, were in full force, and were not repealed, or in any manner affected by that instrument—if, by force of these laws, he was incapable of throwing off his allegiance to the State, and derived no right to do so by virtue of the treaty, it follows that he still retains the capacity he possessed before the treaty," etc.

That capacity was the right to claim citizenship of the State of New Jersey, with all its privileges and immunities, with their accompanying obligations, amongst which was allegiance to her Sovereignty, which he could not throw off.

In another case decided by the same Court, in February, 1796, nine years before *Ware*, etc., vs. *Hylton*, etc., 3 *Dallas*, 199, Chase, Justice, in delivering his opinion, says:

"The first point raised by the counsel for the plaintiff in error was, that the Legislature of Virginia had no right to make the law of the 20th of October, 1777, above in part recited. If this objection is established, the judgment of the Circuit Court must be reversed, because it destroys the defendant's plea in bar, and leaves him without defence to the plaintiff's action.

"I would also remark, that the law of Virginia was made after the Declaration of Independence by Virginia, and also by Congress, and several years before the Confederation of the United States, which, although agreed to by Congress on the 15th of November, 1777, and assented to by ten States in 1778, was only finally completed and ratified on the first of March, 1781.

"I am of opinion that the exclusive right of confiscating, during the war, all and every species of British property, within the territorial limits of Virginia, resides only in the Legislature of that Commonwealth. * * * * It is worthy of remembrance, that delegates and representatives were elected by the people of the several counties and corporations of Virginia, to meet in general Convention, for the purpose of framing a new Government, by the authority of the people only; and that the said Convention met on the sixth of May, and continued in session until the fifth of July, 1776; and, in virtue of their delegated power, established a Constitution or form of Government, to regulate and determine by whom, and in what manner, the authority of the people of Virginia was thereafter to be executed. As the people of that country were the genuine source and fountain of all power that could be rightfully exercised within its limits, they had therefore an unquestionable right to grant it to whom they pleased, and under what restrictions or limitations they thought proper. The people of Virginia, by their Constitution or fundamental law, granted and delegated all their supreme civil power to a Legislature, an Executive, and a Judiciary; the first to make; the second to execute; and the last to declare or expound the laws of the Commonwealth. This abolition of the old Government, and this establishment of a new one, was the highest act of power that any people can exercise. From the moment the people of Virginia exercised this power, all dependence on, and connection with, Great Britain, absolutely and forever ceased; and no formal Declaration of Independence was necessary, although a decent respect for the opinions of mankind required a Declaration of the causes which impelled the separation, and was proper to give notice of the event to the nations of Europe. I hold it as unquestionable, that the Legislature of Virginia, established as I have stated by the authority of the people, was forever thereafter invested with the supreme and Sovereign power of the State, and with authority to make any laws in their discretion, to affect the lives, liberties, and property of all the citizens of that Commonwealth. * * The Legislative power of every nation can only be restrained by its own Constitution; and it is the duty of its Courts of Justice not to question the validity of any law made in pursuance of the Constitution. There is no question but the act of the Virginia Legislature (of the 20th of October, 1777), was within the authority granted to them by the people of that country; and this being admitted, it is a necessary result that the law is obligatory on the Courts of Virginia, and, in my opinion, on the Courts of the United States. If Virginia, as a Sovereign State, violated the ancient or modern law of nations in making the law of the 20th of October, 1777, she was answerable in her political capacity to the British nation, whose subjects have been injured in consequence of that law. * * * * * * * * * In June, 1776, the Convention of Virginia was a free, Sovereign, and Independent State; and on the fourth of July, 1776, following, the United States, in Congress assembled, declared the thirteen United Colonies free and Independent States; and that, as such, they had full power to levy war, conclude peace, etc. I consider this as a Declaration, not that the United Colonies JOINTLY, in a *collective* capacity, were Independent States, etc., but that each of them was a Sovereign and Independent State; that is, that each of them had a right to govern itself by its own authority and its own laws, without any control from any other power upon earth!"

Is authority clearer, stronger, or higher, needed to show the utter groundlessness of Judge Story's argument? If so let us turn to what Chief Justice Marshall said, in delivering the decision of the Supreme Court of the United States, in the great case of *Gibbons* vs. *Ogden*, in 1824. Here it is:

"As preliminary to the very able discussion of the Constitution which we have heard from the bar, and as having some influence on its construction, reference has been made to the political situation of these States anterior to its formation. It has been said that they were Sovereign, were completely Independent, and were connected with each other only by a league. This is true!"*

Judge Marshall here distinctly affirms, judicially affirms, from the Bench of the Supreme Court of the United States, that the States were separate and distinct Sovereignties when the Articles of Confederation were entered into, and that these articles were but a league between Sovereign Powers.

Prof. Norton. Judge; these authorities seem to be strong and to the point.

Mr. Stephens. Strong! Why, sir, there is no answer to them. Judge Story's account of the matter, and his whole argument built upon it, has not a single fact to rest upon; and unless something can be offered in reply, not to me, but to these authorities, I shall take up no more time in establishing the correctness of the assumption with which I set out, that is, that the States, in forming their first political Union, from which the present sprung, entered into it, as free, Sovereign, Independent Powers, or, in other words, in the further prosecution of our inquiry, we may now take it as an established fact, that Mr. Curtis was right, in saying that "the Parties to this instrument (the Articles of Confederation) were free, Sovereign, political Communities, each possessing within itself powers of Legislation and Government over its own citizens, which any political society can possess."

This is equivalent to saying, that the first Constitution was a Compact between Sovereign States, and that the ultimate Paramount authority or Sovereignty under that union remained and resided with the States severally.

---

* *Peters's Con. Rep.* vol. v, p. 565.

COLLOQUY III.

HISTORY OF THE UNION TRACED—ANALYSIS OF THE ARTICLES OF CONFEDERATION—THE DEFECTS IN THEM TREATED OF—THE CALL OF THE FEDERAL CONVENTION TO REMODEL THEM—THE SOLE OBJECT OF THIS CONVENTION WAS TO REVISE THE ARTICLES OF CONFEDERATION AND NOT TO CHANGE THE BASIS OR CHARACTER OF THE UNION—THIS APPEARS FROM THE CALL ITSELF AS WELL AS THE RESPONSES OF THE STATES TO IT—THERE WAS NO INTENTION TO CHANGE THE FEDERAL CHARACTER OF THE UNION.

It, then, being historically and judicially established that the thirteen States, as separate and distinct Sovereign Powers, declared their Independence, and as such entered into their first Union under the Articles of Confederation of 1777 or 1781, according as we may consider the date of the agreement to the terms of the Union by their deputies in Congress, or the time when these terms were acceded to and ratified by all the States; it being further established that citizenship and allegiance were within and under the control of each State under that Confederation as with all other nations; and that each of the States severally, at this period in our history, had full power to confiscate and do what all other Sovereign States by the laws of nations may of right do; and that the right of Eminent Domain which ever accompanies and distinguishes Sovereignty in its fullest extent, was possessed by them severally as separate, distinct States, it now devolves upon us to trace the history of this Union, so formed, from that time to this. If Sovereignty, beyond question, resided with the

States severally at that time, has it ever been changed or parted with by them since? If it has, it must be shown, and shown by evidence and authority of a conclusive character. Sovereignty cannot pass by implication. If the States were Sovereign when they entered into the Articles of Confederation, they must still remain so, unless they parted with that Sovereignty in those articles, or in the new articles—the new Constitution, as it was called—of 1787, which are the basis of the present Union. Now, in this instrument, the new Constitution of 1787, did the States surrender the Sovereignty which they undeniably and beyond all question possessed in 1783? In this instrument have they parted with their control over the citizenship and allegiance of their citizens respectively? This is the great question. In investigating it, as I have said, we must look not only into the instrument itself, but into the old Constitution, to understand correctly the evils arising under its operation and the remedies applied.

Here, again, I premise by assuming an unquestionable position, and that is, that all grants by Sovereignty are to be strictly construed. Nothing can pass by inference or implication against Sovereignty. It is a fundamental maxim of public law that in construing grants from the Sovereign power, nothing is to be taken by implication against the power granting; nothing will pass to the grantee but by clear and express words. This is true of all grants, even of private rights, from the Sovereign power, and much more stringently is the rule to be adhered to in grants, purporting to surrender Sovereign powers themselves.* It is likewise a universal principle and maxim of political law, that Sovereign States cannot

---

* *Broom's Legal Maxims*, p. 260. *Vattel*, *2d Book*, Chap. xvii, Sec. 305–308.

be deprived of any of their rights by implication; nor in any manner whatever but by their own voluntary consent or by submission to a conqueror.*

Now let us examine the Articles of Confederation, as they were styled, and see the nature and extent of the powers delegated by them.† The stipulations entered into by these Articles, as appear from their face, may be divided into two classes:

First, mutual Covenants between the parties, which, at that time, we have seen, were beyond question separate, distinct, Sovereign States.

Secondly, delegations of power by the several Parties to the Compact to all the States, to be exercised by them jointly, in a general Congress of the States.

The mutual Covenants between the States, upon analysis, may be stated as follows:

1st. The style of the Confederacy was to be "The United States of America."

2d. Each State retained its Sovereignty, freedom and Independence, and every power and right which is not expressly delegated to the United States.

3d. The object of the Confederation was for their mutual defence, the security of their liberties and their mutual and general welfare, binding themselves to assist each other against all force offered to or attacks made upon them, or any of them, on account of religion, Sovereignty, trade, or any other pretence whatever.

4th. In determining all questions in Congress each State was to have one vote.

5th. Each State was to maintain its own Delegates.

6th. The free inhabitants of each State, Paupers, Vaga-

---

* *Tucker's Blackstone*, vol. i, Appendix, p. 143.

† See *Appendix* B.

bonds and Fugitives from Justice excepted, were to be entitled to all privileges and immunities of free citizens in the several States.

7th. All Fugitives from Justice from one State into another were to be delivered up on demand.

8th. Full faith and credit were to be given to the records of each State in all the others.

9th. Congress was to grant no title of nobility.

10th. No person holding any office was to receive a present from a foreign power.

11th. No State was to form any agreement or alliance with a foreign power without the consent of the States in Congress assembled.

12th. No two or more States were to form any alliance between themselves, without the like consent of the States in Congress assembled.

13th. No State, without the like consent of Congress, was to keep war ships or an army in time of peace, but each was to keep a well organized and disciplined militia with munitions of war.

14th. No State was to lay any duty upon foreign imports which would interfere with any treaty made by Congress.

15th. No State was to issue letters of marque or to engage in war without the consent of the Congress, unless actually invaded or menaced with invasion.

16th. When land forces were raised, each State was to raise the quota required by Congress, arm and equip them, at the expense of all the States, and to appoint all officers of and under the rank of colonel.

17th. Each State was to levy and raise the quota of tax required by Congress.

18th. The faith of all the States was pledged to pay all the bills of credit emitted, or money borrowed, on their joint account, by the Congress.

19th. It was agreed and covenanted that Canada might accede to the Union, so formed, if she chose to do so.

20th (and lastly). Each State was to abide by the determination of all the States, in Congress assembled, on all questions which, by the Confederation, were submitted to them. The Articles of Confederation were to be inviolably observed by every State, and the Union was to be perpetual. No article of the Confederation was to be altered without the consent of every State.

So much for the mutual covenants.

Secondly. The Delegations of power by each of the States to all the States, in general Congress assembled, upon a like analysis, may be stated as follows:—

1st. The sole and exclusive power to determine on war and peace, except in case a State should be invaded or menaced with invasion.

2d. To send and receive Ambassadors.

3d. To make Treaties, with a Proviso, etc.

4th. To establish rules for Captures.

5th. To grant Letters of Marque and Reprisal.

6th. To appoint Courts for Trial of Piracies and other crimes, specified.

7th. To decide Questions of Dispute, between two or more States, in a prescribed manner.

8th. The sole and exclusive power to coin Money, and regulate the value.

9th. To fix the standard of Weights and Measures.

10th. To regulate trade with the Indian Tribes.

11th. To establish Post-Offices.

12th. To appoint all officers of land forces, except Regimental.

13th. To appoint all officers of the Naval Forces.

14th. To make rules and regulations for the Government of Land and Naval Forces.

15th. To appropriate and apply public money for public expenses, the common defence and general welfare.

16th. To borrow money and emit bills of credit.

17th. To build and equip a navy.

18th. To agree upon the number of land forces, and make requisitions upon the States, for their quotas, in proportion to the number of white inhabitants in each State.

The foregoing powers were delegated, with this limitation—the war power, the treaty power, the power to coin money, the power to regulate the value thereof, the power of fixing the quotas of money to be raised by the States, the power to emit bills of credit, the power to borrow money, the power to appropriate money, the power to regulate the number of land and naval forces, the power to appoint a commander-in-chief for the army or navy, were never to be exercised, unless nine of the States were assenting to the same.

These are the general provisions of the Articles of Confederation of 1777–1781.

JUDGE BYNUM. They are much more numerous and embrace a great many more subjects than I was aware of.

MR. STEPHENS. They embrace nearly the entire ground covered by the present Constitution. That is apparent to all who will carefully compare the provisions of both instruments. But the present object, before going into an examination of a like analysis of the provisions of the new Constitution, is to trace the workings of the old one, the evils or mischiefs discovered in its practical operation, and the remedies sought to be applied in the new. What then were the striking defects in the old system, so far as the want of additional powers was concerned and the remedy which the new Constitution supplied ? Without any fear of successful contradiction, it may be said that these consisted of but two. One was the want of power on the part of the States in Congress assembled, to regulate trade with foreign nations, and between the States, as well as with the Indian Tribes; and the other was the want of a like power to lay taxes directly upon the people of the several States, or to raise revenue by levying duties upon imports, without resorting to requisitions, or quotas, upon the States, in their organized political capacity. This is abundantly clear from the history of the times, and the action of the States in Congress assembled, under the Articles of Confederation. The first movement for additional power, or a change of the Constitution, in any respect, was in Congress, on the 3d of February, 1781.* This was an adoption by the States, in Congress assembled, of the following resolution:

"*Resolved*, That it be recommended to the several States, as indispensably necessary, that they vest a power in Congress to levy, for the use of the United States, a duty of five per cent. *ad valorem*, at the time and place of importation, upon all goods, wares, and merchandise, of foreign growth or manufacture, which may be imported into any of the said States, from any foreign port, island, or plantation, after the 1st day of May, 1781; except arms, ammunition, clothing, and other articles imported on account of the United States, or any of them; and except wool cards, and cotton cards, and wire for making them; and, also, except salt, during the war.

"Also, a like duty of five per cent. on all prizes and prize goods, condemned in the court of admiralty of any of these States, as lawful prize.

"That the moneys arising from said duties be appro-

---

* *Elliot's Debates*, vol. i, p. 92.

priated to the discharge of the principal and interest of the debts already contracted, or which may be contracted, on the faith of the United States, for supporting the present war.

"That the said duties be continued until the said debts shall be fully and finally discharged."

This proposition was not concurred in by the States, and it is useless to trace its history and final rejection.

The second effort at amendment was in 1783, after the war was over, and the independence of the States acknowledged. On the 18th of April, 1783, Congress adopted the following resolution:

"*Resolved, by nine States,* that it be recommended to the several States as indispensably necessary to the restoration of public credit, and to the punctual and honorable discharge of the public debts, to invest the United States, in Congress assembled, with the power to levy, for the use of the United States, the following duties upon goods imported into the said States from any foreign port, island, or plantation," etc.* Then follows a long list of articles on which it was asked to vest the United States, in Congress assembled, with the power to levy duties upon, and the rate of duty proposed.

This request of Congress for additional powers, though accompanied by an able and strong letter from Congress to the States, asking them to make "the constitutional change" proposed, was never acceded to by the States, and no farther notice of it is necessary here.

On the 30th of April, 1784, Congress again "recommended to the Legislatures of the several States to vest the United States, in Congress assembled, for the term of fifteen years," etc., with certain specified powers over

---

* *Elliot's Debates*, vol. i, p. 93.

commerce with foreign nations. This proposition was also rejected by the States. Several States agreed to it, but it lacked the necessary number to carry it into effect.

The next movement to effect a change in the Articles of Confederation was by Mr. Monroe, in Congress, July, 1785. His proposition was for the States to vest in the United States, in Congress assembled, "the power of regulating trade." Congress never acted upon this proposition. "It was deemed, in the language of the day, that any proposition for perfecting the Articles of Confederation should originate with the State Legislatures."* Accordingly, Mr. Madison went into the Legislature of Virginia, and under his auspices a movement was made in that body, in December, 1785, with a view to vest in the United States, in Congress assembled, the powers that had been previously proposed by the Congress. This first movement in the Virginia Legislature failed; but subsequently, on the 21st of January, 1786, that body passed the following resolution: "*Resolved*, That Edmund Randolph, James Madison, Jr., Walter Jones, St. George Tucker, Meriwether Smith, David Ross, William Ronald, and George Mason, Esquires, be appointed Commissioners, who, or any five of whom, shall meet such Commissioners as may be appointed by the other States in the Union, at a time and place to be agreed on, to take into consideration the trade of the United States; to examine the relative situation and trade of the said States; to consider how far a uniform system in their commercial regulations may be necessary to their common interest and their permanent harmony; and to report to the several States such an act relative

---

* *Elliot's Debates*, vol. i, p. 111.

to this great object as when unanimously ratified by them, will enable the United States, in Congress assembled, to provide for the same; That the said Commissioners shall immediately transmit to the several States copies of the preceding resolution, with a circular letter requesting their concurrence therein, and proposing a time and place for the meeting aforesaid."*

Four other States responded to this resolution of the Virginia Legislature, to wit: New York, New Jersey, Pennsylvania, and Delaware. They all appointed Commissioners, as suggested by Virginia. These Commissioners met in convention at Annapolis, in Maryland, 11th September, 1786. They did nothing, however, but make a report to the Legislatures appointing them and recommending the calling of a General Convention of all the States, to meet at Philadelphia on the second Monday in May, 1787, "to take into consideration the situation of the United States; to devise such further provisions as shall appear to them necessary to render the Constitution of the Federal Government adequate to the exigencies of the Union; and to report such an Act for that purpose to the United States, in Congress assembled, as when agreed to by them, and afterwards confirmed by the Legislatures of every State, will effectually provide for the same."†

As a reason for this course, they say "they are the more naturally led to this conclusion, as, in the course of their reflections on the subject, they have been induced to think that the power of regulating trade is of such comprehensive extent, and will enter so far into the general system of the Federal Government, that, to give it efficacy, and to obviate questions and doubts con

* *Elliot's Debates*, vol. i, p. 115. † *Elliot's Debates*, vol. i, p. 118.

cerning its precise nature and limits, may requre a correspondent adjustment of other parts of the Federal system."

This communication was addressed to the States from whom the parties held their commissions, and copies of it were likewise sent to the United States, in Congress assembled, and to the Executives of all the States. The Congress took up the subject on the 21st of February, 1787, and came to the following resolution upon it:

"*Resolved*, That, in the opinion of Congress, it is expedient that, on the second Monday in May next, a Convention of Delegates, who shall have been appointed by the several States, be held at Philadelphia, for the sole and express purpose of revising the Articles of Confederation, and reporting to Congress and the several Legislatures, such alterations and provisions therein as shall, when agreed to in Congress, and confirmed by the States, render the Federal Constitution adequate to the exigencies of Government, and the preservation of the Union."

It was under this resolution of Congress that the ever-memorable Federal Convention of 1787 was called and met. The initiative step to this movement was the resolution of the 21st of January, 1786, of the Virginia Legislature. Mr. Madison was the author of that resolution, though it was offered by Mr. Tyler, father of the late Ex-President Tyler. Mr. Madison's agency in first starting this movement is what has given him the title of father of the present Constitution. In none of these proceedings, either in Congress, or in the Virginia Legislature, or in the communication of the Commissioners at Annapolis, is there any intimation of a wish or desire to change the nature of the Government, then existing, in any of its essential Federative features. It does, however, very clearly appear, from the letter of the Commissioners, that, in granting additional powers to the United States, in Congress assembled, it might and would be, in their opinion, proper to make "a correspondent adjustment of other parts of the Federal system." This, doubtless, referred to a division of the powers vested in the States, jointly, under the then Constitution. These were mostly, as we have seen, committed to one body—to the Congress of the States.

Already, the idea had begun to develop itself, of introducing a new feature in the Federal plan—that of dividing the powers delegated, into Legislative and Executive departments, each distinct from the Judicial; and also dividing the Legislative department into two branches, or houses; and, further still, of allowing the Federal machinery to act directly upon the citizens of the States in special cases, and not on the States in their corporate capacity, as had been in all former Confederacies. This idea, at first, was not fully developed. All new truths are slow of development. Mankind, generally, at first, see new truths indistinctly; as the man we read of in the Scriptures, who, having been born blind, when his eyes were opened, at first, "saw men, as trees, walking." This new feature, or new features, in the Federal plan is but dimly shadowed forth in the letter of the Commissioners, wherein they speak of some necessary correspondent adjustment of the Federal system. Mr. Jefferson, soon after, gives the idea more form and substance, in a letter to Mr. Madison, written at Paris, 16th of December, 1786. Here is his letter:—

"I find, by the public papers, that your Commercial Convention failed in point of Representation. If it should produce a full meeting in May, and a broader reformation, it will still be well. To make us one nation, as to foreign concerns, and keep us distinct in domestic ones, gives the outline of the proper division of powers between the general and particular Governments. But, to enable the Federal head to exercise the powers, given it, to best advantage, it *should be organized, as the particular ones are,* into Legislative, Executive and Judiciary. The first and last are already separated. The second should be. When last with Congress, I often proposed to members to do this, by making of the Committee of the States an Executive Committee, during the recess of Congress; and, during its session, to appoint a committee to receive and despatch all Executive business, so that Congress itself should meddle only with what should be Legislative. But I question if any Congress (much less all successively) can have self-denial enough to go through with this distribution. The distribution, then, should be imposed on them."*

This, as far as I have been able to discover, after no inconsiderable research, is the first embodied conception of the general outline of those proper changes of the old Constitution or Articles of Confederation, which were subsequently, as we shall see, actually and in fact, ingrafted on the old system of Confederations; and which makes the most marked difference between ours, and all other like systems. Of all the Statesmen in this country, none ever excelled Mr. Jefferson in grasp of political ideas, and a thorough understanding of the principles of human Government.

This is a brief, but unquestionable, history of the complaints under the old system. The great leading object, at the time, with Congress, was to get additional power to regulate trade, and to raise revenue directly by law,

---

* *Jefferson's Complete Works*, vol. ii, p. 66.

Engraved by H.B. Hall from an original Portrait by G. Stuart.

THOMAS JEFFERSON.

Th: Jefferson

operating on the individual citizens of the States, and not on the States in their corporate character. Under the Articles of Union, as they then were, Congress could regulate trade, as we have seen, with the Indian tribes, but not between the States respectively, or with foreign nations; nor could they raise revenue, as we have seen, except by requisitions upon the States. The main and leading objects were to get the Federal Constitution amended in these particulars. Could these new ideas and new principles be incorporated in a system strictly Federal? This was the great problem of that day. Congress gave consent to the calling of a Convention of the States, as desired, *for the sole and express purpose* of revising the Articles of Confederation, to the attainment, if possible, of these ends and objects. No intimation was given, in any of the proceedings that led to the call of this Convention, of any wish, much less a desire, to change the character of the Federal system, or to transform it from a Confederate Republic, as it was then acknowledged to be, into a consolidated nation. It is important to pay strict attention to the proceedings at this time. The Convention was called, not to change the nature of the General Government, but to delegate to it some few additional powers, and to adjust its machinery, in accordance with these additional powers. It was with this view, and for this purpose, with this "sole and express purpose," that the States, in Congress, gave the movement their sanction. Now, then, how did this matter proceed? How did the States, in their Sovereign capacities, respond to this call for a Convention, to change the Articles of their Confederation, so as to remedy the evils complained of? Each of the States, be it remembered, at that time, was a perfect State, clothed with all the attributes of Sovereignty. In our inquiries into the nature and extent of the changes in the fundamental law, especially so far as they trenched upon the Sovereign powers of the States, proposed by that Convention, it is of the utmost importance to know what the States did, both anterior to the call of the Convention, and subsequently.

Let us, then, direct our special attention to the responses of each of the States to the call itself. Here are the responses of all of them.* We will take them up singly and separately.

FIRST, GEORGIA.

The response of my own State is seen in the following ordinance:

"An ordinance for the appointment of deputies from this State for the purpose of revising the Federal Constitution.

"Be it ordained, by the Representatives of the State of Georgia, in General Assembly met, and by authority of the same, that William Few, Abraham Baldwin, William Pierce, George Walton, William Houston, and Nathaniel Pendleton, Esqrs., be, and they are hereby, appointed Commissioners, who, or any two or more of them, are hereby authorized, as deputies from this State, to meet such deputies as may be appointed and authorized by other States, to assemble in Convention at Philadelphia, and to join with them in devising and discussing all such alterations and further provisions as may be necessary to render the Federal Constitution adequate to the exigencies of the Union, and in reporting such an Act for that purpose to the United States in Congress assembled, as, when agreed to by them, and duly confirmed by the several States, will effectually provide for the same. In

* *Elliot's Debates*, vol. i, pp. 126–138.

case of the death of any of the said Deputies, or of their declining their appointments, the Executive is hereby authorized to supply such vacancies."

By virtue of this ordinance, the Governor of the State issued commissions, or credentials, to the several Delegates thus appointed. I read one of these. The others are exactly similar to it.

"The State of Georgia, by the grace of God, free, Sovereign, and Independent:

"To the HON. WILLIAM FEW, ESQR.:

"*Whereas*, you, the said William Few, are, in and by an Ordinance of the General Assembly of our said State, nominated and appointed a Deputy to represent the same in a Convention of the United States, to be assembled at Philadelphia, for the purposes of devising and discussing all such alterations and further provisions as may be necessary to render the Federal Constitution adequate to the exigencies of the Union—

"You are, therefore, hereby commissioned to proceed on the duties required of you in virtue of the said ordinance.

"Witness our trusty and well-beloved George Matthews, Esq., our Captain-General, Governor, Commander-in-chief, under his hand and our great seal, this 17th day of April, in the year of our Lord 1787, and of our Sovereignty and Independence the eleventh."

Signed by the Governor and countersigned by his Secretary.

From this it clearly appears that Georgia responded to the call for a Convention of her Co-Sovereign States, with the sole view of discussing and making such alterations in their then Federal Constitution as might be deemed proper and necessary for the better providing for the exigencies of "the Union." That is, the continued

Union of Sovereign Confederated States. Nothing could have been further from the intention of Georgia, or the Congress, than a dissolution of that Union by a general merger of all the people of the United States in one Nation. The object was to preserve the Union as it existed, and not to destroy it.

How utterly demolishing this record is to the reported statement of Mr. Pinckney, quoted by Judge Story, "that no one of the distinguished band of patriots of that day ever thought of the separate independence of the several States." The commission of Governor Mathews shows beyond cavil that at least one of those distinguished patriots, and at least one of those States, not only thought of such an idea, but acted upon it, as a known, fixed, and acknowledged fact. This fact was set forth in the credentials by which the Delegates from Georgia were received by their associates from all the other States. They were received into the Federal Convention, as Delegates from a State *claiming* at least to be Free, Sovereign, and Independent; and, being so received, all the other parties which so received them should be held to be forever estopped from denying the character of the powers or authority under which they were received and acted. This commission shows, too, that this claim of Sovereignty and Independence was from the date that her Delegates in Congress, in her name, and by her Paramount authority, had joined the Delegates from all the other States in proclaiming the great fact in their general Declaration on the ever memorable 4th of July, 1776.

"The 17th of April," says Governor Mathews, "in the year of our Lord, 1787, and of *our* Sovereignty and Independence the eleventh."

The responses of all the States which did respond (and

all did respond except Rhode Island), are no less significant than that of Georgia. It is quite a labor to go through with them all, but the important bearing they have upon the great questions we are now considering, requires not only that we should look into them, but examine them thoroughly, and scan them closely. These establish very essential facts, to which we should look in our inquiry. They are the deep footprints of truth, impressed upon our earlier history, which assertion can never obliterate, argument cannot remove, sophistry cannot obscure, time cannot erase, and which even wars can never destroy! However upheaved the foundations of society may be by political convulsions, these will stick to the very fragments of the rocks of our primitive formation, bearing their unerring testimony to the ages to come!

The responses of all the States show conclusively the great indisputable fact that they all, at that time, claimed to be Sovereign and Independent, and that their *sole object* in going into Convention at that time was barely to provide for such changes as could be made in their then Constitution, as experience had shown to be proper, and not to change its Federal character. Let us examine each of them closely.

SECOND, MASSACHUSETTS.*

The response of your State, Judge, appears from the following commission to her Delegates:

"By his excellency, James Bowdoin, Esq., Governor of the Commonwealth of Massachusetts.

"To the Hon. Francis Dana, Elbridge Gerry, Nathaniel Gorham, Rufus King, and Caleb Strong, Esqs., greeting·

---

* For all these responses, see *Elliot's Debates*, vol. i, pp. 126–138.

"*Whereas*, Congress did, on the 21st day of February, A. D., 1787, Resolve, 'That, in the opinion of Congress, it is expedient that, on the second Monday in May next, a Convention of Delegates, who shall have been appointed by the several States, be held at Philadelphia, for the *sole and express purpose* of revising the Articles of Confederation, and reporting to Congress and the several Legislatures such alterations and provisions therein as shall, when agreed to in Congress, and confirmed by the States, render the Federal Constitution adequate to the exigencies of government and the preservation of the Union:'

"*And whereas*, the General Court have constituted and appointed you their Delegates, to attend and represent this Commonwealth in the said proposed Convention, and have, by a resolution of theirs of the 10th of March last, requested me to commission you for that purpose:

"Now, therefore, know ye, That, in pursuance of the resolutions aforesaid, I do, by these presents, commission you, the said Francis Dana, Elbridge Gerry, Nathaniel Gorham, Rufus King, and Caleb Strong, Esqrs., or any three of you, to meet such Delegates as may be appointed by the other, or any of the other States in the Union, to meet in Convention at Philadelphia, at the time and for the purposes aforesaid.

"In testimony whereof, I have caused the public seal of the Commonwealth aforesaid to be hereunto affixed.

"Given at the Council Chamber, in Boston, the ninth day of April, A. D., 1787, and in the eleventh year of the Independence of the United States of America."

THIRD, CONNECTICUT.

The response of your State, Professor, is seen in the following act of its General Assembly of the second Thursday of May, 1787:

"An Act for appointing Delegates to meet in Convention of the States to be held at Philadelphia, on the second Monday of May instant.

"*Whereas*, the Congress of the United States, by their Act of the 21st February, 1787, have recommended that, on the second Monday of May instant, a Convention of Delegates, who shall have been appointed by the several States, be held at Philadelphia, for the *sole and express purpose* of revising the Articles of Confederation:

"Be it enacted by the Governor, Council, and Representatives, in General Court assembled, and by the authority of the same, That the Hon. William Samuel Johnson, Roger Sherman, and Oliver Ellsworth, Esqrs., be, and they hereby are, appointed Delegates to attend the said Convention, and are requested to proceed to the City of Philadelphia, for that purpose, without delay; and the said Delegates, and, in case of sickness or accident, such one or more of them as shall attend the said Convention, is, and are hereby authorized and empowered to represent this State therein, and to confer with such Delegates appointed by the several States, *for the purposes mentioned in the said* Act of Congress, that may be present and duly empowered to sit in said Convention, and to discuss upon such alterations and provisions, agreeably to the general principles of Republican Government, as they shall think proper to render the Federal Constitution adequate to the exigencies of government and the preservation of the Union; and they are further directed, pursuant to the said Act of Congress, to report such alterations and provisions as may be agreed to by a majority of the United States represented in Convention, to the Congress of the United States, and to the General Assembly of this State."

FOURTH, NEW YORY.

The State of New York, by a joint resolution of her Legislature, passed the 6th of March, 1787, responded as follows:

"*Resolved*, That the Hon. Robert Yates, John Lansing, Jr., and Alexander Hamilton, Esqs., be, and they are hereby declared duly nominated and appointed Delegates, on the part of this State, to meet such Delegates as may be appointed on the part of the other States, respectively, on the second Monday in May next, at Philadelphia, for the *sole and express purpose* of revising the Articles of Confederation, and reporting to Congress, and to the several Legislatures, such alterations and provisions therein as shall, when agreed to in Congress, and confirmed by the several States, render the Federal Constitution adequate to the exigencies of government and the preservation of the Union."

To these proceedings Governor Clinton, Governor of the State, officially certified in the following words:

"In testimony whereof I have caused the privy seal of the said State to be hereunto affixed this ninth day of May, in the eleventh year of the Independence of the said State."

FIFTH, NEW JERSEY.

The State of New Jersey responded as follows:

"To the Hon. David Brearly, William Churchill Houston, William Patterson, and John Neilson, Esqs., greeting:

"The Council and Assembly, reposing especial trust and confidence in your integrity, prudence, and ability, have, at a joint meeting, appointed you, the said David Brearly, William Churchill Houston, William Patterson, and John Neilson, Esqs., or any three of you, Commissioners, to meet such Commissioners as have been, or may be, appointed by the other States in the Union, at the City of Philadelphia, in the Commonwealth of Pennsylvania, on the second Monday in May next, for the *purpose* of taking into consideration the state of the Union as to *trade and other important* objects, and of devising such other provisions as shall appear to be necessary to render the Constitution of the Federal Government adequate to the exigencies thereof.

"In testimony whereof, the great seal of the State is hereunto affixed. Witness, William Livingston, Esq., Governor, Captain-General, and Commander-in-chief, in and over the State of New Jersey, and territories thereunto belonging, Chancellor and Ordinary in the same, at Trenton, the 23d day of November, in the year of our Lord, 1786, and of our Sovereignty and Independence the eleventh."

SIXTH, PENNSYLVANIA.

The State of Pennsylvania responded as follows:

"An Act appointing Deputies to the Convention, intended to be held in the City of Philadelphia, for the Purpose of revising the Federal Constitution.

"Sec. 1. Whereas, the General Assembly of this Commonwealth, taking into their serious consideration, the representations heretofore made to the Legislatures of the several States in the Union, by the United States in Congress assembled, and also weighing the difficulties under which the Confederated States now labor, are fully convinced of the necessity of revising the Federal Constitution, for the purpose of making such alterations and amendments as the exigencies of our public affairs require: And, whereas, the Legislature of the State of Virginia have already passed an Act of that Commonwealth, empowering certain Commissioners to meet at the City of Philadelphia, in May next, a Convention of

Commissioners or Deputies from the different States; and the Legislature of this State are fully sensible of the important advantages which may be derived to the United States, and every of them, from co-operating with the Commonwealth of Virginia, and the other States to the Confederation, in the said design.

"Sec. 2. Be it enacted, and it is hereby enacted, by the Representatives of the freemen of the Commonwealth of Pennsylvania, in General Assembly met, and by the authority of the same, That Thomas Mifflin, Robert Morris, George Clymer, Jared Ingersoll, Thomas Fitzsimmons, James Wilson, and Gouverneur Morris, Esqrs., are hereby appointed Deputies from this State, to meet in the Convention of the Deputies of the respective States of North America, to be held at the City of Philadelphia, on the 2d day in the month of May next; and the said Thomas Mifflin, Robert Morris, George Clymer, Jared Ingersoll, Thomas Fitzsimmons, James Wilson, and Gouverneur Morris, Esqrs., or any four of them, are hereby constituted and appointed Deputies from this State, with powers to meet such Deputies as may be appointed and authorized by the other States, to assemble in the said Convention, at the city aforesaid, and join with them in devising, deliberating on, and discussing, all such *alterations* and *further provisions* as may be necessary to render the *Federal Constitution* fully adequate to the exigencies of the Union, and in reporting such act or acts, for that purpose, to the United States in Congress assembled, as, when agreed to by them, and duly confirmed by the several States, will effectually provide for the same.

"Sec. 3. And be it further enacted by the authority aforesaid, That, in case any of the said Deputies hereby nominated shall happen to die, or to resign his or their said appointment or appointments, the supreme executive council shall be, and hereby are, empowered and required to nominate and appoint other person or persons, in lieu of him or them so deceased, or who has or have so resigned, which person or persons, from and after such nomination and appointment, shall be, and hereby are, declared to be vested with the same powers respectively as any of the Deputies nominated and appointed by this Act is vested with by the same; provided always, that the council are not hereby authorized, nor shall they make any such nomination or appointment, except in vacation and during the recess of the General Assembly of the State."

This Act passed December 30th, 1786. By a supplemental Act passed the 28th day of March, 1787, Dr. Franklin was appointed as an additional Delegate.

SEVENTH, DELAWARE.

The State of Delaware responded as follows:

"His Excellency, Thomas Collins, Esqr., President, Captain-General, and Commander-in-chief, of the Delaware State.

"To all to whom these presents shall come, Greeting: Know ye, that, among the laws of the said State, passed by the General Assemby of the same, on the 3d day of February, in the year of our Lord, 1787, it is thus enrolled:—In the eleventh year of the Independence of the Delaware State.

"An Act appointing Deputies from this State to the Convention proposed to be held in the City of Philadelphia, for the Purpose of revising the Federal Constitution.

"*Whereas*, the General Assembly of this State are fully convinced of the necessity of *revising the Federal Constitution*, and adding thereto such further provisions as may render the same more adequate to the exigencies of the Union; and, whereas, the Legislature of Virginia have already passed an Act of that Commonwealth, appointing and authorizing certain Commissioners to meet, at the City of Philadelphia, in May next, a Convention of Commissioners or Deputies from the different States; and this State being willing and desirious of co-operating with the Commonwealth of Virginia, and the other States in the Confederation, in so useful a design:—

"Be it, therefore, enacted by the General Assembly of Delaware, that George Read, Gunning Bedford, John Dickinson, Richard Basset, and Jacob Broom, Esqrs., are hereby appointed Deputies from this State, to meet in the Convention of the Deputies of other States, to be held at the City of Philadelphia, on the 2d day of May next; and the said George Read, Gunning Bedford, John Dickinson, Richard Basset, and Jacob Broom, Esqrs., or any three of them, are hereby constituted and appointed Deputies from this State, with powers to meet such Deputies as may be appointed and authorized by the other States to assemble in the said Convention at the city aforesaid, and to join with them in devising, deliberating on, and discussing, such *alterations* and further *provisions* as may be necessary to render the Federal Constitution adequate to the exigencies of the Union; and in reporting such Act or Acts, for that purpose, to the United States in Congress assembled, as, when agreed to by them, and duly confirmed by the several States, may effectually provide for the same. So always and provided, that such alterations or further provisions, or any of them, do not extend to that part of the 5*th Article* of the Confederation of the said State, finally ratified on the 1st day of March, in the year 1781, which declares that, '*In determining* questions in the United States in Congress assembled, each State shall have one vote.' And be it enacted, That in case any of the said Deputies hereby nominated shall happen to die, or resign his or their appointment, the President or Commander-in-chief, with the advice of the privy council, in the recess of the General Assembly, is hereby authorized to supply such vacancies.

"In testimony whereof, I have hereunto subscribed my name, and caused the great seal of the said State to be affixed to these presents, at New Castle, the 2d day of April, in the year of our Lord, 1787, and in the 11th year of the Independence of the United States of America."

EIGHTH, MARYLAND.

The State of Maryland responded as follows:

"An Act for the Appointment of, and conferring Powers on, Deputies from this State to the Federal Convention.

"Be it enacted by the General Assembly of Maryland, That the Hon. James McHenry, Daniel of St. Thomas Jenifer, Daniel Carroll, John Francis Mercer, and Luther Martin, Esqrs., be appointed and authorized, on behalf of this State, to meet such Deputies as may be appointed and authorized, by any other of the United States, to assemble in Convention at Philadelphia, for the purpose of revising the Federal system, and to join with them in considering such alterations and further provisions as may be necessary to render the Federal Constitution adequate to the exigencies of the Union; and in reporting such an Act for that purpose, to the United States in Congress asssembled, as, when agreed to by them, and duly confirmed by the several States, will effectually provide for the same; and the said Deputies, or such of them as shall attend the said Convention, shall have full power to represent this State for the purposes aforesaid; and the said

Deputies are hereby directed to report the proceedings of the said Convention, and any Act agreed to therein, to the next Session of the General Assembly of this State."

NINTH, VIRGINIA.

The State of Virginia responded as follows:

"An Act for appointing Deputies from this Commonwealth to a Convention proposed to be held in the City of Philadelphia, in May next, for the purpose of revising the Federal Constitution.

"*Whereas,* the Commissioners who assembled at Annapolis, on the 14th day of September last, for the purpose of devising and reporting the means of enabling Congress to provide effectively for the Commercial interests of the United States, have represented the necessity of extending the revision of the Federal system to all its defects, and have recommended that Deputies, for that purpose, be appointed by the several Legislatures, to meet in Convention, in the City of Philadelphia, on the 2d day of May next,—a provision which was preferable to a discussion of the subject in Congress, where it might be too much interrupted by the ordinary business before them, and where it would, besides, be deprived of the valuable counsels of sundry individuals who are disqualified by the Constitution or laws of particular States, or restrained by peculiar circumstances from a seat in that Assembly: and whereas the General Assembly of this Commonwealth, taking into view the actual situation of the Confederacy, as well as reflecting on the alarming representations made, from time to time, by the United States in Congress, particularly in their Act of the 15th day of February last, can no longer doubt that the crisis is arrived at which the good people of America are to decide the solemn question—whether they will, by wise and magnanimous efforts, reap the just fruits of that independence which they have so gloriously acquired, and of that Union which they have cemented with so much of their common blood—or whether, by giving way to unmanly jealousies and prejudices, or to partial and transitory interests, they will renounce the auspicious blessings prepared for them by the Revolution, and furnish to its enemies an eventful triumph over those by whose virtues and valor it has been accomplished: And whereas the same noble and extended policy, and the same fraternal and affectionate sentiments, which originally determined the Citizens of this Commonwealth to unite with their brethren of the other States in establishing a Federal Government, cannot but be felt with equal force now as motives to lay aside every inferior consideration, and to concur in such further concessions and provisions as may be necessary to secure the great objects for which that Government was instituted, and to render the United States as happy in peace as they have been glorious in war:—

"Be it, therefore, enacted by the General Assembly of the Commonwealth of Virginia, That Seven Commissioners be appointed, by joint ballot of both Houses of Assembly, who, or any three of them, are hereby authorized, as Deputies from this Commonwealth, to meet such Deputies as may be appointed and authorized by other States, to assemble in Convention at Philadelphia, as above recommended, and to join with them in devising and discussing all such alterations and further provisions as may be necessary to render the Federal Constitution adequate to the exigencies of the Union; and in reporting such an Act, for that purpose, to the United States in Congress, as, when agreed to by them, and duly confirmed by the several States, will effectually provide for the same.

"And be it further enacted, That, in case of the death of any of the said Deputies, or of their declining their appointments, the Executive is hereby authorized to supply such vacancies; and the Governor is requested to transmit forthwith a copy of this Act to the United States in Congress, and to the Executives of each of the States in the Union."

Under this Act, Deputies were appointed, as provided; at the head of the list of whom was placed George Washington.

TENTH, NORTH CAROLINA.

The State of North Carolina responded, as appears from the following Commission to her Deputies given by the Governor:

"To the Hon. Alexander Martin, Esq., greeting:

"*Whereas*, our General Assembly, in their late session, holden at Fayetteville, by adjournment, in the month of January last, did, by joint ballot of the Senate and House of Commons, elect Richard Caswell, Alexander Martin, William Richardson Davie, Richard Dobbs Spaight, and Willie Jones, Esqrs., Deputies to attend a Convention of Delegates from the several United States of America, proposed to be held at the City of Philadelphia, in May next, for the purpose of *revising* the Federal Constitution:

"We do, therefore, by these presents, nominate, commissionate, and appoint you, the said Alexander Martin, one of the Deputies for and in behalf, to meet with our other Deputies at Philadelphia on the 1st of May next, and with them, or any two of them, to confer with such Deputies as may have been, or shall be appointed by the other States, for the purpose aforesaid: To hold, exercise, and enjoy the appointment aforesaid, with all powers, authorities, and emoluments, to the same belonging, or in any wise appertaining, you conforming in every instance to the Act of our said Assembly, under which you are appointed.

"Witness, Richard Caswell, Esq., our Governor, Captain-General, and Commander-in-Chief, under his hand and our seal, at Kinston, the 24th day of February, in the eleventh year of our independence, A. D. 1787."

Similar Commissions were given to each of the other Delegates appointed.

ELEVENTH, SOUTH CAROLINA.

The State of South Carolina responded as follows:

"By his Excellency, Thomas Pinckney, Esq., Governor and Commander-in-Chief, in and over the State aforesaid:

"To the Hon. John Rutledge, Esq., greeting:

"By virtue of the power and authority invested by the Legislature of this State, in their Act passed the 8th day of March last, I do hereby commission you, the said John Rutledge, as one of the Deputies appointed from this State, to meet such Deputies or Commissioners as may be appointed and authorized by other of the United States to assemble in Convention, at the City of Philadelphia, in the month of May next, or as soon thereafter as may be, and to join with such Deputies or Commissioners (they being duly authorized and empowered) in devising and discussing all such alterations, clauses, articles, and provisions, as may be thought necessary to render the Federal Constitution entirely adequate to the actual situation and future good government of the Confederated States; and that you, together with the said Deputies or Commissioners, or a majority of them, who shall be present (provided the State be not represented by less than two), do join in reporting such an act to the United States, in Congress assembled, as, when approved and agreed to by them, and duly ratified and confirmed by the several States, will effectually provide for the exigencies of the Union.

"Given under my hand and the Great Seal of the State, in the City of Charleston, this 10th day of April, in the year of our Lord 1787, and of the Sovereignty and Independence of the United States of America, the eleventh."

Signed by the Governor, and countersigned by the Secretary.

TWELFTH, NEW HAMPSHIRE.

The State of New Hampshire responded, in the language of the following Act of her Legislature:

"An Act for appointing Deputies from this State to the Convention proposed to be holden in the City of Philadelphia in May, 1787, for the purpose of revising the Federal Constitution.

"*Whereas,* in the formation of the Federal Compact, which frames the bond of union of the American States, it was not possible, in the infant state of our Republic, to devise a system which, in the course of time and experience, would not manifest imperfections that it would be necessary to reform:

"And whereas, the limited powers, which, by the Articles of Confederation, are vested in the Congress of the United States, have been found far inadequate to the enlarged purposes which they were intended to produce; and whereas, Congress hath, by repeated and most urgent representations, endeavored to awaken this, and other States of the Union, to a sense of the truly critical and alarming situation in which they may inevitably be involved, unless timely measures be taken *to enlarge the powers of Congress*, that they may thereby be enabled to avert the dangers which threaten our existence as a free and independent people; and whereas, this State hath been ever desirous to act upon the liberal system of the general good of the United States, without circumscribing its views to the narrow and selfish objects of partial convenience; and has been at all times ready to make every concession, to the safety and happiness of the whole, which justice and sound policy could vindicate:

"Be it therefore enacted, by the Senate and House of Representatives in General Court convened, that John Langdon, John Pickering, Nicholas Gilman, and Benjamin West, Esqs., be, and hereby are, appointed Commissioners; they, or any two of them, are hereby authorized and empowered, as Deputies from this State, to meet at Philadelphia said Convention, or any other place to which the Convention may be adjourned, for the purposes aforesaid, there to confer with such Deputies as are, or may be, appointed by the other States for similar purposes, and with them to discuss and to procure and decide upon the most effectual means to remedy the defects of our Federal Union, and to procure and secure the enlarged purposes which it was intended to effect, and to report such an Act to the United States in Congress, as, when agreed to by them, and duly confirmed by the several States, will effectually provide for the same."

From all these responses of the States, to the call for a Convention of the States, it clearly appears that the *sole* object of all was to change and modify the Articles of Confederation, so as better to provide for the wants and exigencies of "the Union," which must have meant the Union then existing, and which we have seen was a Union of Sovereign States. The object was not to change the

Federative character of that Union. This is an important point to be kept constantly in view, and never lost sight of. The Convention was called with this *sole* view, and the call was responded to by every State with this sole view.

Under the call and appointment of Delegates, as we have seen, the Convention did meet in Philadelphia, on the second Monday in May (14th of that month), 1787. Washington, a Deputy or Delegate from the State of Virginia, was chosen the President of the Convention. The Convention remained in session until the 17th of September thereafter—four months and three days. It was assembled as a Convention of the States. The Delegates represented distinct, separate, and acknowledged Sovereign powers. The vote upon all questions was taken by States, without respect to the number of Delegates from the several States respectively. Here is the Journal of their proceedings from the day of their meeting to their adjournment.* The result of their deliberations and actions was such changes in the Federal Constitution as were set forth in the paper which they presented to the States. This paper is what has ever since been known as the present Constitution of the United States. Now the great question that we have to consider is the nature and character of the alterations in the old fundamental law, or Constitution, the Articles of Confederation, which the new Constitution made. Is the *Federative feature* of "the Union" changed in it? This is the great question. If the Union, as it existed before, was a Compact between Sovereign States, as has been most conclusively shown, is there any thing upon the face of the proceedings of the Convention, or upon the face of the new Constitution, which shows, either

---

* *Elliot's Debates*, vol. i, pp. 139–318.

expressly or by implication, that any change of the character of the Union in this respect was either intended, contemplated, or, in fact, effected? Was there any change as to where ultimate Sovereignty and Paramount authority under our Institutions then rested or resided? Before the meeting of this Convention these were unquestionably acknowledged to dwell with the people of the States severally. Was any change in this particular effected by the new Constitution?

Prof. Norton. Do you wish an answer to your question now?

Mr. Stephens. Yes. It is best to have all points settled as we go.

Prof. Norton. Then, for myself, I will say, that, as I understand it, there was a thorough and radical change effected in the new Constitution in the very particular you refer to, and such change as utterly overthrows the whole theory which I clearly perceive it is your object to endeavor to establish, by the conclusions you are successively reaching. But what say you to adjourning for the present and resuming the subject hereafter?

Mr. Stephens. Certainly. A little relaxation will be quite agreeable to me. This, recollect, is Liberty Hall. The rules of the establishment are that all its inmates do just as they please. It is now about the usual time for me to take my accustomed evening walk. You, gentlemen, can all remain here and entertain yourselves with books, or in any other way you prefer, or join me in a stroll, just as your several inclinations lead.

Judge Bynum. We have had enough of books for the present. I am for the walk.

Prof. Norton. So am I.

Major Heister. Well, I certainly have no disposition either to secede or to be seceded from. It is against my principles. So we will all join you in the walk.

COLLOQUY IV.

THE NATURE OF THE UNION NOT CHANGED UNDER THE CONSTITUTION—ULTIMATE SOVEREIGNTY UNDER IT RESIDES WHERE IT DID UNDER THE CONFEDERATION—JUDGE STORY ON THE FIRST RESOLUTION OF THE FEDERAL CONVENTION—THE CONSTITUTION, AS THE CONFEDERATION, IS A GOVERNMENT OF STATES AND FOR STATES—THIS APPEARS FROM THE PREAMBLE ITSELF—THE UNION OF THE STATES WAS CONSOLIDATED BY THE CONSTITUTION, AND NOT ABROGATED AS IT WOULD HAVE BEEN BY A GENERAL MERGER OF THE STATE SOVEREIGNTIES—IT FORMS A CONFEDERATED REPUBLIC—SUCH A REPUBLIC IS FORMED BY THE UNION OF SEVERAL SMALLER REPUBLICS EACH RESPECTIVELY PUTTING LIMITED RESTRAINTS UPON THEMSELVES BY VOLUNTARY ENGAGEMENTS WITHOUT ANY IMPAIRMENT OF THEIR SEVERAL SOVEREIGNTIES, ACCORDING TO MONTESQUIEU AND VATTEL.

Mr. Stephens. Well, Professor, I believe we are all ready for your views upon the subjects discussed in our last talk upon the nature of the Government of the United States. I hope you are in good condition after a night's rest. You had something to say in answer to my last question, when we adjourned yesterday evening.

Prof. Norton. Yes. You asked if there was any change of Sovereignty effected by the Constitution, or, in other words, as I understood your question, whether the States, severally, did not retain their ultimate absolute Sovereignty under the Constitution, as fully and completely, as they did under the Articles of Confederation?

Mr. Stephens. Certainly, that was the purport of my question.

Prof. Norton. To this I replied, that I thought there was a change, and a radical change, in this respect, in the New Constitution from the Old, as you call it. In presenting my views on this point I, too. will premise so far as to say, that I never did agree with Judge Story in his historical account of the Declaration of Independence, and his argument founded thereon, that the people of the United States became one nation at that time, or during their Colonial existence. I have always agreed with Mr. Curtis and Mr. Motley, that the Declaration of Independence was made by the Colonies jointly, but for the independence of each separately. That they were so acknowledged to be separate Independent Sovereign States by Great Britain, in the Treaty of Peace, and that the first Union formed by the States, during their common struggle for that separate independence, was a Confederation between distinct separate Sovereign Powers. Further, that that Union was a Confederation of States. It was a bare *League*, founded upon Compact between distinct Powers, acknowledging each other to be Sovereign in all respects whatsoever; and I also hold it to be true, that the Convention of 1787 was called with *the sole* view of revising those articles of Union between the States for the purpose of making it a firm National Government between them as States for all external purposes, without changing the Federative basis of the Union. I do not question the material facts of our history as far as you have gone; nor can it be questioned that the States, in responding to this call for the Convention, understood it in that light. This, their respective responses, you have collated and read, conclusively show. But my position is, that after the Convention met, upon a conference and a free interchange of views with themselves, they found the defects in the old system to be so numerous and thorough (extending not only to the want of power in Congress to regulate trade, and the power to pass laws to operate directly on the people of the States in the collection of revenue, without resorting to requisitions on the States in their corporate or political capacities, but running through the whole system), that it was necessary, in order to do any thing efficiently, to abandon their instructions entirely, and with them, to abandon all idea of *remodelling* the Confederation. With these views and under these convictions, as I understand it, they determined to form and present to the whole American people a plan of government for them as one people or Nation, based upon the principle of a social Compact, and not upon any idea of a Compact between States, as the Articles of Confederation were, at that time, universally acknowledged to be. In other words, the Convention, as I maintain, came to the conclusion that the only cure or remedy for the innumerable defects and evils of the Articles of Confederation was a total abandonment of them, and all ideas of any government founded upon Compact between States, and to substitute in lieu of it a government of the whole people of all the States as one Nation.

My views on this subject are very well expressed by Mr. Motley, in that part of his article which you have referred to, but did not read. Here it is:—

"But there were patriotic and sagacious men in those days, and their efforts at last rescued us from the condition of a Confederacy. The Constitution of the United States was an organic law, enacted by the Sovereign people of that whole territory, which is commonly called, in geographies and histories, the United States of America. It was empowered to act directly, by its own Legislative, Judicial, and Executive machinery, upon every individual in the country. It could seize his property, it could take his life, for causes of which itself was the

Judge. The States were distinctly prohibited from opposing its decree or from exercising any of the great functions of Sovereignty. The Union alone was supreme, any thing in the Constitution and laws of the State to the contrary notwithstanding. Of what significance, then, was the title of 'Sovereign' States, arrogated, in later days, by communities which had voluntarily abdicated the most vital attributes of Sovereignty? * * *

"It was not a Compact. Whoever heard of a Compact to which there were no parties? or, whoever heard of a Compact made by a single party with himself? Yet the name of no State is mentioned in the whole document; the States themselves are only mentioned to receive commands or prohibitions, and the 'people of the United States' is the single party by whom alone the instrument is executed.

"The Constitution was not drawn up by the States, it was not promulgated in the name of the States, it was not ratified by the States. The States never acceded to it, and possess no power to secede from it. It was 'ordained and established' over the States by a power superior to the States—by the people of the whole land, in their aggregate capacity, acting through Conventions of Delegates, expressly chosen for the purpose within each State, independently of the State Governments, after the project had been framed."

This position of Mr. Motley, in the main, accords with my own, and it perfectly accords with another statement of Judge Story, with which I do fully agree, also; and that is when he says: "In the Convention that formed the Constitution of the United States, the first Resolution adopted by that body was 'that a National Government ought to be established, consisting of a Supreme, Legislative, Judiciary, and Executive.' And from this fundamental proposition sprung the subsequent organization of the whole Government of the United States." "It is then our duty (says Judge Story) to examine and consider the grounds on which this proposition rests, since it lies at the bottom of all our Institutions, State as well as National." I read from vol. ii, Book iii, ch. vii, § 518. I will not ask you to reply to me specially, but what reply have you to make to these positions of Mr. Motley and Judge Story. What say you to Judge Story's argument on this view of the subject?

MR. STEPHENS. In the first place I say, I am no less amazed at the statement of Judge Story, in the extract you have just read, than I was at the statement in the extract read by Judge Bynum from him before. It is, indeed, wonderful to me how Judge Story could have said, that from the *first* resolution passed by the Convention, which he quotes correctly, and which he speaks of as a fundamental proposition, the subsequent organization of the whole Government of the United States sprung. I shall show you, most conclusively, that this statement, and the whole argument built upon it, by him or others, have just as little ground to stand upon as his other statement and argument had, by your own admission. He says it is our duty to examine and consider the grounds on which this (his fundamental proposition) rests. Let us then so examine and so consider it, since in his judgment and yours it seems it lies at the bottom of all our Institutions, State as well as National. It certainly does lie at the bottom of his as well as your whole argument attempting to show that the Constitution of the United States established a National and not a Federal Government, and that it is not a Compact between Sovereign States.

Now, what grounds has this argument or consideration of the subject to rest upon? These and these only: The first Resolution passed by the Convention was as Judge Story states it, but it was not the first acted upon. It was the last of a series of three. The Convention was in committee of the whole, having under consideration a plan of Government, submitted by Governor Randolph, of Virginia. The series of Resolutions, of which the one alluded to by Judge Story is the last, was offered by Gouverneur Morris, of Pennsylvania, to be substituted in lieu of the first Resolution in the plan offered by Governor Randolph. Here are these Resolutions constituting this series:*

"1. *Resolved*, That a Union of the States, merely Federal, will not accomplish the objects proposed by the Articles of Confederation, namely, common defence, security of liberty, and general welfare.

"2. *Resolved*, That no treaty or treaties among any of the States, as Sovereign, will accomplish or secure their common defence, liberty, or welfare.

"3. *Resolved*, That a National Government ought to be established, consisting of a supreme Judicial, Legislative, and Executive."

The first two of these resolutions were not agreed to. It was said, that if the first of this series of resolutions was agreed to, the business of the Convention was at an end. The first two, therefore, were dropped. The last was taken up and adopted—but how adopted or in what sense, very clearly appears from Mr. Yates's account of it.† "This last Resolve," he says, "had also its difficulties; the term *supreme* required explanation. It was asked, whether it was intended to annihilate State Govern-

* *Elliot's Debates*, voi. i, p. 391. *Madison Papers* vol. ii, p. 747.

† *Elliot's Debates*, vol. i, p. 392.

ments? It was answered, only so far, as the powers intended to be granted to the new Government, should clash with the States, when the latter were to yield."

The resolution, with this explanation and understanding, then passed in Committee, eight States only being present. But the refusal of the Committee to agree to the other two, or, rather, their abandonment without a division, shows very clearly, to all fair and right-thinking minds, that it was not the intention of the Convention, by the adoption of this third resolution in Committee, to abandon the Federal system, and institute a National Government, as Judge Story argues; and that the Convention did not intend or indicate any purpose, thereby, to travel out of, or beyond their powers, which confined them, in the main, to the sole purpose of revising and amending the terms of their Union, on the basis of a Confederation of Sovereign States. Now, when these first two resolutions, which contained the gist of the whole question, had been abandoned without a count, it is easy to conceive that any one might have supposed that the object of this resolution, after the explanation given, was barely to declare that such changes in the Articles of Confederation were intended by it, as Mr. Jefferson had foreshadowed—that is, that, in the changes to be made, there should be a division, in the powers delegated, into Legislative, Judicial and Executive, without any departure from the *Federal basis* of the Union. This is, also, strengthened by the fact that Delaware voted for the resolution. It is well known that that State never would have voted for the resolution, with the construction put upon its words which Judge Story puts upon them. The introduction of the word *National* may not have struck the minds of the Delegates from Delaware and others, as bearing, or being intended to bear, the import now sought to be given to it, or which, upon close scrutiny, legitimately belongs to it. National was a word often loosely used in application to the Government under the Confederation, and even by the strictest adherents to the Sovereignty of the States. In the letter read yesterday from Mr. Jefferson, he spoke of the Government being so modelled as to make us one Nation as to all foreign powers, and yet separate and distinct Nations, as to ourselves. This Unity, or Nationality, as to foreign powers, was to be founded upon a *Federal basis* or Compact between the internal Nationalities. It is no strain of presumption, therefore, to suppose that this word was understood in this sense by many who voted for that resolution.

But the great controlling fact in the case, one that removes every particle of ground upon which Judge Story builds his entire theory of the Government, is, that subsequently, on the 20th of June, when the report of the Committee of the Whole was before the Convention, for consideration; after the whole plan, submitted by Governor Randolph, had been gone through with; after the ideas and objects of the members, generally, had been developed; and after the bearing of this word *National*, or the sense in which some used it, had been fully disclosed, and when eleven States were present, it was moved, by Mr. Ellsworth, of Connecticut, to strike out this resolution, that had been previously agreed to, as before stated, and to insert the following:—

"*Resolved*, That the Government of the *United States* ought to consist of a Supreme Legislative, Judiciary and Executive."*

This resolution was agreed to; and, after this action

* *Elliot's Debates*, vol. i, p. 183.

of the Convention upon this resolution, the word "National," wherever it occurred, throughout Governor Randolph's whole plan, was stricken out, and the "Government of the United States," or its equivalent, inserted. So, the "*fundamental proposition*," upon which Judge Story built his whole superstructure, is completely knocked from under him. The grounds, upon which it temporarily rested for the short space of twenty-one days, were completely removed by the Convention itself. The truth is, the debates between the 30th of May and the 20th of June, had disclosed the fact that there were quite a number of Delegates in the Convention, who were in favor of doing what Judge Story would make the impression, or seems really to think, that they had done. They were, as clearly appears from Gouverneur Morris's first resolution, for doing away with the *Federal* system entirely, and for establishing one great National Government; or, in other words, they were for abandoning the whole idea of a Federal Union, and incorporating the several State Sovereignties into one National Sovereignty.

Among these, none were more prominent or zealous than Governor Randolph and Mr. Madison, of Virginia, Mr. Morris and Mr. Wilson, of Pennsylvania, Mr. King, of Massachusetts, and Mr. Hamilton, of New York. These differed widely amongst themselves, as to the form of Government which should be instituted upon this National basis. Governor Randolph and Mr. Wilson seemed to have been for a Consolidated Democratic Republic, with two Houses for Legislation, and an Elective Executive. In this view, Mr. Madison concurred. Mr. Hamilton and Mr. Morris were also for one single National Republic, but based upon different principles. Some thought their scheme looked toward Monarchy,

but justice requires it to be stated, that nothing that fell from them, or either of them, in the debates, authorizes such a conclusion. They were all, however,—Randolph, Madison, Morris, Hamilton, Wilson and King—for a great National Republic, with a total departure from the Federal system. While the Nationals in the Convention were so divided, an overwhelming majority of the Delegates, as well as a majority of the States, were utterly opposed to either of their systems. Nothing could induce them to depart from the Federal system, or cause them to yield the equality of the States, as Sovereigns, in the Union, and the equality of their votes in all measures that might be passed upon by the new Government, as it was in the old. It was after this disclosure that the States agreed to the resolution of Mr. Ellsworth, to strike out "National Government," wherever it occurred in Governor Randolph's plan, and substitute for it, "Government of the United States." It was thus settled by the Convention, in their final action upon this very *first* resolution, that the work of their hands, whatever might be its details, was to be a plan, or organization, or Constitution, or Articles of Compact, call you it what you may, of a Government of States, of Sovereign States, formed and instituted by States and for States.

JUDGE BYNUM. You do not mean to say that the Government of the United States, under the Constitution as it was adopted, is nothing but a Government of States and for States?

MR. STEPHENS. I mean to say that it is a Government instituted *by* States and *for* States, and that all the functions it possesses, even in its direct action on the individual citizens of the several States, spring from and depend upon a Compact between the States constituting it. It is, therefore, a Government of *States and for States.* The final action upon the very first resolution, as we have seen, shows that the object of the Convention was to form a Government of States. "The Government of the United States" ought to consist, they declared, "of a Supreme Legislature, Judiciary and Executive." This is the same as if they had declared "the Government of the States United, ought to consist," etc. The first Constitution, we have seen, was a Government of States. The States in Congress assembled passed all laws, made all treaties, and exercised all powers vested in them jointly. No measure could be passed without the equal voice of each State, however small. Delaware had the same influence as New York, Massachusetts, or Virginia, and in this respect I maintain there is no *essential* change in the *new* Constitution. Examine it! Sift it, and dissect it as you may, and you will find it to be nothing but a Government of States, as much so, in principle, as the *old* Confederation. The powers to be exercised by the States jointly, Legislatively, Judicially, and Executively, have been enlarged, and it does not require so many States now to determine many questions as before; but under the present Constitution no measure can be passed, no law can be enacted, if a majority of the States oppose it.

JUDGE BYNUM. Why, Mr. Stephens, that is a most extraordinary position.

MR. STEPHENS. Extraordinary! My dear sir, is it not undeniably true? Has not each State an equal vote in the Senate? Can any law be passed if a majority of the States in the Senate withhold their sanction? The Senators, two to each State, are selected by the States, severally, in their corporate and Sovereign capacity. Can any treaty be made, if any more than a bare third of the States in the Senate refuse to agree to it? Can any man be appointed to any office of dignity or profit, if a majority of the States in the Senate vote against it? If the Electoral Colleges fail to choose a President, does not the election devolve upon the House of Representatives, where the election is by States, each State casting one vote only? If they fail to elect a Vice President does not the election devolve on the Senate, where no one can be chosen if a majority of the States vote against him? Can the Government be worked at all if a majority of the States in the Senate refuse their co-operation? If a majority of the States were to refuse to elect Senators would not the Government, of necessity, cease to exist? The Supreme Court of the United States has so held. Chief Justice Marshall, delivering the opinion, in the case of *Cohens* vs. *Virginia*, uses this language:*

"It is true, that if all the States, or a majority of them, refuse to elect Senators, the Legislative powers of the Union will be suspended!"

Hamilton, in the Convention from New York, when the Constitution was before that body for approval or disapproval, in reply to arguments going to show that the State authorities would be endangered by the powers conferred on the General Government, declared that "the Union is dependent on the will of the State Governments for its Chief Magistrate and for its Senate."† "The States," said Mr. Hamilton, "can never lose their powers till the whole people of America are robbed of their liberties." His great mind never gave utterance to a mightier truth!

Is it not entirely proper and correct, therefore, to say, of

---

* *Peters's Condensed Reports*, vol. v, p. 107. † *Elliot's Debates*, p. 353.

a Government that cannot be carried on rightfully at all against the will of a majority of the States, that it is a Government of States, and nothing but a Government of States?

JUDGE BYNUM. That is certainly a strong way of putting it, but, then, under the Constitution of the United States, there is a House of Representatives elected by the people of the States according to population. The larger or more populous States, have a great preponderance over the smaller or less populous ones, in that branch of the Congress; and even in the Senate the vote is not taken by States; it is taken *per capita*. Each Senator may vote as he pleases, and it often happens that the two Senators from a State, vote differently upon the same question; so that a law may pass without a majority of the States voting for it, and a treaty may be ratified without a majority of two thirds of the States voting for it.

MR. STEPHENS. That is also true, but it does not interfere in the least with what I have said, and maintain, that no law or measure can be passed if a majority of the States, through their Senators who represent their Sovereignty, vote against it. Under the system the power is with the States. If the Senators of a State be divided, the voice of that State is simply not heard on the question, exactly as it was under the Confederation, and in the Convention that formed the Constitution.* It is in such case as if the State voluntarily absented herself from the vote, and let the other States decide it. In this there is no change in the new system from the old. Under the Articles of Confederation, when the Delegation from a State was equally divided on any

---

* *Elliot's Debates*, vol. v, p. 285.

question, the vote of that State was not counted. It had no effect. The States, in forming the new Constitution, did make one concession, and that was that a House of Representatives, to be elected by the people in the several States, in proportion to population, on a certain basis, known ever as the Federal basis, might join in Legislation. But they never did yield their right to an equal vote in the Senate, or, that it might by possibility be without their power as States, to defeat any measure that the popular branch might adopt or pass. In this particular, relating only to the machinery and operation of the system, there is a change in the new Constitution from the old, but none in the principle. The equal voice of all the States, as States, on all questions coming before the Congress of States, now as before, though divided into two Houses, is still retained in the Senate. The right and power of holding a complete and absolute *veto* in the hands of a majority of the States, over the House, or the popular branch of the Congress, was, and is, retained in the States. This was the great point on which the Convention, that framed the Constitution, came near breaking up without agreeing to any thing. The Nationals, as they were called, insisted upon changing the principle of an equality of votes, on the part of the States, in the Senate. The Federals were willing to yield a change, as to the votes in the House, but would never yield their right to an equal voice in one, or the other of the branches of the Congress. They were determined to maintain an equality of political power in the States severally, in whatever form of Constitution might be adopted. It was at this stage of the proceedings that Dr. Franklin moved for prayers. On the first test vote on the motion to allow each State an equal vote in the Senate, the States stood five for it, and five against it, with one divided.* Eleven States only were present. New Hampshire was absent. It was at this stage of the proceedings, that Mr. Bedford, from Delaware, declared

"That all the States at present are equally Sovereign and Independent, has been asserted from every quarter in this House. Our deliberations here are a confirmation of the position, and I may add to it that each of them acts from interested, and many from ambitious motives. * * * The small States never can agree to the Virginia plan, and why, then, is it still urged? * * Let us then do what is in our power—*amend and enlarge the Confederation*, but not alter the Federal system."

The Virginia plan was Governor Randolph's National plan. It was after this dead lock, at which the Convention had come, between the Nationals and the State Sovereignty advocates, or Federals, as they were then called—between those who were in favor of what was called a National Government proper, and those in favor of the continued Union of the several States on a Federal basis—a Government National for external purposes, but leaving ultimate Sovereignty with the several States—after this speech of Mr. Bedford and like speeches of others—after it was seen that nothing could be done on the National line, that a Grand Committee was raised, consisting of one Member from each State, to see if any Compromise could be effected. The Committee consisted of Mr. Gerry, of Massachusetts, Mr. Ellsworth, of Connecticut, Mr. Yates, of New York, Mr. Patterson, of New Jersey, Dr. Franklin, of Pennsylvania, Mr. Bedford, of Delaware, Mr. Martin, of Maryland, Mr. Davie, of North

---

* *Elliot's Debates*, vol. i, p. 193.

Carolina, Mr. Rutledge, of South Carolina, and Mr. Baldwin, of Georgia.

Mr. Yates has given an exceedingly interesting account of the proceedings of this Grand Committee.* "The Grand Committee," says he, "met July 3d. Mr. Gerry was chosen Chairman. The Committee proceeded to consider in what manner they should discharge the business with which they were intrusted. By the proceedings in the Convention, they were so equally divided on the important question of *representation in the two branches*, that the idea of a conciliatory adjustment must have been in contemplation of the House in the appointment of this Committee. But still, how to effect this salutary purpose was the question. Many of the members, impressed with the utility of a General Government, connected with it the indispensable necessity of a representation from the States *according to their numbers and wealth;* while others, equally tenacious of the rights of the States, would admit of no representation but such as *was strictly Federal*, or, in other words, *equality of suffrage*. This brought on a discussion of the principles on which the House had divided, and a lengthy recapitulation of the arguments advanced in the House in support of these opposite propositions. As I had not openly explained my sentiments on any former occasion on this question, but constantly, in giving my vote, *showed my attachment to the National Government on Federal principles, I took this occasion to explain my motives.*

"These remarks gave rise to a motion of Dr. Franklin, which, after some modification, was agreed to, and made the basis of the following report of the Committee:

"'The Committee to whom was referred the eighth

---

* *Elliot's Debates*, vol. i, p. 477.

resolution reported from the Committee of the whole House, and so much of the seventh as had not been decided on, submit the following report:

"'That the subsequent propositions be recommended to the Convention, on condition that both shall be generally adopted.

"'That in the first branch of the Legislature, each of the States now in the Union be allowed one member for every forty thousand inhabitants of the description reported in the seventh resolution of the Committee of the whole House. That each State, not containing that number, shall be allowed one member.

"'That bills for raising or apportioning money, and for fixing salaries of the officers of Government of the United States, shall originate in the first branch of the Legislature, and shall *not* be *altered* or *amended* by the *second* branch; and that no money shall be drawn from the public treasury but in pursuance of appropriations to be originated in the first branch.

"'That in the second branch of the Legislature, *each State shall have an equal vote.*'"

This report was the *basis* of the great compromise, as it was called, between the two distinct parties in the Convention—the Nationals and the Federals. It discloses the nature and the extent of the contest. At first it would seem that it was a fair adjustment of the question—not so thought the vigilant sentinels and guardians of the Sovereignty of the States; for it conceded the absolute power of the popular branch of the Congress over the States in the Senate on one class of measures. That a majority of the States would not yield. The right of the States to hold an absolute negative in their own hands, in all cases, they would not give up. The first part of this report, after being discussed, and after it was ascertained that it could never receive the sanction of a majority of the States, was recommitted to a committee of five. Their report was also discussed, and likewise failed to receive the sanction of a majority of the States. The subject was then recommitted to another Grand Committee, consisting of one from each State, whose final report was agreed to. That fixed the number of members to which each State should be entitled in the first House of Representatives, and provided for future apportionments according to population, etc., as it stands in the Constitution. The clause in the *first* report, that gave the House of Representatives *absolute* power over *money, bills*, etc., was abandoned. The *latter part* of the *first* report, securing to the States severally an *equal vote* in the *Senate*, was not touched afterwards. It stood as first reported, that in the Senate, or second branch of the Congress, each State should have an equal vote. This, however, was not finally *adopted* without another struggle. Before the question was taken on agreeing to it, it was moved that instead of an *equality* of votes, the States should be represented in the second branch as follows: New Hampshire, by two members; Massachusetts, four; Rhode Island, one; Connecticut, three; New York, three; New Jersey, two; Pennsylvania, four; Delaware, one; Maryland, three; Virginia, five; North Carolina, three; South Carolina, three; Georgia, two; making, in the whole, thirty-six."*

This, by several, was thought to be a fair settlement of the dispute, allowing the Sovereign States still to be represented as such, but not equally. Mr. Wilson, Mr. Madison, and the Nationals generally, favored it as a last hope of getting as near what they desired as possi-

* *Elliot's Debates*, vol. i, p. 205.

ble. Some of the Federals were not disinclined to accede to it as a compromise; amongst these was Mr. Gerry, of Massachusetts; but not so the unyielding advocates of State Sovereignty. "Mr. Ellsworth asked two questions: one of Mr. Wilson, whether he had ever seen a good measure fail in Congress for want of a majority of the States in its favor; the other of Mr. Madison, whether a negative lodged with the majority of the States, even the smallest could be more dangerous than the qualified negative proposed to be lodged in a single Executive Magistrate, who must be taken from some one State."*

"Mr. Sherman, of Connecticut, urged the equality of votes, not so much as a security for the small States as for the State Governments, which could not be preserved unless they were represented."†

"Mr. Dayton declared the smaller States can never give up their equality; for himself, he would in no event yield that security for their rights."‡

"Dr. Johnson, of Connecticut, would consent for numbers to be represented in the one branch, but the States must be in the other."§

So the final report of the Second Grand Committee on this subject was adopted, which retained to the States an equal vote in the Senate, the same equality under the new Constitution which they had under the former Articles of Confederation. It was well ascertained that without this security the smaller States would not confederate further upon any basis; and that all attempts at remodelling the Confederation would inevitably fail unless all views of getting them to surrender this right were abandoned. They were so abandoned. The com-

---

* *Madison Papers*, vol. ii, p. 1106. † *Madison Papers*, vol. ii, p. 1098.
‡ *Madison Papers*, vol. ii, p. 1098. § *Madison Papers*, vol. ii, p. 987.

plete negative of a majority of the States in the Senate was retained. So the bond of this "more perfect Union" was written. In this, as in the old, each State, as a State, has an equal vote in the last resort upon all measures.*

Mr. Curtis, in his "*History of the Constitution*," speaking of this feature in the Constitution, says: "It is a part of the Constitution which it is vain to try by any standard of theory; for it was the result of a mere compromise of opposite theories and conflicting interests."† It was, without question, a compromise between the contending parties in the Convention, to the extent that the unyielding advocates of a strictly Federal system did, by it, consent to a Popular Representation from the several States, in the House, but with the full reservation, on the part of the States, of a complete and absolute negative, in the Senate, on all the acts of the popular Branch thus conceded; and it is utterly vain to attempt, by any bare theory or speculation, to make any thing else of it. This feature, itself, conclusively establishes the Federal character of the Government—not upon any theory, but by the "inexorable logic" of the fact itself. It, more-

* Mr. Bancroft maintains that the idea which formed the basis of this Great Compromise of the Constitution, as he calls it, originated with Mr. Jefferson. In the adoption of the Articles of Confederation, in 1776–7, there was no little difficulty encountered in establishing the rule of voting in Congress—some insisting that the vote should be by Delegates *per capita*, and some by Colonies alone, without respect to numbers or wealth—each Colony to have an equal vote on all questions. This is the way it was then settled; but in referring to the debates then had, Mr. Bancroft gives this account of it: "The vote, said Sherman, of Connecticut, should be taken two ways—call the Colonies, and call the individuals, and have a majority of both. This idea he probably derived from Jefferson, who enforced in private, as the means to save the Union, that any proposition might be negatived by the Representatives of a majority of the people, or of a majority of the Colonies. Here is the thought out of which the great compromise of our Constitution was evolved."—*Bancroft*, vol. ix, p. 53.

† *Curtis on the Constitution*, vol. ii, p. 167.

over, totally annihilates all bare theories or speculations, however ingeniously put forth, in whatever speciousness of garb or rhetoric, going to show that the Government of the United States is a Government of the People of the Whole Country, as one community or Nation.

Upon such a theory, what a caricature of a National Representative Government it would be! Just consider its structure a moment under such a theory! The six New England States, Maine, New Hampshire, Massachusetts, Rhode Island, Connecticut and Vermont, according to the census of 1860, had a population, all together, of three millions one hundred and thirty-five thousand three hundred and eighty-three. New York, alone, by the same census, had a population of three millions eight hundred and eighty thousand seven hundred and thirty-five! This single State had over a half a million more population than the other six, all together! And yet, under the Constitution, the three millions of people in these six States have six times the power in the Government that the three millions and a half have who are in New York. Or take another view. This little over three millions of people, in these six New England States, have just as much power in the Administration of the Government as the thirteen and a half millions have who constitute the aggregate population of the six States of New York, Pennsylvania, Virginia, Ohio, Indiana and Illinois. That is, they have just as much power in passing or defeating any measure whatever.

All this is perfectly consistent with the fact of its being a strictly Federal Government, limited, in its action, to strictly Federal objects. But, upon the supposition, idea, or theory, that it is a Government of the entire population of the United States, as one community or Nation, with control over internal State affairs, the whole matchless framework of our ancestors—the Constitution—which, as it was made, deserves the just admiration of the world—would become, in its practical workings, nothing but a frightful political monstrosity! Well might the New England States, looking to no higher motives than their interest and power, be satisfied to have such a theory established, so long as they could hold on to the present structure. If that theory, however, should, unfortunately for Public Liberty, ever be established, a *Reconstruction*, of a very different character from that we now hear so much about, will, sooner or later, be inevitable!

But, no, sirs; this is not a Government of the People of this Country as one Nation.

It is still, under the Constitution, as it was under the Articles of Confederation, a Government of States, and for States. It was so agreed to in the Convention. It was so nominated in the bond. It was so submitted to the States for their approval and ratification, and not to the people of the whole country, in the aggregate, as you, with Mr. Motley and others, maintain; but it was so submitted to the States, in their political organizations, and by them, as States, it was so agreed to and ratified. Each State retained the absolute power to govern its own people in its own way, in all their domestic relations, without any interference by the people of the other States, or the Federal Government, except in the specified cases set forth in the Constitution.

Prof. Norton. Why, does not the Preamble to the Constitution say: "We, the people of the United States," etc., and does not this show clearly that it was submitted to the whole people, and by them acted upon, ratified and adopted, and not by the States, as States?

MR. STEPHENS. My dear sir, it shows no such thing; and it is a wonder to me how any one should ever have entertained such an idea.

PROF. NORTON. Why, does it not say: "We, the people of the United States, in order to form a more perfect Union," etc?

MR. STEPHENS. Yes; but what is the meaning of "We, the people of the United States," as they here stand? The meaning and sense of words must always be understood from the connection in which they are found. We have abundant and conclusive evidence that they could not have been intended to mean, in the connection where they here stand, what you would have them imply. Because, the very authority of the Delegates—their credentials—which, we have seen, stated that what they should do, should be referred back to the States, should be submitted to them, and should not be binding, unless approved by them, severally and respectively. And, besides, we know that this preamble, as it unanimously passed the Convention, on the 7th of August, 1787, was in these words:—*

"We, the people of the States of New Hampshire, Massachusetts, Rhode Island and Providence Plantations, Connecticut, New York, New Jersey, Pennsylvania, Delaware, Maryland, Virginia, North Carolina, South Carolina, and Georgia, do ordain, declare, and establish the following Constitution," etc.

This shows what was the meaning of the Convention. It was we the people of each State. The change in the phraseology was made by a sub-committee on style, not by the Convention, except in their agreement to the Report of said committee. Why was it made? For a very obvious

---

* *Elliot's Debates*, vol. i, p. 230.

reason. It was not known which of the States would ratify it. Hence it was exceedingly inappropriate to set forth in advance the States by name. By the terms of the Constitution, Article VII,* it was to go into operation between such of the States as might ratify it, if as many as nine or more should do so. The committee on style readily perceived that it would be exceedingly out of place, to have, in the preamble to the organic law, terms embracing a people, or States, who might not put themselves under it. For instance, Rhode Island and North Carolina did not ratify the Constitution for some time. During this period they were entirely out of the Union. They might have remained out until now. Suppose they had. How oddly would this preamble to the Constitution have read: "We the people of New Hampshire, Rhode Island, North Carolina, etc., in order to form a more perfect Union," etc., when the people of Rhode Island and North Carolina had done no such thing. To preserve symmetry in their work, and retain the same idea was what the Committee did in their change of phraseology. As they put it, it would embrace the people of such States only as should adopt it. They would then be the people of the States, respectively, which would *thereby* be United. States United and United States mean the same thing.

Upon a close scrutiny of the change of language in the Preamble, as it was at first adopted by the Convention, and as it was reported by the committee on style, some exceedingly interesting views are suggested, but these are far from favoring the inference usually drawn from it. Let me call your special attention to them, for they have a direct and important bearing upon the point

---

* See *Appendix* C.

now before us. The words, as agreed to at first, in Convention, as we have seen, were:

"We, the people of the States of New Hampshire, Massachusetts, Rhode Island and Providence Plantations, Connecticut, New York, New Jersey, Pennsylvania, Delaware, Maryland, Virginia, North Carolina, South Carolina, and Georgia, do ordain, declare, and establish the following Constitution for the government of ourselves and our posterity."*

Now look closely to the words substituted, and weigh nicely the import of the words left out, as well as those inserted. As the clause was changed by the committee on style, and afterwards unanimously adopted in the Convention, it reads as follows:

"We, the people of the United States, in order to form a more perfect Union, establish justice, insure domestic tranquillity, provide for the common defence, promote the general welfare, and secure the blessings of liberty to ourselves and our posterity, do ordain and establish this Constitution for the United States of America."†

The most striking difference in phraseology between the two, is that which sets forth the object in forming "a more perfect Union," etc., to be, to "ordain and establish this Constitution," not for the *people* in any sense, but for States as political societies. As the words originally stood, the inference *might* have been drawn from the bare words themselves, that the object was to form a government for the people in the aggregate. "We, the people of the States of New Hampshire, Massachusetts, etc., * * * do ordain and establish the following Constitution for the government of ourselves and our posterity." From these words, I say, the in-

* *Elliot's Debates*, vol. i, p. 231. † *Elliot's Debates*, vol i, p. 298.

ference *might* have been drawn that the object was to form a government for the people in the aggregate, but this inference is completely rebutted by the change of phraseology. As it stands, the instrument "is ordained and established" as a *Constitution for States*—for the United States. The same as if it read "for the States of this Union."

The change, in this particular, is very important, and the very Preamble, which is so often alluded to, for a directly opposite purpose, conclusively shows that the Government was intended to be, and is a Government of States, and for States, as I said. In the change of phraseology the introduction of the word *Union* has a wonderful significance of itself. The new Constitution was proposed "in order to form a *more perfect Union*," that is, it was to make more perfect "the Union" then existing. That, we have seen, was a Union of States under the Articles of Confederation. It was to revise these Articles, to enlarge the powers under them, or, in other words, to perfect that Union, that the Convention was called; and that was the object aimed at in all their labors to the conclusion of their work as set forth in this Preamble. So much for the evidence furnished by the Preamble.

But to put the matter beyond all cavil the last clause of the Constitution settles that question. That clause is in these words:

"The ratification of the Conventions of nine States shall be sufficient for the establishment of this Constitution between the States so ratifying the same."*

The word, *between*, was put in on special motion, which shows how closely words were watched, weighed, and guarded at the time.† This shows, beyond all doubt or

* See *Constitution*, *Appendix* C. † *Elliot's Debates*, vol. i, p. 277.

cavil, that it was to be acted upon by States as States, and not by the people of all the States in one aggregate mass. That, you will permit me, most respectfully and good-humoredly, to say, as it seems to me, is one of the most preposterous ideas that ever entered into the head of a sensible man.

Why the very last act of the Convention, in giving a finishing touch to the Constitution, and thereby impressing upon it forever their understanding of their own work, that it was a Union of States, is in these words :

" Done in Convention, by the unanimous consent of the States present, the 17th day of September, in the year of our Lord, 1787, and of the Independence of the United States of America the twelfth. In witness whereof we have hereunto subscribed our names."*

The Delegates signing their names by States.

The Constitution was then sent, with a letter, to the States in Congress assembled, requesting that it should be submitted by them to the several State Legislatures, for them to provide for its submission to Conventions in the several States, to be acted on by them, and to go into effect *between* such States as should ratify it, if so many as nine or more should so ratify it.†

Congress, immediately upon the receipt of the report of the Convention, passed the following resolution :

"*Resolved unanimously,* That the said report, with the resolutions and letter accompanying the same, be transmitted to the several Legislatures, in order to be submitted to a Convention of Delegates in each State, by the people thereof, in conformity to the resolves of the Convention made and provided in that case.‡"

---

* *Elliot's Debates*, vol. i, p. 317. † *Elliot's Debates*, vol. i, p. 306.
‡ *Elliot's Debates*, vol. i, p. 319.

These are facts about which there can be no dispute or doubt.

What, then, becomes of Mr. Motley's statement that "the Constitution was not drawn up by the States! It was not promulgated in the name of the States! It was not ratified by the States! The States never acceded to it! It was 'ordained and established' *over* the States by the people of the whole land in their aggregate capacity, acting through Conventions of Delegates expressly chosen for the purpose within each State, *independently of the State Governments* after the project had been framed!"

Was a grave statement of historical facts ever more reckless or more directly in conflict with indisputable public records? By whose authority did the Convention meet that framed the Constitution but that of the several States? Whose work was the Constitution so framed but that of the States themselves through their appointed Deputies or Delegates, as the Constitution declares on its very face? By whose authority were the State Conventions called to act upon it in their Sovereign capacity but the authority of the State Governments, the State Legislatures? How can it be said that the Constitution was established *over* the States by a power superior to the States, when the paper itself declares it to be a Constitution "for the United States," that is, for the States that were to be united by it, and to be established, not *over*, but "*between the States so ratifying*" it? Yes, "*between* the *States* so *ratifying*" it? The States, as States, through Conventions of their people, embodying the Sovereignty of each State severally, were to ratify it, before it could have any binding force or effect upon any one of them or their people.

Yes, I repeat, *between* the States so ratifying it! That is the language of the Constitution itself, and there will stand as an everlasting refutation of the assertion of Mr. Motley and all others of like character, by whomsoever made, without further comment by me!

PROF. NORTON. Why were the words "We, the people," introduced in the preamble at all, if your views be correct? Does not this show clearly, that it was expected and intended, that the whole people should act on it through their State Conventions? Was it not, therefore, virtually submitted to them for their approval and adoption? Why was it not simply referred back to the State Legislatures?

MR. STEPHENS. For the clearest reason in the world. It was because ultimate, absolute Sovereignty resided with the people of each State respectively. The additional Sovereign powers, which were proposed to be delegated to the States jointly under the Constitution, such as the taxing power, and the power to regulate trade, with the right to pass laws acting directly upon the citizens of the Sovereign States, etc., could only be delegated by the people in their Sovereign capacity. This delegation could be made only by a Convention of the people for that purpose. These powers, by their then existing Constitutions, were vested in their State Legislatures. The Legislatures of the several States, at that time, had the sole power to tax, to regulate trade, etc. These powers had to be *resumed* by the people of each State separately, and taken by them from that set of agents and delegated to another set of agents. No power short of the Sovereignty itself, in each State, could do this; or in other words, as ultimate Sovereignty resided in the people of the States respectively, all new delegations of power, as well as all changes of agents in whom the delegated powers were to be intrusted, could only be made by the people themselves of each state in their Sovereign capacity. This is the whole of it in a nutshell.

The Legislatures of the States were not competent to make this delegation of additional powers to the United States, because they were acting under delegated powers themselves. They were possessed of no power, except such as the people of the States, in their Sovereign capacity, had delegated to them, and amongst those delegated powers, with which they were clothed, none had been granted, empowering them to make this new delegation of powers to the General Government. It was for this reason, amongst others, that Mr. Hamilton, in the twenty-second number of the *Federalist*, showed why the Constitution should be submitted to *Conventions* in the several States, instead of to the Legislatures. This is why he said its foundation ought to be deeper than "the mere sanction of delegated authority," why the fabric "ought to rest on the solid basis of the consent of the people." All political power, said he, "ought to flow, immediately, from that pure original fountain of all legitimate authority."

Among the advocates in the Convention for submitting the Constitution to the people of the States, or rather to Conventions in the States, representing the people directly upon this question, none was more zealous or conspicuous, than Mr. Mason, of Virginia, one of the strongest State Sovereignty men in the body.

"He considered a reference of the plan, to the authority of the people, as one of the most important and essential of the resolutions. The Legislatures have no power to ratify it. They are the mere creatures of the State Constitutions, and cannot be greater than their Creators. And he knew of no power in any of the Constitutions—he knew there was no power in some of them—that could be competent to this object. Whither, then, must we resort? To the people, with whom all power remains, etc. It was of great moment, he observed, that this doctrine should be cherished, as the basis of free Government."*

Mr. Curtis, in his *History of the Constitution*, gives, somewhat, more elaborate reasons, but all based upon the same principle. He says:

"The States, in their corporate capacities, and through the agency of their respective Governments, were parties to a Federal system, which they had stipulated with each other, should be changed only by unanimous consent. The Constitution, which was now in the process of formation, was a system, designed for the acceptance of the people of all the States, if the assent of all could be obtained; but it was also designed for the acceptance of a less number than the whole of the States, in case of a refusal of some of them; and it was at this time highly probable that at least two of them would not adopt it. Rhode Island had never been represented in the Convention; and the whole course of her past history, with reference to enlargements of the powers of the Union, made it quite improbable, that she would ratify such a plan of Government, as was now to be presented to her. The State of New York had, through her Delegates, taken part in the proceedings, until the final decision, which introduced into the Government a system of popular representation; but two of those Delegates, entirely dissatisfied with that decision, had withdrawn from the Convention, and had gone home to prepare the State for the rejection of the scheme. The previous conduct of the State had made it not at all unlikely that their efforts would be successful. Nor were there wanting other indications of the most serious dissatisfaction, on the part of

* *Madison Papers*, vol. v, to *Elliot's Debates*, p. 352.

men of great influence in some of the other States. Unanimity had already become hopeless, if not impracticable; and it was necessary, therefore, to look forward to the event of an adoption of the system by a less number than the whole of the States, and to make it practicable for a less number to form the new Union for which it provided. This could only be done by presenting it for ratification to the people of each State, who possessed authority to withdraw the State Government from the Confederation, and to enter into new relations with the people of such other States as might, also, withdraw from the old and accept the new system."*

The whole of this view rests upon the acknowledged principle, that Sovereignty, under our system, or that Paramount authority, which can rightfully make and unmake Constitutions, and which has the uncontrolled right to resume and re-invest, by delegation, the exercise of Sovereign Powers at will, subject only to the laws of Nations, *resided at that time* with the several States. It suggests a very pertinent inquiry, and that is, if any number of States, by virtue of this ultimate, absolute Sovereignty, had the undoubted right, as he clearly admits they had, to withdraw at that time from the old Union, which was declared upon its face to be perpetual, why could not a like number, or any number, of the same States, by virtue of the same ultimate, absolute Sovereignty, in like manner, in 1861, withdraw from the new Union, wherein no such pledge for perpetuity was given or required?

But I will not anticipate by a digression here. We are now on the point, whether the principles, on which the Confederation was based, that is, a Compact or Union

---

* *Curtis's History of the Constitution.* vol. ii, bk 4, ch. 8, pp. 181, 182

between States, were changed by the adoption of the new Constitution. Whether the present Government of the United States is a National Government proper, that is, whether it is a Government of the whole people consolidated into one Nation, or whether it still retains all the original Federative features of the first articles of Confederation. And, whether ultimate Sovereignty or Paramount authority still resides under the Constitution where it did under the Confederation.

We have seen that Judge Story's first resolution of the Convention has not a single leg to stand upon.* We have, also, seen that all arguments drawn from "We, the people," in the Preamble to the Constitution, are quite as legless and groundless.†

PROF. NORTON. What do you do with Washington's letter, where he says, that the great object with the Convention was to consolidate the Union?

MR. STEPHENS. Do with it! Why I show from that the same principles I show from all the facts of our history. That shows that the object of the Convention had been to perfect the terms of the Union, which was the sole object for which the Convention had been called.

PROF. NORTON. Does he not say, that the object was the Consolidation of the Union? And does not that clearly show that he considered the Sovereignty of all the States merged in the Union under the Constitution?

MR. STEPHENS. By no means. So far from it, it shows most clearly directly the contrary. That letter, you must recollect, was not prepared by Washington, but by the Convention that framed the Constitution. It was prepared and reported with the Constitution. It was taken up and adopted, paragraph by paragraph, the same

---

* *Ante*, p. 123–4. † *Ante*, p. 140–41.

day, and immediately after the adoption of the seventh Article of the Constitution, which I have just read.* It was contemporaneous action with it, and by the same body of men, and cannot, therefore, be presumed to have any thing in it intended to be inconsistent with that Article of the Constitution. The letter was one from the Convention that had just finished its labors, which they authorized Washington to send to the States, in Congress assembled, for the purpose of presenting them with the result of their work. It is in these words.†

"We have now the honor to submit to the consideration of the United States, in Congress assembled, that Constitution which has appeared to us the most advisable.

"The friends of our country have long seen and desired that the power of making war, peace, and treaties; that of levying money and regulating commerce; and the correspondent executive and judicial authorities, shall be fully and effectually vested in the General Government of the Union. But the impropriety of delegating such extensive trust to one body of men is evident. Thence results the necessity of a different organization. It is obviously impracticable, in the Federal Government of these States, to secure all rights of Independent Sovereignty to each, and yet provide for the interest and safety of all. Individuals entering into society must give up a share of liberty to preserve the rest. The magnitude of the sacrifice must depend as well on situation and circumstances as on the object to be obtained. It is at all times difficult to draw with precision the line between those rights which must be surrendered, and those which may be reserved. And, on the present occasion, this difficulty was increased by a difference,

---

* *Journal of the Convention. Elliot's Debates*, vol. i, p. 305.

† *Elliot's Debates*, vol. i, pp. 305, 306.

among the several States, as to their situation, extent, habits, and particular interests.

"In all our deliberations on this subject, we kept steadily in our view that which appeared to us the greatest interest of every true American—the consolidation of the Union, in which is involved our prosperity, felicity, safety—perhaps our National existence. This important consideration, seriously and deeply impressed on our minds, led each State in the Convention to be less rigid in points of inferior magnitude, than might have been otherwise expected. And thus the Constitution which we now present is the result of a spirit of amity, and of that mutual deference and concession which the peculiarity of our political situation rendered indispensable.

"That it will meet the full and entire approbation of every State is not, perhaps, to be expected. But each will doubtless consider that, had her interest alone been consulted, the consequences might have been particularly disagreeable and injurious to others. That it is liable to as few exceptions as could reasonably have been expected, we hope and believe; that it may promote the lasting welfare of that country so dear to us all, and secure her freedom and happiness, is our most ardent wish."

Washington signed this letter as President of the Convention, and addressed it to the United States, in Congress assembled. Who were these States thus addressed? Thirteen Sovereignties, as we have seen, between whom there was a well-known Union existing, founded upon Articles of Confederation. These States thus addressed were then in Congress assembled, under the terms of that Union. The body of men addressing them was a Convention of Delegates from each of these States, which had met in pursuance of a resolution of that Congress, as we have seen, for the sole and express purpose of revising the Articles of the Union which then existed between them as separate and distinct Sovereign Powers. This letter simply informed the States thus assembled what they had done in the premises, and that they thought that the work of their hands, so sent them in accordance with their instructions, was the best that could be done with the great business intrusted to their charge. They say, and say truly, that the great object with them in their deliberations was the *consolidation* of the Union. This, of course, was not its abrogation and dissolution, or the formation of a new and different one. The object was to *strengthen* the Union of States. That was the only Union existing, and the only Union to which they could have referred. The object was to strengthen or consolidate the bonds of that Union, and not to weaken them, much less to sever and utterly destroy them, as would be the import of the word according to your construction. The object was to render the Union of States more perfect or better calculated to accomplish the ends for which it was at first formed. Is not this perfectly clear and true beyond all question? Could any thing be more preposterous or absurd than to suppose that such a body of men, so called together, would, in giving an account of their labors to the body calling them, have stated that the great object with them had been to do the very reverse of what they had been called to do? Can any one believe that Washington could ever have been induced to sign a letter with such design and intention? If the Federal character of the Government had been intended to be abandoned in the plan they proposed, would not these very words have been necessarily left out? Do not the words of themselves, in their connection with their contemporaneous action, under all the circumstances and surroundings, most conclusively rebut the inference that you and others draw from them, and establish beyond the shadow of doubt that the object was not to merge the Sovereignty of all the States into one, and to abandon the Union of Sovereign States by the establishment of a great National Government?

Look, also, to other words in the same letter. "It is obviously impracticable in *the Federal* Government of *these States* to secure *all rights* of Independent *Sovereignty* to *each*," etc. Many Sovereign powers had been delegated under the Articles of Confederation. More were now proposed to be delegated in the same way. This required "a *different organization*." That is, a division of the departments into which *all* the powers were to be intrusted. A change of machinery in operating the system, and not a change of the basis of the system. The difficulty attending these changes "was increased by a difference among the States." "This important consideration, etc., led *each State* in the Convention," etc. Does not the whole of this paper most clearly show that the Convention meant by it simply to say that their great object was to strengthen and make more perfect the bonds of the Federal Union then existing? and that they thought that object would be accomplished by the States adopting the plan proposed. "That it will meet the full and entire approbation of every State," they say, "is not perhaps to be expected."

In what respect, in tone or sentiment, touching the character of the Union to be consolidated, does this letter differ from a similar one sent to the States by Congress with the first Articles of Union, in 1777? In that, amongst other things, Congress said, "that to form a permanent Union, accommodated to the opinions and wishes of the Delegates of so many States, differing in habits, produce, commerce, and internal police, was found to be a work which nothing but time and reflection, conspiring with a disposition to conciliate, could mature and accomplish. Hardly is it to be expected that any plan, in the variety of provisions essential to our Union, should exactly correspond with the maxims and political views of every particular State. Let it be remarked, that after the most careful inquiry and the fullest information, this is proposed as the best which could be adapted to the circumstances of all, and as that alone which affords any tolerable prospect of general ratification. Permit us, then, earnestly to recommend these Articles to the immediate and dispassionate attention of the Legislatures of the respective States. Let them be candidly reviewed under a sense of the difficulty of combining, in one general system, the various sentiments and interests of a continent, divided into so many Sovereign and Independent communities, under a conviction of the absolute necessity of uniting all our councils, and all our strength, to maintain and defend our common liberties."* Does the letter of the Convention look any more to the abrogation of State Sovereignties than the letter of Congress to the States in 1777?

Here is also a letter from Roger Sherman and Oliver Ellsworth, two very distinguished Delegates to the Convention from Connecticut, written on the 26th of September, 1787, and addressed to the Governor of their State, making a report to him of the action of the Convention, and the result of their labors. This shows clearly that their understanding of the letter of the Convention to Congress was in accordance with the views now presented.

---

* *Elliot's Debates*, vol. i, p. 69.

"We have the honor to transmit to your Excellency," they say, "a printed copy of the Constitution formed by the Federal Convention, to be laid before the Legislature of the State.

"The general principles which governed the Convention, in their deliberations on the subject, are stated in their address to Congress.

"We think it may be of use to make some further observations on particular parts of the Constitution.

"The Congress is differently organized; yet the whole number of members, and this State's proportion of suffrage, remain the same as before.

"The equal representation of the States in the Senate, and the voice of that branch in the appointment to offices, will secure the rights of the lesser as well as of the greater States.

"Some additional powers are vested in Congress, which was a principal object that the States had in view in appointing the Convention. Those powers extend only to matters respecting the common interests of the Union, and are specially defined, so that the particular States retain their Sovereignty in all other matters.

"The objects for which Congress may apply moneys are the same mentioned in the eighth article of the Confederation, viz.: for the common defence and general welfare, and for payment of the debts incurred for those purposes. It is probable that the principal branch of revenue will be duties on imports. What may be necessary to be raised by direct taxation is to be apportioned on the several States, according to the number of their inhabitants; and although Congress may raise the money by their own authority, if necessary, yet that authority need not be exercised, if each State will furnish its quota.

"The restraint on the Legislatures of the several States respecting emitting bills of credit, making any thing but money a tender in payment of debts, or impairing the obligation of contracts by *ex post facto* laws, was thought necessary as a security to commerce, in which the interest of foreigners, as well as of the citizens of different States, may be affected.

"The Convention endeavored to provide for the energy of Government on the one hand, and suitable checks on the other hand, to secure the rights of the particular States, and the liberties and properties of the citizens. We wish it may meet the approbation of the several States, and be a means of securing their rights and lengthening out their tranquillity. With great respect, we are, Sir, your Excellency's obedient, humble servants."*

Could any thing be more pertinent or conclusive, upon these points, than this letter?

But we have numerous contemporaneous letters from Washington to divers persons, which throw a flood of light upon the subject, and show clearly his understanding of that letter of Congress to have been in accordance with the views I have presented. These letters also show what little weight is to be given to Mr. Motley's assertion that the States never acceded to the Constitution as a Compact between them. On this point we have in these letters authority higher than that of Mr. Motley. What the States did do, we shall see. Whether their action can be properly termed *accession* or not, has been a matter on which men have differed. Mr. Motley is on one side, while General Washington, Mr. Jefferson, Governor Randolph, Judge Marshall, Mr. Madison, and a host of others, are on the other side.

---

* *Elliot's Debates*, vol. i, p. 491.

In a letter of General Washington to Bushrod Washington, on the 10th of November, 1787, while the Constitution was before the States for consideration, he says:*

"Let the opponents of the proposed Constitution in this State be asked—and it is a question they certainly ought to have asked themselves—what line of conduct they would advise it to adopt, if nine other States, of which I think there is little doubt, should *accede* to the Constitution?"

In the same volume, on page 304, is a letter from General Washington to Mr. Madison, dated the 10th of January, 1788. In this he says:

"But of all the arguments that may be used at the Convention which is to be held, the most prevailing one I expect will be that nine States *at least* will have *acceded* to it."

Here is a letter from Washington to Charles C. Pinckney, dated the 28th of June, 1788, in which he says:†

"No sooner had the citizens of Alexandria, who are Federal to a man, received the intelligence by the mail last night, than they determined to devote this day to festivity. But their exhilaration was greatly increased, and a much keener zest given to their enjoyment, by the arrival of an Express, two hours before day, with the news that the Convention of New Hampshire had, on the 21st instant, *acceded to the new Confederacy* by a majority of eleven voices—that is to say, fifty-seven to forty-six. * * * From the local situation, as well as the other circumstances of North Carolina, I should be truly astonished if that State should withdraw itself from the Union. On the contrary, I flatter myself with a confident expecta-

---

* *Washington's Writings*, vol. ix, page 278.

† *Washington's Writings*, vol. ix, pp. 389, 390.

Painted by G. Stuart — Engraved by A.B. Welter, Phila.

Go: Washington

tion that more salutary counsels will certainly prevail. At present there is more doubt how the question will be immediately disposed of in New York; for it seems to be understood that there is a majority in the Convention opposed to the adoption of the new Federal system."

In General Washington's Speech to Congress, on the 8th of January, 1790, he spoke of the adoption of the Constitution by North Carolina, as "the recent *accession* of that State to the Constitution." The Senate, in their reply to his Speech, use the same word.*

But why continue these extracts? Are they not quite sufficient to show that General Washington—he who stood at the head of that band of patriots who framed the Constitution for a more perfect Union between the States—entertained different ideas of the nature of the action of the States upon it from those of Mr. Motley? He says the States *acceded* to it. Mr. Motley says they did not. There the matter may rest, upon that point. But these letters also throw quite a flood of light, as I said, upon the true meaning of the words, "a Consolidation of the Union," which we have just been speaking of. They show that Washington clearly understood the new system to be a Federal system, as the old one was. That there was no change of the *locus* of ultimate absolute Sovereignty under it. That the Union, which was perfected and consolidated, was to be still a Union of States, each Sovereign as before, and not a Union of the entire people of the whole country, as Mr. Motley contends. Washington emphatically styles it, "the new Confederacy"—"the new Federal System." Mr. Motley says, that the present Government is no Confederacy, that "we had already enough of a Confederacy." Here

* *Annals of Congress*, vol. i, pp. 932–935.

again, he is directly at issue with Washington. Washington speaks of the new system, as of the old, and styles it "the new Confederacy." Here, again, I will leave the issue between Mr. Motley and General Washington.

Prof. Norton. Mr. Stephens, without wishing to interrupt you, I should like to ask you a question just here.

Mr. Stephens. It will not interrupt me at all. I am ready to give my views at any time upon any point; and there is no better time than when the point is suggested to the mind in the course of investigation. The object of our inquiry is the nature of the Government of the United States—whether it be the Government of one people as a Nation, or whether it be *Federal*—that is, a Government of States. What is it you would ask?

Prof. Norton. Well, then, I should like to know if it was not generally thought at the time that the consolidation of the Union, mentioned in the letter of the Convention to Congress, would merge the Sovereignty of all the States into one? Was it not because of this general belief that Yates and Lansing, of New York, and Luther Martin, of Maryland, quit the Convention? and was not this the reason that Governor Randolph and Mr. Mason, from Virginia, refused to vote for or sign the Constitution, and that Patrick Henry exerted all the powers of his eloquence against its adoption by the State of Virginia? I have always so understood it. Where I got the impression I do not know. But was not this the case?

Mr. Stephens. There was, as you say, strong opposition to the Constitution upon the grounds you state. Mr. Lansing and Mr. Yates, from New York, did quit the Convention because of their dissatisfaction with its proceedings. So did Luther Martin. Mr. Mason, of

Virginia, and Governor Randolph, of Virginia, both refused to vote for it, and both refused to sign it; as also did Mr. Gerry, from Massachusetts. But they all acted from different motives, and assigned different reasons for their conduct.

Lansing and Yates quit the Convention because they were for an equality of votes on the part of the States in both Houses of Congress. Yates had agreed to the adjustment proposed by the first grand Committee of Conference, as we have seen. That report met with so little favor, was so violently denounced by Mr. Madison and others, that he immediately left, supposing it would not be adopted. His colleague left with him.*

Other equally strong State Sovereignty and State Rights men remained; and, by the final action of the Convention, an equality of votes in the Senate was secured to the States, as we have seen. They were perfectly satisfied that the Federal system was still retained by this adjustment.

Luther Martin was unyielding upon the point of equality of suffrage on the part of the States in both Houses of Congress. Indeed he was unalterably opposed to many of the new and additional powers delegated by the Constitution. He was opposed to the Executive and Judiciary Departments, as constituted, and to the prohibitions on the States against emitting Bills of Credit or passing laws impairing the obligations of contracts. He thought the Government, notwithstanding the opinion of its friends to the contrary, would end in despotism, and so warned his countrymen, in eloquence of the highest order.†

Mr. Mason and Mr. Gerry opposed several features in

---

* *Elliot's Debates*, vol. i, p. 479.

† *Elliot's Debates*, vol. i, pp. 344, 389.

the new plan and thought it departed too far from a strictly Federal alliance.*

Governor Randolph, on the other hand, opposed the new plan and refused to sign it, because, in his judgment, it did not depart from the Federal system.

Mr. Curtis says, that Governor Randolph thought the Constitution was "a system containing far greater restraints upon the powers of the States than he believed expedient or safe," etc.† This is certainly a mistake. Just the contrary is the fact. Governor Randolph, in assigning his reasons for not voting for the Constitution and withholding his signature from it, in a letter to the Speaker of the House of Representatives of Virginia, says, amongst other things:

"It follows, too, that the General Government ought to be the supreme arbiter for adjusting every contention among the States. In all their connections, therefore, with each other, and particularly in commerce, which will probably create the greatest discord, it ought to hold the reins."

Governor Randolph was opposed to many features of the Constitution, such as the Executive department. The whole was summed up in this.

"But, now, sir, permit me to declare, that in my humble judgment, the powers by which alone the blessings of a General Government can be accomplished, cannot be interwoven in the Confederation, without a change in its very essence, or, in other words, that the Confederation must be thrown aside."‡

This shows that Governor Randolph did not consider that there was a general merger of the Sovereignty of

---

* *Elliot's Debates*, vol. i, p. 492.

† *Curtis's History of the Constitution*, vol. i, p. 481.

‡ *Elliot's Debates*, vol. i, p. 486.

all the States in the Union, which the Convention had consolidated, as we have seen. It clearly shows that, in his opinion, the Federative system was still retained in the new Constitution, as it existed under the old. He had put forth the utmost of his strength in the Convention, for what he called a National Government. One based upon the abandonment of the Federal system. His views were embodied in his plan of Government, and in his Resolution, which proposed to give the power to the General Government to judge as between it and the States of infractions of the Constitution, which, we have seen, was negatived, and Martin's Resolution agreed to instead. The essence of Confederation was abandoned in his plan; but his plan, in this particular, was not adopted. The new Constitution continued upon the same Federative basis, and simply sought to make the Union upon that basis more perfect. At this Governor Randolph was disappointed and chagrined—hence his lamentations and opposition. He was elected to the Convention, in Virginia, to which the Constitution was submitted, pledged to go against its ratification, mainly for this very reason; but when he found that there was no hope, whatever, of getting Virginia and the other States to adopt such a National Government as he wanted, or to depart in the slightest degree from the essence of the Federative system, he then ceased his opposition to the Constitution, as it was, and voted for its ratification.

But still there was a very general and strong opposition, throughout all the States, upon the grounds you state. It was urged by many, "That the Union, upon the Federal basis, was proposed to be abandoned, and a new Union to be formed by a consolidation of the separate Sovereignties of the States." In the glowing language of the day it was asserted "That a Government, so organized, and absorbing all the powers of the States, would produce from their ruins one consolidated Government, founded upon the destruction of the several Governments of the States." "The powers of Congress, under the Constitution, are complete and unlimited over the purse and the sword, and are perfectly independent of and supreme over the State Governments, whose intervention, on these great points, is utterly destroyed. By virtue of the power of taxation Congress may command the whole or any part of the properties of the people. They may impose what imposts upon Commerce, they may impose what land taxes, and taxes, excises, and duties on all instruments, etc., to any extent they please. When the spirit of the people shall be gradually broken, when the National Government shall be firmly established, and when a numerous standing army shall render opposition vain, the Congress may complete the system of Despotism in renouncing all dependence on the people by continuing themselves," and successors in power forever.*

Patrick Henry did head this opposition with all his might in the Convention of Virginia. His grounds were various. He saw but little in any of its features that he liked. The Executive Department, in his judgment, "*squinted* towards Monarchy." His chief objection to it, however, was the want of a Bill of Rights, and because it was not expressly stated on the face of the Constitution that the Sovereignty of the States was retained or reserved, as it had been in the Articles of Confederation. It was in vain that he was told, by many as strongly in favor of State Sovereignty as he could be,

* *Story on the Constitution*, vol. i, pp. 272, 273.

that the whole system, upon its face, was one of delegated powers, and that none could be claimed, or exercised, except those delegated. That, as a matter of course, all which were not delegated were retained and reserved,—that Sovereignty, not being expressly parted with, still remained with the States. He, however, thought that what had been aimed at, and so assiduously attempted by the Nationals in the Convention, would be ultimately attained by them by implication and construction, if the Constitution should be adopted and put in operation without numerous amendments which he proposed. With these amendments he declared his willingness to agree to the Constitution, notwithstanding his strong objections to various other features in the new organization. The principles of most of these amendments, proposed by him, were afterwards adopted. He was, then, far advanced in years, and though his opposition to the Constitution, after the adoption of the amendments, "abated in a measure, yet he remained fearful, to the end of his life, that the final result would be the destruction of the rights of the Sovereignty of the States."*

With unsurpassed eloquence, Patrick Henry possessed one of those wonderful minds which, by a sort of instinct or supernatural faculty, scents the approaches of power, even in the distance. This instinct, or far-seeing superhuman endowment, prompted him to sound the alarm when the Constitution was at first presented to him.

This is all true, but it is also true that his opposition, and that of all others at the time, sprung rather from apprehensions of evils that would result from *constructions* that would be put upon the Constitution, than from any

---

* Patrick Henry. *New American Encyclopædia.*

thing that appeared upon its face, or from powers under it claimed by its framers or advocates. Power, it was said by the opponents of the Constitution, was ever insidious in its approaches, and the lines between the Sovereign powers delegated in the Constitution to the States jointly, to be exercised by them jointly, and those retained to the several States, were not drawn with sufficient clearness and distinctness. The whole opposition was argumentative. The reply, on all hands, even by those who had contended in the Convention for an abandonment of the Federal system, was that this system had not been abandoned in the plan proposed—that enlarged powers had been delegated and new machinery for the exercise of those powers had been introduced, but no change in the nature or character of the Government. This, we have just seen, was Washington's position. His name was a host in itself. It was also the position of Hamilton, of King, of Wilson, of Madison, of Morris, of Randolph, and all the Nationals of the Convention, as we shall see. What was *argued* would be the legitimate tendency and ultimate results of a Government so organized was strenuously *denied* by the friends and advocates of the Constitution. This is abundantly clear from the history of the times. Not a supporter or defender of the Constitution advocated it upon the grounds that the Sovereignty of the States was parted with under it. So thoroughly Federal was the Constitution admitted to be by its advocates everywhere that they universally took to themselves the name of Federalists. Washington, we have just seen, said that the people of Alexandria "*were Federal to a man;*" that is they were all for the Constitution, believing and understanding it to be Federal in its nature and character. That series of Articles, eighty-five in number, which have become historic, written by Hamilton, Madison, and Jay (all national before), urging upon the people reasons for adopting the Constitution, were styled "the Federalist." The Constitution was universally called the "Federal Constitution." The seat of Government was to be known as "The Federal City." So strongly and deeply impressed was this idea and understanding upon the minds of the people that it assumed solid embodiment in outward forms, representations, and symbols. In Boston, after the ratification of the Constitution by Massachusetts, "there issued from the gates of Faneuil Hall an imposing procession of five thousand citizens, embracing all the trades of the town and its neighborhood, each with its appropriate decorations, emblems and mottoes. In the centre of this long pageant, to mark the relation of every thing around it to maritime commerce, and *the relation of all to the new Government*, was borne the SHIP 'FEDERAL CONSTITUTION,' with full colors flying and attended by the merchants, captains and seamen of the Port." "This was the first of a series of similar pageants which took place in the other principal cities of the Union in favor of the ratification of the Constitution."*

In Baltimore they had a ball, an illumination, and a grand procession of trades. In this procession was borne a miniature ship, "The Federalist."†

"The ratification of Virginia took place on the 25th of June. The news of this event was received in Philadelphia on the 2d of July. The press of the city was at once filled with rejoicings over the action of Virginia. She was the tenth pillar in the Temple of Liberty. She was Virginia—the oldest and foremost of the States—land of statesmen, whose Revolutionary services

---

* *Curtis's History of the Constitution*, vol. ii, p. 540.

† *Curtis's History of the Constitution*, vol. ii, p. 543.

were household words in all America—birthplace and home of Washington! We need not wonder, when she had come so tardily, so cautiously into the support of the Constitution, that men should have hailed her *accession* with enthusiasm! The people of Philadelphia had been some time preparing a public demonstration in honor of the adoption of the Constitution by nine States. Now that Virginia was added to the number, they determined that all possible magnificence and splendor should be given to this celebration, and they chose for it the anniversary of the National Independence.

"A taste for allegory appears to have been quite prevalent among the people of the United States at this period. Accordingly, the Philadelphia Procession of July 4, 1788, was filled with elaborate and emblematical representations. It was a long pageant of banners of trades and devices. A decorated car bore the Constitution, framed as a banner and hung upon a staff. Then another decorated car carried the American Flag. Then followed the Judges, in their robes, and all the public bodies, preceding a grand Federal Edifice, which was carried by a carriage drawn by ten horses. On the floor of this edifice were in chairs ten gentlemen representing *the citizens of the United States at large*, to whom the *Federal Constitution* had been committed before its ratification. When it arrived at 'Union Green,' *they gave up their seats* to ten others, representing *ten States*, which had ratified the instrument."*

What force was there, in this stage representation, to the popular mind of the process through which the Constitution passed in its ratification? The first ten gentlemen, representing the citizens of all the ten States at

* *Curtis's His. Con.*, vol. ii, p. 543.

large, each acting for themselves, in their several Sovereign capacities, after having given it their several sanction, then turning it over to ten others, representing the ten States for whom it had been so ordained and established, for them to hold, keep, preserve, and maintain, not *over* them, but between them, and *over* the Government instituted by it!

These demonstrations, devices, mottoes, and symbols, clearly show how the great mass of the people, in all the States, understood the new Constitution. It was nothing but a more perfect bond of Union between States. Federal was the watchword of the day in Boston, New York, Philadelphia, Baltimore, Richmond, and Charleston. It was the grand symbolized idea throughout the whole length and breadth of the land. There can be no doubt that the people thought they were adopting a Federal Constitution—forming a Federal Union.

Now, then, what is the meaning of this word Federal, which entered so deeply into the thoughts, the hearts, and understandings of the people at that day. Here words are things! Dr. Johnson, the highest authority of that day, in his *Dictionary*, thus defines the word :—Federal—(*Fœdus, Lat.*) relating to a League or Contract. Federate, he defines (*Federatus, Lat.*) leagued, joined in a Confederacy.

The great American lexicographer, Noah Webster, says of this word "*Federal*," that it is derived from the Latin word "*Fœdus*," which means a League. A League he defines to be "an Alliance or Confederacy between Princes or States for their mutual aid or defence." And, in defining the meaning of the word Federal, he uses this language: "Consisting in a Compact between States or Nations; founded on alliance by contract or mutual agreement; as, a Federal Government, such as that of the United States."

Dr. Worcester, in his new *Dictionary*, another standard work with philologers of the first rank, says, of this word "*Federal*," that it is from the Latin "*Fœdus*," "a Compact." He defines it thus: "1. Relating to a League or Compact;" etc. "2. Relating to, or joined in, a Confederacy, as Communities or States; Confederate;—particularly, belonging to the Union, or the United States."

Federal, from its very origin and derivation, therefore, has no meaning, and can have none, dissociated from Compact or Agreement of some sort, and it is seldom ever used to qualify any Compacts or Agreements except those between States or Nations. So that Federal and Confederate mean substantially the same thing. When applied to States they both imply and import a Compact between States. Washington, in one of his letters, which I have just read, spoke of the new Government as "a Confederacy." In another, to Sir Edward Newenham, dated the 20th July, 1788, he speaks of the new Government then ratified by enough States to carry it into effect as a "Confederated Government."* In his response to the reply of the Senate to his first speech to Congress after the new Government was organized, in 1789, he expressed his happiness in the conviction that "the Senate would at all times co-operate in every measure which may tend to promote the welfare of *this Confederated Republic*."† These are the terms by which he characterized "the Union," after the present Constitution was formed and after it was in operation. There is no difference between the words Federal and Confederated as thus used and applied. We see that Washington used them both, at different times, to signify the same thing, that is, the Union of the American States under the Constitution.

* *Washington's Writings*, vol. ix, p. 398.

† *Annals of Congress*, vol. i, p. 38.

It being *universally* admitted, then, by the advocates of the Constitution at the time of its adoption, that it was Federal in its character, and that the Government under it would be a Confederated or Federal Republic, which means the same thing, let us see what is the nature and very essence of all such Governments. Dropping Dic tionaries, let us go to writers upon the Laws of Nations. Here is Montesquieu. In Book ix, chap. 1, he speaks first of Republics generally. These may exist either under Democratic or Aristocratic Constitutions.

"If a Republic," a single Republic, he means, "is small, it is destroyed by a foreign force; if it be large, it is ruined by an internal imperfection. * * * * *

"It is, therefore, very probable, that mankind would have been at length obliged to live constantly under the Government of a single person, had they not contrived a kind of Constitution that has all the internal advantages of a Republican, together with the external force of a Monarchical Government. I mean a Confederate Republic.

"This form of Government is a Convention, by which several small States agree to become members of a larger one which they intend to form. It is a kind of assemblage of societies, that constitute a new one, capable of increasing by means of new associations, till they arrive to such a degree of power, as to be able to provide for the security of the united body. * * * *

"The State" (that is the State formed by the Confederation) "may be destroyed on one side, and not on the other; the Confederacy may be dissolved, and the Confederates preserve their Sovereignty.

"As this Government is composed of petty Republics, it enjoys the internal happiness of each; and with respect to its external situation, it is possessed, by means of the association, of all the advantages of large monarchies."

This, by the highest authority, is the form and nature of all Federal or Confederated Republics. The Government of the United States, in the judgment of Washington, belongs to that class. All the States of the Union were small Republics within themselves. By entering the Union for foreign and inter State purposes, they did not, therefore, according to Montesquieu, forfeit or part with their separate sovereignty. On the same subject, Vattel, another writer, universally admitted to be authority of high order, says:

"Several Sovereign and Independent States may unite themselves together by a perpetual Confederacy, without ceasing to be, each individually, a perfect State. They will together constitute a Federal Republic; their joint deliberations will not impair the Sovereignty of each member, though they may, in certain respects, put some restraint on the exercise of it in virtue of voluntary engagements."* That, I maintain, was exactly what the States of our Union did, by the adoption of the Constitution.

I am, however, anticipating a little. We have not yet examined the new and additional powers delegated in the Constitution to see if they, by their own force and proper effect, of necessity changed the character of the Union before existing, nor have we yet examined into the acts of the States upon that measure itself. I have been drawn into what I have thus said rather in advance, in answer to your question touching the general opinion at the time, that the new Government was to be a consolidation of the Sovereignty of the States. This, I think, is quite enough to satisfy you that whatever apprehensions were indulged in by many as to results from abuse of powers, yet it was universally admitted by the advocates of the Constitution that a Federal Republic was to be established by it, and not a National Consolidation.

---

* *Vattel's Laws of Nations*, p. 3.

COLLOQUY V.

THE CONSTITUTION OF THE UNITED STATES—ANALYSIS OF ITS PROVISIONS, MUTUAL COVENANTS, AND DELEGATIONS OF POWER, AS IN THE ARTICLES OF CONFEDERATION.

Mr. Stephens. Let us now look into the Constitution itself,* and see the nature of the Government instituted by it, so far as appears from the words, and the terms used in it;—keeping closely in mind all the antecedent facts—these are mainly—the separate Sovereignty of the States, by whose Delegates it was framed—the old law—the articles of Confederation—the evils complained of under them, and the remedies proposed. Keep in mind the purpose for which the Convention was called, the instructions and powers, under which the Delegation from each State acted, as well as what the Convention said of their work, after it was done, in transmitting it to the States, then in Congress assembled. Recollect, also, what Ellsworth and Sherman said of it, and what Washington, in his own name, said of it. All these matters should be kept constantly in view in our examination of the terms of the Constitution. With these facts, then, thoroughly impressed upon the mind, let us enter upon an examination of the Instrument itself.

Upon an analysis of the entire provisions of the Constitution, from the beginning to the end, similar to the analysis made of the Articles of Confederation, we see that the whole may be divided and arranged:

* See *Appendix* C.

First, into mutual Covenants and Agreements between the States, and

Secondly, the delegation of specific powers, by the States severally, to the States jointly, to be exercised by them jointly, in the mode and manner specifically set forth in the mutual Covenants, as stated.

The mutual Covenants relate partly to the new organization, and the general division of the exercise of the powers granted or delegated to the different departments; and partly to restrictions upon the several States, and duties or obligations assumed by them, just as under the former, or old Constitution.

The Covenants of the First Class, for a clearer understanding, by proper analysis, may be further subdivided under appropriate heads, and in classification arranged accordingly. Those relating to the new organization and division of powers being placed by themselves, in order, and those relating to the restraints upon the several States and the duties and obligations assumed by them as States, being, also, arranged by themselves, in like order.

Now, then, upon opening the Constitution, at the head of it, we find the Preamble, of which we have spoken. That is in these words:

"CONSTITUTION OF THE UNITED STATES OF AMERICA.

"We the People of the United States, in order to form a more perfect Union, establish Justice, insure domestic Tranquillity, provide for the common defence, promote the general Welfare, and secure the Blessings of Liberty to ourselves and our Posterity, do ordain and establish this CONSTITUTION for the United States of America."

From this, as has been shown, it clearly appears that it was the intention of those who framed what follows, that it was to be a Constitution for States, or, in other words, a Compact between States. No more on that point here.

First, then, in our examination into the body and substance of the Instrument, let us arrange all the mutual Covenants or Agreements in their order, according to the plan of analysis as stated.

Those relating to the new organization and the machinery of the Government, and the distribution of Powers, may be placed as follows:

FIRST.—COVENANTS RELATING TO THE LEGISLATIVE DEPARTMENT.

1st. "All Legislative Powers herein granted shall be vested in a Congress of the United States, which shall consist of a Senate and House of Representatives."

2d. "The House of Representatives shall be composed of Members chosen every second Year by the People of the several States, and the Electors in each State shall have the Qualifications requisite for Electors of the most numerous Branch of the State Legislature."

3d. "No Person shall be a Representative who shall not have attained to the Age of twenty-five Years, and been seven Years a Citizen of the United States, and who shall not, when elected, be an Inhabitant of that State in which he shall be chosen."

4th. "Representatives and direct Taxes shall be apportioned among the several States which may be included within this Union, according to their respective Numbers, which shall be determined by adding to the whole Number of free Persons, including those bound to Service for a Term of Years, and excluding Indians not taxed, three fifths of all other Persons. The actual Enumeration shall be made within three Years after the first Meeting of the Congress of the United States, and within every subsequent Term of ten Years, in such Manner as they shall by Law direct. The Number of Representatives shall not exceed one for every thirty Thousand, but each State shall have at Least one Representative; and until such enumeration shall be made, the State of New Hampshire shall be entitled to chuse three, Massachusetts eight, Rhode-Island and Providence Plantations one, Connecticut five, New-York six, New Jersey four, Pennsylvania eight, Delaware one, Maryland six, Virginia ten, North Carolina five, South Carolina five, and Georgia three."

5th. "When vacancies happen in the Representation from any State, the Executive Authority thereof shall issue Writs of Election to fill such Vacancies."

6th. "The House of Representatives shall chuse their Speaker and other Officers; and shall have the sole Power of Impeachment."

7th. "The Senate of the United States shall be composed of two Senators from each State, chosen by the Legislature thereof, for six Years; and each Senator shall have one Vote."

8th. "Immediately after they shall be assembled in Consequence of the first Election, they shall be divided as equally as may be into three Classes. The Seats of the Senators of the first Class shall be vacated at the Expiration of the second Year, of the second Class at the Expiration of the fourth Year, and of the third Class at the Expiration of the sixth Year, so that one third may be chosen every second Year; and if Vacancies happen by Resignation, or otherwise, during the Recess of the Legislature of any State, the Executive thereof may make temporary Appointments until the next Meeting of the Legislature, which shall then fill such Vacancies."

9th. "No Person shall be a Senator who shall not have

attained to the Age of thirty Years, and been nine Years a Citizen of the United States, and who shall not, when elected, be an Inhabitant of that State for which he shall be chosen."

10th. "The Vice President of the United States shall be President of the Senate, but shall have no Vote, unless they be equally divided."

11th. "The Senate shall chuse their other Officers, and also a President *pro tempore*, in the Absence of the Vice President, or when he shall exercise the Office of President of the United States."

12th. "The Senate shall have the sole Power to try all Impeachments. When sitting for that Purpose, they shall be on Oath or Affirmation. When the President of the United States is tried, the Chief Justice shall preside: And no Person shall be convicted without the Concurrence of two thirds of the Members present."

13th. "Judgment in Cases of Impeachment shall not extend further than to removal from Office, and Disqualification to hold and enjoy any Office of honour, Trust or Profit under the United States: but the Party convicted shall nevertheless be liable and subject to Indictment, Trial, Judgment and Punishment, according to Law."

14th. "The Times, Places and Manner of holding Elections for Senators and Representatives, shall be prescribed in each State by the Legislature thereof; but the Congress may at any time by Law make or alter such Regulations, except as to the place of chusing Senators."

15th. "The Congress shall assemble at least once in every Year, and such Meeting shall be on the first Monday in December, unless they shall by Law appoint a different Day."

16th. "Each House shall be the Judge of the Elections, Returns and Qualifications of its own Members, and a

Majority of each shall constitute a Quorum to do Business; but a smaller Number may adjourn from day to day, and may be authorized to compel the attendance of absent Members, in such Manner, and under such Penalties as each House may provide."

17th. "Each House may determine the Rules of its Proceedings, punish its Members for disorderly Behaviour, and, with the Concurrence of two thirds, expel a Member."

18th. "Each House shall keep a Journal of its Proceedings, and from time to time publish the same, excepting such Parts as may in their Judgment require Secrecy; and the Yeas and Nays of the Members of either House on any question shall, at the Desire of one fifth of those Present, be entered on the Journal."

19th. "Neither House, during the Session of Congress, shall, without the Consent of the other, adjourn for more than three days, nor to any other Place than that in which the two Houses shall be sitting."

20th. "The Senators and Representatives shall receive a Compensation for their Services, to be ascertained by Law, and paid out of the Treasury of the United States. They shall in all Cases, except Treason, Felony and Breach of the Peace, be privileged from Arrest during their Attendance at the Session of their respective Houses, and in going to and returning from the same; and for any Speech or Debate in either House, they shall not be questioned in any other Place."

21st. "No Senator or Representative shall, during the Time for which he was elected, be appointed to any civil Office under the Authority of the United States, which shall have been created, or the Emoluments whereof shall have been encreased during such time; and no Person holding any Office under the United States, shall be a Member of either House during his Continuance in Office."

22d. "All Bills for raising Revenue shall originate in the House of Representatives; but the Senate may propose or concur with Amendments as on other Bills."

23d. "Every Bill which shall have passed the House of Representatives and the Senate, shall, before it become a Law, be presented to the President of the United States; If he approve he shall sign it, but if not he shall return it, with his Objections to that House in which it shall have originated, who shall enter the Objections at large on their Journal, and proceed to reconsider it. If after such Reconsideration two thirds of that House shall agree to pass the Bill, it shall be sent, together with the Objections, to the other House, by which it shall likewise be reconsidered, and if approved by two thirds of that House, it shall become a Law. But in all such Cases the Votes of both Houses shall be determined by Yeas and Nays, and the Names of the Persons voting for and against the Bill shall be entered on the Journal of each House respectively. If any Bill shall not be returned by the President within ten Days (Sundays excepted) after it shall have been presented to him, the Same shall be a law, in like Manner as if he had signed it, unless the Congress by their Adjournment prevent its Return, in which Case it shall not be a Law."

24th. "Every Order, Resolution, or Vote to which the Concurrence of the Senate and House of Representatives may be necessary (except on a question of Adjournment) shall be presented to the President of the United States; and before the same shall take effect, shall be approved by him, or being disapproved by him, shall be repassed by two thirds of the Senate and House of Representatives, according to the Rules and Limitations prescribed in the Case of a Bill."

SECOND.—COVENANTS RELATING TO THE EXECUTIVE DEPARTMENT.

1st. "The Executive Power shall be vested in a President of the United States of America. He shall hold his Office during the Term of four Years, and, together with the Vice-President, chosen for the same Term, be elected, as follows:"

2d. "Each State shall appoint, in such Manner as the Legislature thereof may direct, a Number of Electors, equal to the whole Number of Senators and Representatives to which the State may be entitled in the Congress: but no Senator or Representative, or Person holding an Office of Trust or Profit under the United States, shall be appointed an Elector."

[* The Electors shall meet in their respective States, and vote by Ballot for two Persons, of whom one at least shall not be an Inhabitant of the same State with themselves. And they shall make a List of all the Persons voted for, and of the Number of Votes for each; which List they shall sign and certify, and transmit sealed to the Seat of the Government of the United States, directed to the President of the Senate. The President of the Senate shall, in the Presence of the Senate and House of Representatives, open all the Certificates, and the Votes shall then be counted. The Person having the greatest Number of Votes shall be the President, if such Number be a Majority of the whole Number of Electors appointed; and if there be more than one who have such Majority, and have an equal Number of Votes, then the House of Representatives shall immediately chuse by Ballot one of them for President; and if no Person have a Majority, then from the five highest on the List the said House shall in like Manner chuse the President. But in chusing the President, the Votes shall be taken by States, the Representation from each State having one Vote; A Quorum for this Purpose shall consist of a Member or Members from two thirds of the States, and a Majority of all the States shall be necessary to a Choice. In every Case, after the Choice of the President, the Person having the greatest Number of Votes of the Electors shall be the Vice President. But if there should remain two or more who have equal Votes, the Senate shall chuse from them by Ballot the Vice President.]

---

* This clause within brackets has been superseded and annulled by the 12th amendment.

3d. "The Congress may determine the Time of chusing the Electors, and the Day on which they shall give their Votes; which Day shall be the same throughout the United States."

4th. "No Person except a natural born Citizen, or a Citizen of the United States, at the time of the Adoption of this Constitution, shall be eligible to the Office of President; neither shall any Person be eligible to that Office who shall not have attained to the Age of thirty five Years, and been fourteen Years a Resident within the United States."

5th. "In Case of the Removal of the President from Office, or of his Death, Resignation, or Inability to discharge the Powers and Duties of the said Office, the same shall devolve on the Vice President, and the Congress may by Law provide for the Case of Removal, Death, Resignation, or Inability, both of the President and Vice President, declaring what Officer shall then act as President, and such Officer shall act accordingly, until the Disability be removed, or a President shall be elected."

6th. "The President shall, at stated Times, receive for his Services, a Compensation, which shall neither be encreased or diminished during the Period for which he shall have been elected, and he shall not receive within that Period any other Emolument from the United States, or any of them."

7th. "Before he enter on the Execution of his Office, he shall take the following Oath or Affirmation:—

"'I do solemnly swear (or affirm) that I will faithfully execute the Office of President of the United States, and will to the best of my Ability, preserve, protect and defend the Constitution of the United States.'"

8th. "The President shall be Commander in Chief of the Army and Navy of the United States, and of the

Militia of the several States, when called into the actual Service of the United States; he may require the Opinion, in writing, of the principal Officer in each of the executive Departments, upon any Subject relating to the Duties of their respective Offices, and he shall have Power to grant Reprieves and Pardons for Offences against the United States, except in Cases of Impeachment."

9th. "He shall have Power, by and with the Advice and Consent of the Senate, to make Treaties, provided two thirds of the Senators present concur; and he shall nominate, and by and with the Advice and Consent of the Senate, shall appoint Ambassadors, other public Ministers and Consuls, Judges of the supreme Court and all other Officers of the United States, whose Appointments are not herein otherwise provided for, and which shall be established by Law: but the Congress may by Law vest the Appointment of such inferior Officers, as they think proper, in the President alone, in the Courts of Law, or in the Heads of Departments."

10th. "The President shall have power to fill up all Vacancies that may happen during the Recess of the Senate, by granting Commissions which shall expire at the End of their next Session."

11th. "He shall from time to time give to the Congress Information of the State of the Union, and recommend to their Consideration such Measures as he shall judge necessary and expedient; he may, on extraordinary Occasions, convene both Houses, or either of them, and in Case of Disagreement between them, with respect to the Time of Adjournment, he may adjourn them to such Time as he shall think proper; he shall receive Ambassadors and other public Ministers; he shall take Care that the Laws be faithfully executed, and shall Commission all the officers of the United States."

12th. "The President, Vice President and all civil Officers of the United States, shall be removed from office on Impeachment for, and Conviction of, Treason, Bribery, or other high Crimes and Misdemeanors."

THIRD.—COVENANTS RELATING TO THE JUDICIAL DEPARTMENT.

1st. "The judicial Power of the United States, shall be vested in one supreme Court, and in such inferior Courts as the Congress may from time ordain and establish. The Judges, both of the supreme and inferior Courts, shall hold their offices during good Behavior, and shall, at stated Times, receive for their Services, a Compensation, which shall not be diminished during their Continuance in Office."

2d. "The judicial Power shall extend to all Cases, in Law and Equity, arising under this Constitution, the Laws of the United States, and Treaties made, or which shall be made, under their Authority;—to all Cases affecting Ambassadors, other public Ministers, and Consuls;—to all Cases of admiralty and maritime Jurisdiction;—to Controversies to which the United States shall be a Party;—to Controversies between two or more States;—between a State and Citizens of another State;—between Citizens of different States,—between Citizens of the same State claiming Lands under Grants of different States, and between a State, or the Citizens thereof, and foreign States, Citizens or subjects."

3d. "In all Cases affecting Ambassadors, other public Ministers and Consuls, and those in which a State shall be Party, the supreme Court shall have original jurisdiction. In all the other Cases before mentioned, the supreme Court shall have appellate Jurisdiction, both as to Law and Fact, with such Exceptions, and under such Regulations as the Congress shall make."

4th. "The Trial of all Crimes, except in Cases of Impeachment, shall be by Jury; and such Trial shall be held in the State where the said Crimes shall have been committed; but when not committed within any State, the Trial shall be at such Place or Places as the Congress may by Law have directed."

NOW THE COVENANTS OF THE SECOND CLASS IN ORDER.

1st. "No State shall enter into any Treaty, Alliance, or Confederation; grant Letters of Marque and Reprisal; coin Money; emit Bills of Credit; make any Thing but gold and silver Coin a Tender in Payment of Debts; pass any Bill of Attainder, ex post facto Law, or Law impairing the Obligation of Contracts, or grant any Title of Nobility."

2d. "No State shall, without the consent of the Congress, lay any Imposts or Duties on Imports or Exports, except what may be absolutely necessary for executing it's inspection Laws: and the net Produce of all Duties and Imposts, laid by any State on Imports or Exports, shall be for the Use of the Treasury of the United States; and all such Laws shall be subject to the Revision and Controul of the Congress."

3d. "No State shall, without the Consent of Congress, lay any Duty of Tonnage, keep Troops, or Ships of War in time of Peace, enter into any Agreement or Compact with another State, or with a foreign Power, or engage in War, unless actually invaded, or in such imminent Danger as will not admit of Delay."

4th. "Full Faith and Credit shall be given in each State to the public Acts, Records, and judicial Proceedings of every other State. And the Congress may by general Laws prescribe the Manner in which such Acts, Records and Proceedings shall be proved, and the Effect thereof."

5th. "The Citizens of each State shall be entitled to all Privileges and Immunities of Citizens in the several States."

6th. "A Person charged in any State with Treason, Felony, or other Crime, who shall flee from Justice, and be found in another State, shall on demand of the executive authority of the State from which he fled, be delivered up, to be removed to the State having Jurisdiction of the Crime."

7th. "No Person held to Service or Labour in one State, under the Laws thereof, escaping into another, shall, in Consequence of any Law or Regulation therein, be discharged from such Service or Labour, but shall be delivered up on Claim of the Party to whom such Service or Labour may be due."

8th. "All Debts contracted and Engagements entered into, before the Adoption of this Constitution, shall be as valid against the United States under this Constitution, as under the Confederation."

9th. "This Constitution, and the Laws of the United States which shall be made in Pursuance thereof; and all Treaties made, or which shall be made, under the authority of the United States, shall be the supreme Law of the Land; and the Judges in every State shall be bound thereby, any Thing in the Constitution or Laws of any State to the Contrary notwithstanding."

10th. "The Senators and Representatives before mentioned, and the Members of the several State Legislatures, and all executive and judicial Officers, both of the United States and of the several States, shall be bound by Oath or Affirmation, to support this Constitution; but no religious Test shall ever be required as a Qualification to any Office or public Trust under the United States."

11th. "The United States shall guarantee to every

State in this Union a Republican Form of Government, and shall protect each of them against Invasion, and on Application of the Legislature, or of the Executive (when the Legislature cannot be convened) against domestic Violence."

These are all the Covenants between the States, arranged in order by analysis, as stated, except two, which may more properly be set forth, after we examine the enumeration of the Powers delegated and the terms used in their delegation.

These are as follows: First, specific grants of power; and secondly, certain limitations upon the Powers so granted or delegated.

FIRST.—THE SPECIFIC POWERS DELEGATED.

"The Congress shall have power"

1st. "To lay and collect Taxes, Duties, Imposts and Excises, to pay the Debts and provide for the common Defence and general Welfare of the United States; but all Duties, Imposts and Excises shall be uniform throughout the United States;"

2d. "To borrow Money on the credit of the United States;"

3d. "To regulate Commerce with foreign Nations, and among the several States, and with the Indian Tribes;"

4th. "To establish an uniform Rule of Naturalization, and uniform Laws on the subject of Bankruptcies throughout the United States;"

5th. "To coin Money, regulate the Value thereof, and of foreign Coin, and fix the Standard of Weights and Measures;"

6th. "To provide for the Punishment of counterfeiting the Securities and current Coin of the United States,"

7th. "To establish Post Offices and post Roads;"

8th. "To promote the progress of Science and useful Arts, by securing for limited Times to Authors and Inventors the exclusive Right to their respective Writings and Discoveries;"

9th. "To constitute Tribunals inferior to the supreme Court;"

10th. "To define and punish Piracies and Felonies committed on the high Seas, and Offences against the Law of Nations;

"Treason against the United States, shall consist only in levying War against them, or in adhering to their Enemies, giving them Aid and Comfort. No Person shall be convicted of Treason unless on the Testimony of two Witnesses to the same overt Act, or on Confession in open Court."

11th. "The Congress shall have Power to declare the Punishment of Treason, but no Attainder of Treason shall work Corruption of Blood, or Forfeiture except during the Life of the Person attainted."

12th. "To declare War, grant Letters of Marque and Reprisal, and make Rules concerning Captures on Land and Water;"

13th. "To raise and support Armies, but no Appropriation of Money to that Use shall be for a longer Term than two Years;"

14th. "To provide and maintain a Navy;"

15th. "To make Rules for the Government and Regulation of the land and naval Forces;"

16th. "To provide for calling forth the Militia to execute the Laws of the Union, suppress Insurrections and repel Invasions;"

17th. "To provide for organizing, arming, and disciplining, the Militia, and for governing such Part of them as may be employed in the Service of the United States, reserving to the States respectively, the Appointment of the Officers, and the Authority of training the Militia according to the Discipline prescribed by Congress;"

18th. "To exercise exclusive Legislation in all Cases whatsoever, over such District (not exceeding ten Miles square) as may, by Cession of particular States, and the Acceptance of Congress, become the Seat of the Government of the United States, and to exercise like Authority over all Places purchased by the Consent of the Legislature of the State in which the Same shall be for the Erection of Forts, Magazines, Arsenals, Dock-Yards, and other needful buildings;—And"

19th. "To make all Laws which shall be necessary and proper for carrying into Execution the foregoing Powers, and all other Powers vested by this Constitution in the Government of the United States, or in any Department or Officer thereof."

20th. "New States may be admitted by the Congress into this Union; but no new State shall be formed or erected within the Jurisdiction of any other State; nor any State be formed by the Junction of two or more States, or Parts of States, without the Consent of the Legislatures of the States concerned as well as of the Congress."

21st. "The Congress shall have Power to dispose of and make all needful Rules and Regulations respecting the Territory or other Property belonging to the United States; and nothing in this Constitution shall be so construed as to Prejudice any Claims of the United States, or of any particular State."

SECONDLY.—LIMITATIONS ON THE POWERS DELEGATED.

1st. "The Migration or Importation of such Persons as any of the States now existing shall think proper to admit, shall not be prohibited by the Congress prior to the Year one thousand eight hundred and eight, but a Tax or Duty may be imposed on such Importation, not exceeding ten dollars for each Person."

2d. "The Privilege of the Writ of Habeas Corpus shall not be suspended, unless when in Cases of Rebellion or Invasion the public Safety may require it."

3d. "No Bill of Attainder or ex post facto Law shall be passed."

4th. "No Capitation, or other direct, Tax shall be laid, unless in Proportion to the Census or Enumeration herein before directed to be taken."

5th. "No Tax or Duty shall be laid on Articles exported from any State."

6th. "No preference shall be given by any Regulation of Commerce or Revenue to the Ports of one State over those of another: nor shall Vessels bound to, or from, one State, be obliged to enter, clear, or pay Duties in another."

7th. "No money shall be drawn from the Treasury, but in Consequence of Appropriations made by Law; and a regular Statement and Account of the Receipts and Expenditures of all public Money shall be published from time to time."

8th. "No title of Nobility shall be granted by the United States: And no Person holding any Office of Profit or Trust under them, shall, without the Consent of the Congress, accept of any present, Emolument, Office, or Title, of any kind whatever, from any King, Prince, or foreign State."

These are all the powers delegated, with their limitations. We come, now, in our classification and arrangement of the entire Constitution, to the two remaining stipulations, which belong properly to the Covenants between the States, but which, in any general classification, may more properly be put at the conclusion of the whole.

These are:

1st. "The Congress, whenever two thirds of both Houses shall deem it necessary, shall propose Amendments to this Constitution, or, on the Application of the Legislatures of two thirds of the several States, shall call a Convention for proposing Amendments, which, in either Case, shall be valid to all Intents and Purposes, as Part of this Constitution, when ratified by the Legislatures of three fourths of the several States, or by Conventions in three fourths thereof, as the one or the other Mode of Ratification may be proposed by the Congress; Provided that no Amendment, which may be made prior to the Year one thousand eight hundred and eight, shall in any Manner affect the first and fourth Clauses in the Ninth Section of the first Article; and that no State, without its Consent, shall be deprived of its equal Suffrage in the Senate."

2d. "The Ratification of the Conventions of nine States, shall be sufficient for the Establishment of this Constitution between the States so ratifying the Same.

"DONE in Convention by the Unanimous Consent of the States present the Seventeenth day of September, in the Year of our Lord one thousand seven hundred and Eighty-seven, and of the Independence of the United States of America the Twelfth.

"IN WITNESS whereof We have hereunto subscribed our Names.

"GEORGE WASHINGTON—
"*Presidt and Deputy from Virginia.*

NEW HAMPSHIRE.

John Langdon, Nicholas Gilman.

MASSACHUSETTS.

Nathaniel Gorham, Rufus King,

CONNECTICUT.

Wm. Saml. Johnson, Roger Sherman.

NEW YORK.

Alexander Hamilton.

NEW JERSEY.

Will: Livingston, David Brearley,
Wm. Paterson, Jona. Dayton.

PENNSYLVANIA.

B. Franklin, Thomas Mifflin,
Robt. Morris, Geo: Clymer,
Thos: Fitzsimons, Jared Ingersoll,
James Wilson, Gouv: Morris.

DELAWARE,

Geo: Read, Gunning Bedford, Jun'r,
John Dickinson, Richard Bassett.
Jaco: Broom,

MARYLAND.

James M'Henry, Dan: of St. Thos. Jenifer.
Danl Carroll,

VIRGINIA.

John Blair, James Madison, Jr.,

NORTH CAROLINA.

Wm. Blount, Rich'd Dobbs Spaight.
Hu. Williamson,

SOUTH CAROLINA.

J. Rutledge, Charles Cotesworth Pinckney,
Charles Pinckney, Pierce Butler.

GEORGIA.

William Few, Abr. Baldwin.
Attest: WILLIAM JACKSON, *Secretary* ."

We have thus gone through with the whole of the original Constitution, as it, at first, came from the hands of the Convention; we have examined it from the beginning to the end—from the Preamble to the signatures of the Delegates. We see that the members of each

Delegation signed it in behalf of the State represented by them. The subsequent amendments, we may, hereafter, examine.

The articles, sections, and clauses, as arranged by the Committee on Style, have not been followed in this analysis. But every section, clause and word, are set forth in it, as the original stands engrossed in the Archives of State, at Washington.* The order of their arrangement only is changed. This does not mar the sense, in the slightest particular, in a single instance, but gives a clearer conception, it appears to me, of the whole instrument, taken together; as all instruments, in writing, should be, to be thoroughly and correctly understood. Now, after scanning the whole, taken together, what section, clause, phrase or word, on the face of the Constitution itself, shows any intention, on the part of the framers, to merge the separate Sovereignty of all the States into one, under it; and, by its adoption, to establish a National Government, instead of perfecting and continuing, under a new organization, with enlarged powers, the Federal Union, then existing between the States, and for the remedying of which, the Convention was called? It was made, we see, by States. It was to be established, we see, not *over*, but *between*, the States ratifying it.

Is not the leading idea, throughout the whole instrument, that the new Government was to be a Compact between States, as the old one was? States pervade the whole instrument. The Senators are to be elected by the Legislatures of the *several States*. The House of Representatives is to be composed of members, chosen by the people of the several States; and to be chosen by

---

* *Edition of the Constitution by Hickey*, p. 31.

electors, possessing such qualifications as *each State, for itself,* may prescribe for the electors of the most numerous branch of its own State Legislature. Thus providing that every member of the Legislative body should be chosen, in the one branch, directly by the States, as such, and in the other branch, by constituencies, to be formed and controlled absolutely by the States, severally.

"Representatives and taxation shall be apportioned among the *several States.*"

"*Each State shall have, at least, one Representative.*" When vacancies happen "in *any State,*" etc.

The Congress shall have power to regulate commerce with foreign nations, "and among the *several States.*" "The migration and importation of such persons as any of the *States,*" etc.

"No preference shall be given," etc., "to the ports of *one State* over those of another," etc. "Nor shall vessels, bound to or from *one State,* be obliged to enter, clear, or pay duties in another."

"No *State* shall enter into any treaty," etc.

"No *State* shall, without the consent of *the Congress,* lay any imposts," etc.

"No *State* shall," without the like consent of the Congress, "lay any duty of tonnage, keep troops or ships of war in time of peace, enter into any agreement or compact with another *State,* or with a foreign Power, or engage in war, unless actually invaded," etc.

Nothing appears more prominent in the whole instrument than *States.* The very first Article in the Constitution declares that all Legislative powers under it shall be vested in "*a Congress of the United States.*" The term "Congress of the United States" was familiar to all at that day. It was well known to mean "The United States in Congress assembled." Congress means a meeting or an assemblage. A Congress of States means a Meeting or Assemblage of States. The title of Congress, under the Confederation, had been "The United States of America in Congress assembled." The same title is still retained. To this very day, the enacting clause of every law, passed by "the Congress," under the Constitution, is in these words:—

"*Be it enacted by the Senate and House of Representatives of the United States of America in Congress assembled.*"

Every law that has been passed, from the beginning, under this Constitution, as under the Articles of Confederation, derives its *sole* authority, as its face shows, from States in Congress assembled!

The whole operation of the Government, from its first starting, depended upon the action of the States. The election of President and Vice President, from the first to the last, depended entirely upon the States, as States, and, also, the election of Senators. Nor can there be a House of Representatives in the Congress without the co-operation of the States! The General Government, created by the instrument, has no authority, as appears from its face, to enter any State, or take jurisdiction over a foot of her soil, even for the erection of forts and arsenals, etc., except by her consent, first had and obtained by contract or purchase. This shows that the Right of Eminent Domain, the indisputable attribute and accompaniment of Sovereignty, remained with the States, severally, even over such places as might thus pass, in fee, from them, or their citizens, to the United States, as in like purchases, in all cases whatsoever.

What is there, then, in this whole instrument, that looks towards such a consolidation of the whole people of this country into one community or Nation, as Mr. Motley contends, and as you maintain?

Judge Bynum. Does not what is said about Treason look that way?

Mr. Stephens. Not at all; if it be true that the Constitution was a Compact between Sovereign States. That is the point in issue. All such inferences, as you refer to, depend upon this primary and essential fact, touching the nature and character of the Government. Nothing is clearer than that Sovereign States may agree, by Compact, between themselves, that certain acts of the citizens of each, against all jointly, shall be deemed and held to be criminal against them jointly, and punished by their joint authority. Such is the case, in this Constitution, as to counterfeiting the current coin and securities of the United States, and divers other offences. The granting of power to punish such offences against the joint authority of all, while the Compact lasts, does not, in the least, in itself, compromit the Sovereignty of each, or change the allegiance of her citizens; which, independently of the Compact, must, by acknowledgment, be admitted to be due to her Paramount authority. The Articles of Confederation delegated the power to punish piracy.

So, it is perfectly consistent with the reserved Sovereignty of each party to such a Compact, to agree among themselves that levying war upon all of them, or adhering to their enemies, giving them aid and comfort, by the citizens of any one of them, shall be considered Treason against all; inasmuch as such an act would, unquestionably, be Treason against the State, of which such persons are citizens, in the breach, which it would necessarily involve, of their allegiance, due to the Paramount authority of the State, in entering into such a Compact, which, by its very nature, is to be binding upon each State, and all her citizens, as the Supreme law, so long as it may last.

It is perfectly competent for Sovereign States to make such an agreement, or compact, as this, without compromitting their Sovereignty, or changing, in the least degree, the ultimate, absolute allegiance of all their citizens, which, by the laws of Nations, is due to their Paramount authority. This is just what the Constitution did on that subject, if it be a Compact between Sovereign States, and that is the point of our inquiry.

In further illustration of the view I was presenting, to show that it is such a Compact, and that no such inference, as you would draw from the words about treason, is at all maintainable, I call your special attention to the fact that there is, in the Constitution, no Covenant, or Delegation of power to the Congress, to define, or punish treason, generally, as all Sovereigns, without doubt, have power to do. That is left with the States, severally, and a solemn Compact entered into, that all persons, charged with treason against any one of the States, fleeing into another State, shall, upon demand, etc., be given up, etc. This shows, clearly, that the general allegiance of the citizens of the several States was not intended to be transferred, by this clause of the Constitution, to the United States. Indeed, there is not a word about allegiance in the whole of it.

Moreover, all that is said upon the subject, in this clause, is only an enlargement in one sense, and a restriction in another, of powers under the Articles of Confederation. There is no change of principle in the nature of the Government, in this particular, in the new Constitution, from the old.

Under the Articles of Confederation, the States, in Congress assembled, had power, as we have seen, to make "Rules for the Government of the land and naval forces," etc. By virtue of this clause they had power not only to punish, but to define what acts should constitute treason against the joint authority of all the States, when committed by any one in the land or naval forces. It was under this clause, doubtless, or under the Rules and Articles of War, established by virtue of it, that Arnold would have been executed, if he had not made his escape. But no one thought that, because Arnold, a citizen of the State of Connecticut, was held and deemed to be guilty of treason against the United States, that, therefore, his allegiance, and the allegiance of all the people of Connecticut, and the allegiance of all the people of all the States, was necessarily, thereby, under the Confederation, transferred from the States, severally, to the United States. We have seen that the Supreme Court of the United States has decided the very reverse, or, that the allegiance of the citizens of the States, severally, during the Confederation, was due to their States respectively.* Hence it follows that it was perfectly consistent, with a full reservation of power to the States, severally, over the allegiance of their citizens, to enter into just such a Compact, as I maintain this to be. This part of the Constitution, as I have said, is but an enlargement, in one sense, and a restriction, in another, of powers delegated under the Articles of Confederation. It is enlarged, so as to embrace all citizens of the States, respectively, whether in the land or naval forces or not; and restricted in this, that the offence, defined in the Constitution to be Treason against the United States, shall consist, only, in levying war against them, or in adhering to their enemies, giving them aid and comfort, with a limitation as to the extent of the punishment. A farther restriction is

* *Ante*, p. 76.

that a person charged with treason, now, cannot be tried by Military Courts. The trial, in all cases, must be by the Civil Courts. The crime can only exist, when the act is committed by the citizens of any State, not only against her, but against all the other States with which she stands united by a solemn Compact.

The Paramount Sovereignty of each State to command the allegiance of her citizens, in case she should exercise it—in severing, as in making, the Compact—cannot be transferred by inference or implication. This, as we have seen, can pass, only, by express terms of surrender.* There is no such express surrender in the Constitution, nor can any intention to make such be inferred, even upon taking the whole Constitution together. None, at least, from this clause of the Constitution. Is there any other that even looks that way?

PROFESSOR NORTON. If it were not for what you said, in the beginning, about the clause which declares that this Constitution, and the laws of the United States, which shall be made in pursuance thereof, and all treaties made, or which shall be made, under the authority of the United States, shall be the supreme law of the land, etc., I should certainly say that that does look that way. But, from what you have said, I suppose you hold that it does not.

MR STEPHENS. Most assuredly I do; and for the reasons before given. This clause contains no delegation of power,—makes no acknowledgment of a surrender of any. It simply declares a fact, or truth, which results from the nature of the Compact. The same fact, here declared, was admitted to exist under the Articles of the Confederation. They were equally the supreme law

---

* *Ante*, p. 83.

of the land, while they lasted, as the Constitution now is.* They were just as obligatory, upon the States, as the Constitution is. So said Mr. Hamilton and Mr. Madison, and so held Mr. Justice Chase, on the Supreme Court Bench, as we have seen.† This clause, as Mr. Hamilton said, is only a limitation inserted out of abundant caution. That limitation was to rebut the very inference that you would draw. It was inserted to make it clear that not only was the *allegiance* of the citizens of the several States not transferred, by virtue of any thing in the Constitution, to the United States, but that even *obedience* to their laws, etc., could be enjoined, only so far as these laws were made in *pursuance of the Constitution!*

The great difference between this clause, offered in substance by Luther Martin, and the one offered by the Nationals, and for which Martin's was substituted, was, that theirs gave to the United States the power or right to *judge* as *between them* and the *States* severally upon Constitutional infractions, while his refused to delegate this power, leaving it, therefore, with the States, where it was before.

PROF. NORTON. If this be so, please, then, explain, if you can, why the next clause was added, which requires the members of the several State Legislatures, and all Executive and Judicial officers of the States, to take an oath to support the Constitution?

MR. STEPHENS. This can be easily done, and in no more pertinent language, perhaps, than Mr. Madison used in answering the same question, when asked, while the Constitution was before the people for their consideration. In the forty-third number of the Federalist, he says:‡

"It has been asked why it was thought necessary

* *Ante*, pp. 45–48 † *Ibid.* ‡ *Dawson's Edition*, p. 317.

that the State magistracy should be bound to support the Federal Constitution, and unnecessary that a like oath should be imposed on the officers of the United States in favor of the State Constitutions. Several reasons might be assigned for the distinction. I content myself with one which is obvious and conclusive. The members of the Federal Government will have no agency in carrying the State Constitutions into effect. The members of the State Governments, on the contrary, will have an essential agency in giving effect to the Federal Constitution. The election of the President and Senate will depend, in all cases, on the Legislatures of the several States." etc.

This is the reason Mr. Madison assigned for it. Whether it was a conclusive reason for the propriety of putting this clause in or not, yet his giving it, when he did, and as he did, is conclusive proof that no inference can be drawn from the clause, as it stands in the Constitution, that it was intended, by virtue of it, any more than by virtue of the other clause just before it, to transfer the allegiance of the citizens of the several States to the United States; and, thereby, form a National Government instead of a Federal one. Mr. Madison, recollect, was one of the extremest in the Convention for a National Government, and not a Federal one; but here, in speaking of the nature of the Government which was finally agreed upon, he calls it "*the Federal Government*," and the Constitution he styles "the Federal Constitution."

This oath was opposed by Mr. Wilson, one of the leading Nationals in the Convention. "He said he was not fond of oaths. He considered them a left-handed security. A good Government did not need them, and a bad one could not or ought not to be supported."* He, certainly, did not regard it as you do.

---

* *Madison Papers, Elliot's Debates*, vol. v, p. 352.

But, as also quite pertinent in further answer to your question, I refer to what Mr. Madison said, in the next number of the Federalist, upon the general nature of the powers delegated under the Constitution, from which it clearly appears that he did not consider the nature of the new Government *essentially* changed, in any *particular*, from what it was under the Confederation.

"If the new Constitution," says he, "be examined with accuracy and candor, it will be found that the change which it proposes consists much less in the addition of NEW POWERS to the Union, than in the invigoration of its ORIGINAL POWERS. The regulation of commerce, it is true, is a new power; but that seems to be an addition which few oppose, and from which no apprehensions are entertained. The powers relating to war and peace, armies and fleets, treaties and finances, with the other more *considerable powers*, are all vested in the existing Congress by the Articles of Confederation. The proposed change does not enlarge these powers; it only substitutes a more effectual mode of administering them. The change relating to taxation may be regarded as the most important; and yet the present Congress have as complete authority to REQUIRE of the States indefinite supplies of money for the common defence and general welfare, as the future Congress will have to require them of individual citizens; and the latter will be no more bound than the States themselves have been, to pay the quotas respectively taxed on them."*

From both these extracts from the Federalist, it clearly appears that Mr. Madison, who is styled the father of the Constitution, did not consider that the Federative nature and character of the previously existing Union between the States was essentially changed in any particular by

* *Mr. Madison, Federalist,* No. 44, p. 324, *Dawson's Edition.*

the new Constitution, framed with the view of perfecting that Union.

"The change," says he, "consists much less in the addition of *new powers* to the Union than in the invigoration of its original powers!" Words of what import are these, coming from the source they did? And how true we shall find them to be upon examining closely the analysis of the various provisions of the two instruments, the Articles of Confederation and the Constitution which we have made? What are the new powers delegated in the Constitution?

These, upon examining the analysis in each case and comparing them, will be found to be

1st. The power to raise revenue by duties upon imposts and taxes directly upon the people without resort to requisitions upon the States.

2d. The power to make the rules for aliens to be admitted to citizenship in the several States, uniform in all the States, and like uniform rules regulating bankruptcy.

3d. The power to promote the progress of science and useful arts by securing, for limited times, to authors and inventors, the exclusive right to their writings and discoveries.

4th. The power to regulate commerce with Foreign Nations, among the several States, and with the Indian Tribes.

This, Mr. Madison puts amongst the new powers. Though, in fact, it was but an enlargement of a previously existing power in the Congress. By the Articles of the Confederation, the Congress had power to regulate trade with the Indian Tribes. This power in the Constitution was only enlarged by extending it to Foreign Nations and among the several States as well as the Indian Tribes. It is in principle not a new power, but an old one, extended and enlarged.

Besides these four there is hardly a new power delegated in the new Constitution of sufficient importance to need special notice.

The Covenants between the States, imposing restraints and assuming obligations, run almost in the same language throughout both instruments.

Amongst the new restraints the most important are

1st. That no State shall emit bills of credit or make any thing but gold and silver a legal tender in the payment of debts; pass any bill of attainder; or *ex post facto* law, or law impairing the obligation of contracts, or grant any title of nobility.

2d. No State shall, without the consent of Congress, lay any imposts or duty upon imports, exports, etc.

The prohibitions against any of the States forming alliances, etc., making war, etc., are nearly the same in both.

One striking feature in the new Constitution is that the States under it have entire control over their *militia.*

The Congress, under the Constitution, has no power over them, except to provide by law for organizing, arming, disciplining them; and for calling them out for specific purposes and governing them when in the service of the United States. But the States have retained to themselves severally the power of training and officering and sending them forth upon any call made for them.

By the Articles of Confederation the Congress had the appointment of all the officers of the *militia* when in service, from the regimental officers up. By the Constitution the power is reserved to the States to appoint all the officers of the *militia,* whether in service or not, from the lowest to the highest.

Great stress, by many, has been put upon the Judicial Department in the new system. This, however, is no new feature. Under the Articles of Confederation there was a Judiciary provided. It is enlarged in the new Constitution, that is all. There is no change in principle in this particular.

Of all the new obligations assumed by the States, the most important, and one without which, it was universally admitted, the Constitution could not be formed, is that which provides for the rendition of fugitives from service from one State to another. We shall have much to say of this hereafter. It was, however, only an enlargement of the principle in the Articles of Confederation on which fugitives from justice were to be delivered up. And Mr. Madison truly said, after his enumeration, that all the other *more considerable powers* under the Constitution were vested in the Congress under the Articles of Confederation. If the States then, under the Confederation, retained their Sovereignty severally, why do they not under this Constitution?

Did their people, by adopting this Constitution, understand that, thereby, they were surrendering the separate Sovereignty of the States? That, for which the war of the Revolution had been fought, and for the maintenance of which the Confederation had been formed? Did they understand that, thereafter, there were to be no more States United by a Compact of Union between them, but that all the people of the whole land, by the ratification of this Constitution, were to be merged into one body-politic, into one Community, one Nation under a social Compact? Does the Constitution, on its face, taken altogether or in any part, admit any such construction? Does not the clause next to the last, which provides for future changes or amendments in it, utterly refute and negative forever every such idea or supposition; or rather every such gross heresy?

In this it is expressly stipulated, that upon all future changes, or amendments, the States, as States, shall act, and that it shall require the concurrence of three fourths of all the States, in their State organization, and by their State Governments, to make any alteration or amendment. It is especially stipulated, that no amendment shall ever be made, which shall deprive the States of their equal suffrage in the Senate! Does not this clearly show where ultimate Sovereign power rests under this system? That is, that it *remains* with the States severally, now, just as it did under the Confederation.

Can this clause of the Constitution admit of any other version or reading without the grossest violation of the plainest import of language? Was not that the understanding of it by its authors and framers? If not, what mockery is there in the last of the mutual Covenants in our classification? That is in these words:

"The United States shall guarantee to every State in this Union a Republican form of Government, and shall protect each of them against invasion, and on application of the Legislature, or of the Executive (when the Legislature cannot be convened) against domestic violence."

Is not this the language of Confederation? The language of Compact? The language of Alliance between Sovereign States? Alliance for mutual safety and protection against foes without, as well as foes within? Do not all the States United, under this Compact, by this clause, guarantee its own Institutions to each State in the Alliance thus formed? Not that the clause confers any power on the States jointly to interfere in any manner or form, or in any contingency, in changing, modelling, moulding, or shaping the Institutions of any State according to their joint will or pleasure! No more palpable, or gross a perversion of the meaning of words could be made, than such a construction as that. But does it not clearly set forth a solemn obligation on the part of her Confederates to maintain, sustain and secure, by their joint authority and means, to each State, such Republican Institutions as each State, for itself, in its own Sovereign will, may adopt?

My dear Sirs, what is a State? Did not the framers of this instrument understand the meaning of the words they used? Is it not a body-politic—a Community organized with all the functions and powers of Government within itself?

Vattel says: "Nations, or States, are bodies-politic. Societies of men, united together for the purpose of their mutual safety and advantage by the efforts of their combined strength. Such society has her affairs and her interests; she deliberates and takes resolutions in common, thus becoming a moral person, who possesses an understanding and a will peculiar to herself and is susceptible of obligations and rights."*

Were not the States for which this Constitution was framed, and by which it was adopted as a bond of Union, such bodies politic? Such "several Sovereign and independent States," as, according to the same author previously quoted, "may unite themselves together by a perpetual Confederacy, without ceasing to be, each, a *perfect State*," and without any impairment, as he says, of "the Sovereignty of each?"†

Were they not just such States as, Montesquieu says, may form "a Confederate Republic," in which case "the Confederacy may be dissolved, and the Confederates preserve their Sovereignty?" Were they not such States as, Cicero says, ought to possess within themselves princi-

* *Preliminaries to Treatise on the Laws of Nations*, p. **49.**

† *Ante*, p. 169.

ples of indestructibility? "A State," says he,* "should "be so constituted as to live forever! For a Commonwealth there is no natural dissolution, as there is for a man to whom death not only becomes necessary, but often desirable." When "a State," however, "is put an end to, it is destroyed, extinguished," annihilated!

There is nothing, says this profound philosopher, in another place, "in which human virtue can more closely resemble the Divine Powers, than in establishing new States, or in preserving those already established!"

Were States ever more Providentially, yea, Divinely, established, than these had been? Under their whole superstructure, in their Declaration of Independence, lie the great truths, announced by political bodies for the first time in the history of the world, of the capacity and right of man to self-government. That all Governments "derive their just powers from the consent of the governed," and that, "whenever any Government becomes destructive of the ends" for which it is established, "it is the right of the people to alter or abolish it, and to institute a new Government, laying its foundation on such principles, and organizing its powers in such forms, as to them may seem most likely to effect their safety and happiness." This is asserted to be the inalienable right of all Peoples and all States! On these immutable principles, the Governments of these States had been established, separately, and severally. Were States ever established that so well deserved to live forever?

Was there ever a grander exhibition of this highest of all bare human virtues, according to Cicero, than was presented by the Patriot Fathers of 1787, in forming this Constitution? Was not their main, chief, and lead-

---

* *Cicero on the Commonwealth.*

ing object throughout, and the object of the Union under it, to *preserve*, and to *perpetuate*, as far as possible by human agency, these separate and several States so established? Is not this apparent from the whole work? Is it not apparent from the face of the instrument, from its Alpha to its Omega? In other words, is not the Constitution, upon its face, as made, without looking into the subsequent amendments, *Federal* in its *every feature*, from beginning to end?

What say you?

PROF. NORTON. I will postpone what I have to say until you get through.

MR. STEPHENS. Well, then, the next step with me, after this examination of the Constitution itself, will be to look into the action of the several States upon it, and see whether they considered it as uniting and consolidating the whole people of the country, over which it was to extend, into one Nation, or whether they considered it, as Washington did, a consolidation of the Union of States, joined together by it, into one Great Confederated Republic.

COLLOQUY VI.

THE ACTION OF THE SEVERAL STATES ON THE CONSTITUTION—DEBATES IN THE SEVERAL STATE CONVENTIONS—COMMENTS THEREON.

MR. STEPHENS. The next step, then, in our inquiry and investigation, will be to look into the action of the several States upon this Constitution, when it was submitted to their Legislatures, by the Congress, as requested by the Convention, and see how it was understood by them, and what construction was put upon it by its supporters and advocates. Whether it was considered by them as a surrender of the Sovereignty of the several States, or simply as a new Constitutional Compact, between the States, upon the same Federal basis, as the former Articles of their Union had been.

We will take them up in their order of ratification. In each case, looking first into the the action of the State, and, secondly, into the debates, where any have been preserved, as part of the *res gestæ*, showing the understanding of the States, in their ratification, as appears from the record.

FIRST, DELAWARE.

The Legislature of the State of Delaware called a Convention of her people to consider the Constitution, and take action upon it, according to the request of Congress. In the Convention of this State, there seems to have been no division and no discussion. At least, none of the debates in that body, if any were had, have been preserved. Here is the action of the Convention.

"We, the Deputies of the People of the Delaware State, in Convention met, having taken into our serious consideration the Federal Constitution, proposed and agreed upon by the Deputies of the United States, in a General Convention, held at the City of Philadelphia, on the seventeenth day of September, in the year of our Lord one thousand seven hundred and eighty-seven, have approved, assented to, ratified, and confirmed, and by these presents do, in virtue of the power and authority to us given, for and in behalf of ourselves and our constituents, fully, freely, and entirely approve of, assent to, ratify, and confirm, the said Constitution.

"Done in Convention, at Dover, this seventh day of December, in the year aforesaid, and in the year of the Independence of the United States of America, the twelfth."*

In this very act of ratification, we see it styled, by the Sovereign people of Delaware, "The Federal Constitution." Indeed, no one can doubt, for a moment, from the Course of her Delegates, in the Philadelphia Convention, that the People of Delaware understood the Constitution, as they here style it, to be Federal in its character, and that the Sovereignty of the State was still retained.

SECOND, PENNSYLVANIA.

The next State in order was Pennsylvania. In this, as in the case of Delaware, let us look *first* into the action of the State and then into the debates, as far as we have them, to see what light they throw upon this action. First, then, the action of the Convention is in these words.

---

* *Elliot's Debates*, vol. i, p. 319.

"In the Name of the People of Pennsylvania.

"Be it known unto all men, that we, the Delegates of the people of the Commonwealth of Pennsylvania, in General Convention assembled, have assented to and ratified, and by these presents do, in the name and by the authority of the same people, and for ourselves, assent to and ratify the foregoing Constitution for the United States of America. Done in Convention at Philadelphia, the twelfth day of December, in the year of our Lord one thousand seven hundred and eighty-seven, and of the independence of the United States of America the twelfth. In witness whereof, we have hereunto subscribed our names."*

No allusion in this is made to the character of the instrument or of the understanding of the members of the Convention of it, farther than their styling it a "Constitution *for the United States* of America." That is a Constitution *for States* United, and not for the whole mass of the people of these States in the aggregate. This of itself is quite enough to show that they considered it Federal or Federative in its character!

But we are not left in doubt or to inference on this point. The debates in the Convention of Pennsylvania have been in part preserved. The speeches of Mr. Wilson, at least, who had been in the Federal Convention that framed the Constitution, and who was also in the State Convention that ratified it, we have. These, it is true, are all of these debates that we have, but they throw much light upon the subject.

Mr. Wilson, recollect, was one of the ablest and most zealous of the Nationals in the Federal Convention. But when their plan failed, he, as Hamilton, Morris, King,

* *Elliot's Debates*, vol. i, p. 319.

and Madison, gave the Constitution agreed upon, his warm support. What he said, therefore, in the State Convention, touching the character, or nature of the Constitution, which was finally agreed upon, is entitled to great weight, and particularly all his disclaimers, as to its being a Consolidation of the whole people of the country into one single grand National Republic. Let us, then, in the second place, see what was his judgment of it, as given to the Pennsylvania Convention. In opening the deliberations of that body, he said:*

"The system proposed, by the late Convention, for the Government of the United States, is now before you. Of that Convention, I had the honor to be a member. As I am the only member of that body, who has the honor to be also a member of this, it may be expected that I should prepare the way for the deliberations of this Assembly, by unfolding the difficulties, which the late Convention was obliged to encounter; by pointing out the end which they proposed to accomplish; and by tracing the general principles which they have adopted for the accomplishment of that end." * * *

"A very important difficulty arose from comparing the extent of the country to be governed, with the kind of Government, which it would be proper to establish in it. It has been an opinion, countenanced by high authority, 'that the natural property of small States is to be governed as a Republic; of middling ones, to be subject to a monarchy; and of large empires, to be swayed by a despotic prince;—and that the consequence is, that, in order to preserve the principles of the established Government, the State must be supported in the extent it has acquired; and that the spirit of the State will alter in proportion

* *Elliot's Debates*, vol. ii, p. 418.

as it extends or contracts its limits.' (*Montesquieu*, b. viii, c. 20.) This opinion seems to be supported, rather than contradicted, by the history of the Governments in the old world. Here, then, the difficulty appeared in full view. On one hand, the United States contain an immense extent of Territory; and, according to the foregoing opinion, a despotic Government is best adapted to that extent. On the other hand, it was well known, that, however the citizens of the United States might with pleasure submit to the legitimate restraints of a Republican Constitution, they would reject with indignation the fetters of despotism. What, then, was to be done? The idea of a *Confederate Republic* presented itself. This kind of Constitution has been thought to have 'all the internal advantages of a Republican, together with the external force of a monarchical Government.' (*Montesquieu*, b. ix, c. 1, 2; *Paley*, 199, 202.)

"Its description is 'a Convention, by which several States agree to become members of a larger one, which they intend to establish. It is a kind of *assemblage of societies* that constitute *a new one*, capable of increasing by means of further association.' (*Montesquieu*, b. ix, c. 1.) The expanding quality of such Government is peculiarly fitted for the United States, the greatest part of whose territory is yet uncultivated.

"But while this form of Government enables us to surmount the difficulty last mentioned, it conducted us to another of which I am now to take notice. It left us almost without precedent or guide, and, consequently, without the benefit of that instruction which, in many cases, may be derived from the Constitution, and history, and experience, of other nations. Several associations have frequently been called by the name of Confederate States, which have not, in propriety of language, deserved it. The Swiss Cantons are connected only by alliances. The United Netherlands are, indeed, an assemblage of societies; but this assemblage constitutes *no new one,* and, therefore, it does not correspond with the full definition of a Confederate Republic. The Germanic body is composed of such disproportioned and discordant materials, and its structure is so intricate and complex, that little useful knowledge can be drawn from it. Ancient history discloses, and barely discloses, to our view, some Confederate Republics—the Achæan League, the Lycian Confederacy, and the Amphictyonic Council. But the facts recorded concerning their Constitutions are so few and general, and their histories are so unmarked and defective, that no satisfactory information can be collected from them, concerning many particular circumstances, from an accurate discernment and comparison of which, alone, legitimate and practical inferences can be made, from one Constitution to another. Besides, the situation and dimension of those Confederacies, and the state of society, manners, and habits, in them, were so different from those of the United States, that the most correct descriptions could have supplied but a very small fund of applicable remark. Thus, in forming *this system,* we were deprived of many advantages, which the history and experience of other ages and other countries would, in other cases, have afforded us." * * *

"To be left without guide or precedent was not the only difficulty in which the Convention was involved, by proposing to their constituents a plan of a *Confederated Republic.* They found themselves embarrassed with another, of peculiar delicacy and importance. I mean, that of drawing a proper line between the National Government and the Governments of the several States. It was easy to discover a proper and satisfactory principle on the subject. Whatever object of Government is *confined*, in its *operation* and effects, *within* the bounds of a particular State, should be considered as belonging to the Government of that State; whatever object of Government extends, in its *operation* or effects, *beyond* the bounds of a *particular* State, should be considered as belonging to the Government of the United States. But though this principle be sound and satisfactory, its application to particular cases would be accompanied with much difficulty, because, in its application, room must be allowed for great discretionary latitude of construction of the principle. In order to lessen or remove the difficulty arising from discretionary construction on this subject, *an enumeration of particular instances*, in which the application of the principle ought to take place, has been attempted with much industry and care. It is only in mathematical science that a line can be described with mathematical precision. But I flatter myself, that, upon the strictest investigation, the *enumeration* will be found to be *safe* and unexceptionable, and accurate, too, in as great a degree as accuracy can be expected in a subject of this nature. Particulars under this head will be more properly explained, when we descend to the minute view of the enumeration, which is made in the proposed Constitution.

"After all, it will be necessary that, on a subject so peculiarly delicate as this, much prudence, much candor, much moderation, and much liberality should be exercised and displayed, both by the *Federal Government*, and by the Governments of the *several States*. It is to be hoped that those virtues of Government will be exercised and displayed, when we consider that the powers of the *Federal Government*, and those of the *State Governments*, are drawn from sources equally pure." * * *

"The United States may adopt any one of four different systems. They may become consolidated into one Government, in which the separate existence of the States shall be entirely absolved. They may reject any plan of Union or association, and act as separate and unconnected States. They may form two or more Confederacies. They may unite in one Federal Republic. Which of these systems ought to have been formed by the Convention?"

After giving his opinion against the first three, he concludes thus:

"The remaining system which the *American States* may adopt, is a *Union of them* under one *Confederate Republic.* It will not be necessary to employ much time, or many arguments, to show that this is the most eligible system that can be proposed. By adopting this system, the vigor and decision of a wide spreading monarchy, may be joined to the freedom and beneficence of a contracted Republic. The extent of territory, the diversity of climate and soil, the number, and greatness, and connection, of lakes and rivers, with which the United States are intersected, and almost surrounded,—all indicate an enlarged Government to be fit and advantageous for them. * * * If those opinions and wishes are as well founded as they have been general, the late Convention were justified in proposing to their constituents *one Confederate Republic,* as the best system of a National Government for the United States." * * *

In another speech, on 1st December, 1787, as the discussion progressed, he said: "We have heard much about a consolidated Government. I wish the honorable gentleman would condescend to give us a definition of what he meant by it. I think this the more necessary, because I apprehend that the term, in the numerous times it has been used, has not always been used in the same sense. It may be said, and I believe it has been said, that a consolidated Government is such as will absorb and destroy the Governments of the several States. If it is taken in this view, the plan before us is not a consolidated Government, as I showed on a former day, and may, if necessary, show further on some future occasion. On the other hand, if it is meant that the General Government will take from the State Governments their power in *some particulars*, it is confessed, and evident, that this will be its operation and effect."

Again, on the 4th of December, he said:—"The very manner of introducing this Constitution, by the recognition of the authority of the people, is said to change the principles of the present Confederation, and to introduce a *Consolidating* and absorbing Government.

"In this Confederated Republic, the Sovereignty of the States, it is said, is not preserved. We are told that there cannot be two Sovereign powers, and that a subordinate Sovereignty is no Sovereignty.

"It will be worth while, Mr. President, to consider this objection at large. When I had the ho or of speaking formerly on this subject, I stated, in as concise a manner as possible, the leading ideas that occurred to me, to ascertain where the Supreme and Sovereign power resides. It has not been, nor, I presume, will it be denied, that somewhere there is, and of necessity must be, a Supreme, absolute, and uncontrollable authority. This, I believe, may justly be termed the *Sovereign* power; for, from that gentleman's (Mr. Findley) account of the matter, it cannot be Sovereign unless it is Supreme; for, says he a subordinate Sovereignty is no Sovereignty at all. I had the honor of observing, that, if the question was asked, where the Supreme power resided, different answers would be given by different writers. I mentioned that Blackstone would tell you that, in Britain, it is lodged in the British Parliament; and I believe there is no writer, on this subject, on the other side of the Atlantic, but supposed it to be vested in that body. I stated, further, that, if the question was asked of some politician, who had not considered the subject with sufficient accuracy, where the Supreme power resided in our Government, he would answer, that it was vested in the State Constitutions. This opinion approaches near the truth, but does not reach it; for the truth is, that the Supreme, absolute, and uncontrollable authority *remains with the people.* I mentioned, also, that the practical recognition of this *truth* was reserved for the honor of this country. I recollect no Constitution founded on this principle; but we have witnessed the improvement, and enjoy the happiness of seeing it carried into practice. The great and penetrating mind of Locke seems to be the only one that pointed towards even the theory of this great truth.

"When I made the observation that some politicians would say the Supreme power was lodged in our State Constitutions, I did not suspect that the honorable gentleman from Westmoreland (Mr. Findley) was included in that description; but I find myself disappointed; for I imagined his opposition would arise from another consideration. His position is, that the *Supreme power* resides in the *States,* as *Governments;* and mine is, that it resides in *the people,* as the fountain of Government; *that the people have not—that the people meant not*—and *that the people ought not—to part with it to any Government whatsoever.* In their hands it remains secure. They can delegate it in such proportions, to such bodies, on such terms, and under such limitations, as they think proper. I agree with the members in opposition, that there cannot be two Sovereign powers on the same subject. * * * This, I say, is the inherent and unalienable right of the people; and as an illustration of it, I beg to read a few words from the Declaration of Independence, made by the Representatives of the United States, and recognised by the whole Union.

"'We hold these truths to be self-evident, that all men are created equal; that they are endowed by their Creator with certain inalienable rights; that among these are life, liberty, and the pursuit of happiness; that, to secure these rights, Governments are instituted among men, *deriving their just powers from the consent of the governed;* that, whenever any form of Government becomes destructive of these ends, it is the right of the people to alter, or abolish it, and institute a new Government, laying its foundation on such principles, and organizing its powers in such forms, as to them shall seem most likely to effect their safety and happiness.'

"This is the broad basis on which our Independence was placed: on the same certain and solid foundation this system is erected. * * *

"It is mentioned that this Federal Government will annihilate and absorb all the State Governments. I wish to save, as much as possible, the time of the house; I shall not, therefore, recapitulate what I had the honor of saying last week on this subject. I hope it was then shown that, instead of being abolished (as insinuated), from the very nature of things, and from the organization of the system itself, the State Governments must exist, or the General Government must fall amidst their ruins. Indeed, so far as to the forms, it is admitted they may remain; but the gentlemen seem to think their power will be gone.

"I shall have occasion to take notice of this power

hereafter; and, I believe, if it was necessary, it could be shown that the State Governments, as States, will enjoy as much power, and more dignity, happiness, and security, than they have hitherto done. * * * *

"I say, Sir, that it was the design of this system to take *some power* from the State Governments, and to place it in the General Government. It was also the design that the people should be admitted to the exercise of some powers, which they did not exercise under the *present* Federation. It was thought proper that the citizens, as well as the States, should be represented. How far the representation in the Senate is a representation of States, we shall see by and by, when we come to consider that branch of the Federal Government.

"This system, it is said, unhinges and eradicates the State Governments, and was systematically intended so to do. To establish the intention, an argument is drawn from Article 1st, Section 4th, on the subject of elections. I have already had occasion to remark upon this, and shall, therefore, pass on to the next objection.

"That the last clause of the 8th Section of the 1st Article, gives the power of Self-preservation to the General Government, independent of the States; for, in case of their abolition, it will be alleged, in behalf of the General Government, that Self-preservation is the first law, and necessary to the exercise of all other powers.

"Now, let us see what this objection amounts to. Who are to have this Self-preserving power? The Congress. Who are Congress? It is a body that will consist of a Senate and a House of Representatives. Who compose this Senate? Those who are elected by the Legislature of the different States. Who are the electors of the House of Representatives? Those who are qualified to vote for the most numerous branch of the Legislature in the separate States. Suppose the State Legislatures annihilated; where is the criterion to ascertain the qualification of electors? and unless this be ascertained, they cannot be admitted to vote; if a State Legislature is not elected, there can be no Senate, because the Senators are to be chosen by the *Legislatures only.*

"This is a plain and simple deduction from the Constitution; and yet the objection is stated as conclusive, upon an agreement expressly drawn from the last clause of this section.

"It is repeated, with confidence, 'that this is not a *Federal Government,* but a complete one, with Legislative, Executive, and Judicial powers; it is a Consolidating Government.' I have already mentioned the misuse of the term; I wish the gentleman would indulge us with his definition of the word. If, when he says it is a consolidation, he means so far as relates to the general objects of the Union; so far it was intended to be a consolidation, and on such a consolidation, perhaps, our very existence, as a nation, depends. If, on the other hand (as something, which has been said, seems to indicate), he (Mr. Findley) means that it will absorb the Governments of the individual States,—so far is this position from being admitted, that it is *unanswerably controverted.* * * *

"Sir, I think there is another subject with regard to which this Constitution deserves approbation. I mean the accuracy with which the *line is drawn* between the powers of the *General Government* and those of the *particular State Governments.* We have heard some general observations, on this subject, from the gentlemen who conduct the opposition. They have asserted that these powers are unlimited and undefined. These words are as easily pronounced as *limited* and *defined.*

They have already been answered by my honorable colleague (Mr. M'Kean), therefore I shall not enter into an explanation. But it is not pretended that the line is drawn with mathematical precision; the inaccuracy of language must, to a certain degree, prevent the accomplishment of such a desire. Whoever views the matter in a true light, will see that the powers are as minutely enumerated and defined as was possible, and will also discover that the general clause, against which so much exception is taken, is nothing more than what was necessary to render effectual the particular powers that are granted.

"But let us suppose—and this supposition is very easy in the minds of the gentlemen on the other side,—that there is some difficulty in ascertaining where the true line lies. Are we, therefore, thrown into despair? Are *disputes* between the *General* Government and the *State* Governments to be necessarily the consequence of inacuracy? I hope, sir, they will not be the enemies of each other, or resemble comets in conflicting orbits, mutually operating destruction; but that their motion will be better represented by that of the planetary system. where each part moves harmoniously within its proper sphere, and no injury arises by interference or opposition. Every part, I trust, will be considered as a part of the United States. Can any cause of distrust arise here? Is there any increase of risk? Or, rather, are not the *enumerated powers as well defined here, as in the present Articles of Confederation?*"

Again, on the 11th December, 1787, he said:

"It is objected to this system, that under it there is no Sovereignty left in the State Governments. I have had occasion to reply to this already; but I should be glad to know at what period the State Governments became possessed of the Supreme power. On the principle on which I found my arguments,—*and that is the principle of this Constitution,—the Supreme* power *resides* in the *people.* * * *

"We are next told, by the honorable gentlemen in opposition (as, indeed, we have been from the beginning of the debates in this Convention, to the conclusion of their speeches, yesterday), that this is a Consolidated Government, and will abolish the State Governments.

"Definitions of a Consolidated Government have been called for; the gentlemen gave us what they termed definitions, but it does not seem, to me, at least, that they have, as yet, expressed clear ideas upon that subject. I will endeavor to state their different ideas upon this point. The gentleman from Westmoreland (Mr. Findley), when speaking on this subject, says, that he means, by a consolidation, 'that Government which puts the thirteen States into one.'

"The honorable gentleman from Fayette (Mr. Smilie), gives you this definition: 'What I mean, by a Consolidated Government, is one that will transfer the Sovereignty from the State Governments to the General Government.'

"The honorable member from Cumberland (Mr. Whitehill), instead of giving you a definition, sir, tells you again, that 'it is a Consolidated Government, and we have proved it so.'

"These, I think, sir, are the different descriptions given to us of a Consolidated Government. As to the first, that it is a Consolidated Government, that puts the thirteen United States into one,—if it is meant that the General Government will destroy the Governments of the States, I will admit that such a Government would not suit the people of America. It would be improper for this Country, because it could not be proportioned to its extent, on the principles of freedom. But *that description does not apply to the system before you.* This, instead of placing the State Governments in jeopardy, is founded on their existence. On this principle its organization depends; it must stand or fall, as the State Governments are *secured or ruined!* Therefore, though this may be a very proper description of a Consolidated Government, yet it must be disregarded, as inapplicable to the proposed Constitution. *It is not treated with decency* when such insinuations are offered against it."*

So much for the debates in the Pennsylvania Convention. It is to be regretted that no part of these debates has been preserved but the speeches of Mr. Wilson, from which these extracts have been read. From these, however, it abundantly appears that the nature and character of the Government to be instituted under the Constitution of the United States was thoroughly discussed. It appears clearly, that there was strong opposition to many of its features, but, what is of very great importance in our investigation, it is equally clear that Mr. Wilson, and the majority who acted with him in that Convention, held the Constitution to be strictly Federal, and that the Government instituted by it was a Federal Government, or Confederated Republic. Whatever may have been his original views as to a consolidation of the States into one National Republic, he distinctly and frankly avowed that the Constitution which had been agreed upon did not effect that result. He declared further, that according to his understanding of the Constitution, the State Governments, as States under it, would enjoy as much power, and more dignity, happiness, and *security*, than

* *Elliot's Debates*, vol. ii, pp. 481-82,—502-503.

they had done before. He insisted that no cause of distrust should arise from apprehensions on that score; for the powers of the Federal Government, said he, with emphasis, were as well defined in the Constitution as under the Articles of Confederation. His whole powers seem to have been put forth to demonstrate that it was not a Consolidated Government, as the opponents of it argued that it would be construed to be. He declared that it was not treating the Constitution with *decency*, to make such insinuations against it. These speeches of Mr. Wilson, without doubt, controlled the majority of the Pennsylvania Convention, who gave the Constitution their sanction. They show clearly what must have been the understanding of the friends and advocates of the Constitution as to its nature, and as to the nature of the Union thereby established, when they styled it, in their ordinance of ratification, "a Constitution for States." These speeches of Mr. Wilson were also extensively published in the newspapers of the day. They were widely circulated in other States, and, Mr. Curtis says, had great influence on the action of other State Conventions.

Let us, however, proceed with the other States. The next in order is New Jersey.

THIRD, NEW JERSEY.

The Legislature of this State called a Convention of her people, to which the Constitution was referred. That Convention came to the following Resolutions and Ordinance.*

"In Convention of the State of New Jersey, (18 December, 1787.)

"*Whereas,* A Convention of Delegates from the follow-

* *Elliot's Debates*, vol. i, p. 320.

ing States, viz.: New Hampshire, Massachusetts, Connecticut, New York, New Jersey, Pennsylvania, Delaware, Maryland, Virginia, North Carolina, South Carolina and Georgia, met at Philadelphia, for the purpose of deliberating on, and forming, a Constitution for the United States of America,—finished their session on the 17th day of September last, and reported to Congress the form which they had agreed upon, in the words following, viz.:

"*And whereas*, Congress, on the 28th day of September last, unanimously did resolve, 'That the said report, with the Resolutions and letter accompanying the same, be transmitted to the several Legislatures, in order to be submitted to a Convention of Delegates, chosen in each State by the people thereof, in conformity to the resolves of the Convention made and provided in that case;'

"*And whereas*, The Legislature of this State did, on the 29th day of October last, resolve in the words following, viz.: '*Resolved*, unanimously, That it be recommended to such of the inhabitants of this State as are entitled to vote for Representatives in General Assembly, to meet in their respective counties on the fourth Tuesday in November next, at the several places fixed by law for holding the annual elections, to choose three suitable persons to serve as delegates from each county in a State Convention, for the purposes hereinbefore mentioned, and that the same be conducted agreeably to the mode, and conformably with the rules and regulations, prescribed for conducting such elections;—

"'*Resolved*, unanimously, That the persons so selected to serve in State Convention, do assemble and meet together on the second Tuesday in December next, at Trenton, in the county of Hunterdon, then and there to take into consideration the aforesaid Constitution, and if approved of by them, finally to ratify the same in behalf and on the part of this State, and make report thereof to the United States in Congress assembled, in conformity with the resolutions thereto annexed.

"'*Resolved,* That the sheriffs of the respective counties of this State shall be, and they are hereby, required to give as timely notice as may be, by advertisements, to the people of their counties, of the time, place and purpose of holding elections, as aforesaid.'

"*And whereas,* The Legislature of this State did also, on the 1st day of November last, make and pass the following act, viz.: 'An Act to authorize the people of this State to meet in Convention, deliberate upon, agree to, and ratify, the Constitution of the United States proposed by the late General Convention,—Be it enacted by the Council and General Assembly of this State, and it is hereby enacted by the authority of the same, That it shall and may be lawful for the people thereof, by their Delegates, to meet in Convention to deliberate upon, and, if approved of by them, to ratify, the Constitution for the United States proposed by the General Convention held at Philadelphia, and every act, matter and clause, therein contained, conformably to the resolutions of the Legislature passed the 29th day of October, 1787,—any law, usage, or custom, to the contrary in any wise notwithstanding;'

"Now be it known, That we, the Delegates of the State of New Jersey, chosen by the people thereof, for the purposes aforesaid, having maturely deliberated on and considered the aforesaid proposed Constitution, do hereby, for and on the behalf of the people of the said State of New Jersey, agree to, ratify, and confirm, the same and every part thereof.

"Done in Convention, by the unanimous consent of the

members present, this 18th day of December, in the year of our Lord 1787, and of the independence of the United States of America, the twelfth."

There was no opposition to the Constitution in the Convention of New Jersey. It was unanimously adopted. But the action of the Convention shows how they understood it. They agreed to and ratified it as "a Constitution *for the United States* of America."

FOURTH, GEORGIA.

The next State in order is Georgia. Here is her action, embodied in the Ordinance of 2d January, 1788, referred to before.*

"In Convention, Wednesday, January 2d, 1788.

"To all to whom these presents shall come, greeting:

"*Whereas*, the form of a Constitution for the Government of the United States of America, was, on the 17th day of September, 1787, agreed upon and reported to Congress, by the Deputies of the said United States, convened in Philadelphia, which said Constitution is written in the words following, to wit:

"*And whereas*, the United States in Congress assembled did, on the 28th day of September, 1787, *Resolve*, unanimously, 'That the said report, with the resolutions and letter accompanying the same, be transmitted to the several Legislatures, in order to be submitted to a Convention of Delegates chosen in each State by the people thereof, in conformity to the resolves of the Convention made and provided in that case;'—

"*And whereas*, the Legislature of the State of Georgia did, on the 26th day of October, 1787, in pursuance of the above-recited resolution of Congress, *Resolve*, That a

* *Elliot's Debates*, vol. i, p. 323.

Convention be elected on the day of the next general election, and in the same manner that representatives are elected; and that the said Convention consist of not more than three members from each county; and that the said Convention should meet at Augusta, on the fourth Tuesday in December then next, and as soon thereafter as convenient, proceed to consider the said report and resolutions, and to adopt or reject any part or the whole thereof;

"Now know ye, that we, the Delegates of the people of the State of Georgia, in Convention met, pursuant to the resolutions of the Legislature aforesaid, having taken into our serious consideration the said Constitution, have assented to, ratified, and adopted, and by these presents do, in virtue of the powers and authority to us given by the people of the said State for that purpose, for and in behalf of ourselves and our constituents, fully and entirely assent to, ratify, and adopt the said Constitution.

"Done in Convention, at Augusta, in the said State, on the 2d day of January, in the year of our Lord, 1788, and of the Independence of the United States the twelfth."

In the Georgia Convention there was no opposing voice. The Constitution was unanimously assented to, ratified, and adopted as "a Constitution for the Government of the United States of America." A Government of States. A Federal Republic.

FIFTH, CONNECTICUT.

We come now, Professor, to your State. First, we will look at the words of her ratification. These are as follows:

"In the name of the People of the State of Connecticut. We, the Delegates of the people of said State, in General

Convention assembled, pursuant to an Act of the Legislature in October last, have assented to, and ratified, and by these presents do assent to, ratify, and adopt the Constitution reported by the Convention of Delegates in Philadelphia, on the 17th day of September, A. D., 1787, for the United States of America.

"Done in Convention, at Hartford, this 9th day of January, A. D., 1788. In witness whereof, we have hereunto set our hands."*

Connecticut ratified the Constitution as a form of Government for States. This shows the understanding of the Convention so far as these words, used in the ratification, go. But we are not left to bare inference or argument from them. We have seen what Roger Sherman and Oliver Ellsworth, two of the Delegates from this State, had said of the Constitution in their letter to the Governor of the State, on the adjournment of the Federal Convention. In that they stated distinctly, that the Sovereignty of the States was retained.† But besides this we have the debates in the ratifying Convention.

Let us look into these, then, in the second place. There were several men of great ability in this Convention. Amongst whom no one was more prominent than Mr. Ellsworth himself. He was afterwards Chief Justice of the Supreme Court of the United States. On him, as a member of the Philadelphia Convention, devolved the part of opening the discussion in the body then assembled, to consider the Constitution. His opening words were as follows:

"MR. PRESIDENT:—It is observable that there is no preface to the proposed Constitution, but it evidently presupposes two things; one is the necessity of a *Federal Government*; the other is the *inefficiency* of the *old* Articles of Confederation."

---

* *Elliot's Debates*. vol. i. p. 321.

† *Ante*, p. 154.

After going through with a detail of the structure of the Government proposed, he concluded by saying: "The Constitution before us is a complete system of Legislative, Judicial, and Executive power. It was designed to supply the *defects* of the former system; and I believe, upon a full discussion, it will be found to answer the *purposes* for which it was designed."*

PROF. NORTON. I always thought that Judge Ellsworth held that the Constitution was not a Federal Compact between the States, but that it established a complete National Government over the whole people of the United States. How is this? Have I been in error on this point? I have certainly seen him quoted to that effect.

MR. STEPHENS. The quotation you refer to, is one that has often been made from one of his speeches in this Convention—about the coercion of laws under the Constitution, instead of the coercion of arms. But no such idea, as you suppose, was intended to be conveyed by the speech, and none such appears in it taken, altogether. Here is that speech. It was in reply to objections that the powers delegated by the Constitution were of themselves inconsistent with the nature of a *Federal Government.* He combated that idea, and maintained that States, by compact, might delegate power to act directly upon their citizens. Here is his speech on that subject. "But, says the honorable objector, if Congress levies money, they must legislate. I admit it. Two legislative powers, says he, cannot legislate on the same subject in the same place. I ask, why can they not? It is not enough to say they cannot. I wish for some reason. I grant that both cannot legislate upon the same object at the same time, and carry into effect laws which are contrary to each other. But the Constitution excludes

* *Elliot's Debates*, vol. ii, p. 185–190.

every thing of this kind. Each Legislature has its province; their limits may be distinguished. * * * Two several Legislatures have in fact existed, and acted at the same time, and in the same territory. It is in vain to say they cannot exist, when they actually have done it. In the time of the war, we had an army. Who made the laws for the army? By whose authority were offenders tried and executed? Congress. By their authority a man was taken, tried, condemned, and hanged, in this very city. He belonged to the army; he was a proper subject of military law; he deserted to the enemy; he deserved his fate."*

In this way he maintained that there would be no change in principle in the operation of laws passed by the Congress, under the Constitution, in levying taxes directly upon the people, from laws that had been passed by the Congress, under the Confederation, in other cases. The great benefit that would flow from the extension, in the Constitution, of this principle, that had been acted on to a limited extent, under the Confederation, he proceeded to explain with great force, and showed its perfect practicability under a Federal system. The point was the collection of revenues by levies on the people, instead of requisitions on the States. Afterwards comes the part from which the extract you refer to is taken. Here is the whole of it. "Hence, we see," says he, "how necessary, for the Union, is a coercive principle. No man pretends the contrary; we all see and feel this necessity. The only question is, shall it be a coercion of law, or a coercion of arms? There is no other possible alternative. Where will those who oppose a coercion of law come out? Where will they end? A necessary consequence of their principles is a war of the States,

* *Elliot's Debates*, vol. ii, p. 196.

one against the other. I am for coercion by law—that coercion which acts only upon *delinquent individuals. This Constitution does not attempt to coerce Sovereign bodies, States, in their political capacity.* No coercion is applicable to such bodies, but that of an armed force. If we should attempt to execute the laws of the Union by sending an armed force against a *delinquent State,* it would involve the good and bad, the innocent and guilty, in the same calamity. But this legal coercion singles out the guilty individual, and punishes him for breaking the laws of the Union."*

He was speaking of the great advantage that would result from delegating to the Congress power to pass laws that would operate directly upon the people, and not upon the States in their corporate capacities. This, he maintained, would be a great improvement in the Federal system, especially in the collection of taxes. And he contended further, that it really involved no new principle; that the Congress had, by virtue of the Articles of Confederation, acted upon the same principle, *so far as persons in the land and naval forces were concerned.* Nothing in this speech is inconsistent with his and Mr. Sherman's joint letter to Governor Huntingdon touching the reserved Sovereignty of the States. Indeed, in this very speech, he says the Constitution does not attempt to coerce Sovereign bodies, States, in their political capacity. There is no trace, in the debates in the Connecticut Convention, of a contrary opinion being entertained. The general doctrine of all the friends of the Constitution in this Convention was, not only that it established a Federal Government, but that the rights of the States were amply secured by it. This was the

* *Elliot's Debates*, vol. ii, p. 197.

judgment of Governor Huntingdon, who was a member of the Convention. It was the judgment of Richard Law, who said: "Consider that this General Government rests upon the State Governments for its support. It is like a vast and magnificent bridge, built upon thirteen strong and stately pillars. Now, the rulers, who occupy the bridge, cannot be so *beside themselves* as to knock away the pillars which support the whole fabric."*

Oliver Wolcott, he who was afterwards Secretary of the Treasury, and the devoted political friend of Mr. Hamilton, said: "The Constitution effectually secures the States in their several rights. It must secure them, for its own sake; for they are the pillars which uphold the general system. The Senate, a constituent branch of the general Legislature, without whose assent no public act can be made, are appointed by the States, and will secure the rights of the several States." "So well guarded is this Constitution throughout, that it seems impossible that the rights either of *the States* or of the people should be destroyed."†

This is quite enough to show what the Convention of Connecticut thought of the Constitution, and hence we see in their ratification they use the same words; they adopt it as a Constitution "for the United States of America.

SIXTH, MASSACHUSETTS.

We now come, Judge, to your State. It is tedious to go through with all these dry, musty records. But it is essential to our investigation; they are the title-deeds of our political inheritance of Constitutional Liberty. From them alone can we arrive at the truth touching the object of our inquiry. I call your special attention, Judge, to the action of your own

* *Elliot's Debates*, vol. ii, p. 201. † *Elliot's Debates*, vol. ii, p. 201.

State in the premises. No better or more conclusive proof could be adduced to establish the fact that Massachusetts, at the time, considered the Union perfected by the Constitution to be a Federal one between States, than her own action on the adoption of it furnishes.

First, the ratification itself. It is in these words:—

"Commonwealth of Massachusetts.

"The Convention having impartially discussed, and fully considered, the Constitution for the United States of America, reported to Congress by the Convention of Delegates from the United States of America, and submitted to us by a resolution of the General Court of the said Commonwealth, passed the 25th day of October, last past,—and acknowledging, with grateful hearts, the goodness of the Supreme Ruler of the Universe in affording the people of the United States, in the course of his providence, an opportunity, deliberately and peaceably, without fraud or surprise, of entering into an explicit and solemn compact with each other, by assenting to and ratifying a new Constitution, in order to form a more perfect Union, establish justice, insure domestic tranquillity, provide for the common defence, promote the general welfare, and secure the blessings of liberty to themselves and their posterity,—do, in the name and in behalf of the people of the Commonwealth of Massachusetts, assent to and ratify the said Constitution for the United States of America.

"And as it is the opinion of this Convention, that certain amendments and alterations in the said Constitution would remove the fears, and quiet the apprehensions, of many of the good people of this Commonwealth, and more effectually guard against an undue administration of the Federal Government,—the Convention do therefore recommend that the following alterations and provisions be introduced into the said Constitution:—

"I. That it explicitly declare that all powers not expressly delegated by the aforesaid Constitution are reserved to the several States, to be by them exercised.

"II. That there shall be one representative to every thirty thousand persons, according to the census mentioned in the Constitution, until the whole number of the representatives amounts to two hundred.

"III. That Congress do not exercise the powers vested in them by the 4th Section of the 1st Article, but in cases where a State shall neglect or refuse to make the regulations therein mentioned, or shall make regulations subversive of the rights of the people to a free and equal representation in Congress, agreeably to the Constitution.

"IV. That Congress do not lay direct taxes but when the moneys arising from the impost and excise are insufficient for the public exigencies, nor then until Congress shall have first made a requisition upon the States to assess, levy, and pay, their respective proportions of such requisition, agreeably to the census fixed in the said Constitution, in such way and manner as the Legislatures of the States shall think best; and in such case, if any State shall neglect or refuse to pay its proportion, pursuant to such requisition, then Congress may assess and levy such State's proportion, together with interest thereon at the rate of six per cent. per annum, from the time of payment prescribed in such requisition.

"V. That Congress erect no company of merchants with exclusive advantages of commerce.

"VI. That no person shall be tried for any crime by which he may incur an infamous punishment, or loss of life, until he be first indicted by a grand jury, except in such cases as may arise in the government and regulation of the land and naval forces.

"VII. The Supreme Judicial Federal Court shall have

no jurisdiction of causes between citizens of different States, unless the matter in dispute, whether it concerns the realty or personalty, be of the value of three thousand dollars at the least; nor shall the Federal Judicial powers extend to any actions between citizens of different States, where the matter in dispute, whether it concerns the realty or personalty, is not of the value of fifteen hundred dollars at least.

"VIII. In civil actions between citizens of different States, every issue of fact, arising in actions at common law, shall be tried by a jury, if the parties, or either of them, request it.

"IX. Congress shall at no time consent that any person, holding an office of trust or profit under the United States, shall accept of a title of nobility, or any other title or office, from any king, prince, or foreign State.

"And the Convention do, in the name and in behalf of the people of this Commonwealth, enjoin it upon their representatives in Congress, at all times, until the alterations and provisions aforesaid have been considered, agreeably to the fifth article of the said Constitution, to exert all their influence, and use all reasonable and legal methods, to obtain a ratification of the said alterations and provisions, in such manner as is provided in the said article.

"And that the United States, in Congress assembled, may have due notice of the assent and ratification of the said Constitution by this Convention, it is *Resolved*, That the assent and ratification aforesaid be engrossed on parchment, together with the recommendation and injunction aforesaid, and with this resolution; and that his Excellency, John Hancock, Esqr., President, and the Hon. William Cushing, Esqr., Vice President of the Convention, transmit the same, countersigned by the Secretary of the Convention, under their hands and seals, to the United States in Congress assembled."*

Here we see potent words! The instrument is recognized as a new Constitution! New in contradistinction to the old one! That was the Articles of Confederation. It is distinctly declared to be a Compact to form a more perfect Union—a more perfect Union, of course, between the same parties. Those parties were the several States, or the people of the several States, in their Sovereign character. We see it was adopted as "a Constitution for the United States of America"—not, as I have often said, for the whole American people, but for the American States united by the Compact. The Government, we see, was to be Federal. The Supreme Court of the United States is styled "the Supreme Judicial Federal Court." The whole proceedings, from beginning to end, show upon their face Federal action and Federal engagements. The instrument, ratified, was directed to be sent "to the United States in Congress assembled." But this is not all. The Constitution did not pass the Convention of Massachusetts without violent opposition. What was said pro and con is upon record. These sayings, at the time, constitute a part of the *res gestæ*, and are to be taken with it, if necessary, for a clearer explanation of the understanding of the Resolutions they came to.

There were great men in that Convention, Men who were the lights of the age in which they lived. Samuel Adams, Fisher Ames, Rufus King, Theophilus Parsons, James Bowdoin, and John Hancock, were there. The questions involved were deemed of the most momentous character. None of greater importance had engaged the attention of Massachusetts' statesmen, since the ever-

* *Elliot's Debates*, vol. i, pp. 322, 323.

memorable struggles over their Charter, in 1685 and 1774, and which finally ended in the war of the Revolution, and establishment of the complete Independence and Sovereignty of the Commonwealth. By many it was thought, that this Sovereignty would be endangered by the adoption of this new Constitution. At the head of this class was the renowned Samuel Adams. With him, stood conspicuously, Singletary, Bodman, Widgery, Taylor, Nason, and Choate.

They doubtless had in mind the insidious encroachments upon their ancient rights, by the crown of Great Britain, through the instrumentality of a Randolph and Andrews, in 1683–85. The reply of the Deputies of Massachusetts, to the proposition of the crown at that time, was not forgotten. "The civil liberties of New England are part of the inheritance of their fathers; and shall we give that inheritance away? Is it objected that we shall be exposed to greater sufferings? Better suffer than sin. It is better to trust the God of our fathers, than to put confidence in Princes! If we suffer, because we dare not comply with the wills of men against the will of God, we suffer in a good cause, and shall be accounted Martyrs in the next generation, and at the great day! The Deputies consent not, but adhere to their former Bills!"*

They did not lose sight of the fact, that these fathers did become Martyrs, and that their self-sacrifice was amply vindicated in the Revolution of 1688, and in the re-establishment of their charter. It was also fresh in their minds, how like attempts to despoil them of their Liberties had been made in their own times by George III, in 1774, and how gloriously their resistance to his encroachments had resulted.

---

* *Bancroft*, vol. ii, pp. 126, 127.

We can easily account, therefore, for the apprehensions awakened in the breasts of such men upon the presentation of this new Constitution. On its face it did not reserve expressly the Sovereignty of the States, severally, as the old one had done. At first a very large majority of the Convention were decidedly opposed to its adoption. The session lasted for a month lacking two days. The debates have been published by order of the State Legislature and make a volume of themselves.

Secondly, then, let us sample these debates to see the prevailing sentiments on both sides.

Mr. Shurtliff. "The Convention says, they aimed at a consolidation of the Union."

Mr. Parsons. "The distinction is between a consolidation of *the States* and a consolidation of *the Union*."

Mr. Jones, of Boston. "The word consolidation has different ideas—as different metals melted into one mass, two twigs tied into one bundle."*

Mr. Ames. "The Senators will represent the Sovereignty of the States. The Representatives are to represent the people."†

Mr. Gore. "The Senate represents the Sovereignty of the States," etc.‡

Mr. Ames again observed, "that an objection was made against the Constitution, because the Senators are to be chosen for *six years*. It has been said, that they will be removed too far from the control of the people, and that, to keep them in proper dependence, they should be chosen annually. It is necessary to premise, that no argument against the new plan has made a deeper impression than this, that it will produce a consolidation of the States. This is an effect which all good men will

* *Debates*, published by order of the State, p. 316.

† *Elliot's Debates*, vol. ii, p. 11. ‡ *Elliot's Debates*, vol. ii, p. 18.

deprecate. For it is obvious, that, if the State powers are to be destroyed, the representation is too small. The trust, in that case, would be too great to be confided to so few persons. The objects of Legislation would be so multiplied and complicated, that the Government would be unwieldy and impracticable. The *State Governments* are *essential parts* of the system, and the defence of this article is drawn from its tendency to their preservation. The *Senators* represent the *Sovereignty of the States;* in the other House, individuals are represented. The Senate may not originate bills. It need not be said that they are principally to direct the affairs of wars and treaties. *They are in the quality of ambassadors of the States,* and it will not be denied that some permanency in their office is necessary to a discharge of their duty. Now, if they were chosen yearly, how could they perform their trust? If they would be brought by that means more immediately under the influence of the people, then they will represent the State Legislatures less, and become the representatives of individuals. This belongs to the other House. The absurdity of this, and its repugnancy to the Federal principles of the Constitution, will appear more fully, by supposing that they are to be chosen by the people at large. If there is any force in the objection to this article, this would be proper. But whom, in that case, would they represent?—Not the Legislatures of the States, but the people. This would totally obliterate the Federal features of the Constitution. What would become of the State Governments, and on whom would devolve the duty of defending them against the encroachments of the Federal Government? A consolidation of the States would ensue, which, it is conceded, would *subvert* the *new Constitution,* and against which this very article, so much condemned, is our best security. Too much provision cannot be made against a consolidation. The State Governments represent the wishes, and feelings, and local interests, of the people. They are the safeguard and ornament of the Constitution; they will protract the period of our liberties; they will afford a shelter against the abuse of power, and will be the *natural avengers of our violated rights.*

"A very effectual *check* upon the power of the Senate is provided. A third part is to retire from office every two years. By this means, while the Senators are seated for six years, they are admonished of their responsibility to the State Legislatures. If one third new members are introduced, who feel the sentiments of their States, they will awe that third whose term will be near expiring. This article seems to be an excellence of the Constitution. and affords just ground to believe that it will be, in practice as in theory, a *Federal Republic.*"*

Mr. Bodman (in speaking of the clause conferring the general powers of the Congress in levying and collecting taxes, etc.,) remarked, "It had been said that the Sovereignty of the States remains with them. He thought this section endangered that Sovereignty, and the powers in that section ought to have been more clearly defined, as to the right or power of the Government to use force in collecting the taxes, etc."†

Mr. Singletary "Thought that no more power could be given to a despot than to give up the purse strings of the people."‡

Mr. Choate. "Gentlemen say this section (8th, giving general powers to Congress) is as clear as the sun, and that all power is retained that is not given. But where

---

* *Elliot's Debates*, vol. ii, p. 45 *et seq.* *Debates* published by order of Massachusetts Legislature, pp. 144, 145.

† *Mass. Debates*, p. 159. ‡ *Mass. Debates*, p. 159.

is the Bill of Rights, which shall check the power of Congress; which shall say, thus far shall ye come, and no farther."*

Mr. Porter asked "If a better rule of yielding power could be shown than in the Constitution; for what we do not give," said he, "we retain."†.

Mr. Sumner. "But some gentlemen object further and say the delegation of these great powers will destroy the State Legislatures; but, I trust, this never can take place, for the General Government depends on the State Legislatures for its very existence. The President is to be chosen by Electors, under the Regulations of the State Legislatures. The Senate is to be chosen by the State Legislatures, and the Representative body by the people, under like Regulations of the Legislative body in the different States. If gentlemen consider this, they will, I presume, alter their opinion; for nothing is clearer than that the existence of the Legislatures in the different States, is essential to the very being of the General Government. I hope, sir, we shall all see the necessity of a *Federal Government*, and not make objections unless they appear to us to be of some weight."‡

Mr. Parsons, after speaking of the several kinds of Government, said, "The Federal Constitution establishes a Government of the last description, and, in this case, the *people divest themselves of nothing!* The Government, and the powers which the Congress can administer, are the *mere result of a Compact*, etc. * * *

"But if gentlemen will still insist that these powers are a grant from the people, and, consequently, improper, let it be observed that it is now too late to impede the grant. It is already completed. The Con-

---

* *Mass. Debates*, p. 180. † *Mass. Debates*, p. 159.
‡ *Mass. Debates*, p. 162.

gress, under the Confederation, are already invested with it by solemn Compact. They have power to demand what moneys and forces they judge necessary, for the common defence, and general welfare. *Powers as extensive as those proposed in this Constitution.* * * *

"It has been objected that we have no Bill of Rights. If gentlemen, who make this objection, would consider what are the supposed inconveniences resulting from a want of a declaration of rights, I think they would soon satisfy themselves that the objection has no weight. Is there a single natural right that we enjoy uncontrolled by our own Legislature, that Congress can infringe? Not one! Is there a single *political right secured to us, by our Constitution,* against the attempts of our own Legislature, which we are deprived of in this Constitution? Not one that I can recollect."*

Mr. Rufus King (who had been in the Philadelphia Convention and who was, while the question was open, for a National Government proper instead of a Federal one) said:

"To conclude, sir, if we mean to support an efficient Federal Government, which, under the *old* Confederation, can never be the case, the proposed Constitution is, in my opinion, the only one that can be *substituted.*"†

It was on the 30th of January, after the Convention had been in session for three weeks, and after it was well ascertained that the Constitution could not get the approval of a majority of that body without some declaration accompanying it setting forth the understanding with which it was adopted, that John Hancock, the President, left the chair and offered his proposition, which was, in substance, for its adoption in the form in which it stands.

---

* *Mass. Debates*, p. 199. † *Elliot's Debates*, vol. ii, p. 57.

After this proposition was so brought forward, the venerable Samuel Adams, and quite a number with him, yielded their former opposition. He expressed himself thus:—

"As your Excellency was pleased yesterday to offer, for the consideration of this Convention, certain propositions intended to accompany the ratification of the Constitution before us, I did myself the honor to bring them forward by a regular motion, not only from the respect due your Excellency, but from a clear conviction, in my own mind, that they would tend to effect the salutary and important purposes which you had in view—'the removing the fears and quieting the apprehensions of many of the good people of this Commonwealth, and the more effectually guarding against an undue administration of the Federal Government.'

"I beg leave, sir, more particularly to consider those propositions, and, in a very few words, to express my own opinion, that they must have a strong tendency to ease the minds of gentlemen who wish for the immediate operation of some essential parts of the proposed Constitution, as well as the most speedy and effectual means of obtaining alterations in some other parts of it, which they are solicitous should be made. I will not repeat the reasons I offered when the motion was made, which convinced me that the measure now under consideration will have a more speedy, as well as a more certain influence, in effecting the purpose last mentioned, than the measure proposed in the Constitution before us.

"Your Excellency's first proposition is, 'that it be explicitly declared, that all powers not expressly delegated to Congress are reserved to the several States, to be by them exercised.' This appears, to my mind, to be a *summary of a bill of rights,* which gentlemen are anxious to obtain. It removes a doubt which many have entertained respecting the matter, and gives assurance that, if any law made by the Federal Government shall be extended beyond the power granted by the proposed Constitution and inconsistent with the Constitution of this State, it will be an error, and adjudged by the courts of law to be void. It is *consonant* with the second article in the present Confederation, that each state *retains its Sovereignty,* freedom, and independence, and every power, jurisdiction, and right, which is not, by this Confederation, expressly delegated to the United States in Congress assembled. I have long considered the watchfulness of the people over the conduct of their rulers the strongest guard against the encroachments of power; and I hope the people of this country will always be thus watchful."*

Amongst others, Fisher Ames followed, in a speech of some length, in which he said:

"There was not any Government, which he knew to subsist, or which he had ever heard of, that would bear a comparison with the new Constitution. Considered merely as a literary performance, it was an honor to our country: Legislators have at length condescended to speak the language of philosophy; and, if we adopt it, we shall demonstrate to the sneering world, who deride liberty, because they have lost it, that the principles of our Government are as free as the spirit of our people.

"I repeat it, our debates have been profitable, because, upon every leading point, we are at last agreed. Very few among us now deny that a Federal Government is necessary to save us from ruin; that the Confederation is not that Government; and that the proposed Constitution, connected with the amendments, is worthy of

---

* *Elliot's Debates,* vol. ii, pp. 130, 131.

being adopted. The question recurs, Will the amendments prevail, and become part of the system? In order to obtain such a system, as the Constitution and the amendments, there are but three ways of proceeding—to reject the whole, and begin anew; to adopt this plan, upon condition that the amendments be inserted into it; or to adopt his Excellency's proposition."*

President Hancock concluded the debate. "I give my assent," said he, "to the Constitution, in full confidence that the amendments proposed will soon become a part of the system. These amendments, being no wise local, but calculated to give security and ease alike to *all the States*, I think that all will agree to them."

The Constitution was then ratified, as we have seen, by only *nineteen* majority. The whole number of the Convention was three hundred and fifty-five.

Governor Hancock, in his message to the Legislature, 27th February, 1788, communicating the action of the Convention, said:

"The objects of the proposed Constitution are, defence against external enemies, and the promotion of tranquillity and happiness *amongst the States*. * * *

"The amendments proposed by the Convention are intended to obtain a Constitutional security of the prinples to which they refer themselves, and must meet the wishes of all the States. I feel myself assured, that they will very early become a part of the Constitution, and when they shall be added to the proposed plan, I shall consider it the most perfect system of Government, as to the objects it embraces, that has been known amongst mankind."†

With this record in hand, who can doubt as to how

---

* *Elliot's Debates, Massachusetts Convention*, vol. ii, pp. 155, 156.

† *Massachusetts Debates*, published by order of the Legislature.

Massachusetts understood what she was doing? Is it not clear, beyond question, that she ratified the new Constitution in place of the old? That she considered it a Compact, between States, as much as the Articles of Confederation? Was there a single supporter or advocate of it in the Convention, who did not hold it to be strictly Federal in its character? Did they not all understand its great object to be, as Governor Hancock said, defence against foreign enemies, and the promotion of tranquillity and happiness *amongst States?* Were not all their apprehensions quieted by the early adoption of their first great amendment, and nearly all the rest? Can there be a reasonable doubt on the question?

But we will proceed to the next State in order.

SEVENTH, MARYLAND.

The action of the State of Maryland is recorded in these words:

"In Convention of the Delegates, of the people of the State of Maryland, April 28, 1788.

"We, the Delegates of the people of the State of Maryland, having fully considered the Constitution of the United States of America, reported to Congress, by the Convention of Deputies, from the United States of America, held in Philadelphia, on the 17th day of September, in the year 1787, of which the annexed is a copy, and submitted to us by a resolution of the General Assembly of Maryland, in November Session, 1787, do, for ourselves, and in the name, and on behalf of the people of this State, assent to, and ratify the said Constitution.

"In witness whereof, we have hereunto subscribed our names."*

In this State there was no material division of senti-

---

* *Elliot's Debates*, vol. i, p. 324.

ment. There was little or no discussion. The vote on it was sixty-three to eleven.* It was simply assented to, and ratified as the "Constitution of the United States of America." The Convention of Maryland styled it a Constitution of States.

EIGHTH, SOUTH CAROLINA.

The next State, in order, is South Carolina. First, as to the action of her Convention. That is set forth in these words:

"In Convention of the people of the State of South Carolina, by their representatives, held in the City of Charleston, on Monday, the 12th day of May, and continued by divers adjournments to Friday, the 23d day of May, Anno Domini, 1788, and in the twelfth year of the Independence of the United States of America.

"The Convention, having maturely considered the Constitution, or form of Government, reported to Congress by the Convention of Delegates from the United States of America, and submitted to them by a resolution of the Legislature of this State, passed the 17th and 18th days of February last, in order to form a more perfect Union, establish justice, insure domestic tranquillity, provide for the common defence, promote the general welfare, and secure the blessings of liberty to the people of the said United States, and their posterity,—Do, in the name and behalf of the people of this State, hereby assent to and ratify the said Constitution.

"Done in Convention, the 23d day of May, in the year of our Lord, 1788, and of the Independence of the United States of America the twelfth.

"*And whereas*, it is essential to the preservation of the

---

* *Elliott's Debates*, vol. ii, p. 549.

rights reserved to the several States, and the freedom of the people, under the operations of a General Government, that the right of prescribing the manner, time, and places of holding the elections to the Federal Legislaure, should be forever inseparably annexed to the Sovereignty of the several States,—This Convention doth declare, that the same ought to remain, to all posterity, a perpetual and fundamental right in the local, exclusive of the interference of the General Government, except in cases where the Legislatures of the States shall refuse or neglect to perform and fulfil the same, according to the tenure of the said Constitution. This Convention doth also declare, that no section or paragraph of the said Constitution warrants a construction, that the States do not retain every power not expressly relinquished by them, and vested in the General Government of the Union.

"*Resolved,* That the General Government of the United States ought never to impose direct taxes, *but* where the moneys arising from the duties, imposts, and excise, are insufficient for the public exigencies, *nor then until* Congress shall have made a requisition upon the States to assess, levy, and pay, their respective proportions of such requisitions; and in case any State shall neglect or refuse to pay its proportion, pursuant to such requisition, then Congress may assess and levy such State's proportion, together with interest thereon, at the rate of six per centum per annum, from the time of payment prescribed by such requisition.

"*Resolved,* That the third section of the sixth article ought to be amended by inserting the word 'other' between the words 'no' and 'religious.'

"*Resolved,* That it be a standing instruction to all such Delegates as may hereafter be elected to represent this State in the General Government, to exert their utmost abilities and influence to effect an alteration of the Constitution, conformably to the aforegoing resolutions.

"Done in Convention, the 23d day of May, in the year of our Lord, 1788, and of the Independence of the United States of America the twelfth."*

In these proceedings we see, clearly, that the under standing was that the Constitution was Federal in its character. The Congress is styled "The Federal Legislature," and, in the accompanying paper, proposing amendments, the reserved Sovereignty of the several States is mentioned as a matter understood, and an express declaration that the Constitution had been assented to and ratified, with the understanding that no section or paragraph of the Constitution warranted a construction that the States did not retain every power not expressly relinquished by them. This was in the nature of a Protocol, which went up with the paper, forever fixing the understanding of the State, with which she had entered into the Compact; and the understanding with which her ratification was accepted by the other States.

Secondly, let us look into the debates. Very few speeches, made in this Convention, have been preserved. No one disputed the character of the Government. The speeches related, mostly, to particular powers delegated. From one of them we perceive, however, that there was spirited opposition made by a respectable minority. This was headed by Patrick Dollard, of Prince Fredericks. He said, "My constituents are highly alarmed at the large and rapid strides which this new Government has taken towards despotism. They say it is big with political mischiefs, and pregnant with a greater variety of impending woes to the good

---

* *Elliot's Debates*, vol. i, p. 325.

people of the Southern States, especially South Carolina, than all the plagues supposed to issue from the poisonous box of Pandora!"*

On the question of ratification, the vote stood 149 to 73.

The most important debate in South Carolina, on the Constitution, was in the Legislature, on the proposition to call a Convention to take it into consideration. In this body, as in the Convention, there was a respectable and spirited minority against the Constitution, though the call for a Convention was unanimous. In the debate on that question, Hon. Rawlins Lowndes concluded his speech by saying "He wished for no other epitaph, than to have inscribed on his tomb, 'Here lies the man that opposed the Constitution, because it was ruinous to the liberty of America!'"†

These apprehensions and forebodings were, doubtless, awakened by the utterance of such sentiments as those which fell from General Pinckney, in this discussion, which Judge Story quotes. He did maintain that the States, severally, were never Sovereign, but in this position he was not sustained, either by the Legislature, or the Convention, as we have have seen by the Protocol of the latter.

NINTH, NEW HAMPSHIRE.

The next State, in order, is New Hampshire. Her action is set forth in the following words:

"In Convention of the Delegates of the People of the State of New Hampshire, June the 21st, 1788.

"The Convention, having impartially discussed and fully considered the Constitution for the United States of America, reported to Congress by the Convention

---

* *Elliot's Debates*, vol. iv, p. 337. † *Elliot's Debates*, vol. iv, p. 311.

of Delegates from the United States of America, and submitted to us by a resolution of the General Court of said State, passed the 14th day of December last past, and acknowledging, with grateful hearts, the goodness of the Supreme Ruler of the Universe in affording the people of the United States, in the course of His providence, an opportunity, deliberately and peaceably, without fraud or surprise, of entering into an explicit and solemn compact with each other, by assenting to and ratifying a new Constitution, in order to form a more perfect Union, establish Justice, insure domestic tranquillity, provide for the common defence, promote the general welfare, and secure the blessings of liberty to themselves and their posterity,—Do, in the name and behalf of the people of the State of New Hampshire, assent to and ratify the said Constitution for the United States of America. And as it is the opinion of this Convention, that certain amendments and alterations, in the said Constitution would remove the fears and quiet the apprehensions of many of the good people of this State, and more effectually guard against an undue administration of the Federal Government,—The Convention do, therefore, recommend that the following alterations and provisions be introduced in the said Constitution:—

"I. That it be explicitly declared that all powers not expressly and particularly delegated by the aforesaid Constitution, are reserved to the several States, to be by them exercised.

"II. That there shall be one representative to every thirty thousand persons, according to the census mentioned in the Constitution, until the whole number of representatives amount to two hundred.

"III. That Congress do not exercise the powers vested in them, by the fourth section of the first article, but in cases when a State shall neglect or refuse to make the regulations therein mentioned, or shall make regulations subversive of the rights of the people to a free and equal representation in Congress; nor shall Congress in any case make regulations contrary to a free and equal representation.

"IV. That Congress do not lay direct taxes, but when the moneys arising from impost, excise, and their other resources, are insufficient for the public exigencies; nor then, until Congress shall have first made a requisition upon the States to assess, levy, and pay, their respective proportions of such requisition, agreeably to the census fixed in the said Constitution, in such way and manner as the Legislature of the State shall think best; and in such case, if any State shall neglect, then Congress may assess and levy such State's proportion, together with the interest thereon, at the rate of six per cent. per annum, from the time of payment prescribed in such requisition.

"V. That Congress shall erect no company of merchants with exclusive advantages of commerce.

"VI. That no person shall be tried for any crime, by which he may incur an infamous punishment, or loss of life, until he first be indicted by a grand jury, except in such cases as may arise in the Government and regulation of the land and naval forces.

"VII. All common-law cases, between citizens of different States, shall be commenced in the common law courts of the respective States; and no appeal shall be allowed to the Federal court, in such cases, unless the sum or value of the thing in controversy amount to three thousand dollars.

"VIII. In civil actions, between citizens of different States, every issue of fact, arising in actions at common-law, shall be tried by jury, if the parties, or either of them, request it.

"IX. Congress shall at no time consent that any person, holding an office of trust or profit under the United States, shall accept any title of nobility, or any other title or office, from any king, prince, or foreign State.

"X. That no standing army shall be kept up in time of peace, unless with the consent of three fourths of the members of each branch of Congress; nor shall soldiers, in time of peace, be quartered upon private houses, without the consent of the owners.

"XI. Congress shall make no laws touching religion, or to infringe the rights of conscience.

"XII. Congress shall never disarm any citizen, unless such as are or have been in actual rebellion.

"And the Convention do, in the name and in behalf of the people of this State, enjoin it upon their representatives in Congress, at all times, until the alterations and provisions aforesaid have been considered, agreeably to the fifth article of the said Constitution, to exert all their influence, and use all reasonable and legal methods, to obtain a ratification of the said alterations and provisions, in such manner as is provided in the article.

"And that the United States, in Congress assembled, may have due notice of the assent and ratification of the said Constitution by this Convention, it is *Resolved*, That the assent and ratification aforesaid be engrossed on parchment, together with the recommendation and injunction aforesaid, and with this resolution; and that John Sullivan, Esqr., President of the Convention, and John Langdon, Esqr., President of the State, transmit the same, countersigned by the Secretary of Convention, and the Secretary of State, under their hands and seals, to the United States in Congress assembled."*

---

* *Elliot's Debates*, vol. i, pp. 325–327.

New Hampshire followed the precedent of Massachusetts, and adopted her form of proceedings throughout, in almost the same words. No farther comment is necessary on these. What has just been said on the Massachusetts ratification is applicable with all its force to that of New Hampshire. But one speech, made in the Convention of this State, has been preserved, and that throws no light upon the object of our inquiry. The action of the Convention, however, abundantly shows that the new Constitution was understood to be Federal it its character as the old one was.

TENTH, VIRGINIA.

We come now to Virginia, the mother of States, as she has properly been called.

First, we will look into her action, then into the debates.

The words of her ratification are as follows:—

"We, the Delegates of the people of Virginia, duly elected in pursuance of a recommendation from the General Assembly, and now met in Convention, having fully and freely investigated and discussed the proceedings of the Federal Convention, and being prepared as well as the most mature deliberation hath enabled us, to decide thereon,—Do, in the name and in behalf of the people of Virginia, declare and make known, that the powers granted under the Constitution, being derived from the people of the United States, may be resumed by them, whensoever the same shall be perverted to their injury or oppression, and that every power not granted thereby remains with them, and at their will; that, therefore, no right, of any denomination, can be cancelled, abridged, restrained, or modified, by the Congress, by the Senate or House of Representatives, acting in any capacity, by the President, or any department or officer of the United States, except in those instances in which power is given by the Constitution for those purposes; and that, among other essential rights, the liberty of conscience, and of the press, cannot be cancelled, abridged, restrained, or modified, by any authority of the United States. With these impressions, with a solemn appeal to the Searcher of all hearts for the purity of our intentions, and under the conviction that whatsoever imperfections may exist in the Constitution ought rather to be examined in the mode prescribed therein, than to bring the Union into danger by a delay with a hope of obtaining amendments previous to the ratifications,—We, the said Delegates, in the name and in behalf of the people of Virginia, do, by these presents, assent to and ratify the Constitution recommended, on the 17th day of September, 1787, by the Federal Convention, for the Government of the United States, hereby announcing to all those whom it may concern, that the said Constitution is binding upon the said people, according to an authentic copy hereto annexed, in the words following.

"Done in Convention, this 26th day of June, 1788."*

The language here used by the Convention of Virginia, in her adoption of the Constitution, styles the instrument a Constitution "for the Government of the United States." The form of expression is the same as that used by Georgia. The meaning is the same in both. It was to be a Constitution for the Government of States in their foreign and inter State affairs. It is to be noted that in it they expressly declare and make known that the powers granted under it may be resumed by them whensoever they may be perverted to their injury.

Judge Bynum. The language is, that the powers granted

* *Elliot's Debates*, vol. i, p. 327.

under it being derived from the *people* of the *United States*, may be resumed by *them*. How does that mean that the people of Virginia can resume these powers by themselves?

Mr. Stephens. The meaning of the people of the United States here, is, the people of the States severally. This is clear. The delegation of the powers was by the States severally. Whoever delegates can resume. The right to resume or recall attends all delegations of all sorts. Where there is a separate or several delegation there cannot be a joint resumption. The resumption must be by the party making the delegation. But the debates in the Convention remove all doubts as to their understanding upon this point. These are the *res gestæ* that fully explain it.

Secondly, then, let us look into the debates.

In Virginia, as in Massachusetts, the Constitution underwent a thorough discussion. The Convention was in session nearly a month. Many of the ablest men of the State were members of it. Men who had first put the ball of the Revolution in motion. Patrick Henry was there. George Mason, Bushrod Washington, Henry Lee of Westmoreland, George Nicholas, Edmund Pendleton, Edmund Randolph, James Monroe, James Madison, and John Marshall. A brighter galaxy of talent, statesmanship and oratory was never assembled in the Old Dominion. The debates fill a large volume by themselves. Here it is. Let us glean from these discussions the leading ideas of the advocates as well as the opponents of the Constitution on the main point of our inquiry, that is, the nature and character of the Government instituted by it. As in Massachusetts, so in Virginia, the opposition was able and formidable. The greatest orator of the age headed it.

"This proposal of altering our Federal Government," said Patrick Henry, "is of a most alarming nature! Make the best of this new Government—say it is composed by any thing but inspiration—you ought to be extremely cautious, watchful, jealous of your liberty; for, instead of securing your rights, you may lose them forever." * *

"I have the highest veneration for those gentlemen; but, sir, give me leave to demand, What right had they to say, '*We, the people?*' My political curiosity, exclusive of my anxious solicitude for the public welfare, leads me to ask, who authorized them to speak the language of, '*We, the people,*' instead of, 'We, the States?' States are the characteristics and the soul of a Confederation! If the States be not the agents of this Compact, it must be one great, consolidated, National Government, of all the States!"*

Edmund Pendleton, President of the Convention, answered: "'*We, the people,*' possessing all power, form a Government, such as we think will secure happiness: and suppose, in adopting this plan, we should be mistaken in the end; where is the cause of alarm on that quarter? In the same plan we point out an easy and quiet method of reforming what may be found amiss. No, but, say gentlemen, we have put the introduction of that method in the hands of our servants, who will interrupt it from motives of self-interest. What then? We will resist, did my friend say? conveying an idea of force. Who shall dare to resist the people? No, *we will assemble in Convention; wholly recall our delegated powers*, or reform them so as to prevent such abuse." * * *

"This is the only Government founded in real Compact.

---

* *Elliot's Debates*, vol. iii, pp. 21–22.

There is no quarrel between Government and liberty; the former is the shield and protector of the latter."*

"This Constitution is said to have beautiful features," said Mr. Henry, subsequently, "but, when I come to examine these features, sir, they appear to me horribly frightful! Among other deformities, it has an awful squinting; it squints towards monarchy; and does not this raise indignation in the breast of every true American?"†

"We are told," said he, "that this Government, collectively taken, is without an example; that it is National in this part, and Federal in that part, etc. We may be amused, if we please, by a treatise of political anatomy. In the brain it is National; the stamina are Federal; some limbs are Federal, others National. The Senators are voted for by the State Legislatures; so far it is Federal. Individuals choose the Members of the first branch; here it is National. It is Federal in conferring general powers, but National in retaining them. It is not to be supported by the States; the pockets of individuals are to be searched for its maintenance. What signifies it to me that you have the most curious anatomical description of it in its creation? To all the common purposes of legislation, it is a great Consolidation of Government. You are not to have the right to legislate in any but trivial cases; you are not to touch private contracts; you are not to have the right of having arms in your own defence; you cannot be trusted with dealing out justice between man and man. What shall the States have to do? Take care of the poor, repair and make highways, erect bridges, and so on, and so on? Abolish the State Legislatures at once. What purposes should they be

---

* *Elliot's Debates*, vol. iii, p. 37.

† *Elliot's Debates*, vol. iii, p. 58.

continued for? Our Legislature will, indeed, be a ludicrous spectacle—one hundred and eighty men marching in solemn, farcical procession, exhibiting a mournful proof of the lost liberty of their country, without the power of restoring it. But, sir, we have the consolation that it is a mixed Government; that is, it may work sorely on your neck, but you will have some comfort by saying, that it was a *Federal* Government in its origin.

"I beg gentlemen to consider: lay aside your prejudices. Is this a *Federal Government?* Is it not a consolidated Government for almost every purpose? Is the Government of Virginia a State Government after this Government is adopted? I grant that it is a republican Government, but for what purposes? For such trivial domestic considerations as render it unworthy the name of a Legislature. I shall take leave of this political anatomy, by observing that it is the most extraordinary that ever entered into the imagination of man. If our political diseases demand a cure, this is an unheard-of medicine. The honorable member, I am convinced, wanted a name for it. Were your health in danger, would you take new medicine? I need not make use of these exclamations; for every member in this committee must be alarmed at making new and unusual experiments in Government."*

Mr. Lee answered: "But, sir, this is a Consolidated Government, he tells us; and most feelingly does he dwell on the imaginary dangers of this pretended Consolidation. I did suppose that an honorable gentleman, whom I do not now see (Mr. Madison), had placed this in such a clear light that every man would have been satisfied with it.

"If this were a consolidated Government, ought it not

* *Elliot's Debates*, vol. iii, pp. 171–172.

to be ratified by a *majority* of the *people as individuals*, and *not as States?* Suppose Virginia, Connecticut, Massachusetts, and Pennsylvania, had ratified it; these four States, being a majority of the people of America, would, by their adoption, have made it binding on all the States, had this been a Consolidated Government. But it is only the Governments of those seven States who have adopted it. If the honorable gentleman will attend to this, we shall hear no more of Consolidation." * * *

"I say, that this new system shows, in stronger terms than words could declare, that the liberties of the people are secure. It goes on the principle *that all power is in the people*, and that rulers have no powers but what are enumerated in that paper. When a question arises with respect to the legality of any power, exercised or assumed by Congress, it is plain on the side of the governed: *Is it enumerated in the Constitution?* If it be, it is legal and just. It is otherwise arbitrary and unconstitutional. Candor must confess that it is infinitely more attentive to the liberties of the people than any State Government.

"[Mr. Lee then said, that, under the State Governments, the people reserved to themselves certain enumerated rights, and that the rest were vested in their rulers; that, consequently, the powers reserved to the people were but an inconsiderable exception from what were given to their rulers; but that, in the Federal Government, the rulers of the people were vested with certain defined powers, and that what were not delegated to those rulers were retained by the people. The consequence of this, he said, was, that the limited powers were only an exception to those which rested in the people, and that they knew what they had given up, and could be in no danger. He exemplified the proposition in a familiar manner. He observed, that, if a man delegated certain powers to an agent, it would be an insult upon common sense to suppose that the agent could legally transact any business for his principal which was not contained in the commission whereby the powers were delegated; but that if a man empowered his representative or agent to transact all his business except certain enumerated parts, the clear result was, that the agent could lawfully transact every possible part of his principal's business, except the enumerated parts; and added, that these plain propositions were sufficient to demonstrate the inutility and *folly* (were he permitted to use the expression) of bills of rights.]"*

Governor Randolph, who had favored a National Government in the Convention, replied as follows: "The liberty of the press is supposed to be in danger. If this were the case, it would produce extreme repugnancy in my mind. If it ever will be suppressed in this country, the liberty of the people will not be far from being sacrificed. Where is the danger of it? He says that every power is given to the General Government that is not reserved to the States. Pardon me if I say the reverse of the proposition is true. I defy any one to prove the contrary. Every power not given it by this system is left with the States."†

John Marshall (afterwards Chief Justice), in reply to Mr. Henry, said: "We are threatened with the loss of our liberties by the possible abuse of power, notwithstanding the maxim, that those who give may take away. It is the *people* that give power, and *can take it back.* What shall restrain them? They are the masters who give it, and of whom their servants *hold it.*"‡

George Nicholas said: "But it is objected to for want

* *Elliot's Debates*, vol. iii, p. 186. † *Elliot's Debates*, vol iii, p. 203.
‡ *Elliot's Debates*, vol. iii, p. 233.

of a bill of rights. It is a principle universally agreed upon, that all powers not given are retained. Where, by the Constitution, the General Government has general powers for any purpose, its powers are absolute. Where it has powers with some exceptions, they are absolute only as to those exceptions. In either case, the people retain what is not conferred on the General Government, as it is by their positive grant that it has any of its powers. In England, in all disputes between the king and people, recurrence is had to the enumerated rights of the people, to determine. Are the rights in dispute secured? Are they included in Magna Charta, Bill of Rights, etc.? If not, they are, generally speaking, within the king's prerogative. In disputes between the Congress and the people, the reverse of the proposition holds. Is the disputed right enumerated? If not, Congress cannot meddle with it." * * *

"Mr. Nicholas concluded, by making a few observations on the general structure of the Government, and its probable happy operation. He said that it was a Government calculated to suit almost any extent of territory. He then quoted the opinion of the celebrated Montesquieu, from vol. i, b. 9, where that writer speaks of a Confederate Republic as the only safe means of extending the sphere of a Republican Government to any considerable degree."*

Mr. Madison said: "The powers of the General Government relate to external objects, and are but few. But the powers in the States relate to those great objects which immediately concern the prosperity of the people. Let us observe, also, that the powers in the General Government are those which will be exercised mostly in time

---

* *Elliot's Debates*, vol. iii, p. 247.

of war, while those of the State Governments will be exercised in time of peace. I should not complete the view which ought to be taken of this subject, without making this additional remark,—that the powers vested in the proposed Government are not so much an augmentation of powers in the General Government, as a change rendered necessary for the purpose of giving efficacy to those which were vested in it before. It cannot escape any gentleman, that this power, in theory, exists in the Confederation as fully as in this Constitution. The only difference is this—that now they tax States, and by this plan they will tax individuals. There is no theoretic difference between the two. But in practice there will be an infinite difference between them. The one is an ineffectual power; the other is adequate to the purpose for which it is given. This change was necessary for the public safety.

"Let us suppose, for a moment, that the acts of Congress, requiring money from the States, had been as effectual as the paper on the table; suppose all the laws of Congress had complete compliance; will any gentleman say that, as far as we can judge from past experience, the State Governments would have been debased, and all consolidated and incorporated into one system? My imagination cannot reach it. I conceive that had those acts that effect, which all laws ought to have, the States would have retained their Sovereignty."*

George Mason (in opposition) said:

"The objection was, that too much power was given to Congress—power that would finally destroy the State Governments more effectually by insidious, underhanded means, than such as could be openly practiced."†

* *Elliot's Debates*, vol. iii, pp. 259, 260, Virginia State Convention.

† *Elliot's Debates*, vol. iii, p. 415.

Mr. Marshall replied: "When the Government is drawn from the people, and depending on the people for its continuance, oppressive measures will not be attempted, as they will certainly draw on their authors the resentment of those on whom they depend. On this Government, thus *depending on ourselves for its existence*, I will rest my safety, notwithstanding the danger depicted by the honorable gentleman. I cannot help being surprised that the worthy member thought this power so dangerous."*

He then concluded by observing, that "the power of governing the militia was not vested in the States, by implication, because, being possessed of it antecedent to the adoption of the Government, and not being divested of it by any grant or restriction in the Constitution, they must necessarily be as fully possessed of it as ever they had been. And it could not be said that any of the States derived any powers from that system, but retained them, though not acknowledged in any part of it."†

Mr. Henry again spoke, as follows: "A bill of rights may be summed up in a few words. What do they tell us? That our rights are reserved. Why not say so? Is it because it will consume too much paper? Gentlemen's reasoning against a bill of rights does not satisfy me—without saying which has the right side, it remains doubtful. A bill of rights is a favorite thing with the Virginians, and the people of the other States, likewise. It may be their prejudice, but the Government ought to suit their geniuses; otherwise, its operation will be unhappy. A bill of rights, even if its necessity be doubtful, will exclude the possibility of dispute; and, with great submission, I think the best way is to have no dispute.

* *Elliot's Debates*, vol. iii, p. 420.

† *Elliot's Debates*, vol. iii, p. 421.

In the present Constitution, they are restrained from issuing general warrants to search suspected places, or seize persons not named, without evidence of the commission of a fact, etc. There was certainly some celestial influence governing those who deliberated on that Constitution; for they have, with the most cautious and enlightened circumspection, guarded those indefeasible rights which ought ever to be held sacred!"*

Mr. George Nicholas, in answer, said: "That, though there was a declaration of rights in the Government of Virginia, it was no conclusive reason that there should be one in this Constitution; for, if it was unnecessary in the former, its omission in the latter could be no defect. They ought, therefore, to prove that it was essentially necessary to be inserted in the Constitution of Virginia. There were five or six States in the Union which had no bill of rights, separately and distinctly as such; but they annexed the substance of a bill of rights to their respective Constitutions. These States, he further observed, were as free as this State, and their liberties as secure as ours. If so, gentlemen's arguments from the precedent were not good. In Virginia, all powers were given to the Government without any exception. It was different in the General Government, to which certain special powers were delegated for certain purposes. He asked which was the more safe. Was it safer to grant general powers than certain limited powers?" * * *

"A bill of rights," continued he, "is only an acknowledgment of the pre-existing claim to rights in the people. They belong to us as much as if they had been inserted in the Constitution. But it is said that, if it be doubtful, the possibility of dispute ought to be precluded. Admit-

---

* *Elliot's Debates*, vol. iii, p. 448.

ting it was proper for the Convention to have inserted a bill of rights, it is not proper here to propose it as the condition of our *accession* to the Union. Would you reject this Government for its omission, dissolve the Union, and bring miseries on yourselves and posterity? I hope the gentleman does not oppose it on this ground solely. Is there another reason? He said that it is not only the general wish of this State, but all the States, to have a bill of rights. If it be so, where is the difficulty of having this done by way of subsequent amendment? We shall find the other States willing to accord with their own favorite wish. The gentleman last up says that the power of legislation includes every thing. A general power of legislation does. But this is a special power of legislation. Therefore, it does not contain that plenitude of power which he imagines. They cannot legislate in any case but those particularly enumerated. No gentleman, who is a friend to the Government, ought to withhold his assent from it for this reason."*

Mr. Henry continued his strenuous opposition in the following language: "The Honorable gentleman (Gov. Randolph), who was up some time ago, exhorts us not to fall into a repetition of the defects of the Confederation. He said, we ought not to declare that each State retains every power, jurisdiction, and right, which is not expressly delegated, because experience has proved the insertion of such a restriction to be destructive, and mentioned an instance to prove it. That case, Mr. Chairman, appears to me to militate against himself. * * * They can exercise power, by implication, in one instance as well as in another. Thus, by the gentleman's own argument, they can exercise the power, though it be not dele-

---

* *Elliot's Debates*, vol. iii, p. 451.

gated. * * * We have nothing local to ask. We ask rights which concern the general happiness. Must not justice bring them into the concession of these? The honorable gentleman was pleased to say that the new Government, in this policy, will be equal to what the present is. If so, that amendment will not injure that part. * * * *

"He speaks of war and bloodshed. Whence do this war and bloodshed come? I fear it, but not from the source he speaks of. I fear it, sir, from the operation and friends of the Federal Government. He speaks with contempt of this amendment. But whoever will advert to the use made, repeatedly, in England, of the prerogative of the king, and the frequent attacks on the privileges of the people, notwithstanding many Legislative acts to secure them, will see the necessity of *excluding implications*. Nations who have trusted to logical deductions have lost their liberty! * * * *

"The worthy member who proposed to ratify has also proposed that what amendments may be deemed necessary should be recommended to Congress, and that a committee should be appointed to consider what amendments were necessary. But what does it all come to at last? That it is a vain project, and that it is indecent and improper! I will not argue unfairly, but I will ask him if amendments are not unattainable? Will gentlemen, then, lay their hands on their hearts, and say that they can adopt it in this shape? When we demand this security of our privileges, the language of Virginia is not that of respect! Give me leave to deny! She only asks amendments previous to her adoption of the Constitution. * * *

"He tells you of the important blessings which, he imagines, will result to us and mankind in general from the adoption of this system. I see the awful immensity of the dangers with which it is pregnant! I see it! I feel it! I see beings of a higher order anxious concerning our decision! When I see beyond the horizon that bounds human eyes, and look at the final consummation of all human things, and see those intelligent beings which inhabit the ethereal mansions, reviewing the political decisions and revolutions which, in the progress of time, will happen in America, and the consequent happiness or misery of mankind, I am led to believe that much of the account, on one side or the other, will depend on what we now decide! Our own happiness alone is not affected by the event! All nations are interested in the determination! We have it in our power to secure the happiness of one half of the human race! Its adoption may involve the misery of the other hemisphere!"*

Just at this point in Mr. Henry's speech, the heavens blackened with a gathering tempest, which burst with so terrible a fury as to put the whole House in such disorder that he could proceed no farther! It was the last speech that Patrick Henry made in that Convention!

Did he possess a superhuman vision, or had he caught something of the spirit of the ancient prophets, which enabled him to see farther into the future, and understand better the workings of political systems controlled by human passion, than any of his many great and equally patriotic colleagues, in that renowned body of sages and statesmen? Did he see farther in the future than Pendleton, Madison, or Marshall, when he said, "I see it! I feel it!" Did he get glimpses of the terrible scenes of the last seven years? or, of the still more horrible ones yet ahead of us—?

---

* "Here a violent storm arose, which put the House in such disorder, that Mr. Henry was obliged to conclude."—*Reporter*. *Elliot's Debates*, vol. iii, p. 625.

Mr. Nicholas replied, by urging "that the language of the proposed ratification would secure every thing which gentlemen desired, as it declared that all powers vested in the Constitution were derived from the people, and might be resumed by them whensoever they should be perverted to their injury and oppression; and that every power not granted thereby remained at their will. No danger whatever could arise; for, says he, these expressions will become a *part of the contract.* The Constitution *cannot be binding on Virginia,* but with these conditions. If thirteen individuals are about to make a contract, and one agrees to it, but at the same time declares that he understands its meaning, signification, and intent, to be (what the words of the contract plainly and obviously denote), that it is not to be construed so as to impose any supplementary condition upon him, and that *he* is to be exonerated from it *whensoever* any such imposition shall be attempted,—I ask whether, in this case, these conditions, on which he has assented to it, would not be binding on the other twelve? In like manner these conditions will be binding on Congress. They can exercise no power that is not expressly granted them."*

On the question of ratification, the vote stood 89 to 79, being only ten majority in its favor.†

Immediately afterwards the amendments, which had been agreed upon to be proposed, were taken up and adopted, without opposition. They were twenty in number. Very similar, in many respects, to those incorporated by Massachusetts in her ratification. The first, and most important, was in these words:

"1st. That each State in the Union shall, respectively, retain every power, jurisdiction, and right, which

* *Elliot's Debates*, vol. iii., pp. 625, 626.

† *Elliot's Debates*, vol. iii, p. 654.

is not by this Constitution delegated to the Congress of the United States, or to the departments of the Federal Government."*

These proceedings conclusively show how the Convention of Virginia understood the Constitution. That is, that it was Federal in its character, and that the Government under it was to be a Federal Government, one founded upon Compact between Sovereign States. Not a member of the Convention advocated the Constitution upon any other principles. The opposition of Patrick Henry, George Mason, and others, was altogether argumentative, and sprung mainly from apprehensions that the Constitution would not be construed as its friends maintained that it would be, and that powers not delegated would be assumed, by construction and implication. These proceedings also show clearly, that Virginia understood by the declaration, in her ratification, that her people had the right to resume the powers that they had delegated, in case these powers, in their judgment, should be perverted to their injury.

ELEVENTH, NEW YORK.

The next State, in order, is New York. First we will see what was done by her Convention. Here is her ratification.

"We, the Delegates of the people of the State of New York, duly elected, and met in Convention, having maturely considered the Constitution for the United States of America, agreed to on the 17th day of September, in the year 1787, by the Convention then assembled at Philadelphia, in the Commonwealth of Pennsylvania (a copy whereof precedes these presents), and having,

---

* *Elliot's Debates*, vol. iii, p. 659.

also, seriously and deliberately considered the present situation of the United States,—Do declare and make known,—

"That all power is originally vested in, and consequently derived from the people, and that Government is instituted by them for their common interest, protection, and security.

"That the enjoyment of life, liberty, and the pursuit of happiness, are essential rights, which every Government ought to respect and preserve.

"That the powers of Government may be re-assumed by the people, whensoever it shall become necessary to their happiness; that every power, jurisdiction, and right, which is not by the said Constitution clearly delegated to the Congress of the United States, or the departments of the Government thereof, *remains to the people of the several States,* or to their respective State Governments, to whom they may have granted the same; and that those clauses, in the said Constitution, which declare that Congress shall not have or exercise certain powers, do not imply that Congress is entitled to any powers not given by the said Constitution; but such clauses are to be construed either as exceptions to certain specified powers, or as inserted merely for greater caution.

"That the people have an equal, natural, and unalienable right, freely and peaceably, to exercise their religion, according to the dictates of conscience; and that no religious sect, or society, ought to be favored or established by law in preference to others.

"That the people have a right to keep and bear arms; that a well regulated militia, including the body of the people *capable of bearing arms,* is the proper, natural, and safe defence of a free State.

"That the militia should not be subject to martial law, except in time of war, rebellion or insurrection.

"That standing armies, in time of peace, are dangerous to liberty, and ought not to be kept up, except in cases of necessity, and that at all times the military should be under strict subordination to the civil power.

"That, in time of peace, no soldier ought to be quartered in any house without the consent of the owner, and in time of war only by the civil magistrate, in such manner as the laws may direct.

"That no person ought to be taken, imprisoned, or disseized of his freehold, or be exiled, or deprived of his privileges, franchises, life, liberty, or property, but by due process of law.

"That no person ought to be put twice in jeopardy of life or limb, for one and the same offence; nor, unless in case of impeachment, be punished more than once for the same offence. That every person restrained of his liberty is entitled to an inquiry into the lawfulness of such restraint, and to a removal thereof if unlawful; and that such inquiry, or removal, ought not to be denied or delayed, except when, on account of public danger, the Congress shall suspend the privilege of the writ of *Habeas Corpus*. That excessive bail ought not to be required, nor excessive fines imposed, nor cruel or unusual punishments inflicted.

"That (except in the government of the land and naval forces, and of the militia, when in actual service, and in cases of impeachment) a presentment, or indictment, by a grand jury, ought to be observed, as a necessary preliminary to the trial of all crimes cognizable by the judiciary of the United States; and such trial should be speedy, public, and by an impartial jury of the county where the crime was committed; and that no person can be found guilty without the unanimous consent of such jury. But in cases of crimes not committed within any county of any of the United States, and in cases of crimes not committed within any county in which a general insurrection may prevail, or which may be in the possession of a foreign enemy, the inquiry and trial may be in such county as the Congress shall by law direct; which county, in the two cases last mentioned, should be as near as conveniently may be to that county in which the crime may have been committed;—and that, in all criminal prosecutions, the accused ought to be informed of the cause and nature of his accusation, to be confronted with his accusers and the witnesses against him, to have the means of producing his witnesses, and the assistance of counsel for his defence; and should not be compelled to give evidence against himself.

"That the trial by jury, in the extent that it obtains by the common law of England, is one of the greatest securities to the rights of a free people, and ought to remain inviolate.

"That every freeman has a right to be secure from all unreasonable searches and seizures of his person, his papers, or his property; and, therefore, that all warrants to search suspected places, or seize any freeman, his papers, or property, without information upon oath, or affirmation of sufficient cause, are grievous and oppressive; and that all general warrants (or such in which the place or person suspected are not particularly designated) are dangerous, and ought not to be granted.

"That the people have a right peaceably to assemble together, to consult for their common good, or to instruct their representatives, and that every person has a right to petition, or apply to the Legislature, for redress of grievances.

"That the freedom of the press ought not to be violated, or restrained.

"That there should be, once in four years, an election of the President and Vice President, so that no officer, who may be appointed by the Congress, to act as President, in case of the removal, death, resignation, or inability, of the President and Vice President, can in any case continue to act beyond the termination of the period for which the last President and Vice President were elected.

"That nothing contained in the said Constitution is to be construed to prevent the Legislature of any State from passing laws at its discretion, from time to time, to divide such State into convenient districts, and to apportion its Representatives to and amongst such districts.

"That the prohibition contained in the said Constitution, against *ex post facto* laws, extends only to laws concerning crimes.

"That all appeals in causes determinable according to the course of the common law, ought to be by writ of error, and not otherwise.

"That the judicial power of the United States, in cases in which a State may be a party, does not extend to criminal prosecutions, or to authorize any suit by any person against a State.

"That the judicial power of the United States, as to controversies between citizens of the same State, claiming lands under grants from different States, is not to be construed to extend to any other controversies between them, except those which relate to such lands, so claimed, under grants of different States.

"That the jurisdiction of the Supreme Court of the United States, or of any other Court to be instituted by the Congress, is not in any case to be increased, enlarged, or extended, by any faction, collusion, or mere suggestion; and that no treaty is to be construed so to operate as to alter the Constitution of any State.

"Under these impressions, and declaring that the rights aforesaid cannot be abridged, or violated, and that the explanations aforesaid, are consistent with the said Constitution, and in confidence that the amendments, which shall have been proposed to the said Constitution, will receive an early and mature consideration. We, the said delegates, in the name and in the behalf of the people of the State of New York, do, by these presents, assent to, and ratify the said Constitution. In full confidence, nevertheless, that, until a Convention shall be called and convened, for proposing amendments to the said Constitution, the militia of this State will not be continued in service out of this State for a longer term than six weeks, without the consent of the Legislature thereof; that the Congress will not make or alter any regulation in this State, respecting the times, places, and manner, of holding elections for Senators or Representatives, unless the Legislature of this State shall neglect or refuse to make laws or regulations for the purpose, or from any circumstance, be incapable of making the same; and that in those cases, such power will only be exercised until the Legislature of this State shall make provision in the premises; that no excise will be imposed on any article of the growth, production, or manufacture of the United States, or any of them, within this State, ardent spirits excepted; and that Congress will not lay direct taxes within this State, but when the moneys arising from the impost and excise shall be insufficient for the public exigencies, nor then, until Congress shall first have made a requisition upon this State, to assess, levy, and pay, the amount of such requisition, made agreeably to the census fixed in the said Constitution, in such way and manner as the Legislature of this State shall judge best; but that, in such case, if the State shall neglect or refuse to pay its proportion, pursuant to such requisition, then the Congress may assess and levy this State's proportion, together with interest, at the rate of six per centum per annum, from the time at which the same was required to be paid.

"Done, in Convention, at Poughkeepsie, in the county of Duchess, in the State of New York, the 26th day of July, in the year of our Lord 1788."*

A careful perusal of these proceedings leaves no doubt as to how the Convention of New York understood the Constitution. They recognized it as a Constitution for States. As Virginia, New York accompanied her ratification with the express declaration that the powers of Government may be resumed by the people whensoever it shall become necessary to their happiness, etc. "*Under these impressions*, and declaring that the *rights aforesaid* (after the enumeration of many, especially the reserved rights of the people of the several States as States) cannot be *abridged* or *violated*," a majority of the members of the Convention gave it their assent and ratification. So much for what was done.

Secondly, let us examine the *res gestæ*—the debates.

In New York the opposition was stronger in numbers, comparatively, than in Virginia. On the final vote on the ratification there was but three majority in its favor. Some of the ablest men of the State were in the Convention. At the head of the list may be placed the venerable Robert R. Livingston, the Chancellor of the State. Next to him stood Alexander Hamilton, who had been in the Philadelphia Convention.

Now let us, as in the other State Conventions, sample the debates in this. The Constitution here, as in Massa-

* *Elliot's Debates*, vol. i, pp. 327–329.

chusetts and Virginia, was thoroughly discussed. How was it understood by its advocates?

Chancellor Livingston opened the discussion. After some general remarks "he next adverted to the form of the Federal Government. He said that, though justified when considered as a mere diplomatic body, making engagements for its respective States, which they were to carry into effect, yet, if it was to enjoy legislative, judicial, and executive powers, an attention as well to the facility of doing business as to the principles of freedom, called for a division of those powers."*

In another speech afterwards, he says:

"The gentleman from Duchess appears to have misapprehended some of the ideas which dropped from me. My argument was, that a Republic might very properly be formed by a *league of States*, but that the laws of the general Legislature must act, and be enforced upon individuals. I am contending for this *species of Government*. The gentlemen who have spoken in opposition to me have either misunderstood or perverted my meaning; but, sir, I flatter myself, it has not been misunderstood by the Convention at large.

"If we examine the history of the Federal Republics, whose legislative powers were exercised only in States, in their collective capacity, we shall find in their fundamental principles the seeds of domestic violence and consequent annihilation. This was the principal reason why I thought the *old* Confederation would be forever impracticable."† He was for a Government founded on a Compact or League of States, with authority to act on the individual citizens of each State, and maintained that such was the form of Government then presented.

---

* *Elliot's Debates*, vol. ii, p. 215.

† *Elliot's Debates*, vol. ii, p. 274.

Again, he said:

"Let us take a view of the present Congress. The gentleman is satisfied with our present Federal Government, on the score of corruption. Here he has confidence. Though each State may delegate seven, they generally sent no more than three; consequently thirty-nine men may transact any business under the old Government; while the new Legislature, which will be, in all probability, constantly full, will consist of ninety-one. But, says the gentleman, our present Congress have not the same powers. I answer, They have the very same. Congress have the power of making war and peace, of levying money and raising men; they may involve us in a war at their pleasure; they may negotiate loans to any extent, and make unlimited demands upon the States. Here the gentleman comes forward, and says, that the States are to carry these powers into execution; and they have the power of non-compliance. But is not every State bound to comply? What power have they to control Congress in the exercise of those rights which they have pledged themselves to support? It is true they have broken, in numerous instances, the compact by which they were obligated; and they may do it again; but will the gentleman draw an argument of security from the facility of violating their faith? Suppose there should be a majority of creditor States, under the present Government; might they not combine, and compel us to observe the covenants by which we had bound ourselves?

"We are told that this Constitution gives Congress the power over the purse and the sword. Sir, have not all good Governments this power? Nay, does any one doubt that, under the old Confederation, Congress holds the purse and the sword? How many loans did they procure, which we are bound to pay! How many men did they raise, whom we are bound to maintain! How will gentlemen say, that that body, which is indeed extremely small, can be more safely trusted than a much larger body possessed of the same authority? What is the ground of such entire confidence in the one—what the cause of so much jealousy of the other?"*

Mr. Williams, in opposition, spoke as follows: "Sir, I yesterday expressed my fears that this clause would tend to annihilate the State Governments. I also observed, that the powers granted by it were indefinite, since the Congress are authorized to provide for the common defence and general welfare, and to pass all laws necessary for the attainment of these important objects. The Legislature is the highest power in a Government. Whatever they judge necessary for the proper administration of the powers lodged in them, they may execute without any check or impediment. Now, if the Congress should judge it a proper provision, for the common defence and general welfare, that the State Governments should be essentially destroyed, what, in the name of common sense, will prevent them? Are they not Constitutionally authorized to pass such laws? Are not the terms, *common defence and general welfare*, indefinite, undefinable terms? What checks have the State Governments against such encroachments? Why, they appoint the Senators once in six years. So do the electors of Germany appoint their Emperor. And what restraint have they against tyranny in their head? Do they rely upon any thing but arms, the *ultima ratio?* And to this most undesirable point must the States recur in order to secure their rights."†

Mr. Hamilton, on the other side, said: "Sir, the most

---

* *Elliot's Debates*, vol. ii, p. 278–279.

† *Elliot's Debates*, vol. ii, p. 338.

powerful obstacle to the members of Congress betraying the interest of their constituents, is the State Legislatures themselves, who will be standing bodies of observation, possessing the confidence of the people, jealous of Federal encroachments, and armed with every power to check the first essays of treachery. They will institute regular modes of inquiry. The complicated domestic attachments, which subsist between the State Legislators and their electors, will ever make them vigilant guardians of the people's rights. Possessed of the means and the disposition of resistance, the spirit of opposition will be easily communicated to the people, and, under the conduct of an organized body of leaders, will act with weight and system. Thus, it appears that *the very structure of the Confederacy* affords the surest preventions from error, and the most powerful checks to misconduct."*

Again, he said: "The gentlemen are afraid that the State Governments will be abolished. But, sir, their existence does not depend upon the laws of the United States. *Congress can no more abolish the State Governments, than they can dissolve the Union.* The whole Constitution is repugnant to it, and yet the gentleman would introduce an additional useless provision against it."†

Mr. Lansing, doubting, expressed himself as follows: "I know not that history furnishes an example of a Confederated Republic coercing the States composing it, by the mild influence of laws operating on the individuals of those States. This, therefore, I suppose to be a new experiment in politics; and, as we cannot always accurately ascertain the results of political measures, and, as reasoning on them has been frequently found fallacious,

---

* *Elliot's Debates*, vol. ii, pp. 266–267.
† *Elliot's Debates*, vol. ii, p. 319.

we should not too confidently predict those to be produced by the new system."*

Mr. Hamilton, in a general exposition of the Constitution, said: "*We contend that the radical vice in the old Confederation is, that the laws of the Union apply only to States in their corporate capacity.* Has not every man, who has been in our Legislature, experienced the truth of this position? It is inseparable from the disposition of bodies, who have a Constitutional power of resistance, to examine the merits of a law. This has ever been the case with the Federal requisitions. In this examination, not being furnished with those lights which directed the deliberations of the general Government, and incapable of embracing the general interests of the Union, the States have almost uniformly weighed the requisitions by their own local interests, and have only executed them so far as answered their particular convenience or advantage. * * * It has been observed, to coerce the States is one of the maddest projects that was ever devised. A failure of compliance will never be confined to a single State. This being the case, can we suppose it wise to hazard a civil war? Suppose Massachusetts, or any large State, should refuse, and Congress should attempt to compel them, would they not have influence to procure assistance, especially from those States which are in the same situation as themselves? What picture does this idea present to our view? A complying State at war with a non-complying State; Congress marching the troops of one State into the bosom of another; this State collecting auxiliaries, and forming, perhaps, a majority against its Federal head. Here is a nation at war with itself. Can any reasonable man be well dis-

* *Elliot's Debates*, vol. ii, p. 219.

posed towards a Government which makes war and carnage the only means of supporting itself—a Government that can exist only by the sword? Every such war must involve the innocent with the guilty. This single consideration should be sufficient to dispose every peaceable citizen against such a Government. But can we believe that one State will ever suffer itself to be used as an instrument of coercion? The thing is a dream; it is impossible. Then we are brought to this dilemma—either a Federal standing army is to enforce the requisitions, or the Federal treasury is left without supplies, and the Government without support. What, sir, is the cure for this great evil? Nothing, but to enable the national laws to operate on individuals, in the same manner as those of the States do. This is the true reasoning upon the subject, sir. The gentlemen appear to acknowledge its force; and yet, while they yield to the principle, they seem to fear its application to the Government."*

Again, he said: "The State Governments possess inherent advantages, which will ever give them an influence and ascendancy over the National Government, and will forever preclude the possibility of Federal encroachments. That their liberties, indeed, can be subverted by the Federal head, is repugnant to every rule of political calculation. Is not this arrangement, then, sir, a most wise and prudent one? Is not the present representation fully adequate to our present exigencies, and sufficient to answer all the purposes of the Union? I am persuaded than an examination of the objects of the Federal Government will afford a conclusive answer."†

Mr. Jay, afterwards Chief Justice of the United States, said: "Sir, it seems to be, on all sides, agreed that a

---

* *Elliot's Debates*, vol. ii, pp. 231, 232, 233.

† *Elliot's Debates*, vol. ii, p. 239.

strong, energetic, Federal Government is necessary for the United States. It has given me pleasure to hear such declarations come from all parts of the House. If gentlemen are of this opinion, they give us to understand that such a Government is the favorite of their desire; and also, that it can be instituted; that, indeed, it is both necessary and practicable; or why do they advocate it."*

Mr. R. Morris said: "I am happy, Mr. Chairman, to perceive that it is a principle *on all sides conceded*, and adopted by this committee, that an energetic Federal Government is essential to the preservation of our Union; and that a Constitution *for these States* ought to unite firmness and vigor in the National operations, with the full securities of our rights and liberties."†

Mr. Hamilton, again, said: "I insist that it never can be the interest or desire of the National Legislature to destroy *the State Governments*. It can derive no advantage from such an event; but, on the contrary, would lose an indispensable support, a necessary aid in executing the laws, and conveying the influence of Government to the doors of the people. The Union is dependent on the will of the State Governments for its Chief Magistrate, and for its Senate. The blow aimed at the members must give a fatal wound to the head; and the destruction of the States must be at once a political suicide." * * *

"The States can never lose their powers till the whole people of America are robbed of their liberties. These must go together; they must support each other, or meet one common fate."‡

"With regard to the *jurisdiction* of the two Governments, I shall certainly admit that the Constitution ought

---

* *Elliot's Debates*, vol. ii, p. 282. † *Elliot's Debates*, vol. ii, p. 296.
‡ *Elliot's Debates*, vol. ii, p. 355.

to be so formed as not to prevent the States from providing for their own existence; and I maintain that it is so formed, and that their power of providing for themselves is sufficiently established. This is conceded by one gentleman, and in the next breath the concession is retracted. He says, Congress have but one exclusive right in taxation—that of duties on imports; certainly, then, their other powers are only concurrent. But, to take off the force of this obvious conclusion, he immediately says, that the laws of the United States are supreme; and that where there is one supreme, there cannot be concurrent authority; and further, that where the laws of the Union are supreme, those of the States must be subordinate, because there cannot be two supremes. This is curious sophistry. That two supremes cannot act together, is false. They are inconsistent only when they are aimed at each other, or at one indivisible object. The laws of the United States are supreme, as to all their proper, constitutional objects; the laws of the States are supreme in the same way. These supreme laws may act on different objects without clashing, or they may operate on different parts of the same object, with perfect harmony. Suppose both Governments should lay a tax, of a penny on a certain article: had not each an independent and uncontrollable power to collect its own tax? The meaning of the maxim, there cannot be two supremes, is simply this—two powers cannot be supreme over each other. This meaning is entirely perverted by the gentleman. But it is said disputes between collectors are to be referred to the Federal courts. This is again wandering in the field of conjecture. But suppose the fact certain: is it not to be presumed that they will express the true meaning of the Constitution and the laws? Will they not be bound to consider the concurrent jurisdiction; to declare that both the taxes shall have equal operation; that both the powers, in that respect, are Sovereign and co-extensive? If they transgress their duty, we are to hope that they will be punished. Sir, we can reason from probabilities alone. When we leave common sense, and give ourselves up to conjecture, there can be no certainty, no security in our reasonings.

"I imagine, I have stated to the committee abundant reasons to prove the entire *safety of the State Governments* and of the people."*

This is quite sample enough of the debates in New York Convention, (which lasted for more than a month) to show how the leading advocates of the Constitution in that State understood it, and especially how Mr. Hamilton understood it. His own copious and elaborate speeches abundantly show that he considered the plan, finally adopted by the Philadelphia Convention, to be a Federal Constitution. And his greatest efforts were put forth against those who argued that a different construction might be put upon it. In all of the speeches I have read, he speaks of the Government as Federal, and in one he styles it a Confederacy. As such, he gave it his zealous support, though it was not such a one as he wished to see organized. Nor was it one in which he had much real confidence. The idea on which it was based was not his own; failing in his own, he patriotically took the plan adopted, and threw his whole soul in its support as an experiment.

TWELFTH, NORTH CAROLINA.

The next State in order is North Carolina. She remained out of the Union for some time. As in the other cases we will look first into her action, and then the debates. Her ratification is in these words:

---

* *Elliot's Debates*, vol. ii, p. 355.

"In Convention:

"*Whereas*, the General Convention, which met in Philadelphia, in pursuance of a recommendation of Congress, did recommend to the citizens of the United States a Constitution, or form of Government, in the following words, namely: *Resolved*, That this Convention, in behalf of the freemen, citizens, and inhabitants of the State of North Carolina, do adopt and ratify the said Constitution and form of Government.

"Done, in Convention, this twenty-first day of November, one thousand seven hundred and eighty-nine."

The proceedings in North Carolina are short. Upon their face there is nothing that would indicate the understanding of the members of the Convention as to the nature and character of the Government instituted by the Constitution they adopted. In the debates, the points discussed related mostly to the details of the Constitution. But quite enough, however, appears in them to show the general understanding.

Secondly, let us look into the debates in this Convention, as we have in those of the other States.

Mr. Davie, who was in the Philadelphia Convention, opened the discussion, and amongst other things, said:

"Another radical vice in the old system which was necessary to be corrected, and which will be understood without a long deduction of reasoning, was, that it legislated on States, instead of individuals; and that its powers could not be executed but by fire or by the sword—by military force, and not by the intervention of the civil magistrate. Every one who is acquainted with the relative situation of the States, and the genius of our citizens, must acknowledge that, if the Government was to be carried into effect by military force, the most dreadful consequences would ensue. It would render the citizens of America the most implacable enemies to one another. If it could be carried into effect against the small States, yet it could not be put in force against the larger and more powerful States. It was, therefore, abundantly necessary that the influence of the magistrate should be introduced, and that the laws should be carried home to individuals themselves.

"In the formation of this system, many difficulties presented themselves to the Convention.

"Every member saw that the existing system would ever be ineffectual, unless its laws operated on individuals, as military coercion was neither eligible nor practicable." * * *

"Mutual concessions were necessary to come to any concurrence. A plan that would promote the exclusive interests of a few States would be injurious to others. Had each State obstinately insisted on the security of its particular local advantages, we should never have come to a conclusion. Each, therefore, amicably and wisely relinquished its particular views. The Federal Convention have told you, that the Constitution, which they formed, 'was the result of a spirit of amity, and of that mutual deference and concession which the peculiarity of their political situation rendered indispensable.' I hope the same laudable spirit will govern this Convention in their decision on this important question.

"The business of the Convention was to amend the Confederation, by giving it additional powers. The present form of Congress being a single body, it was thought unsafe to augment its powers, without altering its organization. The act of the Convention is but a mere proposal, similar to the production of a private pen. I think it a Government which, if adopted, will cherish and protect the happiness and liberty of America; but I hold my mind open to conviction. I am ready to recede from my opinion, if it be proved to be ill-founded. I trust that every man here is equally ready to change an opinion he may have improperly formed. The weakness and inefficiency of the old Confederation produced the necessity of calling the Federal Convention. Their plan is now before you; and, I hope, on a deliberate consideration, every man will see the necessity of such a system. It has been the subject of much jealousy and censure out of doors. I hope gentlemen will now come forward with their objections, and that they will be thrown out and answered with candor and moderation. * * * A consolidation of the States is said by some gentlemen to have been intended. They insinuate that this was the cause of their giving this power of elections. If there were any seeds in this Constitution which might, one day, produce a consolidation, it would, sir, with me, be an insuperable objection, I am so perfectly convinced that so extensive a country as this, can never be managed by one consolidated Government. The Federal Convention were as well convinced as the members of this House, that the State Governments were absolutely necessary to the existence of the Federal Government. They considered them as the great massy pillars on which this political fabric was to be extended and supported; and were fully persuaded that, when they were removed, or should moulder down by time, the General Government must tumble into ruin. A very little reflection will show that no department of it can exist without the State Governments.

"Let us begin with the House of Representatives. Who are to vote for the Federal Representatives? Those who vote for the State Representatives. If the State Government vanishes, the General Government must vanish also. This is the foundation on which this Government was raised, and without which it cannot possibly exist.

"The next department is the Senate. How is it formed? By the States themselves. Do they not choose them? Are they not created by them? And will they not have the interest of the States particularly at heart? The States, sir, can put a final period to the Government, as was observed by a gentleman who thought this power over elections unnecessary. If the State Legislatures think proper, they may refuse to choose Senators, and the Government must be destroyed."*

Besides this act of ratification and the speeches of Mr. Davie, we have a set of Resolutions which were passed by the Convention, recommending six amendments to the Constitution, which fully explain their understanding of the Constitution.

The first of these is as follows:

"1. Each State in the Union shall respectively retain every power, jurisdiction, and right, which is not by this Constitution delegated to the Congress of the United States, or to the departments of the General Government; nor shall the said Congress, nor any department of the said Government, exercise any act of authority over any individual in any of the said States, but such as can be justified under some power particularly given in this Constitution; but the said Constitution shall be considered at all times a solemn instrument, defining the extent of their authority, and the limits of which they cannot rightfully in any instance exceed."†

This is quite sufficient to show that the people of North Carolina understood the Constitution they adopted

* *Elliot's Debates*, vol. iv, pp. 21, 22, 23, 58.

† *Elliot's Debates*, vol iv, p. 249.

to be Federal in its character. That is the object of our inquiry.

THIRTEENTH, RHODE ISLAND.

We come now to Rhode Island, the last of the States which acted upon the Constitution. Her proceedings are very voluminous. Nothing but the importance of the question at issue could induce me to ask you to attend to their reading. Their very length, however, shows how completely Federal they were, and guarding against every possible danger to their Sovereignty.

Here is the Document by which she became a member of the United States, under their present Union:

"We, the Delegates of the people of the State of Rhode Island and Providence Plantations, duly elected, and met in Convention, having maturely considered the Constitution for the United States of America, agreed to on the seventeenth day of September, in the year one thousand seven hundred and eighty-seven, by the Convention then assembled at Philadelphia, in the Commonwealth of Pennsylvania (a copy whereof precedes these presents), and having also seriously and deliberately considered the present situation of this State, do declare and make known,—

"I. That there are certain natural rights of which men, when they form a social Compact, cannot deprive or divest their posterity,—among which are the enjoyment of life and liberty, with the means of acquiring, possessing, and protecting property, and pursuing and obtaining happiness and safety.

"II. That all power is naturally vested in, and consequently derived from, the people; that magistrates, therefore, are their trustees and agents, and at all times amenable to them.

"III That the *powers* of Government *may be resumed*

by the people whensoever it shall become necessary to their happiness. That the rights of the States respectively to nominate and appoint all State officers, and every other power, jurisdiction, and right, which is not by the said Constitution clearly delegated to the Congress of the United States, or to the Departments of Government thereof, remain to the people of the several States, or their respective State Governments, to whom they may have granted the same; and that those clauses in the Constitution which declare that Congress shall not have or exercise certain powers, do not imply that Congress is entitled to any powers not given by the said Constitution; but such clauses are to be construed as exceptions to certain specified powers, or as inserted merely for greater caution.

"IV. That religion or the duty which we owe to our Creator, and the manner of discharging it, can be directed only by reason and conviction, and not by force and violence; and, therefore, all men have a natural, equal, and unalienable right to the exercise of religion according to the dictates of conscience; and that no particular religious Sect, or Society, ought to be favored or established by law, in preference to others.

"V. That the legislative, executive, and judiciary powers of Government should be separate and distinct; and, that the members of the two first may be restrained from oppression, by feeling and participating the public burdens, they should, at fixed periods, be reduced to a private station, returned into the mass of the people, and the vacancies be supplied by certain and regular elections, in which all, or any part of the former members to be eligible, or ineleligible, as the rules of the Constitution of Government and the laws shall direct.

"VI. That elections of representatives in Legislature

ought to be free and frequent: and all men having sufficient evidence of permanent common interest with, and attachment to, the community, ought to have the right of suffrage; and no aid, charge, tax, or fee, can be set, rated, or levied, upon the people, without their own consent, or that of their representatives so elected, nor can they be bound by any law to which they have not in like manner consented for the public good.

"VII. That all power of suspending laws, or the execution of laws, by any authority, without the consent of the representatives of the people in the Legislature, is injurious to their rights, and ought not to be exercised.

"VIII. That, in all capital and criminal prosecutions, a man hath the right to demand the cause and nature of his accusation, to be confronted with the accusers and witnesses, to call for evidence, and be allowed counsel in his favor, and to a fair and speedy trial by an impartial jury in his vicinage, without whose unanimous consent he cannot be found guilty, (except in the government of the land and naval forces,) nor can he be compelled to give evidence against himself.

"IX. That no freeman ought to be taken, imprisoned, or disseized of his freehold, liberties, privileges, or franchises, or outlawed, or exiled, or in any manner destroyed, or deprived of his life, liberty, or property, but by the trial by jury, or by the laws of the land.

"X. That every freeman, restrained of his liberty, is entitled to a remedy, to inquire into the lawfulness thereof, and to remove the same if unlawful, and that such remedy ought not to be denied or delayed.

"XI. That in controversies respecting property, and in suits between man and man, the ancient trial by jury, as hath been exercised by us and our ancestors, from the time whereof the memory of man is not to the contrary, is one of the greatest securities to the rights of the people, and ought to remain sacred and inviolable.

"XII. That every freeman ought to obtain right and justice, freely and without sale, completely and without denial, promptly and without delay; and that all establishments, or regulations contravening these rights are oppressive and unjust.

"XIII. That excessive bail ought not to be required, nor excessive fines imposed, nor cruel or unusual punishments inflicted.

"XIV. That every person has a right to be secure from all unreasonable searches and seizures of his person, his papers, or his property; and, therefore, that all warrants to search suspected places, to seize any person, his papers, or his property, without information upon oath or affirmation of sufficient cause, are grievous and oppressive; and that all general warrants (or such in which the place or person suspected are not particularly designated) are dangerous, and ought not to be granted.

"XV. That the people have a right peaceably to assemble together, to consult for their common good, or to instruct their representatives; and that every person has a right to petition or apply to the Legislature for redress of grievances.

"XVI. That the people have a right to freedom of speech, and of writing, and publishing their sentiments. That freedom of the press is one of the greatest bulwarks of liberty, and ought not to be violated.

"XVII. That the people have a right to keep and bear arms; that a well regulated militia, including the body of the people capable of bearing arms, is the proper, natural, and safe defence of a free State; that the militia shall not be subject to martial law, except in time of war, rebellion, or insurrection; that standing armies, in time of peace, are dangerous to liberty, and ought not to be kept up, except in cases of necessity; and that, at all times, the military should be under strict subordination to the civil power; that, in time of peace, no soldier ought to be quartered in any house without the consent of the owner, and in time of war only by the civil magistrates, in such manner as the law directs.

"XVIII. That any person religiously scrupulous of bearing arms ought to be exempted upon the payment of an equivalent to employ another to bear arms in his stead.

"*Under these impressions*, and declaring that *the right aforesaid* cannot be abridged or violated, and that the explanations aforesaid are consistent with the said Constitution, and in confidence that the amendments hereafter mentioned will receive an early and mature consideration, and, conformably to the fifth article of said Constitution, speedily become a part thereof,—We, the said Delegates, in the name and in the behalf of the people of the State of Rhode Island and Providence Plantations, do, by these presents, asssent to and ratify the said Constitution. In full confidence, nevertheless, that, until the amendments hereafter proposed and undermentioned shall be agreed to and ratified, pursuant to the aforesaid fifth article, the militia will not be continued in service out of this State, for a longer term than six weeks, without the consent of the Legislature thereof; that the Congress will not make or alter any regulation in this State respecting the times, places, and manner of holding elections for Senators or Representatives, unless the Legislature of this State shall neglect or refuse to make laws or regulations for the purpose, or from any circumstance, be incapable of making the same; and that, in those cases, such power will only be exercised until the Legislature of this State shall make provision in the premises; that the Congress will not lay direct taxes within this State, but when the moneys arising from impost, tonnage, and excise, shall be insufficient for the public exigencies, nor until the Congress shall have first made a requisition upon this State to assess, levy, and pay, the amount of such requisition made, agreeably to the census fixed in the said Constitution, in such way and manner as the Legislature of this State shall judge best; and that Congress will not lay any capitation or poll tax.

"Done in Convention, at Newport, in the County of Newport, in the State of Rhode Island and Providence Plantations, the twenty-ninth day of May, in the year of our Lord one thousand seven hundred and ninety, and in the fourteenth year of the Independence of the United States of America."*

We have now gone through with the action of all the States upon the Constitution. We have examined the records themselves, and not mere assertions touching them. This concludes that sketch of the history of the Union, as it is called, which I proposed. In it we see, that it was first formed by separate and distinct Colonies for the common maintenance of the chartered rights of each. When this failed, it became a Union of separate, distinct States, by Articles of Confederation, for the support and maintenance of the Independence and Sovereignty of each. The absolute right of local Self Government, or State Sovereignty, was the primal and leading idea throughout. We have seen that these States, as Sovereign, responded to a call of a General Federal Convention, to revise the first Articles of Confederation. The present Constitution was the result of their labors. We have seen that it was submitted to the Legislatures of

* *Elliot's Debates*, vol. i, pp. 334–335.

each State, in their separate State organizations, to be referred by them to a Convention, in each State, of the people thereof, that they, in their Sovereign majesty, might approve or reject each, separately, for themselves, as States, and that it was to be established between such States only as should ratify it, and then only in case as many as nine should ratify it.

We have seen that the State Conventions did so act upon it separately and severally, and adopt it as a Constitution for the States, so to be united thereby, each believing it to be a Federal Constitution, and that all powers not delegated were reserved to the States; but, to quiet apprehensions on this point, a majority of them, in their acts of ratification, demanded an amendment which should make this express declaration, and it was in *confidence* that this should be done, that they assented to it. Which we shall see was immediately afterwards done.

We have further gone into the debates in the several State Conventions, and seen what were the leading ideas of both friends and opponents as to the nature and character of the Constitution. While many apprehended danger to the Sovereignty of the separate States from *constructions* and *implications*, yet on all hands it was *universally* admitted that it purported to be a Federal Constitution; and it was with this *avowed understanding of its nature*, by every *advocate* and *supporter* it had in every State in the Union, even by Hamilton, Morris, Wilson, King, Madison, and Randolph, who had favored a National Government proper, in the Federal Convention, instead of the plan embodied in the Constitution. The leading idea in all the Conventions was that a Confederate Republic was to be established by it upon the model set forth in Montesquieu. According to that model an artificial State is created for Foreign or National, as well as inter State purposes, and these only, by several small Republics, thus Confederating, for their common defence and happiness; each retaining its separate Sovereignty, and the artificial State so created by them being, at all times, subject to their will and power. That this artificial State so created may be dissolved, and yet the separate Republics survive, retaining, at all times, their State organization and Sovereignty. This model of a Confederate Republic, by Montesquieu, was the leading idea with the advocates of the system, as appears from their debates, in every State where we have access to them.

Now, then, after this review, is it not clear that the United States are, or constitute, a Confederated Republic (as Washington styled it), bound together by the solemn Compact of Union, entered into by the several members thereof, under the Constitution? The legitimate consequences flowing from this great truth, if it be a truth, will be the subject of a farther talk when I hear what you have to say in reply to the premises. I am now through for the present.

Is not the Constitution, as appears not only from the history of its formation thus given, but from its face, **a Compact between Sovereign States?**

COLLOQUY VII.

WEBSTER ON THE CONSTITUTION—COMMENTS.

PROF. NORTON. When I declined replying to your question, I preferred to wait until you got through with all you had to say or offer in reference to the action of the several States upon the adoption of the Constitution. My object was to reply to all together. This I will now endeavor to do, and as my opinions upon the whole subject have been so much better expressed by Mr. Webster, the great recognized Expounder of the Constitution, you will allow me to let him reply to you instead of my undertaking to do it myself. This whole subject was thoroughly and ably discussed in the United States Senate, in 1833, I think, upon a set of Resolutions presented to that body by Mr. Calhoun, in the days of Nullification. Have you these Resolutions and Mr. Webster's speech upon them?

MR. STEPHENS. Yes. Here are Mr. Calhoun's Resolutions you refer to. They were offered by him on the 22d January, 1833, the day after what was called the Force Bill, against South Carolina, was introduced into the Senate.* The Force Bill was taken up first. Mr. Calhoun spoke against that. But Mr. Webster, in rising to speak, when that measure was before the Senate, did not reply to Mr. Calhoun upon it, but called for the reading of these Resolutions, and directed his whole

* *Niles's Register*, vol. xliii, *Appendix*, p. 170.

argument against them. This was on the 16th February, 1833.* Here is his speech. The Resolutions are in these words:

"*Resolved,* That the people of the several States, composing these United States, are united as Parties to a Constitutional Compact, to which the people of each State acceded as a separate Sovereign community, each binding itself by its own particular ratification; and that the Union, of which the said Compact is the bond, is a Union *between the States* ratifying the same.

"*Resolved,* That the people of the several States, thus united by the Constitutional Compact, in forming that instrument, and in creating a General Government to carry into effect the objects for which they were formed, delegated to that Government, for that purpose, certain definite powers, to be exercised jointly, reserving, at the same time, each State to itself, the residuary mass of powers, to be exercised by its own separate Government; and that whenever the General Government assumes the exercise of powers not delegated by the Compact, its acts are unauthorized, and are of no effect; and that the same Government is not made the final judge of the powers delegated to it, since that would make its discretion, and not the Constitution, the measure of its powers; but that, as in all other cases of Compact among Sovereign parties, without any common judge, each has an equal right to judge for itself, as well of the infraction as of the mode and measure of redress.

"*Resolved,* That the assertions, that the people of these United States, taken collectively as individuals, are now, or ever have been, united on the principle of the social Compact, and, as such, are now formed into one

* *Niles's Register*, vol. xliii, *Appendix*, p. 170.

nation or people, or that they have ever been so united in any one stage of their political existence; that the people of the several States composing the Union have not, as members thereof, retained their Sovereignty; that the allegiance of their citizens has been transferred to the General Government; that they have parted with the right of punishing treason through their respective State Governments; and that they have not the right of judging in the last resort as to the extent of the powers reserved, and of consequence of those delegated,—are not only without foundation in truth, but are contrary to the most certain and plain historical facts, and the clearest deductions of reason; and that all exercise of power on the part of the General Government, or any of its departments, claiming authority from such erroneous assumptions, must of necessity be unconstitutional,—must tend, directly and inevitably, to subvert the Sovereignty of the States, to destroy the Federal character of the Union, and to rear on its ruins a consolidated Government, without Constitutional check or limitation, and which must necessarily terminate in the loss of liberty itself."

PROF. NORTON. Yes, these are the Resolutions I refer to, and now let me read such parts of Mr. Webster's speech against them as I think utterly demolish them and the whole superstructure of your argument, which is but an attempt to sustain the principles set forth in these Resolutions.

MR. STEPHENS. Only so far as they maintain the proposition that the Constitution of the United States is a Compact between the States, and that the Government instituted by it is a Federal or Confederated Republic. This is the position which I maintain that I have established.

PROF. NORTON. Well, then, only to the extent of utterly

Engraved by A.B. Walter Phila.

Dan'l Webster

demolishing that position will I read from Mr. Webster's speech.

"The Resolutions," said Mr. Webster, "introduced by the gentleman, were apparently drawn up with care, and brought forward upon deliberation. I shall not be in danger, therefore, of misunderstanding him, or those who agree with him, if I proceed at once to these Resolutions, and consider them as an authentic statement of those opinions upon the great Constitutional question, by which the recent proceedings in South Carolina are attempted to be justified.

"These Resolutions are three in number.

"The third seems intended to enumerate, and to deny, the several opinions expressed in the President's proclamation, respecting the nature and powers of this Government. Of this third Resolution, I purpose, at present, to take no particular notice.

"The first two Resolutions of the honorable member affirm these propositions, viz.:—

"1. That the political system under which we live, and under which Congress is now assembled, is a Compact, to which the people of the several States, as separate and Sovereign communities, are the parties.

"2. That these Sovereign parties have a right to judge, each for itself, of any alleged violation of the Constitution by Congress; and in case of such violation, to choose, each for itself, its own mode and measure of redress.

"It is true, sir, that the honorable member calls this a 'Constitutional' Compact; but still he affirms it to be a Compact between Sovereign States. What precise meaning, then, does he attach to the term *Constitutional?* When applied to Compacts between Sovereign States, the term *Constitutional* affixes to the word *Compact* no definite idea. Were we to hear of a Constitutional league or treaty between England and France, or a Constitutional Convention between Austria and Russia, we should not understand what could be intended by such a league, such a treaty, or such a Convention. In these connections, the word is void of all meaning; and yet, sir, it is easy, quite easy, to see why the honorable gentleman has used it in these Resolutions. He cannot open the book, and look upon our written frame of Government, without seeing that it is called a *Constitution*. This may well be appalling to him. It threatens his whole doctrine of Compact, and its darling derivatives, Nullification and Secession, with instant confutation. Because, if he admits our instrument of Government to be a *Constitution*, then, for that very reason, it is not a Compact between Sovereigns; a Constitution of Government and a Compact between Sovereign powers being things essentially unlike in their very natures, and incapable of ever being the same. Yet the word Constitution is on the very front of the instrument. He cannot overlook it. He seeks, therefore, to compromise the matter, and to sink all the substantial sense of the word, while he retains a resemblance of the sound. He introduces a new word of his own, viz., Compact, as importing the principal idea, and designed to play the principal part, and degrades *Constitution* into an insignificant, idle epithet, attached to *Compact*. The whole then stands as a '*Constitutional Compact!*" And in this way he hopes to pass off a plausible gloss, as satisfying the words of the instrument. But he will find himself disappointed. Sir, I must say to the honorable gentleman, that, in our American political grammar, CONSTITUTION is a noun substantive; it imports a distinct and clear idea of itself; and it is not to lose its importance and dignity, it is not to be turned into a poor, ambiguous, senseless, unmeaning adjective, for the purpose of accommodating any new set of political notions. Sir, we reject his new rules of syntax altogether. We will not give up our forms of political speech to the grammarians of the school of Nullification. By the Constitution, we mean, not a 'Constitutional Compact,' but, simply and directly, the Constitution, the fundamental law; and if there be one word in the language which the people of the United States understand, this is that word.* We know no more of a Constitutional Compact between Sovereign powers, than we know of a *Constitutional* indenture of copartnership, a *Constitutional* deed of conveyance or a *Constitutional* bill of exchange. But we know what the *Constitution* is; we know what the plainly written, fundamental law is; we know what the bond of our Union and the security of our liberties is; and we mean to maintain and to defend it, in its plain sense and unsophisticated meaning.

"The sense of the gentleman's proposition, therefore, is not at all affected, one way or the other, by the use of this word. That proposition still is, that our system of Government is but a Compact between the people of separate and Sovereign States.

"Was it Mirabeau, Mr. President, or some other master of the human passions, who has told us that words are things? They are indeed, things, and things of mighty influence, not only in addresses to the passions and high-wrought feelings of mankind, but in the discussion of legal and political questions also; because a just conclusion is often avoided, or a false one reached, by the adroit substitution of one phrase, or one word, for another. Of this, we have, I think, another example in the Resolutions before us.

---

* *Ante*, p. 51, *et seq.*

"The first Resolution declares that the people of the several States '*acceded*' to the Constitution, or to the Constitutional Compact, as it is called. This word 'accede,' not found either in the Constitution itself, or in the ratification of it by any one of the States, has been chosen for use here, doubtless, not without a well-considered purpose.

"The natural converse of *accession* is *secession;* and, therefore, when it is stated that the people of the States acceded to the Union, it may be more plausibly argued that they may secede from it. If, in adopting the Constitution, nothing was done but acceding to a Compact, nothing would seem necessary, to break it up, but to secede from the same Compact. But the term is wholly out of place.* Accession, as a word applied to political associations, implies coming into a league, treaty, or confederacy, by one hitherto a stranger to it; and secession implies departing from such league or confederacy. The people of the United States have used no such form of expression in establishing the present Government. They do not say that they *accede* to a league, but they declare that they *ordain and establish* a Constitution. Such are the very words of the instrument itself; and in all the States, without an exception, the language used by their Conventions was, that they '*ratified the* Constitution;' some of them employing the additional words 'assented to' and 'adopted,' but all of them ratifying.'

"There is more importance than may, at first sight, appear, in the introduction of this new word by the honorable mover of these resolutions. Its adoption and use are indispensable to maintain those premises from which his main conclusion is to be afterwards drawn.

---

* *Ante*, p. 155, *et seq.*

But before showing that, allow me to remark, that this phraseology tends to keep out of sight the just view of a previous political history, as well as to suggest wrong ideas as to what was actually done when the present Constitution was agreed to. In 1789, and before this Constitution was adopted, the United States had already been in a Union, more or less close, for fifteen years. At least as far back as the meeting of the first Congress, in 1774, they had been, in some measure, and for some National purposes, united together. Before the Confederation of 1781, they had declared independence jointly, and had carried on the war jointly, both by sea and land; and this not as separate States, but as one people.* When, therefore, they formed that Confederation, and adopted its articles as articles of perpetual Union, they did not come together for the first time; and, therefore, they did not speak of the States as *acceding* to the Confederation, although it was a league, and rested on nothing but plighted faith for its performance. Yet, even then, the States were not strangers to each other; there was a bond of Union already subsisting between them; they were associated United States; and the object of the Confederation was to make a stronger and better bond of Union. Their representatives deliberated together on these proposed Articles of Confederation, and, being authorized by their respective States, finally 'ratified' and confirmed them. Inasmuch as they were already in Union, they did not speak of *acceding* to the new Articles of Confederation, but of *ratifying* and *confirming* them; and this language was not used inadvertently, because, in the same instrument, accession is used in its proper sense, when applied to

* *Ante*, p. 66, *et seq.*

Canada, which was altogether a stranger to the existing Union. 'Canada, says the eleventh article, '*acceding* to this Confederation, and joining in the measures of the United States, shall be admitted into the Union.'

"Having thus used the terms *ratify* and *confirm*, even in regard to the old Confederation, it would have been strange, indeed, if the people of the United States, after its formation, and when they came to establish the present Constitution, had spoken of the States, or the people of the States, as *acceding* to this Constitution. Such language would have been ill suited to the occasion. It would have implied an existing separation, or disunion, among the States, such as had never existed since 1774. No such language, therefore, was used. The language, actually employed, is *adopt*, *ratify*, *ordain*, *establish*.

"Therefore, sir, since any State, before she can prove her right to dissolve the Union, must show her authority to undo what has been done; no State is at liberty to *secede*, on the ground that she and other States have done nothing but *accede*. She must show that she has a right to *reverse* what has been *ordained*, to *unsettle* and *overthrow* what has been *established*, to *reject* what the people have *adopted*, and to *break up* what they have *ratified*; because these are the terms which express the transactions which have actually taken place. In other words, she must show her right to make a revolution.

"If, Mr. President, in drawing these Resolutions, the honorable member had confined himself to the use of Constitutional language, there would have been a wide and awful *hiatus* between his premises and his conclusions. Leaving out the two words *Compact* and *accession*, which are not Constitutional modes of expression, and stating the matter precisely as the truth is, his first Resolution would have affirmed that *the people of the several States ratified this Constitution, or form of Government.* These are the very words of South Carolina herself, in her act of ratification. Let, then, his first Resolution tell the exact truth; let it state the fact precisely as it exists; let it say that the people of the several States ratified a Constitution, or form of Government, and then, sir, what will become of his inference in his second Resolution, which is in these words, viz.: 'That, as in all other cases of Compact among Sovereign parties, each has an equal right to judge for itself, as well of the infraction as of the mode and measure of redress?' It is obvious, is it not, sir? that this conclusion requires for its support quite other premises; it requires premises which speak of *accession* and of *Compact* between Sovereign powers; and, without such premises, it is altogether unmeaning.

"Mr. President, if the honorable member will truly state what the people did in forming this Constitution, and then state what they must do if they would now undo what they then did, he will unavoidably state a case of revolution. Let us see if it be not so. He must state, in the first place, that the people of the several States adopted and ratified this Constitution, or form of Government; and, in the next place, he must state that they must have a right to undo this; that is to say, that they have a right to discard the form of Government which they have adopted, and to break up the Constitution which they have ratified. Now, sir, this is neither more nor less than saying that they have a right to make a revolution. To reject an established Government, to break up a political Constitution, is revolution.

"I deny that any man can state accurately what was done by the people, in establishing the present Constitution, and then state accurately what the people, or any part of them, must now do to get rid of its obligations, without stating an undeniable case of the overthrow of Government. I admit, of course, that the people may, if they choose, overthrow the Government. But, then, that is revolution. The doctrine now contended for is, that, by *Nullification* or *Secession*, the obligations and authority of the Government may be set aside or rejected, without revolution. But that is what I deny; and what I say is, that no man can state the case with historical accuracy, and in Constitutional language, without showing that the honorable gentleman's right, as asserted in his conclusion, is a revolutionary right merely; that it does not and cannot exist under the Constitution, or agreeably to the Constitution, but can come into existence only when the Constitution is overthrown. This is the reason, sir, which makes it necessary to abandon the use of Constitutional language for a new vocabulary, and to substitute, in the place of plain historical facts, a series of assumptions. This is the reason why it is necessary to give new names to things, to speak of the Constitution, not as a Constitution, but as a Compact, and of the ratifications by the people, not as ratifications, but as acts of accession.

"Sir, I intend to hold the gentleman to the written record. In the discussion of a Constitutional question, I intend to impose upon him the restraints of Constitutional language. The people have ordained a Constitution; can they reject it without revolution? They have established a form of Government; can they overthrow it without revolution? These are the true questions.

"Allow me, now, Mr. President, to inquire further into the extent of the propositions contained in the Resolutions, and their necessary consequences.

"Where Sovereign communities are parties, there is

no essential difference between a Compact, a Confederation, and a League. They all equally rest on the plighted faith of the Sovereign party. A League, or Confederacy, is but a subsisting or continuing treaty.

"The gentleman's Resolutions, then, affirm, in effect, that these twenty-four United States are held together only by a subsisting treaty, resting for its fulfilment and continuance on no inherent power of its own, but on the plighted faith of each State; or, in other words, that our Union is but a league; and, as a consequence from this proposition, they further affirm that as Sovereigns are subject to no superior power, the States must judge, each for itself, of any alleged violation of the league; and if such violation be supposed to have occurred, each may adopt any mode or measure of redress which it shall think proper.

"Other consequences naturally follow, too, from the main proposition. If a league between Sovereign powers have no limitation as to the time of its duration, and contain nothing making it perpetual, it subsists only during the good pleasure of the parties, although no violation be complained of. If, in the opinion of either party, it be violated, such party may say that he will no longer fulfil its obligations on his part, but will consider the whole League or Compact at an end, although it might be one of its stipulations that it should be perpetual. Upon this principle, the Congress of the United States, in 1798, declared null and void the treaty of alliance between the United States and France, though it professed to be a perpetual alliance.

"If the violation of the League be accompanied with serious injuries, the suffering party, being sole judge of his own mod and measure of redress, has a right to indemnify himself by reprisals on the offending members of the League; and reprisals, if the circumstances of the case require it, may be followed by direct, avowed, and public war.

"The necessary import of the Resolution, therefore, is, that the United States are connected only by a League; that it is in the good pleasure of every State to decide how long she will choose to remain a member of the League; that any State may determine the extent of her own obligations under it, and accept or reject what shall be decided by the whole; that she may also determine whether her rights have been violated, what is the extent of the injury done her, and what mode and measure of redress her wrongs may make it fit and expedient for her to adopt. The result of the whole is, that any State may secede at pleasure; that any State may resist a law which she herself may choose to say exceeds the power of Congress; and that, as a Sovereign power, she may redress her own grievances, by her own arm, at her own discretion. She may make reprisals; she may cruise against the property of other members of the League; she may authorize captures, and make open war.

"If, sir, this be our political condition, it is time the people of the United States understood it. Let us look for a moment to the practical consequences of these opinions. One State, holding an Embargo law unconstitutional, may declare her opinion, and withdraw from the Union. *She* secedes. Another, forming and expressing the same judgment on a law laying duties on imports, may withdraw also. *She* secedes. And as, in her opinion, money has been taken out of the pockets of her citizens illegally, under pretence of this law, and as she has power to redress their wrongs, she may demand satisfaction; and, if refused, she may take it with a strong hand. The gentleman has himself pronounced the collection of duties, under existing laws, to be nothing but robbery. Robbers, of course, may be rightfully dispossessed of the fruits of their flagitious crimes; and, therefore, reprisals, impositions on the commerce of other States, foreign alliances against them, or open war, are all modes of redress justly open to the discretion and choice of South Carolina; for she is to judge of her own rights, and to seek satisfaction for her own wrongs, in her own way.

"But, sir, a third State is of opinion, not only that these laws of imposts are Constitutional, but that it is the absolute duty of Congress to pass and to maintain such laws; and that by omitting to pass and maintain them, its Constitutional obligations would be grossly disregarded. She, herself, relinquished the power of protection, she might allege, and allege truly, and gave it up to Congress, on the faith that Congress would exercise it; if Congress now refuse to exercise it, Congress does, as she may insist, break the condition of the grant, and thus manifestly violate the Constitution; and for this violation of the Constitution, *she* may threaten to secede also. Virginia may secede, and hold the fortresses in the Chesapeake. The Western States may secede, and take to their own use the public lands. Louisiana may secede, if she choose, form a foreign alliance, and hold the mouth of the Mississippi. If one State may secede, ten may do so, twenty may do so, twenty-three may do so. Sir, as these secessions go on, one after another, what is to constitute the United States? Whose will be the army? Whose the navy? Who will pay the debts? Who fulfil the public treaties? Who perform the Constitutional guaranties? Who govern this District and the Territories? Who retain the public property?

"Mr. President, every man must see that these are all questions which can arise only *after a revolution.* They presuppose the breaking up of the Government. While the Constitution lasts, they are repressed; they spring up to annoy and startle us only from its grave.

"The Constitution does not provide for events which must be preceded by its own destruction. SECESSION, therefore, since it must bring these consequences with it, is REVOLUTIONARY, and NULLIFICATION is equally REVOLUTIONARY. What is revolution? Why, sir, that is revolution which overturns, or controls, or successfully resists the existing public authority; that which arrests the exercise of the supreme power; that which introduces a new Paramount authority into the rule of the State. Now, sir, this is the precise object of Nullification. It attempts to supersede the supreme legislative authority. It arrests the arm of the executive magistrate. It interrupts the exercise of the accustomed judicial power. Under the name of an ordinance, it declares null and void, within the State, all the revenue laws of the United States. Is not this revolutionary? Sir, so soon as this ordinance shall be carried into effect, *a revolution* will have commenced in South Carolina. She will have thrown off the authority to which her citizens have heretofore been subject. She will have declared her own opinions and her own will, to be above the laws and above the power of those who are intrusted with their administration. If she makes good these declarations, she is revolutionized. As to her, it is as distinctly a change of the supreme power, as the American Revolution of 1776. That revolution did not subvert Government in all its forms. It did not subvert local laws and municipal administrations. It only threw off the dominion of a power claiming to be superior, and to have a right, in many important respects, to exercise legislative authority. Thinking this authority to have been usurped or abused, the American Colonies, now the United States, bade it defiance, and freed themselves from it by means of a revolution. But that revolution left them with their own municipal laws still, and the forms of local Government. If Carolina now shall effectually resist the laws of Congress; if she shall be her own judge, take her remedy into her own hands, obey the laws of the Union when she pleases, and disobey them when she pleases, she will relieve herself from a Paramount power as distinctly as the American Colonies did the same thing in 1776. In other words, she will achieve, as to herself, a revolution.

"But, sir, while practical Nullification in South Carolina would be, as to herself, actual and distinct revolution, its necessary tendency must also be to spread revolution, and to break up the Constitution, as to all the other States. It strikes a deadly blow at the vital principle of the whole Union. To allow State resistance to the laws of Congress to be rightful and proper, to admit Nullification in some States, and yet not expect to see a dismemberment of the entire Government, appears to me the wildest illusion, and the most extravagant folly. The gentleman seems not conscious of the direction or the rapidity of his own course. The current of his opinions sweeps him along, he knows not whither. To begin with Nullification, with the avowed intent, nevertheless, not to proceed to secession, dismemberment, and general revolution, is as if one were to take the plunge of Niagara, and cry out that he would stop half-way down. In the one case, as in the other, the rash adventurer must go to the bottom of the dark abyss below, were it not that the abyss has no discovered bottom.

"Nullification, if successful, arrests the power of the law, absolves citizens from their duty, subverts the foundation both of protection and obedience, dispenses with oaths and obligations of allegiance, and elevates another authority to supreme command. Is not this revolution? And it raises to supreme command four and twenty distinct powers, each professing to be under a General Government, and yet each setting its laws at defiance at pleasure. Is not this anarchy, as well as revolution? Sir, the Constitution of the United States was received as a whole, and for the whole country. If it cannot stand altogether, it cannot stand in parts; and if the laws cannot be executed everywhere, they cannot long be executed anywhere. The gentleman very well knows that all duties and imposts must be uniform throughout the country. He knows that we cannot have one rule or one law for South Carolina, and another for other States. He must see, therefore, and does see, and every man sees, that the only alternative is a repeal of the laws throughout the whole Union, or their execution in Carolina as well as elsewhere. And this repeal is demanded because a single State interposes her veto, and threatens resistance! The result of the gentleman's opinion, or rather the very text of his doctrine, is, that no act of Congress can bind all the States, the Constitutionality of which is not admitted by all; or, in other words, that no single State is bound, against its own dissent, by a law of imposts. This is precisely the evil experienced under the old Confederation, and for remedy of which this Constitution was adopted. The leading object in establishing this Government, an object forced on the country by the condition of the times, and the absolute necessity of the law, was to give to Congress power to lay and collect imposts *without the consent of particular States*. The Revolutionary debt remained unpaid; the National treasury was bankrupt; the country was destitute of credit; Congress issued its requisitions on the States, and the States neglected them; there was no power of coercion but war; Congress could not lay imposts, or other taxes, by its own authority; the whole General Government, therefore, was little more than a name. The Articles of Confederation, as to purposes of revenue and finance, were nearly a dead letter. The country sought to escape from this condition, at once feeble and disgraceful, by constituting a Government which should have power, of itself, to lay duties and taxes, and to pay the public debt, and provide for the general welfare; and to lay these duties and taxes in all the States, without asking the consent of the State Governments. This was the very power on which the new Constitution was to depend for all its ability to do good; and without it, it can be no Government, now or at any time. Yet, sir, it is precisely against this power, so absolutely indispensable to the very being of the Government, that South Carolina directs her ordinance. She attacks the Government in its authority to raise revenue, the very mainspring of the whole system; and if she succeed, every movement of that system must inevitably cease. It is of no avail that she declares that she does not resist the law as a revenue law, but as a law for protecting manufactures. It is a revenue law; it is the very law, by force of which the revenue is collected; if it be arrested in any State, the revenue ceases in that State; it is, in a word, the sole reliance of the Government for the means of maintaining itself and performing its duties.

"Mr. President, the alleged right of a State to decide Constitutional questions for herself, necessarily leads to force, because other States must have the same right, and because different States will decide differently; and when these questions arise between States, if there be no superior power, they can be decided only by the law of force. On entering into the Union, the people of each State gave up a part of their own power to make laws for themselves, in consideration that, as to common objects, they should have a part in making laws for other States. In other words, the people of all the States agreed to create a common Government, to be conducted by common counsels. Pennsylvania, for example, yielded the right of laying imposts in her own ports, in consideration that the new Government, in which she was to have a share, should possess the power of laying imposts on all the States. If South Carolina now refuses to submit to this power, she breaks the condition on which other States entered into the Union. She partakes of the common counsels, and therein assists to bind others, while she refuses to be bound herself. It makes no difference in the case, whether she does all this without reason or pretext, or whether she sets up as a reason, that, in her judgment, the acts complained of are unconstitutional. In the judgment of other States, they are not so. It is nothing to them that she offers some reason, or some apology for her conduct, if it be one which they do not admit. It is not to be expected that any State will violate her duty without some plausible pretext. That would be too rash a defiance of the opinion of mankind. But if it be a pretext which lies in her own breast; if it be no more than an opinion which she says she has performed, how can other States be satisfied with this? How can they allow her to be judge of her own obligations? Or, if she may judge of her obligations, may they not judge of their rights also? May not the twenty-three entertain an opinion as well as the twenty-fourth? And if it be their right, in their own opinion, as expressed in the common council, to enforce the law against her, how is she to say that her right and her opinion are to be every thing, and their right and their opinion nothing?

"Mr. President, if we are to receive the Constitution as the text, and then to lay down in its margin the contradictory commentaries which have been, and which may be, made by different States, the whole page would be a polyglot indeed. It would speak with as many tongues as the builders of Babel, and in dialects as much confused, and mutually as unintelligible. The very instance now before us presents a practical illustration. The law of the last session is declared unconstitutional in South Carolina, and obedience to it is refused. In other States, it is admitted to be strictly Constitutional. You walk over the limits of its authority, therefore, when you pass a State line. On one side it is law, on the other side a nullity; and yet it is passed by a common Government, having the same authority in all the States.

"Such, sir, are the inevitable results of this doctrine. Beginning with the original error, that the Constitution of the United States is nothing but a Compact between Sovereign States; asserting, in the next step, that each State has a right to be its own sole judge of the extent of its own obligations, and, consequently, of the Constitutionality of laws of Congress; and, in the next, that it may oppose whatever it sees fit to declare unconstitutional, and that it decides, for itself, on the mode and measure of redress—the argument arrives, at once, at the conclusion, that what a State dissents from, it may nullify; what it opposes, it may oppose by force; what it decides for itself, it may execute by its own power; and that, in short, it is, itself, supreme over the legislation of Congress, and supreme over the decisions of the national judicature; supreme over the Constitution of the country; supreme over the supreme law of the land. However it seeks to protect itself against these plain inferences, by saying that an unconstitutional law is no law, and that it only opposes such laws as are unconstitutional, yet, this does not, in the slightest degree, vary the result; since it insists on deciding this question for itself; and, in opposition to reason and argument, in opposition to practice and experience, in opposition to the judgment of others, having an equal right to judge, it says, only, 'Such is my opinion, and my opinion shall be my law, and I will support it by my own strong hand. I denounce the law; I declare it unconstitutional; that is enough; it shall not be executed. Men, in arms, are ready to resist its execution. An attempt to enforce it shall cover the land with blood. Elsewhere, it may be binding; but here it is trampled under foot.'

"This, sir, is practical Nullification.

"And now, sir, against all these theories and opinions, I maintain:—

"1. That the Constitution of the United States is not a League, Confederacy or Compact, between the people of the several States in their Sovereign capacities; but a Government proper, founded on the adoption of the people, and creating direct relations between itself and individuals.

"2. That no State authority has power to dissolve these relations; that nothing can dissolve them but revolution; and that, consequently, there can be no such thing as Secession without revolution.

"3. That there is a supreme law, consisting of the Constitution of the United States, and Acts of Congress, passed in pursuance of it, and treaties; and that, in cases not capable of assuming the character of a suit in law or equity, Congress must judge of, and, finally, interpret, the supreme law, so often as it has occasion to pass acts of legislation; and, in cases capable of assuming, and actually assuming, the character of a suit, the Supreme Court of the United States is the final interpreter.

"4. That an attempt by a State to abrogate, annul, or nullify an Act of Congress, or to arrest its operation within her limits, on the ground that, in her opinion, such law is unconstitutional, is a direct usurpation on the just powers of the General Government, and on the equal rights of other States; a plain violation of the Constitution, and a proceeding essentially Revolutionary in its character and tendency.

"Whether the Constitution be a Compact between States in their Sovereign capacities, is a question which must be mainly argued from what is contained in the instrument itself. We all agree that it is an instrument which has in some way been clothed with power. We all admit that it speaks with authority. The first question then is, what does it say of itself? What does it purport to be? Does it style itself a League, Confederacy, or Compact between Sovereign States? It is to be remembered, sir, that the Constitution began to speak only after its adoption. Until it was ratified by nine States, it was but a proposal, the mere draught of an instrument. It was like a deed drawn, but not executed. The Convention had framed it; sent it to Congress, then sitting under the Confederation; Congress had transmitted it to the State Legislatures; and by these last it was laid before Conventions of the people in the several States. All this while it was inoperative paper. It had received no stamp of authority, no sanction; it spoke no language. But when ratified by the people in their respective Conventions, then it had a voice, and spoke authentically. Every word in it had then received the sanction of the popular will, and was to be received as the expression of that will. What the Constitution says of itself, therefore, is as conclusive as what it says on any other point. Does it call itself a 'Compact?' Certainly not. It uses the word *Compact* but once, and that is when it declares that the States shall enter into no Compact. Does it call itself a 'League,' a 'Confederacy,' a 'subsisting Treaty between the States?' Certainly not. There is not a particle of such language in all its pages. But it declares itself a CONSTITUTION. What is a *Constitution?* Certainly not a League, Compact, or Confederacy, but *a fundamental law.* That fundamental regulation which determines the manner in which the public authority is to be executed, is what forms the *Constitution* of a State. Those primary rules which concern the body itself, and the very being of the political society, the form of Government, and the manner in which power is to be exercised,—all, in a word, which form together the *Constitution of a State,* these are the fundamental laws. This, sir, is the language of the public writers. But do we need to be informed, in this country, what a *Constitution* is? Is it not an idea perfectly familiar, definite, and well settled? We are at no loss to understand what is meant by the Constitution of one of the States; and the Constitution of the United States speaks of itself as being an instrument of the same nature. It says, this *Constitution* shall be the law of the land, any thing in any State *Constitution* to the contrary, notwithstanding. And it speaks of itself, too, in plain contradistinction from a Confederation; for it says that all debts contracted, and all engagements entered into, by the United States, shall be as valid under this *Constitution* as under the *Confederation.* It does not say, as valid under this

Compact, or this League, or this Confederation, as under the former Confederation, but as valid under this *Constitution.*

"This, then, sir, is declared to be a *Constitution.* A Constitution is the fundamental law of the State; and this is expressly declared to be the supreme law. It is as if the people had said, 'We prescribe this fundamental law,' or 'this supreme law,' for they do say that they establish this Constitution, and that it shall be the supreme law. They say that they *ordain* and *establish* it. Now, sir, what is the common application of these words? We do not speak of *ordaining* Leagues and Compacts. If this was intended to be a Compact or League, and the States to be parties to it, why was it not so said? Why is there found no one expression, in the whole instrument, indicating such intent? The old Confederation was expressly called a *League;* and into this League it was declared that the States, as States, severally entered. Why was not similar language used in the Constitution, if a similar intention had existed? Why was it not said, 'the States enter into this new League,' 'the States form this new Confederation,' or 'the States agree to this new Compact?' Or why was it not said, in the language of the gentleman's Resolution, that the people of the several States acceded to this Compact in their Sovereign capacities? What reason is there for supposing that the framers of the Constitution rejected expressions appropriate to their own meaning, and adopted others wholly at war with that meaning?

"Again, sir, the Constitution speaks of that political system which is established as 'the Government of the United States.' Is it not doing a strange violence to language to call a League or a Compact between Sovereign powers a *Government?* The Government of a State is that organization in which the political power resides. It is the political being created by the Constitution or fundamental law. The broad and clear difference between a Government and a League or Compact is, that a Government is a body politic; it has a will of its own; and it possesses powers and faculties to execute its own purposes. Every Compact looks to some power to enforce its stipulations. Even in a Compact between Sovereign communities, there always exists this ultimate reference to a power to insure its execution; although, in such case, this power is but the force of one party against the force of another; that is to say, the power of war. But a *Government* executes its decisions by its own supreme authority. Its use of force in compelling obedience to its own enactments is not war. It contemplates no opposing party having a right of resistance. It rests on its power to enforce its own will; and when it ceases to possess this power, it is no longer a Government.

"Mr. President, I concur so generally in the very able speech of the gentleman from Virginia, near me (Mr. Rives), that it is not without diffidence and regret, that I venture to differ with him on any point. His opinions, sir, are redolent of the doctrines of a very distinguished school, for which I have the highest regard, of whose doctrines I can say, what I can also say of the gentleman's speech, that while I concur in the results, I must be permitted to hesitate about some of the premises. I do not agree that the Constitution is a Compact between States in their Sovereign capacities. I do not agree, that, in strictness of language, it is a Compact at all. But I do agree that it is founded on consent or agreement, or on Compact, if the gentleman prefers that word, and means no more by it than voluntary consent or agreement. The Constitution, sir, is not a contract, but the result of a contract; meaning by contract no more than assent. Founded on consent, it is a Government proper. Adopted by the agreement of the people of the United States, when adopted, it has become a Constitution. The people have agreed to make a Constitution; but, when made, that Constitution becomes what its name imports. It is no longer a mere agreement. Our laws, sir, have their foundation in the agreement or consent of the two Houses of Congress. We say, habitually, that one House proposes a bill, and the other agrees to it; but the result of this agreement is not a Compact, but a law. The law, the statute, is not the agreement, but something created by the agreement; and something which, when created, has a new character, and acts by its own authority. So the Constitution of the United States, founded in or on the consent of the people, may be said to rest on Compact or consent; but it is not itself the Compact, but its result. When the people agree to erect a Government, and actually erect it, the thing is done, and the agreement is at an end. The Compact is executed, and the end designed by it attained. Henceforth, the fruit of the agreement exists, but the agreement itself is merged in its own accomplishment; since there can be no longer a subsisting agreement or Compact to form a Constitution or Government, after that Constitution or Government has been actually formed and established.

"It appears to me, Mr. President, that the plainest account of the establishment of this Government presents the most just and philosophical view of its foundation. The people of the several States had their separate State Governments; and between the States there also existed a Confederation. With this condition of things the people were not satisfied, as the Confederation had been found not to fulfil its intended objects. It was proposed, therefore, to erect a new, common Government, which should possess certain definite powers, such as regarded the prosperity of the people of all the States, and to be formed upon the general model of American Constitutions. This proposal was assented to, and an instrument was presented to the people of the several States for their consideration. They approved it, and agreed to adopt it, as a Constitution. They executed that agreement; they adopted the Constitution as a Constitution, and henceforth it must stand as a Constitution until it shall be altogether destroyed. Now, sir, is not this the truth of the whole matter? And is not all that we have heard of Compact between Sovereign States the mere theoretical and artificial mode of reasoning upon the subject? a mode of reasoning which disregards plain facts for the sake of hypothesis?

"Mr. President, the nature of Sovereignty, or Sovereign power, has been extensively discussed by gentlemen on this occasion, as it generally is when the origin of our Government is debated. But I confess myself not entirely satisfied with arguments and illustrations drawn from that topic. The Sovereignty of Government is an idea belonging to the other side of the Atlantic. No such thing is known in North America. Our Governments are all limited. In Europe, Sovereignty is of feudal origin, and imports no more than the state of the Sovereign. It comprises his rights, duties, exemptions, prerogatives, and powers. But with us, all power is with the people. They alone are Sovereign; and they erect what Governments they please, and confer on them such powers as they please. None of these Governments is Sovereign, in the European sense of the word, all being restrained by Constitutions. It seems to me, therefore, that we only perplex ourselves when we attempt to explain the relations existing between the General Government and the several State Governments, according to those ideas of Sovereignty which prevail under systems essentially different from our own.

"But, sir, to return to the Constitution itself, let me inquire what it relies upon for its continuance and support. I hear it often suggested, that the States, by refusing to appoint Senators and Electors, might bring this Government to an end. Perhaps that is true; but the same may be said of the State Governments themselves. Suppose the Legislature of a State, having the power to appoint the Governor and the Judges, should omit that duty, would not the State Government remain unorganized? No doubt, all elective Governments may be broken up by a general abandonment, on the part of those intrusted with political powers, of their appropriate duties. But one popular Government has, in this respect, as much security as another. The maintenance of this Constitution does not depend on the plighted faith of the States, as States, to support it; and this again shows that it is not a League. It relies on individual duty and obligation.

"The Constitution of the United States creates direct relations between this Government and individuals. This Government may punish individuals for treason, and all other crimes in the code, when committed against the United States. It has power, also, to tax individuals in any mode, and to any extent; and it possesses the further power of demanding from individuals military service. Nothing, certainly, can more clearly distinguish a Government from a Confederation of States than the possession of these powers. No closer relations can exist between individuals and any Government

"On the other hand, the Government owes high and solemn duties to every citizen of the country. It is bound to protect him in his most important rights and interests. It makes war for his protection, and no other Government in the country can make war. It makes peace for his protection, and no other Government can make peace. It maintains armies and navies for his defence and security, and no other Government is allowed to maintain them. He goes abroad beneath its flag, and carries over all the earth a National character imparted to him by this Government, and which no other Government can impart. In whatever relates to war, to peace, to commerce, he knows no other Government. All these, sir, are connections as dear and as sacred as can bind individuals to any Government on earth. It is not, therefore, a Compact between States, but a Government proper, operating directly upon individuals, yielding to them protection on the one hand, and demanding from them obedience on the other.

"There is no language in the whole Constitution applicable to a Confederation of States. If the States be parties, as States, what are their rights, and what their respective covenants and stipulations? And where are their rights, covenants, and stipulations expressed? The States engage for nothing, they promise nothing. In the Articles of Confederation, they did make promises, and did enter into engagements, and did plight the faith of each State for their fulfilment; but in the Constitution there is nothing of that kind. The reason is, that, in the Constitution, it is the *people* who speak, and not the States. The people ordain the Constitution, and therein address themselves to the States, and to the Legislatures of the States, in the language of injunction and prohibition. The Constitution utters its behests in the name and by authority of the people, and it does not exact from States any plighted public faith to maintain it. On the contrary, it makes its own preservation depend on individual duty and individual obligation. Sir, the States cannot omit to appoint Senators and Electors. It is not a matter resting in State discretion or State pleasure. The Constitution has taken better care of its own preservation. It lays its hand on individual conscience and individual duty. It incapacitates any man to sit in the Legislature of a State, who shall not first have taken his solemn oath to support the Constitution of the United States. From the obligation of this oath, no State power can discharge him. All the members of all the State Legislatures are as religiously bound to support the Constitution of the United States as they are to support their own State Constitution. Nay, sir, they are as solemnly sworn to support it as we ourselves are, who are members of Congress.

"No member of a State Legislature can refuse to proceed, at the proper time, to elect Senators to Congress, or to provide for the choice of Electors of President and Vice President, any more than the members of this Senate can refuse, when the appointed day arrives, to meet the members of the other House, to count the votes for those officers, and ascertain who are chosen. In both cases, the duty binds, and with equal strength, the conscience of the individual member, and it is imposed on all by an oath in the same words. Let it then never be said, sir, that it is a matter of discretion with the States whether they will continue the Government, or break it up by refusing to appoint Senators and to elect Electors. They have no discretion in the matter. The members of their Legislatures cannot avoid doing either, so often as the time arrives, without a direct violation of their duty and their oaths; such a violation as would break up any other Government.

"Looking still further to the provisions of the Constitution itself, in order to learn its true character, we find its great apparent purpose to be, to unite the people of all the States under one General Government, for certain definite objects, and, to the extent of this Union, to restrain the separate authority of the States. Congress only can declare war; therefore, when one State is at war with a foreign nation, all must be at war. The President and the Senate only can make peace; when peace is made for one State, therefore, it must be made for all.

"Can any thing be conceived more preposterous, than that any State should have power to nullify the proceedings of the General Government respecting peace and war? When war is declared by a law of Congress, can a single State nullify that law, and remain at peace? And yet she may nullify that law as well as any other. If the President and Senate make peace, may one State, nevertheless, continue the war? And yet, if she can nullify a law, she may quite as well nullify a treaty.

"The truth is, Mr. President, and no ingenuity of argument, no subtilty of distinction, can evade it, that, as to certain purposes, the people of the United States are one people. They are one in making war, and one in making peace; they are one in regulating commerce, and one in laying duties of imposts. The very end and purpose of the Constitution was to make them one people in these particulars; and it has effectually accomplished its object. All this is apparent on the face of the Constitution itself. I have already said, sir, that to obtain a power of direct legislation over the people, especially in regard to imposts, was always prominent as a reason for getting rid of the Confederation, and forming a new Constitution. Among innumerable proofs of this, before the assembling of the Convention, allow me to refer only to the report of the Committee of the old Congress, July, 1785.

"But, sir, let us go to the actual formation of the Constitution; let us open the Journal of the Convention itself; and we shall see that the very first resolution which the Convention adopted, was, 'THAT A NATIONAL GOVERNMENT OUGHT TO BE ESTABLISHED, CONSISTING OF A SUPREME LEGISLATURE, JUDICIARY AND EXECUTIVE.'

"This, itself, completely negatives all idea of League, and Compact, and Confederation. Terms could not be chosen more fit to express an intention to establish a National Government, and to banish forever all notion of a Compact between Sovereign States.

"This resolution was adopted on the 30th of May, 1787. Afterwards, the style was altered; and, instead of being called a National Government, it was called the Government of the United States; but the substance of this resolution was retained, and was at the head of that list of resolutions which was afterwards sent to the Committee who were to frame the instrument.

"It is true, there were gentlemen in the Convention, who were for retaining the Confederation, and amending its Articles; but the majority was against this, and was for a National Government. Mr. Paterson's propositions, which were for continuing the Articles of Confederation, with additional powers, were submitted to the Convention, on the 15th of June, and referred to the Committee of the Whole. The resolutions forming the basis of a National Government, which had once been agreed to in the Committee of the Whole, and reported, were recommitted to the same Committee, on the same day. The Convention, then, in Committee of the Whole, on the 19th of June, had both these plans before them;

that is to say, the plan of a Confederacy, or Compact, between the States, and the plan of a National Government. Both these plans were considered and debated, and the Committee reported, 'That they do not agree to the propositions offered by the Honorable Mr. Paterson, but that they again submit the resolutions formerly reported.' If, sir, any historical fact in the world be plain and undeniable, it is that the Convention deliberated on the expediency of continuing the Confederation, with some amendments, and rejected that scheme, and adopted the plan of a National Government, with a Legislature, an Executive and a Judiciary of its own. They were asked to preserve the League; they rejected the proposition. They were asked to continue the existing Compact between States; they rejected it. They rejected Compact, League, and Confederation, and set themselves about framing the Constitution of a National Government; and they accomplished what they undertook.

"If men will open their eyes fairly, to the lights of history, it is impossible to be deceived on this point. The great object was to supersede the Confederation, by a regular Government; because, under the Confederation, Congress had power only to make requisitions on States; and if States declined compliance, as they did, there was no remedy but war against such delinquent States. It would seem, from Mr. Jefferson's correspondence, in 1786 and 1787, that he was of opinion that even this remedy ought to be tried. 'There will be no money in the treasury,' said he, 'till the Confederacy shows its teeth;' and he suggests that a single frigate would soon levy, on the commerce of a delinquent State, the deficiency of its contribution. But this would be war; and it was evident that a Confederacy could not long hold together, which should be at war with its members. The Constitution was adopted to avoid this necessity. It was adopted that there might be a Government which should act directly on individuals, without borrowing aid from the State Governments. This is as clear as light itself, on the very face of the provisions of the Constitution, and its whole history tends to the same conclusion. Its framers gave this very reason for their work in the most distinct terms. Allow me to quote but one or two proofs, out of hundreds. That State, so small in territory, but so distinguished for learning and talent, Connecticut, had sent to the General Convention, among other members, Samuel Johnston and Oliver Ellsworth. The Constitution having been framed, it was submitted to a Convention of the people of Connecticut for ratification on the part of that State; and Mr. Johnston and Mr. Ellsworth were also members of this Convention. On the first day of the debates, being called on to to explain the reasons which led the Convention, at Philadelphia, to recommend such a Constitution, after showing the insufficiency of the existing Confederacy, inasmuch as it applied to States, as States, Mr. Johnston proceeded to say:—

"'The Convention saw this imperfection in attempting to legislate for States in their political capacity, that the coercion of law can be exercised by nothing but a military force. They have, therefore, gone upon entirely new ground. They have formed one new nation out of the individual States. The Constitution vests in the General Legislature a power to make laws in matters of National concern; to appoint judges to decide upon these laws; and to appoint officers to carry them into execution. This excludes the idea of an armed force. The power which is to enforce these laws is to be a legal power, vested in proper magistrates. The force which is to be employed is the energy of law; and this force is to operate only upon individuals who fail in their duty to their country. This is the peculiar glory of the Constitution, that it depends upon the mild and equal energy of the magistracy for the execution of the laws.'

"In the further course of the debate, Mr. Ellsworth said,—

"'In Republics, it is a fundamental principle, that the majority govern, and that the minority comply with the general voice. How contrary, then, to Republican principles, how humiliating, is our present situation! A single State can rise up, and put a *veto* upon the most important public measures. We have seen this actually take place; a single State has controlled the general voice of the Union; a minority, a very small minority, has governed us. So far is this from being consistent with republican principles, that it is, in effect, the worst species of monarchy.

"'Hence we see how necessary for the Union is a coercive principle. No man pretends the contrary. We all see and feel this necessity. The only question is, shall it be a coercion of law, or a coercion of arms? There is no other possible alternative. Where will those who oppose a coercion of law come out? Where will they end? A necessary consequence of their principles is a war of the States one against another. I am for coercion by law; that coercion which acts only upon delinquent individuals. This Constitution does not attempt to coerce Sovereign bodies, States, in their political capacity. No coercion is applicable to such bodies, but that of an armed force. If we should attempt to execute the laws of the Union by sending an armed force against a delinquent State, it would involve the good and bad, the innocent and guilty, in the same calamity. But this legal coercion singles out the guilty individual and punishes him for breaking the laws of the Union.'*

"Indeed, sir, if we look to all contemporary history, to the numbers of the *Federalist*, to the debates in the Conventions, to the publications of friends and foes, they all agree, that a change had been made from a Confederacy of States to a different system; they all agree, that the Convention had formed a Constitution for a National Government. With this result some were satisfied, and some were dissatisfied; but all admitted that the thing had been done. In none of these varied productions and publications did any one intimate that the new Constitution was but another Compact between States in their Sovereign capacities. I do not find such an opinion advanced in a single instance. Everywhere, the people were told that the old Confederation was to be abandoned, and a new system to be tried; that a proper Government was proposed, to be founded in the name of the people, and to have a regular organization of its own. Everywhere, the people were told that it was to be a Government with direct powers to make laws over individuals, and to lay taxes and imposts without the consent of the States. Everywhere, it was understood to be a popular Constitution. It came to the people for their adoption, and was to rest on the same deep foundation as the State Constitutions themselves. Its most distinguished advocates, who had been themselves members of the Convention, declared that the very object of submitting the Constitution to the people was to preclude the possibility of its being regarded as a mere Compact. 'However gross a heresy,' say the writers of the *Federalist*, 'it may be to maintain that a party to a *Compact* has a right to revoke

* See *Ellsworth*, *ante*, p. 153, and *Speech*, *ante*, pp. 229, 230.

that *Compact,* the doctrine itself has had respectable advocates. The possibility of a question of this nature proves the necessity of laying the foundations of our National Government deeper than in the mere sanction of delegated authority. The fabric of American Empire ought to rest on the solid basis of THE CONSENT OF THE PEOPLE.'*

"Such is the language, sir, addressed to the people, while they yet had the Constitution under consideration. The powers conferred on the new Government were perfectly well understood to be conferred, not by any State, or the people of any State, but by the people of the United States. Virginia is more explicit, perhaps, in this particular, than any other State. Her Convention assembled to ratify the Constitution, 'in the name and behalf of the people of Virginia, declare and make known, that the powers granted under the Constitution, *being derived from the people of the United States,* may be resumed by them whenever the same shall be perverted to their injury or oppression.'† * * *

"Is this language which describes the formation of a Compact between States? or language describing the grant of powers to a new Government, by the whole people of the United States?

"Among all the other ratifications, there is not one which speaks of the Constitution as a Compact between States. Those of New Hampshire and Massachusetts express the transaction, in my opinion, with sufficient accuracy. They recognize the Divine goodness 'in affording THE PEOPLE OF THE UNITED STATES an opportunity of entering into an explicit and solemn Compact with each other, *by assenting to and ratifying a new Con-*

---

* *Ante,* p. 155. † *Ante,* p. 269.

stitution.' You will observe, sir, that it is THE PEOPLE, and not the States, who have entered into this Compact; and it is the PEOPLE of all the United States. These Conventions, by this form of expression, meant merely to say, that the people of the United States had, by the blessing of Providence, enjoyed the opportunity of establishing a new Constitution, *founded in the consent of the people.* This consent of the people has been called, by European writers, the *social Compact;* and, in conformity to this common mode of expression, these Conventions speak of that assent, on which the new Constitution was to rest, as an explicit and solemn Compact, not which the States had entered into with each other, but which the *people* of the United States had entered into.

"Finally, sir, how can any man get over the words of the Constitution itself? 'WE, THE PEOPLE OF THE UNITED STATES, DO ORDAIN AND ESTABLISH THIS CONSTITUTION.'* These words must cease to be a part of the Constititution, they must be obliterated from the parchment on which they are written, before any human ingenuity or human argument can remove the popular basis on which that Constitution rests, and turn the instrument into a mere Compact between Sovereign States!"

PROF. NORTON. Now, sir, I think this speech is a complete answer to all that you have said or can say on the subject. I adopt it because it is so compact, so solid and conclusive. What can you say in reply to it. Whatever you may think of Story as a historian or a statesman, I feel quite assured, from your estimation of Mr. Webster, of which you have given so many of the highest proofs, that his authority will, at least, have some

---

* *Ante*, p. 140: "*For the United States of America.*" The first words are not to be obliterated, neither are the last. All taken together show, that it was a Constitution for States and not the people in the aggregate.

weight with you. If I mistake not, you always regarded him as one of the ablest of our statesmen. His noble bust in the library there is a reminder of that estimate. Well do I remember how you and I strove to make him President in 1852.

Mr. Stephens. Yes, I remember that contest well; and it is true that I ever regarded Mr. Webster as one of the ablest of our statesmen: this the bust and the picture in the hall fully attest. In many respects I considered him the first man in this country, and, indeed, the first man of the age in which he lived. In mental power, in grasp of thought, and in that force and manner of expression which constitute eloquence, he had no superior. Intellectually he was a man of huge proportions, and his patriotism was of the loftiest and purest character. Such was and is my estimation of him. I was exceedingly anxious *to see* him President, and *what* a President he would have made! You did well, therefore, in selecting his argument on this subject. It is the embodiment of all that can be said upon your side of the question. It was the characteristic of Mr. Webster to leave nothing unsaid, on his side of any subject he spoke on, that could be said to strengthen it, and all that could be said, he always said better than any body else. Hence, whether at the bar, on the hustings, or in the Senate, his speeches were always the best that were made on his side. It used to be a remark, often made by our Chief Justice Lumpkin, who was a man himself of wonderful genius, profound learning, and the first of orators in this State, that Webster was always foremost amongst those with whom he acted on any question, and that even in books of selected pieces, whenever selections were made from Webster, those were the best in the book. This, I think, was not too great a eulogium upon his transcendent powers and varied abilities. But it is not the lot of any man to be perfect. I am far from believing Mr. Webster free from political errors. And this speech of his, which, by many (his biographer included, I believe), is considered the greatest of his life, you will allow me to say, contains more errors of this sort than any he ever made. His premises being erroneous, his conclusions must be of the the same character. The superstructure is grand. It is the work of a master genius. But the foundations are not solid. It was this speech, by the by, which gave him the appellation of the "Great Expounder of the Constitution," with the Consolidationists of that day. In it he did throw all the might of his Gigantic and Titan powers. But the subject was an overmatch for him; the undertaking was too great for even him. Facts were too stubborn. His whole soul was in the subject, and he strove to establish what he wished rather than what actually existed. His effort was to make facts bend to theory. This could not be done. This speech, I readily admit, is the best and ablest that ever was made upon that side of the question. It stands as a monument of genius and eloquence. As such it may well take its place by the side of the great argument of Hume in defence of the Prerogatives of the Crown, claimed by the Stuarts, or of Sir Robert Filmer's famous productions in favor of the Divine Right of Kings, or Sir George McKenzie's "*Jus Regium.*"

Much of the answer to this speech, you perceive, has been anticipated. For instance, what is said about "we, the people," etc., near the conclusion, has been sufficiently explained in our investigations. The broad assertion that all parties agreed that the Convention had formed a National Government and had not continued the Federal system, doubtless made a deep impression at the time upon those not conversant with the history of the facts, but it can have no effect upon us who have travelled so carefully through the records of those days. Equally unimpressively falls upon us the declaration that in "*none of the productions* and publications of those days did any one intimate that the *new* Constitution was but *another Compact between States*." We have seen that such was the opinion of Washington, Madison, Hamilton, Rufus King, Ellsworth, Morris, and Randolph; that is, they all held that the Government established by it was *Federal*. This implies Compact; and we have seen that it was the opinion of *all* the advocates of the Constitution in *every* one of the Conventions of the States that ratified it, that the Federative character of the Union was preserved! No advocate of the Constitution in any State admitted that the Federal System was abandoned in it, and no writer in the *Federalist* admitted it!

What is said in this speech about Mr. Paterson's proposition in the Convention that formed the Constitution for continuing the Articles of Confederation, which was offered on the 15th of June and rejected on the 19th of the same month, needs this explanation, and this only. Mr. Paterson's proposition was for *continuing requisitions* on the *States as States*, and for leaving all Legislative powers in the Congress composed of but *one body as before*.

His proposition ignored the division of the Legislative body into two Houses, which was a leading object of a large majority of the States in the new organization. His proposition was rejected, *not because* it proposed to *continue* the *Federal System*, but because it *did not* propose to continue it under a *proper organization*. That the Convention, by the rejection of his plan, did not intend to abandon the Federal system, has been conclusively shown by the vote on the 20th of June. That vote ordered the word "National" to be stricken out of Governor Randolph's plan and "the Government of the United States" to be inserted in lieu of it.* It is also worthy of note in this connection, that this plan of Mr. Paterson, which Mr. Webster admits was nothing but a continuation of the Articles of Confederation, had in it these clauses:

"6. *Resolved,* That the Legislative, Executive and Judicial powers within the several States ought to be bound by oath to support the Articles of Union.

"7. *Resolved,* That all Acts of the United States, in Congress assembled, made by virtue and in pursuance of the powers hereby vested in them and by the Articles of Confederation, and all treaties made and ratified under the authority of the United States, shall be the supreme law of the respective States, as far as those acts or treaties shall relate to the said States or their citizens; and that the judiciaries of the several States shall be bound thereby in their decisions every thing in the respective laws of the individual States to the contrary notwithstanding."†

This, you perceive, is the substance of the clause in the present Constitution which was afterwards offered by Mr. Martin, as has been seen, and upon which Mr. Webster relies so much in his argument to show that a *National* Government and not a *Federal* one was instituted by the Constitution. This fact I wish you to bear in mind at this point in connection with what has been before said on that subject, as it clearly shows that no person in the Convention put such construction upon these words as Mr. Webster puts upon them. This clause was not thought by Mr. Paterson or Mr. Martin, or any body else

* *Journal of Convention, Elliot's Debates,* vol. i, pp. 182, 183.

† *Journal of Convention, Elliot's Debates,* vol. i, p. 177.

in the Convention, to be at all inconsistent with a continuation of the former Articles of Union, which Mr. Webster admits was but a bare League or Compact between States. We have seen that Mr. Hamilton and Mr. Madison, and Judge Chace, were of the same opinion. This much I say in passing.

Now, in full answer to the main points in this truly great argument of Mr. Webster, following your example, I will read the reply to it by Mr. Calhoun. Great as Mr. Webster's was in my judgment, this speech of Mr. Calhoun was a complete refutation of its principles and a clear vindication of the correctness of his Resolutions that Mr. Webster made such powerful assault upon.

Before taking it up, however, allow me to say, that I think Mr. Calhoun was greatly misunderstood in his day and time. He was generally regarded as an enemy to the Union. This was certainly a great mistake. He was, in my judgment, as ardent a friend of the Union as Mr. Webster was. Both were as true patriots as ever lived. They only differed as to the nature of the Union, and the principles upon which it should be maintained. Mr. Calhoun held that it could be maintained and perpetuated consistently with the preservation of Constitutional liberty only on the principle of the recognition of the ultimate Sovereign rights of the States. These doctrines he advocated with an earnestness which showed the profound convictions of his judgment as well as his fearful apprehensions from the ascendancy of opposite principles. By many he was regarded as an alarmist. Sergeant S. Prentiss is reported to have said of him that "he claims our confidence by his very fears, and like the needle he trembles into place." Whether Prentiss ever made the remark or not, the figure is no less characteristic of the reported author than of him to whom it is said to have been applied. Amongst the many great men with whom he was associated, Mr. Calhoun was by far the most philosophical statesman of them all. Indeed, with the exception of Mr. Jefferson, it may be questioned if in this respect the United States has ever produced his superior. Government he considered a science, and in its study his whole soul was absorbed. His Treatise on the Constitution of the United States is the best that was ever penned upon that subject, and his Disquisition on Government generally, is one of the few books of this age, that will outlive the language in which it was written. He studied the controlling principles of all systems, their organic laws, and the inevitable results of their action. Webster, Clay, and Jackson, all his rivals to some extent, were much more practical in their ideas as well as actions. He was regarded as too much of an abstractionist, dealing in incomprehensible metaphysical distinctions. But no better reply to this charge and no better introduction to the speech I propose to read can be made, than the reply he made himself, to this charge, a few days before, in the Senate.

"The Senator from Delaware" (Mr. Clayton), said Mr. Calhoun, "calls this metaphysical reasoning, which, he says, he cannot comprehend. If, by metaphysics, he means that scholastic refinement which makes distinctions without difference, no one can hold it in a more utter contempt than he (Mr. Calhoun); but if, on the contrary, he means the power of analysis and combination—that power which reduces the most complex idea into its elements, which traces causes to their first principles, and by the power of generalization and combination, unites the whole into one harmonious system; then, so far from deserving contempt, it is the highest attribute of the human mind. It is the power which raises man above the brute—which distinguishes his faculties from mere sagacity, which he holds in common with inferior animals. It is this power which has raised the astronomer, from being a mere gazer at the stars, to the high intellectual eminence of a Newton or a La Place; and astronomy itself, from a mere observation of insulated facts, into that noble science which displays to our admiration the system of the universe. And shall this high power of the mind, which has effected such wonders, when directed to the laws which control the material world, be forever prohibited, under a senseless cry of metaphysics, from being applied to the high purpose of political science and legislation. He held them to be subject to laws as fixed as matter itself, and to be as fit a subject for the application of the highest intellectual power. Denunciation may, indeed, fall upon the philosophical inquirer into these first principles, as it did upon Galileo and Bacon, when they first unfolded the great discoveries which have immortalized their names; but the time will come, when truth will prevail in spite of prejudice and denunciation; and when politics and legislation will be considered as much a science as astronomy and chemistry."*

---

* *Niles's Register*, vol. xliii, *Sup.*, p. 163.

Engraved by H.B. Hall from a Daguerreotype by Brady.

JOHN CALDWELL CALHOUN.

J. C. Calhoun

COLLOQUY VIII.

CALHOUN ON THE CONSTITUTION—COMMENTS.

Mr. Stephens. Following your example, I said I would read Mr. Calhoun's speech in reply to the main and leading ideas of Mr. Webster in the speech made by him which you have just read.

Here is that reply of Mr. Calhoun, or so much as bears upon the points at issue between them. It was delivered in the Senate, on the 26th of February, 1833.*

* * * * * *

"The Senator from Massachusetts," said Mr. Calhoun, "in his argument against the Resolutions, directed his attack almost exclusively against the first; on the ground, I suppose, that it was the basis of the other two, and that, unless the first could be demolished, the others would follow of course. In this he was right. As plain and as simple as the facts contained in the first are, they cannot be admitted to be true without admitting the doctrines for which I, and the State I represent, contend. He commenced his attack with a verbal criticism on the Resolution, in the course of which he objected strongly to two words, 'Constitutional' and 'accede.' To the former, on the ground that the word, as used (Constitutional Compact), was obscure—that it conveyed no definite meaning—and that Constitution was a noun-substantive, and not an adjective. I regret that I have

---

* *Niles's Register*, vol. xliii, *Sup.*, p. 259.

exposed myself to the criticism of the Senator. I certainly did not intend to use any expression of doubtful sense, and if I have done so, the Senator must attribute it to the poverty of my language, and not to design I trust, however, that the Senator will excuse me, when he comes to hear my apology. In matters of criticism, authority is of the highest importance, and I have an authority of so high a character, in this case, for using the expression which he considers so obscure and so unconstitutional, as will justify me even in his eyes. It is no less than the authority of the Senator himself—given on a solemn occasion (the discussion on Mr. Foote's Resolution), and doubtless with great deliberation, after having duly weighed the force of the expression."

[Here Mr. Calhoun read from Mr. Webster's speech, in the debate on the Foote Resolutions, in 1830.]

"'Nevertheless, I do not complain, nor would I countenance any movement to alter this arrangement of representation. It is the original bargain—the Compact—let it stand—let the advantage of it be fully enjoyed. The Union itself is too full of benefits to be hazarded in propositions for changing its original basis. I go for the Constitution, as it is, and for the Union, as it is. But I am resolved not to submit, in silence, to accusations, either against myself, individually, or against the North, wholly unfounded and unjust—accusations which impute to us a disposition to evade the CONSTITUTIONAL COMPACT, and to extend the power of the Government over the internal laws and domestic condition of the States.'

"It will be seen by this extract," proceeded Mr. Calhoun, "that the Senator not only used the phrase 'Constitutional Compact,' which he now so much condemns, but, what is still more important, he calls the Constitution a Compact—a bargain—which contains important admissions, having a direct and powerful bearing on the main issue, involved in the discussion, as will appear in the sequel. But, strong as his objection is to the word 'Constitutional,' it is still stronger to the word 'accede,' which, he thinks, has been introduced into the Resolution with some deep design, as I suppose, to entrap the Senate into an admission of the doctrine of State Rights. Here, again, I must shelter myself under authority. But I suspect the Senator, by a sort of instinct (for our instincts often strangely run before our knowledge), had a prescience, which would account for his aversion for the word, that this authority was no less than Thomas Jefferson himself, the great apostle of the doctrines of State Rights. The word was borrowed from him. It was taken from the Kentucky Resolution, as well as the substance of the resolution itself. But I trust I may neutralize whatever aversion the authorship of this word may have excited in the mind of the Senator, by the introduction of another authority—that of Washington, himself—who, in his speech to Congress, speaking of the admission of North Carolina into the Union, uses this very term, which was repeated by the Senate in their reply. Yet, in order to narrow the ground between the Senator and myself as much as possible, I will accommodate myself to his strange antipathy against the two unfortunate words, by striking them out of the Resolution, and substituting, in their place, those very words which the Senator himself has designated as Constitutional phrases. In the place of that abhorred adjective 'Constitutional,' I will insert the very noun substantive 'Constitution;' and, in the place of the word 'accede,' I will insert the word 'ratify,' which he designates as the proper term to be used.

"As proposed to be amended, the Resolution would read:—

"'*Resolved*, That the people of the several States composing these United States are united as parties to a Compact, under the title of the Constitution of the United States, which the people of each State ratified as a separate and Sovereign community, each binding itself by its own particular ratification; and that the Union of which the said Compact is the bond, is a Union *between* the States ratifying the same.'

"Where, sir, I ask, is that plain case of revolution? Where that hiatus, as wide as the globe, between the premises and the conclusion, which the Senator proclaimed would be apparent, if the Resolution was reduced into Constitutional language? For my part, with my poor powers of conception, I cannot perceive the slightest difference between the Resolution, as first introduced, and as it is proposed to be amended in conformity to the views of the Senator. And, instead of that hiatus between the premises and conclusion, which seems to startle the imagination of the Senator, I can perceive nothing but a continuous and solid surface, sufficient to sustain the magnificent superstructure of State Rights. Indeed, it seems to me that the Senator's vision is distorted by the medium through which he views every thing connected with the subject; and that the same distortion which has presented to his imagination this hiatus, as wide as the globe, where not even a fissure exists, also presented that beautiful and classical image of a strong man struggling in a bog, without the power of extricating himself, and incapable of being aided by any friendly hand; while, instead of struggling in a bog, he stands on the everlasting rock of truth.

"Having now noticed the criticisms of the Senator, I shall proceed to meet and repel the main assault on the Resolution. He directed his attack against the strong point, the very horn of the citadel of State Rights. The Senator clearly perceived that, if the Constitution be a Compact, it was impossible to deny the assertions contained in the Resolutions, or to resist the consequences which I had drawn from them, and, accordingly, directed his whole fire against that point; but, after so vast an expenditure of ammunition, not the slightest impression, so far as I can perceive, has been made. But to drop the simile, after a careful examination of the notes which I took of what the Senator said, I am now at a loss to know whether, in the opinion of the Senator, our Constitution is a Compact or not, though the almost entire argument of the Senator was directed to that point. At one time he would seem to deny directly and positively that it was a Compact, while at another he would appear, in language not less strong, to admit that it was.

"I have collated all that the Senator has said upon this point; and, that what I have stated may not appear exaggerated, I will read his remarks in juxtaposition. He said that:

"'The Constitution means a Government, not a Compact.' 'Not a Constitutional Compact, but a Government.' 'If Compact, it rests on plighted faith, and the mode of redress would be to declare the whole void.' 'States may secede, if a League or Compact.'

"I thank the Senator for these admissions, which I intend to use hereafter.

"'The States agreed that each should participate in the Sovereignty of the other.'

"Certainly, a very correct conception of the Constitution; but where did they make that agreement but by the Constitution, and how could they agree but by Compact?

"'The system, not a Compact between States in their Sovereign capacity, but a Government proper, founded on the adoption of the people, and creating individual relations between itself and the citizens.'

"This, the Senator lays down as a leading, fundamental principle to sustain his doctrine, and, I must say, with strange confusion and uncertainty of language; not, certainly, to be explained by any want of command of the most appropriate words on his part.

"'It does not call itself a Compact, but a Constitution. The Constitution rests on Compact, but it is no longer a Compact.'

"I would ask, to what Compact does the Senator refer, as that on which the Constitution rests? Before the adoption of the present Constitution, the States had formed but one Compact, and that was the old Confederation; and, certainly, the gentleman does not intend to assert that the present Constitution rests upon that. What, then, is his meaning? What can it be, but that the Constitution itself is a Compact? And how will his language read, when fairly interpreted, but that the Constitution was a Compact, but is no longer a Compact? It had, by some means or another, changed its nature, or become defunct.

"He next states that—

"'A man is almost untrue to his country who calls the Constitution a Compact.'

"I fear the Senator, in calling it a 'Compact, a bargain,' has called down this heavy denunciation on his own head. He finally states that—

"'It is founded on Compact, but not a Compact.' 'It is the result of a Compact.'

"To what are we to attribute this strange confusion of words? The Senator has a mind of high order, and perfectly trained to the most exact use of language. No man knows better the precise import of the words he uses. The difficulty is not in him, but in his subject. He who undertakes to prove that this Constitution is not a Compact, undertakes a task which, be his strength ever so great, must oppress him by its weight. Taking the whole of the argument of the Senator together, I would say that it is his impression that the Constitution is not a Compact, and will now proceed to consider the reason which he has assigned for this opinion.

"He thinks there is an incompatibility between Constitution and Compact. To prove this, he adduces the words 'ordain and establish,' contained in the preamble of the Constitution. I confess I am not capable of perceiving in what manner these words are incompatible with the idea that the Constitution is a Compact. The Senator will admit that a single State may ordain a Constitution; and where is the difficulty, where the incompatibility, of two States concurring in ordaining and establishing a Constitution? As between the States themselves, the instrument would be a Compact; but in reference to the Government, and those on whom it operates, it would be ordained and established—ordained and established by the joint authority of two, instead of the single authority of one.

"The next argument which the Senator advances to show that the language of the Constitution is irreconcilable with the idea of its being a Compact, is taken from that portion of the instrument which imposes prohibitions on the authority of the States. He said that the language used, in imposing the prohibitions, is the language of a superior to an inferior; and that, therefore, it was not the language of a Compact, which implies the equality of the parties. As a proof, the Senator cited several clauses of the Constitution which provide that no State shall enter into treaties of alliance and confederation, lay imposts, etc., without the assent of Congress. If he had turned to the Articles of the old Confederation, which he acknowledges to have been a Compact, he would have found that those very prohibitory Articles of the Constitution were borrowed from that instrument; that the language, which he now considers as implying superiority, was taken *verbatim* from it. If he had extended his researches still further, he would have found that it is the habitual language used in treaties, whenever a stipulation is made against the performance of any act. Among many instances, which I could cite, if it were necessary, I refer the Senator to the celebrated treaty negotiated by Mr. Jay with Great Britain, in 1793, in which the very language used in the Constitution is employed.

"To prove that the Constitution is not a Compact, the Senator next observes that it stipulates nothing, and asks, with an air of triumph, 'Where are the evidences of the stipulations between the States?' I must express my surprise at this interrogatory, coming from so intelligent a source. Has the Senator never seen the ratifications of the Constitution by the several States? Did he not cite them on this very occasion? Do they contain no evidence of stipulations on the part of the States? Nor is the assertion less strange that the Constitution contains no stipulations.

"So far from regarding it in the light in which the Senator regards it, I consider the whole instrument but a mass of stipulations. What is that but a stipulation to which the Senator refers when he states, in the course of his argument, that each State had agreed to participate in the Sovereignty of the others.

"But the principal argument on which the Senator relied to show that the Constitution is not a Compact, rests on the provision, in that instrument, which declares that 'this Constitution, and laws made in pursuance thereof, and treaties made under their authority, are the supreme laws of the land.' He asked, with marked emphasis, 'Can a Compact be the supreme law of the land?' His argument, in fact, as conclusively proves that treaties are not Compacts as that the Constitution is not a Compact. I might rest the issue on this decisive answer; but, as I desire to leave not a shadow of doubt on this important point, I shall follow the gentleman in the course of his reasoning.

"He defines a Constitution to be a fundamental law, which organizes the Government, and points out the mode of its action. I will not object to the definition, though, in my opinion, a more appropriate one, or, at least, one better adapted to American ideas, could be given. My objection is not to the definition, but to the attempt to prove that the fundamental laws of a State cannot be a Compact, as the Senator seems to suppose. I hold the very reverse to be the case; and that, according to the most approved writers on the subject of Government, these very fundamental laws which are now stated not only not to be Compacts, but inconsistent with the very idea of Compacts, are held invariably to be Compacts; and, in that character, are distinguished from the ordinary laws of the country. I will cite a single authority, which is full and explicit on this point, from a writer of the highest repute.

"Burlamaqui says, vol. ii, part 1, chap. i, secs. 35, 36, 37, 38:

"'It entirely depends upon a free people to invest the Sovereigns, whom they place over their heads, with an authority either absolute or limited by certain laws. These regulations, by which the supreme authority is kept within bounds, are called *the fundamental laws of the State.* The fundamental laws of a State, taken in their full extent, are not only the decrees by which the entire body of the nation determine the form of Government, and the manner of succeeding to the Crown, but are likewise covenants between the people and the person on whom they confer the Sovereignty, which regulate the manner of governing, and by which the supreme authority is limited.

"'These regulations are called fundamental laws, because they are the basis, as it were, and foundation of the State on which the structure of the Government is raised, and, because the people look upon these regulations as their principal strength and support.

"'The name of laws, however, has been given to these regulations in an improper and figurative sense, for, properly speaking, they are *real covenants.* But as these covenants are obligatory between the contracting parties, they have the force of laws themselves.'

"The same, vol. ii, part 2, ch. i, secs. 19 and 22, in part.

"'The whole body of the nation, in whom the supreme power originally resides, may regulate the Government by a fundamental law, in such manner, as to commit the exercise of the different parts of the supreme power to different persons or bodies, who may act independently of each other in regard to the rights committed to them, but still subordinate to the laws from which those rights are derived.

"'And these fundamental laws are real covenants, or what the civilians call *pacta conventa,* between the differ ent orders of the republic, by which they stipulate that each shall have a particular part of the Sovereignty, and that this shall establish the form of Government. It is evident that, by these means, each of the contracting parties acquires a right, not only of exercising the power granted to it, but also of preserving that original right.'

"A reference to the Constitution of Great Britain, with which we are better acquainted than with that of any other European Government, will show that that is a Compact. Magna Charta may certainly be reckoned among the fundamental laws of that kingdom. Now, although it did not assume, originally, the form of a Compact, yet, before the breaking up of the meeting of the Barons which imposed it on King John, it was reduced into the form of a covenant, and duly signed by Robert Fitzwater and others, on the one part, and the King on the other.

"But we have a more decisive proof that the Constitution of England is a Compact, in the resolution of the Lords and Commons, in 1688, which declared:

"'King James the Second, having endeavored to subvert the Constitution of the kingdom, by breaking the original contract between the King and people, and having, by the advice of Jesuits and other wicked persons, violated the fundamental law, and withdrawn himself out of the kingdom, hath abdicated the Government, and that the throne is thereby become vacant.'

"But why should I refer to writers upon the subject of Government, or inquire into the Constitution of foreign States, when there are such decisive proofs that our Constitution is a Compact? On this point the Senator is estopped. I borrow from the gentleman, and thank him for the word. His adopted State, which he so ably represents on this floor, and his native State, the States of Massachusetts and New Hampshire, both declared, in their ratification of the Constitution, that it was a Compact. The ratification of Massachusetts is in the following words:"

[Here Mr. Calhoun called special attention to the ratification of the State of Massachusetts, in which the Constitution is spoken of as a "SOLEMN COMPACT."]*

"The ratification of New Hampshire is taken from that of Massachusetts, and almost in the same words. But proof, if possible, still more decisive, may be found in the celebrated resolutions of Virginia on the alien and sedition law, in 1798,† and the responses of Massachusetts and the other States. These resolutions expressly assert that the Constitution is a Compact between the States, in the following language:

"'That this Assembly doth explicitly and peremptorily declare, that it VIEWS THE POWERS OF THE FEDERAL GOVERNMENT, AS RESULTING FROM THE COMPACT, TO WHICH THE STATES ARE PARTIES, AS LIMITED BY THE PLAIN SENSE AND INTENTION OF THE INSTRUMENT CONSTITUTING THAT COMPACT, AS NO FARTHER VALID THAN THEY ARE AUTHORIZED BY THE GRANTS ENUMERATED IN THAT COMPACT; AND THAT IN CASE OF A DELIBERATE, PALPABLE, AND DANGEROUS EXERCISE OF OTHER POWERS NOT GRANTED BY THE SAID COMPACT, THE STATES WHO ARE PARTIES THERETO HAVE THE RIGHT, AND ARE IN DUTY BOUND, TO INTERPOSE FOR ARRESTING THE PROGRESS OF THE EVIL, AND FOR MAINTAINING WITHIN THEIR RESPECTIVE LIMITS THE AUTHORITIES, RIGHTS, AND LIBERTIES APPERTAINING TO THEM.

"'That the General Assembly doth also express its deep regret that a spirit has, in sundry instances, been manifested by the Federal Government to enlarge its

---

* *Ante*, p. 233. † See *Appendix* E.

powers by forced constructions of the Constitutional Charter, which defines them; and that indications have appeared of a design to expound certain general phrases (which, having been copied from the very limited grant of powers in the former Articles of Confederation, were the less liable to be misconstrued), so as to destroy the meaning and effect of the particular enumeration which necessarily explains and limits the general phrases, and so as to CONSOLIDATE THE STATES, BY DEGREES, INTO ONE SOVEREIGNTY, THE OBVIOUS TENDENCY AND INEVITABLE RESULT OF WHICH WOULD BE, TO TRANSFORM THE PRESENT REPUBLICAN SYSTEM OF THE UNITED STATES INTO AN ABSOLUTE, OR, AT BEST, A MIXED MONARCHY!'

"They were sent to the several States. We have the replies of Delaware, New York, Connecticut, New Hampshire, Vermont, and Massachusetts, not one of which contradicts this important assertion on the part of Virginia; and, by their silence, they all acquiesce in its truth. The case is still stronger against Massachusetts, which expressly recognizes the fact that the Constitution is a Compact."

[Here Mr. Calhoun read from the answer of Massachusetts, in which the Constitution is called *a solemn Compact.*]

"Now, I ask the Senator himself—I put it to his candor to say, if South Carolina be estopped on the subject of the protective system, because Mr. Burke and Mr. Smith proposed a moderate duty on hemp, or some other article, I know not what, nor do I care, with a view of encouraging its production (of which motion, I venture to say, not one individual in a hundred in the State ever heard), whether he and Massachusetts, after this clear, full, and solemn recognition that the Constitution is a Compact (both on his part and that of his State), be not forever estopped on this important point?

"There remains one more of the Senator's arguments, to prove that the Constitution is not a Compact, to be considered. He says it is not a Compact, because it is a Government; which he defines to be an organized body, possessed of the will and power to execute its purposes by its own proper authority; and which, he says, bears not the slightest resemblance to a Compact. But I would ask the Senator, Whoever considered a Government, when spoken of as the agent to execute the powers of the Constitution, and distinct from the Constitution itself, as a Compact? In that light it would be a perfect absurdity. It is true that, in general and loose language, it is often said that the Government is a Compact, meaning the Constitution which created it, and vested it with authority to execute the powers contained in the instrument; but when the distinction is drawn between the Constitution and the Government, as the Senator has done, it would be as ridiculous to call the Government a Compact, as to call an individual, appointed to execute the provisions of a contract, a contract; and not less so to suppose that there could be the slightest resemblance between them. In connection with this point, the Senator, to prove that the Constitution is not a Compact, asserts that it is wholly independent of the State, and pointedly declares that the States have not a right to touch a hair of its head; and this, with that provision in the Constitution that three-fourths of the States have a right to alter, change, amend, or even to abolish it, staring him in the face.

"I have examined all of the arguments of the Senator intended to prove that the Constitution is not a Compact; and I trust I have shown, by the clearest demonstration, that his arguments are perfectly inconclusive, and that his assertion is against the clearest and most solemn evidence—evidence of record, and of such a character that it ought to close his lips forever.

"I turn now to consider the other, and, apparently, contradictory aspect in which the Senator presented this part of the subject: I mean that in which he states that the Government is founded in Compact, but is no longer a Compact. I have already remarked, that no other interpretation could be given to this assertion, except that the Constitution was once a Compact, but is no longer so. There was a vagueness and indistinctness in this part of the Senator's argument, which left me altogether uncertain as to its real meaning. If he meant, as I presume he did, that the Compact is an executed, and not an executory one—that its object was to create a Government, and to invest it with proper authority—and that, having executed this office, it had performed its functions, and, with it, had ceased to exist, then we have the extraordinary avowal that the Constitution is a dead letter—that it had ceased to have any binding effect, or any practical influence or operation.

"It has, indeed, often been charged that the Constitution has become a dead letter; that it is continually violated, and has lost all its control over the Government; but no one has ever before been bold enough to advance a theory on the avowed basis that it was an executed, and, therefore, an extinct instrument. I will not seriously attempt to refute an argument, which, to me, appears so extravagant. I had thought that the Constitution was to endure forever; and that, so far from its being an executed contract, it contained great trust powers for the benefit of those who created it, and of a future generations,—which never could be finally executed during the existence of the world, if our Government should so long endure.

"I will now return to the first Resolution, to see ho the issue stands between the Senator from Massachuset and myself. It contains three propositions. First, that the Constitution is a Compact; second, that it was formed by the States, constituting distinct communities; and, lastly, that it is a subsisting and binding Compact between the States. How do these three propositions now stand? The first, I trust, has been satisfactorily established; the second, the Senator has admitted, faintly, indeed, but still he has admitted it to be true. This admission is something. It is so much gained by discussion. Three years ago even this was a contested point. But I cannot say that I thank him for the admission; we owe it to the force of truth. The fact that these States were declared to be free and independent States at the time of their independence; that they were acknowledged to be so by Great Britain in the treaty which terminated the war of the Revolution, and secured their independence; that they were recognized in the same character in the old Articles of the Confederation; and, finally, that the present Constitution was formed by a Convention of the several States; afterwards submitted to them for their respective ratifications, and was ratified by them separately, each for itself, and each, by its own act, binding its citizens,—formed a body of facts too clear to be denied, and too strong to be resisted.

"It now remains to consider the third and last proposition contained in the Resolution,—that it is a binding and a subsisting Compact between the States. The Senator was not explicit on this point. I understood him, however, as asserting that, though formed by the States, the Constitution was not binding between the States as distinct communities, but between the American people in the aggregate; who, in consequence of the adoption of the Constitution, according to the opinion of the Senator, became one people, at least to the extent of the delegated powers. This would, indeed, be a great change. All acknowledge that, previous to the adoption of the Constitution, the States constituted distinct and independent communities, in full possession of their Sovereignty; and, surely, if the adoption of the Constitution was intended to effect the great and important change in their condition which the theory of the Senator supposes, some evidence of it ought to be found in the instrument itself. It professes to be a careful and full enumeration of all the powers which the States delegated, and of every modification of their political condition. The Senator said that he looked to the Constitution in order to ascertain its real character; and, surely, he ought to look to the same instrument in order to ascertain what changes were, in fact, made in the political condition of the States and the country. But, with the exception of 'we, the people of the United States,' in the preamble, he has not pointed out a single indication in the Constitution, of the great change which as he conceives, has been effected in this respect.

"Now, sir, I intend to prove, that the only argument on which the gentleman relies on this point, must utterly fail him. I do not intend to go into a critical examination of the expression of the preamble to which I have referred. I do not deem it necessary. But if it were, it might be easily shown that it is at least as applicable to my view of the Constitution as to that of the Senator; and that the whole of his argument on this point rests on the ambiguity of the term thirteen United States; which may mean certain territorial limits, comprehending within them the whole of the States and Territories of the Union. In this sense, the people of the United

States may mean *all* the people living within these limits, without reference to the States or Territories in which they may reside, or of which they may be citizens; and it is in this sense only, that the expression gives the least countenance to the argument of the Senator.

"But it may also mean, *the States united*, which inversion alone, without further explanation, removes the ambiguity to which I have referred. The expression in this sense, obviously means no more than to speak of the people of the several States in their united and confederated capacity; and, if it were requisite, it might be shown that it is only in this sense that the expression is used in the Constitution. But it is not necessary. A single argument will forever settle this point. Whatever may be the true meaning of the expression, it is not applicable to the condition of the States as they exist under the Constitution, but as it was under the old Confederation, before its adoption. The Constitution had not yet been adopted, and the States, in ordaining it, could only speak of themselves in the condition in which they then existed, and not in that in which they would exist under the Constitution. So that, if the argument of the Senator proves any thing, it proves, not (as he supposes) that the Constitution forms the American people into an aggregate mass of individuals, but that such was their political condition before its adoption, under the old Confederation, directly contrary to his argument in the previous part of this discussion.

"But I intend not to leave this important point, the last refuge of those who advocate consolidation, even on this conclusive argument. I have shown that the Constitution affords not the least evidence of the mighty change of the political condition of the States and the country, which the Senator supposed it effected; and I intend now, by the most decisive proof, drawn from the instrument itself, to show that no such change was intended, and that the people of the States are united under it as States, and not as individuals. On this point there is a very important part of the Constitution entirely and strangely overlooked by the Senator in this debate, as it is expressed in the first Resolution, which furnishes conclusive evidence not only that the Constitution is a Compact, but a subsisting Compact, binding between the States. I allude to the seventh Article, which provides that the ratification of the Conventions of nine States shall be sufficient for the establishment of this Constitution '*between the States* so ratifying the same.' Yes, '*between the States*.' These little words mean a volume. Compacts, not laws, bind *between* States; and it here binds, not as between individuals, but between *the States*: the States *ratifying*; implying, as strong as language can make it, that the Constitution is what I have asserted it to be—a Compact, ratified by the States, and a subsisting Compact, binding the States ratifying it.

"But, sir, I will not leave this point, all-important in establishing the true theory of our Government, on this argument alone, as demonstrative and conclusive as I hold it to be. Another, not much less powerful, but of a different character, may be drawn from the tenth amended Article, which provides that the powers not delegated to the United States by the Constitution, nor prohibited by it to the States, are reserved to the States respectively or to the people. The Article of Ratification, which I have just cited, informs us that the Constitution, which delegates powers, was ratified by the States, and is binding between them. This informs us to whom the powers are delegated,—a most important fact in determining the point immediately at issue between the Senator and myself. According to his views, the Constitution created a union between individuals, if the solecism may be allowed, and that it formed, at least to the extent of the powers delegated, one people, and not a Federal Union of the States, as I contend; or, to express the same idea differently, that the delegation of powers was to the American people in the aggregate (for it is only by such delegation that they could be constituted one people), and not to the *United States*,—directly contrary to the Article just cited, which declares that the powers are delegated to the United States. And here it is worthy of notice, that the Senator cannot shelter himself under the ambiguous phrase, 'to the people of the United States,' under which he would certainly have taken refuge, had the Constitution so expressed it; but fortunately for the cause of truth and the great principles of Constitutional liberty for which I am contending, 'people,' is omitted: thus making the delegation of power clear and unequivocal to the *United States*, as distinct political communities, and conclusively proving that all the powers delegated are reciprocally delegated by the States to each other, as distinct political communities.

"So much for the delegated powers. Now, as all admit, and as it is expressly provided for in the Constitution, the *reserved* powers are reserved 'to the States *respectively*, or to the people.' None will pretend that, as far as they are concerned, we are one people, though the argument to prove it, however absurd, would be far more plausible that that which goes to show that we are one people to the extent of the delegated powers. This reservation 'to the people' might, in the hands of subtle and trained logicians, be a peg to hang a doubt upon; and had the expression 'to the people' been connected, as fortunately it is not, with the delegated instead of the reserved powers, we should not have heard of this in the present discussion.

"I have now established, I hope, beyond the power of controversy, every allegation contained in the first Resolution—that the Constitution is a Compact formed by the people of the several States, as distinct political communities, and subsisting and binding between the States in the same character; which brings me to the consideration of the consequences which may be fairly deduced, in reference to the character of our political system, from these established facts.

"The first and most important is, they conclusively establish that ours is a Federal system—a system of States arranged in a Federal Union, each retaining its distinct existence and Sovereignty. Ours has every attribute which belongs to a Federative System. It is founded on Compact; it is formed by Sovereign communities, and is binding between them in their Sovereign capacity. I might appeal, in confirmation of this assertion, to all elementary writers on the subject of Government, but will content myself with citing one only. Burlamaqui, quoted with approbation by Judge Tucker, in his Commentary on Blackstone, himself a high authority, says:"

[Here Mr. Calhoun quotes from Tucker's Blackstone as follows]:

"'Political bodies, whether great or small, if they are constituted by a people formerly independent, and under no civil subjection, or by those who justly claim independence from any civil power they were formerly subject to, have the civil supremacy in themselves, and are in a State of equal right and liberty with respect to all other States, whether great or small. No regard is to be had in this matter to names, whether the body-politic be called a kingdom, an empire, a principality, a dukedom, a country, a republic, or free town. If it can exercise justly all the essential parts of civil power within itself, independently of any other person or body-politic,—and no other has any right to rescind or annul its acts,—it has the civil supremacy, how small soever its territory may be, or the number of its people, and has all the rights of an independent State.*

"'This independence of States, and their being distinct political bodies from each other, is not obstructed by any alliance or confederacies whatsoever, about exercising jointly any parts of the supreme powers, such as those of peace and war, in league offensive and defensive. Two States, notwithstanding such treaties, are separate bodies, and independent.†

"'These are, then, only deemed politically united, when some one person or council is constituted with a right to exercise some essential powers for both, and to hinder either from exercising them separately. If any person or council is empowered to exercise all these essential powers for both, they are then one State:‡ such is the State of England and Scotland, since the Act of Union made at the beginning of the eighteenth century, whereby the two kingdoms were incorporated into one, all parts of the supreme power of both kingdoms being thenceforward united, and vested in the three Estates of the realm of Great Britain; by which entire coalition, though both kingdoms retain their ancient laws and usages in many respects, they are as effectually united and incorporated, as the several petty kingdoms, which composed the heptarchy, were before that period.

"'But when only a portion of the supreme civil power

* *Vattel*, B. I, c. i, § 4.

† *Vattel*, B. I, c. i, § 10.

‡ *Vattel*, B. I, c. i, § 10.

is vested in one person or council for both, such as that of peace and war, or of deciding controversies between different States, or their subjects, while each, within itself, exercises other parts of the supreme power, independently of all the others—in this case they are called *Systems of States*, which Burlamaqui defines to be an assemblage of perfect Governments, strictly united by some common bond, so that they seem to make but a single body with respect to those affairs which interest them in common, though each preserves its Sovereignty, full and entire, independently of all others. And in this case, he adds, the Confederate States engage to each other only to exercise, with common consent, certain parts of the Sovereignty, especially that which relates to their mutual defence against foreign enemies. But each of the Confederates retains an entire liberty of exercising, as it thinks proper, those parts of the Sovereignty which are not mentioned in the treaty of Union, as parts that ought to be exercised in common.* And of this nature is the American Confederacy, in which each State has resigned the exercise of certain parts of the supreme civil power which they possessed before (except in common with the other States included in the Confederacy), reserving to themselves all their former powers, which are not delegated to the United States by the common bond of Union.

"'A visible distinction, and not less important than obvious, occurs to our observation, in comparing these different kinds of Union. The kingdoms of England and Scotland are united into one kingdom; and the two contracting States, by such an incorporate Union, are, in the opinion of Judge Blackstone, totally annihilated,

* *Burlamaqui*, B. ii, Part ii, c. i, § 40–44.

without any power of revival; and a third arises from their conjunction, in which all the rights of Sovereignty, and particularly that of Legislation, are vested. From whence he expresses a doubt, whether any infringements of the fundamental and essential conditions of the Union would, of itself, dissolve the Union of those kingdoms; though he readily admits that, in the case of a *Federate* alliance, such an infringement would certainly rescind the Compact between the Confederated States. In the United States of America, on the contrary, each State retains its own antecedent form of Government; its own laws, subject to the alteration and control of its own Legislature only; its own executive officers and council of State; its own courts of Judicature, its own judges, its own magistrates, civil officers, and officers of the militia; and, in short, its own civil State, or body politic, in every respect whatsoever. And by the express declaration of the 12th article of the amendments to the Constitution, the powers not delegated to the United States by the Constitution, nor prohibited by it to the States, are reserved to the States respectively, or to the people. In Great Britain, a new *civil State* is created by the annihilation of two antecedent civil States; in the American States, a general *Federal* council and administration is provided, for the joint exercise of such of their several powers as can be more conveniently exercised in that mode than any other, leaving their *civil State* unaltered; and all the other powers, which the States antecedently possessed, to be exercised by them respectively, as if no Union or connection were established between them.

"'The ancient Achaia seems to have been a Confederacy founded upon a similar plan; each of those little States had its distinct possessions, territories, and boundaries; each had its Senate or Assembly, its magistrates and judges; and every State sent Deputies to the General Convention, and had equal weight in all determinations. And most of the neighboring States which, moved by fear of danger, acceded to this Confederacy, had reason to felicitate themselves.

"'These Confederacies, by which several States are united together by a perpetual league of alliance, are chiefly founded upon this circumstance, that each particular people choose to remain their own masters, and yet are not strong enough to make head against a common enemy. The purport of such an agreement usually is, that they shall not exercise some part of the Sovereignty, there specified, without the general consent of each other. For the leagues, to which these systems of States owe their rise, seem distinguished from others (so frequent among different States), chiefly by this consideration, that, in the latter, each confederate people determine themselves, by their own judgment, to certain mutual performances; yet so that, in all other respects, they design not, in the least, to make the exercise of that part of the Sovereignty, whence these performances proceed, dependent on the consent of their allies, or to retrench any thing from their full and unlimited power of governing their own States. Thus, we see that ordinary treaties propose, for the most part, as their aim, only some particular advantage of the States thus transacting—their interests happening, at present, to fall in with each other—but do not produce any lasting union as to the chief management of affairs. Such was the treaty of alliance between America and France, in the year 1778, by which, among other articles, it was agreed that neither of the two parties should conclude either truce or peace with Great Britain, without the formal consent of the other, first obtained, and whereby they mutually engaged not to lay down their arms until the independence of the United States should be formally or tacitly assured by the treaty or treaties which should terminate the war. Whereas, in these confederacies of which we are now speaking, the contrary is observable, they being established with this design, that the several States shall forever link their safety, one with another; and, in order to their mutual defence, shall engage themselves not to exercise certain parts of their Sovereign power, otherwise than by a common agreement and approbation. Such were the stipulations, among others, contained in the Articles of Confederation and perpetual Union between American States, by which it was agreed that no State should, without the consent of the United States, in Congress assembled, send any embassy to, or receive any embassy from, or enter into any conference, agreement, alliance or treaty with, any king, prince or State; nor keep up any vessels of war, or body of forces, in time of peace; nor engage in any war, without the consent of the United States in Congress assembled, unless actually invaded; nor grant commissions to any ships of war, or letters of marque and reprisal, except after a declaration of war by the United States in Congress assembled, with several others; yet each State, respectively, retains its Sovereignty, freedom and independence, and every power, jurisdiction and right which is not expressly delegated to the United States in Congress assembled. The promises made in these two cases, here compared, run very differently; in the former, thus: I will join you, in this particular war, as a confederate, and the manner of our attacking the enemy shall be concerted by our common advice; nor will we desist from war, till the particular end thereof, the establishment of the independence of the United States, be obtained. In the latter, thus: None of us who have entered into this alliance, will make use of our right as to the affairs of war and peace, except by the general consent of the whole confederacy. We observed before that these Unions submit only some certain parts of the Sovereignty to mutual direction; for it seems hardly possible that the affairs of different States should have so close a connection, as that all and each of them should look on it as their interest to have no part of the chief Government exercised without the general concurrence. The most convenient method, therefore, seems to be, that the particular States reserve to themselves all those branches of the supreme authority, the management of which can have little or no influence in the affairs of the rest.' "

"If we compare our present system," continued Mr. Calhoun, "with the old Confederation, which all acknowledge to have been *Federal* in its character, we shall find that it possesses all the attributes which belong to that form of Government as fully and completely as that did. In fact, *in this particular*, there is but a single difference, and that not essential, as regards the point immediately under consideration, though very important in other respects. The Confederation was the act of the State Governments, and formed a union of Governments. The present Constitution is the act of the States themselves, or, which is the same thing, of the people of the several States, and forms a union of them as Sovereign communities. The States, previous to the adoption of the Constitution, were as separate and distinct political bodies as the Governments which represent them, and there is nothing in the nature of things to prevent them from uniting under a Compact, in a Federal Union, without being blended in one mass, any more than uniting the Governments themselves, in like manner, without merging them in a single Government. To illustrate what I have stated by reference to ordinary transactions, the Confederation was a contract between agents—the present Constitution a contract between the principals themselves; or, to take a more analogous case, one is a League made by ambassadors; the other, a League made by Sovereigns—the latter no more tending to unite the parties into a single Sovereignty than the former. The only difference is in the solemnity of the act and the force of the obligation. * *

"We will now proceed to consider some of the conclusions which necessarily follow from the facts and positions already established. They enable us to decide a question of vital importance under our system: Where does Sovereignty reside? If I have succeeded in establishing the fact that ours is a Federal system, as I conceive I conclusively have, that fact of itself determines the question which I have proposed. It is of the very essence of such a system, that the Sovereignty is in the parts, and not in the whole; or, to use the language of Mr. Palgrave, 'The parts are the units in such a system, and the whole the multiple; and not the whole the unit and the parts the fractions.' Ours, then, is a Government of twenty-four Sovereignties, united by a Constitutional Compact, for the purpose of exercising certain powers through a common Government as their joint agent, and not a Union of the twenty-four Sovereignties into one, which, according to the language of the Virginia Resolutions, already cited, would form a Consolidation. And here I must express my surprise that the Senator from Virginia should avow himself the advocate of these very Resolutions, when he distinctly maintains the idea of a Union of the States in one Sovereignty, which is expressly condemned by these Resolutions as the essence of a Consolidated Government.

"Another consequence is equally clear, that, whatever modifications were made in the condition of the States under the present Constitution, they extended only to the exercise of their powers by Compact, and not to the Sovereignty itself, and are such as Sovereigns are competent to make: it being a conceded point, that it is competent to them to stipulate to exercise their powers in a particular manner, or to abstain altogether from their exercise, or to delegate them to agents, without in any degree impairing Sovereignty itself. The plain state of the facts, as regards our Government, is, that these States have agreed by Compact to exercise their Sovereign powers jointly, as already stated; and that, for this purpose, they have ratified the Compact in their Sovereign capacity, thereby making it the Constitution of each State, in nowise distinguished from their own separate Constitutions, but in the super-added obligation of Compact—of faith mutually pledged to each other. In this Compact, they have stipulated, among other things, that it may be amended by three fourths of the States: that is, they have conceded to each other by Compact the right to add new powers or to subtract old, by the consent of that proportion of the States, without requiring, as otherwise would have been the case, the consent of all: a modification no more inconsistent, as has been supposed, with their Sovereignty, than any other contained in the Compact. In fact, the provision to which I allude furnishes strong evidence that the Sovereignty is, as I contend, in the States severally, as the amendments are effected, not by any one three fourths, but by any three fourths of the States, indicating that the Sovereignty is in each of the States.

"If these views be correct, it follows, as a matter of course, that the allegiance of the people is to their several States, and that treason consists in resistance to the joint authority of the *States* united, not, as has been absurdly contended, in resistance to the Government of the United States, which, by the provision of the Constitution, has only the right of punishing. * *

"Having now said what I intended in relation to my first Resolution, both in reply to the Senator from Massachusetts, and in vindication of its correctness, I will now proceed to consider the conclusions drawn from it in the second Resolution—that the General Government is not the exclusive and final judge of the extent of the powers delegated to it, but that the States, as parties to the Compact, have a right to judge, in the last resort, of the infractions of the Compact, and of the mode and measure of redress.

"It can scarcely be necessary, before so enlightened a body, to premise that our system comprehends two distinct Governments—the General and State Governments, which, properly considered, form but one—the former representing the joint authority of the States in their Confederate capacity, and the latter that of each State separately. I have premised this fact simply with a view of presenting distinctly the answer to the argument offered by the Senator from Massachusetts to prove that the General Government has a final and exclusive right to judge, not only of delegated powers, but also of those reserved to the States. That gentleman relies for his main argument on the assertion that a Government, which he defines to be an organized body, endowed with both will, and power, and authority in *proprio vigore* to execute its purpose, has a right inherently to judge of its powers. It is not my intention to comment upon the definition of the Senator, though it would not be difficult to show that his ideas of Government are not very American. My object is to deal with the conclusion, and not the definition. Admit then, that the Government has the right of judging of its powers, for which he contends. How, then, will he withhold, upon his own principle, the right of judging from the State Governments, which he has attributed to the General Government? If it belongs to one, on his principle, it belongs to both; and if to both, when they differ, the veto, so abhorred by the Senator, is the necessary result: as neither, if the right be possessed by both, can control the other.

"The Senator felt the force of this argument, and, in order to sustain his main position, he fell back on that clause of the Constitution which provides that 'this Constitution, and the laws made in pursuance thereof, shall be the supreme law of the land.'

"This is admitted; no one has ever denied that the Constitution, and the laws made in *pursuance* of it, are of Paramount authority. But it is equally undeniable that laws *not* made in pursuance are not only not of Paramount authority, but are of no authority whatever, being of themselves null and void; which presents the question, who are to judge whether the laws be or be not pursuant to the Constitution?* and thus the difficulty, instead of being taken away, is removed but one step further back. This the Senator also felt, and has attempted to overcome, by setting up, on the part of Congress and the judiciary, the final and exclusive right of judging, both for the Federal Government and the States, as to the extent of their respective powers. That I may do full justice to the gentleman, I will give his doctrine in his own words. He states,—

"'That there is a supreme law, composed of the Constitution, the laws passed in pursuance of it, and the

* This, according to Martin's proposition was just what was refused to the General Government. See *ante*, p. 46.

treaties; but in cases coming before Congress, not assuming the shape of cases in law and equity, so as to be subjects of judicial discussion, Congress must interpret the Constitution so often as it has occasion to pass laws; and in cases capable of assuming a judicial shape, the Supreme Court must be the final interpreter.'

"Now, passing over this vague and loose phraseology, I would ask the Senator upon what principle can he concede this extensive power to the Legislative and Judicial departments, and withhold it entirely from the Executive? If one has the right it cannot be withheld from the other. I would also ask him on what principle—if the departments of the General Government are to possess the right of judging, finally and conclusively, of their respective powers—on what principle can the same right be withheld from the State Governments, which, as well as the General Government, properly considered, are but departments of the same general system, and form together, properly speaking, but one Government? This was a favorite idea of Mr. Macon, for whose wisdom I have a respect increasing with my experience, and who I have frequently heard say, that most of the misconceptions and errors in relation to our system, originated in forgetting that they were but parts of the same system. I would further tell the Senator, that, if this right be withheld from the State Governments; if this restraining influence, by which the General Government is confined to its proper sphere, be withdrawn, then that department of the Government from which he has withheld the right of judging of its own powers (the Executive), will, so far from being excluded, become the *sole* interpreter of the powers of the Government. It is the *armed* interpreter, with powers to execute its own construction, and without the aid of which the construction of the other departments will be impotent.

"But I contend that the States have a far clearer right to the sole construction of their powers than any of the departments of the Federal Government can have. This power is expressly reserved, as I have stated on another occasion, not only against the several departments of the General Government, but against the United States themselves. I will not repeat the arguments which I then offered on this point, and which remain unanswered, but I must be permitted to offer strong additional proof of the views then taken, and which, if I am not mistaken, are conclusive on this point. It is drawn from the ratification of the Constitution by Virginia, and is in the following words:

"'We, the Delegates of the people of Virginia, duly elected in pursuance of a recommendation from the General Assembly, and now met in Convention, having fully and freely investigated and discussed the proceedings of the Federal Convention, and being prepared, as well as the most mature deliberation hath enabled us, to decide thereon, do, in the name and in behalf of the people of Virginia, declare and make known that the powers granted under the Constitution, being derived from the people of the United States, may be resumed by them, whensoever the same shall be perverted to their injury or oppression, and that every power not granted thereby remains with them, and at their will; that, therefore, no right, of any denomination, can be cancelled, abridged, restrained, or modified, by the Congress, by the Senate or House of Representatives, acting in any capacity, by the President, or any department or officer of the United States, except in those instances in which power is given by the Constitution for those purposes; and that, among other essential rights, the liberty of conscience, and of the press, cannot be cancelled, abridged, restrained, or modified by any authority of the United States. With these impressions, with a solemn appeal to the Searcher of all hearts for the purity of our intentions, and under the conviction that whatsoever imperfections may exist in the Constitution ought rather to be examined in the mode prescribed therein, than to bring the Union in danger by a delay, with the hope of obtaining amendments previous to the ratifications,—We, the said Delegates, in the name and in the behalf of the people of Virginia, do, by these presents, assent to and ratify the Constitution recommended, on the 17th day of September, 1787, by the Federal Convention for the Government of the United States, hereby announcing to all those whom it may concern, that the said Constitution is binding upon the said people, according to an authentic copy hereto annexed, in the words following,' etc.

"It thus appears that this sagacious State (I fear, however, that her sagacity is not so sharp-sighted now as formerly) ratified the Constitution, with an explanation as to her reserved powers; that they were powers subject to her own will, and reserved against every department of the General Government—Legislative, Executive, and Judicial—as if she had a prophetic knowledge of the attempts now made to impair and destroy them: which explanation can be considered in no other light than as containing a condition on which she ratified, and, in fact, making part of the Constitution of the United States—extending as well to the other States as herself. I am no lawyer, and it may appear to be presumption in me to lay down the rule of law which governs in such cases, in a controversy with so distinguished an advocate as the Senator from Massachusetts.

But I shall venture to lay it down as a rule in such cases, which I have no fear that the gentleman will contradict, that, in case of a contract between several partners, if the entrance of one on condition be admitted, the condition enures to the benefit of all the partners. But I do not rest the argument simply upon this view Virginia proposed the tenth amended article, the one in question, and her ratification must be at least received as the highest evidence of its true meaning and interpretation.

"If these views be correct—and I do not see how they can be resisted—the rights of the States to judge of the extent of their reserved powers stands on the most solid foundation, and is good against every department of the General Government; and the judiciary is as much excluded from an interference with the reserved powers as the Legislative or Executive departments. To establish the opposite, the Senator relies upon the authority of Mr. Madison, in the *Federalist*, to prove that it was intended to invest the Court with the power in question. In reply, I will meet Mr. Madison with his own opinion, given on a most solemn occasion, and backed by the sagacious Commonwealth of Virginia. The opinion to which I allude will be found in the celebrated Report of 1799, of which Mr. Madison was the author. It says:

"'But it is objected, that the JUDICIAL AUTHORITY is to be regarded as *the sole expositor of the Constitution in the last resort;* and it may be asked for what reason the declaration by the General Assembly, supposing it to be theoretically true, could be required at the present day, and in so solemn a manner.

"'On this objection it might be observed, *first,* that there may be instances of usurped power, which the forms of the Constitution would never draw within the control of the Judicial department; *secondly*, that, if the decision of the judiciary be raised above the authority of the Sovereign parties to the Constitution, the decisions of the other departments, not carried by the forms of the Constitution before the judiciary, must be equally authoritative and final as the decisions of this department. But the proper answer to this objection is, that the Resolution of the General Assembly relates to those great and extraordinary cases in which all the forms of the Constitution may prove ineffectual against infractions dangerous to the essential rights of the parties to it. The Resolution supposes that dangerous powers, not delegated, may not only be usurped and executed by the other departments, but that the Judicial department, also, may exercise or sanction dangerous powers beyond the grant of the Constitution; and, consequently, that the ultimate right of the parties to the Constitution to judge whether the Compact was dangerously violated, must extend to violations by one delegated authority as well as by another; by the judiciary as well as by the executive or the Legislature.'"*

"But why should I waste words in reply to these or any other authorities, when it has been so clearly established that the rights of the States are reserved against each and every department of the Government, and no authority in opposition can possibly shake a position so well established? Nor do I think it necessary to repeat the argument which I offered when the bill was under discussion, to show that the clause in the Constitution which provides that the judicial power shall extend to all cases in law or equity arising under this Constitution, and to the laws and treaties made under its authority, has no bearing on the point in controversy; and that even the boasted power of the Supreme Court to decide

* See *Appendix* E.

a law to be unconstitutional, so far from being derived from this or any other portion of the Constitution, results from the necessity of the case—where two rules of unequal authority come in conflict—and is a power belonging to all courts, superior and inferior, State and General, Domestic, and Foreign.

"I have now, I trust, shown satisfactorily, that there is no provision in the Constitution to authorize the General Government, through any of its departments, to control the action of a State within the sphere of its reserved powers; and that, of course, according to the principle laid down by the Senator from Massachusetts himself, the Government of the States, as well as the General Government, has the right to determine the extent of their respective powers, without the right on the part of either to control the other. The necessary result is the veto, to which he so much objects; and to get clear of which, he informed us, was the object for which the present Constitution was formed. I know not whence he has derived his information, but my impression is very different, as to the immediate motives which led to the formation of that instrument. I have always understood that the principle was, to give to Congress the power to regulate commerce, to lay impost duties, and to raise a revenue for the payment of the public debt and the expenses of the Government; and to subject the action of the citizens, individually, to the operation of the laws, as a substitute for force. If the object had been to get clear of the veto of the States, as the Senator states, the Convention, certainly, performed their work in a most bungling manner. There was, unquestionably, a large party in that body, headed by men of distinguished talents and influence, who commenced early and worked earnestly to the last, to deprive the States—not directly, for that would have been too bold an attempt, but indirectly—of the veto. The good sense of the Convention, however put down every effort, however disguised and perseveringly made. I do not deem it necessary to give, from the journals, the history of these various and unsuccessful attempts—though it would afford a very instructive lesson. It is sufficient to say that it was attempted, by proposing to give to Congress power to annul the acts of the States which they might deem inconsistent with the Constitution; to give to the President the power of appointing the Governors of the States, with a view of vetoing State laws through his authority; and, finally, to give the judiciary the power to decide controversies between the States and the General Government; all of which failed—fortunately for the liberty of the country—utterly and entirely failed; and in this failure we have the strongest evidence, that it was not the intention of the Convention to deprive the States of the veto power. Had the attempt to deprive them of this power been directly made, and failed, every one would have seen and felt, that it would furnish conclusive evidence in favor of its existence. Now, I would ask, what possible difference can it make in what form this attempt was made? Whether by attempting to confer on the General Government a power incompatible with the exercise of the veto on the part of the States, or by attempting directly to deprive them of the right to exercise it? We have thus direct and strong proof that, in the opinion of the Convention, the States, unless deprived of it, possess the veto power—or, what is another name for the same thing, the right of Nullifiation. I know that there is a diversity of opinion among the friends of State Rights in regard to this power, which I regret, as I cannot but consider it as a power essential to the protection of the minor and local interests of the community, and the liberty and the Union of the country. It is the very shield of State Rights, and the only power by which that system of injustice against which we have contended for more than thirteeen years can be arrested: a system of hostile Legislation—of plundering by law, which must necessarily lead to a conflict of arms, if not prevented.

"But I rest the right of a State to judge of the extent of its reserved powers, in the last resort, on higher grounds—that the Constitution is a Compact, to which the States are parties in their Sovereign capacity; and that, as in all other cases of Compact between parties having no common umpire, each has a right to judge for itself. To the truth of this proposition, the Senator from Massachusetts has himself assented, if the Constitution itself be a Compact—and that it is, I have shown, I trust, beyond the possibility of a doubt. Having established this point, I now claim, as I stated I would do, in the course of the discussion, the admissions of the Senator, and, among them, the right of Secession and Nullification, which he conceded would necessarily follow if the Constitution be, indeed, a Compact.

"I have now replied to the arguments of the Senator from Massachusetts so far as they directly apply to the Resolutions, and will, in conclusion, notice some of his general and detached remarks. To prove that ours is a consolidated Government, and that there is an immediate connection between the Government and the citizen, he relies on the fact that the laws act directly on individuals. That such is the case I will not deny; but I am very far from conceding the point that it affords the decisive proof, or even any proof at all, of the position which the Senator wishes to maintain. I hold it to be perfectly within the competency of two or more States to subject their citizens, in certain cases, to the direct action of each other, without surrendering or impairing their Sovereignty. I recollect, while I was a member of Mr. Monroe's cabinet, a proposition was submitted by the British Government to permit a mutual right of search and seizure, on the part of each Government, of the citizens of the other, on board of vessels engaged in the slave-trade, and to establish a joint tribunal for their trial and punishment. The proposition was declined, not because it would impair the Sovereignty of either, but on the ground of general expediency, and because it would be incompatible with the provisions of the Constitution which establish the judicial power, and which provisions require the judges to be appointed by the President and Senate. If I am not mistaken, propositions of the same kind were made and acceded to by some of the Continental powers.

"With the same view the Senator cited the suability of the States as evidence of their want of Sovereignty; at which I must express my surprise, coming from the quarter it does. No one knows better than the Senator that it is perfectly within the competency of a Sovereign State to permit itself to be sued. We have on the Statute-book a standing law, under which the United States may be sued in certain land cases. If the provision in the Constitution on this point proves any thing, it proves, by the extreme jealousy with which the right of suing a State is permitted, the very reverse of that for which the Senator contends.

"Among other objections to the views of the Constitution for which I contend, it is said that they are novel. I hold this to be a great mistake. The novelty is not on my side, but on that of the Senator from Massachusetts. The doctrine of Consolidation which he maintains is of recent growth. It is not the doctrine of Hamilton, Ames, or any of the distinguished Federalists of the period, all of whom strenuously maintained the Federative character of the Constitution, though they were accused of supporting a system of policy which would necessarily lead to Consolidation. The first disclosure of that doctrine was in the case of M'Culloch; in which the Supreme Court held the doctrine, though wrapped up in language somewhat indistinct and ambiguous. The next, and more open avowal, was by the Senator of Massachusetts himself, about three years ago, in the debate on Foote's resolution. The first official annunciation of the doctrine was in the recent proclamation of the President, of which the bill that has recently passed this body is the bitter fruit.

"It is further objected by the Senator from Massachusetts, and others, against the doctrine of State Rights, as maintained in this debate, that, if it should prevail, the peace of the country would be destroyed. But what if it should not prevail? Would there be peace? Yes, the peace of despotism: that peace which is enforced by the bayonet and the sword; the peace of death, where all the vital functions of liberty have ceased. It is this peace which the doctrine of State Sovereignty may disturb by that conflict, which, in every free State, if properly organized, necessarily exists between liberty and power; but which, if restrained within proper limits, gives a salutary exercise to our moral and intellectual faculties. In the case of Carolina, which has caused all this discussion, who does not see, if the effusion of blood be prevented, that the excitement, the agitation, and the inquiry which it has caused, will be followed by the most beneficial consequences? The country had sunk into avarice, intrigue, and electioneering—from which nothing but some such event could rouse it, or restore those honest and patriotic feelings which had almost disappeared under their baneful influence. What Government has ever attained power and distinction without such conflicts? Look at the degraded state of all those nations where they have been put down by the iron arm of the Government.

"I, for my part, have no fear of any dangerous conflict, under the fullest acknowledgment of State Sovereignty: the very fact that the States may interpose will produce moderation and justice. The General Government will abstain from the exercise of any power in which they may suppose three fourths of the States will not sustain them; while, on the other hand, the States will not interpose but on the conviction that they will be supported by one fourth of their co-States. Moderation and justice will produce confidence, attachment and patriotism; and these, in turn, will offer most powerful barriers against the excess of conflicts between the States and the General Government.

"But we are told that, should the doctrine prevail, the present system would be as bad, if not worse, than the old Confederation. I regard the assertion only as evidence of that extravagance of declaration in which, from excitement of feeling, we so often indulge. Admit the power, and still the present system would be as far removed from the weakness of the old Confederation as it would be from the lawless and despotic violence of consolidation. So far from being the same, the difference between the Confederation and the present Constitution would still be most strongly marked. If there were no other distinction, the fact that the former required the concurrence of the States to execute its acts, and the latter, the act of a State to arrest them, would make a distinction as broad as the ocean. In the former, the *vis inertiæ* of our nature is in opposition to the action of the system. Not to act was to defeat. In the latter the same principle is on the opposite side—action is required to defeat. He who understands human nature will see, in this fact alone, the difference between a feeble and illy-contrived Confederation, and the restrained energy of a Federal system. Of the same character is the objection that the doctrine will be the source of weakness. If we look to mere organization and physical power as the only source of strength, without taking into the estimate the operation of moral causes, such would appear to be the fact; but if we take into the estimate the latter, we shall find that those Governments have the greatest strength in which power has been most efficiently checked. The Government of Rome furnishes a memorable example. There, two independent and distinct powers existed—the people acting by Tribes, in which the Plebeians prevailed, and by Centuries, in which the Patricians ruled. The Tribunes were the appointed representatives of the one power, and the Senate of the other; each possessed of the authority of checking and overruling one another, not as departments of the Government, as supposed by the Senator from Massachussetts, but as independent powers,—as much so as the State and General Governments. A shallow observer would perceive, in such an organization, nothing but the perpetual source of anarchy, discord, and weakness; and yet experience has proved that it was the most powerful Government that ever existed; and reason teaches that this power was derived from the very circumstances which hasty reflection would consider the cause of weakness. I will venture an assertion, which may be considered extravagant, but in which history will fully bear me out, that we have no knowledge of any people where the power of arresting the improper acts of the Government, or what may be called the negative power of Government, was too strong,—except Poland, where every freeman possessed a veto. But even there, although it existed in so extravagant a form, it was the source of the highest and most lofty attachment to liberty, and the most heroic courage: qualities that more than once saved Europe from the domination of the crescent and cimeter. It is worthy of remark, that the fate of Poland is not to be attributed so much to the excess of this negative power of itself, as to the facility which it afforded to foreign influence in controlling its political movements.

"I am not surprised that, with the idea of a perfect Government which the Senator from Massachusetts has formed—a Government of an absolute majority, unchecked and unrestrained, operating through a representative body—he should be so much shocked with what he is pleased to call the absurdity of the State *veto*. But let me tell him that his scheme of a perfect Government, as beautiful as he conceives it to be, though often tried, has invariably failed,—has always run, whenever tried, through the same uniform process of faction, corruption, anarchy, and despotism. He considers the representative principle as the great modern improvement in legislation, and of itself sufficient to secure liberty. I cannot regard it in the light in which he does. Instead of modern, it is of remote origin, and has existed, in greater or less perfection, in every free State, from the remotest antiquity. Nor do I consider it as of itself sufficient to secure liberty, though I regard it as one of the indispensable means—the means of securing the people against the tyranny and oppression of their *rulers*. To secure liberty, another means is still necessary—the means of securing the different portions of society against the injustice and oppressions of each other, which can only be effected by *veto*, interposition, or Nullification, or by whatever name the restraining or negative power of Government may be called."

This is quite enough of Mr. Calhoun's reply. I have read all of it that bears directly upon the main points in issue between them. On these points never was a man more completely answered than Mr. Webster was. The argument is a crusher, an extinguisher, an annihilator!

Prof. Norton. Where is Mr. Webster's rejoinder?

Mr. Stephens. He made none. He followed with a few remarks only, disavowing any personal unkind feelings to Mr. Calhoun, explaining how he had used the term "Constitutional Compact," in 1830; and attempting to parry one or two of the blows, but he never made any regular set reply or rejoinder. He never came back at his opponent at all on the real questions at issue. Mr. Calhoun stood master of the arena. This speech of his was not answered then, it has not been answered since, and in my judgment never will be, or can be answered while truth has its legitimate influence, and reason controls the judgment of men!

The power and force of this speech must have been felt by Mr. Webster himself. He was a man of too much reason and logic not to have felt it. This opinion I am the more inclined to from the fact, that he not only did not attempt a general reply to it at the time, but from the further fact, that in after life he certainly, to say the least of it, greatly modified the opinions held by him in that debate.

Prof. Norton. To what do you refer?

MR. STEPHENS. I refer specially to a speech made by him before the Supreme Court of the United States, in 1839, and to his speech at Capon Springs, in Virginia, in 1851, as well as some other matters. But, if it is agreeable to all, we will suspend the investigation for the present, take our evening's walk, and resume the subject to-morrow. Reading aloud is much more exhausting than talking, even with the same tone of voice.

COLLOQUY IX.

SUBJECT CONTINUED—WEBSTER'S SPEECH BEFORE THE SUPREME COURT—HIS LETTER TO BARING BROTHERS & CO—HIS CAPON SPRINGS SPEECH—THE SUPREME COURT ON STATE SOVEREIGNTY—INTERNATIONAL COMITY—DIFFERENCE BETWEEN THE UNION OF THE STATES AND THE UNION OF ENGLAND AND SCOTLAND—EXPOSITION OF THE CONSTITUTION BY THE SENATE IN 1838—CALHOUN'S PRINCIPLES OF 1833 SUSTAINED BY TWO THIRDS OF THE STATES IN 1838—EXPOSITION OF THE CONSTITUTION BY THE SENATE IN 1860—JEFFERSON DAVIS.

Prof. Norton. Well, Mr. Stephens, we are all ready to resume the subject we were last upon. That was the modification of Mr. Webster's opinions upon the issue between him and Mr. Calhoun in their great debate which we have been reviewing.

Mr. Stephens. Yes, I have just looked up the argument of Mr. Webster, before the Supreme Court of the United States, to which I referred. I will first call your attention to that, and then some other expressions of opinion by him, bearing on the same subject. The case the Court had under consideration was the *The Bank of Augusta* vs. *Earle*. In this case the nature of the General Government and the nature of the State Governments in their relations to each other, came up for adjudication. This was in January, 1839, six years after the discussion with Mr. Calhoun in the Senate. Here is what he then said:*

"But it is argued, that though this law of comity exists as between independent Nations, it does not exist

*13 *Peters's Reports*, p. 559.

between the States of this Union. That argument appears to have been the foundation of the judgment in the Court below.

"In respect to this law of comity, it is said, States are not Nations; they have no National Sovereignty; a sort of residuum of Sovereignty is all that remains to them. The National Sovereignty, it is said, is conferred on this Government, and part of the municipal Sovereignty. The rest of the municipal Sovereignty belongs to the States. Notwithstanding the respect which I entertain for the learned Judge, who presided in that Court, I cannot follow in the train of his argument. I can make no diagram, such as this, of the partition of National character between the State and General Governments. I cannot map it out, and say, so far is National, and so far municipal; and here is the exact line where the one begins and the other ends. We have no second La Place, and we never shall have, with his *Mechanique Politique*, able to define and describe the orbit of each sphere in our political system with such exact mathematical precision. There is no such thing as arranging these Governments of ours by the laws of gravitation, so that they will be sure to go on forever without impinging. These institutions are practical, admirable, glorious, blessed creations. Still they were, when created, experimental institutions; and if the Convention which framed the Constitution of the United States had set down in it certain general definitions of power, such as have been alleged in the argument of this case, and stopped there, I verily believe that in the course of the fifty years which have since elapsed, this Government would have never gone into operation.

"Suppose that this Constitution had said, in terms after the language of the Court below—all National Sovereignty shall belong to the United States; all municipal Sovereignty to the several States. I will say, that however clear, however distinct, such a definition may appear to those who use it, the employment of it, in the Constitution, could only have led to utter confusion and uncertainty. *I am not prepared to say that the States have no National Sovereignty.* The laws of some of the States—Maryland and Virginia, for instance—provide punishment for treason. The power thus exercised is, certainly, not municipal. Virginia has a law of alienage; that is, a power exercised against a foreign nation. Does not the question necessarily arise, when a power is exercised concerning an alien enemy—enemy to whom? The law of escheat, which exists in all the States, is also the exercise of a *great Sovereign power.*

"The term 'Sovereignty' does not occur in the Constitution at all. *The Constitution treats States as States,* and the United States as the United States; and, by a *careful enumeration,* declares all *the powers* that are granted to the United States, and *all the rest* are *reserved to the States.* If we pursue, to the extreme point, the powers granted, and the powers reserved, the powers of the General and State Governments will be found, it is to be feared, impinging, and in conflict. Our hope is, that the prudence and patriotism of the States, and the wisdom of this Government, will prevent that catastrophe. For myself, I will pursue the advice of the Court in Deveaux's case; I will avoid nice metaphysical subtilties, and all useless theories; I will keep my feet out of the traps of general definition; I will keep my feet out of all traps; I will keep to things as they are, and go no further to inquire what they might be, if they were not what they are. *The States of this Union, as States, are subject to all the voluntary and customary laws of Nations.*"

[Mr. Webster here referred to, and quoted a passage from *Vattel* (page 61), which, he said, clearly showed, that States connected together as are the States of this Union, must be considered as much component parts of the law of Nations as any others.]*

"If, for the decision of any question, the proper rule is to be found in the law of Nations, that law adheres to the subject. It follows the subject through, no matter into what place, high or low. You cannot escape the law of Nations in a case where it is applicable. The air of every judicature is full of it. It pervades the Courts of law of the highest character, and the Court of pie poudre; aye, even the constable's Court. It is part of the universal law. It may share the glorious eulogy pronounced by Hooker upon law itself: that there is nothing so high as to be beyond the reach of its power, nothing so low as to be beneath its care. If any question be within the influence of the law of Nations, the law of Nations is there. If the law of comity does not exist between the States of this Union, how can it exist between a State and the subjects of any foreign Sovereignty?"

In this carefully prepared argument Mr. Webster significantly says: that in the Constitution nothing is said about "Sovereignty." This is all important. He admitted, in the debate with Mr. Calhoun, that the States were Sovereign before the Constitution was adopted. In this argument he holds the position that the powers delegated to the United States in the Constitution are specific and limited, and that all not delegated are reserved to the States. He states distinctly, that the Constitution treats the States as States. If the States, then, were

* See *Vattel*, here quoted, *ante*, p. 170.

Sovereign anterior to the Constitution, and Sovereignty was not delegated or parted with by them in it, as it could not have been, as the Constitution is silent upon the subject, then of course it is still reserved to the States. If the Sovereignty of the States was not delegated or parted with in the Constitution, was it not of necessity retained by them? He clearly so argues. This is the inevitable conclusion from the rules of inexorable logic. The decision of the Supreme Court in this case was on the line of his argument, and fully sustains his position. They say,

"It has, however, been supposed that the rules of comity between foreign Nations do not apply to the States of this Union; that they extend to one another no other rights than those which are given by the Constitution of the United States; and that the Courts of the General Government are not at liberty to presume, in the absence of all legislation on the subject, that a State has adopted the comity of Nations towards the other States, as a part of its jurisprudence; or that it acknowledges any rights, but those which are secured by the Constitution of the United States. The Court think otherwise. The intimate Union of these States, as members of the same great political family; the deep and vital interests which bind them so closely together; should lead us, in the absence of proof to the contrary, to presume a greater degree of comity, and friendship, and kindness towards one another, than we should be authorized to presume between foreign Nations. And when (as without doubt must occasionally happen) the interest or policy of any State requires it to restrict the rule, it has but to declare its will, and the legal presumption is at once at an end. But until this is done, upon what grounds could this Court refuse to administer the law of international comity between these

States? *They are Sovereign States;* and the history of the past, and the events which are daily occurring, furnish the strongest evidence that they have adopted towards each other the laws of comity in their fullest extent. * *

"But it cannot be necessary to pursue the argument further. We think it is well settled, that by the law of comity among Nations, a corporation created by *one Sovereignty* is permitted to make contracts in another, and to sue in its Courts; *and that the same law of comity prevails among the several Sovereignties of this Union.*"

I read this decision of the Court, not only to show that the Court sustained this view presented by Mr. Webster, in 1839, which was a great modification of the view expressed by him in 1833, that you have read, but to show that it has been decided, solemnly adjudicated by the highest Judicial tribunal in this country, that Sovereignty is still retained by the several States of the Union under the Constitution.

JUDGE BYNUM. The Court in that case barely held that the law of international comity obtained between the States of our Union, as the same doctrine is held by the British Courts between Scotland and England, and yet no one there holds that Scotland is separately Sovereign from England, or that Scotland could dissolve the Compact of their Union.

MR. STEPHENS. The cases are totally different. There is no analogy between them. The decision was not made on any such view. The Sovereignties of England and Scotland are not united by Compact at all. The separate Sovereignties of these countries became united by a union of the Crowns of both, by regular descent in the person of James VI, of Scotland, who became James I, of England, upon the death of Elizabeth. The declaratory Act of the Parliaments of both, setting forth the fact of the Union thus resulting, and the respective rights of each, under it, distinctly states that the two Kingdoms thereafter shall be created into one Kingdom by the name of Great Britain. This was but the declaration of a unity of Sovereignty, which had occurred by the union of Crowns by descent, and not one of Compact at all. This distinction is clearly drawn by Blackstone in his Commentaries.* That was what he called an "*Incorporate Union*," which was very different from a "*Federate alliance.*"

But the difference between the Union of the Sovereignties of England and Scotland and the Federal Union of these States, is fully set forth by Judge Washington, of the Supreme Court of the United States, in the Circuit Court of the Eastern District of Pennsylvania, in the case of *Lonsdale* vs. *Brown*. This decision was made in 1821. In delivering the opinion the judge says, "The Union between England and Scotland is, politically speaking, as intimate as between England and Wales, or between the different counties of either. They form one Kingdom; are subject to the same Government; and are represented in the same legislative body; and although the laws and customs of Scotland in force at the time of the Union were suffered to continue, yet they are alterable by the Parliament of Great Britain, even as they relate to private rights; if the alteration should be deemed for the evident utility of the people of Scotland.

"How different is the Union of these States? They are, in their separate political capacities, Sovereign and independent of each other, except so far as they have united for their common defence and for National purposes. They have each a Constitution and form of Gov-

* *Blackstone's Commentaries*, vol. i, p. 97, note E.

ernment, with all the attributes of Sovereignty. As to matters of National concern they form one Government, are subject to the same laws, and may emphatically be denominated one people. In all other respects, they are as distinct as different forms of Government and different laws can render them. It is true, that the citizens of each State are entitled to all the privileges and immunities of citizens in every other State; that the Sovereignty of the States in relation to fugitives from justice, and from service, is limited; and that each State is bound to give full faith and credit to the public acts, records and judicial proceedings of her sister States. But these privileges and disabilities are mere creatures of the Constitution; and it is quite fair to argue that the framers of that instrument deemed it necessary to secure them by express provisions.

"In the case of *Warder* vs. *Arrell*, 2 Wash. Rep. 282, the question, in part, was, whether the tender laws of Pennsylvania, where the contract was made, ought to be regarded by the Courts of Virginia, where the suit was brought? and throughout the opinions delivered by the judges, Pennsylvania was treated as a foreign country. The president of the Court is express upon this point. He observes that, in cases of contracts, the laws of a foreign country where the contract is made must govern. The same principle applies, though with no greater force, to the different States of America; for though they form a Confederated Government, yet the several States retain their individual Sovereignties, *and with respect to their municipal laws, are to each other foreign.*"*

But in further proof of the modification of the views of Mr. Webster on the subject, I refer to his celebrated

* *Peters's Reports*, vol. ii. App. pp. 689, 690.

letter to the Barings, in London, written the same year. Here it is. In it he uses this language:

"Your first inquiry is, 'whether the Legislature of one of the States has legal and Constitutional power to contract loans at home and abroad?'

"To this I answer, 'that the Legislature of a State has such power; and how any doubt could have arisen on this point it is difficult for me to conceive. Every State is an independent, Sovereign, political community, except in so far as certain powers, which it might otherwise have exercised, have been conferred on a General Government, established under a written Constitution, and exerting its authority over the people of all the States. This General Government is a limited Government. Its powers are specific and enumerated. All powers not conferred upon it still remain with the States and with the people. The State Legislatures, on the other hand, possess all usual and extraordinary powers of Government, subject to any limitations which may be imposed by their own Constitutions, and, with the exception, as I have said, of the operation on those powers of the Constitution of the United States. The powers conferred on the General Government cannot of course be exercised by any individual State; nor can any State pass any law which is prohibited by the Constitution of the United States. * * *

"The security for State loans is the plighted faith of the State, as a political Community. It rests on the same basis as other contracts with established Governments—the same basis, for example, as loans made in the United States under the authority of Congress; that is to say, the good faith of the Government making the loan, and its ability to fulfil its engagements. * * *

"It has been said that the States cannot be sued on

these bonds. But neither could the United States be sued, nor, as I suppose, the Crown of England, in a like case. Nor would the power of suing, probably, give the creditor any substantial additional security. The solemn obligation of a Government, arising on its own acknowledged bond, would not be enhanced by a judgment rendered on such bond. If it either could not, or would not, make provision for paying the bond, it is not probable that it could or would make provision for satisfying the judgment."*

He here distinctly states that every State is an Independent, Sovereign, political Community, except in so far as certain powers, which it might otherwise have exercised, have been conferred on a General Government by a written Constitution, containing certain specified powers. This language is substantially identical with the language of the first Article of the old Confederation.

An important fact in this connection, to be borne in mind, is that there was no vote taken on Mr. Calhoun's Resolutions, in the Senate, in 1833. The matter rested there with the discussion. The controversy that gave rise to it was amicably adjusted, as we shall see. The subject of the discussion, however, was taken up by the press, by public speakers, by the State Legislatures, and by the people generally. The great discussions of 1798, 1799 and 1800, were revived. Old landmarks of principles were traced. The rapid strides of the Federal Government towards consolidation were again stopped.

Mr. Calhoun had, on the 28th of December, 1837, renewed the subject in the Senate. He then brought forward another set of Resolutions on the same subject, covering the same ground, embodying the same principles,

* *Niles's National Register*, vol. lvii, pp. 273-274.

and pressed them to a vote. These Resolutions are as follows:

"I. *Resolved,* That in the adoption of the Federal Constitution, the States adopting the same acted, severally, as free, independent, and Sovereign States; and that each, for itself, by its own voluntary assent, entered the Union with the view to its increased security against all dangers, *domestic* as well as foreign, and the more perfect and secure enjoyment of its advantages, natural, political, and social.

"II. *Resolved,* That, in delegating a portion of their powers to be exercised by the Federal Government, the States retained, severally, the exclusive and sole right over their own domestic institutions and police, to the full extent to which those powers were not thus delegated, and are alone responsible for them; and that any intermeddling of any one or more States, or a combination of their citizens, with the domestic institutions and police of the others, on any ground, political, moral, or religious, or under any pretext whatever, with the view to their alteration or subversion, is not warranted by the Constitution, tending to endanger the domestic peace and tranquillity of the States interfered with, subversive of the objects for which the Constitution was formed, and, by necessary consequence, tending to weaken and destroy the Union itself.

"III. *Resolved,* That this Government was instituted and adopted by the several States of this Union as a common agent, in order to carry into effect the powers which they had delegated by the Constitution for their mutual security and prosperity; and that in fulfilment of this high and sacred trust, this Government is bound so to exercise its powers, as not to interfere with the stability and security of the domestic institutions of the

States that compose this Union; and that it is the solemn duty of the Government to resist, to the extent of its Constitutional power, all attempts by one portion of the Union to use it as an instrument to attack the domestic institutions of another, or to weaken or destroy such institutions.

"IV. *Resolved*, That domestic slavery, as it exists in the Southern and Western States of this Union, composes an important part of their domestic institutions, inherited from their ancestors, and existing at the adoption of the Constitution, by which it is recognized as constituting an important element in the apportionment of powers among the States, and that no change of opinion or feeling, on the part of the other States of the Union in relation to it, can justify them or their citizens in open and systematic attacks thereon, with the view to its overthrow; and that all such attacks are in manifest violation of the mutual and solemn pledge to protect and defend each other, given by the States respectively, on entering into the Constitutional Compact which formed the Union, and as such are a manifest breach of faith, and a violation of the most solemn obligations.

"V. *Resolved*, That the interference by the citizens of any of the States, with the view to the abolition of slavery in this District, is endangering the rights and security of the people of the District; and that any act or measure of Congress designed to abolish slavery in this District, would be a violation of the faith implied in the cessions by the States of Virginia and Maryland, a just cause of alarm to the people of the slaveholding States, and have a direct and inevitable tendency to disturb and endanger the Union.

"*And resolved*, That any attempt of Congress to abolish slavery in any Territory of the United States in which it exists, would create serious alarm, and just apprehension, in the States sustaining that domestic institution; would be a violation of good faith towards the inhabitants of any such territory who have been permitted to settle with, and hold slaves therein, because the people of any such Territory have not asked for the abolition of slavery therein; and because when any such Territory shall be admitted into the Union as a State, the people thereof will be entitled to decide that question exclusively for themselves."*

The first of these Resolutions, which distinctly affirms the great truth set forth in the first of his series in 1833, passed the Senate by the large majority of thirty-two to thirteen, on the third of January, 1838. Congressional Globe, Second Session, Twenty-fifth Congress, page 74. This was certainly the highest authoritative exposition of the subject that could be given. It was the amplest vindication of the merits of Mr. Calhoun's argument in 1833. His argument and Mr. Webster's had gone to the country, and this was the verdict of the States upon the issue presented by them. More than two to one of the Senate of the United States affirmed most positively and solemnly that the Union of the States was Federal, and that in entering into it under the Constitution, the States did so severally as free, independent, Sovereign Powers. That the Union was one of States, formed by States, and not by the people in the aggregate as one nation.

But upon an analysis of the vote upon this Resolution, and the others of the series, this authoritative exposition derives increased importance. For if we look at the vote by States, it will be seen that eighteen States voted for this Resolution, while only six voted against

---

* *Congressional Globe and Appendix*, 2d S., 25th Congress, p. 98.

it. One was divided, and one did not vote.* More than two thirds of the States give this construction to the character of the Government in 1838. It is true, Mr. Webster was then in the Senate, and did not vote for it. But he did not take up the gauntlet thrown down by Calhoun for another contest in debate on the principles thus re-announced. Mr. Clay, however, voted for it, which shows his understanding of the nature of the Government.

On the second of these Resolutions, the vote stood thirty-one to nine on the *per capita* vote. By States the vote was twenty States for it, only four against, one divided, and one not voting.†

Three fourths of the States voted for this Resolution, enough to have amended the Constitution according to its provision, if they had been in Convention for that purpose.

The vote on the third Resolution was thirty-one to eleven. By States the vote was sixteen in favor and only four against it; three were divided, and three not voting. A large majority of the States thus expressly affirmed that the Federal Government was nothing but a common agent of the States, and held all its powers by delegation and in trust.

On the fourth Resolution, the vote stood thirty-four

* *Ayes*,—Alabama, Arkansas, Connecticut, Georgia, Illinois, Kentucky, Louisiana, Mississippi, Missouri, Michigan, Maine, North Carolina, New Hampshire, New York, South Carolina, Pennsylvania, Tennessee, Virginia, 18. *Nays*,—Delaware, Indiana, Massachusetts, New Jersey, Rhode Island, Vermont, 6. *Divided*,—Ohio, 1. *Not voting*,—Maryland, 1.

† *Ayes*.—Alabama. Arkansas, Connecticut, Delaware, Georgia, Illinois, Kentucky, Louisiana, Maine, Michigan, Mississippi, Missouri, New Hampshire, North Carolina, New York, South Carolina, Tennessee, Virginia, Pennsylvania and Maryland, 20. *Nays*.—Indiana, Massachusetts, New Jersey, Vermont, 4. *Divided*,—Ohio, 1. *Not voting*,—Rhode Island, 1.

for it, and only five against it. By States the vote was eighteen for it, and only two against it, while two were divided, and four not voting.

On the fifth Resolution, the vote was thirty-six to eight. This Resolution was slightly amended, on motion of Mr. Clay, from what it was when at first introduced. On the second clause of it, the vote by States was nineteen for it, three only against it; three divided, and one not voting.

These votes all show conclusively how the Constitution was then understood by the "ambassadors of the States," as Mr. Ames, in the Massachusetts Convention, had styled the Senators. This is the construction of it they put on perpetual record. Could any man desire an ampler vindication of the correctness of his position than Mr. Calhoun had of the truth of his principles, of 1833, thus declared by two thirds of the States themselves, through their ambassadors in the Senate, five years afterwards.

It was after these Resolutions had been passed, after the dicussions that had ensued between 1833 and 1838, after the revival of the principles of 1798–99–1800, which had slumbered so long on these subjects, that Mr. Webster, in 1839, made the speech he did, before the Supreme Court of the United States, and wrote the letter he did to the Baring Brothers & Co., touching the nature of the Government, in both of which he fully admits that the States are Sovereign, except in so far as they have delegated specific Sovereign powers. But "Sovereignty" itself, as he says, not being mentioned in the Constitution, must, as a necessary result, remain with the States, or the people thereof.

But besides all this, as a further proof of Mr. Webster's change of views as to the Constitution being a Compact between the States, I cite you to a later speech made by him at Capon Springs, in Virginia, on the 28th June, 1851. Here it is.* In this he says:

"The leading sentiment in the toast from the Chair is the Union of the States. THE UNION OF THE STATES! What mind can comprehend the consequences of that Union, past, present, and to come? The Union of these States is the all-absorbing topic of the day; on it all men write, speak, think, and dilate, from the rising of the sun to the going down thereof. And yet, gentlemen, I fear its importance has been but insufficiently appreciated."

Further on he says:

"How absurd it is to suppose that when different parties enter into a Compact for certain purposes, either can disregard any one provision, and expect, nevertheless, the other to observe the rest! I intend, for one, to regard, and maintain, and carry out, to the fullest extent, the Constitution of the United States, which I have sworn to support in all its parts and all its provisions. It is written in the Constitution:

"'NO PERSON HELD TO SERVICE OR LABOR IN ONE STATE, UNDER THE LAWS THEREOF, ESCAPING INTO ANOTHER, SHALL, IN CONSEQUENCE OF ANY LAW OR REGULATION THEREIN, BE DISCHARGED FROM SUCH SERVICE OR LABOR, BUT SHALL BE DELIVERED UP ON CLAIM OF THE PARTY TO WHOM SUCH SERVICE OR LABOR MAY BE DUE.'

"That is as much a part of the Constitution as any other, and as equally binding and obligatory as any other on all men, public or private. And who denies this? None but the abolitionists of the North. And pray what is it they will not deny? They have but the one idea; and it would seem that these fanatics at the

---

* *Pamphlet Copy.*

North and the secessionists at the South, are putting their heads together to derive means to defeat the good designs of honest and patriotic men. They act to the same end and the same object, and the Constitution has to take the fire from both sides.

"I have not hesitated to say, and I repeat, that if the Northern States refuse, wilfully and deliberately, to carry into effect that part of the Constitution which respects the restoration of fugitive slaves, and Congress provide no remedy, the South would no longer be bound to observe the Compact. A bargain cannot be broken on one side and still bind the other side. I say to you, gentlemen, in Virginia, as I said on the shores of Lake Erie and in the city of Boston, as I may say again, in that city or elsewhere in the North, that you of the South have as much right to receive your fugitive slaves, as the North has to any of its rights and privileges of navigation and commerce."

Again, said he: "I am as ready to fight and to fall for the Constitutional rights of Virginia, as I am for those of Massachusetts."

In this speech Mr. Webster distinctly held that the Union was a Union of States. That the Union was founded upon Compact. And that a Compact broken on one side could not continue to bind the other.

That this speech shows a modification of the opinions expressed in his speech of 1833, must be admitted by all. He had grown older and wiser. The speech of 1851, was in his maturer years, after the nature of the Government had been more fully discussed by the men of his own generation than it had been in 1830 and 1833. He was too great a man and had too great an intellect not to see the truth when it was presented, and he was too honest and too patriotic a man, not to proclaim a truth when he saw it, even to an unwilling people. In this quality of moral greatness I often thought Mr. Webster had the advantage of his great cotemporaries, Messrs. Clay and Calhoun. Not that I would be understood as saying that they were not men of great moral courage, for both of them showed this high quality in many instances, but that they never gave the world such striking exhibitions of it as he did. It was the glory of his life that his was put to a test, in this particular, that theirs never was. On no occasion that I am aware of did Mr. Clay ever take a position which he did not know that he would be sustained in by the people of Kentucky. So with Mr. Calhoun, as to South Carolina. I do not say that they might not have done it if a sense of duty had required it, but they were either so fortunate or so unfortunate as never to have that issue presented to them.

Webster, on the contrary, often passed this ordeal, and that he passed it with unflinching firmness is one of the grandest features in the general grandeur of his character. Even his detractors have been constrained to render him unwilling homage in this respect.

Theodore Parker, in his tirade on his character, after his death, is an illustration of this. He graphically described, if you recollect, his position, in Faneuil Hall, when he returned to give an account of his stewardship to his constituents, in 1842. Webster, you know, had remained in President Tyler's cabinet after Mr. Tyler had come to an open breach with the Whig party. This was exceedingly displeasing to the Whigs of Massachusetts. His object in so remaining, however, was to preserve peace with England by effecting a settlement of the North Eastern Boundary question. This he saw a prospect of accomplishing, and this, by remaining, he had accomplished. But even this great act could not atone for his disregard of the wishes of his party. They were in the main disaffected, displeased, and indignant. The opposition had assumed a hostile attitude. The crisis in his affairs was gloomy enough. The political elements were gathering against him from every point. The storm had been brewing for some time. Denunciations opened from every quarter. All this Parker vividly described, on the occasion alluded to, and then said (I quote from memory): "The clouds had thickened into blackness all around, and over him, and hurled their thunders fearfully upon his devoted head! But there he stood in Faneuil Hall and thundered back again! It was the ground lightning from his Olympian brain!"

This figure was not too exaggerated for the occasion. It gave a truthful representation of the majesty of the man whom he was endeavoring to depreciate, disparage, and defame. In rendering this homage he was but reenacting the part of the Prophet of Aram, who went out to curse, but was constrained to honor instead.

This was not the only instance in which Mr. Webster exhibited this highest quality of human nature.

On this point you will excuse me for repeating what I said on another occasion:

"One of the highest exhibitions of the moral sublime the world ever witnessed, was that of Daniel Webster, when, in an open barouche in the streets of Boston, he proclaimed, in substance, to a vast assembly of his constituents—unwilling hearers—that 'they had conquered an uncongenial clime; they had conquered a sterile soil; they had conquered the winds and currents of the Ocean; they had conquered most of the elements of nature; but they must yet learn to conquer their prejudices!' I know of no more fitting incident or scene in the life of that wonderful man, '*Clarus et vir Fortissimus*,' for perpetuating the memory of the true greatness of his character, on canvas or in marble, than a representation of him as he then and there stood and spoke! It was an exhibition of moral grandeur surpassing that of Aristides when he said, 'O! Athenians, what Themistocles recommends would be greatly to your interests, but it would be unjust!'"

Such exhibitious of moral courage his great rivals never gave—never had occasion, perhaps, to give. But you see the estimation in which I hold Mr. Webster. I did entertain for him the highest esteem and admiration I did not agree with him in his exposition of the Constitution in 1833, but I did fully and cordially agree with him in his exposition in 1839, and 1851. According to that the Constitution was and is a Compact between the States.

But to return from this digression. Whether Mr. Webster ever did or did not modify the opinions expressed in the speech you have read is not the question before us, that is what is the true construction of the Constitution on the point under immediate consideration. We have seen the exposition of the Supreme Court of the United States, which Mr. Webster maintained was the final arbiter, and we have seen the exposition of the United States Senate, that is the exposition of the States themselves by their ambassadors in 1839. Now, in addition to this, I wish to call your special attention to a like exposition by the same high authority, as late as 1860, not twelve months before the war began.

Mr. Jefferson Davis, of whom and about whom we shall have much to say as we proceed, submitted to the Senate, on the 29th of February, a series of resolutions, declaratory of the principles of the Government on the very subjects out of which the war sprung. He was then Senator from Mississippi. These Resolutions passed the Senate May 24, 1860. Here they are. I call your special attention to the first and second of these.

"1. *Resolved,* That, in the adoption of the Federal Constitution, the States adopting the same, acted severally as free and independent Sovereignties, delegating a portion of their powers to be exercised by the Federal Government for the increased security of each against dangers, domestic as well as foreign; and that any intermeddling by any one or more States, or by a combination of their citizens, with the domestic institutions of the others, on any pretext whatever, political, moral, or religious, with a view to their disturbance or subversion, is in violation of the Constitution, insulting to the States so interfered with, endangers their domestic peace and tranquillity—objects for which the Constitution was formed—and, by necessary consequence, tends to weaken and destroy the Union itself.

"2. *Resolved.* That negro Slavery, as it exists in fifteen States of this Union, composes an important portion of their domestic institution, inherited from their ancestors, and existing at the adoption of the Constitution, by which it is recognized as constituting an important element in the apportionment of powers among the States, and that no change of opinion or feeling on the part of the non-slaveholding States of the Union, in relation to this institution, can justify them or their citizens in open or covert attacks thereon, with a view to its overthrow; and that all such attacks are in manifest violation of the mutual and solemn pledge to protect and defend each other, given by the States respectively on entering into the Constitutional Compact which formed the Union, and are a manifest breach of faith, and a violation of the most solemn obligations.

"3. *Resolved,* That the Union of these States rests on the equality of rights and privileges among its members; and that it is especially the duty of the Senate, which represents the States in their Sovereign capacity, to resist all attempts to discriminate either in relation to persons or property in the Territories, which are the common possessions of the United States, so as to give advantages to the citizens of one State which are not equally assured to those of every other State.

"4. *Resolved,* That neither Congress nor a Territorial Legislature, whether by direct legislation or legislation of an indirect and unfriendly character, possesses power to annul or impair the Constitutional right of any citizen of the United States, to take his slave property into the common Territories, and there hold and enjoy the same while the territorial condition remains.

"5. *Resolved,* That, if experience should at any time prove that the Judicial and Executive authority do not possess means to insure adequate protection to Constitutional rights in a Territory, and if the Territorial Government should fail or refuse to provide the necessary remedies for that purpose, it will be the duty of Congress to supply such deficiency.

"6. *Resolved,* That the inhabitants of a Territory of the United States, when they rightfully form a Constitution to be admitted as a State into the Union, may, then, for the first time, like the people of a State, when forming a new Constitution, decide for themselves whether slavery, as a domestic institution, shall be maintained or prohibited within their jurisdiction; and 'they shall be admitted into the Union, with or without slavery, as their Constitution may prescribe at the time of their admission.'

"7. *Resolved,* That the provision of the Constitution for the rendition of fugitives from service or labor, without the adoption of which the Union could not have been formed, and the laws of 1793 and 1850, which were enacted to secure its execution, and the main features of which, being similar, bear the impress of nearly seventy years of sanction by the highest judicial authority, should be honestly and faithfully observed and maintained by all who enjoy the benefits of our Compact of Union, and that all acts of individuals or of State Legislatures to defeat the purpose or nullify the requirements of that provision, and the laws made in pursuance of it, are hostile in character, subversive of the Constitution, and revolutionary in their effect."

These Resolutions decidedly affirmed that the Constitution was formed by States—independent Sovereignties—that the Government established by it is a Federal Government—one founded on Compact, and that any interference, openly or covertly, directly or indirectly, by any of the States or their citizens, with the black population in any other of the States, or with the domestic institutions of any of the States against their own internal policy, would be a manifest breach of plighted faith—and, further, that all acts of the individual citizens of any of the States, as well as of the Legislatures of any of the States, intended to defeat or nullify that clause of the Constitution requiring the rendition of fugitives from service, were hostile to and subversive of the Constitution itself.

Judge Bynum. Though these Resolutions did pass the Senate, the vote on them was nothing but a party vote. Mr. Davis, in introducing them, was but paving the way for his subsequent course. This was but part of his scheme of Secession, which he and his associates had been concocting for years. Every Republican in the Senate, at the time, voted against these Resolutions, while every Democrat, in like manner, voted for them.

MR. STEPHENS. So you might say of Mr. Calhoun's motives and intentions, in 1838. Such motives, I know, have been attributed to him. Now, I think all accusations of this kind were exceedingly unjust to him, and so, I think in this case, you do great injustice to Mr. Davis.

You are mistaken in saying that the vote upon these Resolutions was a strict party vote. Here is the vote. There were thirty-six Senators in favor of the first Resolution and only nineteen against it;* nearly two to one on the *per capita* vote. Among the yeas I see James A. Pearce, John P. Kennedy and John J. Crittenden. When were they ever considered or looked upon as Democrats in the sense in which you use that term? They certainly did not belong to the same political organization with Mr. Davis at that time, and had no sympathy with its bare party objects. While the *per capita* vote is so striking, if we look at it by States it will appear even more so.† From a view of it, in this respect, it appears that nineteen States voted for the

---

* *Yeas.*—Messrs. Benjamin, Bigler, Bragg, Bright, Brown, Chestnut, C. C. Clay, Clingman, Crittenden, Davis, Fitzpatrick, Green, Gwin, Hammond, Hemphill, Hunter, Iverson, Johnson, of Arkansas, Johnson, of Tennessee, Kennedy, Lane, of Oregon, Latham, Mallory, Mason, Nicholson, Pearce, Polk, Powell, Pugh, Rice, Sebastian, Slidell, Thompson, of New Jersey, Toombs, Wigfall and Yulee,—36. *Nays,*—Messrs. Bingham, Chandler, Clark, Collamer, Dixon, Doolittle, Fessenden, Foot, Foster, Grimes, Hale, Hamlin, Harlan, King, Simmons, Sumner, Ten Eyck, Wade, and Wilson,—19.

† Vote by States on the first Resolution:

Yeas,—Alabama, Arkansas, California, Florida, Georgia, Indiana, Kentucky, Louisiana, Missouri, Mississippi, Minnesota, Maryland, North Carolina, Oregon, Pennsylvania, South Carolina, Texas, Tennessee, and Virginia,—19. *Nays,*—Connecticut, Iowa, Maine, Massachusetts, Michigan, New York, New Hampshire, Rhode Island, Vermont, and Wisconsin,—10. *Divided,*—Ohio and New Jersey,—2. *Not voting,*—Delaware and Illinois,—2.

first Resolution, only ten voted against it, while two were divided, and two did not vote. Had the two absent States, Delaware and Illinois, been present, the vote would have been twenty for it, ten against it, and three divided; for Douglas, of Illinois, would have voted for it, and Trumbull of the same State would have voted against it. Would it not have been a strange spectacle to see twenty of the thirty-three States in Senatorial Council, taking the initiative step for a dismemberment of the Union? Is such a supposition reasonable? Can any one suppose that these States, acting through their Senators, could have had any such design? Does not the object of these Resolutions clearly appear to have been just the reverse? Was not this simply but earnestly to declare the nature of the Government, and the only way in which the Union, under it, could be preserved? The vote on the seventh Resolution, looking to the *per capita* vote, or the vote by States, is equally striking. On the *per capita* the yeas were thirty-six, and nays six. By States the vote was twenty for the Resolution, and only four against it. One State divided, and eight not voting.*

An important fact, in connection with these Resolutions, should ever be borne in mind. That is that every one of these ten States, whose Senators voted against them, had, by their State Legislatures, as we shall see, openly and intentionally disregarded their obliga-

* Vote on the seventh Resolution:

Yeas,—Alabama, Arkansas, California, Florida, Georgia, Indiana, Kentucky, Louisiana, Missouri, Maryland, Minnesota, Mississippi, New Jersey, North Carolina, Oregon, Pennsylvania, South Carolina, Texas, Tennessee, and Virginia,—20. *Nays*,—Massachusetts, Michigan, New Hampshire, and Vermont,—4. *Divided*,—Ohio,—1. *Not voting*,—Connecticut, Delaware, Iowa, Illinois, Maine, New York, Rhode Island and Wisconsin,—8.

tions, under that clause of the Constitution, which required the rendition of fugitives from service, and which acts, on their part, a large majority of the States thus by their resolves declared to be a breach of their plighted faith. Indeed, all these ten States were then under the influence of those who held that the Constitution was but "a Covenant with Death and an agreement with Hell."* Is it just or fair to Mr. Davis to say that he was meditating or planning Secession at that time, any more than it was the design of the nineteen States which actually agreed with him in the sentiments of the Resolutions?

Is it not more in accordance with strict justice, to say nothing of that charity which should ever be exercised in investigations of this sort, to suppose that his object was to preserve the Union by having all the members to conform their action to its plain and unmistakable provisions? If there were any *dis*-union sentiments then existing to whom should they be rightly attributed? Should they be attributed to those States and those Senators who were for maintaining the Union on the principles upon which it was formed, or those who were for maintaining a Government, barely, upon totally different principles? Three of these Resolutions of the series offered by Mr. Davis, and which passed the Senate, I am frank to say, I thought, at the time, though not then in public life, and still think, ought not to have been brought forward.

MAJOR HEISTER. Which ones are they?

MR. STEPHENS. The fourth, fifth, and sixth.

PROF. NORTON. These are the ones that relate to the doctrine of Popular or Squatter Sovereignty, as it was called. What objections had you to them?

---

* *Lunt's Origin of the War*. p. 109.

MR. STEPHENS. My objections related solely to the policy of introducing them. They presented questions which tended to divide and thus weaken the Constitutional Party—the State Rights, State Sovereignty Party—the great party throughout the country, everywhere, whatever cognomen its various subdivisions bore, which was for maintaining the Constitution, and the Union under it, as it was made and handed down to them from their ancestors. It seemed to me to be exceedingly inexpedient and impolitic as a matter of statesmanship to divide those thus cordially united on the more essential and vital principles of the Government, upon questions of so little practical importance, especially at such a crisis as that was in public affairs. The new Anti-Constitutional Party, as it might in my view very properly be styled, was then thoroughly organized under the old but misapplied name of Republican, and it should have been a matter of the utmost importance with the real friends of the Constitution, and Union under it, not to divide their ranks upon such questions as those embraced in these three Resolutions. This, in short, was my view of that subject. The only hope of the new party was in a division of its opponents. In case this division should become complete and irreconcileable I saw that a rupture of that party was an inevitable result, and with its rupture a rupture of the Union, upon the principles upon which it was formed, seemed to me to be equally inevitable. I am equally frank in stating that there were some amongst us who meant to use this question for no purpose whatever, but to produce such a rupture both of the party and of the Union. I did not, however, then or now, think that Mr. Davis belonged to that class. No man, in my opinion, which I give you candidly, is less understood at the North, and perhaps to a great extent, at the South, too, than Mr. Davis, on this question. I may be wrong, but I assure you I never regarded him as a Secessionist, properly speaking; that is, I always regarded him as a strong Union man in sentiment, so long as the Union was maintained on the principles upon which it was founded. He was, without doubt, a thorough State Rights, State Sovereignty man. He believed in the right of Secession; but what I mean to say is, that in my opinion, he was an ardent supporter of the Union on the principles, as he understood them, upon which, and for which, the Union was formed. There were, as I have said, many public men amongst us who after these Resolutions passed the Senate, and after the Presidential canvass was opened upon them, and the various issues presented in the Party platforms of the day, as we shall see, who were openly for Secession in case Mr. Lincoln should be elected upon the principles on which he was nominated. But Mr. Davis, as far as I know or believe, did not belong even to this class. If he was in favor of Secession barely upon the grounds of Mr. Lincoln's election, I am not aware of it. He certainly made no speech or wrote any letter for the public during that canvass that indicated such views or purposes. I never saw a word from him recommending Secession as the proper remedy against threatening dangers until he joined in the general letter of the Southern Senators and Representatives in Congress to their States, advising them to take that course.

This was in December, 1860, and not until after it was ascertained in the Committee of the Senate, on Mr. Crittenden's proposition for quieting the apprehensions and alarm of the Southern States from the accession of Mr. Lincoln to power, that the Republicans, his supporters, would not agree to that measure. It is well known that he and Mr. Toombs both declared their willingness to accept the adoption of Mr. Crittenden's measure as a final settlement of the controversy between the States and sections, if the party coming into power would agree to it in the same spirit and with the same assurance. It was after it was known that this party would not enter into any such settlement, or give any assurance for the future, that Mr. Davis joined other Southern Senators and Representatives advising the Southern States to secede, as the proper remedy for what he and they considered impending dangers to their rights, security, and future welfare. There is nothing in Mr. Davis's life, or public conduct, that I am aware of, that affords just grounds for believing that he ever desired a separation of the States, if the principles of the Union, under the Constitution, had been faithfully adhered to by all the Parties to it. These were the sentiments of all his speeches, in Congress and out of it, as far as I have ever seen, even down to his last most touching leave-taking address to the Senate!

But all this is digressing from the matter before us. We shall have enough of these questions hereafter. The point we are now considering is not the object or motive of Mr. Davis in offering these Resolutions. It is the exposition actually made by the Senate of the United States, nineteen States to ten States, of the real nature and character of the Government. Mr. Davis was but the instrument, the draftsman, through whom this overwhelming majority of the States announced for themselves the nature of the bonds of their Union! This exposition was as late as 1860, and substantially the same that had been given by the same August Body of ambassadors representing their Sovereignty in 1838, twenty-two years before! That exposition was that the Constitution is a Compact between Sovereign States.

So, after this very long talk, wandering the while far from the point, we finally return to the same place at which we had arrived before taking up Mr. Webster's speech. We now stand just where we did then. We have gone through with his great argument and Mr. Calhoun's reply, to which no rejoinder was ever made. We have seen that the Senate, by a nearly three fourths vote of the States, in 1838, and by a vote of nearly two to one, in 1860, sustained that construction of the Constitution which was set forth in the first of Mr. Calhoun's Resolutions in 1833, and which I maintain. The decisions of the Supreme Court referred to, sustain the same view also. We have seen further, that Mr. Webster himself, in his riper years, held that the Union was "*a Union of States.*" That it was founded upon "Compact," and that "a bargain cannot be broken on one side and still bind the other side."

Does it not, therefore, clearly appear from these high authorities, and even upon the authority of Mr. Webster himself, that the Government of the United States is a Federal Government, or as Washington styled it, a Confederated Republic? What further, if any thing, have you to say against this as an indisputably established conclusion?

COLLOQUY X.

NULLIFICATION—GENERAL JACKSON ON THE UNION—JEFFERSON ON THE UNION—KENTUCKY RESOLUTIONS OF 1798—SETTLEMENT OF THE NULLIFICATION ISSUE—THE DEBATES IN THE SENATE—WILKINS, CALHOUN, GRUNDY, BIBB AND CLAY—THE COMPROMISE ON THE PROTECTIVE POLICY OF 1833—THE WORKINGS OF THE FEDERAL SYSTEM UNDER THE PRINCIPLES ON WHICH THAT COMPROMSIE WAS MADE—THE GREAT PROSPERITY THAT FOLLOWED—NO PRESIDENT FROM JEFFERSON TO LINCOLN ELECTED, WHO DID NOT HOLD THE GOVERNMENT TO BE A COMPACT BETWEEN SOVEREIGN STATES—MADISON, MONROE, JOHN QUINCY ADAMS, JACKSON, VAN BUREN, HARRISON, POLK, TAYLOR, PIERCE, AND BUCHANAN, ALL SO HELD IT TO BE—THE SUPREME COURT NOT THE UMPIRE BETWEEN THE STATES AND THE GENERAL GOVERNMENT—MADISON, BIBB, MARSHALL, AND LIVINGSTON ON THIS SUBJECT—GENERAL JACKSON'S EXPLANATION OF THE DOCTRINES OF THE PROCLAMATION—HE HELD THE CONSTITUTION TO BE A COMPACT BETWEEN SOVEREIGN STATES—HIS FAREWELL ADDRESS.

MAJOR HEISTER. I have listened with interest to this discussion as it has progressed thus far. Several new views, I candidly confess, have been presented by you. But I am not prepared to assent to your conclusion as a truth indisputably established. I was never a disciple of the school of either Story, Webster, or Calhoun. I was born, bred, and brought up a Jeffersonian Democrat.

MR. STEPHENS. So was I.

MAJOR HEISTER. Well, then, Andrew Jackson was the embodiment of the principles in which I was reared. I am, therefore, a disciple of the School of the Hero of New Orleans as well as of the Sage of Monticello! I have never devoted much time to the study of the questions and principles you have been discussing, and do not profess any very accurate acquaintance with or information upon them; but I have always understood very well, that General Jackson held, that the Union must be preserved. That he put down Nullification, and the whole theory of the Government attempted to be established by Mr. Calhoun. Now, I am a Union man upon the principles of General Jackson. His proclamation against Nullification is my political text-book. Have you got that Proclamation?

MR. STEPHENS. Yes, here it is, in the Statesman's Manual, vol. 2, page 794.

MAJOR HEISTER. Well, did not General Jackson, in it, denounce the proceedings in South Carolina as treasonable, and did he not, by his Roman firmness and decision, at the time, promptly quell the Rebellion in its incipiency, then brewing in that State, and thus save the Union and maintain the Constitution?

What Story and Motley and Webster said about the Constitution has but little weight with me. If Webster did not answer Calhoun, General Jackson, at least, silenced him, and put an end to Nullification and all other attempts to overthrow the Government, for more than a quarter of a century. Here is the Proclamation, which is, as I have said, my text-book on this subject. It is too long for me to read the whole of it, nor is it necessary. I call your attention to only certain portions of it.

MR. STEPHENS. Before looking into the Proclamation I must set you right on some matters of fact.

MAJOR HEISTER. How so? What matters of fact?

MR. STEPHENS. The statement by you that General Jackson put down Nullification and silenced Mr. Calhoun.

MAJOR HEISTER. Are not these statements correct? Do you join issue on them?

Mr. Stephens. I most certainly do. Nullification in South Carolina, whether it be considered as an incipient Rebellion, or as a proper and peaceable mode of obtaining a redress of grievances as its advocates contended, was never put down or quelled by General Jackson or any body else. Its further prosecution was abandoned by those who initiated it as a mode of redress, when the wrongs and grievances complained of were redressed by Congress, and not till then.

It is not my purpose to defend the doctrine of Nullification, or to say how far General Jackson as President was right in issuing a Proclamation declaring his purpose to execute the laws in that instance. It is proper, however, to state that the primary and leading object of its advocates was not Secession or Disunion. It was just the contrary. But so subtle were the principles upon which it was founded, that it was never understood by the country. South Carolina, as well as a number of the other States, held, that the power to levy duties upon imports, not with a view to revenue, but to protect and aid particular classes, was not delegated to the Congress. Nullification, without Secession, was a remedy she resorted to, to defeat the operation of protective laws passed by the Congress. Many who believed in the perfect right of Secession, and looked upon that as the proper remedy in such cases of abuse of power as South Carolina complained of, were utterly opposed to Nullification. How a State could remain in the Union, *with Senators and Representatives* in Congress, and yet *refuse obedience to the laws of Congress not set aside by the Judiciary as unconstitutional*, was, to this class, utterly incomprehensible! But the merits of this doctrine are not now before us. Suffice it to say I was never an advocate of it. And all I mean now to say on this point is, that whether right or wrong in principle, it was never abandoned until the protective policy, which it was resorted to to change, was abandoned by the Government. The Proclamation did not either put it down or silence its advocates or defenders. Mr. Calhoun's speech, which we have read, was made after that. The giving way was on the part of the Federal Government and not the State Government.

A brief statement of the matter is this. The Nullification Ordinance of South Carolina, which was to test the question, was passed the latter part of November, 1832, to go into effect on the 1st of February, 1833. The Proclamation was issued on the 11th of December, 1832. Congress was in session: on the 21st of January, 1833, a Bill was introduced to meet the provisions of the Nullification Ordinance of the State, by counteracting Legislation and clothing the President with the necessary power to execute it, putting at his disposal the whole of the land and naval forces. This was called the Force Bill. The Constitutionality of the provisions of this Bill was denied by many who did not hold to the doctrine of Nullification. Unusual excitement prevailed. A great debate sprung up—the greatest since the formation of the Government, for then principles were discussed. The speeches of Mr. Webster and Mr. Calhoun constitute part of this debate. Mr. Calhoun offered his Resolutions the day after the Force Bill was introduced. Serious fears were entertained that if the Bill should pass, and become a law, while South Carolina held the position she did, that a collision would take place between the United States forces and the forces of the State; and that war would ensue. For, though South Carolina did not, in her Ordinance, contemplate the use of any force in the *modus operandi* of her chosen remedy, yet she declared her intention to be, to repel force by force, in case the United States should resort to force.

We can get some glimpses as to the position of the parties from the debates in the Senate at this time. Here is the opening of the discussion by Mr. Wilkins, who introduced the Force Bill.*

"Mr. Wilkins. All have agreed that on the first of next month, this solemn epoch will arrive. The ordinance of the State of South Carolina—the test law—that unprecedented law called the Replevin Act—and the law for the protection of the citizens of South Carolina—all looking to one object; all go into operation on that day. He had said all these pointed to one object. To what object did they point? The answer was simple. To nullification of existing laws: To violent resistance to the United States."

"Mr. Calhoun said he could not sit silent and permit such erroneous constructions to go forth. South Carolina had never contemplated violent resistance to the laws of the United States."

"Mr. Wilkins was at a loss to understand how any man could read the various acts of the State of South Carolina, and not say that they must lead, necessarily lead, in their consequences, to violent measures. He understood the Senator from South Carolina (Mr. Calhoun) the other day as acknowledging that there was military array in South Carolina, but contending that it followed and did not precede the array of force by the United States."

"Mr. Calhoun said he admitted that there was military preparation, not array."

"Mr. Wilkins. If we examine the measures taken by the Administration, in reference to the present crisis, it would be found that they were not at all of that military character to justify the measures of South Carolina which it was alleged had followed them."

* *Niles's Register*, vol. xliii. *Supp.* p. 53.

"Mr. Calhoun said that South Carolina was undoubtedly preparing to resist force by force. But let the United States withdraw her forces from its borders, and lay this Bill upon the table, and her preparations would cease."

"Mr. Wilkins resumed: That is, sir, if we do not oppose any of her movements all will be right. If we fold our arms and exhibit a perfect indifference whether the laws of the Union are obeyed or not, all will be quiet!"

"Mr. Calhoun. Who relies upon force in this controversy? I have insisted upon it that South Carolina relied altogether upon civil process, and that, if the General Government resorts to force, then only will South Carolina rely upon force. If force be introduced by either party, upon that party will fall the responsibility."

"Mr. Wilkins. The General Government will not appeal, in the first instance, to force. It will appeal to the patriotism of South Carolina—to that magnanimity of which she boasts so much."

"Mr. Calhoun. I am sorry that South Carolina cannot appeal to the sense of justice of the General Government."

"Mr. Wilkins. The Government will appeal to that political sense which exhorts obedience to the laws of the country, as the first duty of the citizen. It will appeal to the moral force in the community. If that appeal be in vain, it will appeal to the judiciary. If the mild arm of the judiciary be not sufficient to execute the laws, it will call out the civil force to sustain the laws. If that be insufficient, God save and protect us from the last resort. But if the evil does come npon the country, *who* is responsible for it? If *force* be brought in to the aid of law, who, I ask of gentlemen, is responsible for it to the people of the United States? That is the question. Talk of it as you please, mystify matters as you will, theorize as you may, pile up abstract propositions to any extent, at last the question resolves itself into one of obedience or resistance of the laws—in other words, of Union or dis-Union."

Mr. Grundy, of Tennessee, presented the case in these words:

"The true question before the Senate is, shall the State of South Carolina be permitted to put down the revenue laws of the Union, prevent their execution within her limits, and no effort be made by this Government to maintain the majesty of the laws, and to counteract the measures adopted by that State to defeat and evade them."*

The debate so commenced became exceedingly interesting as it progressed. It furnishes a rich mine for exploration at this time. Let us dig a little further into it, and sample some other fragments of its *strata*.

In the Register (*Niles*), vol. xliii, Sup. pages 63 to 80, we have the following specimens, from Judge Bibb, of Kentucky:

"Mr. Bibb said it seemed to him that a false issue was presented. The question of war against South Carolina is presented as the only alternative. The issue was false. The first question is between justice and injustice. Shall we do justice to the States who have united with South Carolina in complaint and remonstrance against the injustice and oppression of the tariff? Shall we cancel the obligations of justice to five other States, because of the impetuosity and impatience of South Carolina under wrong and oppression? The question ought not to be whether we have the physical power to crush South Carolina, but whether it is not our duty to heal her dis-

* *Niles's Register*, vol. lxiii, Supp. page 214.

contents, to conciliate a member of the Union, to give peace and happiness to the adjoining States which have made common cause with South Carolina so far as complaint and remonstrance go. Are we to rush into a war with South Carolina to compel her to remain in the Union? Shall we keep her in the Union by force of arms, for the purpose of compelling her submission to the tariff laws of which she complains? How shall we do this? By the naval and military force of the United States, combined with the militia? Where will the militia come from? Will Virginia, will North Carolina, will Georgia, Mississippi, or Alabama, assist to enforce submission to the tariff laws, the justice and Constitutionality of which they have, by resolutions on your files, denied over and over again? Will those States assist to forge chains by which they themselves are to be bound? Is this to be expected, in the ordinary course of chance and probability? * * *

"My creed is that, by the Declaration of Independence, the States were declared to be free and independent States, thirteen in number, not one Nation—that the old Articles of Confederation united them as distinct States, not as one people:—that the treaty of peace, of 1783, acknowledged their independence as States, not as a single Nation; that the Federal Constitution was framed by States, submitted to the States, and adopted by the States, as distinct Nations or States, not as a single Nation or people.

"By canvassing these conflicting opinions, we shall the better unerstand how far South Carolina has transcended her reserved powers as a Sovereign State—how far we can lawfully make war upon her—and whether we, or South Carolina, are likely to transcend the barriers provided in the Constitution of the United States.

"I do not, said Mr. Bibb, wish to be misunderstood. In these times of political excitement, whatever is spoken or reported, may be misrepresented. He wished it to be understood, that he did not approve of the doctrines of Carolina, in their full extent. But, if we make war upon her, to put down her principles, we must be sure that those principles are bad and dangerous.

"What are her principles? That she has a right to judge, in the last resort, in all questions concerning her rights; or, to put it in still stronger language—if Congress attempts to enforce the revenue laws, she will resume her independence and Sovereignty. He did not approve of this course on the part of South Carolina, under all the circumstances. Still, he would like to know when and where South Carolina surrendered the right to secede from the Union, in case of a dangerous invasion of her rights by the Federal Government. In the solemn declaration of principles with which some of the States accompanied the adoption of the Constitution, this right it declared to be inalienable. There was too much truth in the axiom contained in many State Constitutions, that 'a frequent recurrence to first principles is necessary to the maintenance of liberty.' Here Mr. Bibb read a passage from the Declaration of Independence: 'We hold these truths to be self-evident, that all men are created equal, that they are endowed by their Creator with certain unalienable rights; that among these are life, liberty, and the pursuit of happiness.' Now, if South Carolina has mistaken her injury and her remedy, shall we make war upon her, and put down the principles asserted by the Declaration of Independence. The ratification, by the several States, of the Constitution, adopted the same principles; and they were accepted as forming a part of the Constitution. Mr. Bibb here referred to the declaration accompanying the ratification of the Constitution by the State of New York—that 'all power was derived from the people, and could be resumed by the people whenever it became necessary for their happiness.' They go on to say, 'under these impressions, and declaring that the rights aforesaid cannot be abridged or violated, and that the explanations aforesaid are consistent with the said Constitution; and in confidence, that the amendments which shall have been proposed to the said Constitution, will receive an early and mature consideration, we, the said Delegates, in the name and in the behalf of the people of the State of New York, do, by these presents, assent to, and ratify the said Constitution,' etc.

"The reservations of the State of Rhode Island were of the same tenor; and he went on to read her declaration. * * * Mr. Bibb next adverted to the Articles of the old Confederation. They declared the Union should be perpetual, and that no alteration should be made in the Articles, but by consent of Congress, and of the Legislatures of each State of the Union. Here the Compact was declared to be perpetual, and yet we undertook to arrest it without the consent of any State. The Constitution provides that when nine States have ratified the Constitution, it shall go into operation. Why were the fundamental Articles of the old Confederation violated? How could nine States be supposed to combine, and throw the other four out of the Union? They claimed the right, under the principles adopted in the Declaration of Independence, to alter, reform, and amend their form of Government as much and as often as such change was necessary, in their opinion, to the right ends of Government, the interests of the people. The people have an unalienable, indefeasible right to make a Government which shall be adequate to their ends. Upon this *principle* it was that the *old Compact* was destroyed, and a *new one* made.

"We are now about to make war upon a State, which formed a part of the old Confederaticn, and became a party to the new Constitution, with an express reservation of powers not expressly delegated by her. * * *

"Mr. Bibb asked if it was *possible* that the people of the States, in adopting this Constitution, could have *intended to surrender absolutely and forever the right which they had obtained by a Revolution? So well did they understand the difficulty of shaking off the powers which once enchained us, and so jealous were they of their newly acquired freedom, that they took care to say in the Constitution, that the powers not delegated by them, were reserved to themselves.* * * * It stood on record, that one of the Roman provinces rebelled against the Government, again and again. The leaders were subdued, and many of the Senators of this party, and many of the people were taken or killed. The conquered province sent ambassadors to Rome, and when these ambassadors appeared, the consul asked of them, 'what punishment did they deserve?' The answer of the ambassador was, 'such punishment as he deserves who contends for liberty.' It was demanded of them by the Senate, 'whether, if terms of peace were granted them, they would abide faithfully by them?' They replied emphatically, that 'if the terms were good and just, they would faithfully abide by them, and the peace should be perpetual; but if they were unjust, the peace could barely last until they could return to their homes to tell the people what they were.' The Roman Senate were pleased with the spirit which was thus exhibited, declared that 'they who thus contended for freedom, were worthy to be Roman citizens,' and gave them all which they demanded.

"He wished then an American Senate to imitate their noble example. It was a cause worthy of imitation. He invoked the Senate to sift the complaints of South Carolina, for they alone were worthy to be American citizens who contended zealously for the principles of civil liberty, and are not fit subjects to be denounced and accursed."

This is enough of the general debates to show the temper of the times, the contrariety of sentiments existing in various quarters, and the grounds for the apprehensions so universally prevailing that a collision might ensue and the peace of the country be disturbed.

Meantime hopes were entertained that Congress would abandon the protective policy, and strong efforts were made to get South Carolina to postpone the day of final action on her Ordinance, to give time for Congress to grant the relief sought. Mr. Verplanck, of New York, had introduced a Bill in the House of Representatives reducing the duties. This was on the 28th December, 1832. The State of Virginia, who sympathized thoroughly with South Carolina in her complaints against the injustice of the Tariff laws, but who did not agree with her as to the remedy she had adopted to get rid of them by, sent one of her most distinguished statesmen, Benjamin Watkins Leigh, as a Commissioner to intercede, and to urge South Carolina to rescind her Ordinance, or at least to postpone action on it until the close of the first session of of the next Congress. Mr. Leigh's high mission was successful in part. South Carolina agreed, in view of the prospect of Congress reducing the duties to a *revenue standard*, to postpone action on her Ordinance until the close of that session of Congress, which was on the 4th of March.*

* The following letter was addressed by Governor Hayne to Mr. Leigh. --*Niles's Register*, vol. lxiii, p. 435.

It was at this stage of affairs that Mr. Clay, who was the author of the protective policy known as "the American system," brought forward his celebrated compromise of 1833, upon the subject of the Tariff laws. He gave

---

"Executive Department, *Charleston, 5th February*, 1833.

"Sir :—I have had the honor to receive your letter of the 5th instant, and in compliance with the request therein contained, communicated its contents, together with the Resolutions of the Legislature of Virginia, of which you are the bearer, to General James Hamilton, Jr., the President of the Convention. I have now the pleasure of inclosing you his answer, by which you will perceive, that in compliance with the request conveyed through you, he will promptly re-assemble the Convention, to to whom the Resolutions adopted by the Legislature of Virginia will be submitted, and by whom they will doubtless receive the most friendly and respectful consideration. In giving you this information, it is due to the interest manifested by Virginia, in the existing controversy between South Carolina and the Federal Government, to state, that as soon as it came to be understood that the Legislature of Virginia had taken up the subject in a spirit of friendly interposition, and that a Bill for the modification of the tariff was actually before Congress, it was determined, by the common consent of our fellow citizens, that no case should be made under our Ordinance until after the adjournment of the present Congress. The propriety of a still further suspension, can of course only be determined by the Convention itself. With regard to the solicitude expressed by the Legislature of Virginia, that there should be '*no appeal to force*' on 'the part of either the General Government or of the Government of South Carolina in the controversy now unhappily existing between them,' and that 'the General Government and the Government of South Carolina, and all persons acting under the authority of either, should carefully abstain from any and all acts whatever, which may be calculated to disturb the tranquillity of the country, or endanger the existence of the Union;' it is proper that I should distinctly and emphatically state, that no design now exists, or ever has existed, on the part of the Government of South Carolina, or any portion of the people, to 'appeal to force,' unless that measure should be rendered indispensable in repelling unlawful violence.

"I beg leave to assure you, and through you the people of Virginia, and our other sister States, that no acts have been done, or are contemplated by South Carolina, her constituted authorities, or citizens, in reference to the present crisis, but such as are deemed measures of precaution. Her preparations are altogether defensive in their character, and notwithstanding the concentration of large naval and military forces in this harbor, and the adoption of other measures on the part of the General

notice of his intention to ask leave to introduce such a Bill on the 11th of February, and did bring it forward on the next day, the 12th.

His object was two-fold, as stated by him. One was to preserve the manufacturing interest from that ruin which would attend an immediate repeal of the protective duties; the other was by yielding the principle of protection to prevent that collision between the Federal and State Governments which was then so seriously apprehended.

He said, on introducing it (I read still from *Niles's Register*, vol. xliii, page 411):

"I yesterday, sir, gave notice that I should ask leave to introduce a bill to modify the various acts imposing duties on imports. I, at the same time, added, that I should, with the permission of the Senate, offer an explanation of the principle on which that bill is founded. I owe, sir, an apology to the Senate for this course of action, because, although strictly parliamentary, it is, nevertheless, out of the usual practice of this body; but it is a course which I trust that the Senate will deem to be justified by the interesting nature of the subject. I rise, sir, on this occasion, actuated by no motive of a private nature, by no personal feelings, and for no personal ob-

---

Government, which may be considered as of a character threatening the peace and endangering the tranquillity and safety of the State, we shall continue to exercise the utmost possible forbearance, acting strictly on the defensive, firmly resolved to commit no act of violence, but prepared as far as our means may extend, to resist aggression. Nothing, you may be assured, would give me personally, and the people of South Carolina, more satisfaction than that the existing controversy should be happily adjusted, on just and liberal terms; and I beg you to be assured, that nothing can be further from our desire, than to disturb the tranquillity of the country or endanger the existence of the Union.

"Accept, sir, for yourself, the assurance of the high consideration of yours, respectfully and truly,

"ROBERT Y. HAYNE.

"To the Hon. B. W. Leigh."

jects; but exclusively in obedience to a *sense of the duty which I owe to my country.* I trust, therefore, that no one will anticipate on my part any ambitious display of such humble powers as I may possess. It is sincerely my purpose to present a plain, unadorned, and naked statement of facts connected with the measure which I shall have the honor to propose, and with the condition of the country. * * * In presenting the modification of the Tariff laws, which I am now about to submit, I have two great objects in view. My first object looks to the Tariff. I am compelled to express the opinion, formed after the most deliberate reflection, and on full survey of the whole country, that, whether rightfully or wrongfully, the Tariff stands in imminent danger. If it should even be preserved during this session, it must fall at the next session. By what circumstances, and through what cause, has arisen the necessity for this change in the policy of our country, I will not pretend now to elucidate. Others there are who may differ from the impressions which my mind has received upon this point. Owing, however, to a variety of concurrent causes, the Tariff, as it now exists, is in imminent danger, and if the system can be preserved beyond the next session, it must be by some means not now within the reach of human sagacity. The fall of that policy, sir, would be productive of consequences calamitous indeed. When I look to the variety of interests which are involved, to the number of individuals interested, the amount of capital invested, the value of the buildings erected, and the whole arrangement of the business for the prosecution of the various branches of the manufacturing art which have sprung up under the fostering care of this Government, I cannot contemplate any evil equal to the sudden overthrow of all those interests. History can produce no parallel to the extent of the mischief which would be produced by such a disaster. The repeal of the Edict of Nantes itself was nothing in comparison with it. That condemned to exile, and brought to ruin a great number of persons. The most respectable portion of the population of France were condemned to exile and ruin by that measure. But, in my opinion, sir, the sudden repeal of the Tariff policy would bring ruin and destruction on the whole people of this country. There is no evil, in my opinion, equal to the consequences which would result from such a catastrophe.

"What, sir, are the complaints which unhappily divide the people of this great country? On the one hand, it is said by those who are opposed to the Tariff, that it unjustly taxes a portion of the people and paralyzes their industry; that it is to be a perpetual operation; that there is to be no end to the system; which, right or wrong, is to be urged to their inevitable ruin. And what is the just complaint, on the other hand, of those who support the Tariff? It is, that the policy of the Government is vacillating and uncertain, and that there is no stability in our legislation. Before one set of books are fairly opened, it becomes necessary to close them, and to open a new set. Before a law can be tested by experiment, another is passed. Before the present law has gone into operation, before it is yet nine months old, passed as it was under circumstances of extraordinary deliberation, the fruit of nine months' labor, before we know any thing of its experimental effects, and even before it commences its operations, we are required to repeal it. On one side we are urged to repeal a system which is fraught with ruin: on the other side, the check now imposed on enterprise, and the state of alarm in which the public mind has been thrown, renders all prudent men desirous, looking ahead a little way, to adopt a state of things, on the stability of which they may have reason to count. Such is the state of feeling on the one side and on the other. I am anxious to find out some principle of mutual accommodation, to satisfy, as far as practicable, both parties—to increase the stability of our legislation; and at some distant day—but not too distant, when we take into view the magnitude of the interests which are involved—*to bring down the rate of duties to that revenue standard for which our opponents have so long contended.* The basis on which I wish to found this modification, is one of time; and the several parts of the Bill to which I am about to call the attention of the Senate, are founded on this basis. I propose to give protection to our manufactured articles, adequate protection, for a length of time, which, compared with the length of human life, is very long, but which is short, in proportion to the legitimate discretion of every wise and parental system of Government—securing the stability of legislation, and allowing time for a *gradual reduction, on one side; and, on the other, proposing to reduce the duties to that revenue standard for which the opponents of the system have so long contended.* I will now proceed to lay the provisions of this bill before the Senate, with a view to draw their attention to the true character of the bill."

The bill proposed a gradual reduction of the duties on all articles on which they were then over twenty per cent. for ten years, so that at the end of ten years no duties should be above twenty per cent., which was assumed to be about the revenue standard. After explaining the bill and stating his second object in offering it, he said:

"If there be any who want civil war—who want to see the blood of any portion of our countrymen spilt, I am not one of them—I wish to see war of no kind; but above all, I do not desire to see a civil war. When war begins, whether civil or foreign, no human sight is competent to foresee when, or how, or where, it is to terminate. But when a civil war shall be lighted up in the bosom of our own happy land, and armies are marching, and commanders winning their victories, and fleets are in motion on our coasts—tell me, if you can, tell me if any human being can tell its duration? God alone knows where such a war will end. In what state will be left our institutions? In what state our liberties? I want no war; above all no war at home.

"Sir, I repeat, that I think South Carolina has been rash, intemperate, and greatly in the wrong; but I do not want to disgrace her, nor any other member of this Union. No: I do not desire to see the lustre of one single star dimmed of that *glorious Confederacy*, which constitutes our political sun; still less do I wish to see it blotted out, and its light obliterated forever. Has not the State of South Carolina been one of the members of this Union 'in days that tried men's souls?' Have not her ancestors fought alongside our ancestors? Have we not, conjointly, won together many a glorious battle? If we had to go into a civil war with such a State, how would it terminate? Whenever it should have terminated, what would be her condition? If she should ever return to the Union, what would be the condition of her feelings and affections—what the state of the heart of her people? She has been with us before, when her ancestors mingled in the throng of battle, and as I hope our posterity will mingle with hers for ages and centuries to come in the united defence of liberty, and for the honor and glory of the Union. I do not wish to see her degraded or defaced as a member of this Confederacy.

"In conclusion, allow me to entreat and implore each

individual member of this body to bring into the consideration of this measure, which I have the honor of proposing, the same love of country which, if I know myself, has actuated me; and the same desire of restoring harmony to the Union, which has prompted this effort. If we can forget for a moment—but that would be asking too much of human nature—if we could suffer, for one moment, party feelings and party causes—and as I stand here, before my God, I declare I have looked beyond those considerations, and regarded only the vast interests of this united people—I should hope that, under such feelings and with such dispositions, we may advantageously proceed to the consideration of this bill, and heal, before they are yet bleeding, the wounds of our distracted country."

The introduction of this bill, by Mr. Clay, caused great sensation. It was, perhaps, the most trying period of his life. Public meetings had been held in various places, in the manufacturing States, denouncing any modification of the protective system, and charging a disposition to such legislation to intimidation from the threats of South Carolina.* The Legislatures of Massa-

* The following are some of a series of Resolutions adopted by a Tariff meeting at Boston, January 28, 1833:

"*Resolved*, That any legislation on the subject of the Tariff is highly injudicious at the present crisis.

"*Resolved*, That a surrender of the principle of protection, by a repeal of the Act of 1832, before the date of its operation, and by the same Congress which passed it, can be attributed to no cause but fear of the threats of South Carolina.

"*Resolved*, That when the threats of a single State can intimidate Congress into an abandonment of measures deliberately adopted for the good of the whole, the Union will be virtually dissolved.

"*Resolved*, That we earnestly hope and confidently trust in the wisdom and firmness of Congress, that they will reject a bill which threatens such disgrace and disaster to the country.

"*Resolved*, That the only proper and expedient manner of lessening

chusetts, Rhode Island, Vermont, New Jersey and Pennsylvania, had passed resolutions strongly opposed to any such legislation.* Mr. Clay, on this occasion, had to break with his old political friends, while he was offering up the darling system of his heart upon the altar of his country.

Whatever else may be said of him, no one can deny that Henry Clay was a patriot—every inch of him—a patriot of the highest standard. It is said, that when he was importuned not to take the course he had resolved upon, for the reason amongst others, that it would lessen his chances for the Presidency, his reply was, "I would rather be right than be President." This showed the material he was made of. It was worthy a Marcellus or Cato.

Just so soon as he got through with the speech announcing the introduction of the bill, Mr. Calhoun immediately arose. The scene was intensely interesting as described by those who witnessed it. It was just such a scene as occurred in the same Hall on the 17th day of June, 1850, seventeen years afterwards, when Mr. Webster arose to speak on the turning question of the great adjustment of that year, as we shall see hereafter. All eyes were instantly fixed upon the Senator of South Carolina, as he addressed the Chair. The galleries and lobbies and aisles of the Chamber were crowded. The record of what occurred is thus put up. I still read from the same authority, pages 416–417.

"Mr. Calhoun rose and said he would make but one or

---

the revenue, is to reduce the duties on articles not coming into competition with the products of the industry of this country, and to increase the duties upon such articles as can be supplied by our own labor, to such an extent as shall limit the importations from abroad, and thus diminish the revenue to the amount required."—*Niles's Register.*

* *Statesman's Manual*, vol. 3, p. 1010.

Daguerreotype by Root. Engraved by A. Sealey.

HENRY CLAY.

H. Clay

two observations. Entirely approving of the object for which this bill was introduced, he should give his vote in favor of the motion for leave to introduce it. He who loves the Union must desire to see this agitating question brought to a termination. Until it should be terminated, we could not expect the restoration of peace or harmony, or a sound condition of things, throughout the country. He believed that to the unhappy divisions which had kept the Northern and Southern States apart from each other, the present entirely degraded condition of the country, for entirely degraded he believed it to be, was solely attributable. The general principles of this bill received his approbation. He believed that if the present difficulties were to be adjusted, they must be adjusted on the principles embraced in the bill, of fixing *ad valorem* duties, except in the few cases in the bill to which specific duties were assigned.

"He said that it had been his fate to occupy a position as hostile as any one could in reference to the protecting policy; but, if it depended on his will, he would not give his vote for the prostration of the manufacturing interest. A very large capital had been invested in manufactures, which had been of great service to the country, and he would never give his vote to suddenly withdraw all those duties by which that capital was sustained in the channel into which it had been directed. But he would only vote for the *ad valorem* system of duties, which he deemed the most beneficial and the most equitable. At this time he did not rise to go into a consideration of any of the details of this bill, as such a course would be premature, and contrary to the practice of the Senate. There were some of the provisions which had his entire approbation, and there were some to which he objected. But he looked upon these minor points of difference, as points in the settlement of which no difficulty would occur, when gentlemen met together in that spirit of mutual compromise which, he doubted not, would be brought into their deliberations, without at all yielding the Constitutional question as to the right of protection. [Here there was a tumultuous approbation in the galleries, which induced the Chair to order the galleries to be cleared.]"*

This, sir, was the end of Nullification! The *Euthanasia* of what was looked upon by so many as another Polyphemus, a real "*Monstrum horrendum, informe, ingens, cui lumen ademptum!*" It was neither put down or up, nor was the theory of the Government, on which the doctrine was founded, ever put down or up. It simply was never put to a practical test. There were then no steam cars, much less telegraphic wires, to send the glad news of this adjustment, which was received by shouts at the Capital, throughout the country. Not on the wings of lightning, but as fast as it could be borne by lumbering stages, and puffing steamboats, it was received with rejoicing everywhere by the mass of the people, and by it new energy, new life, and new hope were inspired. At this result no one felt more relieved, or rejoiced, perhaps, than General Jackson himself.

Mr. Clay's bill became a law on the 2d of March, 1833. South Carolina soon after repealed her ordinance. In this way was peace preserved, harmony restored, the Union saved, and the Constitution maintained for further progress in that career of greatness on which the States under it had so gloriously entered. So much on that point.

Major Heister. I stand corrected. I had been under a different impression.

---

* *Niles's Register*, vol. xliii, p. 417.

Mr. Stephens. Well, then, we will proceed to another point. You say you were born, bred and brought up a Jeffersonian Democrat.

Major Heister. Yes, my grandfather was one of the electors of Pennsylvania who cast his vote for Jefferson, in 1800. I was not then born, but I have often heard him speak of that fierce contest and the principles involved. I have never departed from these principles which he so thoroughly instilled into me. By them I have endeavored to live, and by them I hope to die.

Mr. Stephens. Well, then, you will have to give it up as an indisputably established truth, I think, that the Constitution of the United States is a Compact between Sovereignties, because Mr. Jefferson was elected upon this very issue.

The administration of John Adams, who succeeded Washington in the Presidency, in 1797, bearing the popular name of Federal, had endeavored, as was believed and charged, by construction and *implication*, to give that effect to the Constitution which Patrick Henry thought would be done in its practical workings. The party still bearing this name, during Mr. Adams's term of office, claimed virtually, it was said, for the Federal Government, general, absolute power, and maintained that the Supreme Court was the only arbiter between the General Government and State Governments, or the people, on all questions arising from the action of the General Government. They passed the Alien and Sedition laws, and acted generally upon the principle that the Federal Government was a consolidated Union of the people of all the States in one single, great Republic. They still kept the Party name of Federal, because it was popular. This Party name, however, with their avowed principles, was nothing but a mask. It was but "the livery of Heaven," stolen "to serve the Devil in."

It was then that the true friends of a real Federal Government, and not a consolidated one, were aroused from one end of the Union to the other. Mr. Jefferson's opinions were well known. As early as 1798, he had drawn up a set of Resolutions for the Kentucky Legislature, setting forth the true nature of the Government. The first of these Resolutions is in these words:

"*Resolved*, That the several States composing the United States of America, are not united on the principle of unlimited submission to their General Government; but that by Compact under the style and title of a Constitution for the United States, and of amendments thereto, they constituted a General Government for special purposes, delegated to that Government certain definite powers, reserving, each State to itself, the residuary mass of right to their own Self-government; and, that whensoever the General Government assumes undelegated powers, its acts are unauthoritative, void, and of no force; that to this Compact each State acceded as a State; and is an integral party, its co-States forming as to itself the other party; that this Government, created by this Compact, was not made the exclusive or final judge of the extent of the powers delegated to itself; since that would have made its discretion, and not the Constitution, the measure of its powers; but, that as in all other cases of Compact, among parties having no common *judge, each party has an equal right to judge for itself, as well of infractions as of the mode and measure of redress.*"*

This Resolution, and a whole series on the same subject drawn up by him, passed the Legislature of Kentucky, with some slight modifications.

Virginia also took her stand, not less decisive or unmis-

* *Randall's Life of Jefferson*, vol. ii, p. 449. See, also, *Appendix* D

takable. She passed the Resolutions which we have seen quoted in Mr. Calhoun's speech. These Resolutions were sent to all the States. The party in most of the States, claiming to be Federal, replied to them, joining issue with the doctrines set forth in these Resolutions. Virginia, in 1799, took up the subject again and gave it a grave reconsideration. She re-affirmed her Resolutions of the year before with an elaborate report, drawn by Mr. Madison. These Resolutions, and this report of Mr. Madison, contain an exceedingly clear and able exposition of the nature of the Government which no student in our history ought to fail to read and study.* It was upon these that the great contest, fierce it was, as you have said, was waged between the so-called Federalists and the Jeffersonian Party, in 1800. Mr. Jefferson, as the acknowledged leader of the State Sovereignty Party was chosen as the standard bearer of the principles set forth in his own Resolutions. The Party name assumed by the Anti-Centralists, under the lead of Mr. Jefferson, was generally that of Republican; but in some places it was Democratic. But the issue in every State was squarely made upon the issue presented in the Kentucky and Virginia Resolutions, and Mr. Madison's Report of 1799. That was the most memorable epoch in our history, from the adoption of the Constitution down to the breaking out of the war, in 1861. The question as to a proper construction of the Constitution was submitted to the people of the several States, and by them it was decided in favor of Mr. Jefferson's construction, and by that decision it was held to be settled, for more than half a century, that the Government of the United States is a Compact between States. Upon these principles and construction of the Constitution, Mr.

---

* See them in full in *Appendix* E.

Jefferson was re-elected in 1805. Upon them Mr. Madison was elected in 1809, and 1813. Upon them Mr. Monroe was elected in 1817, and in 1821. Upon them Mr. John Quincy Adams (who had renounced the party which had made such a departure from principle during the Presidency of his father) was elected, in 1825. Upon these principles General Jackson was elected in 1829, and re-elected in 1833. Upon them Mr. Van Buren was elected in 1837. Indeed no President was elected, from Mr. Jefferson to Mr. Lincoln, who denied these principles. It is true that, in the election of General Harrison, other questions entered into the contest, but on these principles he was a Republican of the Jeffersonian school.

JUDGE BYNUM. You do not mean to say that General Harrison was a Jeffersonian Democrat?

MR. STEPHENS. I mean to say that he was a Jeffersonian Republican—that he believed in the principles of the Kentucky and Virginia Resolutions of 1798–99. And I mean to say, that no man was elected President of the United States, from 1800 to 1860, from Mr. Jefferson to Mr. Lincoln, who did not.

JUDGE BYNUM. I should like to see how you can show that General Harrison held these doctrines?

MR. STEPHENS. That is easily done. Here is his inaugural. From that I read as follows:

"*Our Confederacy*, fellow-citizens, can only be preserved by the same forbearance. Our citizens must be content with the exercise of the powers with which the Constitution clothes them. The attempt of those of one State to control the domestic institutions of another, can only result in feelings of distrust and jealousy, and are certain harbingers of disunion, violence, civil war, and the ultimate destruction of our free institutions. *Our Confederacy* is perfectly illustrated by *the terms and prin-*

ciples governing a common co-partnership. There a fund of power is to be exercised under the direction of the joint counsels of the *allied members,* but that which has been reserved by the individuals is intangible by the common Government, or the individual members composing it. To attempt it finds no support in the principles of our Constitution. It should be our constant and earnest endeavor mutually to cultivate a spirit of concord and harmony among the various parts of our Confederacy. Experience has abundantly taught us that the agitation by citizens of one part of the Union of a subject not confided to the General Government, but exclusively under the guardianship of the local authorities, is productive of no other consequences than bitterness, alienation, discord, and injury to the very cause which is intended to be advanced. Of all the great interests which appertain to our country, that of Union—*cordial, confiding, fraternal, Union*—is by far the most important, since it *is the only true* and sure guarantee of all others."*

Do you want more pointed or conclusive testimony than this?

Mr. Webster, I will here remark, was General Harrison's Secretary of State, and the presumption is that he must have approved, *at that time* (1841), the general principles of this inaugural, to whatever extent its doctrines may imply a modification of his views expressed in 1833. But I said, and maintain, that no man, from Mr. Jefferson to Mr. Lincoln, was elected to the Presidency, who held contrary principles.

The opinions of Mr. Van Buren, Mr. Polk, Mr. Pierce, and Mr. Buchanan, are well known. General Taylor, as General Harrison, was elected on other issues. No public expression of opinion on these principles was ever made

---

* *Statesman's Manual,* vol. iii, p. 1206.

by him, that I am aware of, except that in the construction of the Constitution he should be governed "by the practice of the earlier Presidents, who had so large a share in its formation."* Washington, Jefferson, Madison, and Monroe must have been alluded to. He was well known, however, in early life, to have belonged to the Jefferson school of politics. Indeed, the very name of Federalist had become so odious to the popular mind throughout the United States, by the abuse of the word by those who applied it to themselves during the administration of the elder Adams, that no man openly professing the principles of that party could ever have been chosen President, from 1800 to 1860. This, I think, may be asserted as an incontrovertible truth. Not only Mr. Jefferson, but every President elected, from him to Mr. Lincoln, held the Constitution to be a Compact between the States! On this point there can be no doubt or question.

Under this construction the Union, or Federal Republic formed by it, grew and flourished as no nation ever did before. Under this construction the States, in number, had increased from thirteen to thirty-three! The territory had been enlarged from less than a million of square miles to nearly three millions! The population had increased from less than four millions to over thirty-one millions! The exports had increased from less than forty millions to upwards of three hundred and sixty millions of dollars per annum! The great mass of internal productions and developments had grown in an increased ratio!

Under this construction South Carolina had acted in 1832. Under this construction the peace of the country was then maintained and our unsurpassed progress was not only not checked or impeded by it, but received new

---

* Inaugural Address, *Statesman's Manual*, vol. iv, p. 1861

impetus, and moved on with greatly increased momentum and brilliancy.

Under the principles of free trade then established, to go into full operation in 1843, the manufacturing interests were not crippled. The industry of the country in none of its departments was paralyzed. New life and new energy sprung up everywhere. The exports of domestic manufactures from 1843 to 1860 increased from about eleven to upwards of thirty millions of dollars *per annum!* The tonnage of shipping increased from a little over two millions to upwards of five millions! The miles of railroad, a system of internal improvement just commenced about the time of Nullification, increased from about five thousand to upwards of twenty-five thousand! The exports of domestic products, staples, etc., increased from less than one hundred to upwards of three hundred millions! The production of cotton alone increased from less than sixty millions to upwards of one hundred and sixty millions of dollars *per annum!*

More than twelve hundred thousand square miles of territory were acquired during this period, between 1843 and 1860, and seven new States, more than half the original number, were admitted into the Union! Within the same period, the genius of Morse had seized the idea of the magnetic telegraph, and had brought that wonderful discovery into practical operation by extending these iron nerves throughout the length and breadth of the country, connecting the most distant points and uniting all together, as if under the influence of a common *sensorium!* Was the material progress, to say nothing of the moral and intellectual, of any nation in the world, greater, in the same space of time than was that of this Confederated Republic, from 1843 to 1860? Under this construction of the Constitution all this prosperity and progress, anterior to and subsequent to Nullification, were achieved; and, I maintain, might have gone on, under the same construction, with like common prosperity and joint happiness, until the system covered the entire continent, to the wonder and amazement of all other peoples and nations of the earth! It was only when this great fundamental law of our political existence was violated, in 1860, by a different construction, the anti-Jeffersonian construction, that disorder, confusion, war, and all its disastrous results ensued. The vital laws of every organism must be obeyed and conformed to, if its health, vigor, and development, are preserved. The whole of our late troubles came from a violation of this essential and vital law of our political existence.

But this is anticipatory. I only meant to say, Major, that if you still hold to the doctrines of Mr. Jefferson, that you must admit that the Constitution is a Compact between States, and that the Government under it is strictly Federal in its character.

We will now take up the Proclamation of General Jackson, to which you referred as your political text-book, and see how it squares with the doctrine of Mr. Jefferson.

Major Heister. Well, that is what I am now anxious to do. For what you have said has rather disturbed my equilibrium—especially, about Jackson's holding the doctrine that the Constitution is a Compact between Sovereign States. Here is the Proclamation. It is, as I said, too long to read entire. In it he holds very different doctrines, according to my understanding. In it he distinctly affirms, as I suppose you will admit, that "the people of the United States formed the Constitution." That they constitute "*one people,*" "*one nation.*" That the *allegiance* of the people of the several States was, by it, transferred to the Government of the United States, and that they *thereby* became American citizens. That no State has any right to nullify a law of Congress, or to secede from the Union. That the *Supreme Court of the United States* had been instituted as an *arbiter* to decide in the *last resort* upon all Constitutional questions touching either the powers of the General Government or the reserved rights of the States; that States, as well as individuals, must be bound by the adjudications of that tribunal, and that any *forcible resistance* to the execution of the laws of Congress, thus expounded, would be *treason*.

These are the principles, in substance, of the Proclamation, as I understand them, on the questions you are discussing, and they seem, to me, to be utterly inconsistent with what you would claim as an indisputably established conclusion, utterly inconsistent with the principles upon which you say he was elected, and I must confess, also, that they seem to me to be utterly inconsistent, too, with the principles of Mr. Jefferson, embodied in the Kentucky resolution, you have read.

I should like to hear what you have to say to these principles, thus set forth in this Proclamation, and how you can reconcile them with the principles upon which you say he was elected?

MR. STEPHENS. I have several things to say in reference to them.

In the first place, what General Jackson said in this Proclamation, should be considered in connection with the exact state of public affairs at the time it was issued. South Carolina had not attempted to secede. Her policy was based upon the idea of remaining in the Union, and yet defeating the execution of the Federal laws upon the tariff within her limits. This was the state of things which called forth the Proclamation. A prominent feature in the Proclamation, which must be borne in mind, in construing all its parts, is this:

"The Ordinance (that is South Carolina's Ordinance of Nullification) is founded, not on the *indefeasible* right of resisting acts which are *plainly unconstitutional*, and too oppressive to be endured; but on the strange position that any one State may not only declare an act of Congress void, but prohibit its execution; that they may do this *consistently with the Constitution;* that the true construction of that instrument permits a State to *retain its place in the Union*, and yet be bound by no other of its laws than those it may choose to consider as Constitutional."

This was the statement by him of the case which prompted the Proclamation, and nothing in the Proclamation should be received as the authoritative exposition of the principles of General Jackson touching the nature of the Government, except such as bear directly upon the case then before him, and as stated by himself. Judges never hold themselves bound by any expressions that fall from them in delivering their opinions upon any matter, except those which bear directly upon the case at bar. These only are authoritative. All else are "*obiter dicta.*"

Applying this rule to this Proclamation, there is in it much of that character. It was evidently hastily penned, and it has in it many not well guarded expressions. Under this character may be considered what was said on the subject of citizenship and allegiance, for we have seen what the Supreme Court, the very tribunal to which he refers as the final arbiter in the last resort, had held upon these subjects.* That it would have been *treason*

---

* *Ante*, p. 76, *et sequens.*

in any of the individual citizens of South Carolina, or any number of them, in their private character, to forcibly resist the laws of the United States, *while the State was a member of the Union with her Sovereign powers unresumed*, no one ever denied. South Carolina did not deny it. She did not contemplate any forcible resistance to these laws. There is nothing in that statement against my position. Upon reading this entire Proclamation by itself, however, I frankly admit that a disciple of the Jefferson school may well say of it as Peter said of some of Paul's epistles, that is, that there "are some things" in it "hard to be understood, which they that are unlearned and unstable wrest, as they do also the other scriptures, unto their own destruction." But that General Jackson himself did not mean what some suppose his words in particular passages imply, will be made clearly to appear before I get through. Just now, in reply to the view given in the Proclamation, as you seem to understand it, but as General Jackson did not, touching the powers of the Supreme Court to decide between the States and the General Government, upon questions involving their respective powers, the answer of Madison, in his report referred to, is conclusive. This was quoted, as we have seen, by Mr. Calhoun.* But, in addition to this, the answer of Judge Bibb, of Kentucky, in the Senate at the time, was so much fuller and so perfectly exhaustive of the subject, you will pardon me for reading extensively from it. It is in the same speech of his I read from before. *Niles's Register*, vol. xliii, pages 62 to 80. Here it is. And in it he says:

"That there are powers, authorities, and liberties, appertaining to the States, which belonged to them as

---

* *Ante*, p. 377.

States, and which they have not surrendered, but reserved, is undeniable. The general principle is clear, that in all Compacts, Leagues, Conventions, and Treaties between Sovereign States, Powers, and Potentates, each party has the right to judge whether a breach has been committed by the other party; and in case of a wilful, deliberate breach, to take such measures for redress as prudence and the discretion of the injured party shall dictate.

"Is the Compact between these States an exception to this general rule? If it is, then the States must, by some action of theirs, have surrendered this portion of their Sovereignty. What part of the Constitution declares such a surrender? There is no such express declaration of surrender. In the various enumerations of powers prohibited to the States, and agreed not to be exercised by them, there is no declaration that they shall not exercise the right, appertaining to them as parties to the Compact, to judge of an excessive, alarming, and dangerous stretch of power by the Federal Government. The abridgment of the powers of the States in this particular not being expressed, cannot be made out by implication, or by construction. The powers not delegated by the States to the United States, nor prohibited to the States by the Constitution, are reserved to the States. So says the Constitution. What clause in the Constitution delegates to the Federal Government *the sole power* of deciding the extent of the grant of powers to itself, as well as the extent of the powers reserved to the States?

"It is said that this power is vested by the Constitution in the Supreme Court of the United States. The provisions are:

"'The *Judicial power* shall extend to all cases in *law*

and equity, arising under this Constitution, the laws of the United States, and treaties made, or which shall be made, under their authority.'

"'This Constitution, and the laws of the United States which shall be made in pursuance thereof, and all treaties made, or which shall be made, under the authority of the United States, shall be the supreme law of the land, and the *Judges* in every State shall be bound thereby, any thing in the Constitution or laws of any State to the contrary, notwithstanding.'

"These are the two provisions of the Constitution which are referred to as delegating the power to the Supreme Court, to be the *sole judge* of the extent of the powers granted, and of the powers reserved; and as denying to the States the Sovereign power of protecting themselves against the usurpation of their reserved powers, authorities, and privileges. If the delegation to the Supreme Court, and prohibition to the States, are not contained in these two clauses, then they are not to be found in the Federal Constitution.

"The latter clause cannot touch the question in debate; for that only declares the supremacy of the Constitution, and the treaties 'and laws made in pursuance thereof.' Powers exercised contrary to the Constitution, acts done contrary to the Constitution, by the exercise of authorities not under, but in violation of the Constitution, and by usurpation of State rights, State authorities, and State privileges, are the subjects under consideration.

"Let us examine the former clause: 'The *Judicial* power shall extend to all cases, in *law* and *equity*, arising under this Constitution.' The case must be of '*Judicial power*;' it must be a case, 'in *law or equity*,' arising under the Constitution. The expression is not to all *cases* arising under the Constitution, treaties, and laws of the United States, but it is 'to all cases in *law and equity.*'

"'Use is the law and rule of speech.' By this law and this rule we must examine the language of the Constitution.

"A judicial power is one subject,—a political power is another and a different subject. A case in law, or a case in equity is one subject,—a political case is another and a different subject.

"Judicial cases in law and equity, arising under the regular exercise of Constitutional powers, by laws and treaties made by authority, are different from political questions of usurpation, surmounting the Constitution, and involving the high prerogatives, authorities, and privileges of the Sovereign parties who made the Constitution.

"In judicial cases arising under a treaty, the Court may construe the treaty, and administer the rights arising under it, to the parties who submit themselves to the jurisdiction of the Court in that case. But the Court must confine itself within the pale of judicial authority. It cannot rightfully exercise the political power of the Government, in declaring the treaty null because the one or the other party to the treaty has broken this or that article; and, therefore, that the whole treaty is abrogated. To judge of the breach of the articles of the treaty, by the Sovereign contracting parties, and in case of breach to dissolve that treaty, and to declare it no longer obligatory, is a political power belonging not to the judiciary. It belongs to other departments of the Government, who will judge of the extent of the injury resulting from the violation, and whether the reparation shall be sought by amicable negotiation, or whether the treaty shall be declared no longer obligatory on the

Government and the people of the injured party. Yet, by the law of Nations, the wilful and deliberate breach of one article is a breach of all the articles, each being the consideration of the others; and the injured party has the right so to treat it.

"By the Act approved on the 7th of July, 1798, the Congress of the United States declared themselves of right freed and exonerated from the stipulations of the treaties, and of the Consular Convention theretofore concluded between the United States and France, and that they should not thenceforth be regarded as legally obligatory on the Government or citizens of the United States—because of the repeated violations on the part of the French Government, etc.

"*Before this declaration*, the Supreme Court of the United States was bound, in cases of judicial cognizance coming before them, to take the treaties as obligatory, and to administer the rights growing out of the treaties between France and the United States. *After that declaration*, the Court was bound to consider the treaties as abrogated. The Courts had no power, before the Act of July, 1798, to inquire into violations, and, therefore, to declare the treaties not obligatory. After that act they had no power to demand evidence of the violations recited and revise the political decision of the Government.

"To declare these treaties no longer obligatory was a *political* power, not a *judicial* power. Yet the violations of these, committed under the authority of the French Government, and the consequent injuries to the citizens and Government of the United States, and the rights of the United States consequent therefrom, before the Act of July, 1798, were 'cases arising under the Constitution,' and treaties of the United States. But the judicial power did not extend to those cases of violation, so as to declare the treaties no longer obligatory. The question whether those violations should or should not abrogate the treaties, did not make a case in law or equity, for the decision of a judicial tribunal. Yet they were cases arising under the Constitution. The power to decide them belonged to the Government of the United States as a political Sovereign; but the judicial power did not extend to them; those cases belonged to the political powers, not to the judicial powers of the Government.

"The British Courts of Admiralty executed upon the commerce of the United States the British orders in council, disclaiming the power to decide whether those orders in council were conformable to the general law of Nations, which every nation is bound to respect and observe. In like manner, the French Courts of Admiralty executed upon the commerce of the United States the Berlin and Milan decrees.

"The British and French Courts had not cognizance to judge the Sovereign powers of the Nations, and to declare those orders and decrees contrary to the law of Nations—that was not a judicial power. So the Courts of the United States, even the Supreme Court, had not the power to declare the treaties between the United States and France, and Great Britain, no longer obligatory upon the citizens and Government of the United States, because of the multiplied wrongs and injuries committed upon the citizens of the United States, under color of those orders in council, and decrees, infracting the laws of Nations, and treaties, and hostile to the rights of the Government of the United States. Those cases, in their effects upon the treaties and amicable relations between the United States and those Governments, did not fall within the judicial power of the Courts of the United States. Those questions did not fall within the description of '*cases in law and equity*,' as used in the Constitution of the United States, in conferring, vesting, and defining the powers of the judicial department. Those political powers belong to other departments of the Government. According to the law and rule of speech established by use, such powers are classed under the denomination of political powers, prerogative powers, not under the head of judicial powers.

"Before I proceed to illustrate, by other examples, the distinctions which I have taken, between *political powers* and *judicial powers*, between *political* questions and cases and *judicial* questions or cases, I will refer to the declaration of one, whose opinions on Constitutional questions I know will command respect; a man to whose opinions I willingly yield my respect, without, however, submitting with that implicit faith which belongs to fools. On the resolution of Mr. Livingston, touching the conduct of President Adams, in causing Thomas Nash, *alias* Jonathan Robbins, to be arrested and delivered over to a British naval officer, without any accusation, or trial, or investigation in a Court of Justice, Mr. Marshall, then a Representative of Virginia, now Chief Justice of the United States, in defending the conduct of the President, thus delivered his opinion in that debate—(*Appendix*, 5 *Wheat*. p. 17.)

"'By extending the judicial power to all cases in law and equity, the Constitution had never been understood to confer on that department any political power whatever. To come within this description, a question must assume a legal form for forensic litigation and judicial decision. There must be parties to come into Court, who can be reached by its process, and bound by its powers; *whose rights admit of ultimate decision by a tribunal to which they are bound* to submit. A case in law or equity may arise under a treaty; where rights of individuals acquired or secured by a treaty, are to be asserted or defended in Courts.' 'But the judicial power cannot extend to political compacts.'*

* Judge Marshall's remarks, here quoted in part, may be very properly given more at large. They are as follows:

"This being established, the inquiry was, to what department was the power in question allotted?

"The gentleman from New York had relied on the second section of the third article of the Constitution, which enumerates the cases to which the judicial power of the United States extends, as expressly including that now under consideration. Before he examined that section, it would not be improper to notice a very material mis-statement of it, made in the Resolutions offered by the gentleman from New York. By the Constitution, the judicial power of the United States is extended to *all cases in law and equity*, arising under the Constitution, Laws, and Treaties of the United States; but the Resolutions declare that judicial power to extend to all *questions* arising under the Constitution, treaties, and laws of the United States. The difference between the Constitution and the Resolutions was material and apparent. A *case in law or equity* was a term well understood, and of *limited* signification. It was a controversy between parties, which had taken a shape for judicial decision. If the judicial power extended to *every question* under the Constitution, it would involve almost every subject proper for Legislative discussion and decision; if to every question under the laws and treaties of the United States, it would involve almost every subject on which the Executive could act. The division of power, which the gentleman had stated, could exist no longer, and the other departments would be swallowed up by the Judiciary. But it was apparent that the Resolutions had essentially misrepresented the Constitution. He did not charge the gentleman from New York with intentional misrepresentation; he would not attribute to him such an artifice in any case, much less in a case where detection was so easy and so certain. Yet this substantial departure from the Constitution, in Resolutions affecting substantially to unite it, was not less worthy of remark for being unintentional. It manifested the course of reasoning by which the gentleman had himself been misled, and his judgment betrayed into the opinions those Resolutions expressed. *By extending the judicial power to all cases in law and equity, the Constitution had never been understood to confer on that department any political power whatever.* To come within this description, a question must assume a legal form for forensic litigation and judicial decision. There must be parties to come into Court, who can be reached by its process, and bound by its power; whose

"This distinction between a political power and a judicial power, is recognized and acted upon by the Supreme Court of the United States, in the case of Williams *vs.* Armroyd, 7 *Cranch*, 423, 433.

"Again, in the case of Marbury *vs.* Madison (1 *Cranch*, 137; 1st *Peters's Condensed Reports*, 279), this distinction between the political powers of Government and the judicial power, is most explicitly avowed and recognized by the Supreme Court.

"The supremacy of that is a judicial supremacy only. It is supreme in reference to the other Courts in questions of a judicial character, brought within the sphere of judicial cognizance by controversies which shall have assumed a legal form for forensic litigation and judicial decision. There must be parties amenable to its process, bound by its power, whose rights admit of ultimate decision by a tribunal to which they are bound to submit. 'Questions in their nature political, or which are by the Constitution and laws submitted to the Executive, can never be made in this Court.'

---

rights admit of ultimate decision by a tribunal to which they are bound to submit.

"A case in law or equity, proper for judicial decision, may arise under a treaty, where the rights of individuals, acquired or secured by a treaty, are to be asserted or defended in Court. As under the fourth or sixth article of the Treaty of Peace with Great Britain, or under those articles of our late treaties with France, Prussia, and other nations, which secure to the subjects of those nations their property within the United States; or, as would be an article, which, instead of stipulating to deliver up an offender, should stipulate his punishment, provided the case was punishable by the laws and in the Courts of the United States. *But the judicial power cannot extend to political compacts;* as the establishment of the boundary line between the American and British dominions; the case of the late guarantee in our treaty with France, or the case of the delivery of a murderer under the twenty-seventh article of our present treaty with Britain."—*Annals of Congress, Sixth Congress*, page 606.

"The decision of the *Executive*, upon *political* questions submitted to its discretion, is *as supreme* as the decision of the Court within its jurisdiction. Neither department ought to invade the jurisdiction of the other,—so said the Supreme Court of the United States, in Marbury *vs.* Madison. * * *

"The twelfth amendment to the Constitution takes away the jurisdiction which had been given to the Supreme Court to hold jurisdiction of a suit against one of the United States by a citizen of another State, or by citizens or subjects of any foreign State; but leaves the jurisdiction conferred over controversies between two or more States. If two States, therefore, have a controversy, which, in its character, makes a case in law or equity proper for judicial cognizance, it may be brought before the Supreme Court. Controversies between two or more States, about territory or limits, may be litigated before the Supreme Court of the United States. But then each State must have an opportunity, as a party, to prosecute or defend her right before the decision can bind her. Those are questions of *meum et tuum*, rights of property which one State claims to the exclusion of the other; not political rights belonging to all the States respectively, where the rights and powers of one State does not exclude but establishes the rights of each and every other. Such rights claimed for all, as belonging equally to each and every of the States respectively, cannot make a controversy in law or equity between two States.

"Political powers not delegated to the Federal Government; political powers reserved to the States, constitute the subjects of the propositions which are affirmed on the one side and denied on the other. The propositions affirmed are, that the powers of the Federal

Government result from the Compact to which the States are parties, that these powers are limited by the plain sense and intention of the instrument constituting that Compact, and no farther valid than they are authorized by the grants enumerated in that Compact; 'and that, in case of a deliberate, palpable, and dangerous exercise of other powers, not granted by the said Compact, the States, who are parties thereto, have the right, and are in duty bound, to interpose for arresting the progress of the evil, and for maintaining, within their respective limits, the authorities, rights, and liberties appertaining to them.'"*

This argument of Judge Bibb, in the United States Senate, I have read so copiously from, was the overwhelming answer given at the time, to what were then supposed to be the doctrines of the Proclamation upon the powers and jurisdiction of the Supreme Court, as an arbiter in the last resort between the General Government and the States as States. It is not only conclusive on these points, but it is completely exhaustive of the whole question of the general powers and jurisdiction of this Court, on which so much has been said and written. With it I conclude what I have to say, as I remarked, on the Proclamation in the first place.

Now, in the second place, I will let General Jackson's own authoritative explanation of those parts you particularly refer to speak for itself. General Jackson had been elected as a Jeffersonian Republican. Many parts of this Proclamation were not understood by his most devoted political friends. It was thought to contain doctrines inconsistent with the teachings of the Fathers of that school. Many who agreed with him thoroughly in his

* *Niles's Register*, vol. xliii. *Supp.* p. 2.

position on Nullification thought that there were principles in that paper, not bearing directly on that question, however, which were inconsistent with the true principles of State Rights and State Sovereignty, and which savored much of the doctrines of the Consolidationists of the elder Adams' times. This called forth from him, through the *Washington Globe* newspaper, an explanation. The explanation was editorial—published not long after the great debate on his Proclamation and Force Bill. It was published, as stated, by authority. Now in this explanation will be found the *best answer* to your question, for it came from *General Jackson himself.* Here it is:

From the "Washington Globe."

"THE PRESIDENT'S PROCLAMATION.

"The editors of the *Richmond Enquirer* and of the *Petersburg Intelligencer*, in appealing to the fearless, honest, disinterested patriotism, which dictated the Proclamation, for an interpretation of those points in which it has suffered misconstruction, evinces the just estimation in which they hold the character of the President. Oracular silence and mystery with regard to his official documents, or Executive acts, form no part of General Jackson's policy. As Chief Magistrate, he does not entertain *a thought* which he would hide from the American people. He, who, from youth to age, has borne his life in his hand, ready to offer it up at any moment in defence of his country, now carries his heart as openly towards those, in whose service it is, and has ever been, so affectionately devoted. With him, dignity of station is nothing. He does not allow the ceremonies of office—the outworks which are everywhere thrown round the Chief Magistracy—to separate him from his fellow-citizens. With a wise man of another age, he thinks that '*plain and round dealing is the* HONOR *of man's nature*'—and the charm of existence to him is the consciousness of doing his duty—and the highest distinction is only valued, as it evinces the public confidence and a proper appreciation of his motives. Nothing, therefore, gives him more pain than the misconstruction to which the opinions expressed in his Proclamation have been subjected, and nothing, we are sure, will give him more pleasure, than to find, when properly understood, that they meet the approbation of the enlightened Republicans, the friends of the Union and State Rights, upon whose principles he has uniformly acted, throughout his public life.

"With these preparatory remarks, we proceed to the reply, which we *are authorized* to give, to the inquiries of the editors of the *Richmond Enquirer* and *Petersburg Intelligencer*.

"The impression that the President had given evidence of a '*dereliction from his principles*' in '*those passages which relate to the great question of the origin and character of our Federal Compact*,' would be fully sustained, if those passages warranted the interpretation given by Dr. Cocke in the Resolution submitted by him to the Senate of Virginia. That Resolution assumed that it was 'SET FORTH IN THE LATE PROCLAMATION OF THE PRESIDENT OF THE UNITED STATES, THAT THE FEDERAL CONSTITUTION RESULTS FROM THE PEOPLE IN THE AGGREGATE, AND NOT FROM THE STATES,' etc., and from this assumption, the Resolution goes on to infer, that 'THIS THEORY OF OUR GOVERNMENT WOULD TEND, IN PRACTICE, TO THE MOST DISASTROUS CONSEQUENCES, GIVING A MINORITY OF STATES, HAVING A MAJORITY OF POPULATION, THE CONTROL OVER THE OTHER STATES,' etc. This is the interpretation of the expression of the President's Proclamation, and the implication of consequences, which has given the alarm to many of the sincere friends of State Rights, who have considered the doctrine thus promulgated, as the doctrine of the old Federal Party. If the interpretation were true, we would not hesitate to admit the justice of the censure. * * But we assert, *authoritatively*, that the inferences made by Mr. Cocke are totally repugnant to the opinions of the President, and the views he meant to inculcate by the passage in the Proclamation, from which they are drawn; and these deductions were repelled, in this print, under the direction of the President, the instant he was apprized they had assumed the shape of a Resolution in the Senate of Virginia. The difficulty in the minds of the editors of the *Richmond Enquirer* and *Petersburg Intelligencer*, arises from the same passage in the Proclamation. We have, therefore, we hope, only to recur to them and give the sense in which they were intended by the President, to give perfect satisfaction in relation to the principles he entertains.

"The first passage, to which we are referred in the articles we quote from the *Richmond Enquirer* and *Petersburg Intelligencer*, is as follows:

"'The people of the United States formed the Constitution, acting through the State Legislatures in making the Compact, to meet and discuss its provisions, and acting in separate Conventions, where they ratified those provisions; but the terms used in its construction, show it to be a Government in which the people of all the States collectively are represented.'

"This is not *theory*, it is simple history,—but the phraseology, like that of the Constitution itself, which it copies *verbatim* in the leading member of the sentence, has been subjected to various interpretations. But the President, in saying that '*The people of the United States formed the Constitution*,' although he used the very language of the Constitution itself, did not leave it open to the construction, which the latitudinarian party have put upon its terms. He followed up the general declaration, by particularizing, that the Constitution originated in *a Compact*, that the *Compact* was the offspring of the people of the several States, acting through their respective State Legislatures, and further, that the Constitution or Government, founded in this *Compact*, received its sanction from the people of the several States, acting through independent separate State Conventions, to ratify its provisions. With such precise definite and positive ascription of the Constitution, in its origin, to *a Compact among the several States*, as the organized agents of several communities of people, and again making the obligatory sanction of the instrument, as derived from *the same independent communities*, depend on its ratification in separate Conventions, it would seem that the idea of its being the work of the whole people, in '*the aggregate*' or *united in one body*, was absolutely precluded. Indeed, as we said before, in commenting on Dr. Cocke's *Resolution*, the simple language of the Constitution in proclaiming its origin in its first words, 'We, the people of the United States,' 'do ordain and establish this Constitution for the United States of America,' does, of itself, imply, what is so precisely specified in the added explanation of the Proclamation. It excludes, by its terms, the idea of a people embodied in a Consolidated Government, by describing them as composing different '*States*,' and by speaking of the '*States*' as '*united*,' it repels the idea that the Union intended, is that of '*the people in the aggregate*,' but of States as forming separate communities. The close of the preamble to the Constitution (which we have quoted above, in connection with its first words) preserve the same idea. The Constitution is declared to be established, not for an *aggregate people*, but '*for the United States of America.*'

"The interpretation, forced by the Resolutions, to which we have referred, on the Proclamation, in spite of its explanations, is precisely that which the friends of a Consolidated Government have attempted to force on the Constitution itself. If this were admitted, the conclusion drawn from it, that it would give '*to a minority of States, having a majority of the population, a control over the other States,*' would inevitably follow. * * * While the Proclamation thus recognizes the Constitution as the *creature of the people of the States severally*, and as only susceptible of change, through the agency of '*two thirds of the States,*' in proposing amendments to be effectuated only by the ratification of three fourths of the States, it is difficult to conceive how any one could infer, from its doctrines, that it concedes to '*a minority of States having the majority of population,*' absolute sway over the Constitution and Government.

"The only other difficulty to which we are referred as requiring explanation, by our friends of the *Richmond Enquirer* and *Petersburg Intelligencer*, will be found in the close of the following passage, which speaks of '*the unity of our political character.*' * * * It would be sufficient here, again, to observe, that it is history which speaks in this passage, and not the President. The facts are indubitably as he states them. And it is only by confounding *the unity, which is derived from a Confederacy among the States* (making them, to a certain extent, 'one Nation'), with the idea of a consolidation of all power in the Federal Government, that an objection is created. 'The unity of our political character,' here spoken of, it is expressly said, is not intended to denote 'an *undivided Sovereignty,'* or *authority in the General Government.* On the contrary, the text shows that it *only refers to that special delegated authority* which is vested in the Constitution out of the powers belonging to the several State communities, united in one common Government for the purpose of establishing a National character, and National relations with the other Nations of the world. And as it was especially the scope of the Constitution, to give *unity* to our political character in its *exterior aspect*, and to confer upon the Government all the attributes of *Nationality,* in regard to *Foreign powers,* it is strange that jealousy should be excited by the use of terms pointing out this design, or by references to various periods of our history, to prove that, in this respect, a connection has always existed among the independent communities composing the Confederacy. * * * We were a Nation under the Articles of Confederation, however feeble the means of the National authority then to bring the energies of the several States to act in unison—and we are, surely, not less a Nation, now that Government has been established to form a more perfect Union, endowed with all the faculties which can constitute us a *Nation in our relations with Foreign powers.* * * * The Proclamation, then, in the passage objected to, has merely spoken the facts *of history—the language of the Constitution,* and of the *Declaration of Independence.* There is no speculative opinion advanced—no theory proposed. And we have endeavored to show, that nothing in these generalities tended, in the slightest degree, to justify the inferences drawn from them, and which have been substituted as the principles of the Proclamation. *But we are authorized to be more explicit, and to say positively, that no part of the Proclamation was meant to countenance principles which have* *been ascribed to it. On the contrary, its doctrines, if construed in the sense they were intended, and carried out, inculcate that the Constitution of the United States is founded on Compact—that this Compact derives its obligation from the agreement, entered into by the people of each of the States, in their political capacity, with the people of the other States*—that the Constitution, which is the offspring of this Compact, has its sanction in the ratification of the people of the several States, acting in the capacity of separate communities—that the majority of the people of the United States, in the aggregate, have no power to alter the Constitution of the General Government, but that change, or amendment can only be proposed in the mode pointed out in the Constitution, and can never become obligatory unless ratified by the people of three fourths of the States through their respective Legislatures or State Conventions. * * * *That in the case of a violation of the Constitution of the United States, and the usurpation of powers not granted by it on the part of the functionaries of the General Government, the State Governments have the right to interpose and arrest the evil, upon the principles which were set forth in the Virginia Resolutions of* 1798, *against the Alien and Sedition Laws*—and finally, that in extreme cases of oppression (every mode of Constitutional redress having been sought in vain), the *right resides with the people of the several States* to organize resistance against such oppression, confiding in a good cause, the favor of heaven, and the spirit of freemen, to *vindicate* the right.

"We beg leave here to submit, in aid of our own, an exposition which touches the points involved in the controverted passages of the Proclamation, and which received the sanction of the President, at the threshold of the controversy that led to the promulgation of that paper. During the progress of the debate on Foot's Resolutions, the editor of this print (who was then connected with a press in Kentucky, which sustained the principles of the Republican party), received from the Postmaster General the speech delivered by Mr. Livingston, accompanied by a letter, saying, that the views contained in it were sanctioned by the President; and might be considered as exhibiting the light in which his administration considered the subject under debate. The following extracts from that speech will serve in illustrating the principles on which the President then took his stand, to explain the more condensed view given of them in his Proclamation."

Reference is made in this explanation to certain extracts from the speech of Mr. Livingston, in the Senate, in the debate on Foot's Resolutions, in 1830. The extracts, published by the *Globe*, I have never seen. The explanation I have read is a republication from the *Globe*, in the *Augusta Constitutionalist*, 11th Oct., 1833. The doctrines of that whole speech, however, it was said, met the approval of General Jackson, at the time it was delivered. Here is that speech, in Supplement to *Niles's Register*, vol. xxxviii. I call your special attention to these portions of it.

"I now approach," said Mr. Livingston, "a graver subject; one, on the true understanding of which the Union, and of course the happiness of our country, depends. The question presented is that of the true sense of that Constitution which it is made our first duty to preserve in its purity. Its true construction is put in doubt—not on a question of power, between its several departments, but on the very basis upon which the whole rests; and which, if erroneously decided, must topple down the fabric, raised with so much pain, framed with so much wisdom, established with so much persevering labor, and for more than forty years the shelter and protection of our liberties, the proud monument of the patriotism and talent of those who devised it, and which, we fondly hoped, would remain to after ages as a model for the imitation of every nation that wished to be free. Is that, sir, to be its destiny? The answer to that question may be influenced by this debate. How strong the motive, then, to conduct it calmly; when the mind is not heated by opposition, depressed by defeat, or elate with fancied victory; to discuss it with a sincere desire, not to obtain a paltry triumph in argument, to gain applause by a tart reply, to carry away the victory by addressing the passions, or gain proselytes by specious fallacies, but, with a mind open to conviction, seriously to search after truth, earnestly, when found, to impress it on others. What we say on this subject will remain; it is not an every day question; it will remain for good or for evil. As our views are correct or erroneous; as they tend to promote the lasting welfare, or accelerate the dissolution of our Union; so will our opinions be cited, as those which placed the Constitution on a firm basis, when it was shaken; or deprecated, if they should have formed doctrines which led to its destruction. * * * *The States existed before the Constitution: they parted only with such powers as are specified in that instrument, ; they continue still to exist, with all the powers they have not ceded, and the present Government, itself, would never have gone into operation, had not the States, in their political capacity, consented. That consent is a Compact of each one with the whole,* not (as has been argued in order to throw a kind of ridicule on this convincing part of the argument of my friend from South Carolina), with the Government which was made by such Compact. It is difficult, therefore, it would appear, with all these characters of a Federative nature, to deny to the present Government the description of *one founded on Compact, to which each State was a party;* and a conclusive proof, if any more were wanted, would be in the fact, that the States adopted the Constitution at different times, and many of them on conditions which were afterwards complied with by amendments. *If it were* strictly a popular Government, in the sense that is contended for, the moment a majority of the people of the United States had consented, it would have bound the rest; and yet, after all the others, except one, had adopted the Constitution, the smallest still held out, and if Rhode Island had not consented to enter into the Confederacy, she would, perhaps, at this time, have been unconnected with us. * * * I place little reliance on the argument, which has been mostly depended on, to show that this is a popular Government. I mean the preamble; which begins with the words, 'We, the people.' It proves nothing more than the fact, that the people of the several States had been consulted, and had given their consent to the instrument. To give these words any other construction, would be to make them an assertion directly contrary to the fact. We know—and it has never been imagined, or asserted, that the people of the United States, collectively, as a whole people, gave their assent, or were consulted in that capacity—the people of each State *were* consulted to know whether *that State* would form a part of the United States, under the Articles of the Constitution, and to that they gave their assent, simply as citizens of that State.

"*It is a Compact, by which the people of each State have consented to take from their own Legislatures some of the powers they had conferred upon them, and to transfer them, with other enumerated powers, to the Government of the United States, created by that Compact.* * * *

"Although, in my opinion, in every case which can lawfully be brought within the jurisdiction of the *Supreme Court*, that tribunal must judge of the Constitutionality of laws on which the question before them depends, and its decrees must be final, whether they affect State rights or not; and, as a necessary consequence, that no State has any right to impede or prevent the execution of such sentence; yet, *I am far from thinking that this Court is created an umpire to judge between the General and State Governments.* I do not see it recorded in the instrument, but I see it recorded that every right not given is retained. In an *extreme case* that has been put, of the United States declaring that a particular State should have but one Senator, or should be deprived of its representation, I see nothing to oblige the State to submit this case to the Supreme Court; on the contrary, I see, by the enumeration of the cases and persons which may be brought within their jurisdiction, that this is not included; in this, the injured State would *have a right at once to declare that it would no longer be bound by a Compact which had been thus grossly violated.*"

The authoritative explanation, by General Jackson, of the doctrines of his Proclamation, which I have just read, and these parts of the speech of Mr. Livingston, which, it was asserted, as we have seen, met his entire approval, *clearly* and *beyond doubt* show that General Jackson held the Constitution to be a *Compact between States*, and that he adhered to the old Republican creed of 1798–99. He was express in his injunction that it should be made known that he held to the right of State interposition in certain cases, upon the principles of the Virginia Resolutions of 1799.

From this speech of Mr. Livingston it also appears that

General Jackson did *not mean*, by *any thing* he said in the Proclamation about the Supreme Court of the United States, to be understood as holding, that that Court had any Constitutional jurisdiction over *political* questions, or such as involved the reserved rights of the States. Mr. Livingston is explicit on this point. He says that the Supreme Court is not an umpire between the States and General Government. In this, he agrees entirely with Judge Bibb. General Jackson, in his Proclamation on this subject, must have meant nothing more, therefore, than that the United States Judiciary was clothed with power to decide the Constitutionality of the Tariff laws, as between citizens, in cases made, so long as the State was a member of the Union. That was the case he was addressing the country upon. But Mr. Livingston expressly says, that, in case of a gross violation of the Constitution, where the matter cannot be brought before that Court, that the State would no longer be bound by the Compact. His position, in this respect, was the same as that of Mr. Webster, at Capon Springs, when he said, "a bargain cannot be broken on one side and still bind the other side."

Neither General Jackson, therefore, nor any thing in his Proclamation, can be brought up as authority against what I claimed as an indisputably established conclusion. That was, that the Government of the United States is founded upon Compact between States, and is therefore strictly Federal in its character, or, in other words, that it is what Washington styled it, a Confederated Republic.

No better or stronger proof need have been *adduced* to establish this conclusion than the Proclamation itself, with the explanation that was given afterwards. If with this alone more had been called for, so far as General Jackson's authority goes, the material could be easily and abundantly supplied. His whole administration furnishes it. His numerous vetoes, and the principles upon which he put them, show him to have been a Republican of the old school. His almost every message, from his inaugural to his Farewell Address, abounds with arguments to prove, if it were necessary, that this Government, in his opinion, is a Confederated Republic. In the very second paragraph of his first inaugural, he speaks of the Constitution as "the Federal Constitution." Further on in the same, he says: "In such measures as I may be called on to pursue, in regard to the rights of the separate States, I hope to be animated by a proper respect for *those Sovereign members of our Union*; taking care not to confound the powers they have reserved to themselves, with those they have granted to the Confederacy."*

The same sentiments pervade all his messages for the eight years of his ever memorable administration, and in his Farewell Address he is no less distinct and emphatic. Listen to his parting words to the people of the United States:

"It is well known," says he, "that there have always been those among us, who wish to enlarge the powers of the General Government; and experience would seem to indicate that there is a tendency on the part of this Government to over-step the boundaries marked out for it by the Constitution. Its legitimate authority is abundantly sufficient for all the purposes for which it was created; and its powers being expressly enumerated, there can be no justification for claiming any thing beyond them. Every attempt to exercise power beyond these limits should be promptly and firmly opposed. For

---

* *Statesman's Manual*, vol. ii, p. 695.

Engraved by A.B. Walter, Phila.

Andrew Jackson

one evil example will lead to other measures still more mischievous; and if the principle of constructive powers, or supposed advantages, or temporary circumstances, shall ever be permitted to justify the assumption of a power not given by the Constitution, the General Government will, before long, absorb all the powers of Legislation, and you will have, in effect, but one Consolidated Government. From the extent of our country, its diversified interests, different pursuits, and different habits, it is too obvious for argument, that a single Consolidated Government would be wholly inadequate to watch over and protect its interests; and every friend of our free institutions should be always prepared to maintain unimpaired, and in full vigor, the *rights and Sovereignty of the States*, and to confine the action of the General Government strictly to the sphere of its appropriate duties."*

How wise, patriotic, and even prophetic, were these admonitions of the Hero of New Orleans, and the Sage of the Hermitage! He was, indeed, both hero and sage! In him was presented the rare combination of both military and civic attainments of a very high order. Highest in eminence above all others of this class in the annals of the world stands Washington! Jackson approached as near this great unapproachable model of the general and statesman combined, as perhaps any ever will or can. He left the impress of his ideas deeply fixed upon the times in which he lived. And no more important admonition did he ever give his countrymen than that in the closing part of the extract from his Farewell Address I have just read. This, with all the solemnity of dying declarations, may be received as the strongest evidence of his opinions that ours is a Confede-

---

* *Statesman's Manual*, vol. ii, p. 952.

racy of Sovereign States, and that our liberties, as well as the preservation of the Union, which was so dear to him, depend upon their preservation as such! His last parting words to his countrymen were, to be prepared to maintain unimpaired, and *in full vigor, the Sovereignty of the States!*

May I not, then, upon his authority, again ask if the conclusion, before stated, that the Constitution is a Compact between Sovereign States, is not indisputably established?

MAJOR HEISTER. Waiving that point, I do not yet see that the right of a State to secede from the Union, in disregard of her obligations under the Compact, follows that conclusion.

MR. STEPHENS. That is another question. We must settle one thing at a time. Do you all now give it up that the Constitution is a Compact between Sovereign States? All being silent we will then take that to be an *established truth,* and proceed a step further.

COLLOQUY XI.

THE GREAT TRUTH ESTABLISHED THAT THE CONSTITUTION IS A COMPACT BETWEEN SOVEREIGN STATES—THE GOVERNMENT OF THE UNITED STATES IS STRICTLY A FEDERAL GOVERNMENT—EACH STATE FOR ITSELF HAS THE RIGHT TO JUDGE OF INFRACTIONS AS WELL AS THE MODE AND MEASURE OF REDRESS—THE RIGHT OF A STATE TO WITHDRAW FROM THE UNION UPON BREACH OF THE COMPACT BY OTHER PARTIES TO IT SPRINGS FROM THE VERY NATURE OF THE GOVERNMENT—THE COMPACT WAS BROKEN BY THIRTEEN STATES OF THE UNION—WEBSTER, STORY, TUCKER, RAWLE, DE TOCQUEVILLE, WADE, GREELEY AND LINCOLN UPON THIS RIGHT TO WITHDRAW OR SECEDE IN SUCH CASE.

MR. STEPHENS. We are then, it seems, by the assent of all, brought to the conclusion, that the Constitution of the United States was formed by separate, distinct, and Sovereign States. This is the conclusion to which we are all, however willingly or reluctantly, compelled to come at last, not only by the testimony of witnesses of the highest order, and by the decisions of the judicial tribunal of the highest authority, the Supreme Court of the United States, Chief Justice Marshall at its head, but by the everlasting records themselves, by all the great facts of our history, which can never be obliterated or effaced.

We have seen that the Union existing between these States, anterior to the formation of the new Constitution, was a Compact, or as Judge Marshall expressed it, nothing but "a league" between Sovereign States.

We have seen that in remodelling the Articles of the old Confederation, it was not the object, or design of any of the parties, to change the nature or character of that

Union; but only to make it more perfect, by an enlargement of the delegation of powers conferred upon the Government thereby established with such changes in its organic structure, touching the mode and manner of exercising them, as might be thought best to attain the object of their delegation.

We have also seen, both by the instrument itself, and by the understanding of all the parties at the time; that this was what was done by the adoption of the present Constitution, and nothing more. In other words we have seen, and come to the conclusion from a review of all the facts, that the Constitution, as the Articles of Confederation, is a Compact between "the Sovereign members of the Union" under it, as General Jackson styles the States.

With these essential points first settled, beyond dispute or question, we are now prepared to go a step further and approach the end of our immediate and important inquiry, touching the nature and character of the Government, so formed and constituted, and to see clearly where, under it, Paramount or ultimate Sovereignty necessarily resides.

That the Government of the United States is a Confederated Republic, or Confederacy, of some sort, and not a Consolidated Government, is now no longer a matter of investigation or question. Whatever other characteristics, peculiar or anomalous, it possesses, it is beyond doubt, cavil, or dispute, Federal in its nature and character.

That it presents, in its structure, several new features, wholly unknown in all former Confederacies of which the world's history furnishes examples, all admit. This was well understood at the time of its formation, as well as ever since. No exactly similar model is to be found amongst all the nations of the earth, or in the annals of mankind, in the past or present. But we have seen the model which was in the minds of its authors at the time it was framed, and which formed the basis of their conceptions and designs. That was the model of a Confederated Republic given by Montesquieu. This model was not only in the minds of the Convention which framed the Constitution, but in the minds of all the Conventions of the States which adopted it. This has been shown from the proceedings of those bodies. That model exhibited several small Republics so united into a larger one, for foreign and inter State purposes, as to present themselves in joint Combination to the world, as one Nation, while as between themselves each one retained unimpaired its own inherent, innate Sovereignty and Nationality.* This was the ideal before all the States of this Union, at the time of the formation of the Constitution. According to this model, which was as far as the wisdom of men then had gone in forming Governments for the preservation of free institutions, and to prevent the principle of universal Monarchical Rule, the action of the larger and conventional State or Nation so, formed for external or foreign purposes, was confined in its internal operations exclusively to the integral members of the Union or Confederation. No power was conferred upon this joint agent of all to interfere, in any way or under any circumstances, with the individual citizens of the separate Republics.

But a new idea had for sometime been in embryo. It was then struggling into birth. Jefferson's brain had first felt the impulse of its quickening life. The framers of the Constitution saw its star, as the wise men of the

* *Montesquieu*, vol. i, Book ix, ch. i, p. 154.

East saw the star of Bethlehem. They did homage to it, even in the manger, where it then lay in its swaddlings, as the political Messiah just born for the regeneration of the down trodden Peoples of the Earth. That idea was to apply a new principle to the model before them, to improve upon it by a division of its Powers, and by extending its operations, without changing the basis upon which it was formed. It was simply for these separate Republics to empower their joint agent, the artificial or conventional Nation of their own creation, to act, in the discharge of its limited functions, directly upon their citizens respectively, and to organize these functions into separate departments, Executive, Judicial and Legislative, as their own separate systems were organized. This, it is true, was a new and a grand development in the progress of the science of Government, which, of all sciences, unfortunately for mankind, is the slowest in progress.

But this was the idea—this the design, and this was just what was done.

The great object was to obviate the difficulties and the evils, so often arising in all former Federal Republics, of resorting to force against separate members, when derelict in the discharge of their obligations under the terms and covenants of their Union. Difficulties of this sort had already been felt under their own Confederation, which they were convened to remedy. Some States had failed to meet the requisitions upon them for their quota of taxes to pay the common expenses, and to sustain the common public credit. By the laws of Nations, the Confederates of States thus derelict, had the clear right to compel a fulfilment of their solemn obligations, though the very act of doing it would necessarily have put an end to the Confederation. The question of coercion in the collection of unpaid requisitions, on the part of some of the States, had been raised during the old Confederation. Jefferson saw that this would be necessary if that system could not be amended. All, however, saw that a resort to force, in such cases, would result in war which might become general, and the loss of the liberties of all might, perhaps, ensue. This newly born idea presented an easy solution of the whole vexed question. It was adopted, by the Parties agreeing in the Compact itself, that in the collection of the taxes for the common defence and general welfare, and in some other cases, this common agent of all the members of the Confederacy, should act directly upon the individual citizens of each, within the sphere of its specific and limited powers, and with a complete machinery of functions, for this purpose, similar to their own. This is the whole of it.

It is this exceedingly simple, but entirely new feature, in Confederated Republics, which has so puzzled and bewildered so many in this as in other countries, as to the nature and character of the United States Government. It is this feature, in the American plan, which struck the learned and philosophic De Tocqueville, who, of all foreigners, seems most deeply to have studied our institutions, and to have become most thoroughly imbued with their spirit and principles.

On this point he says:

"This Constitution, which may at first be confounded with the Federal Constitutions which have preceded it, rests, in truth, upon a wholly novel theory, which may be considered as a great discovery in modern political science. In all the Confederations which preceded the American Constitution of 1789, the allied States, for a common object, agreed to obey the injunctions of a Federal Government; but they reserved to themselves the right of ordaining and enforcing the execution of the laws of the

Union. The American States, which combined, in 1789, agreed, that the Federal Government should not only dictate, but should execute its own enactments. In both cases, the right is the same, but the exercise of the right is different; and this difference produced the most momentous consequences."*

In all this he is perfectly right. The principle thus introduced was a new one. It was unknown to the old world. Unknown to Plato, Aristotle, Cicero, Grotius, Puffendorf, or Montesquieu. It was, indeed, a grand discovery. The honor, the glory of this discovery, was reserved for this Continent, and for those who had first proclaimed the great truth that all "Governments derive their just powers from the consent of the governed." From this simple discovery, did, indeed, follow the most momentous consequences. From it sprang that unparalleled career of prosperity and greatness which marked our history under its beneficent operations for nearly three quarters of a century!

These momentous consequences in rapid growth and development, and the unsurpassed happiness and prosperity, resulted from this simple, but wonderful improvement made by the Fathers, in 1787, upon Montesquieu's model of a Confederated Republic. This new feature, however, in the workmanship of their master-hands has been what has caused so much confusion in the minds of many as to the nature and character of the Government. They do not seem to understand how this new feature is consistent with a strictly Federal System. The difficulty with them seems to arise entirely from the fact, that none such ever existed before. They have no *specific* name for this new development or discovery in the science

* *De Tocqueville's Democracy in America*, vol. i, p. 198.

of Government. Hence the great variety of sentiments in the several State Conventions, some calling it a consolidated Government, and some of its friends styling it a mixed Government—partly Federal and partly National—Federal in its formation and National in its operation. Of this class was Mr. Madison. And hence, also, some in later times have styled it a Compositive Government.*

A little analysis and generalization may enable us to bring order out of this confusion. In one sense it is a National Government. In this, however, there is nothing *new* or *peculiar* in the Government established by the *New* Constitution. In the same sense in which it is National, and none other, was the old Confederation National. The United States, under that, we have seen was called and properly called a Nation, for certain purposes. For the same purposes, and in the same sense, and none other, may they now properly be called a Nation. Their present Government is National in the same sense in which the Governments of all Confederated Republics are National, and none other. The very object in forming all Confederated Republics is to create a *new* and an *entirely artificial* or conventional *State or Nation,* which springs from their joint Sovereignties, and which has no existence apart from them, and which is but the Corporate Agent of all those Sovereignties creating it, and through which alone they are to be known to Foreign Powers, during the continuance of the Confederation. This Conventional Nation is but a Political Corporation. It has no *original* or *inherent* powers whatever. All its powers are derived—all are specific—all are limited—all are delegated—all may be resumed—all may be forfeited

---

* *Wheaton's Elements of International Law*, p. 12.

by misuser, as well as non-user. It is created by the separate Republics forming it. They are the Creators. It is but their Creature—subject to their will and control. They barely delegate the exercise of certain Sovereign powers to their common agent, retaining to themselves, separately, all that absolute, ultimate Sovereignty, by which this common agent, with all its delegated powers, is created. This is the basis, and these are the principles, upon which all Confederated Republics are constructed. The new Conventional State or Nation thus formed is brought into being by the will of the several States or Nations forming it, and by the same will it may cease to exist, as to any or all of them, while the separate Sovereignties of its Creators may survive, and live on forever.

A Government so constructed, being itself founded on Compact between distinct Sovereign States, is necessarily Federal in its nature, while it at the same time gives one national character and position amongst the other Powers of the world, to all the Parties constituting it! In this sense, all Confederated Governments are both Federal and National. The Government of the United States is no exception to the rule. In this sense, Washington, Jefferson, and Jackson, spoke of the United States under the Constitution as a Nation, as well as a Confederated Republic. In this sense, it is properly styled by all a Nation. This was the idea symbolized in the motto, "*E pluribus unum.*"* One from many. That is, one State or Nation—one Federal Republic—from many Republics,

* "E PLURIBUS UNUM, [L.] One composed of many; the motto of the United States, consisting of many States confederated."—Noah Webster, LL. D.

"E PLURIBUS UNUM, [L., *one of many.*] The motto of the United States;—the allusion being to the formation of one Federal Government out of several independent States."—Joseph E. Worcester, LL. D.

States, or Nations. This is what is meant by the Nation when properly applied to the United States. It is not the whole people, in the aggregate constituting one body united on the principles of a social Compact, but that conventional State which springs from and is dependent upon the several State Sovereignties creating it, as in all other cases of Confederated Republics. The bare fact that it operates on the individual citizens of the several States, in specified cases, and has in its organization the requisite functions for this purpose, does not change, in the least, the nature of the Government, if this arrangement is agreed upon in the Compact between the Sovereign Parties to it. That depends entirely upon the great fact which we were so long in establishing, that the Government itself, with all its powers as well as machinery, was founded upon Compact between separate and distinct Sovereign States. If this be so, as has been conclusively established, then the Government, so constructed, must of necessity be Federal, and purely Federal, in its character. This character is not changed by the adoption of any machinery, for its practical workings, which may be thus agreed upon. For it is perfectly competent for independent and Sovereign Nations, by treaty or compact, to make any agreement they please touching the enforcement of such treaties, or the terms of such compacts, over the irrespective citizens or subjects, and by such agencies as they may please jointly to agree upon, without the least impairment whatever of their respective Sovereignties.

The great question, therefore, in this investigation was, is the Constitution a Compact between Sovereignties? If so, the Government established by it is purely, entirely, and thoroughly Federal in its nature, and no more National in any sense than all former Federal Republics.

All those features in its operations directly upon individuals, instead of upon States, which give rise to ideas of Nationality, or of its being of a mixed nature, spring themselves from the Federal Compact. Ours, therefore, is a pure Confederated Republic, upon the model of Montesquieu, with the new principle referred to incorporated into the system, without changing, in the least, the basis of its organization—at least, so thought the Fathers by whom it was established. It is true we have as yet no apt distinctive word in political nomenclature, by which to characterize this *specific* distinctive improvement in the purely Federal systsm. This only shows the barrenness of language. Actualities often precede nomenclature. And, hence, De Tocqueville, perceiving this in our system, said of it, that "the new word, which ought to express this novel thing, does not yet exist." "The human understanding," says he, "more easily invents new things than new words, and we are hence constrained to employ many improper and inadequate expressions." No truer remark was ever made about the Government of the United States. All the difficulty or confusion on the subject, however, relates only to the *name.* It is one of nomenclature, and not substance. That stands out perfectly distinct in all its features, however unlanguaged it, with these features, may yet be. This want of a suitable name applies, also, only to its *specific* character, that name which will perfectly characterize its *specific* difference from other Confederacies, ancient or modern. There is no difficulty as to the proper generic term applicable to it. That is unquestionably Federal. Its *genus,* with all the incidents of the class, is a Federal or Confederated Republic. That is fixed by the fact that it is founded upon Compact—Confederation between distinct Sovereign Powers.

What makes any Government Federal, but the fact that it springs, with all its powers and functions, of whatever character, from covenants and agreements between the Sovereign contracting parties creating it? And is it not as competent for a Sovereign State to agree, that the Federal agent or Government shall act upon her citizens, in specified cases, as it is for her to agree, that the same agent or Government may act upon herself? may pass edicts of equal force and obligation upon her, which she is equally bound by the Compact to execute by her own machinery of laws? Where is the difference? What makes the Union between any States Federal is not the manner of its action, but the *Fœdus*, the Covenant, the Convention, the Compact upon which it is founded!

So much for the nature of the Government of the United States, and the terms by which it may be characterized.

Where, under the system so constituted, does Sovereignty reside? This is now the great and last question. It must reside somewhere. It must reside, as all admit, with the people somewhere. Does it reside with the whole people in mass of all the States together, or with the people of the several States separately? That is the only question. The whole subject is narrowed down to this: Where, in this country, resides that Paramount authority that can rightfully make and unmake Constitutions? In all Confederated Republics, according to Montesquieu, Vattel, and Burlamaqui, it remains with the Sovereign States so Confederated. Is our Confederated Republic an exception to this rule? If so, how does it appear? Is there any thing in its history, anterior to the present Compact of Union, that shows it to be an exception? Certainly not; for the Sovereignty of each State was expressly retained in the first Articles of Union. Is there then any thing in the present Compact itself that shows that it was surrendered by them in that? If so, where is the clause bearing that import? None can be found! Again: if it was thereby surrendered, to whom was it surrendered? to whom did it pass? Did it pass to all the people of the United States? Of course not; for not one particle of power of any sort, much less Sovereignty, is delegated in the Constitution to the people of the United States. All powers therein delegated are to the States in their Sovereign character, under the designation of United States. Is it then surrendered to the United States jointly? Certainly not, for one of the main objects in forming the Compact, as before stated, and as clearly appears from the instrument itself, was, to preserve and perpetuate separate State existence. The guarantee to this effect, from the very words used, implies their Sovereignty. There can be no such thing as a *perfect State* without Sovereignty. It certainly is not parted with by any express terms in that instrument. If it be surrendered thereby it must be by implication only. But how can it be implied from any words or phrases in that instrument? If carried by implication, it must be on the strange assumption that it is an incident only of some one or all of those specific and specially enumerated powers expressly delegated. This cannot be, as that would be making the incident greater than the object, the shadow more solid than the substance. For Sovereignty is the highest and greatest of all political powers. It is itself the source as well as embodiment of all political powers, both great and small. All proceed and emanate from it All the great powers specifically and expressly delegated in the Constitution, such as the power to declare war and make peace; to raise and support armies, to tax and lay excise duties, etc., are themselves but the incidents of Sovereignty. If this great embodiment of all powers was parted with, why were any minor specifications made? Why any enumeration? Was not such specification or enumeration both useless and absurd?

All the implications are the other way. The bare fact that all the powers parted with by the States were delegated only, as all admit, necessarily implies that the greater power delegating still continued to exist.

If, then, this ultimate absolute Sovereignty did reside with the several States separately, as without question it did, up to the formation of the Constitution, and if, in the Constitution, Sovereignty is not parted with by the States in express terms, if, as Mr. Webster said, in 1839, there is not a word about Sovereignty in it, and if, further, this greatest of all political powers cannot justly be claimed as an incident to lesser ones, and thereby carried by implication, then, of course, was it not, most clearly, still retained and reserved to the people of the several States in that mass of residuary rights, in the language of Mr. Jefferson, which was expressly reserved in the Constitution itself?

It is true it was not so expressly reserved in the Constitution at first, because it was deemed, as the debates in the Federal Convention, as well as the State Conventions, clearly show, wholly unnecessary; so general was the understanding that it could not go, by inference or implication, from any thing in the Constitution; or in other words, that it could not be surrendered without express terms to that effect. The general understanding was the universally acknowledged principle in public law, that nothing is held good against Sovereignty by implication. But to quiet the apprehensions of Patrick Henry, Samuel Adams, and the Conventions of a majority of the States, this reservation of Sovereignty was soon after put in the

Constitution amongst other amendments, in plain and unequivocal language. So cautious and guarded were the men of that day that the Government had hardly commenced operations before all inferences that had been drawn against the reserved Sovereignty of the States, from the silence of the Constitution, in this particular and some others, were fully rebutted by several amendments, proposed by the States, in Congress assembled, at their first session. These amendments were preceded by a preamble, which shows that they were both declaratory and restrictive in their object. Here is what was done:—

"The Conventions of a number of the States, having, at the time of their adopting the Constitution, expressed a desire, in order to prevent misconstruction or abuse of its powers, that further declaratory and restrictive clauses should be added: And as extending the ground of public confidence in the Government, will best insure the beneficent ends of its institution;

"*Resolved, by the Senate and House of Representatives of the United States of America, in Congress assembled,* two thirds of both Houses concurring, That the following Articles be proposed to the Legislatures of the several States, as amendments to the Constitution of the United States, all, or any of which Articles, when ratified by three fourths of the said Legislatures, to be valid to all intents and purposes, as part of the said Constitution."*

The language of one of the amendments then proposed, on the subject we are now upon, is as follows: "The powers not *delegated* to the *United States* by the Constitution, nor prohibited by it to the States, are reserved to the States, respectively, or to the people."

---

* *Hickey's Constitution*, p. 33; *United States Statutes at Large*, vol. i, p. 97.

This amendment, which was promptly agreed to by the States unanimously, declares that *all powers* not *delegated* were reserved to the States respectively; this, of course, includes, in the reservation, Sovereignty, which is the source of all powers, those delegated as well as those reserved. This reservation Mr. Samuel Adams said, we have seen in the Massachusetts Convention, was consonant with the like reservation in the first Articles of Confederation. And such was the universal understanding at the time. Most of the other amendments,* then proposed, were likewise agreed to by the States, but not unanimously.

Can any proposition within the domain of reason be clearer, from all these facts, than that the Sovereignty of the States, that great Paramount authority which can rightfully make and unmake Constitutions, resides still with the States? Does not this declaratory amendment, added to the original covenant in the Constitution, which provides for its own amendment, show this beyond all doubt or question? Why were further amendments to it to be submitted to the States for their ratification before they could be binding, but upon the indisputable principle or postulate that Sovereignty, which alone has control of all such matters, still resides with the States severally? There is, my dear sirs, no answer to this.

The Government of the United States, however NEW some of its features are in the machinery of its operation, is no exception to the general rule, applicable to all Federal Republics, as to where the ultimate absolute Sovereign or Paramount authority resides. According to that rule, in *all of them*, it is retained by the Parties to the Compact. Such was the case in the model of

---

* See *Appendix* D.

Montesquieu. Such is the case in all Confederacies of this character, according to Vattel, as we have seen. Such is, necessarily, the case in our system, built upon these models. All unions of separate States, under Compacts of this sort, are founded upon the same essential basis. Sovereignty, with us, therefore, upon these fixed and indisputable principles, *now* resides, as I said before, just where it did in 1776—just where it did in 1778—and just where it did in 1787: that is, with the people of the several States of the Federal Union. This Sovereignty, so residing with them, is the Paramount authority to which allegiance is due. Allegiance, a word brought from the Old World, of Latin origin, from *ligo*, to bind, means the obligation which every one owes to that Power in the State, to which he is indebted for the protection of his rights of person and property. Allegiance and Sovereignty, as we have seen, are reciprocal.* "To whatever Power a citizen owes allegiance, that Power is his Sovereign." To what Power are the citizens of the several States indebted for protection of person and property, in all the relations of life, for the regulation of which Governments are instituted? Certainly not to the Federal Government. That Government, in its operations, has no right to *interfere, in any way whatever*, with the citizens of the several States, but in a few exceptional cases; and then, not for protection, but in the enforcement of laws, which the State would have been bound, by her plighted faith, to execute herself, had not this new feature been introduced into the Federal system. The Government of the United States, in its internal polity, is known to the citizens of the several States only by its requisitions upon individuals, instead of States, except in a very few

---

* *Ante*, p. 25.

specified cases. In its National character, it gives ample protection abroad. This was one of its main objects. In its postal arrangements, it furnishes many conveniences, for which it is duly paid. In these particulars, there is no difference between the Constitution and the first Articles of Confederation. But it was no part of the objects of either to afford protection to the citizens of the States, respectively, in all those relations of life which mark the internal polity of different States and Nations. These, now, as before, all depend upon the Sovereign will of the States. This Sovereign will fixes the *status* of the various elements of Society, as well as their rights. In the States, severally, remains the great right of Eminent Domain, which reserves to them complete jurisdiction and control over the rights of person and property of their entire population. With them remains, untrammelled, the power to establish codes of laws—civil, military, and criminal. They may punish for what crimes they please, and as they please, and the Government of the United States cannot interfere. To their own Legislatures, their own Judiciaries, their own Executives, their own laws, established by their own Paramount authority, do all the citizens of all the States look for whatever protection and security they receive, possess, or enjoy, in all the civil relations of life. In all such matters as require that protection to which allegiance is due, the Government of the United States is unknown to them.

It is true that the States did covenant, in the Constitution, that no State should "pass any law, making any thing but gold and silver coin a legal tender in the payment of debts; pass any bill of attainder, or *ex post facto* law, or law impairing the obligation of contracts;" but this, in no wise, changes the principle. Those provisions were put in by each State, to protect the rights of her citizens against the unjust legislation of other States, and not against her own legislation. By the Constitution, the citizens of each State have all the privileges and immunities of all the citizens of the several States, in their intercourse with each other. Hence, the propriety and wisdom of these provisions. It is, in itself, only a negative protection, and such as each State provided, in the Compact, for the protection of her own citizens, in other States, against the acts of the other States, and not against their own. It was inserted from no such view as that the citizens of the several States were to look to the Federal Government for that protection, in any sense, which is the foundation of all allegiance. The guarantee of rights, in the amendments to the Constitution, such as the right to bear arms, freedom from arrest, etc., apply, exclusively, to the Federal Government. They were but bulwarks, thrown around the citadel of State Rights, to protect the citizens of the respective States from the exercise of unjust powers over them by the General Government. They were not inserted with any view of protecting the citizens of the respective States from the action of their own State Governments.

On the several State authorities, therefore, are all the citizens, of all the States, under our system, entirely dependent for the protection of all those civil rights and franchises, for which, mainly, human societies are organized, and for which, mainly, Governments are instituted by men. To this several State authority, when properly expressed, is the allegiance proper of every citizen due. This is his Sovereign.

These things being so, I think I have made it very clearly appear, why I acted as I did, in going with my State, and obeying her high behest, when she resumed the Sovereign Powers she had delegated to the United

States, by entering into a Compact of Union with them in 1788, and asserted her right to be a free and independent State, which she was acknowledged to be by George the Third of England, in the treaty of peace, in 1783.

The rightfulness of this act, on the part of the State, is not now the question. We will come to that presently. But the question now is, was it not the duty of all her citizens to go with her in her solemn Resolve? Was not every one bound to do so, or become guilty of incivism, the highest of all political offences against the society of which one is a member? Would not every one, refusing to obey the mandate of the State, in such case have subjected himself to *her* laws against *treason* to her Sovereignty? In that case, could the United States, either *de jure* or *de facto*, have saved him or afforded him any protection whatever against the prescribed penalty? By the very *terms* of the *Compact*, if that was still in force, if he had escaped, and gone into another State, he would, necessarily, upon demand, have been delivered up to the State for trial and punishment! But in point of fact, the United States had not an officer, civil or military, within the State. All had retired, either voluntarily or by compulsion. Not an emblem even of their authority was to be found within her borders. To whose authority then could any citizen look for any sort of protection, but the authority of the State? Was not obedience both proper and due to that authority which alone could afford proper protection, both *de jure* and *de facto?*

Now as to the *rightfulness* of the State's thus resuming her Sovereign powers! In doing it she *seceded* from that Union, to which, in the language of Mr. Jefferson, as well as General Washington, she had *acceded* as a Sovereign State. She repealed her ordinance by which she ratified and agreed to the Constitution and became a party to the

Compact under it. She declared herself no longer bound by that Compact, and dissolved her alliance with the other parties to it. The Constitution of the United States, and the laws passed in pursuance of it, were no longer the supreme law of the people of Georgia, any more than the treaty with France was the supreme law of both countries, after its abrogation, in 1798, by the same rightful authority which had made it in the beginning.

In answer to your question, whether she could do this without a breach of her solemn obligations, under the Compact, I give this full and direct answer: she had a perfect right so to do, subject to no authority, but the great moral law which governs the intercourse between Independent Sovereign Powers, Peoples, or Nations. Her action was subject to the authority of that law and none other. It is the inherent right of Nations, subject to this law alone, to disregard the obligations of Compacts of all sorts, by declaring themselves no longer bound in any way by them. This, by universal consent, may be rightfully done, when there has been a breach of the Compact by the other party or parties. It was on this principle, that the United States abrogated their treaty with France, in 1798. The justifiableness of the act depends, in every instance, upon the circumstances of the case. The general rule is, if all the other States—the Parties to the Confederation—faithfully comply with their obligations, under the Compact of Union, no State would be morally justified in withdrawing from a Union so formed, unless it were necessary for her own preservation. Self-preservation is the first law of nature, with States or Nations, as it is with individuals.

But in this case the breach of plighted faith was not on the part of Georgia, or those States which withdrew or attempted to withdraw from the Union. Thirteen of their Confederates had openly and avowedly disregarded their obligations under that clause of the Constitution which covenanted for the rendition of fugitives from service, to say nothing of the acts of several of them, in a like open and palpable breach of faith, in the matter of the rendition of fugitives from justice. These are facts about which there can be no dispute. Then, by universal law, as recognized by all Nations, savage as well as civilized, the Compact, thus broken by some of the Parties, was no longer binding upon the others. The breach was not made by the seceding States. Under the circumstances, *and the facts* of this case, therefore, the legal as well as moral right, on the part of Georgia, according to the laws of Nations and nature, to declare herself no longer bound by the Compact, and to withdraw from the Union under it, was perfect and complete. These principles are too incontestably established to be questioned, much less denied, in the forum of reason and justice.

Hence the broad and unqualified admission of Mr. Webster, that, if the Constitution was a Compact between Sovereign States, the right to secede followed as a matter of course. This right comes not from any thing in the Constitution, but from the great law of Nations, governing all Compacts between Sovereigns. His language, you recollect, was: "where Sovereign communities are parties, there is no essential difference between a Compact, a Confederation, and a League. They all equally rest on the plighted faith of the Sovereign party. A League, or Confederacy, is but a subsisting or continuing treaty."

"If, in the opinion of either party," he added, "it be violated, such party may say that he will no longer fulfil its obligations on his part, but will consider the whole

League or Compact at an end, although it might be one of its stipulations that it should be perpetual."*

The right of a State to secede from the Union upon this principle of the laws of Nations was fully admitted by Mr. Webster, if it be true that the Constitution is a Compact between States; and that too when, even in the *opinion* of any Party to it, the Compact had been broken on the other side. But in this case there is no question as to the fact of the breach on the other side.

Judge Story, who strove so hard to establish the position that the Government of the United States is a National Government, proper and not Federal, is equally explicit in his admission as to the right of Secession, if it be true that the Constitution is a Compact between States. On this point there is no disagreement between him and Mr. Webster. Judge Story first states the position of Judge Tucker, in his Commentaries on the Constitution, as follows:—

"It is a Federal Compact. Several Sovereign and independent States may unite themselves together by a perpetual Confederation, without each ceasing to be a perfect State. They will, together, form a Federal Republic. The deliberations in common will offer no violence to each member, though they may in certain respects put some constraint on the exercise of it in virtue of voluntary engagements. The extent, modifications, and objects of the Federal authority are mere matters of discretion. So long as the separate organization of the members remains, and, from the nature of the Compact, must continue to exist, both for local and domestic, and for Federal purposes, the Union is, in fact as well as in theory, an association of States, or a Confederacy."†

---

* *Ante*, p. 309. † *Story on the Constitution*, vol. i, Book 3, Sec. 311.

This is Story's statement of Tucker's position. It is substantially correct. He afterwards comments on it, as follows:—

"The obvious deductions, which may be, and indeed have been drawn, from considering the Constitution as a Compact between the States, are, that it operates as a mere treaty, or convention between them, and has an obligatory force upon each State no longer than it suits its pleasure, or its consent continues; that each State has a right to judge for itself in relation to the nature, extent, and obligations of the instrument, without being at all bound by the interpretation of the Federal Government, or by that of any other State; and that each retains the power to withdraw from the Confederacy, and to dissolve the connection, when such shall be its choice; and may suspend the operations of the Federal Government, and nullify its acts within its own territorial limits, whenever, in its own opinion, the exigency of the case may require. These conclusions may not always be avowed; but they flow naturally from the doctrines which we have under consideration. They go to the extent of reducing the Government to a mere Confederacy during pleasure; and of thus presenting the extraordinary spectacle of a nation existing only at the will of each of its constituent parts."*

In this, Judge Story fully admits the right of a State to withdraw or secede from the Union, if the Constitution be a Compact between the States as States, even without an open breach of the Compact by the Confederates. He says, it is an obvious deduction from the fact of its being a Government founded on Compact; too clear and logical to give room for doubt or question. He was too thoroughly versed in the laws of nations to raise a point even on this

---

* *Story on the Constitution*, vol. i, Book 3, Sec. 321.

conclusion, if the premises as to the Constitution being a Compact between States be correct. Hence his labored argument in assault upon the premises. Hence his utmost efforts were put forth, with what success we have seen, to show that the States were never Sovereign, and that the Constitution is not a Compact between States, but that it is a social Compact between all the people of the United States in mass as one nation. However extraordinary, in the opinion of Judge Story, would be the spectacle of a nation existing only at the will of each of its constituent parts, yet just such a nation ours is, according to his own frank admission, if it be true that the Constitution is founded upon Compact between Sovereign States, (and this, by common consent between us, is a question now no longer open for consideration.)

Our "Nation," such as it is, is indeed a most extraordinary and wonderful spectacle! This we have abundantly seen in the course of our present investigation; and if Judge Story had more profoundly studied its nature and character, he might have been much more profoundly struck with many even more extraordinary features in it than that one to which he here specially refers.

That one has nothing in it more extraordinary than every other Federal Republic that ever existed. Montesquieu saw in such systems nothing more extraordinary than that under them the world had been saved from universal monarchical rule.

This right of a State to consider herself no longer bound by a Compact which, in her judgment, has been broken by her Confederates, and to secede from a Union, formed as ours was, has nothing about it, either new or novel. It is incident to all Federal Republics. It is not derived from the Compact itself. It does not spring from it at all. It is derived from the same source that the right is derived to abrogate a treaty by either or any of the parties to it. That is seldom set forth in the treaty itself, and yet it exists, whether it be set forth or not. So, in any Federal Compact whatever, the parties may or may not expressly provide for breaches of it. But where no such provision is made, the right exists by the same laws of Nations which govern in all matters of treaties or conventions between Sovereigns. The admission of the right of Secession, under this law, on the part of the several States of our Union, by Mr. Webster and Judge Story, if it be true that the Constitution is a Compact between the States, might be considered ample authority, in answer to your question on that point; since the conclusion, to which we arrived, that it is such a Compact.

But I do not mean to let it rest barely on this.

I maintain that such was the general understanding of the parties to the Constitution at the time it was adopted, as well as that such is its true exposition.

"*Contemporanea Expositio est optima et fortissima in Lege.*" "*The best and surest mode of expoundiug an instrument is by referring to time when, and circumstances under which, it was made.*"*

First, then, I maintain that it is a necessary incident of that Sovereignty which was believed to be reserved to the States severally, in the original Constitution, but which reservation, to quiet the apprehensions of the more cautious, was immediately after inserted in express terms, by way of amendment. It was expressly reserved in the ratifications of Virginia, New York, and Rhode Island. These ratifications were received by the other States, which fixes the construction of all at the time. More-

---

* 2 *Inst.* ii, *Broom's Legal Maxims*, p. 300.

over, the Government was formed, or to be formed, according to the very terms of the Constitution, by the Secession of nine States at least from their former Union, which was declared to be perpetual, and to which their faith was plighted in the most solemn manner, that no changes in the Articles of their Union should ever be made without the unanimous consent of its thirteen members. What is there in the history of the times or in the acts of the parties, which goes to show that the same general opinion, as to the Sovereign right to secede, did not continue to exist in reference to the present Constitution, which required no pledge as to its perpetuity?

Secondly. It is very clear that Mr. Jefferson believed in this right. This, the Kentucky Resolutions fully establish. The large majority by which he was elected, after the fierce contest of 1800, shows that the same opinion must have been then very generally entertained. Even Mr. Hamilton must have believed that this right was incident to the system; for in his urgent appeals to Mr. Jefferson, as early as 1790, for his influence with members of Congress, in aid of the bill for the assumption of the State debts, he presented the strong reason, that if that measure should not pass, there was *great danger of a Secession* of the members from the creditor States, which would end in "*a separation of the States.*"* He was then connected with the Government. He was Secretary of the Treasury. Would he have urged such an argument if he had not believed that those States had a right to withdraw? Moreover, his letter to Mr. Gouverneur Morris, of the 27th of February, 1802, shows very clearly, taken in connection with his whole career, that he did not believe that the Government of the United

---

* *Randall's Life of Jefferson*, vol. i, p. 609.

States had any *inherent Sovereign power* whatever. He looked upon the system as radically defective in this particular. "Perhaps," says he in this letter, "no man in the United States has sacrificed or done more for the present Constitution than myself; and *contrary to all my anticipations of its fate, as you know from the very beginning.* I am still laboring to prop the *frail* and *worthless fabric.* Yet I have the murmurs of its friends no less than the curses of its foes, for my reward."* The worthlessness of the fabric, in his opinion, consisted, as we know, in the want of the energy of a consolidation of the Sovereignties of the several States in one single grand Republic, which he had at first insisted upon in the Federal Convention of 1787. When that failed, he did give the Federal plan agreed upon a zealous and patriotic support. He contributed greatly to its adoption by the States. But he never had confidence in its durability. He thought it would go to pieces by State disintegration. His belief and conviction of the want of power on the part of the General Government, as formed to prevent such disintegration, is shown from all that he said in the New York State Convention, when the Constitution was before that body, and what he wrote on the same subject in the *Federalist* afterwards.

But, *thirdly.* One of the earliest, if not the earliest, commentators on the Constitution, not as a politician, but as a jurist and publicist, was Judge Tucker, Professor of Law in the University of William and Mary, in Virginia. In his edition of Blackstone's Commentaries, there is an appendix by him to the first volume, of considerable length, devoted to the consideration of Governments generally, and particularly the Constitution of the United

---

* *Works of Hamilton,* vol. vi, p. 530.

States. He wrote in 1803. He held, as we have seen, that the Constitution was a Federal Compact between States. And while no more devoted friend to the Union under the Constitution perhaps ever lived, he yet was forced, from this indisputable fact, to what Story said was an obvious deduction—that is, that the right of Secession, on the part of any one or more of the States, was a *necessary incident* from the very nature of the system. His language is this:

"The Constitution of the United States, then, being that instrument by which the Federal Government hath been created, its powers defined and limited, and the duties and functions of its several departments prescribed, the Government, thus established, may be pronounced to be a Confederate Republic, composed of several Independent and Sovereign Democratic States, united for their common defence and security against foreign Nations, and for the purposes of harmony and mutual intercourse between each other; each State *retaining an entire liberty* of exercising, as it thinks proper, all those parts of its Sovereignty which are not mentioned in the Constitution, or Act of Union, as parts that ought to be exercised in common."

"In becoming a member of the Federal Alliance, established between the American States by the Articles of Confederation, she expressly retained her Sovereignty and Independence. The constraints, put upon the exercise of that Sovereignty by those Articles, did not destroy its existence. * * *

"The Federal Government, then, appears to be the organ through which the united Republics communicate with foreign Nations, and with each other. Their submission to its operation is voluntary; its councils, its engagements, its authority, are theirs, modified and united. Its Sovereignty is an emanation from theirs, not a flame, in which they have been consumed, nor a vortex, in which they are swallowed up. Each is still a perfect State, still Sovereign, still independent, and still capable, should the occasion require, to resume the exer cise of its functions, as such, in the most unlimited ex tent. * * *

"But, until the time shall arrive, when the occasion requires a resumption of the rights of Sovereignty by the several States (and far be that period removed, when it shall happen), the exercise of the rights of Sovereignty by the States, individually, is wholly suspended or discontinued in the cases before mentioned; nor can that suspension ever be removed, so long as the present Constitution remains unchanged, but by the dissolution of the bonds of union; an event which no good citizen can wish, and which no good or wise administration will ever hazard."*

A clearer or truer exposition of this feature of the Constitution of the United States was never made in fewer words. This exposition went to the country with the sanction of his high authority, and was not gainsayed or controverted by any writer of distinction, that I am aware of, until Chancellor Kent's Commentaries appeared in 1826, and Story's, in 1833. I do not mean to say that no one of that class of politicians, barely, who figured during the Administration of the elder Adams, denied this right; but that no jurist or publicist of eminence denied it up to that time. Chancellor Kent goes into no argument. He barely deals, as Mr. Motley does, in assertion. This, we have seen, will not do. But, meanwhile, Mr. Rawle, an eminent jurist of Pennsylvania,

* *Tucker's Blackstone*, vol. i, *Appendix*, pp. 170, 171, 175, 187.

wrote an elaborate work upon the Constitution, which was published in 1825. He was United States District Attorney under Washington, and had been offered, by him, the Attorney-Generalship of the United States. He was, also, a firm supporter of the Administration of the elder Adams. This shows the character of the man, and the authority with which his opinions should be received. His investigations brought him to the same conclusion to which Judge Tucker had come. That conclusion is expressed by him in the following language:—

"Having thus endeavored to delineate the general features of this peculiar and invaluable form of Government, we shall conclude with adverting to the principles of its cohesion, and to the provisions it contains for its own duration and extension.

"The subject cannot, perhaps, be better introduced than by presenting, in its own words, an emphatical clause in the Constitution:—

"'The United States shall guarantee, to every State in the Union, a Republican form of Government; shall protect each of them against invasion; and, on application of the Legislature, or of the Executive, when the Legislature cannot be convened, against domestic violence.'

"The Union is an association of the people of Republics; its preservation is calculated to depend on the preservation of those Republics. The principle of representation, although, certainly, the wisest and best, is not essential to the being of a Republic; but, to continue a member of the Union, it must be preserved; and, therefore, the guarantee must be so construed. It depends on the State itself, to retain or abolish the principle of representation; because it depends on itself, whether it will continue a member of the Union. To deny this right, would be inconsistent with the principles on which all our political systems are founded; which is, that the people have, in all cases, a right to determine how they will be governed.

"This right must be considered as an ingredient in the original composition of the General Government, which, though not expressed, was mutually understood; and the doctrine, heretofore presented to the reader, in regard to the indefeasible nature of personal allegiance, is so far qualified, in respect to allegiance to the United States. It was observed that it was competent for a State to make a Compact with its citizens, that the reciprocal obligations of protection and allegiance might cease on certain events; and it was further observed that allegiance would necessarily cease on the dissolution of the society to which it was due. * * *

"The Secession of a State from the Union depends on the will of the people of such State. The people, alone, as we have already seen, hold the power to alter their Constitution. The Constitution of the United States is, to a certain extent, incorporated into the Constitutions of the several States, by the act of the people. The State Legislatures have only to perform certain organical operations in respect to it. To withdraw from the Union, comes not within the general scope of their delegated authority. There must be an express provision to that effect inserted in the State Constitutions. This is not, at present, the case with any of them, and it would, perhaps, be impolitic to confide it to them. A matter, so momentous, ought not to be intrusted to those who would have it in their power to exercise it lightly and precipitately, upon sudden dissatisfaction or causeless jealousy, perhaps against the interests and the wishes of a majority of their constituents.

"But in any manner by which a Secession is to take place, nothing is more certain than that the act should be deliberate, clear, and unequivocal. The perspicuity and solemnity of the original obligation require correspondent qualities in its dissolution. The powers of the General Government cannot be defeated or impaired by an ambiguous or implied Secession on the part of the State, although a Secession may, perhaps, be conditional. The people of the State may have some reasons to complain ir respect to acts of the General Government; they may, in such cases, invest some of their own officers with the power of negotiation, and may declare an absolute Secession in case of their failure. Still, however, the Secession must in such case be distinctly and peremptorily declared to take place on that event, and in such case—as in the case of an unconditional Secession—the previous ligament with the Union would be legitimately and fairly destroyed. But, in either case, the people is the only moving power."* * * *

"Under the Articles of Confederation the concurrence of nine States was requisite for many purposes. If five States had withdrawn from that Union, it would have been dissolved. In the present Constitution there is no specification of numbers after the first formation. It was foreseen that there would be a natural tendency to increase the number of States with the increase of population then anticipated, and now so fully verified. It *was also known, though it was not avowed, that a State might withdraw itself.* The number would therefore be variable."† * * *

"To withdraw from the Union is a solemn, serious act. Whenever it may appear expedient to the people of a State, it must be manifested in a direct and unequivocal

---

* *Rawle*, pp. 302, 303. † *Rawle*, p. 304.

manner. If it is ever done indirectly, the people must refuse to elect Representatives, as well as to suffer their Legislature to re-appoint Senators. The Senator whose time had not yet expired, must be forbidden to continue in the exercise of his functions.

"But without plain, decisive measures of this nature, proceeding from the only legitimate source, the people, the United States cannot consider their Legislative powers over such States suspended, nor their Executive or Judicial powers any way impaired, and they would not be obliged to desist from the collection of revenue, within such State.

"As to the remaining States, among themselves, there is no opening for a doubt.

"Secessions may reduce the number to the smallest integer admitting combination. They would remain united under the same principles and regulations, among themselves, that now apply to the whole. For a State cannot be compelled by other States to withdraw from the Union, and, therefore, if two or more determine to remain united, although all the others desert them, nothing can be discovered in the Constitution to prevent it.

"The consequences of an absolute Secession cannot be mistaken, and they would be serious and afflicting.

"The Seceding State, whatever might be its relative magnitude, would speedily and distinctly feel the loss of the aid and countenance of the Union. The Union, losing a proportion of the National revenue, would be entitled to demand from it a proportion of the National debt. It would be entitled to treat the inhabitants and the commerce of the separated State, as appertaining to a foreign country. In public treaties already made, whether commercial or political, it could claim no participation, while foreign powers would unwillingly calculate, and slowly transfer to it, any portion of the respect and confidence borne towards the United States."*

Mr. Rawle came to the same logical conclusion upon the subject of Secession that Judge Tucker had come to. He also distinctly asserts that it *was known* at the time, though *not avowed*, that a *State might withdraw itself*. "It was mutually understood," he says. He was a living actor in the scenes.

Fourthly.—It is upon the grounds or assumption that this was the general understanding of the nature of the Government at the time, that we can account for the triumphant success of Mr. Jefferson, in 1800, on the principles of the Virginia and Kentucky Resolutions of 1798–99, and Mr. Madison's Report, referred to before. It is in accordance with this general understanding that we can account for Mr. Hamilton's strong reason for Mr. Jefferson's co-operation in the matter just stated.

It is in accordance with the same general understanding that we can account for what I have seen it stated was the action of the Massachusetts Legislature in 1803, on the acquisition of Louisiana. That State, it is said, then declared, by solemn resolve, "That the annexation of Louisiana to the Union, transcends the Constitutional power of the Government of the United States. It formed a new Confederacy to which the States united by the former *Compact* are not *bound to adhere*."

Whether this Resolution ever was, in fact, passed by the Massachusetts Legislature, or not, I have not been able to ascertain with absolute certainty. Perhaps you, Judge, know whether the statement which has been so generally made be true or not?

JUDGE BYNUM. I am unable to give any information on the subject.

---

* *Rawle*, pp. 305, 306.

MR. STEPHENS. Well, be that as it may, the Legislature of Massachusetts, in 1844, did, without question, pass a series of Resolutions upon the annexation of Texas, of which the following is a part:

"*Resolved*, * * That the project of the annexation of Texas, unless arrested on the threshold, may drive these States into a dissolution of the Union."

On the same subject, on the 22d of February, 1845, the same body adopted another series of Resolutions, in which the following occurs:

"*Resolved*, * * * and as the powers of Legislation granted in the Constitution of the United States to Congress, do not embrace the case of the admission of a foreign State, or foreign territory, by Legislation, into the Union, such an act of admission would have no binding force whatever on the people of Massachusetts."

Here are authentic copies of each of these sets of Resolutions.* They are not at all inconsistent with those said to have been passed on a similar subject in 1803. These Resolutions show clearly the understanding of Massachusetts as late as 1844–45, of the nature of the Compact of our Union. Though she did not see fit to exercise her right to secede or withdraw, she nevertheless unmistakably asserted her right to do so under circumstances then existing, by asserting that she would not be bound by the anticipated action of the General Government in the matter of the annexation of Texas.

Moreover, it is in strict accordance with this general understanding that several of the Eastern States, upon the call of Massachusetts,† assembled by their deputies

* See also *Lunt's History of the Origin of the War*, pp. 467–8.

† *Niles's Register*, vol. vii, p. 161.

in the well-known New England or Hartford Convention, in December, 1814.* These States, it is well known, were greatly disaffected towards the Federal Administration. It was during our last war with Great Britain. They conceived their interest to be improperly sacrificed by the policy pursued in the conduct of the war. The Convention was called to devise some course to be taken by these States for a redress of their common grievances. They did nothing, however, but issue an address setting forth their grievances, and appoint a delegation to present them, with their views, to the Federal authorities at Washington; and provide for another Convention to take further action in the premises. This address went into a very full review of the nature of the Government. In it the following principles are set forth:

"It is as much the duty of the State authorities to watch over the rights reserved, as of the United States to exercise the powers which are delegated."

Further on this language occcurs:

"But in cases of deliberate, dangerous and palpable infractions of the Constitution, affecting the *Sovereignty of a State* and liberties of the people, it is not only the right, but the duty of such a State to interpose its authority for their protection in the manner best calculated to secure that end. When emergencies occur which are either beyond the reach of the judicial tribunals, or too pressing to admit of the delay incident to their forms, *States which have no common umpire must be their own judges, and execute their own decisions.*†"

To this document are signed, amongst others, the venerable names of Nathan Dane, George Cabot, Zephenia Swift, James Hillhouse, and Harrison G. Otis. Dane

---

* *Niles's Register*, vol. vii, p. 269. † *Niles's Register*, vol. vii, p. 306.

was the founder of the Professorship of Law in the Cambridge University, and was the author of the Abridgment of American Law, so often quoted by Judge Story, as well as the author of the celebrated ordinance for the government of the North-western Territory, in 1787. That these States did intend to secede and withdraw from the Union, unless their grievances complained of were redressed, there can be no doubt, and that these eminent jurists thought then that they had a right to do so, is equally clear.

The news, however, of the treaty of peace which had been signed at Ghent, on the 24th day of December, 1814, was soon after received in this country, and put an end to all other proceedings under this movement of these States.

But what is remarkable in the history of that controversy is, that in no debate in Congress were the fundamental doctrines of this address called in question, so far as I have been able to discover. Mr. Madison, then President, made no allusion, in his message to Congress, to this movement. *Niles's Register* contains six able leading editorial articles against this Convention and its proceedings, but in none of them is the right of the States to withdraw from the Union, if they choose to do so, questioned. It is true, the Convention was generally odious, at the time, to the people of a large majority of the States, and has been ever since. This was from the fact that the threatened Secession was in time of war, and a war which had been undertaken mainly, at the instance of these States, in defence of their shipping and navigating interests. It is also true, that some journalists and partisans of the day did charge the movement to be treasonable. But what have not partisan journalists and public speakers, in times of excitement, charged to be treasonable! Almost every matter in the administration of Government, that does not suit their own peculiar views and notions. This charge was not made by any of the officials of the Government, that I am aware of, and what I mean to say is, that the right of a State to withdraw from the Union was never denied or questioned, that I am aware of, by any jurist, publicist, or statesman of character and standing, until Kent's Commentaries appeared, in 1826, nearly forty years after the Government had gone into operation! From the weight of evidence, therefore, the conclusion follows, that in the opinion of the fathers generally, as well as of the great mass of the people throughout the country, the right existed. It has been stated by high authority, that "the right of Secession" is not a plant of Southern origin"—"it first sprung up in the North."* A more accurate statement would be that it was not *sectional* but *continental* in its origin. It was generally recognized in all parts of the Union during the earlier days of the Republic.

Fifthly and lastly, this right, so apparent to all clear and unbiassed minds from all the facts connected with the history and nature of the Government, is fully and clearly recognized by all foreign writers and publicists who have made our institutions their study. Prominent in this class stands De Tocqueville, before alluded to. On this point he says:—

"However strong a Government may be, it cannot easily escape from the consequences of a principle which it has once admitted as the foundation of its Constitution. The Union was formed by the voluntary agreement of the States; and these, in uniting together, have

* *Mr. Buchanan—History of his Administration*, p. 86.

not forfeited their Nationality, nor have they been reduced to the condition of one and the same people. If one of the States chose to withdraw its name from the contract, it would be difficult to disprove its right of doing so, and the Federal Government would have no means of maintaining its claims directly, either by force or by right."*

To the name of De Tocqueville, the names of many of the most eminent writers in Europe, upon our institutions, might be added. Why, however, multiply authorities of this sort to show either the unprejudiced judgment of foreign writers upon the subject, or the general understanding of all parties in this country, during the earlier and better days of the Republic? Men of great ability of our own day—men, who stand high in the Republican ranks at this time, who had and have no sympathy with the late Southern movement, are fully committed to the rightfulness of that movement. Mr. Lincoln himself was fully committed to it. Besides him, I refer you to but two others of this class, now prominent actors in public affairs. They are Senator Wade, of Ohio, at this time the Vice President of the United States, and Mr. Greeley, of the *New York Tribune*, who is "a power behind the throne greater than the throne itself."

Mr. Wade, in the Senate of the United States, on the 23d of February, 1855, used the following language: I read from the *Appendix to the Congressional Globe*, 2d Session, 33d Congress, page 214.

"Who is to be judge, in the last resort, of the violation of the Constitution of the United States by the enactment of a law? Who is the final arbiter? The General Government, or the States in their Sovereignty? Why, sir,

---

* *De Tocqueville's Democracy in America*, vol. i, p. 498.

to yield that point, is to yield up all the rights of the States to protect their own citizens, and to consolidate this Government into a miserable despotism. I tell you, sir, whatever you may think of it, if this bill pass, collisions will arise between the Federal and State jurisdictions—conflicts more dangerous than all the wordy wars which are got up in Congress—conflicts in which the States will never yield; for the more you undertake to load them with acts like this, the greater will be their resistance."

Again, he says, in the same speech:

"I said there were States in this Union whose highest tribunals had adjudged that bill to be unconstitutional, and that I was one of those who believed it unconstitutional: that my State believed it unconstitutional; and that, under the old Resolutions of 1798 and 1799, a State must not only be the judge of that, but of the remedy in such a case."

This is enough to show that he put himself at that time squarely upon the old States' Rights State Sovereignty Jeffersonian platform of 1798 and 1799. Judge Story has told us what the obvious deductions from these principles are.

Let us now see what Mr. Greeley says. I read from the American Conflict, vol. i, page 359. It is taken from the editorial of his own paper, the Tribune, issued as late as the 9th day of November, 1860.

"The telegraph informs us that most of the Cotton States are meditating a withdrawal from the Union, because of Lincoln's election. Very well: they have a right to meditate, and meditation is a profitable employment of leisure. We have a chronic, invincible disbelief in Disunion as a remedy for either Northern or Southern grievances. We cannot see any necessary connection between the alleged disease and this ultra-heroic remedy; still, we say, if any one sees fit to meditate Disunion, let him do so unmolested. That was a base and hypocritic row that was once raised at Southern dictation, about the ears of John Quincy Adams, because he presented a petition for the dissolution of the Union. The petitioner had a right to make the request; it was the Member's duty to present it. And now, if the Cotton States consider the value of the Union debatable, we maintain their perfect right to discuss it. Nay: we hold, with Jefferson, to the unalienable right of communities to alter or abolish forms of government that have become oppressive or injurious; and, if the Cotton States shall decide that they can do better out of the Union than in it, we insist on letting them go in peace. The right to secede may be a revolutionary one, but it exists nevertheless; and we do not see how one party can have a right to do what another party has a right to prevent. We must ever resist the asserted right of any State to remain in the Union, and nullify or defy the laws thereof; to withdraw from the Union is quite another matter. And, whenever a considerable section of our Union shall deliberately resolve to go out, we shall resist all coercive measures designed to keep it in. We hope never to live in a Republic, whereof one section is pinned to the residue by bayonets.

"But, while we thus uphold the practical liberty, if not the abstract right, of Secession, we must insist that the step be taken, if it ever shall be, with the deliberation and gravity befitting so momentous an issue. Let ample time be given for reflection; let the subject be fully canvassed before the people; and let a popular vote be taken in every case, before Secession is decreed. Let the people be told just why they are asked to break up the Confederation; let them have both sides of the question fully presented; let them reflect, deliberate, then vote; and let the act of Secession be the echo of an unmistakable popular fiat. A judgment thus rendered, a demand for separation so backed, would either be acquiesced in without the effusion of blood, or those who rushed upon carnage to defy and defeat it, would place themselves clearly in the wrong."*

What better argument could I make to show the rightfulness of Secession, if the Southern States of their own goodwill and pleasure chose to resort to it, even for no other cause than Mr. Lincoln's election, than is herein set forth in his own pointed, strong, and unmistakable language? It is true, he waives all questions of Compact between the States. He goes deeper into fundamental principles, and plants the right upon the eternal truths announced in the Declaration of Independence. That is bringing up principles which I have not discussed, not because I do not indorse them as sound and correct, to the word and letter, but because it was not necessary for my purpose. Upon these immutable principles the justifiableness of Georgia in her Secession Ordinance of the 19th of January, 1861, will stand clearly established for all time to come. For if, with less than one hundred thousand population, she was such a people in 1776 as had the unquestionable right to alter and change their form of Government as they pleased, how much more were they such a people, with more than ten times the number, in 1861? The same principle applies to all the States which quit the old and joined the new Confederation. Mr. Greeley here speaks of the Union as a *Confederation*, and not a *Nation*. This was, perhaps, the *unconscious* utterance of a *great truth* when the *true spirit* was moving him.

---

* *Greeley's American Conflict*, vol. i, p. 359.

The State of Georgia did not take this step, however, in withdrawing from the Confederation, without the most thorough discussion. It is true it was not a dispassionate discussion. Men seldom, if ever, enter into such discussions with perfect calmness, or even that degree of calmness with which all such subjects ought to be considered. But the subject was fully canvassed before the people. Both sides were strongly presented. In the very earnest remonstrance against this measure made by me, on the 14th of November, 1860, to which you have alluded, was an appeal equally earnest for just such a vote as he suggests in order that the action of the State on the subject might be "the echo of an unmistakable, popular fiat." On the same occasion I did say, in substance, just what he had so aptly said before, that the people of Georgia, in their Sovereign capacity, had the right to secede if they chose to do so, and that in this event of their so determining to do, upon a mature consideration of the question, that I should bow in submission to the majesty of their will so expressed!

This, when so said by me, is what it seems was "the dead fly in the ointment" of that speech; so sadly "marring its general perfume." This was "the distinct avowal of the right of the State to overrule my personal convictions and plunge me," as he says, "into treason to the Nation!"*

Was not the same "dead fly in the ointment" of his article of the 9th of November, only five days before? And if going with my State, in what he declared she had a *perfect right* to do, plunged me into *treason* to the *Nation*, is he not clearly an accessory before the fact by a rule of construction not more strained than that laid down in the trial of State cases by many judges not quite

* *American Conflict*, vol. i, page 343. Also *ante*, p. 22.

so notoriously infamous as Jeffreys? By a rule not more strained than that which would make out treason in the act itself! But I do not admit the rule in its application either to the accessory or the principal.

Now in relation to Mr. Lincoln. He himself, in 1848, announced the same general principles as above announced by Mr. Greeley in 1860. On the 12th day of January, 1848, Mr. Lincoln, in the House of Represenatives, made a speech which I heard. Here is that speech. In it he used this language. I read from the Appendix to the Congressional Globe, First Session, Thirtieth Congress, page 94.

"Any people any where, being inclined and having the power, have the right to rise up and shake off the existing Government, and form a new one that suits them better. This is a most valuable, a sacred right—a right which, we hope and believe, is to liberate the world. Nor is this right confined to cases in which the whole people of an existing Government may choose to exercise it. Any portion of such people that can, may revolutionize, and make their own of so much of the territory as they inhabit. More than this, a majority of any portion of such people may revolutionize, putting down a minority, intermingled with, or near about them, who may oppose their movements. Such minority was precisely the case of the Tories of our own Revolution. It is a quality of revolutions not to go by old lines, or old laws; but to break up both, and make new ones."

Even if Secession was but a *revolutionary right*, and did not spring at all from the nature of the Compact between the States, Mr. Lincoln here distinctly admits the *right,—a "most valuable and sacred right"*—as one of a revolutionary character. If this be a *sacred right, even in this view*, how, in the language of Mr. Greeley, can there exist any *legal* or *moral* right anywhere else to prevent its exercise? There cannot be two antagonistic rights! Rights, like truths, always fit as between themselves! They never jar, impinge, or collide!

Thus the moral and political worlds, when rightly administered, present the same beauty and symmetry which pervade the physical in all its parts, extending throughout creation; and in the practical workings of all *their* parts, produce a perfect concord and harmony, not unlike that symphony of the spheres in the material universe which has gone forth from the time the most distant stars raised the grand chorus in the morning of their birth!

You thus have, gentlemen, a very full review of the grounds upon which my convictions of duty, in regard to the right of Secession, were founded. They arose from my understanding of the nature of the Government of the United States, and where, under the system, that Paramount authority resides, to which ultimate allegiance is due. The conclusion to which I came was, that this ultimate Paramount authority had never been parted with by the States—that, from the *nature* of the Federal Government, and from the very *terms of the Compact* between the States, this Sovereign power was reserved to them, severally. If I erred in that conclusion, you see I erred with many of the brightest intellects, ablest statesmen, and purest patriots of this as well as other countries.

But even if I erred with them on this point, we see it fully and clearly admitted, by very high authority in the ranks of modern Republicanism, that it *does nevertheless still there reside*, according to the great fundamental principles of the American Revolution! In either view, was I not fully justified in the course I took?

I will not ask your judgment upon the matter, how

ever clearly I may think that this exposition of my course shows that I acted rightly and patriotically. I know full well that you have been too thoroughly schooled in different opinions for any one reasonably to expect so radical a change of them in so short a time. Men's opinions or convictions upon such questions do not so readily or easily change. Truths of this character do not bring forth their fruits in a day. They must have time to germinate, grow, and develop, first.

It is better, therefore, to leave these questions for the verdict of posterity—for the enlightened and unimpassioned judgment of mankind. By this, we or our memories must all abide. All that any of us can do in the premises is, to see to it that all the facts, as well as a true account of our actions, shall be transmitted to that august tribunal. This is the work of history. The only anxiety I have on the matter is, that this work shall be faithfully performed—that the record shall be rightly put up. This being done, I entertain no apprehensions as to the verdict and judgment upon it hereafter to be rendered. From these opposing and conflicting priciples, however, as I said in the beginning, the war sprung. These were the latent but real causes.

Now, then, if it is agreeable, we will proceed to consider that immediate and exciting question which brought these organic principles into such terrible physical conflict in the inauguration of the war.

COLLOQUY XII.

CONCLUSION OF THE ARGUMENT—IS A CONFEDERATED GOVERNMENT TOO WEAK TO SECURE ITS OBJECTS—ON THE CONTRARY, IS IT NOT THE STRONGEST OF ALL GOVERNMENTS—THE OPINIONS OF MR. JOHN QUINCY ADAMS AND MR. JEFFERSON—IN SECESSION WAS INVOLVED THIS GREAT RIGHT, WHICH LIES AT THE FOUNDATION OF THE FEDERATIVE SYSTEM OF GOVERNMENT—IT WAS OF INFINITELY MORE IMPORTANCE TO THE SOUTHERN STATES THAN SLAVERY, SO-CALLED, WITH ITS TWO THOUSAND MILLIONS OF CAPITAL INVESTED IN THAT INSTITUTION.

JUDGE BYNUM. Before proceeding further, I wish briefly to say, at this point, that we have no disposition, or at least I have none, to pronounce judgment in the matter under consideration, so far as it relates to your course, or that of others. It was with no such views or feelings, the subject was at first introduced. We all know full well, that whatever opinion we entertain, or might be inclined to express upon it, if expressed, would have but little weight with that great arbiter, by whom the future judgment to which you refer will be rendered.

But you will allow me to say, that I do not see how you, with your ideas of its nature, could consider the Government of the United States "the best the world ever saw." To me it seems very much, as it did to Judge Story, that such an association of States, bound by nothing stronger than their own will and pleasure, would be no Government at all. It would have no adhesive quality between its parts or members. It would have no stability, no durability, no strength; the bonds of union, in that view, it does seem to me, would be no better, as is often said, than a rope of sand. A Government, to be worth any thing, must be strong; it must be held together by force. It must be clothed with power, not only to pass laws, but to command obedience. What would become of the public faith, of the public credit, of the public property? What Nation would put any confidence in such a Government, if its nature and organic structure were so understood abroad? Who would treat with such a country, or enter into any agreements, or conventions, with a Government so constructed, upon any matters of trade, commerce, finance, or any thing else? It would be virtually treating with an ideal power that had no real existence! The solemn agreements entered into one day, by what you call the *bare agent* of a number of separate Sovereignties, might be annulled the next, by any one of these Sovereigns. Such a Government, it seems to me, you will excuse me for saying it, so far from being entitled to the respect even, of any one, would deserve and receive nothing but the contempt of mankind!

MR. STEPHENS. Do not be so quick and broad in your conclusion. Just such Governments, founded upon just such principles, have existed, and have received, you must upon reflection admit, not the contempt but the admiration of mankind! What think you of the Confederations of Greece? They were just such Governments. To whom is the world so much indebted for European civilization at this time, as to the little Republics upon the Archipelago, held together by no other bonds than their *own consent?* By whom were the battles of Marathon, and Salamis, and Platæa, fought? By whom was the progress of Asiatic Empire stayed in its westward march, but by States so united? What people on earth have left more enduring monuments of their greatness in the defence and maintenance of liberty, or the development of art, science, eloquence, or song, than these same small Hellenic States, confederated upon precisely the principles which you consider of so little worth? When did their greatness and glory depart? Not until these principles were departed from.

What think you of the United Netherlands? In maintaining successfully, as they did, the great principles of civil and religious liberty, in the dawn of modern political reformation, did they deserve nothing but the contempt of mankind? On the contrary, will not their glorious achievements live in history amongst the grandest of any age or country? These States were united by no bonds but their own voluntary consent. Passing over many other instances, what think you of our own old Confederation? Did it not carry these States, then thus united, successfully through the War of Independence? A war against one of the greatest powers then existing? A war of seven years' duration? A war jointly waged to establish this very principle? Did not France, Sweden and Prussia, treat with them? Did not England treat with them upon boundary, upon trade, upon commerce, upon matters of public right, upon all matters of public faith, when she knew that the sanction and co-operation of each State was necessary to give absolute validity to some articles of the treaty? Though the public credit was not so well sustained under the machinery of that Confederation as it has been under the new one, yet was it not sufficient to carry them through the most perilous struggle that any States ever passed successfully through? Have we, or mankind, no feelings towards that Confederacy, so constituted, which effected such grand results, but contempt?

Now all these Governments, the Grecian, the Germanic, as well as our own first Confederation, were founded, as you yourself must admit, upon just such a principle as you speak of. The principle of voluntary consent. This is the principle upon which are founded all Confederations. Just such Governments are all Confederated Republics. And these are the only kinds of Governments, as Montesquieu informs us, which have saved the human race from universal monarchical rule. Low as your estimate of them may be, they are the only escape yet discovered by man foi free institutions, among bordering States or Nations. Governments which have done so much for mankind certainly do not deserve, nor have they received from them, such sentiments as you imagine.

But we have seen that our *present system* is a great improvement upon all *former models* of this kind of Confederation. While it is founded upon the same *basis* of *consent* and voluntary agreement, as I hope I have clearly shown, yet it has several new and important features in its organization, unknown before, and to which we are mainly indebted for its unparalleled success in the past. It is because of these new features, all resting upon the same basis as all other Confederations, placing it far above all other systems, that I considered it the best Government the world ever saw.

The same view was entertained by John Hancock, when, in his message to the Legislature of Massachusetts, as we have seen, he said, that if the proposed amendments, which he had himself offered in the State Convention, should be adopted, the chief one of which was the expressly declared reservation of the Sovereignty of the States, he should "consider it the most perfect system of Government as to the objects it embraces that has been known amongst mankind."

A Government, to be worth any thing, as you say, must be strong. Its parts and members must be held together by force of some sort. This I cordially admit. We do not differ as to the force or its extent; we differ only as to its nature and character. Should it be a physical or moral force? In my judgment, the strongest force that can hold the parts or constituent elements of any Government together is the affection of the people towards it. The Universe is held together by force—the greatest of all forces, by Omnipotence itself! This force in the material world, which binds and holds together in indissoluble union all its parts in their respective and most distant orbits throughout the illimitable regions of space, is the simple law of attraction! So should it be with all Governments, especially with those formed by distinct States United or Confederated upon any sort of Compact, Agreement, or Constitution, as ours was, with a view, and a sole view, to their mutual convenience and reciprocal advantage.

These, also, evidently, were the views of Mr. John Quincy Adams. In his celebrated address before the Historical Society of New York, in 1839, in speaking of the Union of these States, he says:

"With these qualifications we may admit the same right as vested in the people of every State in the Union, with reference to the General Government, which was exercised by the people of the United Colonies with reference to the supreme head of the British Empire, of which they formed a part; and under these limitations have the people of each State in the Union a right to secede from the Confederated Union itself. *Here stands the right!* But the indissoluble union between the several States of this Confederated Nation is, after all, not in the *right*, but in the *heart!* If the day should ever come (may Heaven avert it), when the affections of the people of these States shall be alienated from each other; when the fraternal spirit shall give way to cold indifference, or collision of interest shall fester into hatred, the bands of political asseveration will not long hold together parties no longer attached by the magnetism of conciliated interests and kindly sympathies; and far better will it be for the people of the dis-United States, to part in friendship from each other, than to be held together by constraint; then will be the time for reverting to the precedents which occurred at the formation and adoption of the Constitution, to form again a more perfect Union by dissolving that which could no longer bind, and to leave the separated parts to be re-united by the law of political gravitation to the centre!"

The strength of the Union, in the opinion of Mr. Adams, was not in the *right* to hold it together by *physical force*, but in the *moral power* which springs from the *heart* of the people, and which prompts them to sustain it by their own voluntary action. This was also doubtless the opinion of Mr. Jefferson, when he declared the Government of the United States in his judgment, to be the strongest in the world. In his first inaugural, soon after his election, upon the principles of his own Resolutions touching the nature of the Government and the principles upon which it was founded, he said:

"I know, indeed, that some honest men fear that a Republican Government cannot be strong; *that* THIS *Government is not strong enough.* But would the honest patriot, in the full tide of successful experiment, abandon a Government which has so far kept us free and firm, on the theoretic and visionary fear that *this Government*, the *World's best hope*, may by possibility want energy to preserve itself? I trust not. *I believe this, on the contrary, the strongest Government on the Earth!*"*

Its strength, in his opinion, lay not in physical force,

* *Statesman's Manual*, vol. i, p. 150.

but in moral power, in the hearts and affections of its constituent elements. He fully believed in the right of any State to withdraw when the terms of the Compact were broken by the other parties to it, and he believed in the perfect and absolute right of *each party for itself to judge* as well of *infractions of the Compact* as *the mode and measure of redress.*

Indeed, this is the self-adjusting principle of the system. It is the only principle upon which the safety, security and existence even of the separate members can be maintained and preserved, which is the chief object of all Federal Republics.

Your arguments are but a repetition of the views expressed by the advocates of one great consolidated Government, when the new Constitution was under consideration in the Philadelphia Convention. The same that caused Hamilton to look upon the new Constitution which continued the Federal System as "a *frail and worthless fabric,*" though he gave this plan, when he could not get his own, a zealous and patriotic support as an experiment. It was indeed an experiment, a wonderful experiment, and most wonderfully was it performing its high mission, to his utter astonishment as well as that of all others of his class, so long as the primary law of its existence was recognized in its administration.

In illustration of my views of the normal action of the system in its practical workings, with its new features differing, as we have seen, from all former Federal Republics, you will excuse me for calling your attention to what I said on this subject in the House of Representatives on the 12th day of February, 1859.

The views then expressed I still entertain. They were given in a speech made on the admission of Oregon. In that speech, after going at some length into those agitating questions which were then culminating in that crisis which ended in the war which we are now considering, and after speaking of the nature of the Government and urging "a strict conformity to the laws of its existence," as essential not only "for the safety and prosperity of all its members," but for its own preservation, I went on further to speak not only of what it had accomplished, but of the still greater results that might be expected, if it should continue to be administered upon the principles and for the objects upon which and for which it was formed. Here is what was then added:—

"Such is the machinery of our theory of self-government by the people. This is the great novelty of our peculiar system, involving a principle unknown to the ancients, an idea never dreamed of by Aristotle or Plato. The union of several distinct, independent communities upon this basis (the Federal machinery acting directly upon the citizens of the several States within the sphere of its limited powers), is a new principle in human Governments. It is now a problem in experiment for the people of the nineteenth century, upon this continent, to solve. As I behold its workings in the past and at the present, while I am not sanguine, yet I am hopeful of its successful solution. The most joyous feeling of my heart is the earnest hope that it will, for the future, move on as peacefully, prosperously, and brilliantly, as it has in the past. If so, then we shall exhibit a moral and political spectacle to the world something like the prophetic vision of Ezekiel, when he saw a number of distinct beings or living creatures, each with a separate and distinct organism, having the functions of life within itself, all of one external likeness, and all, at the same time, mysteriously connected, with one common animating spirit pervading the whole, so that when the common spirit moved they all moved; their appearance and their work being, as it were, a wheel in the middle of a wheel; and whithersoever the common spirit went, thither the others went, all going together; and when they went, he heard the noise of their motion like the noise of great waters, as the voice of the Almighty! Should our experiment succeed, such will be our exhibition—a machinery of Government so intricate, so complicated, with so many separate and distinct parts, so many independent States, each perfect in the attributes and functions of Sovereignty, within its own jurisdiction, all, nevertheless, united under the control of a common directing power for external objects and purposes, may naturally enough seem novel, strange, and inexplicable to the philosophers and crowned heads of the world!

"It is for us, and those who shall come after us, to determine whether this grand experimental problem shall be worked out; not by quarrelling amongst ourselves; not by doing injustice to any; not by keeping out any particular class of States; but by each State remaining a separate and distinct political organism within itself—all bound together, for general objects, under a common Federal head; as it were, a wheel within a wheel. Then the number may be multiplied without limit; and then, indeed, may the nations of the earth look on in wonder at our career; and when they hear the noise of the wheels of our progress in achievement, in development, in expansion, in glory, and renown, it may well appear to them not unlike the noise of great waters; the very voice of the Almighty—*Vox populi! Vox Dei!*"*

Such was the spectacle presented to my mind by the harmonious workings of our "glorious institutions," (as

* *Congressional Globe*, 2d Session, 35th Congress, p. 124, *Appendix.*

Mr. Webster styled them, in 1839,) under the Constitution of the United States, as I understood its nature and character! That Constitution which sets forth the terms of Union between Free, Sovereign, and Independent States—each retaining its separate Sovereignty, and only delegating such powers to all the rest as are most conducive, by their joint exercise, to its own safety, security, happiness, and prosperity, as well as most conducive to the like safety, security, happiness and prosperity of all the other members of the great American Federal Republic—the work of their own voluntary creation!

The chief strength of the system, in its proper administration, lay, according to my view, in that moral power which brought the several members into Confederation. It lay in the hearts of the people of the several States, and in no right or power of keeping them together by coercion. The right of any member to withdraw, which you consider an element of weakness, was really, in my judgment, one of the greatest elements of strength, looking in its practical workings to the attainment of the objects for which the Union was formed. This right is not only the basis upon which all Confederated Republics must necessarily be formed, but without it there is, and can be, in such systems, no check, no real barrier, nothing, indeed, that can be successfully relied upon to prevent their running, sooner or later, into centralized despotic Empire, to escape from which, the Federative principle was resorted to in the institution of Governments for neighboring States. This right is essential to avoid that final and inevitable result which, without it, must necessarily ensue. Its full recognition, as I have said, becomes the self-adjusting principle of the system by which all its temporary perturbations and irregularities of motion will correct and rectify themselves. No system of Government, as yet discovered, is perfect. All have their defects, their irregularities, their eccentricities of action. The Federate principle resorted to is only an approximation to the hitherto unattained standard. But it is the nearest approximation, up to this time, reached by the wisdom of man. Ours was a long stride nearer the desired goal, by an improvement on this principle, than any that ever existed before.

All Governments of this character are formed upon the assumption that it is for the best interest of all the members of the Confederation to be united on such terms as may be agreed upon, each faithfully performing all its duties and obligations under the Compact. Ours was, certainly, formed on this assumption, and in this belief.

No State, therefore, would withdraw, or be inclined to withdraw, without a real or supposed breach of faith, on the part of her Confederates, or some of them. If the complaint were real, the derelict States would right the wrong, rather than incur the loss attending the failure to do so. For the maintenance of the Union, so long as the objects for which it was formed alone are looked to, is of equal interest to all. If the complaint were imaginary, and a State should withdraw, without a real and substantial cause, the withdrawal would be but for a very brief period of time. It would be but a temporary aberration. For such State would soon find that she had lost more than she had gained in her new position. New burthens would devolve on her. New responsibilities, as well as her just proportion of those resting on her in common with her former Confederates, would have to be assumed; or, in a word, all the disadvantages of isolation, which impelled the Union at first, would be encountered. Under these circumstances and necessary consequences, no Federal Union would remain *long dis-*

severed, where this principle was left to its full normal action, which was really for the benefit and interest of all its members. It is true that none would stand long that was inherently and permanently injurious to any, and none such ought to stand. For it would be in opposition to the very principles and objects upon which, and for which, all such unions are formed.

In what you consider, then, the weakness of our Government, according to my idea of its nature, I repeat, its chief strength, its great beauty, its complete symmetry, its ultimate harmony, and, indeed, its very perfection, mainly consist; certainly, so long as the objects aimed at in its formation are the objects aimed at in its administration. And, on this principle, on the full recognition of the absolute ultimate Sovereignty of the several States, I did consider it the best, and the strongest, and the grandest Government on earth! My whole heart and soul were devoted to the Constitution, and the Union under it, with this understanding of its nature, character, objects, and functions!

When, therefore, the State of Georgia seceded, against my judgment, viewing the measure in the light of *policy*, only, and not of right (for the causes, as we have seen, and shall see more fully, hereafter, were more than ample to justify the act, as a matter of right), I felt it to be my duty to go with her, not only from a sense of the obligations of allegiance, but from other high considerations of patriotism of not much less weight and influence. These considerations pressed upon the mind the importance of maintaining *this principle*, which *lies at the foundation of all Federal systems;* and to which we were mainly indebted, in ours, for all the great achievements of the past. It was under this construction of the nature of our system, that all these achievements had been attained.

This was the essential and vital principle of the system, to which I was so thoroughly devoted. It was that which secured all the advantages of Confederation, without the risk of Centralism and Absolutism; and on its preservation depended, not only the safety and welfare, and even existence, of my own State, but the safety, welfare, and ultimate existence of all the other States of the Union! The States were older than the Union! They made it! It was but their own creation! Their preservation was of infinitely more importance than its continuance! The Union might cease to exist, and yet the States continue to exist, as before! Not so with the Union, in case of the destruction or annihilation of the States! With their extinction, the Union necessarily becomes extinct also! They may survive it, and form another, more perfect, if the lapse of time and changes of events show it to be necessary, for the same objects had in view when it was formed; but it can never survive them! What may be called a Union may spring from the common ruins, but it would not be the Union of the Constitution!—the Union of States! By whatever name it might be called, whether Union, Nation, Kingdom, or any thing else, according to the taste of its dupes or its devotees, it would, in reality, be nothing but that deformed and hideous Monster which rises from the decomposing elements of dead States, the world over, and which is well known by the friends of Constitutional Liberty, everywhere, as the Demon of Centralism, Absolutism, Despotism! This is the necessary reality of that result, whether the Imperial Powers be seized and wielded by the hands of many, of few, or of one!

The question, therefore, with me, assumed a magnitude and importance far above the welfare and destiny of my own State, it embraced the welfare and ultimate destiny of all the States, North as well as South; nay, more, it embraced, in its range, the general interest of mankind, so far, at least, as the oppressed of all other lands and climes were looking to this country, not only for a present asylum against the evils of misrule in their own, but were anxiously and earnestly looking forward to the Federative principles here established, as "the World's best hope," in the great future, for the regeneration, the *renaisance*, of the Nations of the Earth! Such, in my judgment, were the scope and bearing of the question and the principles involved.

Had this foundation principle of the system then been generally acknowledged—had no military force been called out to prevent the exercise of this right of withdrawal on the part of the seceding States—had no war been waged against Georgia and the other States, for their assertion and maintenance of this right, had not this primary law of our entire system of Government been violated in the war so waged, I cannot permit myself to entertain the shadow of a doubt, that the whole controversy, between the States and Sections, would, at no distant day, have been satisfactorily and harmoniously adjusted, under the peaceful and beneficent operation of this very law itself. Just as all perturbations and irregularities are adjusted in the solar system, by the simple law of gravitation, from which alone it sprung in the beginning, and on which alone its continuance, with its wonderfully harmonious workings, depends!

A brief illustration will more clearly unfold this view. Had the right of withdrawal not been denied or resisted, those States, which had openly, confessedly, and avowedly disregarded their obligations, under the Compact, in the matter of the rendition of fugitives from service, and fugitives from justice, appealing, as they did, to "a higher Law" than the Constitution, would have reconsidered their acts, and renewed their covenants under the bonds of Union, and the Federal administration would have abandoned its policy of taking charge of subjects not within the limits of its delegated powers. The first aberrations in the system; that is the disregard of plighted faith, which had caused the second, that is the secession movement, would themselves have been rectified by that very movement! This rectification on the one side would have been attended by a corresponding rectification on the other. This would have been a *necessary* and *inevitable* result, whatever parties, under the influence of passion at the time, may have thought of the nature and permanency of the separation. That is, it would necessarily and inevitably have been the result, if the assumption on which the Union was founded be correct, namely, that it was for the best interest of all the States to be united upon the terms set forth in the Constitution—each State faithfully performing all its obligations, and the Federal Head confining its action strictly to the subjects with which it was charged. On this point, that the Union was best for all, my own convictions were strong and thorough for many reasons, that may be given hereafter. If this postulate was correct, then the ultimate result of this action and re-action in the operation of the system in bringing about a re-adjustment of the parts to their original places, would have been as *inevitable* as the continued harmonious re-adjustment of continual disturbances in the material world is being produced by like action and counter-action continually going on throughout its entire organization, and the whole resulting from the same all-pervading and all-controlling law, the same law continuing the organization which brought it at first into existence

But if, on the contrary, the whole assumption on which the Union was formed was wrong,—if it were not for the true and best interests of all the States, constituted as they were, to be so united,—if it were true, as asserted by the controlling spirits of the derelict States, that the Constitution itself as to them, was but a "covenant with death and an agreement with Hell,"—then, of course, the re-adjustment would not have taken place, and ought not to have taken place. But I did not believe that the masses of the people in these States entertained any such sentiments towards the work of their Fathers!

My opinion was, that it only required those masses to see, feel, and appreciate the great advantages of that Union to them; and to realize the fact that a Compact, broken by them, could not longer be binding upon others, as Mr. Webster had said, to cause them to compel their officials to comply with the terms of an engagement, which, upon the whole, was of so great importance to their best interests. My convictions were equally strong that, when this was done, the masses of the people at the South, influenced by like considerations, would have controlled all opposition to their cheerful and cordial return to their proper places.

There would have been no war, no bloodshed, no sacking of towns and cities, no desolation, no billions of treasure expended, on either side, and no million of lives sacrificed in the unnatural and fratricidal strife; there would have been none of the present troubles about restoration, or reconstruction; but, instead of these lamentable scenes, a new spectacle of wonder would have been presented for the guide and instruction of the astonished Nations of the earth, greater than that exhibited after the Nullification pacification, of the matchless workings of our American Institutions of Self-Government by the people!

You readily perceive, therefore, how thoroughly, looking to the grand results, my entire feelings, heart, and soul, with every energy of mind and body, became enlisted in the success of this cause, when force was invoked, when war was waged to put it down. It was the cause, not only of the Seceding States, but the cause of all the States, and in this view it became, to a great extent, the cause of Constitutional Liberty everywhere. It was the cause of the Federative principle of Government, against the principle of Empire! The cause of the Grecian type of Civilization against the Asiatic! So, at least, I viewed it, with all the earnestness of the profoundest convictions.

The matter of Slavery, so-called, which was the proximate cause of these irregular movements on both sides, and which ended in the general collision of war, as we have seen, was of infinitely less importance to the Seceding States, than the recognition of this great principle. I say Slavery, so-called, because there was with us no such thing as Slavery in the full and proper sense of that word. No people ever lived more devoted to the principles of liberty, secured by free democratic institutions, than were the people of the South. None had ever given stronger proofs of this than they had done, from the day that Virginia moved in behalf of the assailed rights of Massachussetts, in 1774, to the firing of the first gun in Charleston Harbor, in 1861. What was called Slavery amongst us, was but a legal subordination of the African to the Caucasian race. This relation was so regulated by law as to promote, according to the intent and design of the system, the best interests of both races, the Black as well as the White, the Inferior, as well as the Superior. Both had rights secured, and both had duties imposed. It was a system of reciprocal service, and mutual bonds. But even the two thousand million dollars invested in the relation thus established, between private capital and the labor of this class of population, under the system, was but as the dust in the balance, compared with the vital attributes of the rights of Independence and Sovereignty on the part of the several States. For with these whatever changes and modifications, or improvements in this domestic institution, founded itself upon laws of nature, time, and experience, might have shown to be proper in the advancing progress of civilization, for the promotion of the great ends of society in all good Governments—that is the best interest of all classes, without wrong or injury to any—could, and would have been made by the superior race in these States, under the guidance of that reason, justice, philanthropy, and statemanship, which had ever marked their course, without the violent disruption of the entire social fabric, with all its attendant ills, and inconceivable wrongs, mischiefs, and sufferings; and especially without those terrible evils and consequences which must almost necessarily result from such disruptions and re-organizations as make a sudden and complete transfer of political power from the hands of the superior to the inferior race, in their present condition, intellectually and morally, in at least six States of the Union!

The system, as it existed, it is true, was not perfect. All admit this. No human systems are perfect. But great changes had been made in it, as this class of persons were gradually rising from their original barbarism, in their subordinate sphere, under the operation of the system, and from their contact, in this way, with the civilization of the superior race. Other changes would certainly have been made, even to the extinction of the system, if time, with its changes, and the progress of attainments on the part of these people had shown it to be proper—that is, best for both races. For if the system, as designed, was not really the best, or could not have been made the best for both races, or whenever it should have ceased to be so, it could and would have been thoroughly and radically changed, in due time, by the only proper and competent authority to act in the premises.

The erroneous dogma of the greatest good to the greatest number, was not the basis on which this Institution rested. Much less was it founded upon the dogma oi principle of the sole interest or benefit of the white race to the exclusion of considerations embracing the interests and welfare of the other. It was erected upon no such idea as that *might*, barely, gives *right*, but it was organized and defended upon the immutable principles of justice to all, which is the foundation of all good Governments. This requires that society be so organized as to secure the greatest good possible, morally, intellectually, and politically, to all classes of persons within their jurisdictional control, without necessary wrong or detriment to any. This was the foundation principle on which this institution in these States was established and defended.*

These questions are not now, however, before us. We are at present considering the workings of the Federal system, and not the wisdom or policy of the social systems of the several States, or the propriety of the *status* of their constituent elements respectively.

This whole question of Slavery, so-called, was but one relating to the proper *status* of the African as an element of a society composed of the Caucasian and African races, and the *status* which was best, not for the one race or the other, but best, upon the whole, for both.

---

* See *Appendix* F.

Over these questions, the Federal Government had no rightful control whatever.* They were expressly excluded, in the Compact of Union, from its jurisdiction or authority. Any such assumed control was a palpable violation of the Compact, which released all the parties to the Compact, affected by such action, from their obligations under the Compact. On this point there can be no shadow of doubt.

Waiving these questions, therefore, for the present, I repeat that this whole subject of Slavery, so-called, in any and every view of it, was, to the Seceding States, but a drop in the ocean compared with those other considerations involved in the issue. Hence, during the whole war, being thoroughly enlisted in it from these other and higher considerations, but being, at the same time, ever an earnest advocate for its speediest termination by an appeal from the arena of arms to the forum of reason, justice, and right, I was wedded to no idea as a basis of peace, but that of the recognition of the ultimate absolute Sovereignty of all the States as the essential basis of any permanent union between them, or any of them, consistent with the preservation of their ultimate existence and liberties. And I wanted, at no time, any recognition of Independence on the part of the Confederate States, but that of George III., of England. That is, the recognition of the Sovereignty and Independence of each, by name.

The Confederate States had made common cause for this great principle, as the original thirteen States had done in 1776. The recognition of this I regarded as essential to the future well-being, happiness, and prosperity of all the States, in existence and to be formed, as well as

---

* See *Appendix* G

the countless millions of people who are hereafter to inhabit this half of the Western Hemisphere.

With this simple recognition I saw no formidable difficulty likely to arise in the future, from controversies between States or Sections. Whenever the passions of the day passed off, whatever Union or Unions were, or might be, really beneficial to all the States, would have resulted sooner or later, as inevitably as natural laws produce their natural effects. This they do in the moral and political world, if left to their proper and legitimate action, with as much certainty as they do in the material.

With this principle recognized, I looked upon it hereafter, and at no distant day, to become, by the natural law of political affinity—"mutual convenience and reciprocal advantage"—the great Continental Regulator of the Grand Federal Republic of "the United States of America," to whatever limits their boundaries might go, or to whatever extent their number might swell.

APPENDIX.

A.

In Congress, July 4th, 1776.

THE UNANIMOUS DECLARATION OF THE THIRTEEN UNITED STATES OF AMERICA.

When, in the course of human events, it becomes necessary for one people to dissolve the political bands which have connected them with another, and to assume, among the powers of the earth, the separate and equal station to which the laws of nature, and of nature's God entitle them, a decent respect to the opinions of mankind requires that they should declare the causes which impel them to the separation.

We hold these truths to be self-evident, that all men are created equal; that they are endowed by their Creator with certain unalienable rights; that among these, are life, liberty, and the pursuit of happiness. That, to secure these rights, governments are instituted among men, deriving their just powers from the consent of the governed; that, whenever any form of government becomes destructive of these ends, it is the right of the people to alter or to abolish it, and to institute a new government, laying its foundation on such principles, and organizing its powers in such form, as to them shall seem most likely to effect their safety and happiness. Prudence, indeed, will dictate that governments long established, should not be changed for light and transient causes; and, accordingly, all experience hath shown, that mankind are more disposed to suffer, while evils are sufferable, than to right themselves by abolishing the forms to which they are accustomed. But, when a long train of abuses and usurpations, pursuing invariably the same object, evinces a design to reduce them under absolute despotism, it is their right, it is their duty, to throw off such government, and to provide new guards for their future security. Such has been the patient sufferance of these colonies, and such is now the necessity which constrains them to alter their former systems of government. The history of the present king of Great Britain is a history of repeated injuries and usurpations, all having, in direct object, the establishment of an absolute tyranny over these States. To prove this, let facts be submitted to a candid world:

He has refused his assent to laws the most wholesome and necessary for the public good.

He has forbidden his Governors to pass laws of immediate and pressing importance, unless suspended in their operation till his assent should be obtained; and, when so suspended, he has utterly neglected to attend to them.

He has refused to pass other laws for the accommodation of large districts of people, unless those people would relinquish the right of representation in the legislature; a right inestimable to them, and formidable to tyrants only.

He has called together legislative bodies at places unusual, uncomfortable, and distant from the depository of their public records, for the sole purpose of fatiguing them into compliance with his measures.

He has dissolved representative houses repeatedly, for opposing, with manly firmness, his invasions on the rights of the people.

He has refused, for a long time after such dissolutions, to cause others to be elected; whereby the legislative powers, incapable of annihilation, have returned to the people at large for their exercise; the State remaining, in the meantime, exposed to all the danger of invasion from without, and convulsions within.

He has endeavored to prevent the population of these States; for that purpose obstructing the laws for naturalization of foreigners; refusing to pass others to encourage their migration hither, and raising the conditions of new appropriations of lands.

He has obstructed the administration of justice, by refusing his assent to laws for establishing judiciary powers.

He has made judges dependent on his will alone, for the tenure of their offices, and the amount and payment of their salaries.

He has erected a multitude of new offices, and sent hither swarms of officers to harass our people, and eat out their substance.

He has kept among us, in times of peace, standing armies, without the consent of our legislature.

He has affected to render the military independent of, and superior to, the civil power.

He has combined, with others, to subject us to a jurisdiction foreign to our constitution, and unacknowledged by our laws; giving his assent to their acts of pretended legislation:

For quartering large bodies of armed troops among us:

For protecting them, by mock trial, from punishment, for any murders which they should commit on the inhabitants of these States:

For cutting off our trade with all parts of the world:

For imposing taxes on us without our consent:

For depriving us, in many cases, of the benefits of trial by jury:

For transporting us beyond seas to be tried for pretended offences:

For abolishing the free system of English laws in a neighboring province, establishing therein an arbitrary government, and enlarging its boundaries, so as to render it at once an example and fit instrument for introducing the same absolute rule into these colonies:

For taking away our charters, abolishing our most valuable laws, and altering, fundamentally, the powers of our governments:

For suspending our own legislatures, and declaring themselves invested with power to legislate for us in all cases whatsoever.

He has abdicated government here, by declaring us out of his protection, and waging war against us.

He has plundered our seas, ravaged our coasts, burnt our towns, and destroyed the lives of our people.

He is, at this time, transporting large armies of foreign mercenaries to complete the works of death, desolation, and tyranny, already begun, with circumstances of cruelty and perfidy scarcely paralleled in the most barbarous ages, and totally unworthy the head of a civilized nation.

He has constrained our fellow-citizens, taken captive on the high seas, to bear arms against their country, to become the executioners of their friends and brethren, or to fall themselves by their hands.

He has excited domestic insurrections amongst us, and has endeavored to bring on the inhabitants of our frontiers, the merciless Indian savages, whose known rule of warfare is an undistinguished destruction, of all ages, sexes, and conditions.

In every stage of these oppressions, we have petitioned for redress, in the most humble terms; our repeated petitions have been answered only by repeated injury. A prince, whose character is thus marked by every act which may define a tyrant, is unfit to be the ruler of a free people.

Nor have we been wanting in attention to our British brethren. We have warned them, from time to time, of attempts made by their legislature to extend an unwarrantable jurisdiction over us. We have reminded them of the circumstances of our emigration and settlement here. We have appealed to their native justice and magnanimity, and we have conjured them, by the ties of our common kindred, to disavow these usurpations, which would inevitably interrupt our connections and correspondence. They, too, have been deaf to the voice of justice and consanguinity. We must, therefore, acquiesce in the necessity, which denounces our separation, and hold them, as we hold the rest of mankind, enemies in war, in peace, friends.

We, therefore, the Representatives of the UNITED STATES OF AMERICA in GENERAL CONGRESS assembled, appealing to the Supreme Judge of the World for the rectitude of our intentions, do, in the name, and by the authority of the good people of these colonies, solemnly publish and declare, that these United Colonies are, and of right ought to be, free and Independent States; that they are absolved from all allegiance to the British crown, and that all political connection between them and the state of Great Britain, is, and ought to be, totally dissolved; and that, as FREE AND INDEPENDENT STATES, they have full power to levy war, conclude peace, contract alliances, establish commerce, and to do all other acts and things which INDEPENDENT STATES may of right do. And, for the support of this declaration, with a firm reliance on the protection of DIVINE PROVIDENCE, we mutually pledge to each other, our lives, our fortunes, and our sacred honor.

The foregoing declaration was, by order of Congress, engrossed, and signed by the following members:

JOHN HANCOCK.

NEW HAMPSHIRE.

Josiah Bartlett,
William Whipple,
Matthew Thornton.

RHODE ISLAND.

Stephen Hopkins,
William Ellery.

CONNECTICUT.

Roger Sherman,
Samuel Huntington,
William Williams,
Oliver Wolcott.

NEW YORK.

William Floyd,
Philip Livingston,
Francis Lewis,
Lewis Morris.

NEW JERSEY.

Richard Stockton,
John Witherspoon,
Francis Hopkinson,
John Hart,
Abraham Clark.

PENNSYLVANIA.

Robt. Morris,
Benjamin Rush,
Benjamin Franklin,
John Morton,
Geo: Clymer,
James Smith,
George Taylor,
James Wilson,
George Ross.

MASSACHUSETTS BAY.

Samuel Adams,
John Adams,
Robert Treat Paine,
Elbridge Gerry.

DELAWARE.

Cæsar Rodney,
George Read,
Thomas M'Kean.

MARYLAND.

Samuel Chase,
William Paca,
Thomas Stone,
Charles Carroll,
of Carrollton.

VIRGINIA.

George Wythe,
Richard Henry Lee,
Thomas Jefferson,
Benjamin Harrison,
Thomas Nelson, jun.
Francis Lightfoot Lee,
Carter Braxton.

NORTH CAROLINA.

William Hooper,
Joseph Hewes,
John Penn.

SOUTH CAROLINA.

Edward Rutledge,
Thomas Heyward, jun.
Thomas Lynch, jun.
Arthur Middleton.

GEORGIA.

Button Gwinnett,
Lyman Hall,
George Walton.

B.

ARTICLES OF CONFEDERATION AND PERPETUAL UNION BETWEEN THE STATES.

[*The following have been critically compared with the original Articles of Confederation in the Department of State, and found to conform minutely to them in text, letter, and punctuation. It may therefore be relied upon as a true copy.*]

TO ALL TO WHOM THESE PRESENTS SHALL COME, WE, THE UNDERSIGNED DELEGATES OF THE STATES AFFIXED TO OUR NAMES, SEND GREETING.—Whereas the Delegates of the United States of America in Congress assembled did on the 15th day of November in the Year of our Lord 1777, and in the Second Year of the Independence of America agree to certain articles of Confederation and perpetual Union between the States of New Hampshire, Massachusetts-bay, Rhode-Island and Providence Plantations, Connecticut, New-York, New-Jersey, Pennsylvania, Deleware, Maryland, Virginia, North-Carolina, South-Carolina, and Georgia, in the words following, viz.

ARTICLES OF CONFEDERATION AND PERPETUAL UNION BETWEEN THE STATES OF NEW-HAMPSHIRE, MASSACHUSETTS-BAY, RHODE-ISLAND AND PROVIDENCE PLANTATIONS, CONNECTICUT, NEW-YORK, NEW-JERSEY, PENNSYLVANIA, DELAWARE, MARYLAND, VIRGINIA, NORTH-CAROLINA, SOUTH-CAROLINA, AND GEORGIA.

ARTICLE I. The Style of this confederacy shall be "The United States of America."

ARTICLE II. Each State retains its sovereignty, freedom and independence, and every Power, Jurisdiction and right, which is not by this confederation expressly delegated to the united states, in congress assembled.

ARTICLE III. The said states hereby severally enter into a firm league of friendship with each other, for their common defence, the security of their Liberties, and their mutual and general welfare, binding themselves to assist each other, against all force offered to, or attacks made upon them, or any of them, on account of religion, sovereignty, trade, or any other pretence whatever.

ARTICLE IV. The better to secure and perpetuate mutual friendship and intercourse among the people of the different states in this union, the free inhabitants of each of these states, paupers, vagabonds and fugitives from Justice excepted, shall be entitled to all privileges and immunities of free citizens in the several states ; and the people of each state shall have free ingress and regress to and from any other state, and shall enjoy therein all the privileges of trade and commerce, subject to the same duties, impositions and restrictions as the inhabitants thereof respectively, provided that such restriction shall not extend so far as to prevent the removal of property imported into any state, to any other state of which the Owner is an inhabitant; provided also that no imposition, duties or restriction shall be laid by any state, on the property of the united states, or either of them.

If any person guilty of, or charged with treason, felony, or other high misdemeanor in any state, shall flee from Justice, and be found in any of the united states, he shall upon demand of the Governor or executive power, of the state from which he fled, be delivered up and removed to the state having jurisdiction of his offence.

Full faith and credit shall be given in each of these states to the records, acts and judicial proceedings of the courts and magistrates of every other state.

ARTICLE V. For the more convenient management of the general interests of the united states, delegates shall be annually appointed in such manner as the legislature of each state shall direct, to meet in congress on the first Monday in November, in every year, with a power reserved to each state, to recal its delegates, or any of them, at any time within the year, and to send others in their stead, for the remainder of the Year.

No state shall be represented in congress by less than two, nor by more than seven members; and no person shall be capable of being a delegate for more than three years in any term of six years; nor shall any person, being a delegate, be capable of holding any office under the united states, for which he, or another for his benefit receives any salary, fees or emolument of any kind.

Each state shall maintain its own delegates in any meeting of the states, and while they act as members of the committee of the states.

In determining questions in the united states, in congress assembled, each state shall have one vote.

Freedom of speech and debate in congress shall not be impeached or questioned in any Court, or place out of congress, and the members of congress shall be protected in their persons from arrests and imprisonments, during the time of their going to and from, and attendance on congress, except for treason, felony, or breach of the peace.

ARTICLE VI. No state without the Consent of the united states in congress assembled, shall send any embassy to, or receive any embassy from, or enter into any conference, agreement, alliance or treaty with any King prince or state; nor shall any person holding any office of profit or trust under the united states, or any of them, accept of any present, emolument, office or title of any kind whatever, from any king, prince or foreign state; nor shall the united states in congress assembled, or any of them, grant any title of nobility.

No two or more states shall enter into any treaty, confederation or alliance whatever between them, without the consent of the united states in congress assembled, specifying accurately the purposes for which the same is to be entered into, and how long it shall continue.

No state shall lay any imposts or duties, which may interfere with any stipulations in treaties, entered into by the united states in congress assembled, with any king, prince or state, in pursuance of any treaties already proposed by congress, to the courts of France and Spain.

No vessels of war shall be kept up in time of peace by any state, except such number only, as shall be deemed necessary by the united states in congress assembled, for the defence of such state, or its trade: nor shall any body of forces be kept up by any state, in time of peace, except such number only, as in the judgment of the united states, in congress assembled, shall be deemed requisite to garrison the forts necessary for the defence of such state; but every state shall always keep up a well regulated and disciplined militia, sufficiently armed and accoutred, and shall provide and have constantly ready for use, in public stores, a due number of field pieces and tents, and a proper quantity of arms, ammunition and camp equipage.

No state shall engage in any war without the consent of the united states in congress assembled, unless such state be actually invaded by enemies, or shall have received certain advice of a resolution being formed by some nation of Indians to invade such state, and the danger is so imminent as not to admit of a delay, till the united states in congress assembled can be consulted; nor shall any state grant commissions to any ships or vessels of war, nor letters of marque or reprisal, except it be after a declaration of war by the united states in congress assembled, and then only against the kingdom or state and the subjects thereof, against which war has been so declared, and under such regulations as shall be established by the united states in congress assembled, unless such state be infested by pirates, in which case vessels of was may be fitted out for that occasion, and kept so long as the danger shall continue, or until the united states in congress assembled shall determine otherwise.

ARTICLE VII. When land-forces are raised by any state for the common defence, all officers of or under the rank of colonel, shall be appointed by the legislature of each state respectively by whom such forces shall be raised, or in such manner as such state shall direct, and all vacancies shall be filled up by the state which first made the appointment.

ARTICLE VIII. All charges of war, and all other expenses that shall be incurred for the common defence or general welfare, and allowed by the united states in congress assembled, shall be defrayed out of a common treasury, which shall be supplied by the several states, in proportion to the value of all land within each state, granted to or surveyed for any Person, as such land and the buildings and improvements thereon shall be estimated according to such mode as the united states in congress assembled, shall from time to time, direct and appoint. The taxes for paying that proportion shall be laid and levied by the authority and direction of the legislatures of the several states within the time agreed upon by the united states in congress assembled.

ARTICLE IX. The united states in congress assembled, shall have the sole and exclusive right and power of determining on peace and war, except in the cases mentioned in the 6th article—of sending and receiving ambassadors—entering into treaties and alliances, provided that no treaty of commerce shall be made whereby the legislative power of the respective states shall be restrained from imposing such imposts and duties on foreigners, as their own people are subjected to, or from prohibiting the exportation or importation of any species of goods or commodities whatsoever—of establishing rules for deciding in all cases, what captures on land or water shall be legal, and in what manner prizes taken by land or naval forces in the service of the united states shall be divided or appropriated—of granting letters of marque and reprisal in times of peace—appointing courts for the trial of piracies and felonies committed on the high seas and establishing courts for receiving and determining finally appeals in all cases of captures, provided that no member of congress shall be appointed a judge of any of the said courts.

The united states in congress assembled shall also be the last resort on appeal in all disputes and differences now subsisting or that hereafter may arise between two or more states concerning boundary, jurisdiction or any other cause whatever; which authority shall always be exercised in the manner following. Whenever the legislative or executive authority or lawful agent of any state in controversy with another shall present a petition to congress, stating the matter in question and praying for a hearing, notice thereof shall be given by order of congress to the legislative or executive authority of the other state in controversy, and a day assigned for the appearance of the parties by their lawful agents, who shall then be directed to appoint by joint consent, commissioners or judges to constitute a court for hearing and determining the matter in question: but if they cannot agree, congress shall name three persons out of each of the united states, and from the list of such persons each party shall alternately strike out one, the petitioners beginning, until the number shall be reduced to thirteen; and from that number not less than seven, nor more than nine names as congress shall direct, shall in the presence of congress be drawn out by lot, and the persons whose names shall be so drawn or any five of them, shall be commissioners or judges, to hear and finally determine the controversy, so always as a major part of the judges who shall hear the cause shall agree in the determination: and if either party shall neglect to attend at the day appointed, without showing reasons, which congress shall judge sufficient, or being present shall refuse to strike, the congress shall proceed to nominate three persons out of each state, and the secretary of congress shall strike in behalf of such party absent or refusing; and the judgment and sentence of the court to be appointed, in the manner before prescribed, shall be final and conclusive; and if any of the parties shall refuse to submit to the authority of such court, or to appear or defend their claim or cause, the court shall nevertheless proceed to pronounce sentence, or judgment, which shall in like manner be final and decisive, the judgment or sentence and other proceedings being in either case transmitted to congress, and lodged among the acts of congress for the security of the parties concerned: provided that every commissioner, before he sits in judgment, shall take an oath to be administered by one of the judges of the supreme or superior court of the state, where the cause shall be tried, "well and truly to hear and determine the matter in question, according to the best of his judgment, without favour, affection or hope of reward:" provided also that no state shall be deprived of territory for the benefit of the united states.

All controversies concerning the private right of soil claimed under different grants of two or more states, whose jurisdictions as they may respect such lands, and the states which passed such grants are adjusted, the said grants or either of them being at the same time claimed to have originated antecedent to such settlement of jurisdiction, shall on the petition of either party to the congress of the united states, be finally determined as near as may be in the same manner as is before prescribed for deciding disputes respecting territorial jurisdiction between different states.

The united states in congress assembled shall also have the sole and exclusive right and power of regulating the alloy and value of coin struck by their own authority, or by that of the respective states—fixing the standard of weights and measures throughout the United States—regulating the trade and managing all affairs with the Indians, not members of any of the states, provided that the legislative right of any state within its own limits be not infringed or violated—establishing or regulating post-offices from one state to another, throughout all the united states, and exacting such postage on the papers passing thro' the same as may be requisite to defray the expenses of the said office—appointing all officers of the land forces, in the service of the united states, excepting regimental officers—appointing all the officers of the naval forces, and commissioning all officers whatever in the service of the united states—making rules for the government and regulation of the said land and naval forces, and directing their operations.

The united states in congress assembled shall have authority to appoint a committee, to sit in the recess of congress, to be denominated "A Committee of the States," and to consist of one delegate from each state; and to appoint such other committees and civil officers as may be necessary for managing the general affairs of the united states under their direction—to appoint one of their number to preside, provided that no person be allowed to serve in the office of president more than one year in any term of three years; to ascertain the necessary sums of Money to be raised for the service of the united states, and to appropriate and apply the same for defraying the public expenses—to borrow money, or emit bills on the credit of the united states, transmitting every half year to the respective states an account of the sums of money so borrowed or emitted,—to build and equip a navy—to agree upon the number of land forces, and to make requisitions from each state for its quota, in proportion to the number of white inhabitants in such state; which requisition shall be binding, and thereupon the legislature of each state shall appoint the regimental officers, raise the men and cloath, arm and equip them in a soldier like manner, at the expense of the united states; and the officers and men so cloathed, armed and equipped shall march to the place appointed, and within the time agreed on by the united states in congress assembled: But if the united states in congress assembled shall, on consideration of circumstances judge proper that any state should not raise men, or should raise a smaller number than its quota, and that any other state should raise a greater number of men than the quota thereof, such extra number shall be raised, officered, clothed, armed and equipped in the same manner as the quota of such state, unless the legislature of such state shall judge that such extra number cannot be safely spared out of the same, in which case they shall raise officer, cloath, arm and equip as many of such extra number as they judge can be safely spared. And the officers and men so cloathed, armed and equipped, shall march to the place appointed, and within the time agreed on by the united states in congress assembled.

The united states in congress assembled shall never engage in a war, nor grant letters of marque and reprisal in time of peace, nor enter into any treaties or alliances, nor coin money, nor regulate the value thereof, nor ascertain the sums and expenses necessary for the defence and welfare of the united states, or any of them, nor emit bills, nor borrow money on the credit of the united states, nor appropriate money, nor agree upon the number of vessels of war, to be built or purchased, or the number of land or sea forces to be raised, nor appoint a commander in chief of the army or navy, unless nine states assent to the same: nor shall a question on any other point, except for adjourning from day to day be determined, unless by the votes of a majority of the united states in congress assembled.

The Congress of the united states shall have power to adjourn to any time within the year, and to any place within the united states, so that no period of adjournment be for a longer duration than the space of six months, and shall publish the Journal of their proceedings monthly, except such parts thereof relating to treaties, alliances or military operations, as in their judgment require secrecy: and the yeas and nays of the delegates of each state on any question shall be entered on the Journal, when it is desired by any delegate; and the delegates of a state, or any of them, at his or their request shall be furnished with a transcript of the said Journal, except such parts as are above accepted, to lay before the legislatures of the several states.

ARTICLE X. The committee of the states, or any nine of them, shall be authorized to execute, in the recess of congress, such of the powers of congress as the united states in congress assembled, by the consent of nine states, shall from time to time think expedient to vest them with; provided that no power be delegated to the said committee, for the exercise of which, by the articles of confederation, the voice of nine states in the congress of the united states assembled is requisite.

ARTICLE XI. Canada acceding to this confederation, and joining in the measures of the united states, shall be admitted into, and entitled to all the advantages of this union: but no other colony shall be admitted into the same, unless such admission be agreed to by nine states.

ARTICLE XII. All bills of credit emitted, monies borrowed and debts contracted by, or under the authority of congress, before the assembling of the united states, in pursuance of the present confederation, shall be deemed and considered as a charge against the united states, for payment and satisfaction whereof the said united states, and the public faith are hereby solemnly pledged.

ARTICLE XIII. Every state shall abide by the determinations of the united states in congress assembled, on all questions which by this confederation is submitted to them. And the Articles of this confederation shall be inviolably observed by every state, and the union shall be perpetual; nor shall any alteration at any time hereafter be made in any of them; unless such alteration be agreed to in a congress of the united states, and be afterwards confirmed by the legislatures of every state.

And Whereas it hath pleased the Great Governor of the World to incline the hearts of the legislatures we respectively represent in congress, to approve of, and to authorize us to ratify the said articles of confederation and perpetual union. Know Ye that we the undersigned delegates, by virtue of the power and authority to us given for that purpose, do by these presents, in the name and in behalf of our respective constituents, fully and entirely ratify and confirm each and every of the said articles of confederation and perpetual union, and all and singular the matters and things therein contained: And we do further solemnly plight and engage the faith of our respective constituents, that they shall abide by the determinations of the united states in congress assembled, on all questions, which by the said confederation are submitted to them. And that the articles thereof shall be inviolably observed by the states we respectively represent, and that the union shall be perpetual. In witness whereof we have hereunto set our hands in Congress Done at Philadelphia in the state of Pennsylvania the 9th Day of July in the Year of our Lord, 1778, and in the 3d year of the Independence of America.

Josiah Bartlett,	John Wentworth, jun. August 8th, 1778,	On the part and behalf of the state of New Hampshire.
John Hancock, Samuel Adams, Elbridge Gerry,	Francis Dana, James Lovell, Samuel Holten,	On the part and behalf of the state of Massachusetts-Bay.
William Ellery, Henry Marchant,	John Collins,	On the part and behalf of the state of Rhode-Island and Providence Plantations.
Roger Sherman, Samuel Huntington, Oliver Wolcott,	Titus Hosmer, Andrew Adam,	On the part and behalf of the state of Connecticut.
Jas Duane, Fras Lewis,	William Duer, Gouvr Morris,	On the part and behalf of the state of New-York.
Jno Witherspoon,	Nathl Scudder,	On the part and behalf of the state of New-Jersey, November 26th, 1778.
Robt Morris, Daniel Roberdeau, Jona. Bayard Smith,	William Clingan, Joseph Reed, 22d July, 1778,	On the part and behalf of the state of Pennsylvania.
Tho. M'Kean, Feb. 12, 1779, John Dickinson, May 5, 1779,	Nicholas Van Dyke,	On the part and behalf of the state of Delaware.
John Hanson, March 1st, 1781,	Daniel Carroll, March 1st, 1781,	On the part and behalf of the state of Maryland.
Richard Henry Lee, John Banister, Thomas Adams,	Jno Harvie, Francis Lightfoot Lee,	On the part and behalf of the state of Virginia.
John Penn, July 21st, 1778,	Corns Harnett, Jno Williams,	On the part and behalf of the state of North-Carolina.
Henry Laurens, William Henry Drayton, Jno Matthews,	Richd. Hutson, Thos. Heyward, jun.	On the part and behalf of the state of South-Carolina.
Jno Walton, 24th July, 1778,	Edwd Telfair, Edwd Langworthy,	On the part and behalf of the state of Georgia.

C.

CONSTITUTION OF THE UNITED STATES OF AMERICA.

WE the People of the United States, in order to form a more perfect Union, establish Justice, insure domestic Tranquillity, provide for the common defence, promote the general Welfare, and secure the Blessings of Liberty to ourselves and our Posterity, do ordain and establish this CONSTITUTION for the United States of America.

ARTICLE. I.

SECTION. 1. All legislative Powers herein granted shall be vested in a Congress of the United States, which shall consist of a Senate and House of Representatives.

SECTION. 2. [1] The House of Representatives shall be composed of Members chosen every second Year by the People of the several States, and the Electors in each State shall have the Qualifications requisite for Electors of the most numerous Branch of the State Legislature.

[2] No Person shall be a Representative who shall not have attained to the Age of twenty-five Years, and been Seven Years a Citizen of the United States, and who shall not, when elected, be an Inhabitant of that State in which he shall be chosen.

[3] Representatives and direct Taxes shall be apportioned among the several States which may be included within this Union, according to their respective Numbers, which shall be determined by adding to the whole Number of free Persons, including those bound to Service for a Term of Years, and excluding Indians not taxed, three fifths of all other Persons. The actual Enumeration shall be made within three Years after the first Meeting of the Congress of the United States, and within every subsequent Term of ten Years, in such Manner as they shall by Law direct. The Number of Representatives shall not exceed one for every thirty Thousand, but each State shall have at Least one Representative ; and until such enumeration shall be made, the State of New Hampshire shall be entitled to chuse three, Massachusetts eight, Rhode-Island and Providence Plantations one, Connecticut five, New-York six, New-Jersey four, Pennsylvania eight, Delaware one, Maryland six, Virginia ten, North Carolina five, South Carolina five, and Georgia three.

[4] When vacancies happen in the Representation from any State, the Executive Authority thereof shall issue Writs of Election to fill such Vacancies.

[5] The House of Representatives shall chuse their Speaker and other Officers ; and shall have the sole Power of Impeachment.

SECTION. 3. [1] The Senate of the United States shall be composed of two Senators from each State, chosen by the Legislature thereof, for six Years; and each Senator shall have one Vote.

[2] Immediately after they shall be assembled in Consequence of the first Election, they shall be divided as equally as may be into three Classes. The Seats of the Senators of the first Class shall be vacated at the Expiration of the second Year, of the second Class at the Expiration of the fourth Year, and of the third Class at the Expiration of the sixth Year, so that one-third may be chosen every second Year; and if Vacancies happen by Resignation, or otherwise, during the Recess of the Legislature of any State, the Executive thereof may make temporary Appointments until the next Meeting of the Legislature, which shall then fill such Vacancies.

[3] No Person shall be a Senator who shall not have attained to the Age of thirty Years, and been nine Years a Citizen of the United States, and who shall not, when elected, be an Inhabitant of that State for which he shall be chosen.

[4] The Vice President of the United States shall be President of the Senate, but shall have no Vote, unless they be equally divided.

[5] The Senate shall chuse their other Officers, and also a President pro tempore, in the Absence of the Vice President, or when he shall exercise the Office of President of the United States.

[6] The Senate shall have the sole Power to try all Impeachments. When sitting for that Purpose, they shall be on Oath or Affirmation. When the President of the United States is tried, the Chief Justice shall preside: And no Person shall be convicted without the Concurrence of two thirds of the Members present.

[7] Judgment in Cases of Impeachment shall not extend further than to removal from Office, and Disqualification to hold and enjoy any Office of honour, Trust or Profit under the United States: but the Party convicted shall nevertheless be liable and subject to Indictment, Trial, Judgment and Punishment, according to Law.

SECTION. 4. [1] The Times, Places and Manner of holding Elections for Senators and Representatives, shall be prescribed in each State by the Legislature thereof; but the Congress may at any time by Law make or alter such Regulations, except as to the places of chusing Senators.

[2] The Congress shall assemble at least once in every Year, and such Meeting shall be on the first Monday in December, unless they shall by Law appoint a different Day.

SECTION. 5. [1] Each House shall be the Judge of the Elections, Returns and Qualifications of its own Members, and a Majority of each shall constitute a Quorum to do Business; but a smaller Number may adjourn from day to day, and may be authorized to compel the Attendance of absent Members, in such Manner, and under such Penalties as each House may provide.

[2] Each House may determine the Rules of its Proceedings, punish its Members for disorderly Behaviour, and, with the Concurrence of two thirds, expel a Member.

[3] Each House shall keep a Journal of its Proceedings, and from time to time publish the same, excepting such Parts as may in their Judgment require Secrecy; and the Yeas and Nays of the Members of either House on any question shall, at the Desire of one fifth of those Present, be entered on the Journal.

[4] Neither House, during the Session of Congress, shall, without the Consent of the other, adjourn for more than three days, nor to any other Place than that in which the two Houses shall be sitting.

SECTION. 6. [1] The Senators and Representatives shall receive a Compensation for their Services, to be ascertained by Law, and paid out of the Treasury of the United States. They shall in all Cases, except Treason, Felony and Breach of the Peace, be privileged from Arrest during their Attendance at the Session of their respective Houses, and in going to and returning from the same; and for any Speech or Debate in either House, they shall not be questioned in any other Place.

[2] No Senator or Representative shall, during the Time for which he was elected, be appointed to any civil Office under the Authority of the United States, which shall have been created, or the Emoluments whereof shall have been encreased during such time; and no Person holding any Office under the United States, shall be a Member of either House during his Continuance in Office.

SECTION. 7. [1] All Bills for raising Revenue shall originate in the House of Representatives; but the Senate may propose or concur with Amendments as on other Bills.

[2] Every Bill which shall have passed the House of Representatives and the Senate, shall, before it become a Law, be presented to the President of the United States; If he approve he shall sign it, but if not he shall return it, with his Objections to that House in which it shall have originated, who shall enter the Objections at large on their Journal, and proceed to reconsider it. If after such Reconsideration two thirds of that House shall agree to pass the Bill, it shall be sent, together with the Objections, to the other House, by which it shall likewise be reconsidered, and if approved by two thirds of that House, it shall become a Law. But in all such Cases the Votes of both Houses shall be determined by Yeas and Nays, and the Names of the Persons voting for and against the Bill shall be entered on the Journal of each House respectively. If any Bill shall not be returned by the President within ten Days (Sundays excepted) after it shall have been presented to him, the Same shall be a law, in like Manner as if he had signed it, unless the Congress by their Adjournment prevent its Return, in which Case it shall not be a law.

[3] Every Order, Resolution, or Vote to which the Concurrence of the

Senate and House of Representatives may be necessary (except a question of Adjournment) shall be presented to the President of the United States; and before the same shall take Effect, shall be approved by him, or being disapproved by him, shall be repassed by two thirds of the Senate and House of Representatives, according to the Rules and Limitations prescribed in the Case of a Bill.

SECTION. 8. The Congress shall have power

[1] To lay and collect Taxes, Duties, Imposts and Excises, to pay the Debts and provide for the common Defence and general Welfare of the United States; but all Duties, Imposts and Excises shall be uniform throughout the United States;

[2] To borrow Money on the credit of the United States;

[3] To regulate Commerce with foreign Nations, and among the several States, and with the Indian Tribes;

[4] To establish an uniforn Rule of Naturalization, and uniform Laws on the subject of Bankruptcies throughout the United States;

[5] To coin Money, regulate the value thereof, and of foreign Coin, and fix the Standard of Weights and Measures;

[6] To provide for the Punishment of counterfeiting the Securities and current Coin of the United States;

[7] To establish Post Offices and post Roads;

[8] To promote the progress of Science and useful Arts, by securing for limited Times to Authors and Inventors the exclusive Right to their respective Writings and Discoveries;

[9] To constitute Tribunals inferior to the supreme Court;

[10] To define and punish Piracies and Felonies committed on the high Seas, and Offences against the Law of Nations;

[11] To declare War, grant Letters of Marque and Reprisal, and make Rules concerning Captures on Land and Water;

[12] To raise and support Armies, but no Appropriation of Money to that Use shall be for a longer Term than two Years;

[13] To provide and maintain a Navy;

[14] To make Rules for the Government and Regulation of the land and naval Forces;

[15] To provide for calling forth the Militia to execute the Laws of the Union, suppress Insurrections and repel Invasions;

[16] To provide for organizing, arming, and disciplining, the Militia, and for governing such Part of them as may be employed in the Service of the United States, reserving to the States respectively, the Appointment of the Officers, and the Authority of training the Militia according to the Discipline prescribed by Congress;

[17] To exercise exclusive Legislation in all Cases whatsoever, over such District (not exceeding ten Miles square) as may, by Cession of particular States, and the Acceptance of Congress, become the Seat of the Government of the United States, and to exercise like Authority over all Places

purchased by the Consent of the Legislature of the State in which the Same shall be, for the Erection of Forts, Magazines, Arsenals, Dock-Yards, and other needful Buildings ;—And

[18] To make all Laws which shall be necessary and proper for carrying into Execution the foregoing Powers, and all other Powers vested by this Constitution in the Government of the United States, or in any Department or Officer thereof.

SECTION. 9. [1] The Migration of Importation of such Persons as any of the States now existing shall think proper to admit, shall not be prohibited by the Congress prior to the Year one thousand eight hundred and eight, but a Tax or Duty may be imposed on such Importation, not exceeding ten dollars for each Person.

[2] The Privilege of the Writ of Habeas Corpus shall not be suspended, unless when in Cases of Rebellion or Invasion the public Safety may require it.

[3] No Bill of Attainder or ex post facto Law shall be passed.

[4] No Capitation, or other direct, Tax shall be laid, unless in Proportion to the Census or Enumeration herein before directed to be taken.

[5] No Tax or Duty shall be laid on Articles exported from any State.

[6] No Preference shall be given by any Regulation of Commerce or Revenue to the Ports of one State over those of another: nor shall Vessels bound to, or from, one State, be obliged to enter, clear, or pay Duties in another.

[7] No money shall be drawn from the Treasury, but in Consequence of Appropriations made by Law; and a regular Statement and Account of the Receipts and Expenditures of all public Money shall be published from time to time.

[8] No Title of Nobility shall be granted by the United States: And no Person holding any Office of Profit or trust under them, shall, without the Consent of the Congress, accept of any present, Emolument, Office, or Title, of any kind whatever, from any King, Prince, or foreign State.

SECTION. 10. [1] No State shall enter into any Treaty, Alliance, or Confederation; grant Letters of Marque and Reprisal; coin Money; emit Bills of Credit; make any Thing but gold and silver Coin a Tender in Payment of Debts; pass any Bill of Attainder, ex post facto Law, or Law impairing the Obligation of Contracts, or grant any Title of Nobility.

[2] No State shall, without the consent of the Congress, lay any Imposts or Duties on Imports or Exports, except what may be absolutely necessary for executing it's inspection Laws; and the net produce of all Duties and Imposts, laid by any State on Imports or Exports, shall be for the Use of the Treasury of the United States; and all such Laws shall be subject to the Revision and Control of the Congress.

[3] No State shall, without the Consent of Congress, lay any Duty of Tonnage, keep Troops, or Ships of War in time of Peace, enter into any

Agreement or Compact with another State, or with a foreign Power, or engage in War, unless actually invaded, or in such imminent Danger as will not admit of Delay.

ARTICLE. II.

SECTION. 1. [1] The executive Power shall be vested in a President of the United States of America. He shall hold his office during the Term of four Years, and, together with the Vice President, chosen for the same Term, be elected, as follows:

[2] Each State shall appoint, in such Manner as the Legislature thereof may direct, a Number of Electors, equal to the whole Number of Senators and Representatives, to which the State may be entitled in the Congress: but no Senator or Representative, or Person holding an Office of Trust or Profit under the United States, shall be appointed an Elector.

[* The Electors shall meet in their respective States, and vote by Ballot for two Persons, of whom one at least shall not be an Inhabitant of the same State with themselves. And they shall make a List of all the Persons voted for, and of the Number of Votes for each; which List they shall sign and certify, and transmit sealed to the Seat of the Government of the United States, directed to the President of the Senate. The President of the Senate shall, in the Presence of the Senate and House of Representaatives, open all the Certificates, and the Votes shall then be counted. The Person having the greatest Number of Votes, shall be the President, if such Number be a Majority of the whole Number of Electors appointed; and if there be more than one who have such Majority, and have an equal Number of Votes, then the House of Representatives shall immediately chuse by Ballot one of them for President; and if no person have a Majority; then from the five highest on the List the said House shall in like Manner, chuse the President. But in chusing the President, the Votes shall be taken by States, the Representation from each State having one Vote; A Quorum for this Purpose shall consist of a Member or Members from two thirds of the States, and a Majority of all the States shall be necessary to a Choice. In every Case, after the Choice of the President, the Person having the greatest Number of Votes of the Electors, shall be the Vice President. But if there should remain two or more who have equal Votes, the Senate shall chuse from them by Ballot, the Vice President.]

[3] The Congress may determine the Time of chusing the Electors, and the Day on which they shall give their Votes; which Day shall be the same throughout the United States.

---

* This clause within brackets, has been superseded and annulled by the 12th amendment.

[4] No Person except a natural born Citizen, or a Citizen of the United States, at the time of the Adoption of this Constitution, shall be eligible to the Office of President; neither shall any Person be eligible to that Office who shall not have attained to the Age of thirty-five Years, and been fourteen Years a Resident within the United States.

[5] In Case of the Removal of the President from Office, or of his Death, Resignation, or Inability to discharge the Powers and Duties of the said Office, the same shall devolve on the Vice President, and the Congress may by Law provide for the Case of Removal, Death, Resignation, or Inability, both of the President and Vice President, declaring what Officer shall then act as President, and such officer shall act accordingly, until the Disability be removed, or a president shall be elected.

[6] The President shall, at stated Times, receive for his Services, a Compensation, which shall neither be encreased nor diminished during the Period for which he shall have been elected, and he shall not receive within that Period any other Emolument from the United States, or any of them.

[7] Before he enter on the Execution of his Office, he shall take the following Oath or Affirmation :—

"I do solemnly swear (or affirm) that I will faithfully execute the "Office of President of the United States, and will to the best of my "Ability, preserve, protect and defend the Constitution of the United "States."

SECTION. 2. [1] The President shall be Commander in Chief of the Army and Navy of the United States, and of the Militia of the several States, when called into the actual Service of the United States; he may require the Opinion, in writing, of the principal Officer in each of the executive Departments, upon any subject relating to the Duties of their respective Offices, and he shall have Power to grant Reprieves and Pardons for Offences against the United States, except in Cases of Impeachment.

[2] He shall have Power, by and with the Advice and Consent of the Senate, to make Treaties, provided two thirds of the Senators present concur; and he shall nominate, and by and with the Advice and Consent of the Senate, shall appoint Ambassadors, other public Ministers and Consuls, Judges of the Supreme Court, and all other Officers of the United States, whose Appointments are not herein otherwise provided for, and which shall be established by Law: but the Congress may by Law vest the Appointment of such inferior Officers, as they think proper, in the President alone, in the Courts of Law, or in the Heads of Departments.

[3] The President shall have Power to fill up all Vacancies that may happen during the Recess of the Senate, by granting Commissions which shall expire at the End of their next Session.

SECTION. 3. He shall from time to time give to the Congress Information of the State of the Union, and recommend to their Consideration such Measures as he shall judge necessary and expedient; he may, on extraordinary Occasions, convene both Houses, or either of them, and in Case of Disagreement between them, with Respect to the Time of Adjournment, he may adjourn them to such Time as he shall think proper; he shall Receive Ambassadors and other public Ministers; he shall take care that the Laws be faithfully executed, and shall Commission all the officers of the United States.

SECTION. 4. The President, Vice President and all civil Officers of the United States, shall be removed from Office on Impeachment for, and Conviction of, Treason, Bribery, or other high Crimes and Misdemeanors.

ARTICLE. III

SECTION. 1. The judicial Power of the United States, shall be vested in one supreme Court, and in such inferior Courts as the Congress may from time to time ordain and establish. The Judges, both of the supreme and inferior Courts, shall hold their Offices during good Behaviour, and shall, at stated Times, receive for their Services, a Compensation, which shall not be diminished during their Continuance in Office.

SECTION. 2. [1] The judicial Power shall extend to all Cases, in Law and Equity, arising under this Constitution, the Laws of the United States, and Treaties made, or which shall be made, under their Authority;—to all Cases affecting Ambassadors, other public Ministers, and Consuls;—to all Cases of admiralty and maritime Jurisdiction;—to Controversies to which the United States shall be a Party;—to Controversies between two or more States;—between a State and Citizens of another State,—between Citizens of different States,—between Citizens of the same State claiming Lands under Grants of different States, and between a State, or the Citizens thereof, and foreign States, Citi ens or Subjects.

[2] In all Cases affecting Ambassadors, other public Ministers and Consuls, and those in which a State shall be Party, the supreme Court shall have original Jurisdiction. In all the other Cases before mentioned, the supreme Court shall have appellate Jurisdiction, both as to Law and Fact, with such Exceptions, and under such Regulations as the Congress shall make.

[3] The Trial of all Crimes, except in Cases of Impeachment, shall be by Jury; and such Trial shall be held in the State where the said Crimes shall have been committed; but when not committed within any State, the Trial shall be at such Place or Places as the Congress may by Law have directed.

SECTION. 3. [1] Treason against the United States, shall consist only in levying War against them, or in adhering to their Enemies, giving them Aid and Comfort. No Person shall be convicted of Treason unless on the Testimony of two Witnesses to the same overt Act, or on Confession in open Court.

[2] The Congress shall have Power to declare the Punishment of Treason, but no Attainder of Treason shall work Corruption of Blood, or Forfeiture except during the Life of the Person attainted.

ARTICLE. IV.

SECTION. 1. Full Faith and Credit shall be given in each State to the public Acts, Records, and judicial Proceedings of every other State. And the Congress may by general Laws prescribe the Manner in which such Acts, Records and Proceedings shall be proved, and the Effect thereof.

SECTION. 2. [1] The Citizens of each State shall be entitled to all Privileges and Immunities of Citizens in the several States.

[2] A Person charged in any State with Treason, Felony, or other Crime, who shall flee from Justice, and be found in another State, shall on Demand of the executive Authority of the State from which he fled, be delivered up, to be removed to the State having Jurisdiction of the Crime.

[3] No Person held to Service or Labour in one State, under the Laws thereof, escaping into another, shall, in Consequence of any Law or Regulation therein, be discharged from such Service or Labour, but shall be delivered up on Claim of the Party to whom such Service or Labour may be due.

SECTION. 3. [1] New States may be admitted by the Congress into this Union; but no new State shall be formed or erected within the Jurisdiction of any other State; nor any State be formed by the Junction of two or more States, or Parts of States, without the Consent of the Legislatures of the States concerned as well as of the Congress.

[2] The Congress shall have Power to dispose of and make all needful Rules and Regulations respecting the Territory or other Property belonging to the United States; and nothing in this Constitution shall be so construed as to Prejudice any Claims of the United States, or of any particular State.

SECTION. 4. The United States shall guarantee to every State in this Union a Republican Form of Government, and shall protect each of them against Invasion, and on Application of the Legislature, or of the Executive (when the Legislature cannot be convened) against domestic Violence.

ARTICLE. V.

The Congress, whenever two thirds of both Houses shall deem it necessary, shall propose Amendments to this Constitution, or, on the Application of the Legislatures of two thirds of the several States, shall call a Convention for proposing Amendments, which, in either Case, shall be valid to all Intents and Purposes, as Part of this Constitution, when ratified by the Legislatures of three fourths of the several States, or by Conventions in three fourths thereof, as the one or the other Mode of Ratification may be proposed by the Congress; Provided that no Amendment which may be made prior to the Year one thousand eight hundred and eight shall in any Manner affect the first and fourth Clauses in the Ninth Section of the first Article; and that no State, without its Consent, shall be deprived of its equal Suffrage in the Senate.

ARTICLE. VI.

[1] All Debts contracted and Engagements entered into, before the Adoption of this Constitution, shall be as valid against the United States under this Constitution, as under the Confederation.

[2] This Constitution, and the Laws of the United States which shall be made in Pursuance thereof; and all Treaties made, or which shall be made, under the authority of the United States, shall be the supreme Law of the Land; and the Judges in every State shall be bound thereby, any Thing in the Constitution or Laws of any State to the Contrary notwithstanding.

[3] The Senators and Representatives before mentioned, and the Members of the several State Legislatures, and all executive and judicial Officers, both of the United States and of the several States, shall be bound by Oath or Affirmation, to support this Constitution; but no religious Test shall ever be required as a Qualification to any Office or public Trust under the United States.

ARTICLE. VII.

The Ratification of the Conventions of nine States, shall be sufficient for the Establishment of this Constitution between the States so ratifying the Same.

DONE in Convention by the Unanimous Consent of the States present the Seventeenth Day of September in the Year of our Lord one thousand seven hundred and Eighty seven and of the Independence of the United States of America the Twelfth **In Witness** whereof We have hereunto subscribed our Names,

GEO. WASHINGTON—
Presidt and deputy from Virginia.

NEW HAMPSHIRE.

John Langdon, Nicholas Gilman.

MASSACHUSETTS.

Nathaniel Gorham, Rufus King.

CONNECTICUT.

Wm. Saml. Johnson, Roger Sherman.

NEW YORK.

Alexander Hamilton.

NEW JERSEY.

Wil : Livingston,
Wm. Paterson,
David Brearley,
Jona. Dayton.

PENNSYLVANIA.

B. Franklin,
Robt. Morris,
Tho : Fitzsimons,
James Wilson,
Thomas Mifflin,
Geo : Clymer,
Jared Ingersoll,
Gouv : Morris.

DELAWARE.

Geo : Read,
John Dickinson,
Jaco : Broom.
Gunning Bedford, Jun'r,
Richard Bassett,

MARYLAND.

James M'Henry
Danl. Carroll.
Dan : of St. Thos. Jenifer,

VIRGINIA.

John Blair, James Madison, Jr.,

NORTH CAROLINA.

Wm. Blount,
Hu. Williamson.
Rich'd Dobbs Spaight,

SOUTH CAROLINA.

J. Rutledge,
Charles Pinckney,
Charles Cotesworth Pinckney
Pierce Butler.

GEORGIA.

William Few, Abr. Baldwin.

Attest: WILLIAM JACKSON, *Secretary.*"

ARTICLES IN ADDITION TO, AND AMENDMENT OF THE CONSTITUTION OF THE UNITED STATES OF AMERICA,

Proposed by Congress, and ratified by the Legislatures of the several States, pursuant to the fifth article of the original Constitution.

ARTICLE 1.

Congress shall make no law respecting an establishment of religion, or prohibiting the free exercise thereof; or abridging the freedom of speech, or of the press; or the right of the people peaceably to assemble, and to petition the Government for a redress of grievances.

ARTICLE 2.

A well regulated Militia being necessary to the security of a free State, the right of the people to keep and bear Arms, shall not be infringed.

ARTICLE III.

No Soldier shall, in time of peace be quartered in any house, without the consent of the Owner nor in time of war, but in a manner to be prescribed by law.

ARTICLE IV.

The right of the people to be secure in their persons, houses, papers, and effects, against unreasonable searches and seizures, shall not be violated, and no Warrants shall issue, but upon probable cause, supported by Oath or affirmation, and particularly describing the place to be searched, and the person or things to be seized.

ARTICLE V.

No person shall be held to answer for a capital, or otherwise infamous crime, unless on a presentment or indictment of a Grand Jury, except in cases arising in the land or naval forces, or in the Militia, when in actual service in time of War or public danger; nor shall any person be subject for the same offence to be twice put in jeopardy of life or limb; nor shall be compelled in any Criminal Case to be a witness against himself, nor be deprived of life, liberty, or property, without due process of law; nor shall private property be taken for public use, without just compensation.

ARTICLE VI.

In all criminal prosecutions, the accused shall enjoy the right to a speedy and public trial, by an impartial jury of the State and district wherein the crime shall have been committed, which district shall have been previously ascertained by law, and to be informed of the nature and cause of the accusation; to be confronted with the witnesses against him; to have Compulsory process for obtaining Witnesses in his favour, and to have the Assistance of Counsel for his defence.

ARTICLE VII.

In Suits at common law, where the value in controversy shall exceed twenty dollars, the right of trial by jury shall be preserved, and no fact tried by a jury shall be otherwise re-examined in any Court of the United States, than according to the rules of the common law.

ARTICLE VIII.

Excessive bail shall not be required, nor excessive fines imposed nor cruel and unusual punishments inflicted.

ARTICLE IX.

The enumeration in the Constitution, of certain rights, shall not be construed to deny or disparage others retained by the people.

ARTICLE X.

The powers not delegated to the United States by the Constitution, nor prohibited by it to the States, are reserved to the States respectively, or to the people.

ARTICLE XI.

The Judicial power of the United States shall not be construed to extend to any suit in law or equity, commenced or prosecuted against one of the United States by Citizens of another State, or by Citizens or Subjects of any Foreign State.

ARTICLE XII.

The Electors shall meet in their respective states, and vote by ballot for President and Vice President, one of whom, at least, shall not be an inhabitant of the same state with themselves; they shall name in their ballots the person voted for as President, and in distinct ballots the person voted for as Vice-President, and they shall make distinct lists of all persons voted for as President, and of all persons voted for as Vice-President, and of the number of votes for each, which lists they shall sign and certify, and transmit sealed to the seat of the government of the United States, directed to the President of the Senate;—The President of the Senate shall, in presence of the Senate and House of Representatives, open all the certificates and the votes shall then be counted;—The person having the greatest number of votes for President, shall be the President, if such number be a majority of the whole number of Electors appointed; and if no person have such majority, then from the persons having the highest numbers not exceeding three on the list of those voted for as President, the House of Representatives shall choose immediately, by ballot, the President. But in choosing the President, the votes shall be taken by states, the representation from each state having one vote; a quorum for this purpose shall consist of a member or members from two-thirds of the states, and a majority of all the states shall be necessary to a choice. And if the House of Representatives shall not choose a President whenever the right of choice shall devolve upon them, before the fourth day of March next following, then the Vice-President shall act as President, as in the case of the death or other constitutional disability of the President. The person having the greatest number of votes as Vice-President, shall be the Vice-President, if such number be a majority of the whole number of Electors appointed, and if no person have a majority, then from the two highest numbers on the list, the Senate shall choose the Vice-president; a quorum for the purpose shall consist of two-thirds of the whole number of Senators, and a majority of the whole number shall be necessary to a choice. But no person constitutionally ineligible to the office of President shall be eligible to that of Vice-President of the United States.

D.

JEFFERSON'S DRAFT OF KENTUCKY RESOLUTIONS OF 1798.

1 *Resolved*, That the several States composing the United States of America, are not united on the principle of unlimited submission to their General Government; but that, by a compact under the style and title of a Constitution for the United States, and of Amendments thereto, they constituted a General Government for special purposes,—delegated to that Government certain definite powers, reserving, each State to itself, the residuary mass of right to their own self-government; and that whensoever the General Government assumes undelegated powers, its acts are unauthoritative, void, and of no force: that to this compact each State acceded as a State, and is an integral party, its co-States forming, as to itself, the other party: that the Government created by this compact, was not made the exclusive or final judge of the extent of the powers delegated to itself; since that would have made its discretion, and not the Constitution, the measure of its powers; but that, as in all other cases of compact among powers having no common judge, each party has an equal right to judge for itself, as well of infractions as of the mode and measure of redress.

2 *Resolved*, That the Constitution of the United States, having delegated to Congress a power to punish treason, counterfeiting the securities and current coin of the United States, piracies, and felonies committed on the high seas, and offences against the law of nations,

and no other crimes whatsoever; and it being true, as a general principle, and one of the amendments to the Constitution having also declared, that "the powers not delegated to the United States by the Constitution, nor prohibited by it to the States, are reserved to the States respectively, or to the people," therefore the act of Congress, passed on the 14th day of July, 1798, and intituled, "An Act in Addition to the act intituled An Act for the punishment of certain crimes against the United States," as also the act passed by them on the —— day of June, 1798, intituled "An Act to punish frauds committed on the bank of the United States," (and all their other acts which assume to create, define, or punish crimes, other than those so enumerated in the Constitution,) are altogether void, and of no force; and that the power to create, define, and punish such other crimes is reserved, and, of right, appertains solely and exclusively to the respective States, each within its own territory.

3. *Resolved*, That it is true as a general principle, and is also expressly declared by one of the amendments to the Constitution, that "the powers not delegated to the United States by the Constitution, nor prohibited by it to the States, are reserved to the States respectively, or to the people;" and that no power over the freedom of religion, freedom of speech, or freedom of the press being delegated to the United States by the Constitution, nor prohibited by it to the States, all lawful powers respecting the same did of right remain, and were reserved to the States or the people: that thus was manifested their determination to retain to themselves the right of judging how far the licentiousness of speech, and of the press may be abridged without lessening their useful freedom, and how far those abuses which cannot be separated from their use should be tolerated, rather than the use be destroyed. And thus also they guarded against all abridgment by the United States of the freedom of religious opinions and exercises, and retained to themselves the right of protecting the same, as this State, by a law passed on the general demand of its citizens, had already protected them from all human restraint or interference. And that in addition to this general principle and express declaration, another and more special provision has been made by one of the amendments to the Constitution, which expressly declares, that "Congress shall make no law respecting an establishment of religion, or prohibiting the free exercise thereof, or abridging the freedom of speech, or of the press:" thereby guarding in the same sentence, and under the same words, the freedom of religion, of speech, and of the press: insomuch, that whatever violated either, throws down the sanctuary which covers the others, and that libels, falsehood, and defamation, equally with heresy and false religion, are withheld from the cognizance of Federal tribunals. That, therefore, the act of Congress of the United States passed on the 14th day of July, 1798. intituled "An Act in addition to the act intituled An Act for the

punishment of certain crimes against the United States," which does abridge the freedom of the press, is not law, but is altogether void, and of no force.

4. *Resolved*, That alien friends are under the jurisdiction and protection of the laws of the State wherein they are: that no power over them has been delegated to the United States, nor prohibited to the individual States, distinct from their power over citizens. And it being true as a general principle, and one of the amendments to the Constitution having also declared, that "the powers not delegated to the United States by the Constitution, nor prohibited by it to the States, are reserved to the States respectively, or to the people," the act of the Congress of the United States, passed on the —— day of July, 1798, intituled "An Act concerning aliens," which assumes powers over alien friends, not delegated by the Constitution, is not law, but is altogether void, and of no force.

5. *Resolved*, That in addition to the general principle, as well as the express declaration, that powers not delegated are reserved, another and more special provision, inserted in the Constitution from abundant caution, has declared that "the migration or importation of such persons as any of the States now existing shall think proper to admit, shall not be prohibited by the Congress prior to the year 1808:" that this Commonwealth does admit the migration of alien friends, described as the subject of the said act concerning aliens: that a provision against prohibiting their migration, is a provision against all acts equivalent thereto, or it would be nugatory: that to remove them when migrated, is equivalent to a prohibition of their migration, and is, therefore, contrary to the said provision of the Constitution, and void.

6. *Resolved*, That the imprisonment of a person under the protection of the laws of this Commonwealth, on his failure to obey the simple *order* of the President to depart out of the United States, as is undertaken by said act intituled "An Act concerning aliens," is contrary to the Constitution, one amendment to which has provided that "no person shall be deprived of liberty without due process of law;" and that another having provided that "in all criminal prosecutions, the accused shall enjoy the right to public trial, by an impartial jury, to be informed of the nature and cause of the accusation, to be confronted with the witnesses against him, to have compulsory process for obtaining witnesses in his favor, and to have the assistance of counsel for his defence," the same act, undertaking to authorize the President to remove a person out of the United States, who is under the protection of the law, on his own suspicion, without accusation, without jury, without public trial, without confrontation of the witnesses against him, without hearing witnesses in his favor, without defence, without counsel, is contrary to the provision also of the Constitution, is therefore not law, but utterly void, and of no force; that transferring the power of

judging any person, who is under the protection of the laws, from the courts to the President of the United States, as is undertaken by the same act concerning aliens, is against the article of the Constitution which provides that "the judicial power of the United States shall be vested in courts, the judges of which shall hold their offices during good behavior;' and that the said act is void for that reason also. And it is further to be noted, that this transfer of judiciary power is to that magistrate of the General Government who already possesses all the Executive, and a negative on all Legislative powers.

7. *Resolved*, That the construction applied by the General Government (as is evidenced by sundry of their proceedings) to those parts of the Constitution of the United States which delegate to Congress a power "to lay and collect taxes, duties, imposts, and excises, to pay the debts and provide for the common defence and general welfare of the United States," and "to make all laws which shall be necessary and proper for carrying into execution the powers vested by the Constitution in the Government of the United States, or in any department or officer thereof," goes to the destruction of all limits prescribed to their power by the Constitution: that words meant by the instrument to be subsidiary only to the execution of limited powers, ought not to be so construed as themselves to give unlimited powers, nor a part to be so taken as to destroy the whole residue of that instrument: that the proceedings of the General Government under color of these articles, will be a fit and necessary subject of revisal and correction, at a time of greater tranquillity, while those specified in the preceding resolutions call for immediate redress.

8. *Resolved*, That a Committee of conference and correspondence be appointed, who shall have in charge to communicate the preceding resolutions to the Legislatures of the several States; to assure them that this commonwealth continues in the same esteem of their friendship and union which it has manifested from that moment at which a common danger first suggested a common union: that it considers union for specified national purposes, and particularly to those specified in their late Federal compact, to be friendly to the peace, happiness and prosperity of all the States: that faithful to that compact, according to the plain intent and meaning in which it was understood and acceded to by the several parties, it is sincerely anxious for its preservation: that it does also believe, that to take from the States all the powers of self-government and transfer them to a general and consolidated government, without regard to the special delegations and reservations solemnly agreed to in that compact, is not for the peace, happiness or prosperity of these States; and that therefore this commonwealth is determined, as it doubts not its co-States are, to submit to undelegated, and consequently unlimited powers in no man, or body of men on earth: that in cases of an abuse of the delegated powers, the members of the General Government. being chosen by the

people, a change by the people would be the constitutional remedy; but, where powers are assumed which have not been delegated, a nullification of the act is the rightful remedy: that every State has a natural right in cases not within the compact, (casus non fœderis,) to nullify of their own authority all assumptions of power by others within their limits: that without this right, they would be under the dominion, absolute and unlimited, of whosoever might exercise this right of judgment for them: that nevertheless, this commonwealth, from motives of regard and respect for its co-States, has wished to communicate with them on the subject: that with them alone it is proper to communicate, they alone being parties to the compact, and solely authorized to judge in the last resort of the powers exercised under it, Congress being not a party, but merely the creature of the compact, and subject as to its assumptions of power to the final judgment of those by whom, and for whose use itself and its powers were all created and modified: that if the acts before specified should stand, these conclusions would flow from them; that the General Government may place any act they think proper on the list of crimes, and punish it themselves whether enumerated or not enumerated by the Constitution as cognizable by them: that they may transfer its cognizance to the President, or any other person, who may himself be the accuser, counsel, judge and jury, whose *suspicions* may be the evidence, his *order* the sentence, his *officer* the executioner, and his breast the sole record of the transaction: that a very numerous and valuable description of the inhabitants of these States being, by this precedent, reduced, as outlaws, to the absolute dominion of one man, and the barrier of the Constitution thus swept away from us all, no rampart now remains against the passions and the powers of a majority in Congress to protect from a like exportation, or other more grievous punishment, the minority of the same body, the legislatures, judges, governors and counsellors of the States, nor their other peaceable inhabitants, who may venture to reclaim the constitutional rights and liberties of the States and people, or who for other causes, good or bad, may be obnoxious to the views, or marked by the suspicions of the President, or be thought dangerous to his or their election, or other interests, public or personal: that the friendless alien has indeed been selected as the safest subject of a first experiment; but the citizen will soon follow, or rather, has already followed, for already has a sedition act marked him as its prey: that these and successive acts of the same character, unless arrested at the threshold, necessarily drive these States into revolution and blood, and will furnish new calumnies against republican government, and new pretexts for those who wish it to be believed that man cannot be governed but by a rod of iron; that it would be a dangerous delusion were a confidence in the men of our choice to silence our fears for the safety of our rights: that confidence is everywhere the parent of despotism—free government is founded in jealousy, and not in confidence; it is jealousy and not confidence which prescribes limited Constitutions, to bind down those whom we are obliged to trust with power: that our Constitution has accordingly fixed the limits to which, and no further, our confidence may go; and let the honest advocate of confidence read the Alien and Sedition Acts, and say if the Constitution has not been wise in fixing limits to the government it created, and whether we should be wise in destroying those limits. Let him say what the Government is, if it be not a tyranny, which the men of our choice have conferred on our President, and the President of our choice has assented to, and accepted over the friendly strangers to whom the mild spirit of our country and its laws have pledged hospitality and protection: that the men of our choice have more respected the bare *suspicions* of the President, than the solid right of innocence, the claims of justification, the sacred force of truth, and the forms and substance of law and justice. In questions of power, then, let no more be heard of confidence in man, but bind him down from mischief by the chains of the Constitution. That this Commonwealth does therefore call on its co-States for an expression of their sentiments on the acts concerning aliens, and for the punishment of certain crimes hereinbefore specified, plainly declaring whether these acts are or are not authorized by the Federal compact. And it doubts not that their sense will be so announced as to prove their attachment unaltered to limited government, whether general or particular. And that the rights and liberties of their co-States will be exposed to no dangers by remaining embarked in a common bottom with their own. That they will concur with this Commonwealth in considering the said acts as so palpably against the Constitution as to amount to an undisguised declaration that that compact is not meant to be the measure of the powers of the General Government, but that it will proceed in the exercise over these States, of all powers whatsoever: that they will view this as seizing the rights of the States, and consolidating them in the hands of the General Government, with a power assumed to bind the States, (not merely as the cases made Federal, (casus fœderis,) but) in all cases whatsoever, by laws made, not with their consent, but by others against their consent: that this would be to surrender the form of government we have chosen, and live under one deriving its powers from its own will, and not from our authority; and that the co-States, recurring to their natural right in cases not made Federal, will concur in declaring these acts void, and of no force, and will each take measures of its own for providing that neither these acts, nor any others of the General Government not plainly and intentionally authorized by the Constitution, shall be exercised within their respective territories.

9. *Resolved*, That the said committee be authorized to communicate by writing or personal conferences, at any times or places whatever, with any person or persons who may be appointed by any one or more co-

States to correspond or confer with them; and that they lay their proceedings before the next session of Assembly.*

E.

VIRGINIA RESOLUTIONS OF 1798–99.

DEFINING THE RIGHTS OF THE STATES, AND MADISON'S REPORT THEREON.

In the Virginia House of Delegates, Friday, Dec. 21, 1798.

Resolved, That the General Assembly of Virginia, doth unequivocally express a firm resolution to maintain and defend the Constitution of the United States, and the Constitution of this State, against every aggression either foreign or domestic; and that they will support the Government of the United States in all measures warranted by the former.

That this Assembly most solemnly declares, a warm attachment to the Union of the States, to maintain which it pledges its powers; and, that for this end, it is their duty to watch over and *oppose every infraction of those principles which constitute the only basis of that Union*, because a faithful observance of them, can alone secure its existence and the public happiness.

That this Assembly doth explicitly and peremptorily declare, that it views the powers of the Federal Government, as resulting from the compact to which the States are parties, as limited by the plain sense and intention of the instrument constituting that compact, as no further valid than they are authorized by the grants enumerated in that compact; and that, in case of a deliberate, palpable, and dangerous exercise of other powers, not granted by the said compact, the States, who are parties thereto, have the right, and are in duty bound, to interpose, for arresting the progress of the evil, and for maintaining, within their respective limits, the authorities, rights, and liberties, appertaining to them.

That the General Assembly doth also express its deep regret, that a spirit has, in sundry instances, been manifested by the Federal Government, to enlarge its powers by forced constructions of the constitutional charter which defines them; and that indications have appeared of a design to expound certain general phrases (which, having been copied from the very limited grant of powers in the former Articles of Confederation, were the less liable to be misconstrued) so as to destroy the meaning and effect of the particular enumeration which necessarily explains and limits the general phrases, and so as to consolidate the States,

---

* Jefferson's Complete Works, vol. 9, page 464.

by degrees into one Sovereignty, the obvious tendency and inevitable result of which would be, to transform the present Republican system of the United States into an absolute, or, at best, a mixed monarchy.

That the General Assembly doth particularly protest against the palpable and alarming infractions of the Constitution, in the two late cases of the "Alien and Sedition Acts," passed at the last session of Congress; the first of which, exercises a power nowhere delegated to the Federal Government, and which by uniting Legislative and Judicial powers to those of Executive, subverts the general principles of free government, as well as the particular organization and positive provisions of the Federal Constitution; and the other of which acts, exercises in like manner, a power not delegated by the Constitution, but on the contrary, expressly and positively forbidden by one of the amendments thereto; a power, which more than any other, ought to produce universal alarm, because it is levelled against the right of freely examining public characters and measures, and of free communication among the people thereon, which has ever been justly deemed, the only effectual guardian of every other right.

That this State having by its Convention, which ratified the Federal Constitution, expressly declared, that among other essential rights, "the liberty of conscience and the press cannot be cancelled, abridged, restrained, or modified by any authority of the United States," and from its extreme anxiety to guard these rights from every possible attack of sophistry and ambition, having with other States, recommended an amendment for that purpose, which amendment was, in due time, annexed to the Constitution, it would mark a reproachful inconsistency, and criminal degeneracy, if an indifference were now shown, to the most palpable violation of one of the rights, thus declared and secured; and to the establishment of a precedent which may be fatal to the other.

That the good people of this Commonwealth, having ever felt, and continuing to feel the most sincere affection for their brethren of the other States; the truest anxiety for establishing and perpetuating the union of all; and the most scrupulous fidelity to that Constitution, which is the pledge of mutual friendship, and the instrument of mutual happiness; the General Assembly doth solemnly appeal to the like dispositions in the other States, in confidence, that they will concur with this Commonwealth, in declaring, as it does hereby declare, that the acts aforesaid, are unconstitutional; and, that the necessary and proper measures will be taken *by each* for co-operating with this State, in maintaining unimpaired the authorities, rights, and liberties, reserved to the States respectively, or to the people.

That the Governor be desired to transmit a copy of the foregoing resolutions to the Executive authority of each of the other States, with a request, that the same may be communicated to the legislature thereof; and that a copy be furnished to each of the Senators and Representatives representing this State in the Congress of the United States.

Attest: JOHN STEWART.

1798, December 24th. Agreed to by the Senate.

H. BROOKE.

A true copy from the original deposited in the office of the General Assembly. JOHN STEWART, *Keeper of Rolls.*

MR. MADISON'S REPORT ON THE VIRGINIA RESOLUTIONS.

VIRGINIA.—*House of Delegates, Session of* 1799–1800.

Report of the Committee to whom were referred the communications of various States, relative to the resolutions of the last General Assembly of this State, concerning the Alien and Sedition Laws.

Whatever room might be found in the proceedings of some of the States, who have disapproved of the resolutions of the General Assembly of this Commonwealth, passed on the 21st day of December, 1798, for painful remarks on the spirit and manner of those proceedings, it appears to the Committee most consistent with the duty as well as dignity of the General Assembly, to hasten an oblivion of every circumstance, which might be construed into a diminution of mutual respect, confidence and affection, among the members of the Union.

The Committee have deemed it a more useful task to revise, with a critical eye, the resolutions which have met with their disapprobation; to examine fully the several objections and arguments which have appeared against them; and to inquire whether there can be any errors of fact, of principle, or of reasoning, which the candor of the General Assembly ought to acknowledge and correct.

The first of the resolutions is in the words following:

"*Resolved*, That the General Assembly of Virginia doth unequivocally express a firm resolution to maintain and defend the Constitution of the United States, and the Constitution of this State, against every aggression, either foreign or domestic, and that they will support the Government of the United States in all measures warranted by the former."

No unfavorable comment can have been made on the sentiments here expressed. To maintain and defend the Constitution of the United States, and of their own State, against every aggression, both foreign and domestic, and to support the Government of the United States in all measures warranted by their Constitution, are duties which the

General Assembly ought always to feel, and to which, on such an occasion, it was evidently proper to express their sincere and firm adherence.

In their next resolution—"The General Assembly most solemnly declares a warm attachment to the Union of the States, to maintain which, it pledges all its powers; and that, for this end, it is their duty to watch over and oppose every infraction of those principles, which constitute the only basis of that Union, because a faithful observance of them can alone secure its existence and the public happiness."

The observation just made is equally applicable to this solemn declaration of warm attachment to the Union, and this solemn pledge to maintain it; nor can any question arise among enlightened friends of the Union, as to the duty of watching over and opposing every infraction of those principles which constitute its basis, and a faithful observance of which, can alone secure its existence, and the public happiness thereon depending.

The third resolution is in the words following:

"That this Assembly doth explicitly and peremptorily declare, that it views the powers of the Federal Government, as resulting from the compact, to which the States are parties, as limited by the plain sense and intention of the instrument constituting that compact—as no further valid than they are authorized by the grants enumerated in that compact; and that in case of a deliberate, palpable and dangerous exercise of other powers, not granted by the said compact, the States who are parties thereto, have the right, and are in duty bound, to interpose, for arresting the progress of the evil, and for maintaining within their respective limits, the authorities, rights and liberties appertaining to them."

On this resolution, the committee have bestowed all the attention which its importance merits: they have *scanned* it not merely with a strict, but with a severe eye; and they feel confidence in pronouncing, that, in its just and fair construction, it is unexceptionably true in its several positions, as well as constitutional and conclusive in its inferences.

The resolution declares; first, that "it views the powers of the Federal Government, as resulting frrom the compact to which the States are parties," in other words, that the Federal powers are derived from the Constitution; and that the Constitution is a compact to which the States are parties.

Clear as the position must seem, that the Federal powers are derived from the Constitution, and from that alone, the committee are not unapprized of a late doctrine, which opens another source of Federal powers, not less extensive and important, than it is new and unexpected. The examination of this doctrine will be most conveniently connected with a review of a succeeding resolution. The committee satisfy themselves here with briefly remarking, that in all the contemporary discussions and comments which the Constitution underwent, it was constantly justified and recommended, on the ground that the powers not given to the Government, were withheld from it; and, that if any doubt could have existed on this subject, under the original text of the Constitution, it is removed, as far as words could remove it, by the 12th amendment, now a part of the Constitution, which expressly declares, "that the powers not delegated to the United States, by the Constitution, nor prohibited by it to the States, are reserved to the States respectively, or to the people."

The other position involved in this branch of the resolution, namely, that "the States are parties to the Constitution or compact," is, in the judgment of the committee, equally free from objection. It is indeed true, that the term "States," is sometimes used in a vague sense, and sometimes in different senses, according to the subject to which it is applied. Thus, it sometimes means the separate sections of territory occupied by the political societies within each: sometimes the particular governments, established by those societies; sometimes those societies as organized into those particular governments; and lastly, it means the people composing those political societies, in their highest sovereign capacity. Although it might be wished that the perfection of language admitted less diversity in the signification of the same words, yet little inconvenience is produced by it, where the true sense can be collected with certainty from the different applications. In the present instance, whatever different construction of the term "States," in the resolution may have been entertained, all will at least concur in that last mentioned; because in that sense, the Constitution was submitted to the "States," in that sense the "States" ratified it: and in that sense of the term "States," they are consequently parties to the compact from which the powers of the Federal Government result.

The next position is, that the General Assembly views the powers of the Federal Government, "as limited by the plain sense and intention of the instrument constituting that compact," and "as no farther valid than they are authorized by the grants therein enumerated." It does not seem possible, that any just objection can lie against either of these clauses. The first amounts merely to a declaration, that the compact ought to have the interpretation plainly intended by the parties to it; the other to a declaration, that it ought to have the execution and effect intended by them. If the powers granted be valid, it is solely because they are granted; and if the granted powers are valid, because granted, all other powers not granted, must not be valid.

The resolution having taken this view of the Federal compact, proceeds to infer, "That in case of a deliberate, palpable, and dangerous exercise of other powers, not granted by the said compact, the States, who are parties thereto, have the right and are in duty bound to interpose for arresting the progress of the evil, and for maintaining within their respective limits, the authorities, rights, and liberties appertaining to them."

It appears, to your committee to be a plain principle, founded in common sense, illustrated by common practice, and essential to the nature of compacts—that, where resort can be had to no tribunal superior to the authority of the parties, the parties themselves must be the rightful judges in the last resort, whether the bargain made has been pursued or violated. The Constitution of the United States, was framed by the sanction of the States, given by each in its sovereign capacity. It adds to the stability and dignity, as well as to the authority of the Constitution, that it rests on this legitimate and solid foundation. The States, then, being the parties to the constitutional compact, and in their sovereign capacity, it follows of necessity, that there can be no tribunal above their authority, to decide in the last resort, whether the compact made by them be violated; and, consequently, that, as the parties to it, they must themselves decide in the last resort, such questions as may be of sufficient magnitude to require their interposition.

It does not follow, however, that because the States, as sovereign parties to their constitutional compact, must ultimately decide whether it has been violated, that such a decision ought to be interposed, either in a hasty manner, or on doubtful and inferior occasions. Even in the case of ordinary conventions between different nations. where, by the strict rule of interpretation, a breach of a part may be deemed a breach of the whole; every part being deemed a condition of every other part, and of the whole, it is always laid down that the breach must be both wilful and material to justify an application of the rule. But in the case of an intimate and constitutional union, like that of the United States, it is evident that the interposition of the parties, in their sovereign capacity, can be called for by occasions only, deeply and essentially affecting the vital principles of their political system.

The resolution has, accordingly, guarded against any misapprehension of its object, by expressly requiring for such an interposition, "the case of a deliberate, palpable, and dangerous breach of the Constitution, by the exercise of powers not granted by it." It must be a case not of a light and transient nature, but of a nature dangerous to the great purposes for which the Constitution was established. It must be a case, moreover, not obscure or doubtful in its construction, but plain and palpable. Lastly, it must be a case not resulting from a partial consideration, or hasty determination; but a case stampt with a final consideration and deliberate adherence. It is not necessary, because th resolution does not require, that the question should be discussed, how far the exercise of any particular power, ungranted by the Constitution, would justify the interposition of the parties to it. As cases might easily be stated, which none would contend ought to fall within that description—cases, on the other hand, might with equal ease, be stated, so flagrant and so fatal, as to unite every opinion in placing them within the description.

But the resolution has done more than guard against misconstruction, by expressly referring to cases of a deliberate, palpable, and dangerous nature. It specifies the object of the interposition which it contemplates, to be solely that of arresting the progress of the evil of usurpation, and of maintaining the authorities, rights and liberties appertaining to the States, as parties to the Constitution.

From this view of the resolution, it would seem inconceivable that it can incur any just disapprobation from those who, laying aside all momentary impressions, and recollecting the genuine source and object of the Federal Constitution, shall candidly and accurately interpret the meaning of the General Assembly. If the deliberate exercise of dangerous powers, palpably withheld by the Constitution, could not justify the parties to it, in interposing even so far as to arrest the progress of the evil, and thereby to preserve the Constitution itself, as well as to provide for the safety of the parties to it, there would be an end to all relief from usurped power, and a direct subversion of the rights specified or recognized under all the State Constitutions, as well as a plain denial of the fundamental principle on which our independence itself was declared.

But it is objected, that the Judicial authority is to be regarded as the sole expositor of the Constitution in the last resort; and it may be asked for what reason, the declaration by the General Assembly, supposing it to be theoretically true, could be required at the present day, and in so solemn a manner.

On this objection it might be observed: first, that there may be instances of usurped power, which the forms of the Constitution would never draw within the control of the Judicial department; secondly, that if the decision of the Judiciary be raised above the authority of the sovereign parties to the Constitution, the decisions of the other departments, not carried by the forms of the Constitution before the Judiciary, must be equally authoritative and final with the decisions of that department. But the proper answer to the objection is, that the resolution of the General Assembly relates to those great and extraordinary cases, in which all the forms of the Constitution may prove ineffectual against infractions dangerous to the essential rights of the parties to it. The resolution supposes that dangerous powers not delegated, may not only be usurped and executed by the other departments, but that the Judicial department, also, may exercise or sanction dangerous powers beyond the grant of the Constitution; and, consequently, that the ultimate right of the parties to the Constitution, to judge whether the compact has been dangerously violated, must extend to violations by one delegated authority, as well as by another; by the Judiciary, as well as by the Executive, or the Legislative.

However true, therefore, it may be that the Judicial department is, in all questions submitted to it by the forms of the Constitution, to decide in the last resort, this resort must necessarily be deemed the last in relation to the authorities of the other departments of the Government; not in relation to the rights of the parties to the constitutional compact, from which the Judicial as well as the other departments hold their delegated trusts. On any other hypothesis, the delegation of Judicial power would annul the authority delegating it; and the concurrence of this department with the others in usurped powers, might subvert forever, and beyond the possible reach of any rightful remedy, the very Constitution, which all were instituted to preserve.

The truth declared in the resolution being established, the expediency of making the declaration at the present day, may safely be left to the temperate consideration and candid judgment of the American public. It will be remembered, that a frequent recurrence to fundamental principles, is solemnly enjoined by most of the State Constitutions, and particularly by our own, as a necessary safeguard against the danger of degeneracy to which Republics are liable, as well as other Governments, though in a less degree than others. And a fair comparison of the political doctrines not unfrequent at the present day, with those which characterized the epoch of our Revolution, and which form the basis of our Republican Constitutions, will best determine whether the declaratory recurrence here made to those principles, ought to be viewed as unseasonable and improper, or as a vigilant discharge of an important duty. The authority of Constitutions over Governments, and of the sovereignty of the people over Constitutions, are truths which are at all times necessary to be kept in mind; and at no time, perhaps, more necessary than at present.

The fourth Resolution stands as follows:

"That the General Assembly doth also express its deep regret, that a spirit has in sundry instances, been manifested by the Federal Government, to enlarge its powers by forced constructions of the constitutional charter which defines them; and that indications have appeared of a design to expound certain general phrases (which, having been copied from the very limited grant of powers in the former Articles of Confederation, were the less liable to be misconstrued,) so as to destroy the meaning and effect of the particular enumeration which necessarily explains, and limits the general phrases; and so as to consolidate the States by degrees, into one sovereignty, the obvious tendency and inevitable result of which would be to transform the present republican system of the United States into an absolute or at best a mixed monarchy."

The first question here to be considered is, whether a spirit has in sundry instances been manifested by the Federal Government to enlarge its powers by forced constructions of the constitutional charter.

The General Assembly having declared their opinion, merely, by re gretting in general terms, that forced constructions for enlarging the Federal powers have taken place, it does not appear to the committee necessary to go into a specification of every instance to which the resolution may allude. The Alien and Sedition acts being particularl named in a succeeding resolution, are of course to be understood as in cluded in the allusion. Omitting others which have less occupied public attention, or been less extensively regarded as unconstitutional, the resolution may be presumed to refer particularly to the Bank Law, which from the circumstances of its passage, as well as the latitude of construction on which it is founded, strikes the attention with singular force, and the carriage tax, distinguished also by circumstances in its history having a similar tendency. Those instances alone, if resulting from forced construction, and calculated to enlarge the powers of the Federal Government, as the committee cannot but conceive to be the case, sufficiently warrant this part of the resolution. The committee have not thought it incumbent on them to extend their attention to laws which have been objected to, rather as varying the constitutional distribution of powers in the Federal Government, than as an absolute enlargement of them; because instances of this sort, however important in their principles and tendencies, do not appear to fall strictly within the text under review.

The other questions presenting themselves are—1. Whether indications have appeared of a design to expound certain general phrases copied from the "Articles of Confederation," so as to destroy the effect of the particular enumeration explaining and limiting their meaning. 2. Whether this exposition would by degrees consolidate the States into one sovereignty. 3. Whether the tendency and result of this consolidation would be to transform the Republican system of the United States into a monarchy.

1. The general phrases here meant must be those "of providing for the common defence and general welfare."

In the "Articles of Confederation" the phrases are used as follows, in Art. VIII. "All charges of war, and all other expenses that shall be incurred for the common defence and general welfare, and allowed by the United States in Congress assembled, shall be defrayed out of a common treasury, which shall be supplied by the several States, in proportion to the value of all land within each State, granted to, or surveyed for any person, as such land and the buildings and improvements thereon shall be estimated, according to such mode as the United States in Congress assembled, shall from time to time direct and appoint."

In the existing Constitution, they make the following part of Sec. 8: "The Congress shall have power to lay and collect taxes, duties, imposts and excises, to pay the debts, and provide for the common defence and general welfare of the United States."

This similarity in the use of these phrases in the two great Federal charters, might well be considered, as rendering their meaning less liable to be misconstrued in the latter: because it will scarcely be said, that in the former, they were ever understood to be either a general grant of power, or to authorize the requisition or application of money by the old Congress to the common defence and general welfare, except in cases afterwards enumerated. which explained and limited their meaning; and if such was the limited meaning attached to these phrases in the very instrument revised and remodeled by the present Constitution, it can never be supposed that when copied into this Constitution, a different meaning ought to be attached to them.

That, notwithstanding this remarkable security against misconstruction, a design has been indicated to expound these phrases in the Constitution, so as to destroy the effect of the particular enumeration of powers by which it explains and limits them, must have fallen under the observation of those who have attended to the course of public transactions. Not to multiply proofs on this subject, it will suffice to refer to the debates of the Federal legislature, in which arguments have on different occasions been drawn, with apparent effect, from these phrases, in their indefinite meaning.

To these indications might be added, without looking farther, the official report on manufactures by the late Secretary of the Treasury, made on the 5th of December, 1791; and the report of a Committee of Congress, in January, 1797, on the promotion of agriculture. In the first of these it is expressly contended to belong "to the discretion of the National Legislature to pronounce upon the objects which concern the general welfare, and for which, under that description, an appropriation of money is requisite and proper. And there seems to be no room for a doubt, that whatever concerns the general interests of learning, of agriculture, of manufactures, and of commerce, is within the sphere of National Councils, as far as regards an application of money." The latter report assumes the same latitude of power in the National Councils, and applies it to the encouragement of agriculture, by means of a society to be established at the seat of Government. Although neither of these reports may have received the sanction of a law carrying it into effect; yet, on the other hand, the extraordinary doctrine contained in both, has passed without the slightest positive mark of disapprobation from the authority to which it was addressed.

Now, whether the phrases in question be construed to authorize every measure relating to the common defence and general welfare, as contended by some; or every measure only in which there might be an application of money, as suggested by the caution of others; the effect must substantially be the same, in destroying the import and force of the particular enumeration of powers which follow these general phrases in the Constitution. For, it is evident, that there is not a single power whatever, which may not have some reference to the common defence, or the general welfare; nor a power of any magnitude, which, in its exercise, does not involve or admit an application of money. The Government, therefore, which possesses power in either one or other of these extents, is a Government without the limitations formed by a particular enumeration of powers; and consequently, the meaning and effect of this particular enumeration, is destroyed by the exposition given to these general phrases.

This conclusion will not be affected by an attempt to qualify the power over the "general welfare," by referring it to cases where the general welfare is beyond the reach of the separate provisions by the individual States; and leaving to these their jurisdictions in cases, to which their separate provisions may be competent. For, as the authority of the individual States must in all cases be incompetent to general regulations operating through the whole, the authority of the United States would be extended to every object relating to the general welfare, which might, by any possibility, be provided for by the general authority. This qualifying construction, therefore, would have little, if any tendency, to circumscribe the power claimed under the latitude of the term "general welfare."

The true and fair construction of this expression, both in the original and existing Federal compacts, appears to the committee too obvious to be mistaken. In both, the Congress is authorized to provide money for the common defence and general welfare. In both, is subjoined to this authority, an enumeration of the cases, to which their powers shall extend. Money cannot be applied to the general welfare, otherwise than by an application of it to some particular measure, conducive to the general welfare. Whenever, therefore, money has been raised by the general authority, and is to be applied to a particular measure, a question arises whether the particular measure be within the enumerated authorities vested in Congress. If it be, the money requisite for it, may be applied to it; if it be not, no such application can be made. This fair and obvious interpretation coincides with, and is enforced by, the clause in the Constitution, which declares, that "no money shall be drawn from the treasury, but in consequence of appropriations made by law." An appropriation of money to the general welfare, would be deemed rather a mockery than an observance of this constitutional injunction.

2. Whether the exposition of the general phrases here combatted, would not, by degrees, consolidate the States into one Sovereignty, is a question, concerning which the Committee can perceive little room for difference of opinion. To consolidate the States into one sovereignty, nothing more can be wanted than to supersede their respective sovereignties in the cases reserved to them, by extending the sovereignty of the United States, to all cases of the "general welfare," that is to say, to all cases whatever.

3. That the obvious tendency and inevitable result of a consolidation

of the States into one sovereignty, would be to transform the republican system of the United States into a monarchy, is a point which seems to have been sufficiently decided by the general sentiment of America. In almost every instance of discussion relating to the consolidation in question, its certain tendency to pave the way to monarchy, seems not to have been contested. The prospect of such a consolidation has formed the only topic of controversy. It would be unnecessary, therefore, for the committee to dwell long on the reasons which support the position of the General Assembly. It may not be improper, however, to remark two consequences, evidently flowing from an extension of the Federal power to every subject falling within the idea of the "general welfare."

One consequence must be to enlarge the sphere of discretion allotted to the Executive Magistrate. Even within the legislative limits properly defined by the Constitution, the difficulty of accommodating legal regulations to a country so great in extent, and so various in its circumstances, has been much felt; and has led to occasional investments of power in the Executive, which involve perhaps as large a portion of discretion as can be deemed consistent with the nature of the Executive trust. In proportion as the objects of legislative care might be multiplied, would the time allowed for each be diminished, and the difficulty of providing uniform and particular regulations for all, be increased. From these sources would necessarily ensue a greater latitude to the agency of that department which is always in existence, and which could best mould regulations of a general nature, so as to suit them to the diversity of particular situations. And it is in this latitude, as a supplement to the deficiency of the laws, that the degree of executive prerogative materially consists.

The other consequence would be, that of an excessive augmentation of the officers, honors, and emoluments depending on the Executive will. Add to the present legitimate stock all those of every description which a consolidation of the States would take from them, and turn over to the Federal Government, and the patronage of the Executive would necessarily be as much swelled in this case as its prerogative would be in the other. This disproportionate increase of prerogative and patronages must evidently either enable the Chief Magistrate of the Union, by quiet means, to secure his re-election from time to time, and finally, to regulate the succession as he might please; or, by giving so transcendent an importance to the office, would render the elections to it so violent and corrupt, that the public voice itself might call for an hereditary, in place of an elective succession. Whichever of these events might follow, the transformation of the republican system of the United States into a monarchy, anticipated by the General Assembly from a consolidation of the States into one sovereignty, would be equally accomplished; and whether it would be into a mixed or an absolute monarchy, might depend on too many contingencies to admit of any certain foresight.

The resolution next in order is contained in the following terms:

"That the General Assembly doth particularly protest against the palpable and alarming infractions of the Constitution, in the two late cases of the "Alien and Sedition Acts," passed at the last session of Congress; the first of which exercises a power nowhere delegated to the Federal Government; and which, by uniting legislative and judicial powers to those of executive, subverts the general principles of free government, as well as the particular organization and positive provisions of the Federal Constitution; and the other of which acts exercises, in like manner, a power not delegated by the Constitution, but, on the contrary, expressly and positively forbidden by one of the amendments thereto—a power which, more than any other, ought to produce universal alarm, because it is levelled against the right of freely examining public characters and measures, and of free communication among the people thereon, which has ever been justly deemed the only effectual guardian of every other right."

The subject of this resolution having, it is presumed, more particularly led the General Assembly into the proceedings which they communicated to the other States, and being in itself of peculiar importance, it deserves the most critical and faithful investigation; for the length of which no apology will be necessary.

The subject divides itself into,—

First, the "Alien Act."

Secondly, the "Sedition Act."

Of the "Alien Act," it is affirmed by the resolution—1. That it exercises a power nowhere delegated to the Federal Government; 2. That it unites legislative and judicial powers to those of the executive; 3. That this union of powers subverts the general principles of free government; 4. That it subverts the particular organization and positive provisions of the Federal Constitution.

In order to clear the way for a correct view of the first position, several observations will be premised.

In the first place, it is to be borne in mind, that, it being a characteristic feature of the Federal Constitution, as it was originally ratified, and an amendment thereto having precisely declared, "that the powers not delegated to the United States by the Constitution, nor prohibited by it to the States, are reserved to the States respectively, or to the people," it is incumbent in this, as in every other exercise of power by the Federal Government, to prove, from the Constitution, that it grants the particular power exercised.

The next observation to be made is, that much confusion and fallacy have been thrown into the question, by blending the two cases of *aliens, members of a hostile nation; and aliens, members of friendly nations.* These two cases are so obviously and so essentially distinct, that it occasions no little surprise that the distinction should have been disregarded; and the surprise is so much the greater, as it appears that the two cases are actually distinguished by two separate acts of Congress, passed at the same session, and comprised in the same publication; the one providing for the case of "alien enemies;" the other "concerning aliens" indiscriminately, and consequently extending to aliens of every nation in peace and amity with the United States. With respect to alien enemies, no doubt has been intimated as to the Federal authority over them; the Constitution having expressly delegated to Congress the power to declare war against any nation, and of course to treat it and all its members as enemies. With respect to aliens who are not enemies, but members of nations in peace and amity with the United States, the power assumed by the act of Congress is denied to be constitutional; and it is accordingly against this act that the protest of the General Assembly is expressly and exclusively directed.

A third observation is that, were it admitted, as is contended, that the "act concerning aliens" has for its object, not a *penal*, but a *preventive* justice, it would still remain to be proved that it comes within the constitutional power of the Federal Legislature; and, if within its power, that the Legislature has exercised it in a constitutional manner. In the administration of preventive justice, the following principles have been held sacred: that some probable ground of suspicion be exhibited before some judicial authority; that it be supported by oath or affirmation; that the party may avoid being thrown into confinement, by finding pledges or sureties for his legal conduct sufficient in the judgment of some judicial authority; that he may have the benefit of a writ of *habeas corpus*, and thus obtain his release if wrongfully confined; and that he may at any time be discharged from his recognizance, or his confinement, and restored to his former liberty and rights, on the order of the proper judicial authority, if it shall see sufficient cause.

All these principles of the only preventive justice known to American jurisprudence are violated by the Alien Act. The ground of suspicion is to be judged of, not by any judicial authority, but by the Executive magistrate alone. No oath or affirmation is required. If the suspicion be held reasonable by the President, he may order the suspected alien to depart from the territory of the United States, without the opportunity of avoiding the sentence by finding pledges for his future good conduct. As the President may limit the time of departure as he pleases, the benefit of the writ of *habeas corpus* may be suspended with respect to the party, although the Constitution ordains that it shall not be suspended unless when the public safety may require it, in case of Rebellion or invasion,—neither of which existed at the passage of the act; and the party being, under the sentence of the President, either removed from the United States, or being punished by imprisonment, or disqualification ever to become a citizen, on conviction of not obeying the order of removal, he cannot be discharged from the proceedings against him, and restored to the benefits of his former situation, although the *highest judicial authority* should see the most sufficient cause for it.

But, in the last place, it can never be admitted that the removal of aliens, authorized by the act, is to be considered, not as punishment for an offence, but as a measure of precaution and prevention. If the banishment of an alien from a country into which he has been invited as the asylum most auspicious to his happiness,—a country where he may have formed the most tender connections; where he may have invested his entire property, and acquired property of the real and permanent, as well as the movable and temporary kind; where he enjoys, under the laws, a greater share of the blessings of personal security, and personal liberty, than he can elsewhere hope for; and where he may have nearly completed his probationary title to citizenship; if, moreover, in the execution of the sentence against him, he is to be exposed, not only to the ordinary dangers of the sea, but to the peculiar casualties incident to a crisis of war and of unusual licentiousness on that element, and possibly to vindictive purposes, which his emigration itself may have provoked;—if a banishment of this sort be not a punishment, and among the severest of punishments, it will be difficult to imagine a doom to which the name can be applied. And if it be punishment, it will remain to be inquired, whether it can be constitutionally inflicted, on mere suspicion, by the single will of the Executive magistrate, on persons convicted of no personal offence against the laws of the land, nor involved in any offence against the law of nations, charged on the foreign State of which they are members.

One argument offered in justification of this power exercised over aliens is, that, the admission of them into the country being of favor, not of right, the favor is at all times revocable. To this argument it might be answered, that, allowing the truth of the inference, it would be no proof of what is required. A question would still occur, whether the Constitution had vested the discretionary power of admitting aliens in the Federal government or in the State governments.

But it cannot be a true inference, that, because the admission of an alien is a favor, the favor may be revoked at pleasure. A grant of land to an individual may be of favor, not of right; but the moment the grant is made, the favor becomes a right, and must be forfeited before it can be taken away. To pardon a malefactor may be a favor, but the pardon is not, on that account, the less irrevocable. To admit an alien to naturalization, is as much a favor as to admit him to reside in the country; yet it cannot be pretended that a person naturalized can be deprived of the benefits, any more than a native citizen can be disfranchised.

Again, it is said that, aliens not being parties to the Constitution, the rights and privileges which it secures cannot be at all claimed by them.

To this reasoning, also, it might be answered that, although aliens are not parties to the Constitution, it does not follow that the Constitution has vested in Congress an absolute power over them. The parties to the Constitution may have granted, or retained, or modified, the power over aliens, without regard to that particular consideration.

But a more direct reply is, that it does not follow, because aliens are not parties to the Constitution, as citizens are parties to it, that, whilst they actually conform to it, they have no right to its protection. Aliens are not more parties to the laws than they are parties to the Constitution; yet it will not be disputed that, as they owe, on one hand, a temporary obedience, they are entitled, in return, to their protection and advantage.

If aliens had no rights under the Constitution, they might not only be banished, but even capitally punished, without a jury or the other incidents to a fair trial. But so far has a contrary principle been carried, in every part of the United States, that, except on charges of treason, an alien has, besides all the common privileges, the special one of being tried by a jury, of which one half may be also aliens.

It is said, further, that, by the law and practice of nations, aliens may be removed, at discretion, for offences against the law of nations; that Congress are authorized to define and punish such offences; and that to be dangerous to the peace of society is, in aliens, one of those offences.

The distinction between alien enemies and alien friends is a clear and conclusive answer to this argument. Alien enemies are under the law of nations, and liable to be punished for offences against it. Alien friends, except in the single case of public ministers, are under the municipal law, and must be tried and punished according to that law only.

This argument, also, by referring the alien act to the power of Congress to define and *punish* offences against the law of nations, yields the point that the act is of a *penal*, not merely of a preventive operation. It must, in truth, be so considered. And if it be a penal act, the punishment it inflicts must be justified by some offence that deserves it.

Offences for which aliens, within the jurisdiction of a country, are punishable, are—first, offences committed by the nation of which they make a part, and in whose offences they are involved; secondly, offences committed by themselves alone, without any charge against the nation to which they belong. The first is the case of alien enemies; the second, the case of alien friends. In the first case, the offending nation can no otherwise be punished than by war, one of the laws of which authorizes the expulsion of such of its members as may be found within the country against which the offence has been committed. In the second case,—the offence being committed by the individual, not by his nation, and against the municipal law, not against the law of nations,—the individual only, and not the nation, is punishable; and the punishment must be conducted according to the municipal law, not according to the law of nations. Under this view of the subject, the Act of Congress for the removal of alien enemies, being conformable to the law of nations, is justified by the Constitution; and the "act" for the removal of alien friends, being repugnant to the constitutional principles of municipal law, is unjustifiable.

Nor is the act of Congress for the removal of alien friends more agreeable to the general practice of nations than it is within the purview of the law of nations. The general practice of nations distinguishes between alien friends and alien enemies. The latter it has proceeded against, according to the law of nations, by expelling them as enemies. The former it has considered as under a local and temporary allegiance, and entitled to a correspondent protection. If contrary instances are to be found in barbarous countries, under undefined prerogatives, or amid revolutionary dangers, they will not be deemed fit precedents for the Government of the United States, even if not beyond its constitutional authority.

It is said that Congress may grant letters of marque and reprisal; that reprisals may be made on persons as well as property; and that the removal of aliens may be considered as the exercise, in an inferior degree, of the general power of reprisal on persons.

Without entering minutely into a question that does not seem to require it, it may be remarked that reprisal is a seizure of foreign persons or property, with a view to obtain that justice for injuries done by one State, or its members, to another State, or its members, for which a refusal of the aggressors requires such a resort to force, under the law of nations. It must be considered as an abuse of words, to call the removal of persons from a country a seizure, or a reprisal on them; nor is the distinction to be overlooked between reprisals on persons within the country, and under the faith of its laws, and on persons out of the country. But, laying aside these considerations, it is evidently impossible to bring the Alien Act within the power of granting reprisals; since it does not allege or imply any injury received from any particular nation, for which this proceeding against its members was intended as a reparation.

The proceeding is authorized against aliens *of every nation;* of nations charged neither with any similar proceedings against American citizens, nor with any injuries for which justice might be sought, in the mode prescribed by the act. Were it true, therefore, that good causes existed for reprisals against one or more foreign nations, and that neither the persons nor property of its members, under the faith of our laws, could plead an exemption, the operation of the act ought to have been limited to the aliens among us belonging to such nations. To license reprisals against all nations, for aggressions charged on one only, would be a measure as contrary to every principle of justice and public law, as to a wise policy, and the universal practice of nations.

It is said that the right of removing aliens is an incident to the power of war, vested in Congress by the Constitution. This is a former argument in a new shape only, and is answered by repating, that the removal of alien enemies is an incident to the power of war; that the removal of alien friends is not an incident to the power of war.

It is said that Congress are, by the Constitution, to protect each State against invasion; and that the means of *preventing* invasion are included in the power of protection against it.

The power of war, in general, having been before granted by the Constitution, this clause must either be a mere specification for greater caution and certainty, of which there are other examples in the instrument, or be the injunction of a duty, superadded to a grant of the power. Under either explanation, it cannot enlarge the powers of Congress on the subject. The power and the duty to protect each State against an invading enemy would be the same under the general power, if this regard to the greater caution had been omitted.

Invasion is an operation of war. To protect against invasion is an exercise of the power of war. A power, therefore, not incident to war. cannot be incident to a particular modification of war; and as the removal of alien friends has appeared to be no incident to a general state of war, it cannot be incident to a partial state, or a particular modification of war.

Nor can it ever be granted, that a power to act on a case, when it actually occurs, includes a power over all the means that may *tend to prevent* the occurrence of the case. Such a latitude of construction would render unavailing every practical definition of particular and limited powers. Under the idea of preventing war in general, as well as invasion in particular, not only an indiscriminate removal of all aliens might be enforced, but a thousand other things, still more remote from the operations and precautions appurtenant to war, might take place. A bigoted or tyrannical nation might threaten us with war, unless certain religious or political regulations were adopted by us; yet it never could be inferred, if the regulations which would prevent war were such as Congress had otherwise no power to make, that the power to make them would grow out of the purpose they were to answer. Congress have power to suppress insurrections; yet it would not be allowed to follow, that they might employ all the means tending to prevent them; of which a system of moral instruction for the ignorant, and of provident support for the poor, might be regarded as among the most efficacious.

One argument for the power of the General Government to remove aliens would have been passed in silence, if it had appeared under any authority inferior to that of a report made, during the last session of

Congress, to the House of Representatives, by a committee, and approved by the House. The doctrine on which this argument is founded is of so new and so extraordinary a character, and strikes so radically at the political system of America, that it is proper to state it in the very words of the report.

"The act (concerning aliens) is said to be unconstitutional, because to remove aliens is a direct breach of the Constitution, which provides, by the 9th section of the 1st article, that the migration or importation of such persons as any of the States shall think proper to admit, shall not be prohibited by the Congress prior to the year 1808."

Among the answers given to this objection to the constitutionality of the act, the following very remarkable one is extracted:—

"Thirdly, That, as the Constitution has *given to the States* no power to remove aliens, during the period of the limitation under consideration, in the meantime, on the construction assumed, there would be no authority in the county empowered to send away dangerous aliens; which cannot be admitted."

The reasoning here used would not, in any view, be conclusive; because there are powers exercised by most other governments, which, in the United States are withheld by the people both from the General Government and the State Governments. Of this sort are many of the powers prohibited by the declarations of rights prefixed to the Constitutions, or by the clauses, in the Constitutions, in the nature of such declarations. Nay, so far is the political system of the United States distinguishable from that of other countries, by the caution with which powers are delegated and defined, that, in one very important case, even of commercial regulation and revenue, the power is absolutely locked up against the hands of both Governments. A tax on exports can be laid by no constitutional authority whatever. Under a system thus peculiarly guarded, there could surely be no absurdity in supposing that alien friends—who, if guilty of treasonable machinations, may be punished, or, if suspected on probable grounds, may be secured by pledges or imprisonment, in like manner with permanent citizens—were never meant to be subjected to banishment by an arbitrary and unusual process, either under the one Government or the other.

But it is not the inconclusiveness of the general reasoning, in this passage, which chiefly calls the attention to it. It is the principle assumed by it, that the powers held by the States are given to them by the Constitution of the United States; and the inference from this principle, that the powers supposed to be necessary, which are not so given to the State Governments, must reside in the Government of the United States.

The respect which is felt for every portion of the constituted authorities forbids some of the reflections which this singular paragraph might excite; and they are the more readily suppressed, as it may be presumed, with justice perhaps as well as candor, that inadvertence may have had its share in the error. It would be unjustifiable delicacy, nevertheless, to pass by so portentous a claim, proceeding from so high an authority, without a monitory notice of the fatal tendencies with which it would be pregnant.

Lastly, it is said that a law on the same subject with the Alien Act, passed by this State originally in 1785, and re-enacted in 1792, is a proof that a summary removal of suspected aliens was not heretofore regarded, by the Virginia Legislature, as liable to the objections now urged against such a measure.

This charge against Virginia vanishes before the simple remark, that the law of Virginia relates to "suspicious persons, being the subjects of any foreign power or State who shall have *made a declaration of war*, or actually *commenced hostilities*, or from whom the President shall apprehend *hostile designs;*" whereas the act of Congress relates to aliens, being the subjects of foreign powers and States, who have *neither declared war, nor commenced hostilities, nor from whom hostile dangers are apprehended.*

2. It is next affirmed of the Alien Act, that it unites legislative, judicial, and executive powers, in the hands of the President. However difficult it may be to mark, in every case, with clearness and certainty, the line which divides legislative power from the other departments of power, all will agree that the powers referred to these departments may be so general and undefined, as to be of a legislative, not of an executive or judicial nature, and may for that reason be unconstitutional. Details, to a certain degree, are essential to the nature and character of a law; and on criminal subjects, it is proper that details should leave as little as possible to the discretion of those who are to apply and execute the law. If nothing more were required, in exercising a legislative trust, than a general conveyance of authority—without laying down any precise rules by which the authority conveyed should be carried into effect—it would follow that the whole power of legislation might be transferred by the Legislature from itself, and proclamations might become substitutes for law. A delegation of power in this latitude would not be denied to be a union of the different powers.

To determine, then, whether the appropriate powers of the distinct departments are united by the act authorizing the Executive to remove aliens, it must be inquired whether it contains such details, definitions, and rules, as appertain to the true character of a law; especially a law by which personal liberty is invaded, property deprived of its value to the owner, and life itself indirectly exposed to danger.

The Alien Act declares "that it shall be lawful for the President to order all such aliens as he shall judge *dangerous* to the peace and safety of the United States, or shall have reasonable ground to *suspect* are concerned in any treasonable or *secret machinations* against the Government thereof, to depart," etc.

Could a power be well given in terms less definite, less particular, and less precise? To be *dangerous to the public safety*—to be *suspected of secret machinations* against the Government—these can never be mistaken for legal rules or certain definitions. They leave every thing to the President. His will is the law.

But it is not a legislative power only that is given to the President. He is to stand in the place of the judiciary also. His suspicion is the only evidence which is to convict; his order, the only judgment which is to be executed.

Thus it is the President whose will is to designate the offensive conduct; it is his will that is to ascertain the individuals on whom it is charged; and it is his will that is to cause the sentence to be executed. It is rightly affirmed, therefore, that the act unites legislative and judicial powers to those of the Executive.

3. It is affirmed that this union of power subverts the general principle of free government.

It has become an axiom in the science of government, that a separation of the legislative, executive, and judicial departments is necessary to the preservation of public liberty. Nowhere has this axiom been better understood in theory, or more carefully pursued in practice, than in the United States.

4. It is affirmed that such a union of power subverts the particular organization and positive provision of the Federal Constitution.

According to the particular organization of the Constitution its legislative powers are vested in the Congress, its executive powers in the President, and its judicial powers in a supreme and inferior tribunals. The union of any of these powers, and still more of all three, in any one of these departments, as has been shown to be done by the Alien Act, must, consequently, subvert the constitutional organization of them.

That positive provisions, in the Constitution, securing to individuals the benefits of fair trial, are also violated by the union of powers in the Alien Act, necessarily results from the two facts, that the act relates to alien friends, and that alien friends, being under the municipal law only, are entitled to its protection.

The *second* object, against which the resolution protests, is the Sedition Act.

Of this act it is affirmed—1. That it exercises, in like manner, a power not delegated by the Constitution; 2. That the power, on the contrary, is expressly and positively forbidden by one of the amendments to the Constitution; 3. That this is a power which, more than any other, ought to produce universal alarm, because it is levelled against that right of freely examining public characters and measures, and of free communication thereon, which has ever been justly deemed the only effectual guardian of every other right.

1. That it exercises a power not delegated by the Constitution.

Here, again, it will be proper to recollect that the Federal Government being composed of powers specifically granted, with reservation of all others to the States or to the people, the positive authority under which the Sedition Act could be passed must be produced by those who assert its constitutionality. In what part of the Constitution, then, is this authority to be found?

Several attempts have been made to answer this question, which will be examined in their order. The committee will begin with one which has filled them with equal astonishment and apprehension; and which, they cannot but persuade themselves, must have the same effect on all who will consider it with coolness and impartiality, and with a reverence for our Constitution, in the true character in which it issued from the sovereign authority of the people. The committee refer to the doctrine lately advanced, as a sanction to the Sedition Act, "that the common or unwritten law"—a law of vast extent and complexity, and embracing almost every possible subject of legislation, both civil and criminal—makes a part of the law of these States, in their united and national capacity.

The novelty, and, in the judgment of the committee, the extravagance of this pretension, would have consigned it to the silence in which they have passed by other arguments which an extraordinary zeal for the act has drawn into the discussion; but the auspices under which this innovation presents itself have constrained the committee to bestow on it an attention which other considerations might have forbidden.

In executing the task, it may be of use to look back to the colonial state of this country prior to the Revolution; to trace the effect of the Revolution which converted the colonies into independent States; to inquire into the import of the Articles of Confederation, the first instrument by which the union of the States was regularly established; and, finally, to consult the Constitution of 1787, which is the oracle that must decide the important question.

In the state prior to the Revolution, it is certain that the common law, under different limitations, made a part of the colonial codes. But, whether it be understood that the original colonists brought the law with them, or made it their law by adoption, it is equally certain that it was the separate law of each colony within its respective limits, and was unknown to them as a law pervading and operating through the whole, as one society.

It could not possibly be otherwise. The common law was not the same in any two of the colonies; in some, the modifications were materially and extensively different. There was no common legislature, by which a common will could be expressed in the form of a law; nor any common magistracy, by which such a law could be carried into practice. The will of each colony, alone and separately, had its organs for these purposes. This stage of our political history furnishes no foothold for the patrons of this new doctrine.

Did, then, the principle or operation of the great event, which made the colonies independent States, imply or introduce the common law, as a law of the Union?

The fundamental principle of the Revolution was, that the colonies were co-ordinate members with each other, and with Great Britain, of an empire united by a common executive sovereign, but not united by any common legislative sovereign. The legislative power was maintained to be as complete in each American Parliament, as in the British Parliament. And the royal prerogative was in force, in each colony, by virtue of its acknowledging the King for its executive magistrate, as it was in Great Britain, by virtue of a like acknowledgment there. A denial of these principles by Great Britain, and the assertion of them by America, produced the Revolution.

There was a time, indeed, when an exception to the legislative separation of the several component and coequal parts of the empire obtained a degree of acquiescence. The British Parliament was allowed to regulate the trade with foreign nations, and between the different parts of the empire. This was, however, mere practice without right, and contrary to the true theory of the Constitution. The convenience of some regulations, in both cases, was apparent; and as there was no legislature with power over the whole, nor any constitutional pre-eminence among the legislatures of the several parts, it was natural for the legislature of that particular part which was the eldest and the largest, to assume this function, and for the others to acquiesce in it. This tacit arrangement was the less criticized, as the regulations established by the British Parliament operated in favor of that part of the empire which seemed to bear the principal share of the public burdens, and were regarded as an indemnification of its advances for the other parts. As long as this regulating power was confined to the two objects of conveniency and equity, it was not complained of, nor much inquired into. But no sooner was it perverted to the selfish views of the party assuming it, than the injured parties began to feel and to reflect; and the moment the claim to a direct and indefinite power was engrafted on the precedent of the regulating power, the whole charm was dissolved, and every eye opened to the usurpation. The assertion by Great Britain of a power to make laws for the other members of the empire, in all cases whatsoever, ended in the discovery that she had a right to make laws for them in no cases whatever.

Such being the ground of our Revolution, no support or color can be drawn from it for the doctrine that the common law is binding on these States as one society. The doctrine, on the contrary, is evidently repugnant to the fundamental principle of the Revolution.

The Articles of Confederation are the next source of information on this subject.

In the interval between the commencement of the Revolution and the final ratification of these Articles, the nature and extent of the Union was determined by the circumstances of the crisis, rather than by any accurate delineation of the general authority. It will not be alleged that the "common law" could have any legitimate birth, as a law of the United States, during that state of things. If it came, as such, into existence at all, the charter of confederation must have been its parent.

Here, again, however, its pretensions are absolutely destitute of foundation. This instrument does not contain a sentence or a syllable that can be tortured into a countenance of the idea that the parties to it were, with respect to the objects of the common law, to form one community. No such law is named, or implied, or alluded to, as being in force, or as brought into force by that compact. No provision is made by which such a law could be carried into operation; whilst, on the other hand, every such inference or pretext is absolutely precluded by art. 2, which declares "that each State retains its sovereignty freedom, and independence, and every power, jurisdiction, and right, which is not by this Confederation expressly delegated to the United States in Congress assembled."

Thus far it appears that not a vestige of this extraordinary doctrine can be found in the origin or progress of American institutions. The evidence against it has, on the contrary, grown stronger at every step, till it has amounted to a formal and positive exclusion, by written articles of compact, among the parties concerned.

Is this exclusion revoked, and the common law introduced as national law, by the present Constitution of the United States? This is the final question to be examined.

It is readily admitted that particular parts of the common law may have a sanction from the Constitution, so far as they are necessarily comprehended in the technical phrases which express the powers delegated to the Government; and so far, also, as such other parts may be adopted by Congress, as necessary and proper for carrying into execution the powers expressly delegated. But the question does not relate to either of these portions of the common law. It relates to the common law beyond these limitations.

The only part of the Constitution which seems to have been relied on in this case, is the 2d section of art. 3:—"The judicial power shall extend to all cases, in law and equity, arising under this Constitution, the laws of the United States, and treaties made, or which shall be made, under their authority. It has been asked what cases, distinct from those arising under the laws and treaties of the United States, can arise under the Constitution, other than those arising under the common law; and it is inferred that the common law is, accordingly, adopted or recognized by the Constitution.

Never, perhaps, was so broad a construction applied to a text so clearly unsusceptible of it. If any color for the inference could be found, it must be in the impossibility of finding any other cases, in law and equity, within the provisions of the Constitution, to satisfy the expression; and rather than resort to a construction affecting so essentially the whole character of the Government, it would perhaps be more rational to consider the expression as a mere pleonasm or inadvertence. But it is not necessary to decide on such a dilemma. The expression is fully satisfied, and its accuracy justified, by two descriptions of cases, to which the judicial authority is extended, and neither of which implies that the common law is the law of the United States. One of these descriptions comprehends the cases growing out of the restrictions on the legislative power of the States. For example, it is provided that "no State shall emit bills of credit," or "make any thing but gold and silver coin a tender for the payment of debts." Should this prohibition be violated, and a suit between citizens of the same State be the consequence, this would be a case arising under the Constitution before the judicial power of the United States. A second description comprehends suits between citizens and foreigners, of citizens of different States, to be decided according to the State or foreign laws, but submitted by the Constitution to the judicial power of the United States; the judicial power being, in several instances, extended beyond the legislative power of the United States.

To this explanatian of the text, the following observations may be added:—

The expression "cases in law and equity" is manifestly confined to cases of a civil nature, and would exclude cases of criminal jurisdiction. Criminal cases in law and equity would be a language unknown to the law.

The succeeding paragraph in the same section is in harmony with this construction. It is in these words: "In all cases affecting ambassadors, or other public ministers, and consuls; and those in which a State shall be a party, the Supreme Court shall have original jurisdiction. *In all* the other cases, (including cases of law and equity arising under the Constitution,) the Supreme Court shall have *appellate* jurisdiction, both as to law and *fact*, with such exceptions, and under such regulations, as Congress shall make."

This paragraph, by expressly giving an appellate jurisdiction, in cases of law and equity arising under the Constitution, to *fact*, as well as to law, clearly excludes criminal cases, where the trial by jury is secured—because the fact, in such cases, is not a subject of appeal; and, although the appeal is liable to such *exceptions* and regulations as Congress may adopt, yet it is not to be supposed that an *exception* of *all* criminal cases could be contemplated, as well because a discretion in Congress to make or omit the exception would be improper, as because it would have been unnecessary. The exception could as easily have been made by the Constitution itself, as referred to the Congress.

Once more: The amendment last added to the Constitution deserves attention as throwing light on this subject. "The judicial power of the United States shall not be construed to extend to any suit in *law* or *equity*, commenced or prosecuted against one of the United States, by citizens of another state, or by citizens or subjects of any foreign power." As it will not be pretended that any criminal proceeding could take place against a State, the terms *law* or *equity* must be understood as appropriate to *civil* in exclusion of *criminal* cases.

From these considerations, it is evident that this part of the Constitution, even if it could be applied at all to the purpose for which it has been cited, would not include any cases whatever of a criminal nature, and consequently would not authorize the inference from it, that the judicial authority extends to offences against the common law, as offences arising under the Constitution.

It is further to be considered that, even if this part of the Constitution could be strained into an application to every common law case, criminal as well as civil, it could have no effect in justifying the Sedition Act, which is an act of legislative, and not of judicial power: and it is the judicial power only of which the extent is defined in this part of the Constitution.

There are two passages in the Constitution, in which a description of the law of the United States is found. The first is contained in art. 3, sec. 3, in the words following: "This Constitution, the laws of the United States, and treaties made, or which shall be made, under this authority." The second is contained in the second paragraph of art. 6, as follows: "This Constitution, and the laws of the United States which shall be made in pursuance thereof, and all treaties made or which shall be made, under the authority of the United States, shall be the supreme law of the land." The first of these descriptions was meant as a guide to the judges of the United States; the second, as a guide to the judges of the several States. Both of them consist of an enumeration, which was evidently meant to be precise and complete. If the common law had been understood to be a law of the United States, it is not possible to assign a satisfactory reason why it was not expressed in the enumeration.

In aid of these objections, the difficulties and confusion inseparable from a constructive introduction of the common law would afford powerful reasons against it.

Is it to be the common law with or without the British statutes? If without the statutory amendments, the vices of the code would be insupportable.

If with these amendments, what period is to be fixed for limiting the British authority over our laws?

Is it to be the date of the eldest, or the youngest, of the colonies? Or are the dates to be thrown together, and a medium deduced? Or is our independence to be taken for the date?

Is, again, regard to be had to the various changes in the common law made by the local codes of America?

Is regard to be had to such changes subsequent as well as prior to the establishment of the Constitution?

Is regard to be had to future as well as past changes?

Is the law to be different in every State, as differently modified by its code; or are the modifications of any particular State to be applied to all?

And on the latter supposition, which among the State codes forms the standard?

Questions of this sort might be multiplied with as much ease as there would be difficulty in answering them.

These consequences, flowing from the proposed construction, furnish other objections equally conclusive; unless the text were peremptory in its meaning, and consistent with other parts of the instrument.

These consequences may be in relation to the legislative authority of the United States; to the executive authority; to the judicial authority; and to the Governments of the several States.

If it be understood that the common law is established by the Constitution, it follows that no part of the law can be altered by the Legislature. Such of the statutes already passed as may be repugnant thereto, would be nullified; particularly the Sedition Act itself, which boasts of being a melioration of the common law; and the whole code, with all its incongruities, barbarisms, and bloody maxims, would be inviolably saddled on the good people of the United States.

Should this consequence be rejected, and the common law be held, like other laws, liable to revision and alteration by the authority of Congress, it then follows that the authority of Congress is co-extensive with the objects of common law; that is to say, with every object of legislation; for to every such object does some branch or other of the common law extend. The authority of Congress would, therefore, be no longer under the limitations marked out in the Constitution. They would be authorized to legislate in all cases whatsoever.

In the next place, as the President possesses the executive powers of the Constitution, and is to see that the laws be faithfully executed, his authority also must be co-extensive with every branch of the common law. The additions which this would make to his power, though not readily to be estimated, claim the most serious attention.

This is not all: it will merit the most profound consideration, how far an indefinite admission of the common law, with a latitude in con struing it equal to the construction by which it is deduced from the Constitution, might draw after it the various prerogatives, making part of the unwritten law of England. The English Constitution itself is nothing more than a composition of unwritten laws and maxims.

In the third place, whether the common law be admitted as of legal or of constitutional obligation, it would confer on the judicial department a discretion little short of a legislative power.

On the supposition of its having a constitutional obligation, this power in the judges would be permanent and irremediable by the Legislature. On the other supposition, the power would not expire until the Legislature should have introduced a full system of statutory provisions. Let it be observed, too, that, besides all the uncertainties above enumerated, and which present an immense field for judicial discretion, it would remain with the same department to decide what parts of the common law would, and what would not, be properly applicable to the circumstances of the United States.

A discretion of this sort has always been lamented as incongruous and dangerous, even in the colonial and State courts, although so much narrowed by positive provisions in the local codes on all the principal subjects embraced by the common law. Under the United States, where so few laws exist on those subjects, and where so great a lapse of time must happen before the vast chasm could be supplied, it is manifest that the power of the judges over the law would, in fact, erect them into legislators, and that, for a long time, it would be impossible for the citizens to conjecture either what was, or would be, law.

In the last place, the consequence of admitting the common law as the law of the United States, on the authority of the individual States, is as obvious as it would be fatal. As this law relates to every subject of legislation, and would be paramount to the Constitutions and laws of the States, the admission of it would overwhelm the residuary sovereignty of the States, and, by one constructive operation, new-model the whole political fabric of the country.

From the review thus taken of the situation of the American colonies prior to their independence; of the effect of this event on their situation; of the nature and import of the Articles of Confederation; of the true meaning of the passage in the existing Constitution from which the common law has been deduced; of the difficulties and uncertainties incident to the doctrine; and of its vast consequences in extending the powers of the Federal Government, and in superseding the authorities of the State Governments,—the committee feel the utmost confidence in concluding that the common law never was, nor by any fair construction ever can be, deemed a law for the American people as one community; and they indulge the strongest expectation that the same conclusion will be finally drawn by all candid and accurate inquirers into the subject. It is, indeed, distressing to reflect that it ever should have been made a question, whether the Constitution, on the whole face of which is seen so much labor to enumerate and define the several objects of Federal power, could intend to introduce in the lump, in an indirect manner, and by a forced construction of a few phrases, the vast and multifarious jurisdiction involved in the common law—a law filling so many ample volumes; a law overspreading the entire field of legislation; and a law that would sap the foundation of the Constitution as a system of limited and specified powers. A severer reproach could not, in the opinion of the committee, be thrown on the Constitution, on those who framed, or on those who established it, than such a supposition would throw on them.

The argument, then, drawn from the common law, on the ground of its being adopted or recognized by the Constitution, being inapplicable to the Sedition Act, the committee will proceed to examine the other arguments which have been founded on the Constitution.

They will waste but little time in the attempt to cover the act by the preamble to the Constitution, it being contrary to every acknowledged rule of construction to set up this part of an instrument in opposition to the plain meaning expressed in the body of the instrument. A preamble usually contains the general motives or reason for the particular regulations or measures which follow it, and is always understood to be explained and limited by them. In the present instance, a contrary interpretation would have the inadmissible effect of rendering nugatory or improper every part of the Constitution which succeeds the preamble.

The paragraph in art. 1, sect. 8, which contains the power to levy and collect taxes, duties, imposts, and excises, to pay the debts, and provide for the common defence and general welfare, having been already examined, will also require no particular attention in this place. It will have been seen that, in its fair and consistent meaning, it cannot enlarge the enumerated powers vested in Congress.

The part of the Constitution which seems most to be recurred to, in defence of the Sedition Act, is the last clause of the above section, empowering Congress "to make all laws which shall be necessary and proper for carrying into execution the foregoing powers, and all other powers vested by this Constitution in the Government of the United States, or in any department or officer thereof."

The plain import of this clause is, that Congress shall have all the incidental or instrumental powers necessary and proper for carrying into execution all the express powers, whether they be vested in the Government of the United States, more collectively, or in the several departments or officers thereof.

It is not a grant of new powers to Congress, but merely a declaration, for the removal of all uncertainty, that the means of carrying into execution those otherwise granted are included in the grant.

Whenever, therefore, a question arises concerning the constitutionality of a particular power, the first question is, whether the power be expressed in the Constitution. If it be, the question is decided. If it be not expressed, the next inquiry must be, whether it is properly an incident to an express power, and necessary to its execution. If it be, it may be exercised by Congress. If it be not, Congress cannot exercise it.

Let the question be asksd, then, whether the power over the press, exercised in the Sedition Act, be found among the powers expressly vested in Congress. This is not pretended.

Is there any express power, for executing which it is a necessary and proper power?

The power which has been selected, as least remote, in answer to this question, is that "of suppressing insurrections;" which is said to imply a power to prevent insurrections, by punishing whatever may lead or tend to them. But it surely cannot, with the least plausibility, be said, that the regulation of the press, and punishment of libels, are exercises of a power to suppress insurrections. The most that could be said would be, that the punishment of libels, if it had the tendency ascribed to it, might prevent the occasion of passing or executing laws necessary and proper for the suppression of insurrections.

Has the Federal Government no power, then, to prevent as well as to punish resistance to the laws?

They have the power, which the Constitution deemed most proper, in their hands for the purpose. The Congress has power, before it happens, to pass laws for punishing it; and the executive and judiciary have power to enforce those laws when it does happen.

It must be recollected by many, and could be shown to the satisfaction of all, that the construction here put on the terms "necessary and proper" is precisely the construction which prevailed during the discussions and ratifications of the Constitution. It may be added, and cannot too often be repeated, that it is a construction absolutely necessary to maintain their consistency with the peculiar character of the Government, as possessed of particular and definite powers only, not of the general and indefinite powers vested in ordinary governments; for, if the power to suppress insurrections includes the power to punish libels, or if the power to punish includes a power to prevent, by all the means that may have that tendency, such is the relation and influence among the most remote subjects of legislation, that a power over a very few would carry with it a power over all. And it must be wholly immaterial whether unlimited powers be exercised under the name of unlimited powers, or be exercised under the name of unlimited means of carrying into execution limited powers.

This branch of the subject will be closed with a reflection which must have weight with all, but more especially with those who place peculiar reliance on the judicial exposition of the Constitution, as the bulwark provided against an undue extension of the legislative power. If it be understood that the powers implied in the specified powers have an immediate and appropriate relation to them, as means necessary and proper for carrying them into execution, questions on constitutionality of laws passed for this purpose will be of a nature sufficiently precise and determinate for judicial cognizance and control. If, on the other hand, Congress are not limited, in the choice of means, by any such appropriate relation of them to the specified powers, but may employ all such means as they may deem fitted to prevent, as well as to punish, crimes subjected to their authority, (such as may have a tendency only to promote an object for which they are authorized to provide,) every one must perceive that questions relating to means of this sort must be questions for mere policy and expediency; on which legislative discretion alone can decide, and from which the judicial interposition and control are completely excluded.

2. The next point which the resolution requires to be proved is, that the power over the press, exercised by the Sedition Act, is positively forbidden by one of the amendments to the Constitution.

The amendment stands in these words: "Congress shall make no law respecting an establishment of religion, or prohibiting the free exercise thereof, or abridging the freedom of speech, or of the press, or of the right of the people peaceably to assemble, and to petition the Government for a redress of grievances."

In the attempts to vindicate the Sedition Act, it has been contended, 1. That the "freedom of the press" is to be determined by the meaning of these terms in the common law; 2. That the article supposes power over the press to be in Congress, and prohibits them only from abridging the freedom allowed to it by the common law.

Although it will be shown, on examining the second of these positions, that the amendment is a denial to Congress of all power over the press, it may not be useless to make the following observations on the first of them:—

It is deemed to be a sound opinion that the Sedition Act, in its definition of some of the crimes created, is an abridgment of the freedom of publication, recognized by principles of the common law in England.

The freedom of the press, under the common law, is, in the defences of the Sedition Act, made to consist in an exemption from all previous restraint on printed publications, by persons authorized to inspect or prohibit them. It appears to the committee that this idea of the freedom of the press can never be admitted to be the American idea of it; since a law inflicting penalties on printed publications would have a similar effect with a law authorizing a previous restraint on them. It would seem a mockery to say that no laws should be passed preventing publications from being made, but that laws might be passed for punishing them in case they should be made.

The essential difference between the British Government and the American Constitutions will place this subject in the clearest light.

In the British Government, the danger of encroachments on the rights of the people is understood to be confined to the executive magistrate. The Representatives of the people in the Legislature are not only exempt themselves from distrust, but are considered as sufficient guardians of the rights of their constituents against the danger from the Executive. Hence it is a principle, that the Parliament is unlimited in its power; or, in their own language, is omnipotent. Hence, too, all the ramparts for protecting the rights of the people,—such as their Magna Charta, their bill of rights, etc.,—are not reared against the Parliament, but against the royal prerogative. They are merely legislative precautions against executive usurpation. Under such a Government as this, an exemption of the press from previous restraint by licensers appointed by the King, is all the freedom that can be secured to it.

In the United States, the case is altogether different. The people, not the Government, possess the absolute sovereignty. The Legislature, no less than the Executive, is under limitations of power. Encroachments are regarded as possible from the one as well as from the other. Hence, in the United States, the great and essential rights of the people are secured against legislative as well as executive ambition. They are secured, not by laws paramount to prerogative, but by Constitutions paramount to laws. This security of the freedom of the press requires that it should be exempt, not only from previous restraint of the Executive, as in Great Britain, but from legislative restraint also; and this exemption, to be effectual, must be an exemption, not only from the previous inspection of licensers, but from the subsequent penalty of laws.

The State of the press, therefore, under the common law, cannot, in this point of view, be the standard of its freedom in the United States.

But there is another view under which it may be necessary to consider this subject. It may be alleged that, although the security for the freedom of the press be different in Great Britain and in this country,—being a legal security only in the former, and constitutional security in the latter,—and although there may be a further difference, in an extension of the freedom of the press, here, beyond an exemption from previous restraint, to an exemption from subseqnent penalties also, —yet the actual legal freedom of the press, under the common law, must determine the degree of freedom which is meant by the terms, and which is constitutionally secured against both previous and subsequent restraints.

The committee are not unaware of the difficulty of all general questions, which may turn on the proper boundary between the liberty and licentiousness of the press. They will leave it, therefore, for consideration only, how far the difference between the nature of the British Government, and the nature of the American Government, and the practice under the latter, may show the degree of rigor in the former to be inapplicable to, and not obligatory in, the latter.

The nature of Governments elective, limited, and responsible, in all their branches, may well be supposed to require a greater freedom of animadversion, than might be tolerated by the genius of such a Government as that of Great Britain. In the latter, it is a maxim, that the King—an hereditary, not a responsible magistrate—can do no wrong; and that the Legislature, which, in two thirds of its composition, is also hereditary, not responsible, can do what it pleases. In the United States, the executive magistrates are not held to be infallible, nor the Legislatures to be omnipotent; and both, being elective, are both responsible. Is it not natural and necessary, under such different circumstances, that a different degree of freedom in the use of the press should be contemplated?

Is not such an inference favored by what is observable in Great Britain itself? Notwithstanding the general doctrine of the common law, on the subject of the press, and the occasional punishment of those who use it with a freedom offensive to the Government, it is well known that, with respect to the responsible measures of the Government, where the reasons operating here become applicable there, the freedom exercised by the press, and protected by public opinion, far exceeds the limits prescribed by the ordinary rules of law. The ministry, who are responsible to impeachment, are at all times animadverted on, by the press, with peculiar freedom; and during the elections for the House of Commons, the other responsible part of the Government, the press is employed with as little reserve towards the candidates.

The practice in America must be entitled to much more respect. In every State, probably, in the Union, the press has exerted a freedom in canvassing the merits and measures of public men, of every description, which has not been confined to the strict limits of the common law. On this footing the freedom of the press has stood; on this foundation it yet stands; and it will not be a breach, either of truth or of candor, to say that no persons or presses are in the habit of more unrestrained animadversions on the proceedings and functionaries of the State Governments, than the persons and presses most zealous in vindicating the act of Congress for punishing similar animadversions on the Government of the United States.

The last remark will not be understood as claiming for the State Governments an immunity greater than they have heretofore enjoyed. Some degree of abuse is inseparable from the proper use of every thing; and in no instance is this more true than in that of the press. It has accordingly been decided, by the practice of the States, that it is better to leave a few of its noxious branches to their luxuriant growth, than, by pruning them away, to injure the vigor of those yielding the proper fruits. And can the wisdom of this policy be doubtful by any one who reflects that to the press alone, checkered as it is with abuses, the world is indebted for all the triumphs which have been gained by reason and humanity over error and oppression; who reflects that to the same beneficent source the United States owe much of the lights which conducted them to the rank of a free and independent nation and which have improved their political system into a shape so auspicious to their happiness? Had Sedition Acts, forbidding every publication that might bring the constituted agents into contempt or disrepute, or that might excite the hatred of the people against the authors of unjust or pernicious measures, been uniformly enforced against the press, might not the United States have been languishing, at this day, under the infirmities of a sickly Confederation? Might they not, possibly, be miserable colonies, groaning under a foreign yoke?

To these observations one fact will be added, which demonstrates that the common law cannot be admitted as the universal expositor of American terms, which may be the same with those contained in that law. The freedom of conscience, and of religion, is found in the same instrument which asserts the freedom of the press. It will never be admitted that the meaning of the former, in the common law of England, is to limit their meaning in the United States.

Whatever weight may be allowed to these considerations, the committee do not, however, by any means intend to rest the question on them. They contend that the article of the amendment, instead of supposing in Congress a power that might be exercised over the press, provided its freedom was not abridged, meant a positive denial to Congress of any power whatever on the subject.

To demonstrate that this was the true object of the article, it will be sufficient to recall the circumstances which led to it, and to refer to the explanation accompanying the article.

When the Constitution was under the discussions which preceded its ratification, it is well known that great apprehensions were expressed by many, lest the omission of some positive exception, from the powers delegated, of certain rights, and of the freedom of the press particularly, might expose them to danger of being drawn, by construction, within some of the powers vested in Congress; more especially of the power to make all laws necessary and proper for carrying their other powers into execution. In reply to this objection, it was invariably urged to be a fundamental and characteristic principle of the Constitution, that all powers not given by it were reserved; that no powers were given beyond those enumerated in the Constitution, and such as were fairly incident to them; that the power over the rights in question, and particularly over the press, was neither among the enumerated powers, nor incident to any of them; and consequently that an exercise of any such power would be manifest usurpation. It is painful to remark how much the arguments now employed in behalf of the Sedition Act, are at variance with the reasoning which then justified the Constitution, and invited its ratification.

From this posture of the subject resulted the interesting question, in so many of the conventions, whether the doubts and dangers ascribed to the Constitution should be removed by any amendments previous to the ratification, or be postponed, in confidence that, as far as they might be proper, they would be introduced in the form provided by the Constitution. The latter course was adopted; and in most of the States, ratifications were followed by the propositions and instructions for rendering the Constitution more explicit, and more safe to the rights not meant to be delegated by it. Among those rights, the freedom of the press, in most instances, is particularly and emphatically mentioned. The firm and very pointed manner in which it is asserted in the proceedings of the convention of this State will hereafter be seen.

In pursuance of the wishes thus expressed, the first Congress that assembled under the Constitution proposed certain amendments, which have since, by the necessary ratifications, been made a part of it; among which amendments is the article containing, among other prohibitions on the Congress, an express declaration that they should make no law abridging the freedom of the press.

Without tracing farther the evidence on this subject, it would seem scarcely possible to doubt that no power whatever over the press was supposed to be delegated by the Constitution, as it originally stood, and that the amendment was intended as a positive and absolute reservation of it.

But the evidence is still stronger. The proposition of amendments made by Congress, is introduced in the following terms:—

"The conventions of a number of the States, having, at the time of their adopting the Constitution, expressed a desire, in order to prevent misconstruction or abuse of its powers, that further declaratory and restrictive clauses should be added; and as extending the ground of public confidence in the Government, will best insure the beneficent ends of its institution."

Here is the most satisfactory and authentic proof that the several amendments proposed were to be considered as either declaratory or restrictive, and, whether the one or the other, as corresponding with the desire expressed by a number of the States, and as extending the ground of public confidence in the Government.

Under any other construction of the amendment relating to the press, than that it declared the press to be wholly exempt from the power of Congress, the amendment could neither be said to correspond with the desire expressed by a number of the States, nor be calculated to extend the ground of public confidence in the Government.

Nay, more; the construction employed to justify the Sedition Act would exhibit a phenomenon without a parallel in the political world.

It would exhibit a number of respectable States, as denying, first, that any power over the press was delegated by the Constitution; as proposing, next, that no such power was delegated; and, finally, as concurring in an amendment actually recognizing or delegating such a power.

Is then, the Federal Government, it will be asked, destitute of every authority for restraining the licentiousness of the press, and for shielding itself against the libellous attacks which may be made on those who administer it?

The Constitution alone can answer this question. If no such power be expressly delegated, and if it be not both necessary and proper to carry into execution an express power; above all, if it be expressly forbidden, by a declaratory amendment to the Constitution,—the answer must be, that the Federal Government is destitute of all such authority.

And might it not be asked, in turn, whether it is not more probable, under all the circumstances which have been reviewed, that the authority should be withheld by the Constitution, than that it should be left to a vague and violent construction, whilst so much pains were bestowed in enumerating other powers, and so many less important powers are included in the enumeration?

Might it not be likewise asked, whether the anxious circumspection which dictated so many peculiar limitations on the general authority, would be unlikely to exempt the press altogether from that authority? The peculiar magnitude of some of the powers necessarily committed to the Federal Government; the peculiar duration required for the functions of some of its departments; the peculiar distance of the seat of its proceedings from the great body of its constituents; and the peculiar difficulty of circulating an adequate knowledge of them through any other channel;—will not these considerations, some or other of which produced other exceptions from the powers of ordinary Governments, altogether, account for the policy of binding the hands of the Federal Government from touching the channel which alone can give efficacy to its responsibility to its constituents, and of leaving those who administer it to a remedy, for their injured reputations, under the same laws, and in the same tribunals, which protect their lives, their liberties, and their properties? But the question does not turn either on the wisdom of the Constitution, or on the policy which gave rise to its particular organization. It turns on the actual meaning of the instrument, by which it has appeared that a power over the press is clearly excluded from the number of powers delegated to the Federal Government.

3. And in the opinion of the committee, well may it be said, as the resolution concludes with saying, that the unconstitutional power exercised over the press by the Sedition Act, ought, "more than any other, to produce universal alarm; because it is levelled against that right of freely examining public characters, and measures, and of free

communication among the people thereon, which has ever been justly deemed the only effectual guardian of every other right."

Without scrutinizing minutely into all the provisions of the Sedition Act, it will be sufficient to cite so much of section 2d as follows:—"And be it further enacted, that if any shall write, print, utter, or publish, or shall cause or procure to be written, printed, uttered, or published, or shall knowingly and willingly assist or aid in writing, printing, uttering, or publishing, any false, scandalous, and malicious writing or writings against the Government of the United States, or either house of the Congress of the United States, with an intent to defame the said Government, or either house of the said Congress, or the President, or to bring them, or either of them into contempt or disrepute, or to excite against them, or either, or any of them, the hatred of the good people of the United States, etc.,—then such persons, being thereof convicted before any court of the United States having jurisdiction thereof, shall be punished by a fine not exceeding two thousand dollars, and by imprisonment not exceeding two years."

On this part of the act the following observations present themselves:—

1. The Constitution supposes that the President, the Congress, and each of its Houses, may not discharge their trusts, either from defect of judgment or other causes. Hence they are all made responsible to their constituents, at the returning periods of elections; and the President, who is singly intrusted with very great powers, is, as a further guard, subjected to an intermediate impeachment.

2. Should it happen, as the Constitution supposes it may happen, that either of these branches of the Government may not have duly discharged its trust, it is natural and proper, that, according to the cause and degree of their faults, they should be brought into contempt or disrepute, and incur the hatred of the people.

3. Whether it has, in any case, happened that the proceedings of either or all of those branches evince such a violation of duty as to justify a contempt, a disrepute, or hatred among the people, can only be determined by a free examination thereof, and a free communication among the people thereon.

4. Whenever it may have actually happened that proceedings of this sort are chargeable on all or either of the branches of the Government, it is the duty, as well as the right, of intelligent and faithful citizens to discuss and promulgate them freely—as well to control them by the censorship of the public opinion, as to promote a remedy according to the rules of the Constitution. And it cannot be avoided that those who are to apply the remedy must feel, in some degree, a contempt or hatred against the transgressing party.

5. As the act was passed on July 14, 1798, and is to be in force until March 3, 1801, it was of course that, during its continuance, two elec-

tions of the entire House of Representatives, an election of a part of the Senate, and an election of a President, were to take place.

6. That, consequently, during all these elections,—intended, by the Constitution, to preserve the purity or to purge the faults of the administration,—the great remedial rights of the people were to be exercised, and the responsibility of their public agents to be screened, under the penalties of this act.

May it not be asked of every intelligent friend to the liberties of his country, whether the power exercised in such an act as this ought not to produce great and universal alarm? Whether a rigid execution of such an act, in time past, would not have repressed that information and communication among the people which is indispensable to the just exercise of their electoral rights? And whether such an act, if made perpetual, and enforced with vigor, would not, in time to come, either destroy our free system of government, or prepare a convulsion that might prove equally fatal to it?

In answer to such questions, it has been pleaded that the writings and publications forbidden by the act are those only which are false and malicious, and intended to defame; and merit is claimed for the privilege allowed to authors to justify, by proving the truth of their publications, and for the limitations to which the sentence of fine and imprisonment is subjected.

To those who concurred in the act, under the extraordinary belief that the option lay between the passing of such an act, and leaving in force the common law of libels, which punishes truth equally with falsehood, and submits fine and imprisonment to the indefinite discretion of the court, the merit of good intentions ought surely not to be refused. A like merit may perhaps be due for the discontinuance of the corporeal punishment, which the common law also leaves to the discretion of the Court. This merit of intention, however, would have been greater if the several mitigations had not been limited to so short a period; and the apparent inconsistency would have been avoided, between justifying the act, at one time, by contrasting it with the rigors of the common law otherwise in force; and at another time, by appealing to the nature of the crisis, as requiring the temporary rigor exerted by the act.

But whatever may have been the meritorious intentions of all or any who contributed to the Sedition Act, a very few reflections will prove that its baleful tendency is little diminished by the privilege of giving in evidence the truth of the matter contained in political writings.

In the first place, where simple and naked facts alone are in question, there is sufficient difficulty in some cases, and sufficient trouble and vexation in all, in meeting a prosecution from the Government with the full and formal proof necessary in a court of law.

But in the next place, it must be obvious to the plainest minds, that opinions and inferences, and conjectural observations, are not only in many cases inseparable from the facts, but may often be more the objects of the prosecution than the facts themselves; or may even be altogether abstracted from particular facts; and that opinion, and inferences, and conjectural observations, cannot be subjects of that kind of proof which appertains to facts, before a court of law.

Again: it is no less obvious that the intent to defame, or bring into contempt, or disrepute, or hatred,—which is made a condition of the offence created by the act,—cannot prevent its pernicious influence on the freedom of the press. For, omitting the inquiry, how far the malice of the intent is an inference of the law from the mere publication, it is manifestly impossible to punish the intent to bring those who administer the Government into disrepute or contempt, without striking at the right of freely discussing public characters and measures; because those who engage in such discussions must expect and intend to excite these unfavorable sentiments, so far as they may be thought to be deserved. To prohibit the intent to excite those unfavorable sentiments against those who administer the Government, is equivalent to a prohibition of the actual excitement of them; and to prohibit the actual excitement of them is equivalent to a prohibition of discussions having that tendency and effect; which, again, is equivalent to a protection of those who administer the Government, if they should at any time deserve the contempt or hatred of the people, against being exposed to it, by free animadversions on their characters and conduct. Nor can there be a doubt, if those in public trust be shielded by penal laws from such strictures of the press as may expose them to contempt, or disrepute, or hatred, where they may deserve it, that, in exact proportion as they may deserve to be exposed, will be the certainty and criminality of the intent to expose them, and the vigilance of prosecuting and punishing it; nor a doubt that a Government thus intrenched in penal statutes against the just and natural effects of a culpable administration, will easily evade the responsibility which is essential to a faithful discharge of its duty.

Let it be recollected, lastly, that the right of electing the members of the Government constitutes more particularly the essence of a free and responsible Government. The value and efficacy of this right depends on the knowledge of the comparative merits and demerits of the candidates for public trust, and on the equal freedom, consequently, of examining and discussing these merits and demerits of the candidates respectively. It has been seen that a number of important elections will take place while the act is in force, although it should not be continued beyond the term to which it is limited. Should there happen, then, as is extremely probable in relation to some one or other of the branches of the Government, to be competitions between those who are, and those who are not, members of the Government, what will be the situations of the competitors? Not equal; because the characters of the former will be covered by the Sedition Act from animadversions exposing them to disrepute among the people, whilst the latter may be exposed to the contempt and hatred of the people without a violation of the act. What will be the situation of the people? Not free; because they will be compelled to make their election between competitors whose pretensions they are not permitted by the act equally to examine, to discuss, and to ascertain. And from both these situations will not those in power derive an undue advantage for continuing themselves in it; which, by impairing the right of election, endangers the blessings of the Government founded on it?

It is with justice, therefore, that the General Assembly have affirmed, in the resolution, as well that the right of freely examining public characters and measures, and of communication thereon, is the only effectual guardian of every other right, as that this particular right is levelled at by the power exercised in the Sedition Act.

The resolution next in order is as follows:

"That this State having, by its Convention, which ratified the Federal Constitution, expressly declared that, among other essential rights, 'the liberty of conscience and of the press cannot be cancelled, abridged, restrained, or modified, by any authority of the United States;' and, from its extreme anxiety to guard these rights from every possible attack of sophistry and ambition, having, with other States, recommended an amendment for that purpose, which amendment was in due time annexed to the Constitution, it would mark a reproachful inconsistency, and criminal degeneracy, if an indifference were now shown to the most palpable violation of one of the rights thus declared and secured, and to the establishment of a precedent which may be fatal to the other."

To place this resolution in its just light, it will be necesssary to recur to the act of ratification by Virginia, which stands in the ensuing form:

"We, the delegates of the people of Virginia, duly elected in pursuance of a recommendation from the General Assembly, and now met in convention, having fully and freely investigated and discussed the proceedings of the Federal Convention, and being prepared, as well as the most mature deliberation hath enabled us, to decide thereon,—DC, in the name and in behalf of the people of Virginia, declare and make known, that the powers granted under the Constitution, being derived from the people of the United States, may be resumed by them whensoever the same shall be perverted to their injury or oppression; and that every power not granted thereby remains with them, and at their will. That, therefore, no right of any denomination can be cancelled, abridged, restrained, or modified, by the Congress, by the Senate or the House of Representatives, acting in any capacity, by the President, or any department or officer of the United States, except in those instances in which power is given by the Constitution for those purposes; and that, among other essential rights, the liberty of conscience and of the press cannot be cancelled, abridged, restrained, or modified, by any authority of the United States."

Here is an express and solemn declaration by the Convention of the State, that they ratified the Constitution in the sense that no right of any denomination can be cancelled, abridged, restrained, or modified, by the Government of the United States, or any part of it, except in those instances in which power is given by the Constitution; and in the sense, particularly, "that among other essential rights, the liberty of conscience and freedom of the press cannot be cancelled, abridged, restrained, or modified, by any authority of the United States."

Words could not well express, in a fuller or more forcible manner, the understanding of the Convention, that the liberty of conscience and freedom of the press were *equally and completely* exempted from all authority whatever of the United States.

Under an anxiety to guard more effectually these rights against every possible danger, the Convention, after ratifying the Constitution, proceeded to prefix to certain amendments proposed by them, a declaration of rights, in which are two articles providing, the one for the liberty of conscience, the other for the freedom of speech and of the press.

Similar recommendations having proceeded from a number of other States; and Congress, as has been seen, having, in consequence thereof, and with a view to extend the ground of public confidence, proposed, among other declaratory and restrictive clauses, a clause expressly securing the liberty of conscience and of the press; and Virginia having concurred in the ratifications which made them a part of the Constitution,—it will remain with a candid public to decide whether it would not mark an inconsistency and degeneracy, if an indifference were now shown to a palpable violation of one of those rights—the freedom of the press; and to a precedent, therein, which may be fatal to the other—the free exercise of religion.

That the precedent established by the violation of the former of these rights may, as is affirmed by the resolution, be fatal to the latter, appears to be demonstrable by a comparison of the grounds on which they respectively rest, and from the scope of reasoning by which the power of the former has been vindicated.

First. Both of these rights, the liberty of conscience, and of the press, rest equally on the original ground of not being delegated by the Constitution, and consequently withheld from the Government. Any construction, therefore, that would attack this original security for the one, must have the like effect on the other.

Secondly. They are both equally secured by the supplement to the Constitution; being both included in the same amendment, made at the same time and by the same authority. Any construction or argument, then, which would turn the amendment into a grant or acknowledgment of power, with respect to the press, might be equally applied to the freedom of religion.

Thirdly. If it be admitted that the extent of the freedom of the press, secured by the amendment, is to be measured by the common law on this subject, the same authority may be resorted to for the standard which is to fix the extent of the "free exercise of religion." It cannot be necessary to say what this standard would be—whether the common law be taken solely as the unwritten, or as varied by the written law of England.

Fourthly. If the words and phrases in the amendment are to be considered as chosen with a studied discrimination, which yields an argument for a power over the press, under the limitation that its freedom be not abridged, the same argument results from the same consideration, for a power over the exercise of religion, under the limitation that its freedom be not prohibited.

For, if Congress may regulate the freedom of the press, provided they do not abridge it, because it is said only, "they shall not abridge it," and is not said, "they shall make no law respecting it," the analogy of reasoning is conclusive, that Congress may *regulate*, and even *abridge*, the free exercise of religion, provided they do not *prohibit it;* because it is said only, "they shall not prohibit;" and is *not* said, "they shall make no law *respecting*, or no law *abridging* it."

The General Assembly were governed by the clearest reason, then, in considering the Sedition Act, which legislates on the freedom of the press, as establishing a precedent that may be fatal to the liberty of conscience; and it will be the duty of all, in proportion as they value the security of the latter, to take the alarm at every encroachment on the former.

The two concluding resolutions only remain to be examined. They are in the words following:

"That the good people of this Commonwealth, having ever felt, and continuing to feel, the most sincere affection for their brethren of the other States, the truest anxiety for establishing and perpetuating the union of all, and the most scrupulous fidelity to that Constitution which is the pledge of mutual friendship and the instrument of mutual happiness,—the General Assembly doth solemnly appeal to the like dispositions in the other States, in confidence that they will concur with this Commonwealth in declaring, as it does hereby declare, that the acts aforesaid are unconstitutional; and that the necessary and proper measures will be taken, by each, for co-operating with this State, in maintaining, unimpaired, the authorities, rights, and liberties, reserved to the States respectively, or to the people.

"That the Governor be desired to transmit a copy of the foregoing resolutions to the executive authority of each of the other States, with a request that the same may be communicated to the Legislature thereof· and that a copy be furnished to each of the Senators and Representatives representing this State in the Congress of the United States."

The fairness and regularity of the course of proceeding here pursued, have not protected it against objections even from sources too respectable to be disregarded.

It has been said that it belongs to the Judiciary of the United States, and not the State Legislatures, to declare the meaning of the Federal Constitution.

But a declaration that proceedings of the Federal Government are not warranted by the Constitution, is a novelty neither among the citizens nor among the Legislatures of the States; nor are the citizens or the Legislature of Virginia singular in the example of it.

Nor can the declarations of either, whether affirming or denying the constitutionality of measures of the Federal Government, or whether made before or after judicial decisions thereon, be deemed, in any point of view, an assumption of the office of the Judge. The declarations in such cases are expressions of opinion, unaccompanied with any other effect than what they may produce on opinion, by exciting reflection. The expositions of the Judiciary, on the other hand, are carried into immediate effect by force. The former may lead to a change in the legislative expression of the general will—possibly to a change in the opinion of the Judiciary; the latter enforces the general will, whilst that will and that opinion continue unchanged.

And if there be no impropriety in declaring the unconstitutionality of proceedings in the Federal Government, where can there be the impropriety of communicating the declaration to other States, and inviting their concurrence in a like declaration? What is allowable for one, must be allowable for all; and a free communication among the States, where the Constitution imposes no restraint, is as allowable among the State Governments as among other public bodies or private citizens. This consideration derives a weight that cannot be denied to it, from the relation of the State Legislatures to the Federal Legislature as the immediate constituents of one of its branches.

The Legislatures of the States have a right also to originate amendments to the Constitution, by a concurrence of two thirds of the whole number, in applications to Congress for the purpose. When new States are to be formed by a junction of two or more States, or parts of States, the Legislatures of the States concerned are, as well as Congress, to concur in the measure. The States have a right also to enter into agreements or compacts, with the consent of Congress. In all such cases a communication among them results from the object which is common to them.

It is lastly to be seen, whether the confidence expressed by the Constitution, that the *necessary and proper measures* would be taken by the other States for co-operating with Virginia in maintaining the rights reserved to the States, or to the people, be in any degree liable to the objections raised against it.

If it be liable to objections, it must be because either the object or the means are objectionable.

The object, being to maintain what the Constitution has ordained, is in itself a laudable object.

The means are expressed in the terms "the necessary and proper measures." A proper object was to be pursued by the means both necessary and proper.

To find an objection, then, it must be shown that some meaning was annexed to these general terms which was not proper; and, for this purpose, either that the means used by the General Assembly were an example of improper means, or that there were no proper means to which the terms could refer.

In the example, given by the State, of declaring the Alien and Sedition Acts to be unconstitutional, and of communicating the declaration to other States, no trace of improper means has appeared. And if the other States had concurred in making a like declaration, supported, too, by the numerous applications flowing immediately from the people, it can scarcely be doubted that these simple means would have been as sufficient as they are unexceptionable.

It is no less certain that other means might have been employed which are strictly within the limits of the Constitution. The Legislatures of the States might have made a direct representation to Congress, with a view to obtain a rescinding of the two offensive acts; or they might have represented to their respective Senators in Congress their wish that two thirds thereof would propose an explanatory amendment to the Constitution; or two thirds of themselves, if such had been their opinion, might, by an application to Congress, have obtained a Convention for the same object.

These several means, though not equally eligible in themselves, nor probably to the States, were all constitutionally open for consideration. And if the General Assembly, after declaring the two acts to be unconstitutional, (the first and most obvious proceeding on the subject,) did not undertake to point out to the other States a choice among the further measures that might become necessary and proper, the reserve will not be misconstrued by liberal minds into any culpable imputation.

These observations appear to form a satisfactory reply to every objection which is not founded on a misconception of the terms employed in the resolutions. There is one other, however, which may be of too much importance not to be added. It cannot be forgotten that, among the arguments addressed to those who apprehended danger to liberty from the establishment of the General Government over so great a country, the appeal was emphatically made to the intermediate existence of the

State Governments between the people and that Government, to the vigilance with which they would descry the first symptons of usurpation, and to the promptitude with which they would sound the alarm to the public. This argument was probably not without its effect; and if it was a proper one then to recommend the establishment of a Constitution, it must be a proper one now to assist in its interpretation.

The only part of the two concluding resolutions that remains to be noticed, is the repetition, in the first, of that warm affection to the Union and its members, and of that scrupulous fidelity to the Constitution, which have been invariably felt by the people of this State. As the proceedings were introduced with these sentiments, they could not be more properly closed than in the same manner. Should there be any so far misled as to call in question the sincerity of these professions, whatever regret may be excited by the error, the General Assembly cannot descend into a discussion of it. Those who have listened to the suggestion can only be left to their own recollection of the part which this State has borne in the establishment of our national independence, or the establishment of our national Constitution, and in maintaining under it the authority and laws of the Union, without a single exception of internal resistance or commotion. By recurring to the facts, they will be able to convince themselves that the representatsive of the people of Virginia must be above the necessity of opposing any other shield to attacks on their national patriotism, than their own conscientiousness, and the justice of an enlightened public; who will perceive in the resolutions themselves the strongest evidence of attachment, both to the Constitution and the Union, since it is only by maintaining the different Governments, and the departments within their respective limits, that the blessings of either can be perpetuated.

The extensive view of the subject, thus taken by the committee, has led them to report to the House, as *the result of the whole*, the following resolution:—

Resolved, That the General Assembly, having carefully and respectfully attended to the proceedings of a number of the States, *in answer to the Resolutions of December* 21, 1798, *and having accurately and fully re-examined and reconsidered the latter, find it to be their indispensable duty* to adhere to the same, as founded in truth, as consonant with the Constitution, and as conducive to its preservation; and more especially to be their duty to renew, as they do hereby renew, their PROTEST against Alien and Sedition Acts, as palpable and alarming infractions of the Constitution.

F.

EXTRACTS FROM AN ADDRESS BY THE HON. JAMES P HOLCOMBE, DELIVERED BEFORE THE VIRGINIA STATE AGRICULTURAL SOCIETY, AT ITS SEVENTH ANNUAL MEETING, NOVEMBER 4, 1858.

Personal and political liberty are both requisite to develop the highest style of man. They furnish the amplest opportunities for the exercise of that self-control which is the germ and essence of every virtue, and for that expansive and ameliorating culture by which our whole nature is exalted in the scale of being, and clothed with the grace, dignity and authority, becoming the lords of creation. Whenever the population of a State is homogeneous, although slavery may perform some important functions in quickening the otherwise tardy processes of civilization, it ought to be regarded as a temporary and provisional relation. If there are no radical differences of physical organization or moral character, the barriers between classes are not insurmountable. The discipline of education and liberal institutions, may raise the serf to the level of the baron. Against any artificial circumscription seeking to arrest that tendency to freedom which is the normal state of every society of equals, human nature would constantly rise in rebellion. But where two distinct races are collected upon the same territory, incapable from any cause of fusion or severance, the one being as much superior to the other in strength and intelligence as the man to the child, there the rightful relation between them is that of authority upon the one side, and subordination in some form, upon the other. Equality, personal and political, could not be established without inflicting the climax of injustice upon the superior, and of cruelty on the inferior race: for if it were possible to preserve such an arrangement, it would wrest the sceptre of dominion from the wisdom and strength of society, and surrender it to its weakness and folly. "Of all rights of man," says Carlyle' "the right of the ignorant man to be guided by the wiser, to be gently and firmly held in the true course, is the indispensablest. Nature has ordained it from the first. Society struggles towards perfection by conforming to and accomplishing it, more and more. If freedom have any meaning, it means enjoyment of this right, in which all other rights are enjoyed. It is a divine right and duty on both sides, and the sum of all social duties between the two." Under the circumstances I have supposed, no intelligent man could hesitate, except as to the form of subordination: nor has entire equality been ever allowed in society where the inferior race constituted an element of any magnitude. * * * *

But when we are settling the law of a society embracing in its bosom distinct and unequal races, the problem is complicated by elements which create the gravest doubt whether personal liberty will prove a blessing or a curse. It may become a question between the slavery, and the extinction or further deterioration of the inferior race. Thus, if it is difficult to procure the means of subsistence from density of population or other cause, and if the inferior race is incapable of sustaining a competition with the superior in the industrial pursuits of life, a condition of freedom which would involve such competition, must either terminate in its destruction, or consign it to hopeless degradation. If, under these circumstances, a system of personal servitude gave reasonable assurance of preserving the inferior race, and gradually imparting to it the amelioration of a higher civilization, no Christian statesman could mistake the path of duty. Natural law, illuminated in its decision by History, Philosophy, and Religion, would not only clothe the relation with the sanction of justice, but lend to it the lustre of mercy. It will not, I apprehend, be difficult to show that all these conditions apply to African slavery in the United States. Look at the races which have been brought face to face in unmanageable masses, upon this continent, and it is impossible to mistake their relative position. The one still filling that humble and subordinate place, which, as the pictured monuments of Egypt attest, it has occupied since the dawn of history; a race which during the long-revolving cycles of intervening time has founded no empire, built no towered city, invented no art, discovered no truth, bequeathed no everlasting possession to the future, through law-giver, hero, bard, or benefactor of mankind: a race which though lifted immeasurably above its native barbarism by the refining influence of Christian servitude has yet given no signs of living and self-sustaining culture. The other, a great composite race which has incorporated into its bosom all the vital elements of human progress; which, crowned with the traditions of history and bearing in its hands the most precious trophies of civilization, still rejoices in the overflowing energy, the abounding strength, the unconquerable will, which have made it "the heir of all the ages;" and which, with aspirations unsatisfied by centuries of toil and achievement, still vexes sea and land with its busy industry, binds coy nature faster in its chains, embellishes life more prodigally with its arts, kindles a wider inspiration from the fountain lights of freedom, follows knowledge, like a sinking star, beyond the utmost bound of human thought. * * * *

The whole reasoning of modern philanthropy upon this subject has been vitiated, by its overlooking those fundamental moral differences between the races, which constitute a far more important element in the political arrangements of society, than relative intellectual power. It is immaterial how these differences have been created. Their existence is certain; and if capable of removal at all, they are yet likely to endure for such an indefinite period, that in the consideration of any practical problem, we must regard them as permanent. The collective superiority of a race can no more exempt it from the obligations of justice and mercy, than the personal superiority of an individual; but where unequal races are compelled to live together, a sober and intelligent estimate of their several aptitudes and capacities must form the basis of their social and political organization. The intellectual weakness of the black man is not so characteristic, as the moral qualities which distinguish him from his white brother. The warmest friends of emancipation, amongst others the late Dr. Channing, have acknowledged that the civilization of the African must present a different type from that of the Caucasian, and resemble more the development of the East than the West. His nature is made up of the gentler elements. Docile, affectionate, light-hearted, facile to impression, reverential, he is disposed to look without for strength and direction. In the courage that rises with danger, in the energy that would prove a consuming fire to its possessor, if it found no object upon which to spend its strength, in the proud aspiring temper which would render slavery intolerable, he is far inferior to other races. Hence, subordination is as congenial to his moral, as a warm latitude is to his physical nature. Freedom is not "chartered on his manly brow," as on that of the native Indian. Unkindness awakens resentment, but servitude alone carries no sense of degradation fatal to self-respect. * * * *

The mutual good will of distinct classes has, in all ages, been dependent upon a well defined subordination. This opinion is confirmed by the testimony of one of the most eloquent writers of New England, in reference to the workings of its social system as they fell under his personal observation. "I appeal," says Dana, in his Essay on Law as suited to Man, "to those who remember the state of our domestic relations, when the old Scriptural terms of master and servant were in use. I do not fear contradiction when I say there was more of mutual good will then than now; more of trust on the one side and fidelity on the other; more of protection and kind care, and more of gratitude and affectionate respect in return; and because each understood well his place, actually more of a certain freedom, tempered by gentleness and by deference. From the very fact that the distinction of classes was more marked, the bond between the individuals constituting these two, was closer. As a general truth, I verily believe that, with the exception of near-blood relationships, and here and there peculiar friendships, the attachment of master and servant was closer and more enduring than that of almost any other connection in life. The young of this day, under a change of fortune, will hardly live to see the eye of an old, faithful servant fill at their fall; nor will the old domestic be longer housed and warmed by the fireside of his master's child, or be followed by him to the grave. The blessed sun of those good old days has gone down, it may be for ever, and it is very cold." It is through the operation of these kindly sentiments, which it awakens on both sides, that

African slavery reconciles the antagonism of classes that has elsewhere reduced the highest statesmanship to the verge of despair, and becomes the great Peace-maker of our society, converting inequalities, which are sources of danger and discord in other lands, into pledges of reciprocal service, and bonds of mutual and intimate friendship. * * *

If I have at all comprehended the elements which should enter into the determination of this momentous problem of social welfare and public authority, the existence of African Slavery amongst us, furnishes no just occasion for self-reproach; much less for the presumptuous rebuke of our fellow man. As individuals, we have cause to humble ourselves before God, for the imperfect discharge of our duties in this, and in every other relation of life: but for its justice and morality as an element of our social polity, we may confidently appeal to those future ages, which, when the bedimming mists of passion and prejudice have vanished, will examinine it in the pure light of truth, and pronounce the final sentence of impartial History. Beyond our own borders there has been no sober and intelligent estimate of its distinctive features; no just apprehension of the nature, extent, and permanence of the disparities between the races, or of the fatal consequences to the slave, of a freedom which would expose him to the unchecked selfishness of a superior civilization; no conception approaching to the reality of the power which has been exerted by a public sentiment, springing from Christian principle, and sustained by the universal instincts of self-interest, in tempering the severity of its restraints, and impressing upon it the mild character of a patriarchal relation; no rational anticipation of the improvement of which the negro would be capable under our form of servitude, if those who now nurse the wild and mischievous dream of peaceful emancipation, should lend all their energies to the maintenance of the only social system under which his progressive amelioration appears possible. African slavery is no relic of barbarism to which we cling from the ascendency of semi-civilized tastes, habits, and principles; but an adjustment of the social and political relations of the races, consistent with the purest justice, commended by the highest expediency, and sanctioned by a comprehensive and enlightened humanity. It has no doubt been sometimes abused by the base and wicked passions of our fallen nature to purposes of cruelty and wrong; but where is the school of civilization from which the stern and wholesome discipline of suffering has been banished? or the human landscape not saddened by a dark flowing stream of sorrow? Its history, when fairly written, will be its ample vindication. It has weaned a race of savages from superstition and idolatry, imparted to them a general knowledge of the precepts of the true religion, implanted in their bosom sentiments of humanity and principles of virtue, developed a taste for the arts and enjoyments of civilized life, given an unknown dignity and elevation to their type of physical, moral and intellectual man, and for two centuries during which this humanizing process has taken place, made for their subsistence and comfort, a more bountiful provision, than was ever before enjoyed in any age or country of the world by a laboring class. If tried by the test which we apply to other institutions, the whole sum of its results, there is no agency of civilization which has accomplished so much in the same time, for the happiness and advancement of mankind.

G.

A LECTURE BY HON. ROBERT TOOMBS, DELIVERED IN THE TREMONT TEMPLE, BOSTON, MASSACHUSETTS, JANUARY 24, 1856.

SLAVERY—ITS CONSTITUTIONAL STATUS—ITS INFLUENCE ON THE AFRICAN RACE AND SOCIETY.

I propose to submit to you this evening some considerations and reflections upon two points.

1*st*. The constitutional powers and duties of the Federal Government in relation to Domestic Slavery.

2*d*. The influence of Slavery as it exists in the United States upon the Slave and Society.

Under the first head I shall endeavor to show that Congress has no power to limit, restrain, or in any manner to impair slavery: but, on the contrary, it is bound to protect and maintain it in the States where it exists, and wherever its flag floats, and its jurisdiction is paramount.

On the second point, I maintain that so long as the African and Caucasian races co-exist in the same society, that the subordination of the African is its normal, necessary and proper condition, and that such subordination is the condition best calculated to promote the highest interest and the greatest happiness of both races, and consequently of the whole society: and that the abolition of slavery, under these conditions, is not a remedy for any of the evils of the system. I admit that the truth of these propositions, stated under the second point, is essentially necessary to the existence and permanence of the system. They rest on the truth that the white is the superior race, and the black the inferior, and that subordination, with or without law, will be the status of the African in this mixed society, and, therefore, it is the interest of both, and especially of the black race, and of the whole society, that this status should be fixed, controlled, and protected by law. The perfect equality of the superior race, and the legal subordination of the inferior, are the foundations on which we have erected our republican systems

Their soundness must be tested by their conformity to the sovereignty of right, the universal law which ought to govern all people in all centuries. This sovereignty of right is *justice*, commonly called natural justice, not the vague uncertain imaginings of men, but natural justice as interpreted by the written oracles, and read by the light of the revelations of nature's God. In this sense I recognize a "higher law," and the duty of all men, by legal and proper means, to bring every society in conformity with it.

I proceed to the consideration of the first point.

The old thirteen States, before the Revolution, were dependent colonies of Great Britain—each was a separate and distinct political community, with different laws, and each became an independent and sovereign State by the Declaration of Independence. At the time of this declaration slavery was a *fact*, and a fact recognized by law in each of them, and the slave trade was lawful commerce by the laws of nations and the practice of mankind. This declaration was drafted by a slaveholder, adopted by the representatives of slaveholders, and did not emancipate a single African slave; but, on the contrary, one of the charges which it submitted to the civilized world against King George was, that he had attempted to excite "domestic insurrection among us." At the time of this declaration we had no common Government; the Articles of Confederation were submitted to the representatives of the States eight days afterwards, and were not adopted by all of the States until 1781. These loose and imperfect articles of union sufficed to bring us successfully through the Revolution. Common danger was a stronger bond of union than these Articles of Confederation; after that ceased, they were inadequate to the purposes of peace. They did not emancipate a single slave.

The Constitution was framed by delegates elected by the State Legislatures. It was an emanation from the sovereign States as independent, separate communities. It was ratified by conventions of these separate States, each acting for itself. The members of these conventions represented the sovereignty of each State, but they were not elected by the whole people of either of the States. Minors, women, slaves, Indians, Africans, bond and free, were excluded from participating in this act of sovereignty. Neither were all the white male inhabitants, over twenty-one years old, allowed to participate in it. Some were excluded because they had no land, others for the want of good characters, others again because they were non-freemen, and a large number were excluded for a great variety of still more unimportant reasons. None exercised this high privilege except those upon whom each State, for itself, had adjudged it wise, safe, and prudent to confer it.

By this Constitution these States granted to the Federal Government certain well defined and clearly specified powers in order "*to make a more perfect Union, establish justice, insure domestic tranquillity, provide for the common defence and general welfare, and to secure the blessings of liberty to (themselves and their) posterity.*" And with great wisdom and forecast this Constitution lays down a plain, certain, and sufficient rule for its own interpretation, by declaring that "*the powers not herein delegated to the United States by the Constitution, nor prohibited by it to the States, are reserved to the States respectively, or to the people.*" The Federal Government is therefore a limited Government. It is limited expressly to the exercise of the enumerated powers, and of such others only "*which shall be necessary and proper to carry into execution*" these enumerated powers. The declaration of the purposes for which these powers were granted can neither increase or diminish them. If any one or all of them were to fail by reason of the insufficiency of the granted powers to secure them, that would be a good reason for a new grant, but could never enlarge the granted powers. That declaration was itself a limitation instead of an enlargement of the granted powers. If a power expressly granted be used for any other purpose than those declared, such use would be a violation of the grant and a fraud on the Constitution, and therefore it follows, that if anti-slavery action by Congress is not warranted by any express power, nor within any of the declared purposes for which any such power was granted, the exercise of even a granted power to effect that action, under any pretence whatever, would fall under the just condemnation of the Constitution.

The history of the times, and the debates in the convention which framed the Constitution, show that this whole subject was much considered by them, and "perplexed them in the extreme;" and these provisions of the Constitution which related to it, were earnestly considered by the State conventions, which adopted it. Incipient legislation, providing for emancipation, had already been adopted by some of the States. Massachusetts had declared that slavery was extinguished in her limits by her bill of rights; the African slave trade had been legislated against in many of the States, including Virginia and Maryland, and North Carolina. The public mind was unquestionably tending towards emancipation. This feeling displayed itself in the South as well as in the North. Some of the delegates from the present slaveholding States thought that the power to abolish, not only the African slave trade, but slavery in the States, ought to be given to the Federal Government; and that the Constitution did not take this shape, was made one of the most prominent objections to it by Luther Martin, a distinguished member of the convention from Maryland, and Mr. Mason, of Virginia, was not far behind him in his emancipation principles; Mr. Madison sympathized to a great extent, to a much greater extent than some of the representatives from Massachusetts, in this anti-slavery feeling; hence we find that anti-slavery feelings were extensively indulged in by many members of the convention, both from slaveholding and non-slaveholding States. This fact has led to many and grave errors; artful and unscrupulous men have used it much to deceive the northern public. Mere opinions of individual men have been relied upon as authoritative expositions of the Constitution. Our reply to them is simple, direct: they were not the opinions of the collective body of the people, who made, and who had the right to make this Government; and, therefore, they found no place in the organic law, and by that alone are we bound; and, therefore, it concerns us rather to know what was the collective will of the whole, as affirmed by the sovereign States, than what were the opinions of individual men in the convention. We wish to know what was done by the whole, not what some of the members thought was best to be done. The result of the struggle was, that not a single clause was inserted in the Constitution giving power to the Federal Government anywhere, either to abolish, limit, restrain, or in any other manner to impair the system of slavery in the United States: but on the contrary every clause which was inserted in the Constitution on this subject, does in fact, and was intended either to *increase* it, to *strengthen* it, or to *protect* it. To support these positions, I appeal to the Constitution itself, to the contemporaneous and all subsequent authoritative interpretations of it. The Constitution provides for the *increase* of slavery by prohibiting the suppression of the slave trade for twenty years after its adoption. It declares in the 1st clause of the 9th section of the first article, that "*the migration or importation of such persons as any of the States now existing shall think proper to admit, shall not be prohibited by the Congress prior to the year* 1808, *but a tax or duty may be imposed on such importation, not exceeding ten dollars for each person.*" After that time it was left to the discretion of Congress to prohibit, or not to prohibit, the African slave trade. The extension of this traffic in Africans from 1800 to 1808, was voted for by the whole of the New England States, including Massachusetts, and opposed by Virginia and Delaware; and the clause was inserted in the Constitution by votes of the New England States. It fostered an active and profitable trade for New England capital and enterprise for twenty years, by which a large addition was made to the original stock of Africans in the United States, and thereby it *increased* slavery. This clause of the Constitution was specially favored: it was one of those clauses which was protected against amendment by article fifth.

Slavery is *strengthened* by the 3d clause, 2d section of 1st article, which fixes the basis of representation *according to numbers* by providing that the "*numbers shall be determined by adding to the whole number of free persons, including those bound to service for a term of years, and excluding Indians not taken, three-fifths of all other persons.*" This provision *strengthens* slavery by giving the existing slaveholding States many more representatives in Congress than they would have if slaves were considered only as property; it was much debated, but finally adopted, with the full understanding of its import, by a great majority.

The Constitution protects it, impliedly, by withholding all power to injure it, or limit its duration, but it protects it expressly *by the 3d clause of 2d section of the 4th article, by the 4th section of the 4th article, and by the 15th clause of the 1st article.* The 3d clause of the 2d section, 4th article, provides that "no persons held to service or labor in one State by the laws thereof, escaping into another, shall in consequence of any law or regulation therein, be discharged from such service or labor, but shall be delivered up on claim of the party to whom such service or labor may be due." The 4th section of the 4th article provides that Congress shall protect each State "on application of the Legislature (or of the Executive when the Legislature cannot be convened) against domestic violence." The 15th clause of the 8th section of the 1st article, makes it the duty of Congress "to provide for calling forth the militia to execute the laws of the Union, *suppress insurrections*, and repel invasions." The first of these three clauses last referred to protects slavery by following the escaping slave into non-slaveholding States and returning him to bondage; the other clauses place the whole military power of the Republic in the hands of the Federal Government to repress "domestic violence" and "insurrections." Under this Constitution, if he flies to other lands, the supreme law follows, captures, and returns him; if he resists the law by which he is held in bondage, the same Constitution brings its military power to his subjugation. There is no limit to this protection, it must exist as long as any of the States tolerate domestic slavery and the Constitution, unaltered, endures. None of these clauses admit of misconception or doubtful construction. They were not incorporated into the charter of our liberties by surprise or inattention, they were each and all of them introduced into that body, debated, referred to committees, reported upon, and adopted. Our construction of them is supported by one unbroken and harmonious current of decisions and adjudications by the Executive Legislature, and Judicial Departments of the Government, State and Federal, from President Washington to President Pierce. Twenty representatives in the Congress of the United States hold their seats to-day, by the virtue of one of these clauses. The African slave trade was carried on its whole appointed period under another of them. Thousands of slaves have been delivered up under another, and it is a just cause of congratulation to the whole country that no occasion has occurred to call into action the remaining clauses which have been quoted.

These constitutional provisions were generally acquiesced in even by those who did not approve them, until a new and less obvious question sprung out of the acquisition of territory. When the Constitution was adopted the question of slavery had been settled in the northwest territory by the articles of session of that territory by the State of Virginia, and at that time the United States had not an acre of land over which it claimed unfettered jurisdiction except a disputed claim on our southwestern boundary, which will hereafter be considered in its appropriate connection. The acquisition of Louisiana imposed upon Congress the necessity of its government. This duty was assumed and performed for the general benefit of the whole country without challenge or question for nearly seventeen years. Equity and good faith shielded it from criticism. But in 1819, thirty years after the Constitution was adopted, upon application of Missouri for admission into the Union, the extraordinary pretension was, for the first time, asserted by a majority of the non-slaveholding States, that Congress not only had the power to prohibit the extension of slavery into new territories of the Republic, but that it had power to compel new States seeking admission into the Union to prohibit it in their own constitutions and mould their domestic policy in all respects to suit the opinions, whims, or caprices of the Federal Government. This novel and extraordinary pretension subjected the whole power of Congress over the territories to the severest criticism. Abundant authority was found in the Constitution to manage this common domain merely as property; the 2d clause, 3d section of the 4th article, declares "*that Congress shall have power to dispose of and make all needful rules and regulations respecting the territory or other property belonging to the United States; and nothing in this Constitution shall be so construed as to prejudice any claims of the United States or of any particular State.*" But this clause was rightfully adjudicated by the supreme judicial authority not to confer on Congress general jurisdiction over territories, but by its terms to restrain that jurisdiction to their management as property, and even without that adjudication, it would not be difficult to prove the utter disregard of all sound principles of construction of this attempt to expand this simple duty "to dispose of and make all needful rules and regulations concerning the territory and other property of the United States" into this gigantic assumption of unlimited power in all cases whatsoever over the territories. When the Constitution seeks to confer this power, it uses appropriate language; when it wished to confer this power over the District of Columbia and the places to be acquired for forts, magazines, and arsenals, it gives Congress power "to exercise exclusive legislation in all cases whatsoever over them." This is explicit, it is apt language to express a particular purpose, and no ingenuity can construe the clause concerning the territories into the same meaning.

This construction was so clear that Congress was then driven to look for power to govern its acquisitions in the necessity and propriety of it as a means of executing the express power to make treaties. The right to acquire territory under the treaty-making power, was itself an implication, and an implication whose rightfulness was denied by Mr. Jefferson, who exercised it; the right to govern being claimed as an incident of the right to acquire, was then but an implication of an implication, and the power to exclude slavery therefrom, was still another remove from the fountain of all power—express grant. But whether this power to prohibit slavery in the common territories be claimed from the one source or the other, it cannot be sustained upon any sound rule of constitutional construction. The power is not expressly granted. Then unless it can be shown to be both "necessary and proper" in order to the just execution of a granted power, the constitutional argument against it is complete. This remains to be shown by the advocates of this power. Admit the power in Congress to govern the territories until they shall be admitted as States into the Union—derive it either from the clause of the Constitution last referred to, or from the treaty-making power, this power to prohibit slavery is not an incident to it in either case, because it is neither "necessary nor proper" to its execution,—that it is not necessary to execute the treaty-making power, is shown from the fact that the treaty power not only was never used for this purpose, but can be wisely and well executed without it, and has been repeatedly used to increase and protect slavery. The acquisitions of Louisiana and Florida are examples of its use without the exercise of this pretended "necessary and proper" incident. Numerous treaties and conventions, with both savage and civilized nations, from the foundation of the Government, demanding and receiving indemnities for injuries to this species of property, are conclusive against this novel pretension. That it is not necessary to the execution of the power "to make needful rules and regulatious respecting the territory and other property of the United States," is proven from the fact that seven territories have been governed by Congress, and trained into sovereign States without its exercise. It is not proper, because it seeks to use an implied power for other and different purposes from any specified, expressed, or intended by the grantors. The purpose is avowed to be, to limit, restrain, weaken, and finally crush out slavery, whereas the grant expressly provides for strengthening and protecting it. It is not proper, because it violates the fundamental condition of the Union—the equality of the States. The States of the Union are all political equals—each State has the same right as every other State—no more, no less. The exercise of this prohibition violates this equality, and violates justice. By the laws of nations, acquisitions, either by purchase or conquest, even in despotic governments, enure to the benefit of all of the subjects of the State; the reason given for this principle, by the most approved publicists, is, that they are the fruits of the common blood and treasure. This prohibition destroys this equality, excludes a part of the joint owners from an equal participation and enjoyment of the common domain, and against justice and right, appropriates it to the greater number. Therefore, so far from being a necessary and proper means of executing granted powers, it is an arbitrary and despotic usurpation, against the letter, the spirit, and the declared purposes of the Constitution; for its exercise neither "promotes a more perfect union, nor establishes justice, nor insures domestic tranquillity, nor provides for the common defence, nor promotes the general welfare, nor secures the blessings of liberty to ourselves or our posterity," but, on the contrary, puts in jeopardy all these inestimable blessings. It loosens the bonds of union, seeks to establish injustice, disturbs domestic tranquillity, weakens the common defence, and endangers the general welfare by sowing hatreds and discords among our people, and puts in eminent peril the liberties of the white race, by whom and for whom the Constitution was made, in a vain effort to bring them down to an equality with the African or to raise the African to an equality with them. Providence has ordered it otherwise, and vain will be the efforts of man to resist this decree. This effort is as wicked as it is foolish and unauthorized. It does not benefit, but injures the black race; penning them up in the old States will necessarily make them more wretched and miserable, but will not strike a fetter from their limbs. It is a simple wrong to the white race, but it is the refinement of cruelty to the blacks. Expansion is as necessary to the increased comforts of the slave as to the prosperity of the master.

The constitutional construction of this point by the South works no wrong to any portion of the Republic, to no sound rules of construction, and promotes the declared purposes of the Constitution. We simply propose that the common territories be left open to the common enjoyment of all the people of the United States, that they shall be protected in their persons and property by the Federal Government until its authority is superseded by a State Constitution, and then we propose that the character of the domestic institutions of the new State be determined by the freemen thereof. This is justice—this is constitutional equality.

But those who claim the power in behalf of Congress to exclude slavery from the common territories, rely rather on precedent and authority than upon principle to support the pretension. In utter disregard of the facts, they boldly proclaim that Congress has, from the beginning of the Government, uniformly asserted and repeatedly exercised this power. This assertion I will proceed to show is not supported by a single precedent up to 1820. Before that time the general duty to protect this great interest, equally with every other, both in the territories and elsewhere, was universally admitted and fairly performed by every Department of the Government. The act of 1793 was passed to secure the delivery up of fugitives from labor, escaping to the non-slaveholding States; our navigation laws authorized their transportation on the high seas, the Government demanded and frequently received compensation for owners of slaves, for injuries sustained in these lawful voyages by the interference of foreign Governments. It not only protected this property on the high seas, but followed it to foreign lands where it had been driven by the dangers of the sea, and protected it when cast even within the jurisdiction of hostile laws. It was protected against the invasions of Indians by your military power and public treaties. In your statute book are to be found numerous treaties from the beginning of the Government to this time, compelling the Indian tribes to pay for slave property captured or destroyed by them in peace or war, and your laws regulating intercourse with the Indian tribes on our borders made permanent provision for its protection. The treaty of Ghent provides for compensation by the British Government for the loss of slaves, precisely upon the same footing as for all other property, and a New England man, (Mr. John Q. Adams,) ably, faithfully, and successfully, maintained the slaveholders' rights under it at the Court of St. James. Until the year 1820, our territorial legislation was marked by the same general spirit of fairness and equity. Up to that period, no act was passed by Congress asserting the primary constitutional power to prevent any citizen of the United States, owning slaves, from removing with them into our territories, and there receiving legal protection for his property; and until that time such persons did so remove into all the territories owned or acquired by the United States, (except the northwest territory,) and were there adequately protected. This fact alone is a complete refutation of the claim of early precedents. The action of Congress in reference to the ordinance of 1787, does not contravene my position. That ordinance was adopted on the 13th day of July, 1787, before the adoption of the Constitution. It purported on its face to be a perpetual compact between the State of Virginia, the people of that territory, and the then Government of the United States. It was unalterable except by the consent of all the parties; when Congress met for the first time under the new Gov nment on the 4th day of March, 1789, it found the Government established by virtue of this ordinance in actual operation; and on the 7th of August, 1789, it passed an act making the officers of Governor and Secretary of the territory conform to the Federal Constitution. It did nothing more—it made no reference to, it took no action upon the 6th and last section of the ordinance, which prohibited slavery. The division of that territory was provided for in the ordinance; at each division, the whole of the ordinance was assigned to each of its parts. This is the whole sum and substance of the free-soil claim, to legislate precedents. Congress did not assert or exercise the right to alter a compact entered into with the former Government, (the old Confederation,) but gave its assent to the Government already established and provided for in the compact. If the original compact was void for want of power in the old Government to make it, as Mr. Madison supposed, Congress may not have been bound to accept it, it certainly had no power to alter it. From these facts, it is clear, that this legislation for the northwest territory, does not conflict with the principle I assert, and does not furnish a precedent for hostile legislation by Congress against slavery in the territories. That such was neither the principle nor the policy upon which this act of Congress in 1789 was based, is further shown by the subsequent action of the same Congress upon the same subject. On the 2d of April, 1790, Congress, by a formal act, accepted the session by North Carolina of her western lands, (now the State of Tennessee,) with this clause in the deed of session—"that no regulations made, or to be made by Congress, shall tend to emancipate slaves" in the ceded territory, and on the 26th May, 1790, passed a territorial bill for the government of all the territory claimed by the United States south of the Ohio river. The description of this territory included all the lands ceded by North Carolina, and it included a great deal more. Its boundaries were left indefinite because there were conflicting claims to all the rest of the territory. But this act put the whole country south of the Ohio, claimed by the Federal Government, under this pro-slavery clause of the North Carolina deed. The whole action of the first Congress in relation to slavery in the territories was simply this: it acquiesced in a government for the northwest territory, based upon a pre-existing anti-slavery ordinance, established a government for the country ceded by North Carolina in conformity with the pro-slavery clause in her deed of cession, and extended this pro-slavery clause to all the rest of the territory claimed by the United States. This legislation vindicates the first Congress from all imputation of having established the precedent claimed by the advocates of legislative exclusion. On the 7th of April, 1798, (during the administration of President John Adams,) the next territorial act was passed: it was the first act of territorial legislation resting solely upon primary, original, unfettered constitutional power over the subject. It established a government over the territory included within the boundaries of a line drawn due east from the mouth of the Yazoo river to the Chatahoochee river, thence down that river to the thirty-first degree of north latitude, thence west on that line to the Mississippi, then up that river to the beginning. This territory was within the boundary of the United States, as defined by the treaty of Paris, and was held not to be within the boundary of any of the States. The controversy arose out of this state of facts. The charter of Georgia limited her boundary in the South by the Altamaha river. In 1763 (after the surrender of her charter), her limits were extended on the south by the Crown of Great Britain, to the St. Mary's river, and thence on the thirty-first parallel of latitude to the Mississippi river. In 1764, it was claimed, that on the recommendation of the Board of Trade, the boundary was again altered, and that portion of territory lying within the boundaries I have described, was annexed to West Florida, and that thus it stood at the Revolution and the treaty of peace. Therefore the United States claimed it as common property, and in 1798, passed the act now under review for its government. In that act, Congress neither claimed or exercised any power to prohibit slavery. The question came directly before it. The ordinance of 1787, in terms, excluding the anti-slavery clause, was applied to this territory: this is a precedent directly in point, and is directly against the exercise of the power now claimed. In 1802, Georgia ceded her western lands, protecting slavery in her grant, and the Federal Government observed the stipulation. In 1803, we acquired Louisiana from France by purchase. There is no special reference to slavery in the treaty; it was protected only under the general name of property. This acquisition was, soon after the treaty, divided into two territories, the Orleans and Louisiana territories, over both of which governments were established. Slavery was protected by law in the whole territory when we acquired it. Congress prohibited the foreign and domestic slave trade in these territories, but gave the express protection of its laws to slave owners emigrating thither with their slaves. Upon the admission of Louisiana into the Union, a new government was established over the rest of the country, under the name of the Missouri Territory. This act attempted no exclusion; slaveholders emigrated to the country with their slaves, and were protected by their Government. In 1819, Florida was acquired by purchase; its laws recognized and protected slavery at the time of the acquisition. The United States extended the same recognition and protection to it. In all this legislation, embracing every act upon the subject up to 1820, we find no warrant, authority, or precedent, for the prohibition of slavery by Congress in the territories.

When Missouri applied for admission into the Union, an attempt was then made, for the first time, to impose restrictions upon a sovereign State, and admit her into the Union upon an *unequal* footing with her sister States, and to compel her to mould her Constitution, not according to the will of her own people, but according to the fancy of a majority in Congress. The attempt was sternly resisted, and resulted in an act providing for her admission, but containing a clause prohibiting slavery forever in all the territory acquired from France, outside of Missouri, and north 36° 30′ north latitude. The principle of this law was a division of the common territory. The authority to prohibit even to this extent was denied by Mr. Madison, Mr. Jefferson, and other leading men of that day. It was carried by most of the southern representatives combined with a small number of northern votes. It was a departure from principle, but it savored of justice. Subsequently, upon the settlement of our claim to Oregon, it lying north of that line, the prohibition was applied. Upon the acquisition of Texas, the same line of division was adopted. But when we acquired California and New Mexico, the South, still willing to abide by the principle of division, again attempted to divide by the same line. It was almost unanimously resisted by the Northern States; their representatives, by a great majority, insisted upon absolute prohibition and the total exclusion of the people of the Southern States from the whole of the common territories unless they divested themselves of their slave property. The result of a long and unhappy conflict was the legislation of 1850. By it a large body of the representa tives of the non-slaveholding States, sustained by the approbation of their constituents, acting upon sound principles of constitutional construction, duty and patriotism, aided in voting down this new and dangerous usurpation, declared for the equality of the States, and protected the people of the territories from this unwarrantable interference with their rights. Here we wisely abandoned "the shifting grounds of compromise," and put the rights of the people again "upon the rock of the Constitution." The law of 1854 (commonly known as the Kansas-Nebraska act) was made to conform to this policy, and but carried out the principles established in 1850. It righted an ancient wrong, and will restore harmony because it restores justice to the country. This legislation I have endeavored to show is just, fair, and equal; that it is sustained by principle, by authority, and by the practice of our fathers. I trust, I believe, that when the transient passions of the day shall have subsided, and reason shall have resumed her dominion, it will be approved, even applauded, by the collective body of the people, in every portion of our widely extended Republic.

In inviting your calm consideration of the second point in my lecture, I am fully persuaded that even if I should succeed in convincing your reason and judgment of its truth, I shall have no aid from your sympathies in this work; yet, if the principles upon which our social system is founded are sound, the system itself is humane and just as well as necessary. Its permanence is based upon the idea of the superiority by nature of the white race over the African; that this superiority is not transient and artificial, but permanent and natural; that the same power which made his skin unchangeably black, made him inferior, intellectually, to the white race, and incapable of an equal struggle with him in the career of progress and civilization; that it is necessary for his preservation in this struggle, and for his own interest as well as that of the society of which he is a member, that he should be a servant and not a freeman in the commonwealth.

I have already stated that African slavery existed in all of the colonies at the commencement of the American Revolution. The paramount authority of the Crown, with or without the consent of the colonies, had introduced it, and it was inextricably interwoven with the frame-work of society, especially in the Southern States. The question was not presented for our decision whether it was just or beneficial to the African, to tear him away by force or fraud from bondage in his own country and place him in a like condition in ours. England and the Christian world had long before settled that question for us. At the final overthrow of British authority in these States our ancestors found seven hundred thousand Africans among them, already in bondage, and concentrated, from our climate and productions, chiefly in the present slaveholding States. It became their duty to establish governments for themselves and these people; and they brought wisdom, experience, learning, and patriotism to the great work. They sought that system of government which would secure the greatest and most enduring happiness to the whole society. They incorporated no Utopian theories into their system. They did not so much concern themselves about what rights man might possibly have in a state of nature, as what rights he ought to have in a state of society; they dealt with political rights as things of compact, not of birthright, in the concrete and not in the abstract. They held, and maintained, and incorporated into their system as fundamental truths, that it was the right and duty of the State to define and fix, as well as to protect and defend the individual rights of each member of the social compact, and to treat all individual rights as subordinate to the great interests of the whole society. Therefore, they denied "natural equality," repudiated mere governments of men necessarily resulting therefrom, and established governments of laws,—thirteen free, sovereign, and independent Republics. A very slight examination of our State Constitutions will show how little they regarded vague notions of abstract liberty, or natural equality in fixing the rights of the white race as well as the black. The elective franchise, the cardinal feature of our system, I have already shown, was granted, withheld, or limited, according to their ideas of public policy and the interest of the State. Numerous restraints upon the supposed abstract right of a mere numerical majority to govern society in all cases, are to be found planted in all of our Constitutions, State and Federal, thus affirming this subordination of individual rights to the interest and safety to the State.

The slaveholding States, acting upon these principles, finding the African race among them in slavery, unfit to be trusted with political power, incapable as freemen of securing their own happiness, or promoting the public prosperity, recognized their condition as slaves, and subjected it to legal control. There are abundant means of obtaining evidence of the effects of this policy on the slave and society, accessible to all who seek the truth. We say its wisdom is vindicated by its results, and that, under it, the African in the slaveholding States is found in a better position than he has ever attained in any other age or country, whether in bondage or freedom. In support of this point, I propose to trace him rapidly from his earliest history to the present time. The monuments of the ancient Egyptians carry him back to the morning of time—older than the pyramids—they furnish the evidence, both of his national identity and his social degradation before history began. We first behold him a slave in foreign lands; we then find the great body of his race slaves in their native land; and after thirty centuries, illuminated by both ancient and modern civilization, have passed over him, we still find him a slave of savage masters, as incapable as himself of even attempting a single step in civilization—we find him there still, without government or laws of protection, without letters or arts of industry, without religion, or even the aspirations which would raise him to the rank of an idolater, and in his lowest type, his almost only mark of humanity is, that he walks erect in the image of the Creator. Annihilate his race to-day, and you will find no trace of his existence within half a score of years; and he would not leave behind him a single discovery, invention, or thought worthy of remembrance by the human family.

In the Eastern Hemisphere he has been found in all ages, scattered among the nations of every degree of civilization, yet inferior to them all, always in a servile condition. Very soon after the discovery and settlement of America, the policy of the Christian world bought large numbers of these people of their savage masters and countrymen and imported them into the Western world. Here we are enabled to view them under different and far more favorable conditions. In Hayti, by the encouragement of the French Government, after a long probation of slavery, they became free, and led on by the conduct and valor of the mixed races, and by the aid of overwhelming numbers, they massacred the small number of whites who inhabited the island, and succeeded to the undisputed sway of the fairest and best of all the West India Islands under the highest state of cultivation. Their condition in Hayti left nothing to be desired, for the most favorable experiment of the race in self-government and civilization. This experiment has now been tested for sixty years, and its results are before the world. Fanaticism may palliate, but cannot conceal the utter prostration of the race. A war of races began the very moment the fear of foreign subjugation ceased, and resulted in the extermination of the greater number of the mulattoes, who had rescued the African from the dominion of the white race. Revolutions, tumults, and disorders, have been the ordinary pastime of the emancipated blacks; industry has almost ceased, and their stock of civilization acquired in slavery has been already nearly exhausted, and they are now scarcely distinguished from the tribes from which they were torn in their native land.

More recently the same experiment has been tried in Jamaica, under the auspices of England. This was one of the most beautiful, productive, and prosperous of the British colonial possessions. In 1838, England, following the false theories of her own abolitionists, proclaimed total emancipation of the black race in Jamaica. Her arms and her power have watched over and protected them; not only the interest, but the absolute necessities of the white proprietors of the land compelled them to offer every inducement and stimulant to industry; yet the experiment stands before the world a confessed failure. Ruin has overwhelmed the proprietors; and the negro, true to the instincts of his nature, buries himself in filth, and sloth, and crime. Here we can compare the African with himself in both conditions, in freedom and in bondage; and we can compare him with his race in the same climate and following the same pursuits. Compare him with himself under the two different conditions in Hayti and Jamaica, or with his race in bondage in Cuba, and every comparison demonstrates the folly of his emancipation. In the United States, too, we have peculiar opportunities of studying the African race under different conditions. Here we find him in slavery; here we find him also a free man in both the slaveholding and non-slaveholding States. The best specimen of the free black is to be found in the Southern States, in the closest contact with slavery, and subject to many of its restraints. Upon the theory of the anti-slavery men, the most favorable condition in which you can view the African ought to be in the non-slaveholding States of this Union. There we ought to expect to find him displaying all the capabilities of his race for improvement and progress—in a temperate climate, with the road of progress open before him, among an active, industrious, ingenious, and educated people, surrounded by sympathizing friends, and mild, just, and equal institutions, if he fails here, surely it can be chargeable to nothing but himself. He has had seventy years in which to cleanse himself and his race from the leprosy of slavery, yet what is his condition here to-day? He is free: he is lord of himself; but he finds it is truly a "heritage of woe." After this seventy years of education and probation, among themselves, his inferiority stands as fully a confessed fact in the non-slaveholding as in the slaveholding States. By them he is adjudged unfit to enjoy the rights and perform the duties of citizenship—denied social equality by an irreversible law of nature and political rights, by municipal law, incapable of maintaining the unequal struggle with the superior race; the melancholy history of his career of freedom is here most usually found in the records of criminal courts, jails, poor-houses, and penitentiaries. These facts have had themselves recognized in the most decisive manner throughout the Northern States. No town, or city, or State, encourages their immigration; many of them discourage it by legislation; some of the non-slaveholding States have prohibited their entry into their borders under any circumstances whatever. Thus, it seems, this great fact of "inferiority" of the race is equally admitted everywhere in our country. The Northern States admit it, and to rid themselves of the burden, inflict the most cruel injuries upon an unhappy race; they expel them from their borders and drive them out of their boundaries, as wanderers and outcasts. The result of this policy is everywhere apparent; the statistics of population supply the evidence of their condition. In the non-slaveholding States their annual increase, during the ten years preceding the last census, was but a little over one per cent. per annum, even with the additions of the emancipated slaves and fugitives from labor from the South, clearly proving that in this, their most favored condition, when left to themselves, they are scarcely capable of maintaining their existence, and with the prospect of a denser population and a greater competition for employment consequent thereon, they are in danger of extinction.

The Southern States, acting upon the same admitted facts, treat them differently. They keep them in the subordinate condition in which they found them, protect them against themselves, and compel them to contribute to their own and the public interest and welfare; and under this system, we appeal to facts, open to all men, to prove that the African race has attained a higher degree of comfort and happiness than his race has ever before attained in any other age or country. Our political system gives the slave great and valuable rights. His life is equally protected with that of his master: his person is secure from assault against all others except his master, and his master's power in this respect is placed under salutary legal restraints. He is entitled, by law, to a home, to ample food and clothing, and exempted from "excessive" labor; and when no longer capable of labor, in old age and disease, he is a legal charge upon his master. His family, old and young, whether capable of labor or not, from the cradle to the grave, have the same legal rights; and in these legal provisions, they enjoy as large a proportion of the products of their labor as any class of unskilled hired laborers in the world. We know that these rights are, in the main, faithfully secured to them; but I rely not on our knowledge, but submit our institutions to the same tests by which we try those of all other countries. These are supplied by our public statistics. They show that our slaves are larger consumers of animal food than any population in Europe, and larger than any other laboring population in the United States; and that their natural increase is equal to that of any other people; these are true and undisputable tests that their physical comforts are amply secured.

In 1790 there were less than seven hundred thousand slaves in the United States: in 1850 the number exceeded three and one quarter millions. The same authority shows their increase, for the ten years preceding the last census, to have been above twenty-eight per cent., or nearly three per cent. per annum, an increase equal, allowing for the element of foreign immigration, to the white race, and nearly three times that of the free blacks of the North. But these legal rights of the slave embrace but a small portion of the privileges actually enjoyed by him. He has, by universal custom, the control of much of his own time, which is applied, at his own choice and convenience, to the mechanic arts, to agriculture, or to some other profitable pursuit, which not only gives him the power of purchase over many additional necessaries of life, but over many of its luxuries, and, in numerous cases, enables him to purchase his freedom when he desires it. Besides, the nature of the relation of master and slave begets kindnesses, imposes duties, (and secures their performance,) which exist in no other relation of capital and labor. Interest and humanity co-operate in harmony for the well-being of slave labor. Thus the monster objection to our institution of slavery, that it deprives labor of its wages, cannot stand the test of a truthful investigation. A slight examination of the true theory of wages, will further expose its fallacy. Under a system of free labor, wages are usually paid in money, the representative of products—under ours, in products themselves. One of your most distinguished statesmen and patriots, President John Adams, said that the difference to the State was "imaginary." "What matters it (said he) whether a landlord employing ten laborers on his farm, gives them annually as much money as will buy them the necessaries of life, or gives them those necessaries at short hand." All experience has shown that if that be the measure of the wages of labor, it is safer for the laborer to take his wages in products than in their fluctuating pecuniary value. Therefore, if we pay in the necessaries and comforts of life more than any given amount of pecuniary wages will buy, then our laborer is paid higher than the laborer who receives that amount of wages. The most authentic agricultural statistics of England show that the wages of agricultural and unskilled labor in that kingdom, not only fail to furnish the laborer with the comforts of our slave, but even with the necessaries of life, and no slaveholder could escape a conviction for cruelty to his slaves who gave his slave no more of the necessaries of life for his labor than the wages paid to their agricultural laborers by the noblemen and gentlemen of England would buy. Under their system man has become less valuable and less cared for than domestic animals, and noble Dukes will depopulate whole districts of men to supply their places with sheep, and then, with intrepid audacity, lecture and denounce American slaveholders.

The great conflict between labor and capital, under free competition, has ever been how the earnings of labor shall be divided between them. In new and sparsely settled countries, where land is cheap, and food is easily produced, and education and intelligence approximate equality, labor can successfully struggle in this warfare with capital. But this is an exceptional and temporary condition of society. In the Old World this state of things has long since passed away, and the conflict with the lower grades of labor has long since ceased. There the compensation of unskilled labor which first succumbs to capital, is reduced to a point, scarcely adequate to the continuance of the race. The rate of increase is scarcely one per cent. per annum, and even at that rate, population, until recently, was considered a curse; in short, capital has become the master of labor with all the benefits, without the natural burdens of the relation.

In this division of the earnings of labor between it and capital, the southern slave has a marked advantage over the English laborer, and is often equal to the free laborer of the North. Here again we are furnished with authentic data from which to reason. The census of 1850 shows that, on cotton estates of the South, which is the chief branch of our agricultural industry, one half of the arable lands are annually put under food crops. This half is usually wholly consumed on the farm by the laborers and necessary animals; out of the other half must be paid all the necessary expenses of production, often including additional supplies of food beyond the produce of the land, which usually equals one third of the residue, leaving but one third for net rent. The average rent of the land in the older non-slaveholding States, is equal to one third of the gross product, and it not unfrequently amounts to one half of it, (in England it is sometimes even greater,) the tenant, from his portion, paying all expenses of production, and the expenses of himself and family. From this statement it is apparent that the farm laborers of the South receive always as much, and frequently a greater portion of the produce of the land, than the laborer in the New or Old England. Besides, here the portion due the slave, is a charge upon the whole product of capital, and the capital itself; it is neither dependent upon seasons nor subjects to accidents, and survives his own capacity for labor, and even the ruin of his master.

But it is objected that religious instruction is denied the slave. While it is true that religious instruction and privileges are not enjoined by law in all of the States, the number of slaves who are in connection with the different churches abundantly proves the universality of their enjoyment of those privileges. And a much larger number of the race in slavery enjoy the consolation of religion than the efforts of the combined Christian world have been able to convert to Christianity out of all the millions of their countrymen who remained in their native land

The immoralities of the slaves, and of those connected with slavery, are constant themes of abolition denunciation. They are lamentably great; but it remains to be shown that they are greater than with the laboring poor of England, or any other country. And it is shown that our slaves are without the additional stimulant of want to drive them to crime, we have at least removed from them the temptation and excuse of hunger. Poor human nature is here at least spared the wretched fate of the utter prostration of its moral nature at the feet of its physical wants. Lord Ashley's report to the British Parliament, shows that in the capital of that empire, perhaps within hearing of Stafford House and Exeter Hall, hunger alone daily drives thousand of men and women into the abyss of crime.

It is also objected that our slaves are debarred the benefits of education. This objection is also well taken, and is not without force. And for this evil the slaves are greatly indebted to the abolitionists—formerly in none of the slaveholding States, was it forbidden to teach slaves to read and write, but the character of the literature sought to be furnished them by the abolitionists caused these States to take counsel rather of their passions than their reason, and to lay the axe at the root of the evil · better counsels will in time prevail, and this will be remedied. It is true that the slave, from his protected position, has less need of education than the free laborer who has to struggle for himself in the welfare of society; yet, it is both useful to him, his master, and society.

The want of legal protection to the marriage relation is also a fruitful source of agitation among the opponents of slavery. The complaint is not without foundation; this is an evil not yet removed by law, but marriage is not inconsistent with the institution of slavery as it exists among us, and the objection, therefore, lies rather to an incident than the essence of the system. But, in the truth and fact, marriage does exist to a very great extent among slaves, and is encouraged and protected by their owners; and it will be found, upon careful investigation, that fewer children are born out of wedlock among slaves, than in the capitals of two of the most civilized countries of Europe—Austria and France: in the former, one half of the children are thus born—in the latter, more than one fourth. But even in this we have deprived the slave of no pre-existing right. We found the race without any knowledge of or regard for the institution of marriage, and we are reproached with not having as yet secured to it that, with all other blessings of civilization. To protect that and other domestic ties by laws forbidding, under proper regulations, the separation of families, would be wise, proper, and humane, and some of the slaveholding States have already adopted partial legislation for the removal of these evils. But the objection is far more formidable in theory than in practice. The accidents and necessities of life, the desire to better one's condition, produce infinitely a greater amount of separation in families of the white than ever happen to the colored race. This is true, even in the United States, where the general condition of the people is prosperous. But it is still more marked in Europe. The injustice and despotism of England towards Ireland has produced more separation of Irish families, and sundered more domestic ties within the last ten years than African slavery has effected since its introduction into the United States. The twenty millions of freemen in the United States are witnesses of the dispersive injustice of the old world. The general happiness, cheerfulness, and contentment of slaves, attest both the mildness and humanity of the system and their natural adaptation to their condition. They require no standing armies to enforce their obedience; while the evidence of discontent and the appliance of force to repress it, are every where visible among the toiling millions of the earth; even in the northern States of this Union, strikes and mobs, unions and combinations against employers, attest at once the misery and discontent of labor among them. England keeps one hundred thousand soldiers in time of peace, a large navy, and an innumerable police, to secure obedience to her social institutions; and physical force is the sole guarantee of her social order, the only cement of her gigantic empire.

I have briefly traced the condition of the African race through all ages and all countries, and described it fairly and truly under American slavery, and I submit that the proposition is fully proven, that his position in slavery among us is superior to any which he has ever attained in any age or country. The picture is not without shade as well as light; evils and imperfections cling to man and all of his works, and this is not exempt from them. The condition of the slave offers great opportunities for abuse, and these opportunities are frequently used to violate humanity and justice. But the laws restrain these abuses, and punish these crimes in this as well as other relations of life, and they who assume it as a fundamental principle in the constitution of man, that abuse is the unvarying concomitant of power, and crime of opportunity, subvert the foundations of all private morals, and of every social system. Nowhere do these assumptions find a nobler refutation than in the general treatment of the African race by southern slaveholders: and we may, with hope and confidence, safely leave to them the removal of existing abuses, and the adoption of such further ameliorations as may be demanded by justice and humanity. The condition of the African, (whatever may be his interests,) may not be permanent among us; he may find his exodus in the unvarying laws of population. Under the conditions of labor in England and the Continent of Europe domestic slavery is impossible there, and could not exist here, or anywhere else. The moment wages descend to a point, barely sufficient to support the laborer and his family, capital cannot afford to own labor and it must cease. Slavery ceased in England in obedience to this law, and not from any regard to liberty or humanity. The increase of population in this country may produce the same results, and American slavery, like that of England, may find its euthanasia in the general prostration of all labor.

The next aspect in which I propose to examine this question is, its effects upon the material interests of the slaveholding States. Thirty years ago slavery was assailed, mainly on the ground that it was a dear, wasteful, unprofitable labor, and we were urged to emancipate the blacks, in order to make them more useful and productive members of society. The result of the experiment in the West India Islands, to which I have before referred, not only disproved, but utterly annihilated this theory. The theory was true as to the white race, and was not true as to the black, and this single fact made thoughtful men pause and ponder, before advancing further with this folly of abolition. An inquiry into the wealth and productions of the slaveholding States of this Union demonstrates that slave labor can be economically and profitably employed, at least in agriculture, and leaves the question in great doubt, whether it cannot be thus employed in the South more advantageously than any other description of labor. The same truth will be made manifest by a comparison of the production of Cuba and Brazil, not only with Hayti and Jamaica, but with the free races, in similar latitudes, engaged in the same or similar productions in any part of the world. The slaveholding States, with one half of the white population, and between three and four millions of slaves, furnish above three fifths of the annual exports of the Republic, containing twenty-three millions of people; and their entire products, including every branch of industry, greatly exceed *per capita* those of the more populous Northern States. The difference in realized wealth in proportion to population is not less remarkable and equally favorable to the slaveholding States. But this is not a fair comparison, on the contrary it is exceedingly unfair to the slaveholding States. The question of material advantage would be settled on the side of slavery, whenever it was shown that our mixed society was more productive and prosperous than any other mixed society with the inferior race free instead of slave. The question is not whether we could not be more prosperous and happy with these three and a half millions of slaves in Africa, and their places filled with an equal number of hardy intelligent enterprising citizens of the superior race, but it is simply whether while we have them among us, we would be most prosperous with them in freedom or bondage; with this bare statement of the true issue, I can safely leave the question to the facts already heretofore referred to, and to those disclosed in the late census. But the truth itself needs some explanation, as it seems to be a great mystery to the opponents of slavery, how the system is capable at the same time of increasing the comforts and happiness of the slave, the profits of the master, and do no violence to humanity. Its solution rests upon very obvious principles. In this relation, the labor of the country is united with, and protected by its capital, directed by the educated and intelligent, secured against its own weakness, waste, and folly, associated in such form as to give the greatest efficiency in production, and the least cost of maintainance. Each individual free black laborer is the victim not only of his own folly and extravagance, but of his ignorance, misfortunes, and necessities. His isolation enlarges his expenses, without increasing his comforts; his want of capital increases the price of every thing he buys, disables him from supplying his wants at favorable times, or on advantageous terms, and throws him in the hands of retailers and extortioners. But labor united with capital, directed by skill, forecast and intelligence, while it is capable of its highest production, is freed from all these evils, leaves a margin, both for the increased comforts to the laborer, and additional profits to capital. This is the explanation of the seeming paradox.

The opponents of slavery, passing by the question of material interests, insist that its effects on the society where it exists is to demoralize and enervate it, and render it incapable of advancement and a high civilization; and upon the citizen to debase him morally and intellectually. Such is not the lesson taught by history, either sacred or profane, nor the experience of the past or present.

To the Hebrew race were committed the oracles of the Most High; slaveholding priests administered at his altar, and slaveholding prophets and patriarchs received his revelations, and taught them to their own, and transmitted them to all future generations of men. The highest forms of ancient civilization, and the noblest development of the individual man, are to be found in the ancient slaveholding commonwealths of Greece and Rome. In eloquence, in rhetoric, in poetry and painting, in architecture and sculpture, you must still go and search amid the wreck and ruins of their genius for the "pride of every model and the perfection of every master," and the language and literature of both, stamped with immortality, passes on to mingle itself with the thought and the speech of all lands and all centuries. Time will not allow me to multiply illustrations. That domestic slavery neither enfeebles or deteriorates our race; that it is not inconsistent with the highest advancement of man and society, is the lesson taught by all ancient and confirmed by all modern history. Its effects in strengthening the attachment of the dominant race to liberty, was eloquently expressed by Mr. Burke, the most accomplished and philosophical statesman England ever produced. In his speech on conciliation with America, he uses the following strong language: "Where this is the case those who are free are by far the most proud and jealous of their freedom. I cannot alter the nature of man. The fact is so, and these people of the southern colonies are much more strongly, and with a higher and more stubborn spirit attached to liberty than those to the northward. Such were all the ancient commonwealths, such were our Gothic ancestors, and such in our day were the Poles; such will be all masters of slaves who are not slaves themselves. In such a people the haughtiness of domination combines itself with the spirit of freedom, fortifies it, and renders it invincible."

No stronger evidence of what progress society may make with domestic slavery can be desired, than that which the present condition of the slaveholding States presents. For near twenty years, foreign and domestic enemies of their institutions have labored by pen and speech to excite discontent among the white race, and insurrections among the black; these efforts have shaken the National Government to its foundations, and burst the bonds of Christian unity among the churches of the land; yet the objects of their attacks—these States—have scarcely felt the shock. In surveying the whole civilized world, the eye rests not on a single spot where all classes of society are so well content with their social system, or have greater reason to be so, than in the slaveholding States of this Union. Stability, progress, order, peace, content, prosperity, reign throughout our borders. Not a single soldier is to be found in our widely-extended domain to overawe or protect society.

The desire for organic change nowhere manifests itself. Within less than seventy years, out of five feeble colonies, with less than one and a half millions of inhabitants, have emerged fourteen Republican States, containing nearly ten millions of inhabitants, rich, powerful, educated, moral, refined, prosperous, and happy; each with Republican Governments adequate to the protection of public liberty and private rights, which are cheerfully obeyed, supported, and upheld by all classes of society. With a noble system of internal improvements penetrating almost every neighborhood, stimulating and rewarding the industry of our people; with moral and intellectual surpassing physical improvements; with churches, schoolhouses, and colleges daily multiplying throughout the land, bringing education and religious instruction to the homes of all the people, they may safely challenge the admiration of the civilized world. None of this great improvement and progress have been even aided by the Federal Government; we have neither sought from it protection for our private pursuits, nor appropriations for our public improvements. They have been effected by the unaided individual efforts of an enlightened, moral, energetic, and religious people. Such is our social system, and such our condition under it. Its political wisdom is vindicated in its effects on society; its morality by the practices of the patriarchs and the teachings of the apostles; we submit it to the judgment of mankind, with the firm conviction that the adoption of no other system under our circumstances would have exhibited the individual man, bond or free, in a higher development, or society in a happier civilization.

GENERAL INDEX.

VOL. I.

www.ingramcontent.com/pod-product-compliance
Lightning Source LLC
LaVergne TN
LVHW021049110826
845150LV00001B/27

* 9 7 8 1 4 2 5 5 6 7 8 9 7 *